W9-CTR-030

LOEB CLASSICAL LIBRARY
FOUNDED BY JAMES LOEB 1911

EDITED BY
JEFFREY HENDERSON

AELIUS ARISTIDES
II

LCL 545

AELIUS ARISTIDES

ORATIONS 3–4

EDITED AND TRANSLATED BY

MICHAEL TRAPP

HARVARD UNIVERSITY PRESS
CAMBRIDGE, MASSACHUSETTS
LONDON, ENGLAND
2021

First published 2021

Library of Congress Control Number 2016957656
CIP data available from the Library of Congress

ISBN 978-0-674-99736-3

*Composed in ZephGreek and ZephText by
Technologies 'N Typography, Merrimac, Massachusetts.
Printed on acid-free paper and bound by
Maple Press, York, Pennsylvania*

CONTENTS

INTRODUCTION vii

ABBREVIATIONS xxiii

REFERENCES xxv

BIBLIOGRAPHY xxvii

ORATIONS

3. A REPLY TO PLATO: IN DEFENSE OF THE FOUR 1

4. A REPLY TO CAPITO 567

INDEX 619

INTRODUCTION[1]

In *Oration* 2, the first of the three *Platonic Orations*, Aristides had vigorously contested Plato's attack on oratory in the *Gorgias*, reasserting its claim to be a truly scientific activity and a positive element in politics and civic life. In the process, he had touched on Plato's disparaging treatment of the four great Athenian orator-statesmen, Miltiades, Cimon, Themistocles, and Pericles, but only relatively briefly (2.319–43) and as a subordinate part of his defense of the activity itself. He had also used the story of Plato's attempted interventions in the politics of Sicily (as told in the Platonic *Epistles* 7 and 8) to show that Plato himself in his better moments did not really believe what he makes Socrates say in the *Gorgias* about the relative unimportance of preventing the suffering of wrong as opposed to the doing of it.

Orations 3 and 4 both pick up on different aspects of this nexus: *Or.* 3 by expanding on the defense of the Four, *Or.* 4 by defending the invocation of Plato's own practical political record in Sicily.[2] Like *Or.* 2, both of them com-

[1] For a General Introduction to Aristides' life and works, see vol. I (LCL 533), ix–xxxi.

[2] Cf. vol. I, 326–35; in one version of the *Prolegomena*, *Or.* 3 is classified as a *deuterologia* (second speech, supplementary plea—3.436.3 Dindorf = *Hypoth.* H_1 2, 15.5–6 Lenz).

bine defense with a vigorous element of counterattack. Although neither can be given a secure absolute date, any more than *Or.* 2 can, it is clear that, in spite of the standard numeration, *Or.* 4 must have been composed and circulated before *Or.* 3 (where it is indeed placed in some branches of the manuscript tradition).[3]

ORATION 4

Oration 4 (to begin with the chronologically earlier piece) takes the form of a letter to an individual named Capito, responding to a complaint he has reportedly made about the handling of Plato's Sicilian adventures in *Or.* 2 (4.8–9). Aristides begins by reasserting his deep respect for Plato and pointing to the pains he has already taken to highlight it (4.1–7, 10–16). He observes that his strategy of looking for discrepancies between Plato's words in the *Gorgias* and what he says or does elsewhere was a consistent one (witness also his use of *Laws* 829a, 4.17–19), and pleads that his treatment of Plato should be assessed on the strength of his whole performance, not of any individual element of it seen on its own (4.20–26). In the second half of the letter (4.27–51), defense gives way to counterattack, with an increasingly indignant demonstration that, in drawing critical attention to just one episode in Plato's life, Aristides was only doing to him in a very

[3] On dating, see (with caution) Behr, *Aelius Aristides*, 54–56 with n. 52, and 94–95 with n. 2 (arguing for 161–165 AD for *Or.* 3), and Behr, *Complete Works* I, 449 and 460. For the manuscript order, cf. vol. I, xviii.

mild and limited form what he had done much more vigorously and less scrupulously to his satirical targets in the dialogues.

The epistolary character of Aristides' riposte can be seen to some extent in its restricted length, its simple form, and its relatively informal style,[4] but it is brought into focus particularly in 4.32, where Aristides rounds off a substantial quotation from the *Alcibiades I* with a comment on the circumstances in which he is making it: "Does it look as if I am just making work for you? No more than for myself and for my secretary: it is around lamp-lighting time that I am going into this, and it has to be finished before I go to bed." The combination of the reflexive comment on the writing process with the tense used in "going into this" and "has to be" (imperfects in the Greek) puts down a clear epistolary marker.[5]

The addressee, Capito, is not certainly identifiable. The internal evidence of the letter establishes that—at least as Aristides chooses to present things—he has a close student's engagement, rather than just a literary amateur's

4 "Informal" at least in comparison with the much more syntactically elaborate *Orr.* 2 and 3; for stylistic level, length, and structure as epistolary markers, cf., e.g., Demetrius, *De elocutione* 223–29.

5 Epistolary tenses: H. Koskenniemi, *Studien zur Idee und Phraseologie des griechischen Briefes* (Helsinki, 1956), 189–200; H. Weir-Smyth, *Greek Grammar* §1942 (Cambridge, MA, 1984 [1920]). Epistolary reflexivity: M. Trapp, *Greek and Latin Letters* (Cambridge, 2003), 36. Aristides' opening expression of friendly feelings also has an epistolary tinge: Trapp, *Greek and Latin Letters*, 40–41.

one, with Plato (4.28) and perhaps that he is a native of Pergamum (4.22). Behr tentatively identifies him as the Pergamene priest Sextus Julius Capito, who is known from a couple of contemporary inscriptions, but this can count only as a plausible guess.[6] Behr's further suggestion that Capito, as a Pergamene Platonist, can be connected with a larger contemporary phenomenon in the form of a Platonist movement centered on the philosopher Gaius—the so-called "School of Gaius"—though taken up in several recent accounts, must be rejected. John Dillon showed over forty years ago that this supposed "school" is a figment of modern scholarship.[7]

A more revealing facet of the *Oration* is its relationship with the *Letter to Gnaeus Pompeius* by the Augustan-period critic Dionysius of Halicarnassus, composed at least a century and a half previously.[8] The parallel in situation, between Dionysius using a letter to defend the stylistic criticisms he had previously made of Plato in his essay on Demosthenes, and Aristides using one to defend

[6] Behr, *Aelius Aristides*, 59 n. 60; cf. *Inschr. von Pergamon* 8.2.428 and *IGRR* 4.386.

[7] Behr, *Complete Works* I, 479 n. 1, building on T. Sinko, *De Apulei et Albini doctrinae Platonicae adumbratione* (Kraków, 1906) and R. Witt, *Albinus and the History of Middle Platonism* (Cambridge, 1937), demolished in J. Dillon, *The Middle Platonists* (Ithaca, NY, 1977), 266–338. Behr has been followed by R. Fowler, *Imperial Plato* (Las Vegas, 2016), 19, and "Variations of Receptions of Plato During the Second Sophistic," in H. Tarrant et al., eds., *Brill's Companion to the Reception of Plato in Antiquity* (Leiden, 2018), 233.

[8] Cf. Hunter, *Plato and the Traditions of Ancient Literature*, 181–84, and Milazzo, "L'Epistola a Capitone di Elio Aristide, 83–96 (the latter written apparently in ignorance of the former).

his criticism of Plato's arguments in *Or.* 2, is too close for coincidence, especially since it is intensified by the parallel in the characterization of Plato that both authors offer and by the fact that both of them seek to differentiate between a better Plato, whom they declare they admire, and a worse Plato, who they wish would just abandon the less well-judged side of his work. For Dionysius, in the *Demosthenes* and the *Letter*,[9] Plato's is an overwhelmingly great intellect, apt to be carried into stylistic excess (his self-confessed "dithyrambic" mode) by the very abundance of his talent; Aristides in *Or.* 4 proposes the same cause for his inappropriately scornful treatment of other great Greek writers and thinkers. Dionysius, moreover, anticipates Aristides in protesting that in making his criticisms he is only paying Plato back in his own coin; he likewise stigmatizes him for his inappropriate competitiveness (*philotimia*) and indicates *Protagoras*, *Gorgias*, *Parmenides*, and *Republic* as the most discreditable instances.[10]

Aristides surely expected that alert readers would pick up on his evocation of Dionysius in *Or.* 4. This in turn encourages further thoughts about the motives with which he composed and published his letter. On the most straightforward reading, he did so because he really had come under public attack because of what he had said in *Or.* 2, from Capito speaking either for himself or on behalf of a larger local Platonist faction. But another level of concern must be in play, either in addition to this or indeed instead of it. Defending oneself for what one has said in a previous publication is also a good way of reminding a potential

[9] Dion. Hal. *Dem.* 5–7 and 23–32; *Ep. Pomp.* 1–2.
[10] Cf. *Or.* 4.29–45.

readership of that publication's existence, offering guidance on how it ought to be read, and further shaping one's own profile as writer, thinker, and significant player in the world of culture more generally—all of which projects are manifestly under way in *Or.* 4. In the process, moreover, Aristides begins to explore lines of thought that he will develop much more fully when, after whatever lapse in time, he returns to the subject of Plato's hostility to orators and oratory in *Or.* 3.

ORATION 3

Oration 3 is by some way the longest of all Aristides' works (it runs to 694 chapters as against the 466 of *Or.* 2). Its rhetorical form struck ancient commentators as something of a puzzle. A somewhat mangled version of their discussions is preserved in the Aristides *Prolegomena*, which list the reasons for which the work cannot count as symbouleutic, epideictic ("panegyric"), or judicial, and scorn the alternative suggestions that it might represent a mixed form (combining epideictic with judicial) or might be an *anaskeuê* (since that can be only a form of training exercise—*progymnasma*—not a self-standing composition). They conclude instead that "the technographer Theon" provides the key in his recognition of *antirrhêsis* (speech of confutation) as a legitimate self-standing form, or perhaps—since it is not directed toward a living opponent—*antigraphê* (written confutation) might be still better.[11]

The discourse begins with a short prologue, in which

[11] 3.434.5–435.15 and 436.3–437.22 Dindorf = *Hypoth.* H_2 4–9, 170.8–172.9 and H_1 3–8, 158.6–161.10 Lenz. Cf. Lenz, *Aris-*

Aristides underlines his contention that Plato's attack on the Four statesmen in the *Gorgias* was tactically inept and reflected badly on his character (3.1–10). From this he proceeds to a series of individual vindications of each of the Four, in which apology is combined with implicit and explicit encomium (3.11–351), followed by a collective defense highlighting considerations that apply equally to all of them (3.352–510). Woven through the defensive vindications there is a complementary element of counterattack, as Aristides complains about alleged incoherencies and contradictions in Plato's criticism, the meanness of spirit that underlies it, and Plato's own vulnerability to many of the same charges.

The ground is thus well prepared for the turn to the still more direct and personal confrontation with Plato that follows in 3.511–662. To the charge of self-contradiction, Aristides now adds reproaches on the grounds of factual unreliability, fictionalizing, arbitrary and idiosyncratic use of conceptual categories, and a perverse hostility to almost every manifestation of both political greatness and literary culture in the Greek tradition. Behind this, he diagnoses a combination of excessive competitiveness with lofty carelessness over detail, itself grounded in the sheer magnitude of Plato's talent and the confidence it brings him (3.663).

A slightly different tack is then taken in 3.663–91,

---

tides Prolegomena, 5–11. For discussion of the date of Theon, apparently the same man as the author of the surviving *Progymnasmata*, and a reconstruction of the earlier course of the debate over the classification of *Or*. 3, see M. Heath, "Theon and the History of the Progymnasmata," *GRBS* 43 (2002/3): 129–60, at 141–58.

which begin with a complaint that Plato's unfortunate example of disrespect to the greats of the Greek tradition has been followed and made still more discreditable by a current generation of critics, who take him as justifying their own disgraceful attacks on Demosthenes. This is a part of the oration that historically has aroused considerable interest for its mention, under the description of "infidels of Palestine," of contemporary Christians (3.671). These malefactors are mentioned not, as Dindorf for instance believed,[12] as Aristides' main target here, but rather as a comparison designed to emphasize just how misguided and alienated from good Greek values are the critics who mistakenly claim Plato's precedent. The critics themselves, as Aristides makes clear, call themselves "philosophers," even though, as he indignantly argues, they are simply not entitled to the name. There has been further discussion of whether Aristides' sights are here set just on the Cynics of his immediate acquaintance,[13] or whether in fact he has a broader spectrum of philosophers, including scholastic theorizers, in mind;[14] on the strength of passages such as 3.672, the latter seems more likely.

Rather than a loosely-attached digression, this last major component of Aristides' riposte to Plato can plausibly be read as one final challenge, following on from the al-

[12] Dindorf's edition of the *Orations* (1829), 2.397–406 (in the *apparatus*).

[13] So J. Bernays, *Lucian und die Kyniker* (Berlin, 1879), 100–104; Behr, *Aelius Aristides*, 94 n. 2; Behr, *Complete Works* I, 449.

[14] So, approximately, A. Boulanger, *Aelius Aristide et la sophistique dans la province d'Asie au IIe siècle de notre ère* (Paris, 1923), 249–65, esp. 259–65.

ready alarming picture painted in 3.511–662 of his potential alienation from Greek culture. Does Plato, it asks, really wish to throw in his lot thus with the lunatic fringe, whether marginal in its uncouth disrespect or in its bizarrely esoteric theorizing, rather than drawing back to a more comfortable definition of what counts as philosophical (3.680–81) and to a proper accommodation with the other leading lights of Hellenism?[15]

By its end, therefore, *Or.* 3 has widened its focus from the *Gorgias* and the question of Plato's scandalous views about oratory and the great Athenian statesmen, to a broader problematization of the position of philosophy in general and Plato in particular in relation to the mainstream literate culture (*paideia*) that, as self-elected champion of oratory, Aristides implicitly claims to represent with unique authority. It has thus, like *Or.* 2, forwarded not only the argument over oratory but also the construction of Aristides' own profile as guardian of Hellenic values as well as practitioner of a particularly pure and high-minded kind of oratory; his confrontation with the wayward Plato thus builds on and reinforces the image also projected in his unsurpassable praises of the city of Athens in the *Panathenaic Oration* (*Or.* 1).[16]

Like *Or.* 2, therefore, *Or.* 3 deserves its prominent place near the beginning of the corpus of Aristides' collected works, following hard on the *Panathenaic*, which with its combination of oratorical virtuosity and compelling historical subject matter was always going to take first

15 On this stage of the argument, see further Trapp, "With All Due Respect to Plato," 85–113.

16 Cf. vol. I, xv–xviii, 9–10, and 332.

place. There is indeed a notable respect in which, thanks to its focus not on oratory per se, but on its great Athenian practitioners, it clusters well with *Or.* 1. Both of the two review the great achievements of the Persian Wars, the Pentecontaetea, and the opening stages of the Peloponnesian Wars, but *Or.* 1, in order to conform to the collectivist ethos of one of its chief models, the Athenian Funeral Oration,[17] did so without naming the principal participants; this leaves a gap, which *Or.* 3 neatly fills precisely by its concentration on the personalities. The interest consequently attracted by these portions of the oration from ancient (later classical and Byzantine) readers is amply attested by the volume of the surviving scholia devoted to them.[18]

THE TEXT

The manuscript evidence for *Orr.* 3 and 4 is the same as for *Orr.* 1 and 2 (for which see vol. I, xxiii–xxv and xxxi). The text it presents is also by and large in the same general condition: readable and marred by only minor slips and blemishes for long stretches, but also intermittently affected by interpolations of marginal matter (reader's comments, glosses, and paraphrases) that testify, like the volume of scholia, to the relative prominence of these pieces

[17] Cf. vol. I, 8.

[18] Some 225 of the 300 pages of scholia in Dindorf's edition are devoted to the individual defenses of the Four, as compared to the 45 given to the shared defense and the 30-odd to the remaining portions.

in Aristides' collected works.[19] It is notable, however, that the closing pages of *Or.* 3 (3.686–92) show particular signs of damage; this may well indicate a stage in the tradition at which *Orr.* 1 to 4, or perhaps just the three *Platonic Orations*, circulated separately, with *Or.* 3 rather than *Or.* 4 in last position.

Sigla and Stemma

A	Parisinus graecus 2951
A^1	principal hand
A^2	corrections by a later hand
A^c	corrections by Arethas
a	Vaticanus graecus 75 (in *Orr.* 2–4) = A_a
a^1	principal hand
a^2	later corrections and additions
Barocc. 136	Bodleianus Baroccianus 136 (used by Jebb and Dindorf)
Bodl. misc. 57	Bodleianus miscellaneus 57 = Auct. E.4.12
E	Parisinus graecus 2950
E^2	corrections by later hands
L	Laurentianus 60.9
L^{mrg}	addition in the margin
M	Marcianus graecus 423
$M^{rec.}$	later corrections and additions
Marc. gr. 425	Marcianus graecus 425

19 It is ironic that among the surviving *un*interpolated scholia there is one, attached to *Or.* 3.415, that wrongly alleges an interpolation at that point: see p. 347 below.

Monac. 432	Monacensis graecus 432 (used by Reiske and Dindorf)
O	consensus of all or most of AaEMQRTUV
P.Ant.	Antinoopolis Papyri 3.182 (Mertens-Pack 00136.400)
P.Oxy.	Oxyrhynchus Papyri 13.1608 (Mertens-Pack 00019.000)
Ph^{A}	Marcianus graecus 450 (text of Photius, *Bibliotheca*)
Ph^{M}	Marcianus graecus 451 (text of Photius, *Bibliotheca*)
Ph^{M3}	excerpts in margin of Marc. gr. 451 (Photius)
Ph^{s}	readings of other Photius MSS reported by Bekker (1824–25)
Q	Vaticanus graecus 1297
Q^{1}	principal hand
Q^{2}	corrections by a later hand
R	Vaticanus graecus 1298
R^{1}	principal hand
R^{2}	later corrections and additions
R$^{rec.}$	corrections in a 15th-century hand
T	Laurentianus 60.8
T^{1}	principal hand
T^{2}	corrections by a later hand
U	Vaticanus Urbinas graecus 123
V	Marcianus graecus Appendix 8.7
V^{1}	principal hand
V^{2}	corrections and supplements in a later hand
Vat. gr. 76	Vaticanus graecus 76

Σ	scholia
a.c.	before correction
cett.	remainder of the manuscripts
codd.	manuscripts
edd.	consensus of editors/editions
p.c.	after correction

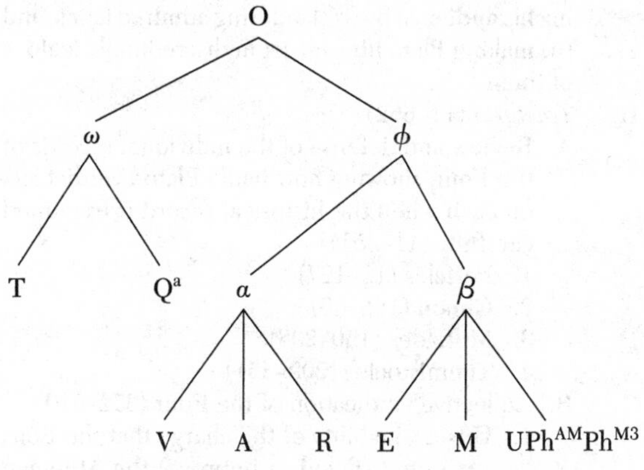

Simplified stemma for *Orr.* 1–4 (after Behr)

ANALYSES

Oration 3. A Reply to Plato: In Defense of the Four

I. Prologue and *prothesis* (1–10)
Plato's attack on the Four in *Gorgias* is astonishing but also inept, because it (a) adds nothing to the force of his criticism of oratory, and (b) risks alienating his audience by (i) slandering admired icons, and (ii) making Plato himself seem discreditably jealous of them.

II. *Tractatio* (11–662)
- A. Review and defense of the individual records of the Four, showing how badly Plato's verdict sits on each when the historical record is examined carefully (11–351)
    1. Pericles (11–127)
    2. Cimon (128–49)
    3. Miltiades (150–208)
    4. Themistocles (209–351)
- B. Collective vindication of the Four (352–510)
    1. Unsustainability of the charge that the Four corrupted (failed to improve) the Athenian demos, and that this failure is proved by the way the demos subsequently turned on them. Counter-examination of Plato's record in improving people (Dionysius? Critias and Alcibiades?) (352–460)
    2. Unfairness of blaming human beings (the Four) for the work of circumstance and for-

tune; Plato here forgetting what he acknowledges elsewhere (e.g., *Laws* 709bc) about causal factors in the world (461–98)

3. Plato's captious criticism of the Four contrasted with the generous praise of Demosthenes (499–510)

C. Counterattack: Plato's deficiencies in argument, authorship, and attitude to Hellenic tradition (511–662)
   1. Self-contradictions between the *Gorgias* and other works, and within the *Gorgias* itself (511–76)
   2. Anachronism and other kinds of factual unreliability in the dialogues, e.g., *Menexenus*, *Symposium*, *Phaedrus* (577–87)
   3. Arbitrary and unreliable use of categories in the evaluation of *technai* in the *Gorgias* —medicine/gymnastics, legislation/justice, sophist/orator (588–604)
   4. Ungenerous, damaging, and unnecessary attacks on the glories of Hellenic tradition—not only the heroes of Greek history but also the treasures of Greek literature (605–62)

III. Excursus (663–91)

Outrageous attack on civilized values in general and Demosthenes in particular, by soi-disant "philosophers," encouraged by what they see as Plato's example. Rejection of their claims to the status of philosopher, and reassertion of Aristides' devotion and respect for the true kind.

IV. Peroration (692–94)
Aristides has honored both the Four and Plato as they deserve but will respect anyone who can prove him wrong in his turn.

Oration 4: Reply to Capito

I. Preliminaries (1–7)
Shared devotion to Plato, so no hard feelings toward Capito for speaking up for him.

II. Capito's complaint (8–9)
Aristides' use of Plato's Sicilian voyages to attack his arguments.

III. Aristides' answer (10–45)

- A. Careful concern to praise Plato, esp. at *Or*. 2.295 (10–16)
- B. Use of *Laws* 829a at *Or.* 2.304–306 (17–19)
- C. Necessary to look at Aristides' whole argument, not just one individual passage (20–26)
- D. Aristides followed the normal rules of argument, and in any case Plato was the one who got abusive first (27–45)
  1. Preliminary statement (27–28)
  2. Plato in *Alc. I*, on Pericles (29–36)
  3. Plato in *Parm.*, on Parmenides (37)
  4. Plato in *Rep.*, on Homer (38–43)
  5. Plato in *Protag.*, on the Sophists (44–45)

IV. Conclusion (46–51)
Concluding contrast of Aristides' treatment of Plato with Plato's of all and sundry.

ABBREVIATIONS

DK	*Die Fragmente der Vorsokratiker*, ed. H. Diels and W. Kranz
Giannantoni	*Socratis et Socraticorum Reliquiae*, ed. G. Giannantoni
GRBS	*Greek, Roman and Byzantine Studies*
IEG	*Iambi et Elegi Graeci*, ed. M. L. West
IGRR	*Inscriptiones Graecae ad Res Romanas Pertinentes*
Jacoby	*Die Fragmente der griechischen Historiker*, ed. F. Jacoby
JHS	*Journal of Hellenic Studies*
Kassel-Austin	*Poetae Comici Graeci*, ed. R. Kassel and C. Austin
Kock	*Comicorum Atticorum Fragmenta*, ed. T. Kock
L-P	*Poetarum Lesbiorum Fragmenta*, ed. E. Lobel and D. L. Page
Page	*Further Greek Epigrams*, ed. D. L. Page
PIR	*Prosopographia Imperii Romani*
PMG	*Poetae Melici Graeci*, ed. D. L. Page
ST	Aelius Aristides, *The Sacred Tales* (*Orr.* 47–52)
SVF	*Stoicorum Veterum Fragmenta*, ed. J. von Arnim
TrGF	*Tragicorum Graecorum Fragmenta*

REFERENCES

Abresch	F. L. Abresch, in *Miscellaneae Observationes Criticae* 5.2 (Amsterdam, 1734), 225–45
Behr	F. W. Lenz and C. A. Behr, *P. Aelii Aristidis Opera Quae Exstant Omnia*, vol. 1 (Leiden, 1976–1980), *Orr.* 1–16
Behr, *Aelius Aristides*	C. A. Behr, *Aelius Aristides and the Sacred Tales* (Amsterdam, 1968)
Behr, *Complete Works*	C. A. Behr, trans., *P. Aelius Aristides. The Complete Works*, 2 vols. (Leiden 1981–6)
Boulanger	A. Boulanger, *Aelius Aristide et la sophistique dans la province d'Asie au IIe siècle de notre ère* (Paris, 1923)
Canter	G. Canter, trans., *Aelii Aristidis . . . orationum tomi tres, nunc primum Latinè versi* (Basel, 1566), or as cited in J. J. Reiske, *Animadversionum volumen quintum* (Leipzig, 1766), 588–624, and in Dindorf 1829
Dindorf	W. Dindorf, *Aristides*, 3 vols. (Leipzig, 1829)
Iunt.	*Orationes Aristidis* (Florence, 1517)

Jebb	S. Jebb, *Aelii Aristides . . . Opera Omnia*, 2 vols. (Oxford, 1722, 1730)
Keil	B. Keil, marginalia to copy of Dindorf, reported by Lenz-Behr
Krauss	H. Krauss, *Aeschinis Socratici Reliquiae* (Leipzig, 1911)
Lenz	F. W. Lenz and C. A. Behr, *P. Aelii Aristidis Opera Quae Exstant Omnia*, vol. 1 (Leiden, 1976–1980), *Orr.* 1–16
Liebel	I. Liebel, *Archilochi Iambographorum Principis Fragmenta*[2] (Vienna, 1818)
Lucarini	C. Lucarini, "Per il testo e il ritmo di Elio Aristide," *Bolletino dei Classici* 39–40 (2018–19): 201–49
Oporinus	J. Oporinus, as cited in Canter 1566 and Dindorf 1829
Pasquali	G. Pasquali, as cited in Lenz-Behr 1976–80
Reiske	J. J. Reiske, *Animadversionum in graecos auctores volumen tertium* (Leipzig, 1761), 185–572, reprinted in Dindorf 1829
Scaliger	J. J. Scaliger, as cited in Dindorf 1829
Stephanus	P. Stephanus, *Aeli Aristidis . . . Orationum tomi tres* (Geneva, 1604)
Valckenaer	L. Valckenaer on Herod. 2.80, as cited in Dindorf 1829
Wyttenbach	D. Wyttenbach, *Plutarchi Chaeronensis Moralia* VI.2 (1810), p. 1047 (note on *Mor.* 174b)

BIBLIOGRAPHY

Dittadi, A. "Difesa della retorica e 'riscrittura' di Platone nei Discorsi Platonici di Elio Aristide." *Rhetorica* 26 (2008): 113–37.

———. "Ἡ ῥητορικὴ τελεωτέρον: il confronto tra retorica e filosofia nei Discorsi Platonici di Elio Aristide (or. 2–4)." In *Aelius Aristide écrivain*, edited by L. Pernot, G. Abbamonte, and M. Lamagna, 59–81. Turnhout, 2016.

Flinterman, J.-J. "'... largely fictions ...': Aelius Aristides on Plato's Dialogues." *Ancient Narrative* 1 (2000–2001): 32–54.

Geffcken, J. "Antiplatonika." *Hermes* 64 (1928): 87–109.

Hunter, R. *Plato and the Traditions of Ancient Literature. The Silent Stream.* Cambridge, 2012.

Karadimas, D. *Sextus Empiricus and Aelius Aristides: The Conflict between Philosophy and Rhetoric in the Second Century AD.* Lund, 1996.

Milazzo, A. *Un dialogo difficile: la retorica in conflitto nei Discorsi Platonici di Elio Aristide.* Hildesheim, 2002.

———. "L'Epistola a Capitone di Elio Aristide (or. 4) e l'Epistola a Pompeo Gemino di Dionigi di Alicarnasso." In *Aelius Aristide écrivain*, edited by L. Pernot, G. Abbamonte, and M. Lamagna, 83–96. Turnhout, 2016.

Pernot, L. "Platon contre Platon: le problème de la rhétorique dans les Discours platoniciens d'Aelius Aristide." In *Contre Platon I: Le Platonisme dévoilé*, edited by M. Dixsaut, 315–38. Paris, 1993.

Trapp, M. "With All Due Respect to Plato: the Platonic Orations of Aelius Aristides." *TAPA* 150 (2020): 85–113.

ORATION 3

A REPLY TO PLATO: IN DEFENSE OF THE FOUR

3

ΠΡΟΣ ΠΛΑΤΩΝΑ ΥΠΕΡ ΤΩΝ ΤΕΤΤΑΡΩΝ

[*Prologue: Plato's Astonishing but Inept Attack (1–10)*]

Παραιτεῖσθαι μὲν οὐκ οἶδ᾽ ὅτι δεῖ περὶ τῶν αὐτῶν πολλάκις, ἄλλως τε καὶ οὐ πρὸς ἄνδρας μέλλοντας ἐρεῖν μᾶλλον ἢ ὑπὲρ ἀνδρῶν καλῶν καὶ ἀγαθῶν, καὶ τούτων οὐκ ὀλίγων, οὐδὲ ἧττον παλαιῶν ἢ Πλάτων, ὅτι μὴ καὶ πρεσβυτέρων ἐκείνου, εἴ τῳ καὶ τοῦτ᾽ ἄξιον αἰδοῦς εἶναι δοκεῖ. παρέστη δέ μοι θαυμάσαι πολλάκις ἄλλα τε δὴ τῶν ἐν Γοργίᾳ καὶ τὴν κατηγορίαν ἣν ἐποιήσατο Μιλτιάδου καὶ Θεμιστοκλέους καὶ Περικλέους καὶ Κίμωνος, καὶ ταῦτ᾽ ἀφελῶς οὕτως καὶ ἀνειμένως, ὃ μηδ᾽ ἂν εἷς εἰκάσειεν πρὶν διακοῦσαι τοῦ λόγου.

2 πρῶτον μὲν γὰρ οὐδὲ τὸ πρᾶγμα ἐπηνάγκαζεν, οὐδ᾽ ἔχοι τις ἂν εἰπεῖν. νὴ Δία, ὁ γὰρ λόγος αὐτῷ διεφθείρετο μὴ τούτους κακῶς εἰπόντι· ἀλλὰ ἐξῆν καὶ χωρὶς τῆς βλασφημίας ταύτης περαίνειν τὴν ὑπόθε-

3

A REPLY TO PLATO: IN DEFENSE OF THE FOUR

Prologue: Plato's Astonishing but Inept Attack (1–10)

I do not think there is any need to apologize repeatedly for the same thing, especially when what one means to do is not to attack anybody but rather to speak in defense of the great and the good, individuals who are not few in number and no less venerable than Plato, indeed even senior to him in age (should this too strike anyone as a claim to respect). The contents of the *Gorgias* never cease to amaze me, in particular Plato's denunciation there of Miltiades, Themistocles, Pericles, and Cimon,[1] all the more because it is delivered with a casual insouciance that one could not even guess at before actually reading the dialogue.

In the first place, Plato's subject matter did not demand 2
this, nor could anyone ever claim that it did. You may protest that his argument would have collapsed if he had not spoken ill of these men, but he could in fact perfectly well have completed his case without these outrageous

[1] *Grg*. 503b–5b.

3 σιν. εἰ μὲν γὰρ τοῦτο εὐθὺς ἐξ ἀρχῆς προὔθετο καὶ
τοῦτ᾽ ἐνεστήσατο ἐξετάσαι τοὺς Ἀθήνησιν πολιτευ-
σαμένους, ἐκ τοῦ πράγματος ἦν ἴσως καὶ περὶ τούτων
λέγειν. νῦν δὲ τί φησι καὶ πρὸς τί προσῆγε[1] τὸν
λόγον; δύο ταύτας εἶναι παρασκευὰς περὶ σῶμα καὶ
ψυχήν, μίαν μὲν πρὸς ἡδονὴν ὁμιλεῖν, τὴν ἑτέραν δὲ
πρὸς τὸ βέλτιστον· καὶ τὴν μὲν πρὸς ἡδονὴν ἀγεννῆ
καὶ κολακείαν εἶναι, τὴν δὲ ἑτέραν σπουδαῖον καὶ
καλόν. ὥστε τίς ἦν βλάβη τῷ λόγῳ μὴ τούτων τῶν
ἀνδρῶν κακῶς ἀκουσάντων; εἴ γε[2] μηδὲν μᾶλλον ἐκινδύνευεν τό γε δήπου πρὸς χάριν ἀντὶ τοῦ τὰ βέλτιστα
λέγειν χρηστὸν νομισθῆναι, ἄλλως τε καὶ τοῦ Καλλικλέους ἀπειρηκότος ἤδη πολλάκις, ὡς αὐτὸς ἐνδεί-
κνυται, καὶ τελευτῶντος εἰπόντος

> σὺ μὲν οὐκ οἶδ᾽ ὅντινά μοι τρόπον δοκεῖς εὖ λέγειν, ὦ Σώκρατες· πέπονθα δὲ τὸ τῶν πολλῶν πάθος, οὐ πάνυ σοι πείθομαι.

4 οὐ γὰρ δὴ τοῦτό γε ἔστιν εἰπεῖν, ὡς εἰ ψέξειεν
ἐκείνους, μᾶλλόν τι πείσειν αὐτὸν ἡγεῖτο καὶ προσ-
5 άξεσθαι. τοὐναντίον γὰρ ἔμοιγε δοκεῖ μᾶλλον ἂν καὶ
παροξῦναι καὶ πλέον θάτερον ποιῆσαι τῇ ἐκείνων
βλασφημίᾳ, ὥστε οὕτω γ᾽ ἄν, ὅ φησιν αὐτός, ἀνεσό-
βει τὴν θήραν, καὶ ταῦθ᾽ ὅπερ ἐβούλετο δηλοῦν ἔχων

[1] προσῆγε Canter προσεῖχε *codd.*

[2] εἴ γε Q^{1}p.c.M^{1}p.c.U^{2} εἰ γὰρ καί OQ^{1}a.c.M^{1}a.c. οὐ γὰρ καί Lenz

insults. If it had been his objective from the outset to re- 3
view the conduct of the politicians of Athens, if this had been what he had set himself to do, then perhaps it would have been relevant to speak about these men along with the rest. But what is it that he actually says, and what is the proposition that he argues for? That there are two kinds of provision relating to the body and soul, one of which has a view to pleasure in its dealings with them and the other to their real best interests: the one which looks to pleasure, he claims, is base "flattery" (*kolakeia*), while the other is something noble and good.[2] Given this, what damage would his argument have suffered if these men had not been bad-mouthed? At all events, the omission would surely not have increased the risk of anyone's thinking that speaking with an eye to gratification rather than speaking for the best was the virtuous course, especially since Callicles had already, as Plato himself underlines, several times given up the argument,[3] and ended up by saying

> Socrates, somehow or other I think that you are right, but as happens to most people, I'm not completely convinced by you.[4]

It certainly cannot be said that Plato thought that he 4
would have a better chance of persuading Callicles and
winning him over if he denounced these men. On the 5
contrary, I think that by his insults against them he would only have provoked him and achieved the opposite result instead, so as, in his own phrase,[5] to scare off his quarry at

[2] *Grg.* 463a–66a. [3] *Grg.* 505c–9c.
[4] *Grg.* 513c. [5] *Lys.* 206a.

6 ἤδη καὶ συνειληφώς. γνοίη δ᾽ ἄν τις ἐξ αὐτῶν τῶν ῥημάτων. προελθὼν γὰρ τοῦ λόγου,

> ἆρ᾽ οὖν—φησίν—οὕτως ἐπιχειρητέον ἡμῖν ἐστιν τῇ πόλει καὶ τοῖς πολίταις θεραπεύειν, ὡς βελτίστους αὐτοὺς τοὺς πολίτας ποιοῦντας;

"πάνυ γ᾽, εἴ σοι ἥδιον," φησὶν ὁ Καλλικλῆς. ὥσθ᾽ ὅταν ὡμολόγητο καὶ συγκεχώρητο ὑπὲρ οὗ πᾶς ἤνυστο λόγος καὶ πρὸς ὃ πάντα ταῦτ᾽ εἶχεν τὴν ἀναφοράν, τίς ἦν ἡ ζημία τῶν ἀνδρῶν μὴ προσκαθάπτεσθαι;

7 νῦν δὲ ὥσπερ ὠδίνων καὶ περιβαλλόμενος κύκλῳ τὴν ἐπ᾽ ἐκείνους ὁδὸν οὕτως ἐπιβούλως ἐλθὼν ἐπὶ τοὺς λόγους φαίνεται. καὶ μὴν τὸ μὲν διάφορον οὐχὶ μικρόν. ἐκεῖνο μὲν γὰρ ἦν ὑπὲρ αὐτῆς τῆς ἀληθείας ἀγωνίζεσθαι, τοῦτο δὲ ἐγὼ μὲν οὐδέποτε ἂν φήσαιμι, ἄλλος δ᾽ ἄν τις εἴποι διαβάλλων οὐ πόρρω κακο-
8 ηθείας εἶναι. καίτοι πῶς οὐκ ἄτοπον τοσοῦτον προέχοντα φιλανθρωπίᾳ καὶ μεγαλοψυχίᾳ τὴν τοῦ βασκαίνειν δοκεῖν παρέχειν λαβὴν ὅσα γε ἐκ τῶν λόγων; θαυμάζω δὲ εἰ κωμῳδίαν μὲν ἔξεστι ποιεῖν, κἂν μὴ ὀνομαστὶ κωμῳδεῖν ἐξῇ, πιστοῦσθαι δὲ οὐκ ἐνῆν τὸν λόγον, εἰ μή τινας εἶπεν κακῶς ὀνομαστί.
9 φέρε γὰρ πρὸς θεῶν, εἰ πρὸ τούτων τῶν ἀνδρῶν ἔτυ-

---

[6] *Grg.* 513e–14a.

[7] For a discussion of this rule, which ancient scholars held to mark a turning point in the development of comedy, but which

a stage when he had already securely proved his point. You can see this from his own words, when a little further on he says, 6

> Ought we not then to set about our treatment of the state and its citizens with the aim of making the citizens themselves as good as possible?

and Callicles replies, "By all means, if that's what you prefer."[6] So, seeing that the proposition on which all his argumentation had been expended and to which all of this material related had been conceded and agreed, what would have been the harm in refraining from adding an attack on these men?

As things actually are, Plato's labor pains, as you might 7
call them, and the long circuitous route he takes to get to these men clearly reveal the malign intent with which he set himself to his argument. The difference is anything but a small one, between striving hard in the service of the truth on the one hand, and on the other—well, I myself would never say as much, but a hostile critic might say it
was not far from malevolent. And yet how can it fail to 8
be absurd for someone so preeminent in generosity and greatness of heart to give a hand-hold, at least as far as his words go, to an appearance of malignant carping? I am amazed that it should be possible to write comedies even if it is forbidden to satirize individuals by name,[7] and yet not possible for Plato to win a reasoned argument without
speaking ill of named individuals. For heaven's sake, what 9

seems to have been an invention of Hellenistic literary scholarship, see S. Halliwell, *JHS* 111 (1991): 54–58 and 63–64, and cf. §631 below; Aristides invokes it again in *Or*. 29.

χεν γενόμενος, ἢ νὴ Δί᾽ εἴ τις ἄλλος τῶν ὑπὲρ τούτους ἄνω τὸν αὐτὸν τοῦτον λόγον ἠγωνίζετο, ἆρ᾽ ἂν οἷός τ᾽ ἦν Μιλτιάδου κατηγορεῖν καὶ Θεμιστοκλέους καὶ τῶν μήπω γεγενημένων; οὐδαμῶς.

10 *ὅτε τοίνυν ἦσαν λόγοι τῷ πράγματι καὶ χωρὶς τῆς περὶ τούτων μνήμης, οὐ μετ᾽ ἀνάγκης ἤκουον οὗτοι κακῶς. ὅτι τοίνυν οὐδ᾽ ἀληθῆ κατ᾽ αὐτῶν εἴρηκεν, ἄνευ τοῦ μηδὲν προσήκειν βλασφημεῖν, εἰ καὶ τὰ μάλιστα ἐλέγχειν ἔμελλε, τοῦτ᾽ ἤδη πειράσομαι δεικνύναι.*

[*Argumentation 1: Vindication of Pericles (11–127)*]

11 *καὶ πρῶτον μὲν τὸν Περικλέα σκεψώμεθα, ἐπειδὴ καὶ*
πρῶτον ἐξετάζειν ἐκεῖνον ἐπεχείρησεν, εἰ ἄρα ἄξιος
ἀνὴρ[3] *ἀκοῦσαι ταῦτα, ἢ τῶν ἰδίων ἕνεκα ἢ τῆς πολι-*
12 *τείας. ἐκεῖνος τοίνυν λέγεται βιῶναι μὲν οὕτω σεμνῶς*
ὥστε μηδὲν τῶν προφητῶν καὶ τῶν ἱερέων τὸν ἐκείνου
βίον διαφέρειν, οὕτω δὲ εἶναι σώφρων ὥστε καὶ βα-
δίζειν τεταγμένα καὶ τὴν ὀρθὴν ὁδὸν σῴζειν κατὰ τὴν
παροιμίαν, διαίτης δὲ τάξιν τὴν μέσην προῃρῆσθαι,
μήτε ὑπερήφανον μήτε ἀνελεύθερον, ὥσπερ τοὺς
πρεσβυτάτους Ἀθηναίων ὁ Πλάτωνος ὑμνεῖ λόγος.
13 *δημοτικὸς δὲ ὢν τῇ προαιρέσει καὶ πράττων ὑπὲρ τοῦ*

[3] *ἀνήρ codd.* ἁνήρ Lucarini

if he just happened to have lived before these individuals in time, or come to that if someone else from an earlier generation than them were arguing the selfsame case: would he be able to denounce Miltiades and Themistocles and the as yet unborn? Of course not.

Since then Plato's case could have been argued even 10
without any mention of these men, there was no necessity for them to be spoken ill of. What I shall now try to demonstrate is that, quite apart from the point that it would have been unseemly to speak ill of them, even if he was sure to expose them by this means, his accusations against them were in fact false as well.

Argumentation 1: Vindication of Pericles (11–127)

Turning first to Pericles, since he was the first that Plato 11
tried to show up,[8] let us consider whether he is a man who deserves to be spoken of like this, either for his private life or for his public career. He is said to have lived with such 12
dignity that his life was indistinguishable from that of a priest or the spokesman of an oracle, and to have had such self-control that he even walked in a disciplined way, in the proverbial straight line.[9] In his style of life he aimed for a middle position, avoiding both excessive pride and excessive humility, like the earliest Athenians Plato praises in his account of them.[10] In his political policy he was a 13

[8] *Grg.* 515d–16d.

[9] Pericles was supposed to have been seen only ever walking one route in Athens—from home to the Agora and the Council Chamber: Plut. *Per.* 7.4.

[10] *Critias* 112c.

πλήθους ἐναντία Θουκυδίδῃ πλεῖστον τῆς ἀγοραίου προπετείας καὶ κομψότητος ἀποσχεῖν, ὅς γε οὐδὲ γελῶν οὐδ' ὑφ' ἑνὸς πώποτε ὀφθῆναι, ἀλλὰ τῆς μὲν πολιτείας τῇ φυλακῇ καὶ τῷ τὸ ἴσον τοῖς ἄλλοις ἔχων ἀνέχεσθαι κοινὸς εἴπερ τις ἀνθρώπων εἶναι, τῷ δὲ ἀξιώματι τῆς γνώμης καὶ τῷ μὴ τῶν αὐτῶν ἡττᾶσθαι τοῖς πολλοῖς ὀλίγοις καταλιπεῖν ἐγγὺς ἐλθεῖν ἑαυτοῦ.

14 χρημάτων τοίνυν τοσοῦτον γενέσθαι κρείττων ὥσθ'— ὅτι μὲν καὶ τοὺς ἀγροὺς ἠφίει τῇ πόλει, παρίημι, μή τις ἄρα εἴπῃ ὡς φόβῳ τῆς διαβολῆς † εἶδεν αὐτό †[4] ἐδόκει γὰρ ὥσπερ ἄλλο τι καὶ τοῦτο σύμβολον τοῦ Περικλέους εἶναι, τὸ ὑπερφρονεῖν χρημάτων,[5] ὥστε καὶ αὐτὸς ποτὲ ἐν τῷ δήμῳ παρρησιαζόμενος καὶ λέγων περὶ τῶν αὐτῷ προσόντων ἀγαθῶν ἕν τι καὶ τοῦτο ἐν πρώτοις ἐτίθει τὴν περὶ ταῦτα μεγαλοψυ-

15 χίαν. οὕτω δ' ἦν παραπλήσιος κατὰ τὸν βίον καὶ τὴν πολιτείαν καὶ τοσοῦτον ἀπεῖχεν τοῦ ζῆν πρὸς τὰς ἑτέρων ἡδονὰς ὥστε φασὶν οἱ γράψαντες περὶ αὐτοῦ διδασκάλου τάξιν πρὸς παῖδας πρὸς τοὺς Ἀθηναίους αὐτὸν ἔχειν, ὥστε ἀπόντος μὲν Περικλέους ἐν ἀταξίᾳ πολλῇ καὶ ῥαθυμίᾳ τὴν ἐκκλησίαν εἶναι πολλάκις, φανέντος δὲ εὐθὺς μεταβάλλεσθαι καὶ σωφρονίζεσθαι πρὸς τὴν ὄψιν, ὥσπερ δεδιότας μή τι γνοίη Πε-

16 ρικλῆς ὧν ἡμάρτανον. ὃ δέ φασιν ὑπάρξαι Σωκράτει σοφιστῶν διαφερόντως, τοῦτ' ἐκείνῳ δημαγωγῶν·

[4] *crucibus notat* Trapp εἶκεν Behr εἶξεν Lenz *lacunam post* διαβολῆς Pasquali [5] τὸ ὑπερφρονεῖν χρημάτων *del.* Behr

friend of the people and opposed Thucydides on their
behalf, but could not have been further from the impetu-
osity and cleverness of the forensic orator—not a single
person ever saw him even so much as laugh. In his watch-
ful care for the state and his acceptance of an equal share
with everyone else, he was a man of the people if anyone
ever was, but in the value of his intellect and his freedom
from the failings of the majority of mankind he let few
indeed rival him. He was so indifferent to material wealth 14
that—well, I forbear to mention that he even gave up his
estates to the city,[11] in case anyone should say that it was
in fear of hostile comments . . . . . this too,[12] contempt for
material possessions, was famed as yet another of Pericles'
hallmarks, to such an extent that once, in the course of a
frank speech in the Assembly in which he was talking
about the blessings he enjoyed, he himself listed high-
mindedness in this regard as among the most prominent
of them. So consistent was he in his personal life and his 15
political conduct, and so far was he from living so as to
please anyone else, that those who wrote about him say
that he played the role of schoolmaster to the Athenians'
children: when Pericles was away, the Assembly frequently
relapsed into chaos and idleness, but when he turned up
it immediately changed and put on a sober appearance, as
if they were afraid that Pericles would find out about what
they had been doing wrong. The quality that they say 16
marked Socrates out from the sophists marked him out

[11] Thuc. 2.13.1.

[12] The dots here indicate an unresolved textual problem (*εἶδεν αὐτό* looks wrong, and some words may also have dropped out), but the overall sense of the sentence is clear.

ἐπαρθέντα μὲν γὰρ τὸν δῆμον καὶ μεῖζον φρονήσαντα δεινότατον εἶναι συστεῖλαι καὶ καθελεῖν, ἀθυμήσαντα δὲ καὶ ταπεινωθέντα ἀναγαγεῖν αὖ τοῖς λόγοις καὶ μεστὸν ἐλπίδων ποιῆσαι, ὥσπερ ἐκεῖνος εἰώθει περὶ τοὺς νέους ποιεῖν.

17 συνελόντι δ' εἰπεῖν σχῆμα τῆς πόλεως ἦν Περικλῆς, οὐ δουλεύων ταῖς τῶν πολλῶν ἐπιθυμίαις, ἀλλ' αὐτὸς ἄρχων τῶν πολλῶν, οὐδ' ὅ τι δόξειεν ἐκείνοις, τοῦτο λέγειν ἀξιῶν, ἀλλ' ὅ τι δόξειεν αὐτῷ, τοῦτ' ἐκείνους πράττειν ἐπαναγκάζων· οὐδ' ἐν κόλακος μοίρᾳ προσκείμενος, ἀλλ' οὐδαμοῦ τοῖς κόλαξι πάροδον τὸ καθ' αὑτὸν διδούς, τῇ μὲν χρηστότητι καὶ ταῖς ἐπιεικείαις ἐν πατρὸς ὢν τάξει τῷ δήμῳ, τῷ δὲ καθείργειν ἅπαντας καὶ πάνθ' ὑφ' αὑτὸν ἔχειν πλέον ἢ τύραννος. ἐξ ὧν, ὡς ἔοικεν, ἔξεστιν σαφῶς ἰδεῖν ὅτι εἴ τις ἄλλος καὶ Περικλῆς ἑκὼν δίκαιος. οὐδαμοῦ γὰρ τὴν πλεονεξίαν ἀντὶ τῶν νόμων ἠγάπησεν, οὐδὲ ὅπως μείζων τῆς τάξεως ἔσται προὐνοήθη, παρὸν αὐτῷ μᾶλλον παντὸς Πεισιστράτου· ἀλλ' ἦν παραπλήσιος κατέχοντι τὴν ἀκρόπολιν ἐπὶ τῷ σῴζειν τοὺς νόμους καὶ τῷ πάντας
18 εὖ ποιεῖν ἐκ μέσου. καίτοι εἰ τὸν Ἀρχέλαον κακίζεις ὡς ἄθλιον καὶ κακοδαίμονα, ὅτι οὐδαμόθεν προσῆκον αὐτῷ τὴν τυραννίδα ἐκτήσατο, ὑπερβὰς τὸ δίκαιον καὶ διαφθείρας οὓς ἥκιστα εἰκὸς ἦν, ᾧ γε ἐξὸν ἐκείνῳ ὁμοίως τυραννεῖν, εἴπερ ἐβούλετο, οὐ ταῦτα ἔδοξεν, ἀλλὰ τοὺς νόμους καὶ τὸ δίκαιον πλείονος ἄξια τοῦ κέρδους ἐποιήσατο, πῶς οὐ τούτῳ συγχαίρειν εἰκὸς ἦν;

from the demagogues: he had the knack, to the highest degree, of calming the demos down and reining it in when it was elated and overreaching itself, and of reviving it with his eloquence and filling it with fresh hope when it was despondent and low, just as Socrates used to do with the young.

In sum, Pericles was the city's fair face: he was not a 17
slave to the desires of the masses, but their ruler; he did not think it was his duty to repeat their views in his speeches, but instead forced them to act in accordance with his; he did not cling to their side like a sycophant, but instead did all he could to prevent sycophants gaining access to them. In his goodness and his decency he was like a father to the people, but in his ability to restrain them all and to keep everything under his control, he was a tyrant and more. All of which, it would seem, makes it plain to see that Pericles was a spontaneously just man if anyone ever was. At no time did he prefer personal gain to legal propriety, nor did he ever plan to rise above his proper rank, even though he had more of an opportunity to do so than any Pisistratus; rather, he was like someone who had seized control of the Acropolis in order to preserve the
laws and do good to all in common. Plato, if you abuse 18
Archelaus as a miserable wretch, because he transgressed the bounds of justice and destroyed those it was least fitting for him to destroy,[13] how could it not be fitting to congratulate a man who, though he had the opportunity to play the tyrant in a similar way, if he had wanted to, nevertheless counted law and justice as more important than personal profit?

[13] *Grg.* 470d–71d, 479d–e.

19 εἰ μὲν τοίνυν περὶ ἄλλου του πράγματος ἢ δόγματος συνέβαινεν εἶναι τὸν λόγον, οὐδ᾽ ἂν αὐτὸς ᾤμην δεῖν καταφεύγειν εἰς μάρτυρας, ἀλλ᾽ ἐπ᾽ ἐμαυτοῦ δεικνύναι τἀληθὲς ὅπως ἔχει· ἐπεὶ δὲ ὑπὲρ ἀνδρῶν πάλαι γεγενημένων ἐξέτασις πρόκειται, ποῖοί τινες ἦσαν καὶ τίνα τάξιν τῆς πολιτείας προείλοντο, δεῖ δή τινος, ὦ Πλάτων, καὶ μάρτυρος, ὦ τῶν μαρτύρων ὑπερορῶν, αὐτὸς δ᾽ οὐδέποτ᾽ ἂν φωραθεὶς οἶμαι προσχρώμενος
20 οὐδενί. τοὺς μὲν οὖν ἄλλους ἅπαντας παραλείψω, πολλοὺς ἂν ἔχων εἰπεῖν, ἕνα δὲ ἀρκοῦντα παρέξομαι, Θουκυδίδην τὸν Ὀλόρου· ὃς οὐ μόνον τῇ τῶν λόγων δυνάμει καὶ σεμνότητι, ἀλλὰ καὶ τῇ τῶν πραγμάτων ἀκριβείᾳ πλεῖστον προέχειν τῶν συγγραφέων δοκεῖ.
21 φέρε δὴ τί τῷ Περικλεῖ μαρτυρεῖ καὶ ποῖόν τινά φησι γενέσθαι τοὺς τρόπους αὐτόν, καὶ πῶς ἄγειν τὸν δῆμον; ἡ γὰρ ἐκείνου φωνὴ γένοιτ᾽ ἂν ἡμῖν ὥσπερ ἂν εἰ αὐτὸν ἐν ὀφθαλμοῖς εἴχομεν τὸν Περικλέα καὶ συνόντες ἑωρῶμεν ὁποῖός τις ἦν.

> ὅσον τε γὰρ χρόνον προὔστη τῆς πόλεως ἐν τῇ εἰρήνῃ μετρίως ἐξηγεῖτο καὶ ὡς ἀσφαλῶς διεφύλαξεν αὐτήν, καὶ ἐγένετο ἐπ᾽ αὐτοῦ μεγίστη· ἐπειδὴ δὲ ὁ πόλεμος κατέστη, ὁ δὲ φαίνεται καὶ ἐν τούτῳ προγνοὺς τὴν δύναμιν. ἐπεβίω δὲ δύο ἔτη καὶ ἓξ μῆνας· καὶ ἐπειδὴ ἀπέθανεν, ἐπὶ πλέον ἔτι ἐγνώσθη ἡ πρόνοια αὐτοῦ εἰς τὸν

---

[14] *Grg.* 471e–72c.

3. IN DEFENSE OF THE FOUR

If we were discussing some other matter or other rep- 19
utations, even I would not think it necessary to resort to
witnesses, but would take it that I should demonstrate
from my own unaided resources what the true state of
affairs was. But since the task before us is to review the
lives of men who lived long ago, so as to establish what sort
of people they were and what political arrangements they
made it their policy to pursue, then we do in fact need
some kind of witness, Plato—you who scorn witnesses,[14]
and I am sure would never be caught out using one yourself! There are many I could mention, but I will leave all 20
the others to one side, and produce just one who will be
quite sufficient: Thucydides son of Olorus, who is held to
be preeminent by far among historians not only for the
power and dignity of his words, but also for the precision
of his material. What evidence does he give concerning 21
Pericles: what sort of character does he say he had, and
how does he say he led the people? As he speaks to us in
his own words, it will be as if we had Pericles himself before our eyes and could see from direct acquaintance what
sort of a person he was:[15]

> For as long as he was in charge of the city in peacetime, he led her with moderation and kept her safe and secure, and she grew great under his leadership. And when the war broke out, here too he clearly estimated her power correctly. He survived its outbreak by two years and six months; and when he died, his foresight in relation to the war was even

[15] Thuc. 2.65.5–11 (with some minor orthographic and other divergences from the text in our manuscripts of Thucydides).

πόλεμον. ὁ μὲν γὰρ ἡσυχάζοντάς τε καὶ τὸ ναυτικὸν θεραπεύοντας καὶ ἀρχὴν μὴ ἐπικτωμένους ἐν τῷ πολέμῳ μηδὲ τῇ πόλει κινδυνεύοντας ἔφη περιέσεσθαι· οἱ δὲ ταῦτά τε πάντα εἰς τοὐναντίον ἔπραξαν καὶ ἄλλα ἔξω τοῦ πολέμου δοκοῦντα εἶναι κατὰ τὰς ἰδίας φιλοτιμίας καὶ ἴδια κέρδη κακῶς ἔς τε σφᾶς αὐτοὺς καὶ τοὺς συμμάχους ἐπολίτευσαν, ἃ κατορθούμενα μὲν τοῖς ἰδιώταις τιμὴ καὶ ὠφέλεια μᾶλλον ἦν, σφαλέντα δὲ τῇ πόλει εἰς τὸν πόλεμον βλάβη καθίστατο. αἴτιον δὲ ἦν ὅτι ἐκεῖνος μὲν δυνατὸς ὢν τῷ τε ἀξιώματι καὶ τῇ γνώμῃ, χρημάτων τε διαφανῶς ἀδωρότατος γενόμενος κατεῖχε τὸ πλῆθος ἐλευθέρως καὶ οὐκ ἤγετο μᾶλλον ὑπ' αὐτοῦ ἢ αὐτὸς ἦγεν, διὰ τὸ μὴ κτώμενος ἐξ οὐ προσηκόντων τὴν δύναμιν πρὸς ἡδονὴν λέγειν, ἀλλ' ἔχων ἐπ' ἀξιώσει καὶ πρὸς ὀργὴν ἀντειπεῖν. ὁπότε γοῦν αἴσθοιτό τι αὐτοὺς παρὰ καιρὸν ὕβρει θαρσοῦντας, λέγων κατέπλησσεν ἐπὶ τὸ φοβεῖσθαι, καὶ δεδιότας αὖ ἀλόγως ἀντικαθίστη πάλιν ἐπὶ τὸ θαρσεῖν· ἐγίγνετο δὲ λόγῳ μὲν δημοκρατία, ἔργῳ δ' ὑπὸ τοῦ πρώτου ἀνδρὸς ἀρχή. οἱ δ' ὕστεροι ἴσοι μᾶλλον αὐτοὶ πρὸς ἀλλήλους ὄντες καὶ ὀρεγόμενοι τοῦ πρῶτος ἕκαστος γίγνεσθαι ἐτράποντο καθ' ἡδονὰς

more clearly recognized. For he had said that they would be victorious if they bided their time and looked after their navy and neither tried to add to their empire in the course of the war, nor took any risks with the city's safety. But they did the exact opposite in every regard, and in other matters which they thought were unrelated to the war were led by personal ambition and personal gain to pursue policies detrimental both to themselves and to their allies, which when successful were a source of advancement and profit to individuals rather than to the city, and when they failed only damaged the city's capacity to fight. The reason for this was that Pericles, because of the power he wielded both from his reputation and from his intelligence, and his manifest and total incorruptibility by bribery, kept the masses in check by his frank speaking. It was not they who led him but he who led them, since he did not speak so as to please them in an effort to acquire power by improper means, but could actually contradict them angrily because of the power he possessed on the strength of his reputation. At all events, whenever he saw that their arrogance had carried them into an inappropriately confident mood, he would use his speeches to jolt them into a more fearful frame of mind, and then again when they were apprehensive he would restore their confidence. This was nominally a democracy, but in actual fact supreme power rested with the first citizen. His successors were more on a level with each other, and as each of them grasped for first position they tended to entrust public policy to

τῷ δήμῳ τὰ πράγματα ἐνδιδόναι, ἐξ ὧν ἄλλα τε πολλὰ ὡς ἐν μεγάλῃ πόλει καὶ ἀρχὴν ἐχούσῃ ἡμαρτήθη καὶ ὁ ἐς Σικελίαν πλοῦς.

22 εἶτα ἐπὶ τούτοις τὸ ἀκροτελεύτιόν ἐστιν

τοσοῦτον τῷ Περικλεῖ ἐπερίσσευσεν τότε, ἀφ' ὧν αὐτὸς προέγνω, καὶ πάνυ ἂν ῥᾳδίως περιγενέσθαι τὴν πόλιν Πελοποννησίων αὐτῶν τῷ πολέμῳ.

23 ταῦθ' ὑπὲρ τῆς Περικλέους προαιρέσεως καὶ πολιτείας ἁνὴρ[6] διεξέρχεται, πρῶτον μὲν κατ' αὐτὸν ἐκεῖνον γεγονὼς καὶ συγγεγονώς, οὐχ ὥσπερ Πλάτων οὐδὲ ἰδὼν αὐτὸν φαίνεται· ἔπειτ' οὐ φιλονικίας ἕνεκεν οὐδεμιᾶς, οὐδ' εἰς ἀγῶνος χρείαν, οὐδὲ εἰς ἓν ὃ προὔθετο πάντα ἀναφέρων, ἀλλ' ἐν ἱστορίᾳ καὶ διηγήσει τἀληθὲς ἁπλῶς οὑτωσὶ παραδιδούς, ὥσπερ ὅταν περὶ τῆς Πελοποννησίων εἰσβολῆς, ἤ τινος ἄλ-
24 λου τῶν ἐφ' αὐτοῦ διηγῆται. εἰ μὲν τοίνυν ἠμφισβητεῖτο τῷ Θουκυδίδῃ περὶ τούτων, ἄλλος ἂν ἦν λόγος· διδόντας δὲ καὶ πειθομένους ἀναγκαίως τοιοῦτον γενέσθαι τὸν Περικλέα, ποῦ τῶν βλασφημιῶν τούτων εἰκὸς ἀξιοῦν, ὡς διάκονος ἀντὶ προστάτου καὶ τῶν ὀψοποιῶν οὐδὲν ἦν βελτίων οὐδ' ἐπιτηδειότερος χρῆ-
25 σθαι πόλει; πολλοῦ μένταν ἄξιον ἦν κολακεία, εἰ Περικλεῖ τοῦτ' ἦν ἐπενεγκεῖν τὸ πρόσρημα· ἐπεὶ σὺ μὴ

[6] ἁνήρ Dindorf ὁ ἀνήρ *vel* ἀνήρ *codd.*

> popular whim, resulting in a long series of mistakes of the kind that a great city with an empire to govern was liable to, culminating in the Sicilian Expedition.

He then puts the finishing touch to his account with these words:[16] 22

> Such was the position of strength that Pericles then enjoyed, on the basis of which he foresaw that Athens would easily come out on top of the Peloponnesians on their own in the war.

This is what this author has to tell us about Pericles' policy and political record. Note first that, unlike Plato who clearly never even saw him, Thucydides was Pericles' contemporary and had personal dealings with him, and secondly that he was not writing out of any sense of rivalry, or to suit the needs of an argument, nor tailoring everything to suit a single personal objective, but recording the plain and simple truth in a historical narrative, as for example when he tells the story of the Peloponnesian invasion,[17] or of any of the other events that took place during 23
his lifetime. Now, if the truth of Thucydides' account were in dispute, it would be another story; but since everyone concedes and is convinced that Pericles necessarily was that sort of person, how can it possibly be reasonable to think that he deserves those insults, to the effect that he was a servant rather than a leader and no better than a 24
caterer and unfit to govern a city? "Flattery" would indeed be something enormously valuable, if the word could properly be used of Pericles. By all means do not attribute 25

[16] Thuc. 2.65.13. [17] Thuc. 2.18–23.

μόριον μόνον κολακείας αὐτῷ προσθῇς, ἀλλὰ καὶ πᾶσαν τὴν κολακείαν φέρων ἀνάθες, καὶ νὴ Δί', εἰ βούλει, τὴν ἰδέαν αὐτήν, ἐφ' ἣν πάντα ἀνάγεις, ἐὰν δείξῃς ὡς ὅτῳ ταῦτα ὑπῆρχεν, τῇ Θεαρίωνος καὶ Μιθαίκου τύχῃ συνεκεκλήρωτο, καὶ τούτων ἀντίστροφος ἦν τὰ πολιτικά. ἀλλ' ἴσως οἱ κόλακες πρότερον τἀληθῆ φανοῦνται λέγοντες ἢ ἡμεῖς, εἴ τι τοιοῦτον ἐκείνῳ προφέρειν ἀξιοῖμεν.

26 *φέρε δὴ πόθεν αὐτῷ πᾶς οὗτος ὁ λόγος ὡρμήθη καὶ πόθεν εἰς τὰς βλασφημίας τὰς κατὰ τῶν ἀνδρῶν ἀφίκετο; ἴσως οὐ χεῖρον ὡς πρὸς παρόντα καὶ συνόντα ποιήσασθαι τοὺς λόγους, ἀναμιμνήσκοντας*[7] *οὑτωσί· ἔφησθα μὴ χρῆναι τὸν ἀγαθὸν πολίτην τὰς ἐπιθυμίας ἐκ παντὸς τρόπου ζητεῖν ἀποπιμπλάναι, μήτ' αὐτὸν ἑαυτοῦ μήτε τῶν πολιτῶν, μηδὲ τοῦτον ὅρον τῆς εὐδαιμονίας τίθεσθαι, ἀλλὰ τὰ βέλτιστα ἀντὶ τῶν ἡδίστων προαιρεῖσθαι· μηδὲ γὰρ εἶναι τὸ ἡδὺ πάντως ἀγαθόν, μηδ' αὖ τὸ ἀγαθὸν τοῦ ἡδέος χάριν, ἀλλὰ τὸ ἡδὺ τοῦ ἀγαθοῦ χρῆναι διώκειν. οὐ ταῦτα κυκλεῖς ἄνω καὶ κάτω; καλῶς γε ποιῶν, ὦ ἑταῖρε, τὸ σὸν δὴ τοῦτο, καὶ τἀληθῆ λέγων. οὐδεὶς ἀντερεῖ μέχρι τούτου, οὔκουν ὅστις γε μὴ κἀμοί. ὅρα*
27 *δή, τάχα γὰρ ἄν τι καὶ ἀλλοῖον ἐκβαίη. Περικλέους*

[7] *ἀναμιμνήσκοντας* Oxon. Coll. Nov. 259 Dindorf *ἀναμιμνήσκοντας αὐτά cett. ἀναμιμνήσκοντας αὐτόν* Reiske

just a part of flattery to him, but go and credit him with the whole thing,[18] and come to that, if you want, with the Form itself, to which you refer everything,[19] if you can really show that the man who had these qualities belonged to the same station in life as Thearion and Mithaecus,[20] and was their counterpart in politics. Actually, you might perhaps catch flatterers telling the truth sooner than me, if I were to think fit to bring any such charge against him.

So where did this whole argument of Plato's start from, 26
and how did he arrive at the insults that he hurled at these men? It might not be a bad idea to address him as if he were here with us, and remind him in the following terms. Plato, you said that the good politician should not seek to fulfill desires at all costs, either his own or those of the citizenry, or to make this the definition of happiness, but rather to prioritize what is for the best over what gives the greatest pleasure, because what gives pleasure is not in all cases good, and one should pursue the pleasant for the sake of the good, rather than the good for the sake of the pleasant. Is this not what you keep repeating over and over?[21] You are quite right to do so, my friend, to quote your own phrase back at you,[22] and you are telling the truth. No one will gainsay you thus far, at any rate not
without gainsaying me as well. But be careful, the result 27

[18] *Grg.* 464b–e. [19] This is a reference to the importance of the so-called "theory of Forms" to Plato's thinking in general, rather than to any specific passage from the *Gorgias*.

[20] A famous Athenian baker and a famous Sicilian chef, mentioned together in *Grg.* 518b. [21] See especially *Grg.* 506c–8a, where Plato makes Socrates sum up the whole course of the argument up to that point. [22] *Grg.* 473a.

μοι λέγεις, ὦ ἄριστε, βίον καὶ πολιτείαν, ὅταν ταῦτα λέγῃς, καὶ οὐκ ἐλέγχεις τὸν ἄνδρα, ἀλλ᾽ ἐπιψηφίζεις, ὡς αὐτὸς καλεῖς, καὶ παρὸν αὐτῷ χρῆσθαι μάρτυρι τῶν λόγων μεθίστης οὐκ οἶδ᾽ ὅπως εἰς τοὺς ἀντιδίκους τὸν ἄνδρα. ἃ γὰρ σὺ διδάσκεις τῷ λόγῳ, ταῦτα ἐπὶ τῶν ἔργων ἐκεῖνος δείξας πρότερος φαίνεται· ὥστ᾽ εἰ μηδὲν προσέθηκας, ἀλλ᾽ ἐν τούτοις ἔστης, πᾶς τις ἂν εὗρεν ἐκ τῶν εἰρημένων τὸν Περικλέα, ὥσπερ τοὺς ἀπὸ τῶν γνωρισμάτων ἐν τοῖς δράμασιν.

28 σκόπει γὰρ πάλιν ἐξ ἀρχῆς ὥσπερ νόμον. οὐ χρὴ τὰς ἐπιθυμίας θεραπεύειν οὐδ᾽ εἰς ἀπέραντον ἐᾶν προϊέναι, ἀλλὰ κρατεῖν τῶν ἡδονῶν τόν γε δὴ χρηστὸν καὶ σώφρονα, καὶ τοὺς πολίτας μὴ συνεθίζειν τὸ
29 πλέον ζητεῖν[8] ἔχειν. ὁ τοίνυν Περικλῆς οὕτως ἦν ἀπὸ πολλοῦ τοῦ δουλεύειν ταῖς ἐπιθυμίαις ἢ τὸ πρὸς ἡδονὴν ζητεῖν ἢ πρὸς πλεονεξίαν, ἀλλὰ μὴ πρὸς τὸ βέλτιστον ἄγειν, ὥστ᾽ ἀπ᾽ αὐτῶν τῶν ἐναντιωτάτων φαίνεται τὴν δόξαν λαβών. αὐτός τε γὰρ τοῦ πλείονος τοσοῦτον ὑπερεῖδεν, ὅσον πλεῖστον ἐξῆν, τῇ τε πόλει συνεβούλευεν μήτε ἀρχὴν ἐπικτᾶσθαι μήτε ἔξω τῶν ἀναγκαίων μηδὲν πραγματεύεσθαι, ἀλλ᾽ ἡσυχαζούσῃ
30 τὸν πόλεμον διαφέρειν. καίτοι ὅτε τὸν πόλεμον μεθ᾽ ἡσυχίας παρῄνει διαφέρειν, σχολῇ γ᾽ ἂν ἄλλως ἐπέτρεψεν πολυπραγμονεῖν εἰκῇ. καὶ μὴν αὐτός γε ἐν τάξει ζῆν, οὐχ ὡς ἥδιστα, προείλετο, καὶ τὸν δῆμον

[8] ζητεῖν *del.* Behr

might be something other than what you want. It is Pericles' life and policies you are describing to me, my dear fellow, when you say this. You are not showing the man up but, as you yourself put it,[23] voting in his favor, and somehow or other managing to shift over into the ranks of your opponents someone who you might have used as a witness in support of your words. The lessons you teach in theory, he had clearly applied in real life before you; so if you had added nothing more, but stopped with this, everyone would have identified Pericles from your words, as if in a recognition scene in a play.

Because look at the matter again from the beginning 28
as if you were scrutinizing a law. The good, self-controlled
man, you insist, should not pander to desires or allow them
to increase without limit, but should instead keep pleasure
under firm control, and he should not let his fellow citizens
grow accustomed to seeking to have more. Well, Pericles 29
was so far from being a slave to desire, or from seeking out
what conduced to pleasure or gain rather than leading his
charges toward what was for the best, that he quite clearly
won his reputation from the exact opposite. He himself
had the most complete disdain for wealth that there could
be, and he advised his city not to add to its empire or take
on any projects beyond what it had to, but instead to conduct the war throughout in a defensive posture. And given 30
that his advice was to carry the war through to its end in a
defensive posture, he would hardly have given them license for any other kinds of random meddling either. He
himself chose to live an orderly life, rather than one in
pursuit of maximum pleasure, and he used to restrain the

[23] *Grg.* 474a, 476a.

31 εἴ ποτ᾽ αἴσθοιτο ὑβρίζοντα κατεῖχεν. πῶς ἄν τις μᾶλλον τοῖς Πλάτωνος λόγοις πειθόμενος φανερὸς γένοιτο, εἰ χρὴ τοῖς Πλάτωνος φῆσαι πείθεσθαι τὸν τοσοῦτον πρότερον Πλάτωνος, ἢ πῶς ἂν Πλάτων μᾶλλον ἐλεγχθείη τἀναντία αὐτὸς ἑαυτῷ λέγων ἢ εἰ φαίνοιτο ἅμα τ᾽ ἀξιῶν μὴ πρὸς ἡδονὴν μηδὲ ἐν κόλακος μοίρᾳ τοῖς δήμοις ὁμιλεῖν, ἀλλὰ πρὸς τὸ βέλτιστον, καὶ Περικλέα κακίζων, ὃς οὐ πρὸς ἡδονήν, ἀλλὰ ἀπὸ τῆς ὀρθοτάτης ἀεὶ γνώμης ὡμίλει; ὅμοιον γὰρ ἐμοὶ δοκεῖ ποιεῖν ὥσπερ ἂν εἰ προειπὼν τοῖς ἀνθρώποις ὅτι οὕτω χρὴ προΐστασθαι τῶν πόλεων, ὡς Περικλέα ποτὲ τῶν Ἀθηναίων ἑωρᾶτε, εἶτ᾽ ἀπηγόρευεν
32 πάλιν μὴ οὕτως ὥσπερ ἐκεῖνος προΐστασθαι. φαίνεται γὰρ βουλομένῳ σκοπεῖν ὀρθῶς κἀν τοῖς λόγοις κἀν τοῖς ἔργοις τὰ κεφάλαια τοῦ διαλόγου πεπληρωκὼς ἁνὴρ,[9] λέγω τοῖς μὲν λόγοις οἷς διεξῄει πρὸς τὸ πλῆθος ἑκάστοτε, τοῖς δὲ ἔργοις ἅ τε αὐτὸς ἐπὶ τοῦ βίου τοῦ καθ᾽ ἡμέραν ἐπεδείκνυτο, ἄξια τῆς παρρησίας ταύτης καὶ κακῶν ὧν ἐπὶ τῶν ἐκείνου καιρῶν ἀπέσχετο ἡ πόλις. μέχρι μὲν γὰρ ἐδημηγόρει Περικλῆς καὶ καθεῖργε τὸ πλῆθος, οὔτ᾽ εἰς Σικελίαν ἀποστόλους ἔπεμπον Ἀθηναῖοι οὔτε μακροὺς καὶ ἀνηνύτους τοῦ πολέμου κύκους περιεβάλλοντο, ἀλλὰ καὶ

[9] ἁνήρ Dindorf ἀνήρ *codd.*

people if he ever saw them growing too full of themselves. How could anyone more clearly conform to Plato's defini- 31
tion—if we are to say that a man who lived so long before Plato can conform to his definition—or how could Plato be more decisively convicted of contradicting himself than if he were to be clearly seen simultaneously demanding that statesmen should not deal with their peoples with hedonistic aims or in the role of flatterers, but aiming for what is best, and at the same time heaping insults on Pericles, whose dealings with his people were based consistently not on hedonistic aims, but on the rightest of right policy? It seems to me that he is doing the same as if, having first told people that statesmen ought to lead their cities in just the way you once saw Pericles leading Athens, he then turned around and said that they should not lead as he did. It is obvious to anyone who is prepared to con- 32
sider the matter that this man satisfied the main stipulations of the dialogue in both word and deed: in word in the speeches that he made to the people on each occasion, and in deed in the actions he himself performed in the day-to-day course of his life, actions which were commensurate with that frank speaking, and on the same scale as the ills from which the city was preserved in his time.[24] Because for as long as Pericles spoke in the Assembly and restrained the mass of the people, the Athenians sent no expeditionary force to Sicily and involved themselves in no great, interminable, and roundabout schemes of military activity, but accepted that even emerging from their

[24] Aristides' striving for rhetorical neatness yields a rather contorted point: the scale of the disasters that Pericles' prudence saved Athens from is proof of the magnitude of his achievement.

τοῦ τείχους ἔξω προϊέναι περίεργον ἐπείθοντο εἶναι καὶ οὐκ ἀσφαλὲς οὐδὲ εἰδότων τὰ ὑπάρχοντα σῴζειν.

33 ἐπειδὴ δὲ ἐτελεύτησεν ἐκεῖνος, ὠνειροπόλουν μὲν Σικελίαν, ἐφίεντο δὲ Ἰταλίας, ὠρέγοντο δὲ Καρχηδόνος καὶ Λιβύης, πάντας δὲ ἀνθρώπους περιεσκόπουν, ἤρκει δὲ οὐδὲν αὐτοῖς, μακροτέραν δὲ τοῦ πολέμου τὴν παρενθήκην ἐποιήσαντο. ὁ δὲ ταῦτα πείθων ἦν, ὦ Πλάτων τε καὶ Σώκρατες, ὁ ὑμέτερος κοινωνὸς μὲν οὐκ ἔστιν εἰπεῖν, ἑταῖρος δὲ καὶ αὐτὸς ἂν φαίης, μᾶλλον δὲ εἴρηκας.

34 πῶς οὖν ἄν τις ταῦτα δικαίως κατηγοροίη Περικλέους, ἢ πῶς οὐκ ἀναγκαίως Ἀλκιβιάδου, ὅστις παραλαβὼν τὴν πόλιν εἰδυῖαν ἀκούειν συμβούλων εἶθ' οὕτως ἐξέμηνεν; Περικλῆς μὲν γὰρ οἶμαι Ἀναξαγόρᾳ συγγενόμενος βελτίων ἢ κατ' ἐκεῖνον ἐγένετο, Ἀλκιβιάδης δ' ἑταίρῳ χρώμενος Σωκράτει μικρά, μᾶλλον δ' οὐδὲν ἀπώνατο τῆς συνουσίας. ὥστ' οὐκ

35 ἀνεκτὸν εἴ τις ἐκεῖνον ἐπαινῶν τούτῳ μέμφεται. Πλάτων τοίνυν ὥσπερ ἐξεπίτηδες ἐναντία τῶν ὄντων λέγων ἢ τοὺς θαυματοποιοὺς μιμούμενος οὐ μόνον Περικλέους κατηγόρηκεν ἃ μὴ προσῆκεν, ἀλλὰ καὶ δεινόν τί φησιν εἶναι, εἴ τις Ἀλκιβιάδην αἰτιάσεται τῶν αὐτῶν τούτων πραγμάτων. ἐκ δὲ τοῦ λόγου φαίνεται τῷ μὲν οὐδ' ὁτιοῦν προσῆκον τῶν αἰτιῶν, τῷ δ'

---

[25] Alcibiades: *Grg.* 519a.

[26] Pericles' association with the philosopher and natural sci-

own fortifications was superfluous and unsafe, and the action of a people who did not know how to preserve what
they already had. But when he was dead, they began to 33
dream of Sicily, to long for Italy, to reach out for Carthage and Libya; their gaze played over every people of the world, nothing was enough for them, and they made the side-show more extensive than the main conflict. The one who persuaded them to this, Plato and Socrates, was a man who cannot be said to have shared your values, but whom you yourself might—and indeed did—call your companion.[25]

How then could these charges justly be brought against 34
Pericles? And how could one escape bringing them against Alcibiades, who inherited an Athens that knew how to listen to its advisers and then drove it mad in this way? Pericles associated with Anaxagoras and, I think, attained a higher level of virtue than him;[26] Alcibiades by contrast, although a companion of Socrates, derived little or rather no profit from the association.[27] So it is intolerable for
someone to praise the latter and blame the former. Yet 35
Plato, as if deliberately turning the truth of the situation on its head or imitating a conjuror, not only charged Pericles with actions that had nothing to do with him, but also says that it is outrageous for anyone to bring the very same charges against Alcibiades.[28] But the argument clearly establishes that the charges do not apply to the former in the

entist Anaxagoras is mentioned by Plato at *Phdr.* 270a and described in more detail in Plut. *Per.* 5.

[27] A fundamental point for defenders of Socrates from Plato *Symp.* and [Plato] *Alc. I* onward, here cleverly turned to his own critical purposes by Aristides.

[28] *Grg.* 519a.

οὐκ ἐλάχιστον μέρος. ὁ μὲν γὰρ ἡσυχάζοντάς τε καὶ τὸ ναυτικὸν θεραπεύοντας, τοῦτο δ' ἦν τὰ ὑπάρχοντα σῴζοντας, καὶ ἀρχὴν μὴ ἐπικτωμένους ἔφη περιέσεσθαι, ὁ δὲ τῶν τὰ πολλὰ πράττειν πεισάντων εἷς ἦν. ἐν οἷς ἄλλα τε πολλὰ καὶ ὁ εἰς Σικελίαν ἡμαρτήθη πλοῦς, ἐξ ὧν πλείους τῶν συμμάχων τοὺς πολεμίους ἐκτήσαντο καὶ τελευτῶντες ἀπήλλαξαν ὡς ἴσμεν.

36 οὔκουν ὁ Περικλῆς ἦν ὁ ποιήσας οἰδεῖν καὶ ὕπουλον εἶναι τὴν πόλιν, οὐδὲ δι' ὃν τῶν ἀρχαίων σαρκῶν, ὡς σὺ φῄς, ἐστερήθησαν, ἀλλ' ὁ τὰς ἐπιθυμίας ἐπαύξων αὐτοῖς καὶ τοῖς τῶν Ἐγεσταίων[10] χρήμασι δελεάζων καὶ τὴν Σικελικὴν τράπεζαν προξενῶν, ἅτε καὶ αὐτὸς ὢν τοιοῦτος καὶ μηδαμοῦ στῆναι τῶν ἐλπίδων ἐῶν τὸν δῆμον, ἀλλ' ἀεὶ μακρότερ' αὐτοῖς ὧν ἐβούλοντό τε καὶ ἐδέοντο ὑποτιθεὶς καὶ τἀναντία τῷ Περικλεῖ πολιτευ-

37 όμενος, μετὰ τὴν ἐκείνου τελευτήν. οὐκοῦν πρίν τινα τῶν ἀντιπάλων ἑλεῖν, ἕνα τῶν φίλων θηρεύσας ἄγεις, καὶ πέπονθας ταυτὸν τῷ Πινδάρου Πηλεῖ, ὃς τῆς τε θήρας διήμαρτεν καὶ τὸν Εὐρυτίωνα φίλτατον ὄντα ἑαυτῷ προσδιέφθειρεν. τὸ δ' αὐτὸ κἀν τοῖς ὕστερον οἶμαι Ἀδράστῳ τῷ Γορδίου φασὶ συμβῆναι.

38 ἐγὼ τοίνυν περὶ μὲν Ἀλκιβιάδου τὰ νῦν οὐδὲν δέο-

[10] Ἐγεσταίων Behr αἰγεσταίων *codd.*

---

[29] As seen above all in his speech in Thuc. 6.15–18.
[30] Thuc. 6.30–7.87.
[31] *Grg.* 518c–e.

slightest degree, whereas the greater proportion of them do apply to the latter. Because the former said that the Athenians would prevail if they remained on the defensive and looked after their fleet, that is, if they held on to what they already had, and did not try to add to their empire, whereas the latter was one of those trying to persuade them to multiply their activities.[29] Among the many mistakes this led to was the Sicilian Expedition, which won them more enemies than it did allies, and ended for them
in the manner we are all well aware of.[30] It was therefore 36
not Pericles who made the city swell up and become ulcerated, and was responsible for them, as you put it, being robbed of their old physique;[31] it was instead the man who whipped up their desires, and lured them on with the wealth of Egesta, and introduced them to Sicilian cuisine, since this was in his own nature too, and who never allowed the Athenians to call a halt in their desires, but was constantly proposing something beyond what they wanted and needed, and pursuing an opposite policy to Pericles'
after his death. Sooner than capturing one of your ene- 37
mies, then, Plato, you have hunted down and brought back one of your friends; the same thing has happened to you as to Pindar's Peleus, when he missed the wild boar and annihilated his dearest friend Eurytion into the bargain.[32] And I think they say the same thing subsequently happened to Adrastus son of Gordius.[33]

There is no need for the moment for me to say anything 38

[32] Fr. 48 Sn-M: Peleus accidentally killed his father-in-law Eurytion in the course of the Calydonian boar hunt.

[33] Hdt. 1.35: the refugee Adrastus accidentally killed Croesus' son Atys, whom he had been detailed to protect.

μαι λέγειν, ἀλλὰ καὶ τοῦθ᾽ ὑπ᾽ αὐτοῦ τοῦ λόγου προήχθην ἄκων εἰπεῖν· εἰ δὲ ἡ γεωμετρία καλὸν καὶ ἡ κατ᾽ αὐτὴν ἰσότης, καὶ δεῖ μὴ τούτων ἀμελεῖν, εὑρίσκω τὸν Περικλέα τὴν ἰσότητα κάλλιστα τιμήσαντα οὐ μόνον ἐν τοῖς ἰδίοις, ἀλλὰ κἀν τοῖς κοινοῖς. ὅσον τε γὰρ χρόνον ἐν τῇ εἰρήνῃ προὔστη, μετρίως ἐξηγεῖτο, φησὶν ὁ τἀκείνου καλῶς εἰδὼς—τοῦτο δ᾽ ἐστὶν ἐναντίον τοῦ βιαίως καὶ πλεονεκτικῶς, ὧν σὺ κατηγορεῖς—ἐπειδή τε[11] ὁ πόλεμος συνέστη, μόνος ᾔδει τί
39 πράττουσιν ὑπάρχει σωθῆναι. οὐκοῦν τῷ μὲν ἅπαντος κέρδους κρείττω παρέχειν ἑαυτὸν δικαιοσύνην ἀσκῶν δῆλος ἦν, τῷ δὲ τὸν ἐν τάξει βίον ἀντὶ τοῦ πρὸς ἡδονὴν προῃρῆσθαι σωφροσύνης πίστιν παρείχετο ἐμφανῆ, καὶ μὴν ἀνδρείας γε ἐν οἷς οὐ πρὸς χάριν οὐδ᾽ ὑποπεπτωκώς, ἀλλ᾽ ὡς οἷόν τε μάλιστα ἐλευθέρως
40 ὡμίλει τῷ δήμῳ. μόνος τοίνυν καὶ τὰ μέλλοντα ἔσεσθαι προειδὼς καὶ τοῖς παροῦσι χρήσασθαι δυνηθεὶς πῶς οὐκ ἂν σοφίας δικαίως δόξαν φέροιτο τῆς γέ που χρησιμωτάτης, εἴ τις ἀνθρωπίνως ἐθέλοι λογίζεσθαι;
41 εἶθ᾽ ὃν ἐξ ἁπάντων τῶν τῆς ἀρετῆς μορίων ὑπάρχει προσειπεῖν, ἀνδρεῖον, δίκαιον, φρόνιμον, σώφρονα, τοῦτον Πλάτων μετὰ τῶν κολάκων ἠρίθμησεν; λάλους γάρ, φησίν, Ἀθηναίους ἐποίησεν καὶ ἀργοὺς καὶ δειλοὺς καὶ φιλαργύρους, εἰς μισθοφορὰν καταστήσας.
42 περὶ μὲν δὴ λάλων, ὦ Πλάτων, καὶ ἀργῶν καὶ δειλῶν αὐτόθεν κατάβαλε,

[11] τε U *cum codd. Thuc.* δέ *cett.*

more about Alcibiades; I was induced into this against my wishes by the needs of the argument. But if geometry and geometrical equality are fine things and emphatically not to be neglected,[34] I find that Pericles had the finest respect for equality not only in his private but also in his public life. For as long as he was head of state in peacetime, he led it with moderation, as the man who knew his life well tells us—and that means the opposite of the violent and greedy manner that you accuse him of—and when war broke out he alone knew what they had to do in order to
remain safe. From his ability to rise above all forms of 39
personal gain, then, it was evident that he practiced the virtue of justice, just as in his choice of a well disciplined life rather than one devoted to pleasure he gave clear proof of self-mastery, and indeed of courage in so far as his dealings with the people were conducted not in a spirit of ingratiation and subservience, but with the highest possible degree of independence. With his unique ability both 40
to foresee the future and to manage the present, how could he fail to deserve a name for what, on the human scale of reckoning, surely counts as the most useful form of wisdom?

Was it then this man, who can have complimentary ep- 41
ithets from all the categories of moral virtue attached to him and be called brave, just, prudent, and self-mastered, that Plato numbered among the flatterers? He made the Athenians garrulous, he says,[35] and idle and cowardly and mercenary, by reducing them to the status of wage earn-
ers. This point, Plato, about their being made garrulous 42
and idle and cowardly, you should let drop on the spot,

[34] *Grg.* 508a. [35] *Grg.* 515e.

μή πού τις καὶ Τρῶας ἐγείρῃσιν θεὸς ἄλλος,

καὶ δῶμεν λαβὴν καθ' ἡμῶν αὐτῶν, προσήκουσαν μὲν ἥκιστα, ὅμως δὲ τὸ τοῦ Ὁμήρου κἀνταῦθα νικᾷ τὸ

ὁπποῖόν κ' εἴπῃσθα ἔπος, τοῖόν κ' ἐπακούσαις.

ἐγὼ μὲν γὰρ οὐδὲν ἂν εἴποιμι φλαῦρον οὐδὲ προαχθείην, μήποθ' οὕτω μανείην· ἀλλ' ἐμαυτοῦ πρότερον τὰ ἔσχατα ἂν καταγνοίην ἢ Πλάτωνα τῶν μεγίστων εὐφημιῶν ἑκὼν ἂν ἀποστερήσαιμι. ἕτεροι δ' εἰσὶν ἴσως τινὲς οἷς ἔλαττον μέλει τῆς σῆς ἀξίας, ἄλλως τε κἂν προφάσεως εὐπροσώπου λάβωνται, ὡς ὑπὲρ ἀνδρῶν οὐδ' αὐτῶν φαύλων οὐδ' ἀξίων κακῶς ἀκούειν ἀμύνονται. ἐπεὶ ὅτι γε ᾔδειν καὶ περὶ τούτων λέγειν, ὡς οὐδὲ τούτοις ἔνοχος Περικλῆς, σιωπῆσαι χαλεπώτερον ἢ πειρωμένῳ δεικνύειν εὑρεῖν ὅ τι χρὴ λέγειν.

43 *πρῶτον μὲν οὖν ὡς οὐ λάλους ἐποίησεν μέγιστον, οἶμαι, κἀνταῦθα σημεῖον τὸ μὴ ἐπὶ τῶν ἐκείνου χρόνων γενέσθαι τῇ πόλει τὴν διαβολὴν ταύτην, ἀλλ' ὕστερον ἡνίκα τὸν μὲν ἤδη λαμπρῶς ἐπόθουν, τοὺς δὲ παρόντας πλείω λαλοῦντας ἢ φρονοῦντας εὕρισκον*

---

36 *Il.* 10.511.

37 *Il.* 20.250 (also alluded to in *Or.* 2.380).

38 A somewhat contorted paragraph. Aristides observes that some people would be delighted to point out that the charge of

Lest some other god should rouse the Trojans too,[36]

and lest we should give our opponents a handle against ourselves—a wholly inappropriate handle, but here too the Homeric principle holds good that

Whatever you say, you may hear said back to you.[37]

I for my part would not want to say anything cheap, and hope never to be so mad as to be induced to; I would rather condemn myself to the most extreme punishment than willingly withhold the highest praise from Plato. But there may be others who have less regard for your worth, especially when they have the attractive excuse of defending individuals who are themselves not worthless and do not deserve to be spoken ill of. At any rate, it is harder for me to keep quiet about the fact that I know very well what to say about these charges, namely that Pericles is not liable to them either, than it would have been to find what I needed to say if I was seeking to prove them.[38]

To begin with the accusation that he made the Athe- 43
nians garrulous: the strongest proof, I think, that he did not is the fact that this slander was not directed against Athens in his own day, but only came later on, at the stage when the Athenians were beginning to feel his loss keenly, and were discovering that the politicians they actually had were better at talking than at thinking, and had not pre-

making empty babblers of the Athenians could be brought far more plausibly against the philosopher Plato than against the politician Pericles. But he is not going to score such a cheap point, even though he easily could if he chose, because he is bursting to make the more important one that neither man deserves the charge, especially not Pericles.

καὶ οὐδαμῶς τὸ τοῦ Περικλέους ἀγαθὸν σῴζοντας. ὥστ' ἐξ αὐτῶν ὧν τοὺς ὕστερον ᾐτιάσαντο καὶ ὧν ὑπὸ τῶν μετ' ἐκεῖνον διεβλήθησαν τά γ' ἐκείνου σεμνύνε-
44 ται. ὥσπερ γὰρ ἰατροῦ χρηστοῦ τελευτήσαντος καὶ κατὰ πολλὴν τὴν ἄδειαν ἤδη διαιτωμένων ὕστερον ἡ νόσος ἐπελθεῖν ἴσχυσεν. ὥστ' ἔκ γε τῶν εἰκότων οὐκ ἀφεῖσθαι μόνον τῆς αἰτίας, ἀλλὰ καὶ κατ' αὐτὸ τοῦτο μειζόνως εὐδοκιμεῖν αὐτῷ προσῆκεν ἀντὶ τοῦ μέχρι τούτου τοῦ χρόνου, ὥσπερ ἡ Διοτίμα δέκα ἔτη τῆς νόσου δυνηθεῖσα ἀναβαλέσθαι τῇ πόλει εἰς εὐεργεσίας μέρος, οἶμαι, κατέθετο καὶ οὐδεὶς ἐκείνην αἰτιᾶται τῶν ὕστερον συμβάντων, ἀλλὰ τοῦ μὲν μὴ πρότερον συμβῆναι πάντες ἂν εἰκότως, τοῦ δὲ ὅλως οὐδείς. οὐ γὰρ ἐκείνη ταῦτα ἐποίησεν, ἀλλ' [ἐκείνη ταῦτα][12] εἰς ὅσον ἐξῆν ἐκώλυσεν· ὥστ' οὐδ' ἂν συμβεβηκὸς εἴη
45 τὴν ἀρχὴν τό γε ἐκείνης μέρος. σὺ δὲ Μαντινικὴν μὲν ξένην καὶ Μιλησίαν ἐπίστασαι κοσμεῖν καὶ οὕστινας ἄν σοι δοκῇ πάνυ ῥᾳδίως μεγάλων ἠξίωσας, τῶν δὲ Ἑλλήνων τοὺς ἄκρους καὶ παρὰ πᾶσι βεβοημένους ἐν φαύλῳ καθαιρεῖς, οὐδὲν διαφερόντως ἢ εἴ τίς τινα τῶν μαγείρων ὡς ἀληθῶς, ἢ καὶ ἄλλο τι τῶν τυχόντων ἀνδραπόδων. αἴτιον δὲ οὐ τὸ ἀγνοεῖν τὴν ἀξίαν,

[12] *del.* Canter Dindorf

---

[39] Pl. *Symp.* 201d.

[40] Diotima of Mantinea is praised in *Symp.* 201d not only for delaying the plague but also for being Socrates' teacher in the

served anything of his virtue. The result of the accusations
they brought against the later figures, and of the slanders
they were subjected to by those who came after him, is
that Pericles' stock actually rises. It was as if a good doctor 44
had died, but they still carried on in a state of complete
confidence until the disease grew strong enough to attack
them again. On any reasonable reckoning, then, he ought
not only to have been acquitted of the charge, but to have
gained a still greater reputation in this regard, on the
strength of what he had achieved up to that point, just as
Diotima, when she was able to delay something of the
Plague in Athens for ten years,[39] could I believe count this
as a good service done, without anyone blaming her for
what happened subsequently. Anyone could reasonably
hold her responsible for the plague's not happening earlier, but nobody just for its happening, because she did not
bring it about, but rather delayed it as far as could be done,
so that it would not have happened at all if it had been up
to her. Plato, when it comes to a foreign woman from 45
Mantinea or Miletus, you know very well how to cry her
up,[40] since you have always found it very easy to make
great claims on behalf of anyone you please, but when it
comes to the greatest of the Greeks, men with worldwide
reputations, you bring them down and treat them like dirt,
for all the world as if someone were putting down a real-
life caterer, or some other random specimen of low-grade
humanity. The reason is not that you do not know what

science of Love (as demonstrated in *Symp.* 201e–12a). Aspasia of Miletus, Pericles' consort, is praised as Socrates' teacher in oratory at *Menex.* 235e–36a (with the evidence of her skill following in 236d–49c).

ἀλλὰ πῶς ἂν εἴποιμι εὐπρεπῶς; σφόδρα τῶν λόγων
γίγνῃ.
46 ἀλλ' ἐκεῖσε ἐπάνειμι, ὅτι πρῶτον μὲν οὐ τῶν Περικλέους καιρῶν, ἀλλὰ τῶν ὕστερόν ἐστι τὸ τῆς λαλιᾶς
ἔγκλημα τοῦτο, ὑπ' ἀνδρῶν οὐδὲν ὁμοίων ἐκείνῳ γενομένων. ἔπειτα καὶ τὸ εἰκὸς οὕτω σῴζεται, ὡς πάντες
μᾶλλον ἢ Περικλῆς ἐπηρκὼς ἂν εἴη λαλεῖν αὐτούς,
καὶ τοσοῦτον ἥττων ἐκείνου ἡ αἰτία—καὶ μηδεὶς θαυ-
μάσῃ τὸ παράδοξον—ὅσῳπερ ἀμείνων ἦν λέγειν, εἰ
δὴ τοῦτό γ' ἀληθές ἐστιν. εἰ μὲν γὰρ αὐτὸς ὅπως
ἔτυχεν τοὺς λόγους μετεχειρίζετο, ἢ κατήγαγεν εἰς
φαῦλον τὸ πρᾶγμα, ὡς παντὶ τῷ βουλομένῳ λαβεῖν
εἶναι, εἰκότως ἂν πολλοὺς ἐδόκει διαφθεῖραι καὶ πεῖσαι λαλεῖν τοῦ φρονεῖν ἀμελήσαντας, ὥσπερ οἵ τι
τῶν ῥᾳδίων ἄλλο προδείξαντες ταχέως πολλοὺς ἐπι-
47 σπῶνται. ὅτε δὲ αὐτὸς ἐν κόσμῳ καὶ νόμῳ καὶ μετὰ
παντὸς τοῦ γιγνομένου καλοῦ τοὺς λόγους ἐδείκνυεν
αὐτοὺς καὶ τὸ τοῦ Λάχητος, εἰ δὲ βούλει Πλάτωνος,
ὁμοῦ συνδιέσῳζεν, οὐδὲν χείρω τῶν λόγων τὸν βίον
παρεχόμενος, πῶς ἂν εἴη διεφθαρκὼς Ἀθηναίους, ἢ
πῶς λάλους εἶναι πεποιηκώς, ὅς γε κἂν τοῖς λόγοις
αὐτοῖς τὸ μηδὲν φαύλως μηδ' εἰκῇ τιμήσας φαίνεται;
τοὐναντίον γὰρ ἔμοιγε πᾶν αὐτοὺς ἐθίσαι δοκεῖ, μήτε
λέγειν ὅπως ἔτυχεν μηδὲν μήτε ποιεῖν ἀπὸ τοῦ πρώτου
48 παραστάντος. τριῶν γοῦν ἕν γέ τι δεῖ λελύσθαι· ἢ
γὰρ οὐδὲν φαῦλον οὐδὲ αἰσχρὸν λάλους εἶναι, ἢ Πε-

41 *Lach.* 188c–e.

they are worth, but that—how can I put this politely?—you are a prisoner of your own argument.

But I will get back to my answer. The first point is that 46
this accusation about empty talkativeness belongs not to Pericles' own times but to those of his successors, and arose over individuals who were not like him at all. Secondly, this line of reply also respects considerations of plausibility, since Pericles was the least likely of all men to incite the Athenians to empty talkativeness; the responsibility belongs to him all the less (let nobody be astonished at the paradox) insofar as he was the better speaker (granted that this is indeed true). If he had set himself about the business of speaking in any old fashion, or belittled the activity as something that all and sundry could master, he might reasonably have been thought to have corrupted large numbers of people by persuading them to babble on without regard for sense, just as those who make a display of some other easy activity rapidly draw many
others along with them. But given that in fact he delivered 47
his own oratory in a well-ordered way that respected convention and displayed all the appropriate attractiveness, and that at the same time he also observed Laches' (or, if you prefer, Plato's) principle in living a life that fully matched up to his words,[41] how could he have corrupted the Athenians and how could he have made them garrulous, since it is clear even in his very words that he valued only what had nothing trivial or inconsequential about it? In my opinion the habits he tried to inculcate into them were the exact opposite: to say nothing haphazardly, and to do nothing on the strength of the first idea to come into
their heads. The conclusion has to be one of three: either 48
that there is nothing mean and shameful about their being

ρικλῆς οὐκ ἂν εἴη λάλους πεποιηκώς, εἴπερ ἦν ἀγαθὸς λέγειν, ἢ δή τοι τό γε τρίτον, Περικλῆς οὐ δεινὸς
λέγειν, οὐδ' ὑπὲρ τοὺς ἄλλους. οὐκοῦν ὡς δεινὸς καὶ
ὡς ὑπὲρ τοὺς ἄλλους λοιπὸν ἂν εἴη διδάσκειν.

49 τίνες οὖν ἂν μᾶλλον ἀξιόχρεῳ γένοιντο ἐπαινέται
καὶ μάρτυρες τῆς ἐκείνου δεινότητος καὶ δυνάμεως ἢ
οἷς συνηθέστερον ψέγειν ἅπαντας ἢ κοσμεῖν; εἰ γὰρ
οὗτοι φανεῖεν διδόντες τὴν ψῆφον, σχολῇ γ' ἂν ἄλλος
50 τις ἀποστεροίη. ἐπὶ δ' ἄλλου μέν τινος πράγματος
σκήπτεσθαι μάρτυρι κωμῳδοδιδασκάλῳ τάχ' ἂν οὐκ
ἰσχυρὸν ἦν, εἰς δὲ λόγων κρίσιν μήποτε οὕτως σεμνὸς
γενοίμην ὥσθ' ὑπεριδεῖν τῶν ἀνδρῶν τούτων ὡς οὐδενὸς ἀξίων. λέγω δὲ ἤδη ταῦτα πρὸς οὓς ἔξεστιν.
τῶν δὲ βεβήλων ὀλίγος ὁ λόγος. πάντως οὐδὲν δεῖ
πύλας αὐτοὺς ἐπιθέσθαι τοῖς ὠσίν, ἀλλ' ἐπίκεινται
πάλαι· τοὺς δὲ λέληθε καὶ αὐτὸ τοῦτο, οὕτω παντάπασιν ἀναισθήτως ἔχουσιν καὶ τοσοῦτόν εἰσι πόρρω
τῶν ἱερῶν.

51 οὐκοῦν τῶν μαρτύρων ἡμῖν τῶν εἰς τοὺς λόγους
κεκλημένων τῷ Περικλεῖ καὶ οἷς οὐκ ἐλάχιστον μετεῖναι φαίημεν ἂν τῆς περὶ ταῦτα ἐμπειρίας, ὁ μὲν τῶν

---

42 Aristides here plays on a line from an "Orphic" poem (*Orphicorum Fragmenta* 334 Kern) also cited three times by Plutarch (*Mor.* 391d, 636d, and fr. 203): "I shall sing to those with understanding; close your doors, you who are profane." The point of insisting that these are words for those who understand the "mysteries of oratory," rather than for a lay public, is presumably that

garrulous; or that Pericles could not have made the Athenians garrulous, if he was a good speaker; or thirdly, that Pericles was not a skilled speaker and was not on a higher level than the others. What still needs to be shown, therefore, is that he was indeed a skilled speaker and was indeed on a higher level than the others.

What more creditable encomiasts and witnesses to his skill and power could there be than those who are more in the habit of censuring all and sundry than of praising them? If it were clear that these people cast their vote for Pericles, then it is hardly likely that anyone else would deny him theirs. In any other matter it might perhaps not be entirely safe to rely on comic poets as a witnesses, but where it is a question of judging verbal ability, may I never become so high and mighty as to despise these individuals as worthless. (I am saying this now to those it is permissible to address; I am not much concerned about the profane. At all events, there is no need for them to close up the doors of their ears,[42] because they are long since shut tight, and some of them do not even realize that this has happened, so completely insensible are they and so very remote from our sacraments.) 49 50

Well, one of these witnesses who we have summoned to give evidence on Pericles' eloquence, and who we might say have no inconsiderable degree of experience in such matters, has called his tongue "the greatest of all 51

Aristides does not want his invocation of comic poets in this particular case to be taken as a general seal of approval. For his otherwise disapproving attitude to comedy, see *Or.* 29, and for the idea of oratory/rhetoric as a holy mystery, compare *Orr.* 33.19–21 and 34.42–44.

Ἑλληνίδων μεγίστην τὴν ἐκείνου γλῶτταν εἴρηκεν, λέγων μὲν ἴσον τι καὶ φωνήν, ἀναμίξας δέ τι τῆς παρὰ τῆς τέχνης πικρίας τοῖς ἀπὸ τῆς ἀληθείας. ὅμως δ᾽ οὐκ ἐξέφυγεν τὸ μὴ οὐ τὰ πρῶτα δοῦναι τῷ ἀνδρί, μηδ᾽ ἐνδείξασθαι τὴν μεγαλοπρέπειαν τὴν περὶ τοὺς λόγους αὐτοῦ· ὁ δ᾽ ἀστράπτειν καὶ βροντᾶν καὶ κυκᾶν αὐτόν φησι δημηγοροῦντα. μὴ γάρ μοι τοῦτο εἴ τι μέμφεται αὐτοῦ, ἀλλ᾽ ὅσον εἰς τὸν παρόντα προσήκει λόγον τῆς μαρτυρίας λάβωμεν, ἔπειτα κἀκεῖνα μικρὸν ὕστερον, ἄν τι δέῃ, πρὸς ἡμῶν ὄντα φανήσεται. ὁ δὲ δὴ τρίτος ἄντικρυς ὥσπερ οὐδὲ κωμῳδίας οὗτός γε ποιητής, ἀλλ᾽ ὡς ἂν εἷς τῶν καλῶν κἀγαθῶν ἀνεπίφθονον αὐτῷ καὶ καθαρὰν τὴν μαρτυρίαν ἀποδέδωκε λέγων ὡς ἐκ δέκα μὲν ποδῶν ᾕρει τοὺς ῥήτορας ἐν τοῖς λόγοις, μόνου δὲ πειθώ τις ἐπεκάθιζεν ἐπὶ τοῖς χείλεσιν· πάντα δ᾽ εἶναι φλυαρίαν πρὸς ἐκεῖνον. φησὶ γοῦν οὑτωσὶ δυσχεραίνων

ῥήτωρ γάρ ἐστιν νῦν τις; ὧν γ᾽ ἐστὶν λέγειν,
ὁ Βουζύγης ἄριστος ἀλιτήριος.

οὕτως ἴσασιν οὕς τε προσήκει διασύρειν ἐπὶ τοῖς λόγοις καὶ οὓς ἄξιον θαυμάσαι.

52 ἆρ᾽ οὖν ὁ τοσοῦτον αἱρῶν τοὺς ῥήτορας, τὴν πειθὼ

[43] Cratinus, fr. 324 Kassel-Austin (cf. *Or*. 2.72).
[44] Ar. *Ach*. 531.
[45] Eupolis, fr. 102 Kassel-Austin.

tongues in Greece."[43] By "tongue" he meant the same as if he had said "voice": he was seasoning the truthful content of his remark with a dash of comic acerbity, but all the same, he did not shrink from granting our man first place or from drawing attention to the magnificence of his eloquence. Another of them said that Pericles "thundered" and "lightened" and "brought turmoil" when he spoke in public.[44] Do not bother to suggest to me that there may be an element of criticism in this; let me for the time being take from this testimony only what is relevant to my present argument, and then a little later, if necessary, it will become clear that the rest of it is actually favorable to my case too. The third witness, speaking not like a comic poet at all but like a man of quality and breeding, simply gave unimpeachable and unqualified evidence in Pericles' favor, with the declaration that when he spoke he "caught up with other orators from ten feet behind" and that with him alone "a kind of persuasion perched upon his lips," and everything else was rubbish in comparison to him.[45] At all events, he voices this complaint:

> Is there any orator now? Of those worth a mention,
> The best is blasted Bouzyges.[46]

That is how well they know which men it is appropriate to satirize for their oratory and which deserve to be admired.

So then, did the man who comprehensively defeated 52

[46] Eupolis, fr. 103 Kassel-Austin; although Aristides seems to quote these as the words of a single speaker, they should probably be divided between two. "Bouzyges" refers to the supposedly choleric Athenian politician Demostratus (cf. Ar. *Lys*. 391–97, with Henderson's notes *ad loc.*).

δὲ ἐπὶ τῶν χειλῶν ἔχων, τοσαύτης δὲ αἰδοῦς παρὰ πάντων τυγχάνων, τοιαῦτα δ᾿ ἀκηκοὼς ὑπὸ τῶν ἅπαντας ἐρευνώντων περὶ τὰ ἄλλα καὶ εἰς αὐτὸ τοῦτο κωμῳδούντων ὡς ἀδυνάτους εἰπεῖν, φλυαρίαν τινὰ καὶ λαλιὰν ἐπεδείκνυτο ἐν ταῖς ἐκκλησίαις, ἢ παντὸς ἀνδρὸς πρᾶγμα διεπράττετο, ἀλλ᾿ οὐ πολλῇ τινι τῇ περιουσίᾳ χρώμενος οὕτω διεγίγνετο, πόρρω μὲν αὐτὸς ὢν τοῦ ληρεῖν, πλεῖστον δὲ τοὺς ἄλλους ἐθίζων
53 ἀπέχειν; σκεψώμεθα γὰρ τί τῆς λαλιᾶς ἐστι καὶ τί τῶν λόγων τῶν ἐμφρόνων. λαλιᾶς μὲν οἶμαι διὰ κενῆς ληρεῖν καὶ εἰς μηδὲν δέον καὶ διατρίβειν τηνάλλως, λόγων δὲ ἀληθινῶν τῶν καιρῶν καὶ τῶν πραγμάτων στοχάζεσθαι καὶ τὸ πρέπον σῴζειν πανταχοῦ. τούτοις γοῦν ἕπεται καὶ τὸ κρατεῖν οἶμαι καὶ τὰς ψυχὰς προσ-
54 άγεσθαι τῶν ἀκουόντων. ὁ τοίνυν Περικλῆς τοσοῦτον νικῶν καὶ τοσαῦτα ἀφ᾿ ὧν ἐνίκα πράττων λάλος μὲν ἥκιστα οἶμαι, λέγειν δὲ ἄριστος εἰκότως ἐνομίζετο. καὶ μὴν ἐν οἷς γε καὶ τοὺς ἄλλους αἰτιῶνται, ἅμα τοῦτόν τ᾿ ἀφιᾶσιν καὶ τίνας ἀντὶ τούτου προσήκει μέμφεσθαι διδάσκουσιν.

55 εἰ δὲ δεῖ καὶ σεμνοτέρου μάρτυρος, σκόπει τί φησιν ὁ Θουκυδίδης ἐν τοῖς περὶ αὐτοῦ λόγοις. εὑρήσεις γὰρ ἁπανταχοῦ μεμνημένον ὡς ἀρίστου λέγειν καὶ οὐδ᾿ ἀμφισβήτησιν δόντα ὅτι μὴ καὶ πράττειν οὗτός γε πρὸς τῷ λέγειν προστίθησιν, ἐπειδὰν πρῶτον αὐτὸν

other orators, and had persuasion on his lips, and won such respect from all, and had so many good things said about him by men who scrutinized everyone in general and particularly satirized their victims for incompetence in oratory, really produce only nonsense and empty chatter in the Assembly, or achieve only what anyone could have achieved? Did he not rather live out his life in a position of immense superiority, far removed himself from empty nonsense, and trying to accustom everyone else to keep
the greatest possible distance from it too? Because let us 53
consider what is characteristic of empty talk and what of sensible oratory. Empty talk, I think, means babbling vacuously and to no good purpose and pointlessly wasting time, whereas true eloquence means aiming for timeliness and relevance, and having a constant regard for what is appropriate. From this flows victory and the ability to win
over an audience heart and soul. Pericles, who was so of- 54
ten victorious in debate and achieved so much on the strength of his victories, I therefore think was the least garrulous of men, and was quite reasonably held to be the best of orators. Moreover in the charges they bring against the others they simultaneously acquit him and show us who ought to be censured instead.

But if another more impressive witness is needed, con- 55
sider what Thucydides says in his account of Pericles.[47] You will find that wherever he mentions him, it is as the best of orators, and he makes it unambiguously clear that he for one is also crediting him with the ability to act as well as to speak when he says that he is preeminent.

[47] Principally 1.127, 1.139–45, 2.22, 2.34–46, 2.55–65 (especially the famous overall verdict on Pericles at 2.65).

56 εἶναι φῇ. καὶ οὗτος ὁ μάρτυς, ὦ χρηστέ, τῶν Ἀντιφῶντος ἑταίρων ἐστὶν καὶ ἅμα ὡς τὸ εἰκὸς καὶ ἐφ' ἑαυτῷ
τι φρονῶν, ἀλλ' ὅμως ἀποδίδωσιν ἐκείνῳ τὰ πρέποντα. ἦ που σοί γε τῷ τὴν Ἀσπασίαν ἐπαινοῦντι
πρὸ τοῦ Ἀντιφῶντος συγχωρητέον ταῦτα.

57 καὶ τί δεῖ Θουκυδίδου λοιπόν; ἥκει γὰρ πρὸς τοὔ-
σχατον τῆς μαρτυρίας ὁ λόγος. αὐτὸς γάρ ἐστι
Πλάτων ἡμῖν ὁ τὴν Ἀσπασίαν ὑμνῶν ὡς διδάσκαλον
θαυμαστὴν ῥητορικῆς, καταφεύγων ἐπὶ τὸν Περικλέα
καὶ δι' ἐκείνου πιστούμενος καὶ διαρρήδην γε οὑτωσὶ
διαφέροντα τῶν Ἑλλήνων αὐτὸν προσειρηκώς· τοσ-
58 οῦτον φαίνεται τῷ Περικλεῖ νέμων εἰς λόγους. καίτοι
οὐ δήπου τοῦ μὲν Ἀσπασίᾳ μετεῖναι λόγων σημεῖον
ἦν Περικλῆς οὕτω λέγων, τῆς δ' αὐτοῦ Περικλέους
δυνάμεως ἑτέρωθεν χρὴ τὸ σύμβολον ζητεῖν· οὐδέ γε
ὑπὲρ μὲν Ἀσπασίας διαφέροντα τῶν Ἑλλήνων αὐτὸν
ἔδει προσειπεῖν, τῷ δὲ καθ' αὑτὸν πράγματι μηδενὸς
59 βελτίω τῶν πολλῶν. καὶ οὐκ ἐνταῦθα μόνον ταῦτ'
εἴρηκεν περὶ τοῦ ἀνδρός, ἀλλὰ καὶ ἑτέρωθι εἰκότως
φησὶν τέλεον τὸν Περικλέα τὴν ῥητορικὴν γενέσθαι
συγγενόμενον Ἀναξαγόρᾳ. ἀλλὰ μή πω πᾶν τοῦτο.
ἀλλ' ὅτι γε ὡμολόγηκεν τέλεον γενέσθαι κατὰ τοὺς
λόγους δῆλον.

---

48 Apparently, an inference from the warm words in praise of the orator Antiphon of Rhamnus at Thuc. 8.68.

49 *Menex.* 235e–36a.

This witness, my dear Plato, is one of Antiphon's faction[48] 56
and at the same time in all probability has some pride in his own ability too, and yet he praises Pericles as he deserves. Given that you yourself praised Aspasia more highly than Antiphon,[49] you certainly ought to agree with this.[50]

Actually, what further need do we have of Thucydides, 57
since the argument of its own accord has brought us the clinching testimony—Plato himself, the man who, in lauding Aspasia to us as a marvelous teacher of oratory, relies on Pericles and uses him to prove his case, and so explicitly describes him as supreme among the Greeks.[51] That is
how highly he clearly rates Pericles as an orator. If Peri- 58
cles' ability to speak thus is the proof of Aspasia's oratorical talent, then presumably we do not have to look elsewhere for the evidence of Pericles' own capacity. Nor, if in support of Aspasia's claims he had to be described as supreme among the Greeks, could he in respect of his own standing
be described as no better than anyone else. And it is not 59
only here that Plato says this about Pericles; elsewhere too he very plausibly says that Pericles achieved perfection in oratory thanks to his association with Anaxagoras.[52] But let us not yet go into all of that. It is at all events clear that Plato agrees that Pericles achieved perfection in eloquence.

50 Another rather strained piece of reasoning: if Thucydides, a pupil of the lesser orator Antiphon, can praise Pericles, who was a pupil of the greater orator Aspasia, then Plato, as himself a pupil (via Socrates) and an admirer of Aspasia, has even more reason to do so.

51 *Menex.* 235d.

52 *Phdr.* 269e–70a.

60 πῶς ἂν οὖν ὁ τοσοῦτον ὑπερέχων καὶ μόνος πᾶσιν
τοῖς κριταῖς νικῶν τὴν τοῦ φλυαρεῖν εἰκῇ καὶ παρὰ
καιρὸν Ἀθηναίους ἀνεῖναι φέροιτ᾽ ἂν δόξαν; ἐγὼ μὲν
γὰρ τοὐναντίον ἡγοῦμαι, σιωπῆς αἴτιον αὐτὸν πλείο-
61 νος ἢ προπετείας καταστῆναι. ἴσμεν γοῦν ὅτι κἀν
ταῖς ἄλλαις δήπου δυνάμεσιν οὗ μὲν πολλοὶ παραπλήσιοι καὶ ἐφάμιλλοι πρὸς ἀλλήλους, πολλὰ τὰ
πράγματα καὶ πλείων ἡ ἔρις, ἐπειδὰν δέ τις εἷς ὑπέρ-
62 σχῃ λαμπρῶς, ἅπαντες ἤδη συγκεχωρήκασιν. οὕτω
δὴ καὶ λέγειν ἐπειδάν τις εἷς ἄκρος ἐγγένηται, στέργειν ἀνάγκη τοὺς πλείους καὶ μὴ πολυπραγμονεῖν,
ἀλλ᾽ ὡς οἷόν τε μάλιστα εὐλαβεῖς καὶ κοσμίους εἶναι
περὶ τοὺς λόγους. οὐ γὰρ ἂν ᾧ γέ τίς ἐστιν βέλτιστος, τούτῳ χείρους ἀπεργάζοιτο, ἄλλως τε καὶ πρὸς
αὐτὰ ταῦτα ἃ βέλτιστός ἐστιν. ὥσπερ γὰρ ἐν τοῖς
κατὰ τὸν βίον πράγμασιν ὅστις ἑαυτὸν κόσμιον
παρέχει καὶ σώφρονα καὶ τοῖς πᾶσιν εὔτακτον, οὐδ᾽
ἂν εἷς εἴποι δήπου τοῦτον ὡς ταύτῃ διαφθείρει τοὺς
ἐντυγχάνοντας, ὅτι μὴ καὶ τοῦ σωφρονεῖν παράδειγμα πάντες ἂν αὐτὸν εἶναι φαῖμεν, εἴπερ αὐτοὶ
μέλλομεν δόξειν σωφρονεῖν, οὕτω κἀν τοῖς λόγοις
ὅστις τὴν τοῦ καλοῦ καὶ πρέποντος φυλακὴν ἔχει καὶ
μηδαμοῦ παρορᾷ τὸ βέλτιον, μηδ᾽ ἀμελεῖ τοῦ περὶ
ταῦτα κόσμου, τὸ σόν, ὦ Πλάτων, ποιεῖ, τό γε σύμπαν τοῦτο ὡς κόσμος ἐκλήθη λογιζόμενος, ἀλλ᾽ οὐχὶ
ἀκοσμία οὐδὲ ἀταξία οὐδὲ τῶν περὶ ταῦτα ὀνομάτων
οὐδέν. καὶ τοὺς κρείττους εἰς ὅσον οἷόν τέ ἐστιν ἐν

How then could someone who enjoyed such superior- 60
ity and in the unanimous view of his judges was the sole
victor still win a reputation for encouraging the people of
Athens in pointless and inappropriate babble? I think that
the reality was quite the reverse, and that he was responsible for reticence much more than for hasty speech. At 61
any rate, we know in the case of other kinds of ability that
when there are many competing with each other on an
equal footing, there is a great deal of trouble and still more
strife, but when some one individual is starkly superior, a
general state of concord prevails. Just so, when some one 62
individual emerges as supreme in oratory, the majority
must accept the fact and not trespass on territory that is
not theirs, but instead must be as circumspect and orderly
as they can in their speech, because a person will not use
the ability in which he is preeminent to make people
worse, especially not in respect of the very qualities in
which he himself is preeminent. No one surely would say
that the person who shows himself to be orderly and self-
controlled and entirely well behaved in his day-to-day
dealings corrupts those he meets by this means; on the
contrary, our own prospects of being thought sensible
would depend on our calling him a model of self-control.
So too in the field of eloquence, anyone who keeps a grip
of beauty and propriety and never lets his attention stray
from what is best or loses his concern for good order in
these matters, is an upholder of your principles, Plato,
since he reflects that the name for this Universe of ours is
"order" (*kosmos*), not "disorder" or "confusion" or any
other such word,[53] and attempts to imitate the higher pow-

[53] *Grg.* 508a.

63 τοῖς ἑαυτοῦ μιμούμενος. οὐκ ἂν οὖν εἴη φλυαρίας αἴτιος οὐδὲ ἡγεμών, οὐδὲ ἀταξίας οὐδὲ τῶν αἰσχρῶν οὐδενός, οὐ μᾶλλόν γε ἢ τὸν γυμναστὴν ἐθίζειν ἀμελεῖν τοῦ σώματός ἐστ' εἰπεῖν ᾧ γε ὅπως τὸ σῶμα
64 καλῶς ἕξει μέλειν ὁ σοφὸς Πλάτων φησίν. ἐὰν δὲ δή τις καὶ τὸν βίον ἐξ ἴσου τοῖς λόγοις καταστήσῃ καὶ μὴ μόνον λέγων εἰς κάλλος, ἀλλὰ καὶ ζῶν ᾖ φανερός, πῶς οὗτος ἐθίζει λαλεῖν ἢ καὶ ἄλλ' ὁτιοῦν ποιεῖν ἄνευ τῆς τοῦ βελτίονος μοίρας; ἐγὼ μὲν οὐκ ἔχω πεισθῆναι. ἀλλὰ δυοῖν ἔμελλον, οἶμαι, θάτερον οἱ τότ' ἐκείνῳ συνόντες ἢ ζηλώσαντες αὐτοῦ τὴν δύναμιν, χρηστόν τι καὶ παραπλήσιον κατὰ τοὺς λόγους ἐπιτηδεύειν, καὶ ὅσῳ μᾶλλον ἐτίμων κἀκεῖνον καὶ τοὺς λόγους, τοσούτῳ κοσμιώτερον καὶ σωφρονέστερον αὑτῶν[13] ἕξεσθαι καὶ πάσης παρανομίας ἀφέξεσθαι, ἢ καὶ παντάπασιν ἀπογνόντες καὶ νομίσαντες κρεῖττον ἢ καθ' αὑτοὺς εἶναι τὸ πρᾶγμα τὴν ἡσυχίαν σχήσειν καθαρῶς, ὡς τὸ μὲν εἶναι ῥήτορα τοῦτο ὄν, ὅπερ ἦν ὁ Περικλῆς, αὑτοῖς δ' οὐκ ἐξ ἴσου τὴν τύχην οὖσαν. ὥστε καὶ οὕτως κἀκείνως ἥκιστα ἔμελλον ἔσεσθαι λάλοι.

65 ὁρῶ δέ τοι καὶ περὶ τὴν τραγῳδίαν Αἰσχύλον μὲν αἰτίαν οὐ σχόντα ὡς εἰσαγάγοι λαλιάν, οὐδὲ τὸν ἥδιστον εἰπεῖν Σοφοκλέα οὐδαμοῦ ταῦτ' ἀκούσαντα ὡς ἐπῆρεν Ἀθηναίους λαλεῖν, ὅτι, οἶμαι, τῆς σεμνότητος ὡς οἷόν τε μάλιστα ἀντείχοντο καὶ κρείττονα ἢ κατὰ

[13] *αὑτῶν* Ph^{M3} Dindorf *αὐτῶν* *codd.*

ers as far as can be done in his own life. He would, then, 63
not instigate or take the lead in empty nonsense or disorder, or in anything shameful at all, any more than one could assert that the man who the wise Plato says is professionally concerned with good physical condition would
train an athlete to neglect his body.[54] If someone puts his 64
life on the same footing as his words and manifestly not only speaks but also lives in pursuit of all that is fine, how on earth can he accustom people to be garrulous, or to do anything at all that is divorced from what is for the best? I for one cannot be persuaded of this. In my opinion, one of two things had to happen to those who associated with Pericles at the time, or sought to emulate his ability: either they had to exercise a good sort of oratory comparable to his, and in proportion as they honored him and his eloquence to surpass themselves all the more in discipline and sobriety and abstain from all forms of transgression, or they had to give up entirely in the belief that the achievement was beyond their powers and simply hold their peace, convinced that to be an orator was to be what Pericles was, and that they themselves did not enjoy a comparable degree of good fortune. Either way, they were certainly not going to be garrulous.

In the field of tragedy, Aeschylus, I observe, was not 65
accused of introducing empty talk, and that most elegant of stylists Sophocles did not ever have it said of him that he incited the Athenians to chatter emptily. This was, I take it, because they maintained the highest possible degree of dignity and displayed moral characters superior to

[54] *Grg.* 463e–64c.

τοὺς πολλοὺς τὰ ἤθη παρείχοντο· Εὐριπίδην δὲ λαλεῖν αὐτοὺς ἐθίσαι καταιτιαθέντα, ἀφελεῖν τι δόξαντα τοῦ βάρους καὶ τῶν καιρῶν, καὶ μετ᾽ ἐκεῖνον αὖ πλεῖν ἢ σταδίῳ λαλίστερα Ἀριστοφάνης μειράκια γενέσθαι φησίν, ἅτ᾽, οἶμαι, τοσοῦτον Εὐριπίδου λειπόμενα κατὰ τὴν ποίησιν. τοῦ γὰρ κόσμου κατὰ μικρὸν ὑπορρέοντος εἰς τοῦτο ἔδει τὸ ἁμάρτημα κατενεχθῆ-
66 ναι καὶ δοκεῖν λαλεῖν μᾶλλον ἢ ποιεῖν. οὕτω δὴ καὶ περὶ τοὺς λόγους τοὺς πολιτικοὺς οὐχ ὁ σεμνότατος οὐδ᾽ ᾧ τῶν ῥημάτων ὁ νοῦς ἡγεῖτο, οὐδ᾽ ὃς ἄνευ μὲν φρονήματος οὐκ ᾤετο δεῖν λέγειν, τὸ φρόνημα δ᾽ ἐξ ἁπάντων ὧν ἑαυτῷ συνῄδει δικαίως ἐκέκτητο, οὐχ οὗτος ἦν ὁ λάλους ἀντὶ κοσμίων ποιήσας, ἀλλὰ οὗτος
67 ὁ κωλύων εἶναι λάλους τὸ καθ᾽ αὑτόν. οὔκουν ὅ γε Ὀδυσσεὺς οὐδὲ ὁ Νέστωρ αἰτίαν ἔσχον ὡς διαφθείροντες τῶν Ἀχαιῶν τὸ στρατόπεδον, ἀλλ᾽ ὁ Θερσίτης μᾶλλον,

ὅς ῥ᾽ ἔπεα φρεσὶν ᾗσιν ἄκοσμά τε πολλά τε ᾔδη
μάψ, ἀτὰρ οὐ κατὰ κόσμον ἐριζέμεναι
βασιλεῦσιν.

διὸ καὶ κατεῖχεν αὐτὸν ὁ τῷ Περικλεῖ προσόμοιος
68 ῥήτωρ καὶ οὐκ εἴα λαλεῖν. σὺ δὲ ποιεῖς παραπλήσιον

---

[55] Cf. Ar. *Ran.* 840–50, 939–70, etc.
[56] *Ran.* 89–91, quoting 91.

the general norm. Euripides, however, was accused of putting the Athenians in the habit of chattering emptily, because he was thought to have taken something away from the gravity and decorum of tragedy.[55] Then after him, in their turn, Aristophanes says that youngsters "more than a mile more talkative" came onto the scene, meaning I take it that their poetry was that far inferior to Euripides';[56] as the sense of decorum gradually deteriorated, it was inevitable that their shortcoming should bring things down to this level and that they should give the impression
of chattering rather than writing poetry. In just the same 66
way in the field of political oratory, it was not the most dignified individual, nor the one whose words were guided by their sense, nor the one who believed that he should not speak unless he was confident, and possessed a justified confidence from everything that he knew about himself, who made his people garrulous instead of well behaved; no, he was the one who as far as depended on him
prevented them from being garrulous. It was not Odys- 67
seus or Nestor who were held responsible for corrupting the Achaean army, but rather Thersites,

> Who knew within his head many words, but
> disorderly;
> vain, and without decency, to quarrel with the
> princes.[57]

That is why the orator who resembled Pericles restrained
him and did not allow him to carry on chattering.[58] You, 68
Plato, are doing the same as if someone were to have ac-

[57] Hom. *Il.* 2.213–14.
[58] *Il.* 2.244–69.

ὥσπερ ἂν εἴ τις τὸν Ὀδυσσέα τότε ᾐτιᾶτο θόρυβον ἐν τῷ στρατοπέδῳ ποιεῖν, ὃς τοὺς ἄλλους τοῦ θορυβεῖν ἔπαυεν· ὥσπερ ἂν εἰ καὶ τὸν Ἡρακλέα φαίης τοὺς ἀνθρώπους ἐθίζειν αὐθάδεις εἶναι καὶ θρασεῖς, ὅτι τοῖς τόξοις καὶ τῷ ῥοπάλῳ περιῄει χρώμενος, τοὐναντίον γε πᾶν ἐθίζων, ὦ χρηστέ, πάντας κοσμίους εἶναι καὶ τοῖς νόμοις ἐμμένειν, καὶ χρῆσθαί γε τοῖς ὀργάνοις τούτοις ὥσπερ ἐκεῖνον ἑώρων μετὰ παντὸς τοῦ
69 βελτίονος. οὕτω καὶ Περικλεῖ μοί τις ἂν ἐγκαλέσαι δοκεῖ λάλους ποιεῖν· ὃς τοσοῦτον ἅπαντας καθεῖργεν ὥστε σιωπᾶν καὶ ἑκόντας καὶ ἄκοντας αὐτῷ· καὶ τοσοῦτον ἀπεῖχεν τοῦ τὸ πλῆθος ἐπαίρειν ὥστε καὶ τοὺς ῥήτορας ἡσυχίαν ἔχοντας ὡς τὰ πολλὰ παρείχετο. ὥστε εἰ μὴ καθ' Ἡρακλέα, κατὰ γοῦν τὸν Ἰόλεων ἦν ἐπικάων, ὡς τὸ τοῦ κωμικοῦ ῥῆμα, τὰς κεφαλὰς τῶν πλειόνων.

70 εἶτα λέγεις ὡς λάλους Ἀθηναίους Περικλῆς ἐποίησεν; ὥσπερ ἂν εἴ τις τὸν διδάσκαλον αἰτιῷτο τοὺς παῖδας λάλους ποιεῖν, ὅτι αὐτοῖς ἅπαντα ἐξηγεῖται. καὶ μὴν ὅ γε αὐτὸς οὗτος οὐδὲ φθέγγεσθαί ποτε αὐτοὺς εἴα, ἀλλὰ καὶ τῶν λόγων αὐτῶν μέρος ἦν αὐτῷ τὸ τὴν ἡσυχίαν ἄγειν εἰδέναι προστάττειν. οὐδὲ γὰρ Σωκράτη φαίην ἂν ἔγωγε ὡς ἐποίησεν Ἀθηναίους λάλους καὶ φιλονείκους, ὅτι πλεῖστα Ἀθηναίων ἐπὶ τῶν τραπεζῶν καὶ τῶν ἐργαστηρίων διελέγετο καὶ πρὸς τοὺς ἀστοὺς καὶ πρὸς τοὺς ξένους· οὐδ' εἰς τοῦτον τὸ τοῦ Ἡσιόδου φέρειν, ἐπιτιμῶντος καὶ διακωλύοντος,

cused Odysseus on that occasion of creating an uproar in the camp, when in fact he was the one preventing the rest of them from raising an uproar. It is as if you were also to say that Heracles got people into the habit of being headstrong and brash, on the grounds that he went around brandishing a bow and arrows and a club, when in fact, my dear Plato, he was training them in exactly the opposite qualities of good behavior and adherence to the laws, and training them to use those weapons as they saw him using them, wholly in the service of what was for the best. That 69
is what I think it would be for someone to accuse Pericles of making people garrulous, when in fact he exercised such a restraining influence on everyone that they all kept silent for him whether they wanted to or not, and when he was so far from inciting the masses that he usually kept the orators quiet as well. So even if he was not like Heracles in this, he was at least like Iolaus in, to quote the comic poet's witticism, "cauterizing the heads of the masses."[59]

Can you really then maintain that Pericles made the 70
Athenians garrulous, as if someone were to accuse a schoolmaster of making his pupils garrulous because he explains everything to them? This same man, what is more, sometimes did not even allow them to speak; it was actually part of his very eloquence to teach them knowledge of how to stay quiet. I for one would not say that Socrates made the Athenians garrulous and quarrelsome either, on the strength of the enormous number of conversations he had in Athens at bankers' tables and in workshops with both citizens and foreigners, and I would not say that Hesiod's censorious prohibition in the line

[59] Plato Comicus, fr. 202 Kassel-Austin.

πὰρ δ' ἴθι χάλκειον θῶκον καὶ ἐπαλέα λέσχην,

ἀλλὰ καὶ τοῖς χαλκείοις ἂν αὐτὸν καὶ τοῖς ἄλλοις ἐργαστηρίοις θαρρούντως κελεύειν προσιέναι, οὗ τι μέλλουσιν τοιοῦτον ἀκούσεσθαι ἢ τῶν νέων ἢ τῶν πρεσβυτέρων τινές. οὐ γὰρ ἂν εἴη φλυαρεῖν ἐθίζεσθαι τὸ τί τῶν χρησίμων ἀκούειν, ὥσπερ γε καὶ αὐτοῦ τοῦ Ἡσιόδου ταῦτα συμβουλεύοντος ἀκούοντες οὐκ ἀπολλύναι τὸν χρόνον ἡγούμεθα οὐδὲ χείρους γίγνεσθαι.
71 εἰ δέ τινες Σωκράτους ἢ Περικλέους ἀκούοντες, εἶτα τῆς ἐκείνων δυνάμεως ἐπιθυμήσαντες κακῶς ἐμιμήσαντο, οὐ τοῦτό γε ἐκείνων αἴτιον. ἐκεῖνοι μὲν γὰρ τοῖς ἀκούουσι λέγοντες τὰ βέλτιστα οὕτως ἐπεδείκνυντο τὴν δύναμιν, οἱ δ' ἁμαρτόντες τοῦ κεφαλαίου καὶ πρὸς οὐδὲν χρήσιμον τοὺς λόγους ἀναλίσκοντες εἰκότως ἂν τὴν μέμψιν φέροιντο καὶ οὐδὲ ταὐτὸν ἂν ἐκείνοις, οἶμαι, δοκοῖεν ποιεῖν, ἀλλ' αὐτὰ τὰ ἐναντιώτατα, ὥσπερ οἱ παρὰ τοὺς νόμους γράφοντες, νόμους δὲ ὅμως ὄνομα οἷς γράφουσι τιθέμενοι. Περικλῆς τοίνυν κάλλιστον νόμον περὶ δημηγοριῶν ἔθη-
72 κεν, μηδαμοῦ τῆς σεμνότητος ὑφίεσθαι. πῶς οὖν τῆς περὶ ταῦτα ὀλιγωρίας αἴτιος;

ἀλλὰ μὴν ὡς αὐτό γε οὐκ ἄτιμον τὸ δύνασθαι λέγειν οὐδ' εἰς ὄνειδος φέρον, οὐδὲ κατηγορίας ἄξιον, οὐδέ γε συγγνώμης, ἀλλά τινος κρείττονος, αἰσχυνοίμην ἂν τοὺς λογίους θεούς, εἰ ζητοίην ἀποδεικνύναι, πλήν γε τοσοῦτον ἂν εἴποιμι,—ἐμοὶ γὰρ εἴη εἴ τις ἄλλος δυσχεραίνει καὶ τρέποιτο ἅπαν εἰς ἐμέ, καὶ

Pass by the smith's bench and the cozy parlor[60]

applies to him. No, Hesiod would order him to march confidently into smithies and other sorts of workshop, where representatives of the young and the old alike could hear the sort of thing he had to say. Because hearing something beneficial would not count as becoming habituated to talking nonsense, just as when we hear this advice from Hesiod we do not think that we are wasting our time or
becoming worse people. If some people listened to Socra- 71
tes or Pericles and then in their desire to acquire their ability imitated them badly, it is no fault of theirs. Socrates and Pericles demonstrated their ability by giving the best possible advice to their audiences, but these mistook the main point and misused their words for bad ends; it would I think be entirely reasonable for them to bear the blame for this and not to be thought to be doing the same as Socrates and Pericles but the complete reverse, like people who draft illegal legislation and yet give the name "laws" to what they have drafted. Pericles on the other hand established the best of all laws for public speaking, never to
relax his dignity. How then can he have been responsible 72
for a casual attitude to these matters?

I would feel ashamed indeed before the gods of eloquence if I were to seek to prove that oratorical ability itself is not worthless or grounds for reproach or deserving of denunciation. This much however I would say (if anyone else feels disgruntled, let it be with me; let him place the whole responsibility on me, and I will not complain at

[60] *Op.* 493.

οὐ μέμψομαι τῷ δαίμονι—ὡς ἐγὼ δεξαίμην ἂν δύνασθαι λέγειν μετὰ χρηστοῦ βίου καὶ σώφρονος εἰς ὅσον οἷόν τε κάλλιστα ἀνθρώπων μᾶλλον ἢ μυριάκις Δαρεῖος ὁ Ὑστάσπου γενέσθαι· καὶ μικρά μοι πάνθ'
73 ὡς ἀληθῶς πρὸς τοῦτο ἤδη φαίνεται. οἶδα δὲ καὶ τὰ Πλάτωνος πράγματα, εἰ μὴ τετυφώμεθα, οὐδὲν ἄλλο σχεδὸν ὄντα ἢ λόγους, καὶ συγχαίρω τῆς λέξεως αὐτῷ, κἂν με προσπαίζων οὑτωσὶ πείθῃ, μὴ πάνυ τούτου φροντίζειν, οὐ πάνυ πείσομαι, ἀλλ' εἴσομαι σφόδρα σπουδάζοντα, καὶ τηνικαῦτα μάλιστα ἡνίκ' ἂν ὡς παίζων λέγῃ. ὥστε τὸν οἴκοι θησαυρὸν διαβάλλοιμεν ἂν εἰ ταῦτα διασύροιμεν. ἀλλ' ὑπὲρ μὲν τούτων οὐδὲ λέγειν ἄξιον, ἀλλὰ τοσούτῳ ἧττον ὅσῳπερ ἂν ᾖ κρεῖττον τὸ δύνασθαι λέγειν.

74 εἶεν. ἀργοὺς δὲ δὴ πῶς ἡμῖν ἐποίησεν Ἀθηναίους Περικλῆς; ἢ σὺ λίαν ἐνεργοὺς ἡμᾶς ποιήσεις, ἀναγκάζων πρὸς ἕκαστον τῶν εἰρημένων ἀποκρίνεσθαι, οὐχ οὗτός ἐστιν ὁ πανταχοῖ κομίζων ἐκείνους; οὐχ οὗτος ὁ μηδαμοῦ καθεύδειν ἐῶν, ἐπὶ μὲν Σάμῳ δέκατος αὐτὸς στρατηγῶν, ἀποκρύψας τοὺς ἄλλους ἅπαντας στρατηγοὺς καὶ δείξας ὄνομα ἄλλως ὄντας, καὶ τοὺς Σαμίους καταστήσας εἰς πολιορκίαν, οὐχ ἡσυχάζων, ἀλλ' ἐκπλέων μέρει τινὶ τῶν νεῶν ἐπὶ Καρίας, καὶ μετὰ ταῦτ' ἀπελθόντος αὐτοῦ θαρρήσαντας ἐπεξελθεῖν καὶ πλέον σχόντας τῶν ἐφορμούντων ἀναστρέψας αὖθις καθείργων ἕως παρεστήσατο, καὶ

61 *Phdr.* 276c–d.

my luck): I would rather possess the ability to speak, along with a good and sober life, in as fair a form as is possible among men, than be Darius son of Hystaspes ten times over, and all else truly seems insignificant to me in comparison with this. I also know, if I have not gone insane, 73
that Plato's own business is effectively nothing other than words. I am as pleased as he is by his prose style, and if he tries to persuade me jestingly that he really does not take this seriously,[61] I really will not believe him; I will know that he is deeply serious about it, above all when he speaks as if in jest. So if I were to ridicule this, I would be slandering all that I myself hold most precious. But the right thing is not to speak in defense of these skills in the first place, since the very superiority of oratorical ability makes it all the less appropriate to do so.

So, now for the claim that Pericles made the Athenians 74
idle. How pray did he bring that about? Or is it me that you are going to make hyperactive, by forcing me to answer each and every one of the charges? Was this not the man who took the Athenians to every corner of the world and never let them sleep, commanding them as one of their ten generals at Samos and eclipsing the other nine so as to show them up as mere names, not sitting tight once he had put the Samians under siege but making an expedition to Caria with a portion of the fleet, and when, after his departure, the Samians regained their confidence and made a sortie and had the better of their besiegers, coming back and bottling them up until he brought them to terms,[62] and then on another occasion when the Euboeans

[62] In 440 BC: Thuc. 1.116–17 (with a verbal echo of 1.116.1 in "commanding them as one of their ten generals").

πάλιν Εὐβοέων ἀποστάντων ἄγων εἰς Εὔβοιαν Ἀθηναίους, καὶ Πελοποννησίων ἀγγελθέντων εἶναι Μεγα-
ροῖ κομίζων αὖθις εἰς Μέγαρα κἀκ τῶν Μεγάρων
75 πάλιν εἰς Εὔβοιαν, ἕως καὶ ταύτην κατεστρέψατο; τί
δ᾽ ἄν τις λέγοι περίπλους Πελοποννήσου καὶ ἀποβά-
σεις πανταχοῖ τῆς πολεμίας καὶ πραγμάτων συν-
76 έχειαν <. . .> οὐδεμιᾶς ἄλλης πόλεως εἰκάσαι;[14] εἶτα
τὸν οὕτως ὀξὺν καὶ ἄγρυπνον καὶ ἥδιστ᾽ ἂν εἶπον
ὑπόπτερον τοῦτον ἢ αὐτὸν ἀργεῖν ἢ ἑτέρους ἐθίζειν
ἐγὼ πεισθῶ; οὐκ ἄρ᾽ ἐπίστασθαι δόξω τῶν πραγμάτων οὐδέν, ὅστις γε μὴ ὅτι Ἀθηναίοις, ἀλλ᾽ οὐδὲ τοῖς
πολεμίοις ἀργεῖν ἐπέτρεπεν, ἀλλὰ κἀκείνους ἐποίησεν
μεταβαλεῖν τοὺς τρόπους, τοσαύτας ἀνάγκας αὐτοῖς
περιίστη τοῦ κινεῖσθαι, καὶ τὸ δικαίως προσῆν, ἔφη
Δημοσθένης. ἀλλ᾽ ὅμως Πλάτων ᾐτιάσατο αὐτὸν ἀργοὺς καὶ δειλοὺς πεποιηκέναι.

77 τί λέγεις, δειλοὺς Περικλῆς, ὦ θεοί, δειλούς, ὃς καὶ
δημηγορῶν εὐθὺς ἐνθένδε ἤρξατο, τῆς μὲν γνώμης,
ἔφη, τῆς αὐτῆς, ὦ Ἀθηναῖοι, ἀεὶ ἔχομαι, μὴ εἴκειν
Πελοποννησίοις. ὃ τίς τῶν εἰς ἐκείνην τὴν ἡμέραν
εἰσάπαξ εἰπεῖν ἐθάρρησεν, οἵ γε καὶ ἡνίκ᾽ ἔσῳζον τὴν
Ἑλλάδα, Λακεδαιμονίοις εἶξαν;[15] ὁ δὲ οὐδὲν προκαλυ-

[14] συνέχειαν <. . .> οὐδεμιᾶς ἄλλης πόλεως εἰκάσαι Lenz συνέχειαν <οἵαν> οὐδεμιᾶς ἄλλης πόλεως εἰκάσαι Reiske συνέχειαν; οὐδεμιᾶς ἄλλης πόλεως <ὡς> εἰκάσαι Behr

[15] εἶξαν αὐτῶν TQA^{2}U^2 εἶξαν αὑτῶν U^{1}aR^2 εἶξαν αὐτοῖν A^{1}M εἶξαν αὐτοῖς R^{1}E αὐτῶν *del.* Trapp

revolted leading the Athenians against Euboea, then when it was reported that the Peloponnesians were at Megara taking them to Megara and from Megara back to Euboea,
until he had subdued her too?[63] Need one mention cir- 75
cumnavigations of the Peloponnese and raids against every part of enemy territory[64] and a continuity of effort . . .
no other city . . . ?[65] Am I then meant to accept that so 76
quick and alert and (as I would be delighted to call him) winged an individual as this was either idle himself or accustomed others to be idle? If I do, people will think that I understand nothing of what he did, seeing that, to say nothing of the Athenians, he did not even allow their enemies to remain idle, but made them too change their ways, and surrounded them with so many compelling incentives to action, and, to quote Demosthenes,[66] quite rightly too.

And yet Plato charges him with having made the Athe- 77
nians idle and cowardly! What are you saying? For heaven's sake, did Pericles make them cowardly? Cowardly, when even in his speechmaking he began straight away with this sentiment: "Athenians, I keep consistently to the same view, that we should not make any concessions to the Peloponnesians."[67] Who in the history of Athens up to that day had had the courage to say as much straight out? Even

[63] 446 BC: Thuc. 1.114. [64] Thuc. 1.111, 2.25, 2.56.

[65] The Greek text is corrupt at this point and has not yet been satisfactorily emended, but the general message—that Pericles kept the Athenians constantly active—is clear. Some version of Reiske's conjecture ("a continuity of effort such as no other city achieved") may well be right.

[66] Dem. *De cor.* (18) 306. [67] Thuc. 1.140.

ψάμενος, οὐδ' ἀναμείνας, εἰ μή τι ἄλλο, τήν γε ἐκ τοῦ προοιμίου παραμυθίαν εὐθὺς ἐν ἀρχῇ τῶν λόγων μάλα ῥᾳδίως ἐξεῖπεν τὸ δοκοῦν αὐτῷ,[16] ὡς ἄν τις αὐτός τε κρείττων ἀξιῶν εἶναι τῶν ἀκουόντων κἀκεί-
78 νους τῶν ἀνταγωνιστῶν. πότερα οὖν φοβεῖσθαι τοὺς πολεμίους καὶ ὑποχωρεῖν, ἢ θαρρεῖν καὶ ὑπερφρονεῖν συνεθίζοντος τὴν φωνὴν εἶναι φῶμεν καὶ τὴν ἀνδρείαν αὐτόθεν δεικνύντος; ἐγὼ μὲν οὕτω μᾶλλον ἡγοῦμαι. εἰ μὲν γὰρ ἢ τὸν πόλεμον κεκινηκέναι, ἢ πραγμάτων αἴτιον αὐτὸν γεγενῆσθαι, ἤ τι τῶν τοιούτων ᾐτιᾶτο, ἀληθῆ μὲν οὐδ' οὕτως—ὕστερον γοῦν ἅπαντες συνεχώρησαν μὴ ἐκεῖθεν λελύσθαι τὰς σπονδάς—εἰρημένα δ' ἂν καὶ ὑπ' ἄλλων ἐδόκει λέγειν. νῦν δὲ πῶς ἔνεστι κατηγορεῖν δειλίαν, οὗ τἀναντία ἤδη τινὲς ᾐτιάσαντο;

79 ἃ γοῦν τῆς Ἀριστοφάνους κωμῳδίας παρεθέμεθα ἀρτίως εἰς ἐκεῖνον ἔχοντα, λέγω τό,

ἤστραπτ',[17] ἐβρόντα, συνεκύκα τὴν Ἑλλάδα,
ἐτίθει νόμους ὥσπερ σκόλια γεγραμμένους,
ὡς χρὴ Μεγαρέας·

ταῦτα οὐ δειλίαν αἰτιώμενά ἐστιν ἐκείνου, ἀλλ' ἴσμεν ἅ γε αἰτιᾶται, ὧν ὄντων μὲν ἀληθῶν τά γ' ἐναντία ψευδῆ· εἰ δὲ μηδὲ ἐκείνων προσήκει τῷ Περικλεῖ μη-

[16] αὐτῷ Jebb αὐτῷ *codd.*
[17] ἤστραπτ' *codd. Aristoph.* ἤστραπτεν *codd.*

when his predecessors saved Greece, they still made concessions to the Spartans. But he without veiling his message in any way and without pausing, if for nothing else, at least for the softening effect of a preamble, right at the beginning of his speech unhesitatingly declared his opinion, like someone who believed himself to be superior to his audience, and them to their adversaries. Are we to say 78
that these were the words of someone who was training his people to fear their enemies and retreat before them, or confidently to despise them, and who was demonstrating his own courage in the process? I for one think the latter. If Plato had accused him of having provoked the war or having been a cause of trouble or something of the kind, that would not have been true either—everyone subsequently agreed that that was not why the truce was broken—but people would have felt that he was repeating a charge made by others as well. But as things actually stand, how is it possible to charge Pericles with cowardice, when the accusation that some people brought against him at the time was quite the opposite?

The lines from Aristophanes' comedy bearing on him 79
that I cited a moment ago, I mean the words

> He lightened, he thundered, he threw Greece into
> turmoil,
> he made laws drafted like drinking songs,
> saying that the Megarians must . . .[68]

are not an accusation of cowardice against him. We know very well what they accuse him of, and if those charges are true, then their opposites must be false; but if none of

[68] *Ach.* 531–33.

δὲν τῶν ἐγκλημάτων, ἀλλὰ καὶ δίκαια καὶ ἀναγκαῖα
ἐβουλεύσατο ὑπὲρ τῶν πραγμάτων, πῶς οὐχ ἅμα τε
αἰτίας ἀφεῖσθαι καὶ πάσης εὐφημίας δίκαιος τυγχά-
80 νειν ἐστίν; ἆρα οὖν πρὸς μὲν Λακεδαιμονίους μόνους
οὕτως εἶχε τὴν γνώμην ὡς ἄν τις ἰδίᾳ φιλονικῶν,
πρὸς δὲ τοὺς ἄλλους ὑφειμένως; ὅστις ἠξίου μὲν
αὐτοῖς ὁρμητήριον ἀποχρῶν εἶναι τὸν Πειραιᾶ, θαυμάζειν δὲ οὐκ εἴα οὔτε βασιλέα οὔτ' ἄλλον τῶν πάντων οὐδένα, ἀπέφαινε δὲ τὴν ἰσχὺν αὐτοῖς ἐξ ἡμισείας οὖσαν πρὸς τοὺς ἄλλους ἅπαντας ἀνθρώπους,
ὡς τοὺς μὲν ἄλλους ἄλλοθι κρατεῖν, τῆς δὲ θαλάττης
81 αὐτοὺς πανταχοῦ. καίτοι ταῦτα πότερον ἀργίαν καὶ
δειλίαν καὶ ἀνανδρίαν καὶ ταπεινότητα καὶ νωθείαν
εἰσάγοντος εἰς τὴν πόλιν καὶ τὰς ψυχὰς αὐτῶν ἦν,
ἢ—δέδοικα μή τι καὶ ἀλλοῖον εἴπῃ τις, πλήν γε ὅσον
οὐκ ὀρθῶς ἐρεῖ.

82 ὥσπερ τοίνυν φῂς ἐκεῖνα ἀκούειν λεγόντων εἰς
Περικλέα, οὕτως ἀντάκουε καὶ τῶν τἀληθῆ περὶ ἐκείνου λεγόντων καὶ οἷς οὐδεὶς ἀντεῖπεν εἰς τήνδε τὴν
ἡμέραν, ἐπειδή γε καὶ αὐτὸς φῂς οὐκ ἀπὸ τῆς σεαυτοῦ γνώμης κατηγορεῖν, ἀλλ' ἀκοήν. ταῦτά γε ὁ Κρὴς
83 δὴ τὸν πόντον, φήσει τις. ἐπειδὴ τοίνυν ἐκεῖνα μὲν
ἀξιοῖς ἀκούειν, ταῦτα δ' οὐ βούλει, φέρε ἐγώ σοι καὶ
ἕτερα μείζω τούτων ἔτι καὶ τελεώτερα ἐπιδείξω τῆς
Περικλέους ἀνδρείας καὶ ῥώμης καὶ φιλοτιμίας στη-

---

69 *Grg.* 515e.

70 A proverbial expression for pretending not to know some-

those charges fits Pericles either, and instead his policies in affairs of state were right and necessary, how can it not be right for him at once to be acquitted of blame and showered with all praise? Did he show this firmness of 80
purpose toward the Peloponnesians alone, like someone pursuing a purely private rivalry with them, and behave submissively toward everyone else? The man who estimated that the Piraeus provided the Athenians with a sufficient base for operations, and did not allow them to go in awe of the king of Persia or anyone else on earth, and made it clear to them that their strength was equivalent to half of that possessed by the whole of the rest of humanity, so that even if that others might hold sway elsewhere, they had mastery of the sea everywhere? Are these the words 81
of someone trying to introduce idleness and cowardice and unmanliness and abjectness and sloth into the city and the character of its citizens, or—well, I am afraid someone may say something even less appropriate than this, except that he will not be right to do so.

You say that you have heard people saying this about 82
Pericles:[69] very well, now listen to those who tell the truth about him, uncontradicted by anyone to this very day, especially as you yourself assert that your accusations are hearsay and do not derive from your own firsthand judgment. Like the Cretan and the sea, someone will say.[70] So, 83
since you see fit to listen to the one set of testimony but do not want to listen to the other, come on, let me now show you other still greater and more decisive evidence of Pericles' courage and strength and ambition. If you can

thing one knows very well: Strabo 10.4.17, Zen. *Prov*. 5.30, 1.131 Leutsch-Schneidewin.

μεῖα, κἂν σὺ δείξῃς ἐνοῦσαν ὑπερβολήν, ἅπαντ᾽ ἔστω λῆρος τὰ παρ᾽ ἡμῶν.

84 νὴ Δία, εἴποι γὰρ ἄν τις ὡς οὐδὲν μέγα οὐδ᾽ ἱκανὸν τὸ πρὸ τοῦ πολέμου θρασύνεσθαι. ἀλλ᾽ ἐκεῖνός γε καὶ τὰς πρεσβείας ἠξίου κατὰ χώραν ἱδρυμένων Πελοποννησίων δέχεσθαι τῇ πόλει, ἐξεστρατευμένων δὲ μὴ καὶ τὸν Μελήσιππον προπεμψάντων. οὕτω σφόδρα δειλὸς ἦν, ἐπειδὴ προσάγειν τοὺς πολεμίους ἐπύθετο, ὥστε ἔργῳ τὰς ἀποκρίσεις ἔδωκεν αὐτῷ περὶ ἁπάντων, παραδοὺς τοῖς ἄξουσιν αὐτὸν ἔξω τῆς

85 χώρας. καὶ τὸ δὴ πάντων ἔσχατον καὶ μέγιστον ἀκοῦσαι, μὴ ὅτι μιμήσασθαι· παρόντος μὲν ἤδη τοῦ πολέμου καὶ συνεστηκότος, τῆς νόσου δὲ ἐπικειμένης, καὶ τῆς μὲν γῆς δῃουμένης, τῶν δὲ ἀνθρώπων ὁσημέραι φθειρομένων καὶ τοσούτων ἤδη κειμένων ὅσων καὶ πολλοστὸν μέρος ἐξέπληξεν ἂν τοὺς πολεμίους, εἰ παρ᾽ ἐκείνοις ἡ συμφορὰ συνέβη, καὶ διὰ ταῦτα δὴ πάντα ἀθύμως καὶ δυσχερῶς ἔχοντας ὁρῶν τοὺς πολλοὺς καὶ περὶ ὧν μὲν ἐψηφίσαντο μετεγνωκότας, ἐπικηρυκεύεσθαι δὲ ἀξιοῦντας Λακεδαιμονίοις καὶ ἑτέρους ὑπὸ τῶν κακῶν γεγενημένους οὐδὲν μᾶλλον ἀνῆκεν, οὐδὲ ἐξέστη τῆς ἀρχαίας γνώμης, οὐδὲ ἐστράφη τὴν ψυχὴν ὑπὸ τῶν συμφορῶν, ἀλλὰ καίπερ τοσοῦτον τῶν ἄλλων τοῖς δεινοῖς πλεονεκτῶν ὥσθ᾽ οἱ μὲν ἄλλοι τοῖς παροῦσι τούτοις ἠθύμουν, ὁ δὲ καὶ τοῦτ᾽ αὐτὸ προσειλήφει μεῖζον τὸ τοὺς πολίτας οὕτως

---

71 Thuc. 2.12.

show that there is any exaggeration in this, then let the whole of my case be dismissed as nonsense.

Someone might indeed say that showing confidence 84
before war actually breaks out is not enough and no great achievement. Pericles however saw fit to receive embassies in Athens while the Peloponnesians remained where they were in their own territory, but refused to do so when they marched out on campaign and sent Melesippus on ahead.[71] So complete a coward was he, when he learned that the enemy were attacking, that he replied comprehensively to Melesippus in deed rather than word, by
handing him over to be escorted out of the country. And 85
the ultimate and greatest of all his deeds, even to hear about, let alone to imitate, was this. The war had broken out and was now upon them, and the plague was pressing in on them, and their territory was being ravaged, and people were dying every day with so many already lying dead that even a fraction of those losses would have paralyzed their enemy if they had fallen victim to that calamity themselves. But when he saw that the mass of the population were demoralized and indignant because of all this, and were having second thoughts about the measures they had voted for, and demanding that negotiations should be opened with the Spartans, when he saw that they had been changed by their sufferings, he was not any the more inclined to let up and did not depart from his former resolve and was not lowered in spirit by what had befallen. Instead, even though he was more disadvantaged by the dire situation than the others, to the extent that while they were disheartened by these circumstances, he also had to bear the greater extra burden of seeing his citizens in such a state that they were useless for practical action, so as not

ἔχοντας ὁρᾶν, ὥστ' ἀπόρους εἶναι χρῆσθαι, καὶ ταῦτα οὐχ ὅσον τοῖς πολεμίοις ὑποπεπτωκέναι, ἀλλὰ κἀκείνῳ δυσμεναίνειν ὡς τῶν παρόντων πραγμάτων αἰτίῳ· πρὸς δυοῖν τοῖν ἀπὸ τῆς τύχης, τῷ πολέμῳ καὶ τῇ νόσῳ, δύο ταῦτα προσειληφότας ὁρῶν αὐτούς, λύπην καὶ παροξυσμὸν εἰς αὐτόν, ἐν μέσοις τοῖς δεινοῖς ἐμβεβηκὼς καὶ πανταχόθεν μεμονωμένος ὡς εἰπεῖν, οὐκ ἔδεισεν οὐδ' ὑπεχώρησεν, οὐδ' ὥσπερ χροιὰν τὴν γνώμην μετέβαλεν, τοῖς τε πολίταις ὁμοῦ καὶ τοῖς πολεμίοις ἀντιτεταγμένος· ἀλλ' ὥσπερ ἂν ἄλλο τι μάθημα διδάσκων αὐτούς, κατὰ ταὐτὰ ἃ καὶ πρότερον διεξῄει, καὶ οὐ διέφθειρεν τὰ δόγματα ἐπὶ τῶν κινδύνων, οὐδὲ ἐπὶ τῆς ἐξουσίας ἐφιλοσόφησεν μόνον, ἀλλ' ὡς περὶ ἀριθμῶν ἢ μέτρων ἐρωτηθεὶς ταὐτὸν ἂν ἀπεκρίνατο καὶ ὕστερον καὶ πρότερον, οὕτω καὶ τότε τὰς αὐτὰς ἠφίει φωνὰς ὑπὲρ τῶν ὅλων πραγμάτων, οὔτε τοῖς δεινοῖς εἴκειν ἀξιῶν οὔτε αὑτῷ μέμφεσθαι, αἰσχύνεσθαί τε ὑπὲρ αὐτῶν ἑτέρων ἅμα τοῖς καιροῖς γεγονότων.

86 ὥστ' ἔμοιγε καὶ τὸν Αἴαντα τὸν πρὸ τῶν νεῶν μαχόμενον καὶ βοῶντα ἐν κουφοτέροις καὶ ῥᾴοσιν εἶναι δοκεῖν. τῷ μὲν γὰρ πρὸς τοὺς Τρῶας ἦν μόνον ἡ μάχη, τὰ δὲ τῶν οἰκείων εὐμενῆ δήπουθεν ὑπῆρχεν, τῷ δ' οὐχ ἧττον πονήρως εἶχε τῶν ἔξω τὰ ἔνδον καὶ πλείων ἦν ὁ φόβος τῶν πολιτῶν ἢ τῶν πολεμίων. ἐν οἷς ἔδειξεν οὐ τοῖς ὀψοποιοῖς ἐοικὼς οὐδὲν Περικλῆς,
87 ἀλλὰ τοῖς ἄκροις τῶν Ἑλλήνων. ὥστ' ἐμοὶ μέν, ὅταν

only to have collapsed before their enemies but also to hate him into the bargain as the one responsible for their present troubles, even though he saw them bearing the double burden of pain and of bitterness toward him in addition to the two blows of fortune constituted by the war and the plague, and was himself up to his waist in adversity and so to speak forsaken on all sides, he did not flinch or retreat or alter his resolve as someone might his complexion, as he confronted both his citizens and the enemy together. Just as if he were teaching them any other kind of lesson, he told them what he had told them before in the selfsame terms.[72] He did not allow his beliefs to become corrupted in times of danger and he did not philosophize only when it was safe to do so, but just as, if he had been asked a question about numbers or measurements, he would have given the same answer both earlier and later, so too at that time he spoke in the same tones on all matters without exception, deeming it wrong either to give way to dangers or to reproach himself, but right for the others to feel ashamed at the way they had changed in time with events.

Given this, I think that Ajax crying out as he fought to 86
protect the ships was in an easier and less oppressive situation:[73] he only had the Trojans to fight, since his own side were presumably well disposed toward him, but in Pericles' case the situation inside the city was as bad as that outside and he had more to fear from his fellow citizens than from the enemy. It was in this situation that Pericles showed that he did not resemble caterers at all, but rather
the greatest of the Greeks. So, whenever I direct my gaze 87

[72] Thuc. 2.59–64. [73] Hom. *Il.* 15.685–88.

βλέψω πρὸς ταύτας τὰς ἀπορίας καὶ τὸν ὄχλον τῶν πραγμάτων αὐτοῦ, κυβερνήτου τινὸς ἔννοιαν παρίστασθαι περικλυζομένης αὐτῷ τῆς νεὼς καὶ τῶν νεφῶν καταρρηγνυμένων ἐπὶ τῶν οἰάκων μένοντος καὶ οὐ μεθιέντος, καὶ πρός γ' ἔτι τῶν ἐμπλεόντων ἀπειλούντων καὶ ἑτοίμων ὄντων διασπάσασθαι, κατέχοντος καὶ νουθετοῦντος καὶ ἅμα ὑπέρ τε τοῦ σκάφους ἀγωνιζομένου καὶ πρὸς τοὺς ἐν τῷ σκάφει.

88 πόθεν οὖν ἔτι χρὴ τὴν ἀνδρείαν θεωρῆσαι; εἴτε γὰρ ἐκ τῶν ἔργων εἴτ' ἀπὸ τῶν λόγων ὁρῶμεν τὸν ἄνδρα, πῶς[18] ἄν τις μᾶλλον ἔδειξεν παντὸς ἀφεστὼς δέους, ἢ πῶς ἄμεινον πρὸς εὐψυχίαν αὐτός τε πεφυκὼς καὶ τοὺς ἄλλους ἄγων, ὅστις οὔτε ἐκείνους ἠξίου φόβῳ τῶν πολεμίων προέσθαι τὰ γνωσθέντα ἐξ ἀρχῆς οὔτ' αὐτὸς ἐκείνων φόβῳ τοὺς ὑπὲρ τῶν δικαίων λόγους
89 ἐγκαταλιπεῖν; εἰ δὲ λέγεις ὅτι οὐκ ἐπεξῆγεν, σκόπει μὴ οὐδεὶς τῶν στρατηγικῶν ταῦτ' ἀποδέξηται τὰ ἐγκλήματα. οὔτε γὰρ ἐν παντὶ καιρῷ οὔτε ἐν ἅπαντι δήπου χωρίῳ συμφαῖεν ἄν, ἀρχὴν δ' οὐ μάχεσθαι χρῆναι πάντως τόν γε δὴ χρηστὸν στρατηγόν, ἀλλὰ μάλιστα μὲν ἥκιστα κινδυνεύειν καὶ τοῖς βουλεύμασι μᾶλλον ἢ ταῖς χερσὶ πολεμεῖν, ὥσπερ καὶ Λακεδαιμονίοις ἐπιχώριον εἶναι δοκεῖ· εἰ δ' αὖ καὶ μάχης δεήσειεν, ἄμεινον μετὰ συμμάχων ἐθέλειν ἢ μόνους καὶ μετὰ πλειόνων ἢ μετὰ ἐλαττόνων καὶ μετὰ κρειττόνων

[18] *ita* Dindorf πῶς γάρ *codd.*

to these intractable problems and the mass of troubles he had to endure, I am put in mind of a helmsman, standing firm at the tiller and not giving way as the clouds burst and his ship is swamped around him, and in addition his crew threaten him and are ready to tear him limb from limb, restraining and reproving them, struggling simultaneously for the safety of his vessel and against those on board it.[74]

Do we need to spend any more time contemplating his 88
courage? Whether one looks at this man on the evidence of his deeds or on the evidence of his words, how could anyone more clearly have shown himself to be detached from all fear, or better endowed with courage in his own nature and better at inculcating it in others, than this man who thought it proper neither for them to abandon their original resolve from fear of the enemy, nor for him to leave off speaking in the cause of right through fear of
them? If you say that he did not lead the Athenians out on 89
campaign, beware of finding this charge rejected by all expert strategists; they would not agree with you over every occasion or indeed over every place. According to them the good general ought assuredly not to fight at all, but should for preference take the fewest possible risks and wage war by good planning rather than physical force, as is reputed to be the Spartans' native practice too; if however there had to be fighting as well, then they would say that it is better to engage in it with allies to support you than on your own, and with a larger number of them rather than a smaller one, and with superior rather than

[74] A sideways glance at Plato's image of the ship of state in *Resp.* 488a–89a, once again suggesting that Pericles fulfills Plato's ideals rather than falling short of them.

ἢ μετὰ χειρόνων, εἰς ὅσον ἂν περιῇ τινί. εἰς ἀνάγκην μὲν γὰρ καταστάντας οὐκ εἰκὸς ἀκριβῶς λογίζεσθαι, ἕως δέ τίς ἐστι κύριος γνώμης, ἄνοια πολλὴ καὶ δυστυχία τῆς ἀσφαλείας ἀφέμενον ὃ τοῖς πολεμίοις συνοίσει, τοῦτ᾽ ἐξεπίτηδες αἱρεῖσθαι. ἐκείνοις γὰρ ἂν ἤδη στρατηγοίη καὶ γίγνοιτο ἂν αὐτοῖς ἀντὶ τοῦ
90 παρ᾽ αὐτοῖς ἡγουμένου. μὴ δὴ τοῦτο λέγωμεν ὡς οὐκ ἐξῆγεν, ἀλλ᾽ εἰ προσῆκον ἐξάγειν καὶ μάχεσθαι παρεώρα, τοῦτο σκοπῶμεν, ἐπεὶ καὶ Λακεδαιμονίους ἀκούομεν δήπου προσκειμένων αὐτοῖς ποτὲ Θηβαίων καὶ κελευόντων ἐξιέναι καὶ μάχεσθαι ἢ χείρους ὁμολογεῖν εἶναι σφῶν, ἀποκρίνασθαι περὶ μὲν τοῦ πότεροι βελτίους τὰς πράξεις κρίνειν τὰς ὑπὲρ τῶν Ἑλλήνων ἑκατέροις πεπραγμένας, μαχεῖσθαι δὲ οὐκ ἐν τῷ τῶν πολεμίων καιρῷ οὐδ᾽ ὅτε ἐκεῖνοι κελεύουσιν, ἀλλ᾽ ἡνίκ᾽ ἂν αὐτοῖς δοκῇ, καὶ οὐ χρήσεσθαι περὶ τούτου συμβούλοις Θηβαίοις. καὶ ταῦτα ἀπεκρίναντο καὶ ταῦτα ἐποίουν Ἀγησιλάου προεστηκότος αὐτῶν, ὃς εἴπερ τις ἄλλος τῶν Ἑλλήνων γενέσθαι ἐδόκει φιλοπόλεμος.

91 ἀλλὰ τί χρῆν ποιεῖν τὸν Περικλέα; εἰπὲ γὰρ ὦ πρὸς θεῶν, μᾶλλον δὲ εἰ στρατηγῶν αὐτὸς ἐτύγχανες ἡμῖν κατ᾽ ἐκείνους τοὺς χρόνους, τί ποιεῖν ἂν ἢ τί λέγειν ᾤου δεῖν, ὄντων μὲν συμπάντων Ἀθηναίων τόσων καὶ τόσων, τῶν δὲ συμμάχων τῶν μὲν ἐν ταῖς νήσοις, τῶν δὲ κατ᾽ ἤπειρον μεμερισμένων, μυριάσιν δὲ ἓξ στρα-

inferior ones, as far as your circumstances permit. When
circumstances compel, it is not reasonable to expect people to calculate precisely, but as long as someone is free to
plan it is the height of folly and ill fortune for him to sacrifice his safety and choose deliberately what is going to
advantage the enemy, because he would then be exercising his command to suit them and becoming their general
by proxy. Let us not say that Pericles did not lead the 90
Athenians out on campaign, but instead let us consider
whether he passed up the opportunity to lead an expeditionary force and fight a campaign when it was appropriate
to do so. We are after all told that, on one occasion when
the Thebans were pressing them hard and telling them
either to march out and fight, or to confess their inferior-
ity, the Spartans replied that, on the question of who were
the better, they should judge by the achievements of both
in defense of Greece, but that they themselves would fight
not in their enemies' time nor when they told them to, but
when they themselves should so decide, and they would
not need the Thebans to advise them on the matter. They
made this answer and took this action when under the
leadership of Agesilaus, who had the reputation of being
a lover of war if any Greek ever did.[75]

But what ought Pericles to have done? Tell me, for 91
heaven's sake, or rather, if you had been our general at that
time, what would you have thought you needed to say or
do, when total Athenian numbers were such and such, and
their allies were divided up some on the islands and some
on the mainland, and the enemy had invaded with an army

[75] The episode is described in Plut. *Ages*. 31 and Diod. Sic. 15.65.

τιᾶς τῶν πολεμίων εἰσβεβληκότων, καὶ τούτων Πελοποννησίων, οὐδὲ γὰρ τοῦτο φαῦλον εἰς προσθήκην, ἀνθρώπων ἱκανῶν καὶ πρὸς ἅπαντας τοὺς Ἕλληνας μάχεσθαι, καὶ οὓς ἐγὼ φαίην ἂν ἡγουμένων γε Ἀθηναίων καὶ Περικλέους οὐ χαλεπῶς ἂν καὶ πᾶσαν γῆν ὑφ᾽ αὑτοῖς ποιήσασθαι. καὶ οὔπω λέγω τὴν νόσον τοσοῦτον πρᾶγμα, ἣ καὶ προσέκειτο ἐλαύνουσα καὶ τοὺς μὲν ὅλως ἀπανηλώκει τῶν ἀνθρώπων, τοὺς δ᾽ ἀχρήστους εἰς τὰ παρόντα ἐπεποιήκει, ἣν καὶ χωρὶς μάχης καὶ πολέμου προσβολῆς οὐχ ἕν τι τῶν ῥᾴστων ἦν ὑπενεγκεῖν.

92 καὶ μὴν οὐδ᾽ ἐκεῖνο ἠγνόει Περικλῆς ὅτι νικήσας μὲν πολλῷ πλείοσιν αὖθις μαχεῖται καὶ πολλοὺς ἄλλους εὑρήσει τοὺς ἀμφισβητοῦντας τοῦ τροπαίου, καθάπερ Κορίνθιοι πρότερον, καὶ κληρονομοῦντας τῶν αὐτῶν τούτων πραγμάτων· ὥστε τὴν Καδμείαν νίκην ἡγεῖτο νικήσειν, ὡς ἑτέρως δὲ πράξας ἀπολεῖν τὴν πόλιν. τοῖς μὲν γὰρ πολεμίοις μέρος ἑκάστοις ἐκινδύνευεν, αὐτοῖς δὲ καὶ τοὔδαφος τῆς πόλεως συνυπέκειτο τῷ κινδύνῳ, καὶ εἷς ὑπὲρ πάντων κύβος ἀνερρίπτετο, σωμάτων, χρημάτων, δόξης, ἡγεμονίας, τοῦ βάθρου τῆς πόλεως, τῶν ἐλπίδων, ὅτου τις ἂν
93 εἴποι παντός. οὔκουν ᾤετο δεῖν οὕτως ἄνισον ἀγῶνα ἀγωνίζεσθαι, οὐδ᾽ ἐπὶ μηδενὶ πλείονι πᾶσι τοῖς οὖσι

---

[76] Perhaps a reference to the fighting between Athens and Corinth in circa 460 BC, described at Thuc. 1.105–6.

of sixty thousand—sixty thousand Peloponnesians what is more (this is no trivial additional detail), men who could have fought against the whole of the rest of Greece, and I would say could under the leadership of Pericles and the Athenians easily have subjugated the whole world? And I have not yet mentioned the huge matter of the Plague, which harried and oppressed them and had already entirely destroyed some of the population, while making others useless for current needs, and which would not have been one of the easiest things to bear, even apart from battle and the onset of war.

Pericles was also well aware that if he should win a 92
victory, he would have to fight many more opponents subsequently and would find many others competing for the trophy, just as the Corinthians had done previously,[76] and laying claim to the same inheritance; consequently, he concluded, any victory would be a Cadmaean one,[77] and if he failed he would destroy his city. Each of the enemy had only a part of his strength at risk, whereas for the Athenians the very ground on which their city stood was imperiled and everything—lives, property, honor, supremacy, the city's foundation, hopes, everything one might think to mention—rode on a single roll of the dice.
He therefore thought that he ought not to engage in such 93
an uneven contest or risk everything he had for no advan-

[77] So called after the fratricidal combat of the brothers Eteocles and Polyneices for the throne of Cadmus' city, Thebes (see, e.g., Plut. *Mor.* 488a); a "Cadmaean victory," like a "Pyrrhic victory," is one that costs the winner(s) as much as or more than the loser(s).

κινδυνεύειν, σωφρονῶν οἶμαι καὶ στρατηγοῦ λογισμῷ
94 χρώμενος. ὁρῶμεν δὲ δήπου καὶ τοὺς παλαιστὰς οὐκ εἰς τὰ τῶν ἀντιπάλων ἰσχυρὰ συγκαθιέντας, οὐδ' ἐξεπίτηδες καθ' ἑαυτῶν παρέχοντας λαβάς, ἀλλ' ἀπὸ τούτων μὲν ὡς οἷόν τε μάλιστα ἀποχωροῦντας, τοῖς δ' ἑαυτῶν πλεονεκτήμασι χρῆσθαι πειρωμένους καὶ τὴν νίκην ἀπὸ τούτων διώκοντας. ἃ καὶ Περικλῆς ἐνθυμούμενος οὐκ ἔδωκεν τοῖς πολεμίοις τοσαύτην κατὰ τῆς πόλεως λαβήν, ἀλλ' ἐάσας ἐκείνους ἐν τῇ Ἀττικῇ ληρεῖν ἑκατὸν νεῶν ἐπίπλουν ἐξήρτυε τῇ Πελοπον-
95 νήσῳ καὶ αὐτὸς ἐμβὰς ἐκόμιζε τὴν στρατιάν. καὶ περιῆν τοῖς μὲν τῆς Ἀττικῆς μέρος τι τετμηκέναι, τοῖς δ' ὡσπερεὶ πᾶσαν τὴν πολεμίαν. ὥστε ἠναγκάζοντο ἤδη φεύγειν ἐκ τῆς Ἀττικῆς οἱ τότε ὡς ἐπὶ ἕρμαιον βαδίζοντες. οὕτως ἃ μὲν οὐκ ἐκίνει, προνοίας, οὐ δειλίας ἦν, ἃ δὲ κἀν τούτοις ὄντας ἠξίου τολμᾶν ἔσχατον δεῖγμα τῆς ἀνδρείας ἔχει τῆς ἐκείνου.

96 καίτοι πῶς οὐκ ἄτοπον, εἰ ὅτι μὲν οὐκ ἐξῆγεν αἰτιασόμεθα, ὅτι δὲ ἔξω τῆς Ἀττικῆς ἦγεν αὐτοὺς οὐ θαυμασόμεθα; καὶ ὅτι μὲν οὐκ ἐμάχετο οὗ μὴ προσῆκεν ἐπιτιμήσομεν, ὅτι δ' ἠπίστατο ποῦ χρὴ τοῦτο ποιεῖν οὐ διαλογιούμεθα; καὶ ὅτι μὲν οὐ τὴν Ἀττικὴν ἐνεπίμπλη πολέμου καὶ ταραχῆς κατηγορήσομεν, ὅτι δὲ εἰς τὴν πολεμίαν ἀπέβαινεν καὶ ἀντιμεθίστη τῇ Πελοποννήσῳ τὴν πολιορκίαν οὐ θήσομεν εἰς λόγον; ἀλλὰ

tage,[78] and in this I believe he both showed good sense and reasoned like a general. It is a matter of common observa- 94
tion that wrestlers do not accommodate themselves to their opponents' strong points or deliberately offer holds against themselves, but rather retreat as far as they can from such behavior, trying to exploit their own advantages and using these as their means to victory. With this in mind, Pericles too declined to give the enemy such a substantial hold against his city, but instead allowed them to waste their time in Attica, while he prepared an expeditionary force of a hundred ships against the Peloponnese, then embarked and led the campaign himself.[79] The one 95
side succeeded in ravaging a mere part of Attica, but the other more or less the whole of their enemies' territory, with the result that those who had initially marched in as if to claim a windfall were then compelled to flee from Attica. Thus the moves Pericles declined to make were a sign of forethought not cowardice, and the daring action he thought that they should take even in this situation is the ultimate proof of his courage.

96 How can it not be absurd for us to make it a matter for censure that he did not lead them on a local sortie, and yet refuse to admire him for leading them outside Attica entirely? To reproach him for refusing to fight when it was not appropriate, yet not to reflect that he understood when it ought to be done? To denounce him for not filling Attica with the turmoil of war, yet not to count it to his credit that he disembarked on enemy territory and turned the siege on the Peloponnese? Are we going to look for

[78] "Risk everything he had" echoes Dem. *Philip.* 4 (10) 3.
[79] Thuc. 2.56.

τὰ μὴ πραχθέντα ἀντὶ τῶν πεπραγμένων ζητήσομεν; καὶ ὅτι μὴ νοσοῦντας μὲν οὐκ ἐξῆγεν οὐ συγγνωσόμεθα, ὅτι δὲ καὶ νοσοῦντας ἐξῆγεν οὐ θαυμασόμεθα; ὅστις οὕτω καμνόντων ἡγεῖτο, ὡς οὐδ' ἂν εἷς τῶν ἐρρωμένων καθαρῶς. οὕτω καὶ τῶν πολεμίων καὶ τῶν πολιτῶν καὶ τοῦ λοιμοῦ καὶ παντὸς ἦν κρείττων
97 πράγματος. καίτοι σχολῇ γ' ἂν Ἀθηναίους ἑαυτῶν ὄντας εἴασεν ἀργεῖν, ἢ ὑποκατακλίνεσθαί τισιν ἀνθρώπων, ὅστις οὐδὲ κάμνειν αὐτοῖς ἐπέτρεπεν, ἀλλ' εἴς γε τὸν περὶ τῆς ἐλευθερίας ἀγῶνα καὶ τὸ μὴ λιπεῖν τὴν τοῦ φρονήματος τάξιν ἠξίου καὶ παρὰ τὴν ὑπάρχουσαν τύχην ἐρρῶσθαι. πρότερον δ' ἔγωγ' ἂν ᾤμην τὸν Μελέαγρον ὀφλῆσαι δειλίας ἢ Περικλέα, ὅν γε καὶ πρὶν γενέσθαι προσεῖπεν ἀπ' αὐτῶν τῶν ἐναντιωτάτων ὁ θεός, προειπὼν αὐτοῦ τῇ μητρὶ λέοντα τέξεσθαι· ἡ δ' ἐπὶ ταύτῃ τῇ ὄψει τίκτει Περικλέα. ὥσθ' ὅρα μὴ λέοντα ξυρεῖν ἐπιχειρῶμεν, οὐ Θρασύμαχον συκοφαντεῖν ἐπιχειροῦντες, ἀλλὰ κωμῳδεῖν Περικλέα, καὶ ταῦτα εἰς δειλίαν, ἔπειτ' αὐτοὶ δόξωμεν ἀνδρειότεροι τοῦ δέοντος εἶναι τοῖς βουλομένοις ἀντικατηγο-

---

80 "Abandon the station that their courage had won them" is Demosthenic: Dem. 13.34 (cf. §§184 and 300 below, and *Or.* 12.53).

81 Meleager in Greek mythology famously refused to be cowed by the prophecy of the Fates to his mother Althaea that he would die when a branch burning in the fire was completely consumed (Apollod. *Bibl.* 1.8.2–3). The prophetic dream of Peri-

what he did not do instead of for what he did do? Will we
decline to forgive him for refusing to lead them out when
they were not afflicted by the plague, yet not admire him
for leading them out even when they were? He who led
them when they were sick better than anyone could lead
an army in full health and strength? Such was his mastery,
over the enemy and his fellow citizens and the plague and
all. He would hardly have permitted the Athenians to re- 97
main idle when in full possession of themselves, or to bow
down before anyone on earth, given that he did not allow
them to do so when they were sick, but instead expected
them in the fight for their freedom, and so as not to abandon the station that their courage had won them,[80] to show
a strength out of proportion to their actual circumstances.
I would have expected Meleager to have fallen victim to a
charge of cowardice sooner than Pericles, seeing that even
before the latter's birth the god foretold him in quite opposite terms, in prophesying to his mother that she would
give birth to a lion, and she on receiving this dream vision
gave birth to Pericles.[81] So let us beware of trying to beard
a lion, in attempting not to criticize Thrasymachus but to
satirize Pericles,[82] and for cowardice into the bargain, and
then of being thought bolder than we ought to be by those
who might wish to accuse us in return, and of it turning

cles' mother Agariste is described at Hdt. 6.131.2, in wording that Aristides echoes here.

[82] An allusion to Pl. *Resp.* 341c ("Do you think I'm crazy enough to try to shave a lion by criticizing Thrasymachus?"—spoken by Socrates).

ρεῖν, καὶ φανῇ τι καὶ δειλίας, εἰ δὲ βούλει, σιωπῆς ἀκίνδυνον γέρας, ὥς τις τῶν Κείων ἔφη ποιητής.

98 ἀλλὰ γὰρ λίνον λίνῳ συνάπτει, φασίν. ὃς γὰρ ἐτόλμησεν εἰπεῖν ὅτι καὶ φιλαργύρους ἀπέφηνεν Περικλῆς ἀνθρώπων καὶ οὑστινασοῦν τί τις ἂν λέγοι; νὴ Δία, πρῶτος γὰρ εἰς μισθοφορὰν κατέστησε τὰ πράγματα. ἐγὼ δὲ εἰμὶ μὲν οὐδ' αὐτὸς τῶν ἐπαινούντων τὸ μισθοφορεῖν, καὶ τούτου σχεδὸν ἔργῳ πεῖραν
99 ἐγὼ δεδωκέναι νομίζω. οὔκουν μέτεστί μοι τοῦ πράγματος οὐδέν, ἀλλὰ καὶ τῶν λόγων προὔστην καθαρώτερον ἢ τῶν φόρων οἶμαι τὸν ὁμώνυμον, εἴ τι δεῖ καὶ νεανιεύσασθαι. ὁ μὲν γὰρ τὸ σύμμετρον τάξας ἑκάστοις οὕτως εὐδοκίμησεν, ἐγὼ δὲ οὔτε πλέον οὔτε ἔλαττον οὐδενὶ πώποτε· ἀλλὰ οὐδ' ὅσαι διαδόσεις πρὸς οὐδεμίαν πώποτε ἀπήντησα, εἰ μή τις ἑκὼν ἔπεμψεν. ἀλλὰ καὶ τὴν Σωκράτους εἴτε χρὴ σοφίαν εἴτε φιλοσοφίαν λέγειν, ἢ καί τι ἄλλο, καὶ τοῦτο ἄγαμαι, τὸ μὴ καπηλεύειν μηδ' ἐπὶ τοῖς βουλομένοις

---

[83] Simonides fr. 582 *PMG*. The original wording and context of Simonides' words are unclear; Aristides' (rather labored) point seems to be that, because it is stupidly over-bold to accuse Pericles of cowardice—as Plato has done—a degree of "cowardice" over this (just keeping quiet about it) may be the safer course.

[84] The saying is used by Plato himself, in a negative version ("you are not joining flax with flax") in *Euthyd.* 298c (cf. Strattis fr. 39 Kassel-Austin, Arist. *Ph.* 207a17). Aristides converts the reproach for inconsistency into the suggestion that Plato is, with

out that it is to cowardice, or if you prefer, to silence (as a certain Cean poet once said),[83] that a risk-free reward attaches.

But Plato joins one thread of flax to another, as the 98
saying goes,[84] in daring to assert that Pericles made them greedy too. But what can one say about someone who dares assert that Pericles made anyone at all greedy? Well, look (the argument would be), he was the first to make state subsidies a feature of public life.[85] Now, I myself do not belong among those who approve of receiving state subsidies either, and I think I have given pretty direct
proof of this in action. So I am not compromised at all in 99
this respect; indeed, if I may be allowed to boast, I have championed oratory in a purer spirit than that in which my namesake supervised the tribute payments.[86] He gained his good reputation from setting a suitable rate for each people, but I have never set a higher or a lower rate for anybody, and indeed I have never attended a single one of the many distributions that there are, unless someone sent me something of his own free will. I admire Socrates' principle—whether one should call it wisdom, or philosophy, or something else besides—of not selling one's wares or putting oneself into the power of those who want to buy

a wrongheaded consistency, compounding one mistake with another.

85 *Grg.* 515e: the maintenance allowance paid to citizens doing jury service.

86 The fifth-century politician, "Aristides the Just": Hdt. 8.79, Thuc. 5.18.5, Plut. *Arist.* 4. For Aristides' sense of his own devotion to oratory as distinctively high-minded and pure, cf. n. 42 above.

ὠνεῖσθαι ποιεῖν ἑαυτόν, μηδ᾽ οὕτω σφόδρα φάσκειν ἑαυτὸν πεπαιδεῦσθαι ὥστε δουλείαν αὑτοῦ καταψηφίζεσθαι.

100 *ἐγὼ μὲν οὖν ὅπερ λέγω περὶ τούτων, οὕτω καὶ χαίρω τῇ μεγαλοπρεπείᾳ παντὸς μᾶλλον, ὥς γε ἐμαυτὸν πείθω· ὁρῶ δὲ ὅτι πολλὰ τῶν πόλεών ἐστιν ὥσπερ ἐφόλκια, οἷς ἀνάγκη συγχωρεῖν ὥσπερ ἐν σώματι. καὶ γὰρ τὰ σώματα καὶ τὰ χείριστα καὶ τὰ κάλλιστα ἀκούω ἐκ τῶν αὐτῶν κεκρᾶσθαι, τῷ δ᾽ ἢ πλείονος ἢ ἐλάττονος τούτων ἕκαστον μετέχειν, τούτῳ κρίνεσθαι τό τε χεῖρον καὶ τὸ βέλτιον. οὕτω δὴ καὶ τὰς πόλεις ἀνάγκη τῆς φύσεως τῆς ἀνθρωπείας ἀπολαύειν, κἂν ὡς βέλτιστα οἰκεῖσθαι δοκῶσιν. ἐπεὶ κἂν τῷδε τῷ παντὶ τοσούτων καλῶν καὶ τοσαύτης ἀγαθῆς τύχης μετειληφότι καὶ οὐδὲν ἔξω δήπουθεν αὑτοῦ λελοιπότι τῶν καλῶν πολλὰ ἂν εὕροις οἷς ἥκιστα ἂν ἡσθείης· ἀλλ᾽ οὐ κατηγορεῖς διὰ ταῦτα τοῦ παντὸς οὐδὲ τοῦ ποιήσαντος, οὐδὲ νομίζεις ἄλλον τινὰ δήπου βελτίω γενέσθαι ποτὲ ἂν αὖθις δημιουργὸν τῶν ὅλων, ἀλλὰ δίδως τῇ φύσει ταῦτα ἐφειλκύσθαι καὶ οὐ πολυπραγ-*
101 *μονεῖς. τί δὴ θαυμαστὸν εἰ καὶ Ἀθήνησί τι τῶν πάντων οὕτως ἔσχεν ὥσπερ ἴσως ἄν που καὶ ἄλλοθι, καὶ συνεχώρησαν οἱ προεστῶτες ἅμα μὲν τὴν τῶν πολλῶν πενίαν καὶ χρείαν ἐπανορθούμενοι, δι᾽ ἣν οὐκ*

---

[87] Plato, *Ap.* 19d–20c, 31b–c, 33a–b; Xen. *Mem.* 1.2.5–8, 1.6.11–14.

from you, or so vehemently insisting on one's own erudition as to condemn oneself to slavery.[87]

I for my part then am convinced in my own mind at 100
least that, in line with what I have said on this matter, I really do prize such nobility of spirit more than anything else. But I also see that cities as it were tow many smaller boats behind them, to which as in the case of a human body some concession has to be made. Because human bodies, I understand, the meanest and the handsomest alike, are all compounded from the same constituents, and the distinction between better and worse is drawn according to the greater or lesser proportion of these constituents that they contain. In just the same way cities too, even if they have the highest reputation for good governance, must necessarily feel the effects of human nature. Even in this Universe around us, which partakes of so many beautiful things and is so richly blessed by fortune, and has left nothing beautiful outside itself, you could find much vehemently to dislike; but you do not on these grounds condemn the Universe or its maker, and you do not think that there could ever be some other better Creator of everything, but instead you grant that such things are a necessary concomitant of nature and make no fuss about it.[88]
Would it be so very surprising if in Athens also some part 101
of the whole was in the same kind of condition as perhaps elsewhere too, and the leading citizens cooperated in alleviating the poverty and want of the masses, which is the

[88] Aristides here echoes Stoic justifications for the presence of apparently negative elements in the perfect universe devised by divine providence: see, e.g., Chrysippus in Gell. *NA* 7.1.7–13 (= *SVF* 2.1170, 54Q Long-Sedley).

ἐλάχιστα τῶν ἁμαρτημάτων συμβαίνει, ἃ κωλύειν μᾶλλον οὕτως ἡγοῦντο, ἅμα δὲ εὐλαβούμενοι μή τι καὶ χεῖρον ἐξεργάσαιντο τῷ καθείργειν παντελῶς αὐτούς. τί γὰρ οὐκ ἦν προσδοκῆσαι ποιήσειν ἀνθρώπους τοσούτους τὸ πλῆθος καὶ οὕτως ὀξεῖς, καὶ χρημάτων τοσούτων παρόντων, εἰ μηδεὶς αὐτοῖς μετεδίδου τὰ μέτρια; ἆρ᾽ οὐ πάντ᾽ ἂν αὐτοῖς ἐπιχειρῆσαι
102 λαβεῖν; ἔτι δὲ ὥσπερ ἐν τοῖς ἰδίοις οἴκοις πᾶς τις οἶμαι βούλεται τῶν προσόντων ἀπολαύειν, οὕτως οὐδὲν ἀπεικὸς καὶ πόλιν ἄλλως τε καὶ ἀρχὴν ἔχουσαν, ἐν οἷς οὐχ ὁ τὸ πᾶν κωλύων ἴσως βέλτιστος, ἀλλ᾽ ὅστις τοῦ μετρίου ποιεῖται λόγον. ἢ τί χρῆν ἢ φόρους ἔτι λαμβάνειν ἢ πράγματα ἔχειν, εἰ μηδὲν ἔμελλον ἀπ᾽ αὐτῶν κουφιεῖσθαι; ὥσθ᾽ ὅταν ταῦτα λέγῃς, οὐ τὸν μισθὸν ἐγκαλεῖς, ἀλλὰ τὴν ἀρχήν.

103 ἐπεὶ ὅτι γε ἀναγκαῖον ἐν πόλει μισθὸς καὶ οὐκ ἔνεστι παρελθεῖν οὐδὲ τῷ σεμνοτάτῳ τὸ μὴ οὐκ ἐπιχορηγῆσαι καὶ φιλανθρωπεύσασθαι οὐδὲν δέομαι μαρτύρων πολλῶν, ἀλλ᾽ εἷς ὁ τῶν Ἑλλήνων ἄριστος ἐξαρκεῖ μοι. τίς οὗτος; αὐτὸς σύ. τῇ γὰρ εὐδαίμονί τε καὶ ἀγαθῇ πόλει—πῶς γὰρ οὐκ εὐδαίμων ἧς γε οἰκιστής ἐστι Πλάτων;—τοὺς φύλακας διδοὺς τάττεις μισθὸν αὐτοῖς δημοσίᾳ, ὡς οὔτε αὐτὸς αἰσχρὸν οὐδὲν συμβουλεύων οὔτ᾽ ἐκείνους ποιήσοντας οὐδετέρους,
104 οὔτε τοὺς δώσειν οὔτε τοὺς λήψεσθαι μέλλοντας. εἰ δὲ

[89] Aristides here plays on *Grg.* 472b–c.

cause of the greater part of the mistakes that are made—mistakes which they thought they had a better chance of preventing by this means—and at the same time combined in taking care not to bring about still worse results by repressing them completely? For what actions could not be expected from such a great mass of the hot-tempered, with such a quantity of money available, if nobody gave them a reasonable share of it? Would they not try to take it all for themselves? Again, just as in his own 102
house I think everyone wants to enjoy what he has, so there is nothing unreasonable in a city feeling the same way, especially an imperial city, in which the best citizen is perhaps not the one who puts a brake on everything, but the one who is alert to the need for moderation. What was the point of continuing to go to the trouble of collecting tribute payments if this was not going to make the people's lives any easier? So when you say this, your complaint is not against the state subsidy, but against the empire.

Because I do not need many witnesses to prove that a 103
city needs its subsidies and that even the haughtiest of its citizens cannot dispense with volunteering funds and performing acts of philanthropy; one witness, the very best in Greece, is enough for me.[89] Who is that? You, Plato. When furnishing your blessed and virtuous city with Guardians—how could a city that has Plato for its founder not be blessed?—you specify payment for them from public resources,[90] as if you yourself were not recommending anything disgraceful and as if neither party among them, neither the prospective givers nor the prospective receivers, were going to do anything disgraceful either. If this 104

[90] *Resp.* 416d–417a.

μὴ ἀργύριον μηδὲ χρυσίον ὁ μισθός ἐστιν, ἀλλ᾽ ἕτερόν τι, ἕτερος λόγος οὗτος. πρὸς γὰρ τὰ σχήματα τῶν πολιτειῶν οἶμαι καὶ τοὺς μισθοὺς εἰκὸς εἶναι. οὐδὲ γὰρ εἰ Βυζάντιοι σιδήρῳ νομίζουσιν, τούτου χάριν εἰσὶ δίκαιοι τῶν Ἑλλήνων καταγελᾶν, οὐδ᾽ ἧττόν τι δοκεῖν ἂν φέρειν μισθόν, ὅτι οὐ χρυσίον οὐδὲ ἀργύριον φέρουσιν· οὐδέ γε εἰ Καρχηδόνιοι σκύτεσιν· εἰ μὴ κἄν τινες ἀργύριον φέρωσιν, ὅτι οὐ τὸ τιμιώτερον αὖ φέρουσι χρυσίον, ἄλλο τι τοῦτ᾽ ἢ μισθὸν εἶναι φήσουσιν. ἀλλ᾽ οὐδ᾽ ἂν εἷς οἶμαι ταῦτα συγχωρήσειεν. οὐδὲ γὰρ τὰς τροφὰς ἅπασι τὰς αὐτὰς αἱρεῖ-
105 σθαι νόμος, δεῖ δὲ ὅμως ἅπασι τροφῶν. οὕτω δὴ κἀνταῦθα μὴ τίς ὁ μισθός, ἀλλ᾽ ὅλως[19] εἰ μισθὸν εἴρηκας· εἰ μὴ καὶ ὁ Εὔνεως προῖκα τὸν οἶνον ἔπεμπε τοῖς Ἀχαιοῖς, ὅτι οὐκ ἀργύριον αὐτῷ διέλυον, ἀλλ᾽ οἱ μὲν χαλκόν, ἄλλοι δ᾽ αἴθωνα σίδηρον. ἀλλ᾽ οὐδ᾽ αὐτὸς
106 ταῦτά γε ἠλαζονεύετο. Περικλῆς τοίνυν οὐκ αὐτὸς κοψάμενος νόμισμα, ἀλλ᾽ ὄντων ἐν ἀκροπόλει χρημάτων ἐκεῖθεν ἔσῳζε τὸν μισθόν. ὥστε οὐδετέρου δίκαιος ἔχειν αἰτίαν, οὔτε τοῦ νομίσματος οὔτε τοῦ μισθοῦ.

107 καὶ τί ταῦτα ἀγωνίζομαι σφόδρα; εἰ γὰρ ὡς οἷόν τε μάλιστα αἰσχρὸν ἡ μισθοφορὰ καὶ τὸ νέμειν, οὐ τῆς Περικλέους ἐστὶ πολιτείας, οὐδ᾽ ἀπὸ τῶν ἐκείνου χρόνων ἤρξατο, ἀλλὰ καὶ τῶν νομοθετῶν τις ἤδη[20]

[19] ὅλως Reiske ὅμως *codd.*
[20] ἤδη Reiske ᾔδει *codd.*

payment is neither silver nor gold, but something else, that is a different point: I think it is perfectly reasonable for forms of payment to be relative to types of constitution. If the people of Byzantium use iron for currency, and the Carthaginians use hides, that does not justify them in laughing at the Greeks, nor in themselves being thought any the less to receive payment just because it is not gold or silver that they receive—unless it is also the case that if some people receive silver they will say that this is something other than a payment, because they are not receiving the most valuable thing, namely gold. I do not think a single person would agree with this. It is not customary either to choose the same forms of nourishment for everybody, but all the same, everyone still needs to be fed. So 105
too in this case, what matters is not what form the payment takes, but whether you have mentioned payment at all—unless it is the case that Euneus sent the Achaeans wine for free, simply because they did not settle up with him with silver, but some "with bronze and some with flashing iron."[91] Not even Euneus himself said anything as idiotic as that. Pericles however maintained the payment of the 106
subsidy not by having coins minted himself, but from the reserves stored on the Acropolis. Consequently, there is no justification for blaming him either for the coinage or for the subsidy.

But why am I arguing so vehemently about this? Even 107
if a state subsidy and its distribution is the most disgraceful thing imaginable, it was not distinctive of Pericles' political program, and did not originate in his times; one of the Founding Fathers, indeed, had already introduced it

[91] Hom. *Il.* 7.467–75.

108 ταῦτα· τοὺς γὰρ ἄλλους σιωπῶ. οὕτω τὰ μὲν ὕστερα
τῆς ἐκείνου πολιτείας ἐγκέκληκεν, ἃ μικρῷ πρόσθεν
ἠλέγχομεν, τὰ δὲ πρεσβύτερα, τὰ περὶ τοῦ νομίσμα-
109 τος, ὥσπερ[21] νῦν αὖ δείκνυται. πῶς ἄν τις ῥᾷον χρήσαιτο ἄνθρωπος λόγοις, ἢ πῶς μετὰ πλείονος ἐξουσίας;

ὅλως δ' ἔγωγε θαυμάζω, εἴ τίς ἐστιν ἁπλούστερος
ἢ δικαιότερος τρόπος ἐξετάσεως εἰ[22] φιλαργύρους
ἐποίησεν Περικλῆς Ἀθηναίους ἢ καὶ ἄλλους τινὰς ἀνθρώπους Ἑλλήνων ἢ καὶ βαρβάρων, ἢ αὐτὸν ἰδεῖν
καὶ σκέψασθαι τὸν Περικλέα ποῖός τις ἦν. ὁ γὰρ τοῦ
Ξενοφῶντος λόγος ἐρρῶσθαί μοι δοκεῖ. ὥσπερ γάρ,
ἔφη, τοὺς παιδοτρίβας ὁρῶμεν τὰ μὲν τῇ φωνῇ τοῖς
παισὶν εἰσηγουμένους, τὸ δὲ πλεῖστον τῷ παραδεῖξαι
προσβιβάζοντας, οὕτω καὶ Σωκράτη φησὶν κρίνειν
110 δίκαιον. οὕτω τοίνυν καὶ Περικλέα δὴ θεασώμεθα,
πῶς αὐτὸς εἶχε πρὸς χρήματα καὶ ποῖόν τινα παρεῖχεν ἑαυτὸν παράδειγμα τοῖς τε Ἀθηναίοις καὶ τοῖς
ἄλλοις Ἕλλησιν κατὰ τοῦτο τὸ μέρος· κἂν μὲν εὑρί-
σκωμεν αὐτὸν ἀγεννῆ καὶ ἀνελεύθερον καὶ τοῦ κέρδους ἥττονα,[23] φῶμεν καὶ τοὺς ἄλλους ταὐτὰ διδάσκειν καὶ διαφθείρειν καὶ παραπλησίους αὑτῷ ποιεῖν·
εἰ δὲ τοσοῦτον ὑπερεῖδεν χρημάτων, ὅσον οὐκ οἶδ' εἴ
τις τῶν πώποτε, πῶς ἐποίει φιλοχρημάτους, ἢ πῶς

[21] *ita* Reiske ὥσπερ ἅ *codd.* ἅ *vel* ἅπερ Lenz
[22] *ita* Reiske εἴ τε *codd.*
[23] ἥττονα *codd.* ἥττω *edd.*

(to say nothing of the others).[92] Thus some of Plato's 108
charges belong later than Pericles' administration, namely
the ones I was disproving a while back, and others belong
earlier, namely the ones concerning coinage, as is now
being shown in its turn. How could anyone be more casual 109
in his use of argument, or allow himself any greater license
than this?

All in all, I would be amazed if there were any simpler
or fairer way of examining whether Pericles made the
Athenians, or any other Greek or foreign people, greedy,
than to look at Pericles himself and consider what sort of
a man he was. Xenophon's principle seems to me to be a
valid one. He says that we see gymnastic trainers explaining some things to their pupils in words, but for the most
part using practical demonstrations to help them progress,
and that this is also the right light in which to judge Socrates.[93] So let us examine Pericles too in this light, to es- 110
tablish what his attitude to money was, and what sort of
personal example he set to the Athenians and the rest of
Greece in this regard. If we find that he was ignoble and
mean and a slave to gain, let us say that he taught the same
to others as well and corrupted them by making them like
himself; but if on the other hand he had a contempt for
money that I do not think was matched by anyone ever,
how could he have made them greedy, or have corrupted

[92] It is not clear what evidence Aristides is relying on here, given that *Ath. pol.* 27.3–4 firmly credits Pericles with the introduction of jury pay (the scholia say he means "Solon or Poliouchos").

[93] In *Mem.* 1.2.17, Xenophon asserts that Socrates taught by personal example as well as by formal lessons but says nothing about gymnastic trainers.

ἑτέρους διέφθειρεν, ἐν οἷς αὐτὸς χρηστὸς ἦν; ὥσπερ ἂν εἰ λέγοις τὸν Ῥαδάμανθυν ἐθίζειν τοὺς ἀνθρώπους ἐπιορκεῖν, ᾧ τοσοῦτον περιῆν εὐσεβείας καὶ δικαιοσύνης ὥστε καὶ τελευτήσας τοῖς ἐκεῖσε ἀφικνουμένοις
111 δικάζειν δοκεῖ περὶ τῶν ἐν τῷ βίῳ πραχθέντων. καὶ σὺ δείξας οὖν πρότερον τὸν Περικλέα μικρὸν καὶ ἀγεννῆ καὶ ταπεινὸν καὶ πρὸς ἀργύριον βλέποντα, τότε δὴ φάθι καὶ τοὺς ἄλλους πεποιηκέναι τοιούτους· ὥσπερ καὶ τοὺς περὶ τῶν γραμμάτων διδασκάλους ἔστιν εἰπεῖν· οὐκέθ' αὕτη Ξενοφῶντος ἡ εἰκών, ἀλλ' αὐτοῦ Πλάτωνος. ὥσπερ γάρ, φησίν, οἱ γραμματισταὶ τοῖς μήπω δεινοῖς γράφειν τῶν παίδων ὑπογράψαντες γραμμὰς τῇ γραφῖδι οὕτω τὸ γραμματεῖον διδόασι καὶ ἀναγκάζουσι γράφειν κατὰ τὴν ὑφήγησιν τῶν γραμμάτων,[24] οὕτω δὴ καὶ ἡ πόλις. ἀλλ'
112 ἡμεῖς ἀντὶ τῆς πόλεως λάβωμεν τὸν Περικλέα. Περικλῆς τοίνυν τὰ μὲν λέγων, ὡς ἔοικεν, ὑφηγεῖτο τοῖς Ἀθηναίοις, ἐν οἷς οὐδὲν ἦν ἀνελεύθερον οὐδὲ ἀγεννές, τὰ δὲ ἐπ' αὐτοῦ τοῦ βίου δεικνὺς ἑαυτὸν καὶ παρέχων
113 σκοπεῖν ὁποῖός τις ἦν. πότερ' οὖν εἰς κάλλος αὐτοῖς ζῆν ὑπέγραφε τοιοῦτος ὢν οἷον ἀκούομεν, ἢ πρὸς κέρδος καὶ τὴν χεῖρα ὑφεικότας καὶ ὡς ἥκιστα ἔμελλον ὀρθῶς πράξειν; καὶ μὴν λέγοντος μὲν αὐτοῦ ἐν ταῖς ἐκκλησίαις ἤκουον κἂν τῷ βουλευτηρίῳ, τὸν δὲ βίον καθ' ἑκάστην ἑώρων δήπου τὴν ἡμέραν. ὥστε εἴπερ ἑώρων πρὸς ἐκεῖνον, ἔμελλον κρείττους εἶναι χρημάτων.

[24] γραμμῶν *fort. scribendum cum codd. Plat.*

others in respects in which he himself was good? It is as if you were to say that Rhadamanthys got people into the habit of breaking their oaths, when in fact he was so superlatively pious and just that even in death he is reputed to judge those arriving on the other side for their deeds in
life.[94] First show, then, that Pericles was petty and mean 111
and unctuous and on the lookout for money, and then say that he made the others the same. Think of what one can say about teachers of reading and writing. This is no longer Xenophon's comparison, but Plato's own: he says that the state's practice is just like that of schoolmasters, who trace faint lines with their stylus for those of their pupils who are not yet good at writing, then hand the tablet over to them like this and make them follow the traces as they write.[95] But for our purposes let us put "Pericles" rather
than "the state." Pericles, then, it seems, showed the Athe- 112
nians the way partly by what he said, in which there was nothing mean or ignoble, and partly by displaying himself in the very way he lived his life and allowing them to consider what sort of a man he was. So, in being the kind of 113
man we are told that he was, was he sketching out for them a life lived with an eye to high moral principle, or a life lived with an eye to gain, with their hands held out, in the way least calculated to let them behave rightly? They heard him speak at meetings of the Assembly and in the Council, and his style of life they could of course observe every day, so if it was to him that they looked, they were bound to be above considerations of money.

[94] As noted by Plato in *Grg.* 523e–24a and 524e–25a.

[95] *Prt.* 326d (spoken by Protagoras, rather than Socrates).

114 φέρε δὴ καὶ περὶ τῶν ἄλλων ἁπασῶν αἰτιῶν αὖ
τούτου σκεψώμεθα καὶ διέλθωμεν τὸν αὐτὸν τρόπον
ὅνπερ περὶ τῆς φιλαργυρίας, κατ᾽ ἀμφοτέρας ταύτας
τὰς εἰκόνας, τήν τε τοῦ παιδοτρίβου καὶ τοῦ γραμμα-
τιστοῦ, καὶ συγκεφαλαιωσώμεθα πάντα ἐν βραχεῖ.
115 λάλους, φησίν, ἐποίησεν· καὶ μὴν οὐκ ἦν αὐτὸς
λάλος. ἀργούς· ὁ δ᾽ ἐνεργὸς ἦν. δειλούς· ὁ δὲ νικῶν
ἀνδρείᾳ φαίνεται. φιλοχρημάτους· ὁ δ᾽ ἥκιστα ἐτίμα
116 χρήματα. πῶς οὖν αὐτὸς ὢν ἀγαθὸς λέγειν, ἱκανὸς
πράττειν, ἀνδρεῖος, κρείττων χρημάτων, ἐποίει λάλους, ἀργούς, δειλούς, ἀνελευθέρους; ἢ γὰρ ὄναρ λέγεις, ἢ γρῖφον, ἢ οὐκ ἔχω τί φῶ. πῶς γὰρ οὐκ ἄτοπον,
εἰ οἷος μὲν αὐτὸς ἦν οὐκ ἐποίει τοιούτους, οἷος δ᾽ ἥκιστα αὐτὸς ἦν, τοιούτους ἀπειργάζετο; ἐμοὶ μὲν γὰρ
τοὐναντίον ἐκ τούτων φαίνεται, τὸ γοῦν καθ᾽ αὑτόν,
πεποιηκὼς δεξιούς, ἐνεργούς, ἀνδρείους, μεγαλοπρε-
πεῖς· εἰ μή τι καὶ κατὰ Σωκράτους χρὴ πιστεύειν, ὅτι
τοὺς νέους διέφθειρεν, ὃς αὐτοῖς παράδειγμα παντὸς
117 ἦν χρηστοῦ. οὐκ ἔστιν ταῦτα, ὦ Πλάτων, ἀλλὰ δυοῖν
θάτερον· ἢ οὐκ ἦσαν Ἀθηναῖοι τοιοῦτοι οἵους σὺ
κατῃτιάσω, ἢ πάντες μᾶλλον ἢ Περικλῆς αἴτιος, εἴπερ γε μήτε φαύλως ἐδείκνυ τὰ παλαίσματα μήτε
ἀσαφεῖς τινὰς ἢ κιβδήλους ἢ σκολιὰς παρεῖχε τὰς
γραμμάς.

118 ἔτι τοίνυν τῶν ἀνωτέρω μνημονεύσωμεν καὶ συλ-
λογισώμεθα, καὶ ταῦτα ἐκ τῶν πεφηνότων. Πλάτων
εἶπεν μὴ δεῖν κολακεύειν τὰ πλήθη· Περικλῆς δέ γε
πλείστῃ παρρησίᾳ χρησάμενος φαίνεται. διαμάχε-

3. IN DEFENSE OF THE FOUR

Let us now consider all Plato's other accusations in turn 114
and go through them in the same way as we did the charge
of greed, in the light of the twin comparisons with the
gymnastics trainer and the schoolmaster, and let us sum
everything up concisely. "He made them garrulous," he 115
says; but in fact Pericles was not himself garrulous. "He
made them lazy"; but in fact he was vigorous. "He made
them cowardly"; but in fact he was manifestly superlatively
brave. "He made them greedy"; but in fact he set minimal
value on money. So how, when Pericles himself was a good 116
speaker, an able doer of deeds, a brave man, and above
considerations of money, did he make the Athenians garrulous, lazy, cowardly, and mean? Either you are describing a dream, or setting a riddle, or I do not know what to
say. Surely it is extraordinary if he did not make them into
the sort of people he was, but did make them into the sort
of people he simply was not. To me at least it is quite clear
that he did the exact opposite, as far as depended on him,
and by these means made them clever, active, brave, and
noble—unless we must also believe of Socrates that he
corrupted the young, when in fact he was an example to
them of everything that is good. That is impossible, Plato, 117
and one of two things must be the case instead: either the
Athenians were not the sort of people you accused them
of being, or the blame lay with anyone sooner than with
Pericles, at any rate if he neither demonstrated their wrestling holds to them incompetently, nor furnished them
with indistinct, debased, or crooked letters.

Let us also recall and summarize the earlier charges, 118
in the light of what has now been established. Plato said
that politicians should not play the flatterer to the masses;
it is clear that Pericles always spoke with the greatest can-

σθαι δεῖν ὑπὲρ τοῦ βελτίονος· ὁ δ' ἐν καιροῖς τοιούτοις ἐμάχετο οἷς ἀρτίως ἡμεῖς ἐπεδείκνυμεν. μὴ ζητεῖν ἀποπιμπλάναι τὰς ἐπιθυμίας· ἐκεῖνος τοίνυν κατεῖχεν καὶ οὐκ ἤγετο μᾶλλον ἢ αὐτὸς ἦγεν. μηδ' ἐκ παντὸς τρόπου συνεθίζειν πλέον ἔχειν, φησὶν ὁ τὸν νόμον τιθείς· ὁ δ' ἀφ' ἑστίας ἀρξάμενος τῆς αὐτὸς αὑτοῦ τὸ σύμμετρον ᾑρεῖτο πρὸ τοῦ πλέονος. [οὐκοῦν ταῦτ' ἐδόκει Πλάτωνι, ταῦτα ποιῶν Περικλῆς φαίνεται.][25] πῶς ἄν τις μᾶλλον κατὰ τοὺς Πλάτωνος λόγους φανείη βεβιωκὼς ἢ πεπολιτευμένος; ἢ τίνα χρῆν ὑπὲρ ἐκείνου πρῶτον εἰπεῖν, εἴ τις ἐπῃτιάσατο; [Πλάτωνα.][26]

119 μέγιστον δὲ κἀκεῖνο σημεῖον τῆς Περικλέους ὀρθότητος ἄνευ τῶν εἰρημένων, καὶ ὡς οὐκ ἐκεῖνος ἦν ὁ διαφθείρας οὐδ' ἐθίσας Ἀθηναίους φιλαργύρους εἶναι, οὐδ' ἐκ παντὸς τρόπου τὸ πλέον ζητεῖν ἔχειν. οὔτε γὰρ τοὺς φόρους Περικλῆς εἰς ἄπειρόν ἐστιν ὁ ἐξαγαγών, ἀλλὰ καὶ ταύτης τῆς ἀμετρίας, ὦ φίλε Σώκρατες, εἰ ζητοίης τὸν αἴτιον, τὸν ἑταῖρον εὑρήσεις τὸν σεαυτοῦ. ἐκεῖνος γάρ ἐστιν ὁ πρὸς τοσοῦτον προαγαγὼν τοὺς φόρους, ὅσον οὐδὲ βουλομένοις φέρειν ἐξῆν, οὔτε σοὶ πειθόμενος οὐδὲν οὔτε τὸν Περικλέα

120 μιμούμενος. ἀλλ' οὐ Περικλῆς τοιοῦτος οὔτ' ἐνταῦθα οὔτε ἄλλοθι, ἀλλ' οὕτω σφόδρα πόρρω τῆς πλεο-

25 *del.* Lenz
26 *del.* Dindorf

dor. He said that they should fight to the finish for what is for the best; Pericles fought his fight in the circumstances I explained just now. He said that they should not seek to satiate their people's desires; Pericles restrained them and took the lead rather than being led. Our legislator also says that politicians should not accustom their people to gaining the advantage at every turn; starting with his own hearth and home, Pericles consistently chose what was proportionate rather than what won an advantage.[96] How could anyone more clearly have shaped his life and his politics to conform to Plato's principles? Or who ought to have been the first to defend him, if someone had accused him?

Leaving aside what has just been said, there is also a 119
very substantial proof of Pericles' rectitude, and of the fact that he did not corrupt the people of Athens or accustom them to being greedy, or to seek to gain an advantage at every turn, in the following consideration. It was not Pericles who infinitely increased the tribute payments either; the man responsible for that disproportion, my dear Socrates, you would discover on investigation to be your very own companion![97] He was the one who increased the tribute payments to such a level that even willing tributaries could not have borne them, without listening to you or
imitating Pericles' example in the least. Pericles was not 120
that sort of person in this case or in any other, but was so very far from thoughts of gain and from advising the Athe-

[96] The next sentence in the Greek text, bracketed opposite, looks like a reader's note ("So this is what Plato believed, and this is what Pericles clearly did").

[97] Alcibiades ([Andocides] 4.11).

νεξίας ἦν καὶ τοῦ συμβουλεύειν Ἀθηναίοις τὰ μὴ προσήκοντα πράγμαθ' ἑαυτοῖς προστίθεσθαι ὥστε τῷ προτέρῳ πολέμῳ κεκρατηκότας αὐτοὺς Πελοποννησίων καὶ ἔχοντας [Μέγαρα][27] *Νίσαιαν καὶ Τροιζῆνα καὶ Πηγὰς καὶ Ἀχαΐαν ἔπεισεν ταῦτα ἀποδόντας εἰρήνην συνθέσθαι. [τοσούτου ἔδει προσδιδάσκειν*
121 *πλέον ἀεί τι τῶν ὑπαρχόντων αὐτοὺς ἔχειν.]*[28] *ὥστ' ἔγωγε νομίζω πρὸς ταῦθ' ὁρῶν καὶ τούτοις τεκμαιρόμενος, εἰ ἐπεβίω Περικλῆς καὶ μὴ πρότερον ᾤχετο ἀπιών, οὐκ ἂν εἰς ἔσχατον κακῶν ἐξοκεῖλαι τοὺς Ἕλληνας, ἀλλ' ἐπειδὴ τοὺς ἄνδρας τῶν Λακεδαιμονίων εἶχον Ἀθηναῖοι καὶ Πύλον, οὐδὲν ἂν αὐτοὺς πλέον ζητῆσαι, ἀλλ' εὐθὺς ἐλευθέρως ἂν ταῦτ' ἀποδόντας ποιῆσαι τοῖς Ἕλλησι κοινὴν εἰρήνην. οὐδὲ γὰρ αὐτὸν τὸν πόλεμον πλεονεξίας ἕνεκα αὐτοῖς προελέσθαι συνεβούλευσεν, ἀλλὰ τοῦ μὴ τῶν ὑπαρχόντων ἀποστῆναι· ἀρχὴν δ' ἐκεῖνός γε οὐδ' ἠξίου γίγνεσθαι πόλεμον, ἀλλὰ δίκῃ διαλύεσθαι περὶ τῶν διαφόρων.*
122 *οὕτω καὶ πόλεμον ἐξ εἰρήνης ᾔδει δέχεσθαι καὶ παρὸν εἰρήνην ἄγειν οὐδαμοῦ τὸν πόλεμον προῃρεῖτο· οὐδὲ τοῦ πλείονος αὐτοὺς ἔχεσθαι συνείθιζεν, ἀλλὰ τοῦ προσήκοντος. καίτοι ταῦτά ἐστιν ἀνδρείας, εὐβουλίας, δικαιοσύνης, τῶν καλλίστων ἐπιδείγματα, ἀλλ' οὐχ ὧν Πλάτων ἀνέθηκεν αὐτῷ.*

[27] *del.* Keil [28] *del.* Behr

---

[98] In 445 BC (Thuc. 1.115 and 4.21). The Greek text adds Megara to the start of this list, in line with *Or.* 1.278, but against

nians to add things to their possessions that were not appropriate to them that in the earlier war, when they had defeated the Peloponnesians and had taken possession of Nisaea and Troezen and Pegae and Achaea,[98] he persuaded them to give them all back and make peace.[99]
Looking at this and judging by these indications, I for one 121
am of the opinion that if Pericles had survived and not departed the scene first, the Greek nation would not have run aground in such an extremity of misfortune as it did; instead, when the Athenians had captured Pylos and its Spartan garrison,[100] they would not have sought any further gain, but would have had the magnanimity to hand them back immediately and make a shared peace for all the Greeks. Pericles had after all not advised them to vote for the war for the sake of gaining an advantage, but so as not to resign what they already had; in fact, he did not even think that there ought to be a war at all, but that they ought
to settle their differences by arbitration. That is how true 122
it is that he both knew how to wage war in succession to peace and, when it was possible to remain at peace, never chose war, and that he made the Athenians accustomed to cling not to prospects of gain but to what belonged to them. All this is proof of the noblest virtues—courage, wise counsel and justice—not of what Plato attributed to him.

the evidence of Thuc. 1.115.1 and 4.21.3; since the addition breaks the grammatical construction, it is probably best deleted here. [99] The next sentence in the Greek text, bracketed opposite, looks like a reader's note, summarizing Aristides' point: "That is how far he was from instructing them always to have something more than they already possessed."

[100] In 425 BC (Thuc. 4.24–41).

123 οἶμαι τοίνυν ἔγωγε καὶ τὴν ἐπωνυμίαν ἣν ἔσχεν ἐκεῖνος ἐν τοῖς Ἕλλησιν, οὐχ ἥνπερ Μίθαικός τε καὶ Θεαρίων, ἀλλὰ τὴν αὐτὴν τῷ Διί, μαρτύριον μέγιστον εἶναι τοῖς ὑπὲρ αὐτοῦ λόγοις καὶ ὡς οὐ τῶν φαύλων τις ἦν. ἢ τῆς μὲν Ἀριστείδου δικαιοσύνης σύμβολον τὴν ἐπωνυμίαν ποιούμεθα—οὐ γὰρ αὐτοί γέ που τάττοντι παρῆμεν αὐτῷ τοὺς φόρους—τῆς δὲ Περικλέους ἀρετῆς τε καὶ φύσεως οὐ ποιησόμεθα τὴν ἐπωνυμίαν σύμβολον, ἣν οὐκ ἀφ᾽ ἑνὸς τῶν τῆς ἀρετῆς μορίων, ἀλλ᾽ ἀπὸ πάντων συλλήβδην ἐκτήσατο; ὅτι γὰρ οὐκ ἀτιμαστέον αὖ τοὺς πολλοὺς οὐδὲ ἀμελητέον τῆς δόξης τῆς παρ᾽ αὐτῶν, ἀλλ᾽ ἔνι τι κἀν τούτοις εὔστοχον θείᾳ τινὶ μοίρᾳ τῆς ἀληθείας ἐφαπτόμενον, αὐτὸς Πλάτων ὁ διδάσκων καὶ λέγων ἐστίν· ἔτι δὲ ἀνωτέρω Πλάτωνος πολλαῖς γενεαῖς ὕμνησεν Ἡσίοδος ποιήσας τὰ ἔπη ταῦτα ἃ πάντες ᾄδουσιν

φήμη δ᾽ οὔτις πάμπαν ἀπόλλυται ἥντινα πολλοὶ
λαοὶ φημίξωσι· θεός νύ τίς ἐστι καὶ αὐτή.

124 οὐκοῦν ἡ φήμη μαρτυρεῖ τῷ Περικλεῖ τὰ κάλλιστα, καὶ θεὸς οὖσα αὐτὴ[29] φησὶν ἐκεῖνον κρείττονα ἢ κατ᾽ ἄνθρωπον γενέσθαι. καὶ μὴν οὐδ᾽ ἐκεῖνό γε ἔστιν εἰπεῖν ὡς ἄρα φαύλως πράττοντες ὑπὸ συμφορῶν Ἀθηναῖοι ταύτην αὐτῷ παρεῖσαν τὴν τιμήν, ὥσπερ χρόνῳ ὕστερον ἔσθ᾽ ἃ καὶ παρ᾽ ἀξίαν συνεχώρησαν ταπει-

29 αὐτή Reiske αὕτη *codd.*

I also think that the epithet Pericles enjoyed among the Greeks, which was not the one borne by Mithaecus and Thearion but the same as is applied to Zeus,[101] offers the weightiest of testimonies in his defense, to prove that he was not one of the worthless. Or are we going to take Aristides' epithet as evidence of his justice—since I take it we were not there with him when he was setting the tribute payments—but not take Pericles' as evidence of his virtuous nature, even though it was given him not on the strength of just one species of virtue but of all of them together? It is Plato himself who maintains in his teaching that we should not scorn the majority or disregard the opinions that emanate from them, but that by some divine dispensation there is in them too an element of shrewdness that can attain to the truth.[102] And even many generations before Plato Hesiod proclaimed as much when he composed those lines that everyone recites: 123

> No rumor ever wholly perishes that many
> folk noise abroad; this too is some kind of goddess.[103]

Reputation then offers the most glowing evidence in Pericles' favor: with the authority of her own divinity she declares him to have been superhuman. Nor can it be said that the Athenians conceded him this honor when setbacks had put them in a bad way, just as later on they agreed to a number of unworthy measures when they had been humiliated by defeat.[104] No, if they ever flourished 124

[101] "The Olympian." [102] *Leg.* 950b–c.

[103] *Op.* 763–64. [104] It is not clear whether this refers to the measures imposed on Athens following its defeat in 404 BC, or to the consequences of its defeat by Demetrius Poliorcetes in 307 BC (Diod. Sic. 20.46.2, Plut. *Demetr.* 10–13).

νωθέντες. ἀλλ' εἴπερ ποτὲ ἄλλοτε ἤκμαζον καὶ τότε
καὶ ἦν ἡ πόλις αὐτοῖς ἐπ' ἐκείνου μεγίστη, ὡς ἂν
ἡμεῖς, ὦ Πλάτων, μεγίστην φαῖμεν. ἀλλ' οὐδέν γε
τοῦτο βλάβος τῷ λόγῳ. τοὺς γὰρ οὕτως ὡς λέγω
πράττοντας ἀνάγκη πλεῖστον ἐφ' αὑτοῖς οἶμαι φρονεῖν καὶ πορρωτάτω μὲν ταπεινότητος, ἐγγυτάτω δὲ
αὐθαδείας εἶναι. τότε τοίνυν αὐτὸν προσεῖπον Ὀλύμ-
125 πιον, τοσοῦτον ἦν τὸ συγκεχωρηκός. καίτοι τί λέγω;
εἰ γὰρ τὰ μάλισθ' ὑπεπεπτώκεσαν,[30] περιετρέπετο καὶ
οὕτως ὁ λόγος Πλάτωνι. ἐκεῖνοι γὰρ ἐκεῖνον ἤδη κο-
λακεύοντες φαίνοιντ' ἄν, οὐ Περικλῆς Ἀθηναίους.
ἀλλὰ οὔτ' Ἀθηναίους Περικλῆς οὔτ' Ἀθηναῖοι Περι-
126 κλέα. πόθεν; ἀλλ' ὁρῶντες ἄνδρα καὶ λέγειν καὶ πράττειν ἄκρον καὶ δουλείας μὲν οὐδαμῶς ἐγγύς, ἄρχειν
δ' ἐπιτηδειότατον καὶ ἱκανώτατον καὶ πάντων ὑπερ-
πεφυκότα τῶν ἄλλων, ἔπαθόν τι Ὁμηρικὸν καὶ παρα-
127 πλήσιον αὐτὸν τοῖς θεοῖς ἐνόμισαν. εἶθ' ὃν οἱ χρώμενοι καὶ συνόντες καὶ μετὰ τῆς πείρας εἰδότες τῆς
αὐτῆς θεοῖς προσηγορίας ἠξίωσαν, τοῦτον ἡμεῖς Θεα-
ρίωνι καὶ Μιθαίκῳ καὶ οὐκ οἶδ' ὅτῳ τῷ[31] τρίτῳ γρα-
φώμεθα τῆς αὐτῆς; οὐκ ἄρ' εὖ φρονεῖν δόξομεν.

[30] ὑπεπεπτώκεσαν Behr ὑποπεπτώκεσαν *codd.*
[31] τῷ *del.* Reiske

at any other time, they were flourishing then, and their city was at its greatest in his day, in our sense of the word "greatest," Plato. But this does no damage to the argument. Because it is inevitable that people whose fortunes are as I have described should have the greatest pride in themselves and be at their furthest from humility and their nearest to conceit. It was at this point in time that they gave him the epithet "Olympian." Such was the degree
of their deference. But what am I saying? Even if they 125
had been utterly dejected, even so Plato's own argument would be turned against him, because it would by now be clear that the Athenians were flattering Pericles, not Pericles the Athenians. But in fact Pericles did not flatter the
Athenians, nor the Athenians Pericles. Why would they? 126
No, seeing a man superlative in both speech and action, with nothing in the least servile about him, ideally suited and equipped to rule and excelling all others, they had a Homeric moment and deemed him comparable to the
gods.[105] Are we then to put into the same category as 127
Thearion and Mithaecus and whoever else might make up a trio with them[106] the man whose acquaintances and associates, who knew him from direct experience, thought worthy of the same mode of address as the gods? If so, people will think we are mad.

[105] Echoing such Homeric phrases as *epieikelon athantoisi* and *athatoisin homoios* (like to the immortals).

[106] Sarambus: *Grg.* 518b.

[*Argumentation 2: Vindication of Cimon (128–49)*]

128 ἀλλὰ νὴ Δία ὁ Κίμων φαῦλός τις ἄνθρωπος, ἢ τοιοῦτος οἷον ἀπεύξαιτ' ἄν τις μὴ γενέσθαι παιδίον αὐτῷ. ἀλλὰ τούτου γε καὶ χάριν ἄν τις Πλάτωνι δικαίως ἔχοι, ὅτι καὶ τοῦτον ἡμῖν εἰς τοὺς ῥήτορας ἐγγράφει. ὡς ἐγὼ μᾶλλον ἂν τοῦτο ἔδεισα, μή τις αὐτὸν τῶν ῥητόρων μὲν ἀποστεροίη, τιθείη δὲ τῶν στρατηγῶν. νῦν δὲ ἀκριβῶς τὸ τοῦ Ὁμήρου συμβαίνει, τὸν αὐτὸν ἂν ἀρκεῖν

μύθων τε ῥητῆρ' ἔμεναι πρηκτῆρά τε ἔργων,

εἰ δὴ καὶ Κίμων ἔσται μεθ' ἡμῶν. οὕτως οὐδὲν ὄνειδος τῇ ῥητορικῇ Κίμων ἐγγραφόμενος.

129 ἐβουλόμην δ' ἂν καὶ πρὸς ἄλλον τινά μοι τὸν ἀγῶνα τυγχάνειν ὄντα καὶ μὴ πρὸς Πλάτωνα, καὶ περὶ τούτου λέγω καὶ περὶ τῶν ἄλλων, ἵνα πᾶσιν οἷς εἶχον ἐχρώμην θαρρούντως καὶ μὴ συνέβαινέν μοι παραπλήσιον ὥσπερ ἂν εἰ πλέων καὶ παρὸν ἐξ οὐρίας κομίζεσθαι, εἶτα ὑφιέμην ὑπὸ δειλίας, ἢ καὶ ἵπποις ἀγωνιζόμενος, ἐξὸν καὶ ταχὺ καὶ τοσοῦτον ὅσον βούλομαι παρενεγκεῖν, εἶτ' ἀνεῖχον ἐξεπίτηδες φειδοῖ τοῦ προειληφότος· οὕτω πολὺ πλείω ποιοῦμαι λόγον μηδὲν ἀπηχὲς εἰς Πλάτωνα τυχεῖν εἰπὼν μηδ' ὡσπερεὶ θρασύνεσθαι δοκεῖν, ἢ ἐκείνων ἕκαστον ἐπαινέσαι. εἰκότως· οὐδὲ γὰρ ἐλάττονος ἄξια χάριτός μοι τὰ

130 πρὸς τοῦτον. οὐ μὴν ἀλλ' εἴ γ' ἄμφω συμβήσεται, καὶ

Argumentation 2: Vindication of Cimon (128–49)

But, our adversary will say, Cimon was certainly a worth- 128
less sort of person, the kind of man you would pray not to have as your son.[107] Yet one might be forgiven for feeling grateful to Plato at least for the fact that we find him enrolling Cimon among the orators. I would have been more frightened at the prospect of someone taking him away from the orators and categorizing him as a general. But as it is, Homer's idea, that the same man could be capable

> Of being a speaker of words and a doer of deeds,[108]

is fully realized if Cimon is included in our ranks. That is how definitely his enrollment is no reproach to oratory.

I could have wished that I was in dispute with someone 129
else rather than Plato, I mean both over Cimon and over
the others, so that I could cheerfully deploy all the resources at my disposal and not find myself experiencing
something akin to striking my sails from cowardice when
at sea and free to run before a following wind, or deliberately holding back so as to spare the man in front when in
a chariot race and in a position to overtake at speed and
go as far into the lead as I desired. That is how very much
more concerned I am that I shouldn't find myself saying
anything discordant about Plato or give the impression of
behaving brashly, than I am to praise each of those men—
and quite reasonably so, since my relationship with Plato
demands no less warmth of feeling. All the same, if it can 130

[107] Cf. §149 below.
[108] *Il.* 9.443.

τὰς κατ᾽ ἐκείνων αἰτίας ἀπολύσασθαι καὶ Πλάτωνι πᾶν ὅσον αἰδοῦς καὶ τιμῆς ἔξεστιν σεσωκέναι, καὶ προσέσται τὸ δίκαιον ἀμφοτέροις, μετρίως ἂν ἔχοι πανταχῇ.

131 ὅτι μὲν τοίνυν οὐχ εἷς τῶν κομψῶν οὐδ᾽ οἷος ὑπελθεῖν καὶ κολακεῦσαι Κίμων ἐγένετο οἱ μηδὲ τὰ πατρῷα ἐθελήσαντες αὐτῷ παραδοῦναι μέχρι πόρρω τῆς ἡλικίας ἐπίτροποι μαρτυροῦσιν· οὕτως εὐήθη καὶ μᾶλλον ἀρχαῖον ἡγοῦντο. ὅτι δ᾽ οὐ παντὸς ἀνδρὸς τὰ Κίμωνος πράγματα οὐδὲ τῆς ἐσχάτης μοίρας, ἀλλὰ καὶ λογίσασθαι περὶ πραγμάτων δεινὸς ἁνὴρ[32] καὶ καταπρᾶξαι, καὶ τοιοῦτος οἷος μὴ μόνον παρ᾽ Ἀθηναίοις εἰκότως εὐδοκιμεῖν, ἀλλὰ καὶ παρὰ Λακεδαιμονίοις οὐ χαλεπῶς ἂν τὰ πρῶτα ἔχειν, ἐφεξῆς ἂν εἴη

132 λέγειν. ἅπαντα μὲν τοίνυν τἀκείνου διηγεῖσθαι ἢ καὶ τὰ τῶν ἄλλων τῶν ὑπολοίπων ἔξω τοῦ καιροῦ παντελῶς γίγνοιτ᾽ ἄν, ἄλλως τε καὶ μηδεμιᾶς αἰτίας εἰρημένης κατ᾽ αὐτῶν πρὸς ἣν ἀπολογεῖσθαι δεῖ, πλήν γε δὴ ὡς διάκονοί τινες ἦσαν. ἃ δ᾽ ἐστὶν ὡσπερεὶ κεφάλαια καὶ ὅσα οὐδὲ βουλομένῳ παρελθεῖν δυνατόν, ταῦτ᾽ εἰρήσεται.

133 ἀνάγκη δὲ ἴσως τοσοῦτον ὑπειπεῖν. εἰ μὲν γὰρ ἅπαντα ταῦθ᾽ ἡμῖν ἐστιν διακονία καὶ νόμους θεῖναι καὶ πολιτείαν καταστῆσαι καὶ στρατοπέδων ἄρξαι καὶ ἀρχὴν ἐπέτειον ἐν πόλει, καὶ προσέτι προβουλεῦσαι, προεδρεῦσαι, πρεσβείαν τελέσασθαι, δικάσαι

[32] ἁνήρ Trapp ἀνήρ *codd.*

be contrived both that I absolve those men from the charges against them and that in the process I preserve all possible respect and honor for Plato, and both sides receive their due, then that would be the respectable outcome all round.

Well then, evidence that Cimon was not one of the 131
smart set, nor the kind of person to ingratiate himself and flatter, is provided by those guardians of his who did not want to hand over his inheritance to him until he was well on into adulthood; that is how naïve, or indeed old-fashioned, they thought him to be. What needs to be said in the next breath is that Cimon's achievements were not commonplace, nor those of a nonentity; no, this was a man skilled both in reasoning things through and in bringing his plans to fruition, and the kind of person not only to enjoy a justifiably high reputation among the Athenians, but also easily to have occupied the first place among the
Spartans as well. Now, it would go entirely beyond what 132
the present occasion allows to detail all his achievements, or those of the remaining figures as well, especially as no charge has been brought against them that requires a defense except that they were some kind of lackeys. But I shall give what you might call the headlines, and everything that I could not omit even if I wanted to.

Perhaps I need to say this much by way of a preface. 133
If we are going to count all of the following as the work of mere lackeys, making laws, establishing constitutions, commanding armies, holding annual magistracies in the city, and in addition framing preliminary decrees, holding presidencies, conducting embassies, judging cases, orga-

δίκας, πανηγύρεις, ἂν οὕτω τύχῃ, κοσμῆσαι, λέγω συνελὼν ἅπασαν πρᾶξιν καὶ προστασίαν, εἰ διακονίαν καὶ ὑπηρεσίαν χρὴ καλεῖν, οἷον δὴ καὶ βασιλείαν αὐτὴν καὶ δυναστείαν ἅπασαν, καὶ ἔτι γ', εἰ βούλει, πρότερον οἰκίας ἄρχοντα μὴ ἄρχειν μᾶλλον ἢ δουλεύειν, καὶ τὸ τοῦ κωμῳδιοποιοῦ βεβαίως καὶ παγίως ἔχει ὡς ἄρ' εἷς εἴη τῆς οἰκίας δοῦλος ὁ δεσπότης· εἰ ταῦθ' οὕτως ὥσπερ ἔφην ἔχει, πρῶτον μὲν ἔγωγε οὐχ ὁρῶ πῶς ἂν μᾶλλον πάντ' ἄνω καὶ κάτω γένοιτο. εἰ γὰρ τἀναντία τοῖς ἐναντίοις ὁριούμεθα, πῶς ἕκαστον ἔθ' ἡμῖν σώσει τὴν αὑτοῦ φύσιν; εἰ γὰρ ἡ ἀρχὴ δουλεία, σχολῇ γ' ἂν ἄλλο τι δουλείαν ἐκφύγοι· κἂν εἴ γε τὴν ἀρχὴν δουλείαν εἶναι τιθείημεν, τί κωλύει καὶ τὴν δουλείαν ἀρχὴν τοῖς αὐτοῖς τούτοις τιθέναι λόγοις; κἀκ τούτου περίεισιν ἡμῖν ἡ θέσις, καὶ οὐδέποτ' ἐν ταὐτῷ μένει, ἀλλ' ἡ μὲν ἀρχὴ δουλεία πρότερον γενομένη δι' ἐκείνης πάλιν ἀρχὴ γίγνεται, ἡ δ' αὖ δουλεία πρότερον ἀρχὴ νομισθεῖσα ὑπ' αὐτῆς τῆς ἀρχῆς ἐπάνεισι δουλεία πάλιν εἶναι. καὶ οὕτω πλανήσεται καὶ μεταχωρήσει τὰ ὀνόματα ταῦτα τῶν ἐναντίων πραγμάτων ὄντα, εἰ δὲ βούλει,
134 τἀναντία τοῦ πράγματος. καὶ μὴν οὐδὲ ὅ τι λοιπὸν ἔσθ' ἡμῖν τούτων περιῃρημένων ῥᾴδιον εὑρεῖν. εἰ γὰρ μὴ προστησόμεθα μήτε πολλῶν μήτε ὀλίγων, μήτε οἰκίας μήτε ἡμῶν αὐτῶν, ὡς ἔπος εἰπεῖν, μηδὲ κινήσει μηδένα ἡμῶν μήτε χρεία πατρίδος μήτε ἑστία πατρῴα μήτ' οἰκέται ὁρῶντες εἰς ἡμᾶς μήτε ἄλλο τῶν ἀνθρωπίνων μηδέν, ἀλλ' οὕτω φυγῇ φευξούμεθα τὰ

nizing festivals if the occasion arises, I mean in sum if we have to call all forms of political activity and leadership the work of lackeys and servants, and indeed kingship itself and all forms of rule, and if you also want at a lower level say that the head of a household is not its head but its slave, and the comic poet's joke, that a household's only slave is its master,[109] is fairly and squarely true; if all of this were to be as I have just said, then for a start I for one cannot see how it would be possible to turn the world upside down more completely. Because if we define things as their opposites, how on earth will anything keep hold of its own true nature? If ruling is slavery, then it would be hard for anything else to escape being slavery either; and what is more, if we were to stipulate that ruling is slavery, what is to stop us stipulating that slavery is rule by the very same reasoning? As a result, our thesis will turn round on itself and never stand still: ruling having formerly been slavery will by being slavery become ruling again, and slavery in turn having formerly been thought of as rule will through being rule return to being slavery again. That is how these names, which are the names of their opposites, or if you prefer, names opposed to the reality, will wander
about and change position. Moreover, it is not easy to see, 134
either, what we are left with if these capacities are stripped away. If we are not going to be in charge either of large or of small numbers, or of a household, or even so to speak of ourselves, and if none of us is going to be moved to action by our country's need or our ancestral hearth or our household servants looking to us or any other human consideration, but instead we are to flee from all activity like

109 Menander, *Monostich.* 168 = fr. 506 Kassel-Austin.

πράγματα καὶ καθεδούμεθα ὥσπερ ἐν μέσῳ τῷ ἀέρι, τῆς γῆς οὐδὲν προσαπτόμενοι, οὐδὲ φροντίζοντες οὐδενὸς πράγματος, οὐδ᾽ ἂν προσαγγέλλῃ τις ἡμῖν ἅπερ τῷ Μελεάγρῳ,

ἄνδρας μὲν κτείνουσι, πόλιν δέ τε πῦρ ἀμαθύνει,
τέκνα δέ τ᾽ ἄλλοι ἄγουσι βαθυζώνους τε γυναῖκας,

ἀλλὰ πάντα ταῦτα ἀνελευθερίαν καὶ ταπεινότητα εἶναι καταγνωσόμεθα, καὶ πρὸς ἅπανθ᾽ ἡμῖν οὗτος ὁ λόγος ἀρκέσει, τὸ διακονεῖν ταῦτ᾽ εἶναι καὶ ὑπηρετεῖν καὶ τὸ ἀδικεῖσθαι κρεῖττον ἢ ἀδικεῖν, ἄλλο τι ἢ τῶν ἀψύχων ἐγγύτατα ζῆν λείπεται, καὶ τοῖς κάμνουσι παραπλησίως, ὅταν αὐτοῖς ὑπὸ τῶν ἰατρῶν ἡσυχάζειν ἐπιταχθῇ;

135 εἰ δ᾽ οὖν καὶ διακονία πάντα ταῦτ᾽ ἐστὶν καὶ οὐδὲν σεμνόν, τί μαθών, ὦ φίλη κεφαλή, αὐτὸς ἡμῖν τοὺς διακόνους μιμῇ, πολιτείαν κατασκευαζόμενος καὶ νόμους συγγράφων, καὶ λέγεις μὲν καὶ τυραννίδα συντελεῖν εἰς νόμων θέσιν, λέγεις δὲ τῇ φιλοσοφίᾳ δυναστείας προσδεῖν καὶ μὴ πρότερον παύσεσθαι κακῶν τὰς πόλεις, πρὶν ἄν σοι τὸ πολυύμνητον δὴ τοῦτο ἢ οἱ βασιλεῖς φιλοσοφήσωσιν, ἢ βασιλεύσωσιν οἱ φιλόσοφοι; ὡς εἰ μὴ ταῦτα συνέλθοι, φιλοσοφία καὶ δύναμις πολιτική, οὐδὲν πλέον εἰς τὸ κοινὸν τοῖς ἀν-
136 θρώποις ἐσόμενον. καὶ τὸ δὴ μέγιστον ἁπάντων, ἐν

this and sit idly down as if suspended in midair, out of contact with the ground, and have no concern for anything, even if someone brings us the same message as they brought Meleager—

> They are killing the men, and fire is razing the city to
> the ground,
> While others lead captive their children and deep-
> girdled wives—[110]

and we are going to dismiss all this as base servility, and treat the proposition that it is the work of lackeys and servants and that being wronged is better than doing wrong as a uniquely adequate principle,[111] what is left to us except to live for all the world like inanimate objects, or like sick people when they are ordered to rest by their doctors?

But, Plato my dear fellow, if all this is the work of lack- 135
eys and nothing to go in awe of, then whatever made you
go and imitate the lackeys yourself by setting up a Republic and drafting Laws? Why do you say that tyranny too has
a contribution to make to the establishment of laws,[112] and
that philosophy needs political power, and that cities will
not find relief from their ills until, in your much-quoted
phrase, either kings practice philosophy, or philosophers
become kings,[113] on the grounds that unless philosophy
and political power coincide, human beings will see no
benefit in their life together? Most significantly of all, in 136

[110] *Il.* 9.593–94.

[111] The position maintained by Socrates throughout the *Gorgias*, from 469b onward.

[112] *Leg.* 709e–10b.

[113] *Resp.* 473c–e.

γὰρ αὐτοῖς οἷς πολιτεύῃ καὶ νομοθετεῖς, ἀφορίζεις μὲν φύλακας τῇ πόλει, οἵτινες τὴν αὐτὴν ἕξουσι τέχνην Κίμωνι, δίδως δὲ αὐτοῖς τὰ πρεσβεῖα τῶν ἄλλων πολιτῶν, οὐκ ὀλίγον τι προκρίνας, καὶ τιμὰς καὶ προεδρίας καὶ ζῶσιν καὶ τελευτήσασιν, ὃς ἂν αὖ τούτων ἄριστος φανῇ, καὶ ὅλως περὶ τούτους διατρίβεις τὰ πλεῖστα, ὡς μίαν οὖσαν ταύτην τῇ πόλει σωτηρίαν, εἰ τὰ τῶν φυλάκων εὐθενοῖ. καὶ οὔτε μισθωτοὺς αὐτοὺς καλεῖς, καίτοι μισθὸν τάξας αὐτοῖς παρὰ τῶν ἄλλων ἐν τῇ πόλει, οὔτε τῶν κοινῶν διακόνους, καὶ ταῦτα ὑπὲρ πάντων ἀγρύπνους μέλλοντας διάξειν καὶ κινδυνεύσειν ἅπαντα κίνδυνον ὑπὲρ τῆς πόλεως ἁπάσης· οὐδ' ἡγήσω μισθοφόροις τισὶ καὶ ξένοις ὡς ἀληθῶς αὐτοὺς προσεοικέναι δόξειν, οὐδ' ἐν Καρῶν σχήματι καὶ μοίρᾳ θρέψεσθαι, πολλὰ πράγματ' ἔχοντας, ὀλίγου καὶ ταῦτα μισθοῦ, ἀλλ' ἱκανὴν αὐτοῖς ἡγεῖ φιλοτιμίαν, ἐὰν τὴν χώραν σῴζειν ἐπίστωνται καὶ ἡ πόλις ἅπασα πρὸς αὐτοὺς ἀποβλέπῃ. εἰ γὰρ αὖ πάντα ταῦτα καλῶς καὶ δικαίως ἔχει σοι καὶ οὐκ ἄχρηστος ἡ σπουδὴ οὐδ' ἀνελεύθερος, οὐδὲ αἰσχύνην ἔχουσα κατεσκευάσθαι τοιαύτην φυλακὴν πόλει καὶ τοιούτους ἄνδρας, ὁποῖοι τοῖς τε φίλοις βοηθεῖν καὶ τοὺς ἐχθροὺς ἀμύνεσθαι δυνήσονται, σκόπει τὸν Κί-

114 *Resp.* 374a ff., with the description of the Guardians' lifestyle at 416d–21c, and the discussion of prizes for heroism at 468b–e. 115 *Resp.* 416d–e.

116 Caria, in southwest Asia Minor, was thought of in the clas-

the community for which you are creating a constitution and drafting a code of laws, you mark off a class of state Guardians, who are to exercise the same skills as Cimon, and you give them precedence over the other citizens, and no small degree of privilege, and you specify honors and distinctions for them in life and in death, for whoever proves himself to be the best;[114] all in all you devote the greater part of your attention to them, evidently assuming that the only way that the state is going to be kept safe is if the Guardians' fortunes flourish. And you do not call them hired hands, even though you specify a wage that is to come to them from the other members of the state,[115] or lackeys in service of the common good, even though they are going to live in perpetual wakefulness on everyone's behalf and run every kind of risk in defense of the state as a whole. Nor did you think that they were going to resemble some kind of foreign mercenaries, no better maintained than a pack of Carians in their appearance or their status,[116] as they toiled for their meager pay, but instead you thought that knowing how to keep their country safe and having the whole state looking to them was enough of a distinction for them. If all these measures of yours are fine and right, and your efforts to secure this sort of protection for the state, and the kind of men who will be able both to help their own people and to protect them against their enemies, are not useless and slavish and do not bring any shame on you, then you should look at

sical period as a particularly fertile source of mercenary soldiers: see, e.g., Hdt. 2.152–54, and the proverb "run your risks with a Carian" (= let someone else do the dangerous work) cited by Plato at *Lach.* 187b and Aristides at *Or.* 1.241.

μωνα μὴ πόρρωθεν, ἀλλ' ἐκ τούτων, καί σοι πάντες οὗτοι μάρτυρες παρεῖναι δόξουσι τῷ ἀνδρί, μὴ διάκονον μηδὲ τῶν πρὸς ἡδονὴν ὁμιλούντων γεγενῆσθαι, ἀλλ' ὡς ἐλευθεριώτατα καὶ ὡς κάλλιστα ἔχειν αὐτῷ τὰ τῆς πολιτείας, καὶ σχεδὸν ὥσπερ σοὶ τὰ τῆς πολιτείας ἔχει τῆς ἀκινδύνου ταύτης.

137 σκέψαι δὴ αὐτὸν μὴ μόνον ὡς τὴν πόλιν καὶ τὴν χώραν ἐφύλαξεν, ἀλλὰ καὶ ἐκ δυοῖν τοῖν ἐσχάτοιν ὅροιν, ὅπως τοῖς τε Ἕλλησι προσηνέχθη καὶ ὅπως τοῖς βαρβάροις· ἐπειδή γε καὶ αὐτῷ σοι δοκεῖ μὴ τὸν αὐτὸν δεῖν ἀμφοτέροις τρόπον, ἀλλὰ τοῖς μὲν ὡς τοῖς ὁμοφύλοις εἰκός, τοῖς δ' ὡς χρὴ τοῖς φύσει πολεμίοις. ἐκεῖνος γὰρ συμβάσης μὲν ἐν Πελοποννήσῳ ταραχῆς οὐ φαύλης οὐδὲ μικρᾶς τινος, ἀλλ' ὥστε Λακεδαιμονίους εἰς πᾶν ἐλθεῖν τῶν εἱλώτων ἐπαναστάντων, καὶ ἅμα τῶν σεισμῶν ἐπικειμένων, ἀγαγὼν Ἀθηναίους τετρακισχιλίους ὁπλίτας, οὓς σὺ τιμᾷς, ὦ Πλάτων, ἔσωσε μὲν τὴν πόλιν αὐτοῖς καὶ τὴν χώραν, ἔλυσε δὲ τοὺς περιστάντας ἅπαντας φόβους, κατέστησε δὲ τὰ
138 ἐν Πελοποννήσῳ πράγματα. τοιοῦτος μὲν πρὸς τοὺς Ἕλληνας καὶ τῶν Ἑλλήνων τοὺς ἀρίστους καὶ ἅμα συμμάχους. πρὸς δὲ τοὺς βαρβάρους καὶ πολεμίους ὁποῖός τις; οὐκ εἰσὶ τῶν Ἑλλήνων οὐδενὶ πλείους οὐδὲ ὀνομαστότεραι πράξεις ἐν τῇ ὑπερορίᾳ, οὐδὲ τρόπαια

---

117 *Resp.* 471a–b. 118 464 BC, as described in Thuc. 1.101–2 and Plut. *Cim.* 16. Plato makes the Athenian in *Leg.* 706a–7b express a preference for a hoplite army over a navy, but not in connection with Cimon's expedition.

Cimon not in the light of any more remote considerations but in the light of these men: you will see that they all rally round to bear witness on his behalf that he was not a lackey nor one of those who make it their aim to give pleasure in their dealings with people, but that his politics were as liberal and as noble as can be imagined, and pretty much like your politics in this state of yours that you have made safe from all danger.

You should consider not only how Cimon protected the 137
city and its territory, but also, thinking of the two extreme points on the scale, how he dealt with both Greeks and barbarians, since you yourself believe as others do that they should not both be dealt with in the same way, but instead that it is only reasonable to treat the former as members of the same tribe and the latter as one ought one's natural enemies.[117] When the combination of a Helot revolt and the simultaneous onset of earthquakes in the Peloponnese brought about a state of turmoil that was neither trivial nor minor, but such as to inspire desperate measures on the part of the Spartans, Cimon took four thousand Athenian hoplites (those hoplites whom you so respect, Plato) and saved their city and their territory for them, dissolving all the fears that surrounded them and
stabilizing the situation in the Peloponnese.[118] That was 138
his behavior toward the Greeks, and the best of the Greeks who were at the same time his allies. How was he toward barbarians and enemies? No Greek has more or more distinguished achievements on foreign soil to his name;[119]

[119] 476–463 BC, as described in Thuc. 1.97–101 and Plut. *Cim.* 12–14; Aristides goes over the same territory, without naming names, in *Or.* 1.189–211.

καλλίω βαρβάρων, οὐδ᾽ ὧν μᾶλλον ἄγασθαι προσήκει τῆς ἀνδρείας ἅμα καὶ τῆς ὑποθέσεως. οὐ γὰρ ἐπειδὴ διήμαρτον ὧν ἤλπισάν τε καὶ προὐθυμήθησαν, καὶ δὴ διὰ τοῦθ᾽ ὥσπερ εὐεργέτας αὐτοὺς ἠξίωσεν ἀφεῖναι, οὐδ᾽ ἠμνημόνησεν τῶν ἱερῶν τῶν ὑπ᾽ ἐκείνων ὑβρισθέντων, οὐδ᾽ ὧν ἐν οἷς ἠδυνήθησαν ἐπεδείξαντο, ἀλλὰ καὶ τούτων ἀξιῶν αὐτοὺς ὀφείλειν δίκην τήν γε[33] ἐσχάτην καὶ ἔτι μειζόνων, ἃ ἄν,[34] εἰ κατώρθωσαν, δῆλοι πᾶσιν ἦσαν ἐξεργασάμενοι, οὐκ ᾤετο δεῖν τὴν ἡσυχίαν ἄγειν οὐδὲ τοῖς ἄλλοις παραινεῖν, οὐδὲ τοῖς θεοῖς αἰσχρῶς ἔχειν τὴν χάριν, ἀγαπῶντας εἰ σῴζονται, ἀλλ᾽ ὃ ποιηταὶ καὶ νομοθέται καὶ παροιμίαι καὶ ῥήτορες καὶ πάντες κελεύουσιν, ἀμύνεσθαι τοὺς ὑπάρξαντας, τοῦτο εἰσηγεῖτο καὶ πρὸς τοῦτ᾽ ἦγεν αὐτούς, οὐχ ὡς ἄν τις τὸ ἥδιστον, ἀλλ᾽ ὡς ἄν τις τὸ δικαιότατον λέγων.

139 πρὸς δὲ τούτοις καὶ τῆς Ἑλλάδος φυλακὴν ἀληθεστάτην ἡγεῖτο οὐκ εἰ καθείρξας αὐτοὺς οἴκοι παρέχοι καθεύδειν ἀσφαλῶς, ἀλλ᾽ εἰ τοῖς βαρβάροις φόβον ἐμβάλοι μηδὲν ἔτι τοιοῦτον ἐνθυμηθῆναι τοῦ λοιποῦ, καὶ εἰ τῆς Ἑλλάδος αὐτοὺς ἀπώσαιτο ὡς δυνατὸν πορρωτάτω. διὰ ταῦτα εἰς τὴν ἐκείνων ἐξῆγε τὸν πόλεμον καὶ περιέπλει μὲν Κύπρον, παρέπλει δὲ Παμφυλίαν, ἐναυμάχει δὲ Φοίνιξιν καὶ Κυπρίοις καὶ οἷ-
140 στισι προσμίξαιεν αὐτῶν. ἐπὶ δὲ Εὐρυμέδοντι ποταμῷ

[33] γε *om.* Monac. 432 Barocc. 136 *del.* Dindorf
[34] ἄν *add.* Keil

no one has won more glorious victories over the barbarians, or done deeds more rightly to be admired at once for their bravery and for the intentions behind them. When the barbarians failed in what they had hoped for and had shown such enthusiasm to achieve, he did not think that this was good reason to let them go as if they had done Greece a favor. He did not forget the holy places that they had violated nor the behavior they had exhibited while they were able, but rather, in the belief that they should pay the most extreme penalty both for these and for the still greater misdeeds it was clear to all they would have committed had they been successful, he did not think it right to remain inactive or advise others to do so, or for the Greeks to shame themselves with offerings of thanks to the gods in contentment simply at being kept safe. No, what he proposed and what he forced them to, enunciating it not as one might the pleasantest of measures but as one might the most just, was the action universally enjoined by poets, lawgivers, proverbs, and orators—to take vengeance on the aggressor.

In addition, he thought that the truest form of defense 139
for Greece would not be allowing the Greeks to sleep secure by keeping the barbarians confined at home, but rather frightening the latter into never conceiving any such design again in the future, and driving them as far away from Greece as possible. For this reason he carried the war into their territory, sailing around Cyprus and along the coast of Pamphylia, and fighting naval engagements with Phoenicians, Cypriots, and whoever dared
close with him. At the River Eurymedon, he set up me- 140

ναυμαχίας καὶ πεζομαχίας μνημεῖα ἔστησεν ἀμφότερα ἡμέρᾳ μιᾷ νικῶν. ὥστε τοῖς προτέροις ἔργοις ἐκπεπληγμένων τῶν ποιητῶν τοῖς ὅτ' ἐπῄεσαν οἱ βάρβαροι πραχθεῖσιν, ὅμως τις ὕμνησεν αὐτῶν εἷς[35] ταῦτα ὕστερον, οὐ πάντα, ἀλλὰ μιᾶς τινος ἡμέρας ἔργα·

ἐξ οὗ τ' Εὐρώπην Ἀσίας δίχα πόντος ἔκρινεν
καὶ πόλιας θνητῶν θοῦρος Ἄρης ἐφέπει,
οὐδενί πω κάλλιον ἐπιχθονίων γένετ' ἀνδρῶν
ἔργον ἐν ἠπείρῳ καὶ κατὰ πόντον ὁμοῦ.
οἵδε γὰρ ἐν γαίῃ Μήδων πολλοὺς ὀλέσαντες
Φοινίκων ἑκατὸν ναῦς ἕλον ἐν πελάγει
ἀνδρῶν πληθούσας, μέγα δ' ἔστενεν Ἀσὶς ὑπ' αὐτῶν
πληγεῖσ' ἀμφοτέραις χερσὶ κράτει πολέμου.

141 καὶ ταῦτα οὐκ ἀπεικότως παρύμνησεν οὐδ' ἐξῆρεν οὕτως ὡς ποιητής. ἐκεῖνα μὲν γὰρ ἐν πύλαις τῆς Ἑλλάδος ἐκινδυνεύετο, τὰ μέν γε ἐν αὐταῖς Πύλαις, τὰ δ' ἐπ' Ἀρτεμισίῳ τῆς Εὐβοίας, ταῦτα δ' ἐν μέσῃ τῇ πολεμίᾳ. καὶ τότε μὲν διείλοντο τὸν κίνδυνον αἱ πόλεις, ταῦτα δὲ ἀμφότερα ἑνὸς ἀνδρὸς καὶ ἑνὸς ἦν στόλου. κἀκεῖνοι μὲν ὥσπερ τὸν κίνδυνον, οὕτω καὶ

[35] εἷς Reiske εἰς *codd.*

---

[120] In or around 466 BC: Thuc. 1.100; Plut. *Cim.* 13; Aristid. *Or.* 1.202–3.

[121] "Simonides" 45 in Page, *Further Greek Epigrams*; attrib-

morials to celebrate a naval and a land victory, both won on a single day.[120] Consequently, although the poets were quite astounded by the earlier deeds done at the time of the barbarian invasion, there was none the less one of them who celebrated these later ones, not all of them, but those done on the single day:

> Since the time when the seas first separated Europe and Asia,
> and since raging Ares has haunted the cities of men,
> no finer deed has ever yet been wrought by mortal man,
> on dry land and on the seas together.
> These men on land slaughtered many of the Medes,
> and captured a hundred Phoenician ships at sea
> with all their crews. Asia groaned loud at their onset,
> stricken on either hand by their martial might.[121]

And it was not unreasonable for him to celebrate these achievements as superior to their rivals, nor was he thereby exaggerating them in poetic style. Those others were hazarded on Greece's doorstep, at The Gates[122] themselves and at Artemisium in Euboea, but these in the midst of enemy territory. On that other occasion the danger was shared out among the cities of Greece, but in this case the achievement was that of one man and one expeditionary 141

uted to Simonides by *Anth. Pal.* (7.296), but cited without an author's name, as an Athenian civic dedication, in Diod. Sic. 11.62. Aristides' version shows a number of minor differences in wording and orthography from those in the other two sources.

[122] Thermopylae ("the Hot Gates").

τὴν τύχην ὡς εἰπεῖν διείλοντο· Ἀθηναῖοι μὲν γὰρ καὶ Θεμιστοκλῆς ἐνίκων ἐπ' Ἀρτεμισίῳ λαμπρῶς, οἱ δ' εἰς Πύλας ἀπαντήσαντες οὐδὲν πλέον κατεπράξαντο τῇ Ἑλλάδι, πλὴν ὅσον τὰ σώματα εἰσήνεγκαν, τῷ θανάτῳ τοὺς βαρβάρους ἐκπλήξαντες, ἐπισχεῖν ὧν ὥρμηντο αὐτοὺς οὐ δυνηθέντες. οὗτοι δέ, φησίν, καὶ κατὰ γῆν καὶ κατὰ θάλατταν ἐνίκων τοὺς πολεμίους, καὶ τοσούτους αἰχμαλώτους εἷλον αὐτῶν ὅσοις ἔργον ἦν καὶ τοῖς ἅπασιν ἀντιστῆναι. διὰ ταῦτα, φησίν, λέγω θαρρῶν

οὐδενί πω κάλλιον ἐπιχθονίων γένετ' ἀνδρῶν
ἔργον ἐν ἠπείρῳ καὶ κατὰ πόντον ὁμοῦ.

142 οὕτως ἀκριβής τις καὶ βέβαιος ἐκεῖνος φύλαξ ἦν τῆς Ἑλλάδος, οὐ μόνον τῆς ἑαυτοῦ πόλεως, καὶ τοιούτους ἐπικούρους, ὦ Πλάτων, τοῖς Ἕλλησιν παρέσχετο. ὥστε ἕως ἔζη Κίμων τεθνάναι περιῆν τοῖς βαρβάροις τῷ φόβῳ τοὺς Ἕλληνας καὶ μὴ σκοπεῖν ὅντινα τῶν παρ' ἡμῶν ὑφ' ἑαυτοῖς ποιήσονται, ἀλλ' ὅπως αὐτοὶ σωθήσονται. ἐξ ὧν τάς τε πόλεις ἁπάσας ἀφεῖσαν καὶ τῆς κάτω χώρας οὐκ ὀλίγης ἀπέστησαν, ὧν τἀναντία ὕστερον συνεχώρησαν Λακεδαιμόνιοι, πρὸς οὓς σὺ βλέπων καὶ ἁμιλλώμενος τοὺς σαυτοῦ συγκροτεῖς, [καὶ][36] οἷς ἡ τῶν εἰς τοὺς πολέμους ἐμπειρία

[36] *del.* Reiske

---

[123] "Auxiliaries" (*epikouroi*) echoes Plato's term for the military class in his ideal state: *Resp.* 414b, etc.

force. Those others moreover (you might say) enjoyed mixed fortunes between them just as they took different shares of the danger: the Athenians and Themistocles won a brilliant victory at Artemisium, while those who joined battle at The Gates achieved nothing to Greece's advantage beyond the contribution of their own bodies; though they may have astonished the barbarians by the manner of their death, they were not able to hold them back in their advance. These men, on the other hand, as the poet says, defeated their enemies on land and at sea, and took enough prisoners to mean that even their whole force would have found it hard to withstand them. This is why, he says, I am confident in declaring that

> No finer deed has ever yet been wrought by mortal
> man,
> on dry land and on the seas together.

That is how meticulous and how steadfast a guardian Cimon was, Plato, not only to his own city, but to the whole of Greece, and that is the kind of "auxiliaries" he furnished them with.[123] Consequently, for as long as Cimon was alive, all that was open to the barbarians was to be mortally afraid of the Greeks and to devote their thoughts not to which of our peoples they might subjugate, but to how they might remain safe themselves. As a result, they surrendered all the cities and abandoned not a little of their coastal territory, all of which the Spartans subsequently agreed to go back on[124]—the same Spartans that you have your eye on and compete with when you are organizing your own military class, whose sole attribute is experience 142

[124] In the so-called Peace of Antalcidas of 387 BC: see Xen. *Hell*. 5.125–34 and Aristid. *Or*. 1.271.

καὶ ἕξις πρόσκειται μόνη. τοσούτῳ κρεῖττον Κίμων ἐφύλαξε τοὺς Ἕλληνας καὶ οὕτω πολλοῦ τινος ἄξιος ἦν καὶ λέγων καὶ πράττων.

143 ἆρ' οὖν ταῦτα ἂν οὕτω κατείργαστο, ἢ νίκας οὕτω πολλὰς καὶ λαμπρὰς καὶ κατὰ γῆν καὶ κατὰ θάλατταν ἐφεξῆς ἀνῃρεῖτο, εἰ δουλεύειν ἠξίου τῷ πλήθει καὶ μὴ τοὐναντίον εἰς ὅσον ἐξῆν ἦρχεν ἀκριβέστατα, ἢ κόσμου καὶ τάξεως χωρὶς ἦγεν τὸ στρατόπεδον καὶ συνεχώρει πᾶν ὃ βούλοιντο, ἀλλὰ μὴ πανταχοῦ πᾶσαν φροντίδα καὶ πρόνοιαν ἐποιεῖτο εὐταξίας καὶ εὐαρμοστίας αὐτῶν καὶ τοῦ πρὸς ἅπαντα ὑπάρχειν εὐκόλους αὐτῷ; ἐγὼ μὲν γὰρ οὐκ ἀσελγαίνοντας οὐδ' ὑβρίζοντας αὐτοὺς οὐδὲ τῶν ἡδονῶν ἡττωμένους, ἀλλ' ὡς οἷόν τε μάλιστα κοσμίους ὄντας καὶ τὴν τάξιν φυλάττοντας, καὶ ὅ φησιν Ὅμηρος αἰδουμένους κρατεῖν ἂν τῶν πολεμίων οἶμαι καὶ χρησίμους εἶναι κἀκείνῳ καὶ σφίσιν αὐτοῖς.

144 καί μοι πάντ' ἐκεῖνα ἤδη λέγε, τὸν ναυπηγὸν ὡς εἰς τάξιν τίθησι τὰ ξύλα, τὸν τέκτονα ὡς εἰς τάξιν τοὺς λίθους, τὸν χοροποιόν, τὸν ὁντιναδήποτε. ὅ τι γὰρ ἂν τούτων εἴπῃς, ὑπὲρ τῆς Κίμωνος ἐρεῖς ἡγεμονίας καὶ πολιτείας. καὶ μὴν ὅτι καὶ τὸ πᾶν τοῦτο κόσμος ἐκλήθη λέγεις ὀρθῶς, ὡς ἔγωγέ φημι, προσ-
145 βιβάζων ἡμᾶς πρὸς τὸ μηδὲν εἰκῇ πράττειν. Κίμων τοίνυν τῆς τοῦ παντὸς ἐπωνυμίας τὸ γιγνόμενον τῇ πόλει διεσώσατο. κοσμίους γὰρ ἅπαντας παρεῖχεν εἰς δύναμιν. τοιαῦτα ἐπολιτεύετο καὶ τοιαῦτα ἐδίδασκεν

and conditioning in war. That is how much better Cimon was at guarding the Greeks and that is how great his worth was both as speaker and as man of action.

Would he have brought all this to such a successful 143
conclusion or would he have won so many and such brilliant victories in succession both on land and at sea, if he had seen fit to subordinate himself to the masses and had not on the contrary as far as was open to him exercised the strictest of command, or if he had led the army without order and structure and agreed to everything they might want, rather than at every turn exercising all care and forethought for their good discipline and harmony, so as to secure their docility toward him in all things? I do not think that they would have defeated the enemy and been useful both to him and to themselves if they had been licentious and violent and enslaved to sensual pleasure, but rather if they were as well disciplined as possible and kept good order and were in Homer's phrase "reverential."[125]

Now give me all those examples of yours, how the ship- 144
wright puts timbers in their proper order, and the builder blocks of stone, and the chorus master, and whoever else.[126] Whatever you say about these, you will be saying in support of Cimon's leadership and policies. I for one, moreover, am ready to declare that you are quite right when you insist, in attempting to motivate us to avoid all disorderly action, that this Universe of ours was given the
name "order" (*kosmos*).[127] Well, Cimon too respected the 145
relevance to his city of this way of naming the Universe, because he made all its citizens orderly to the best of his ability. That was his policy, and that was the lesson he

[125] *Il.* 5.531. [126] *Grg.* 503d–4a. [127] *Grg.* 508a.

κἀν τῇ πόλει τὸν δῆμον κἀν ταῖς στρατείαις τοὺς ἑπομένους.

146 νὴ Δία ἀλλ' ἐξωστράκισαν αὐτόν, ὅπως αὐτοῦ δέκα ἐτῶν τῆς φωνῆς μὴ ἀκούσειαν. καὶ πάλιν γε κατήγαγον πρὶν τὰ δέκα ἐξήκειν ἔτη, ἵν' αὐτοῦ τῆς φωνῆς ἀκούσειαν· οὕτως ἐπόθησαν. σὺ δὲ ὡς μὲν κατέγνωσαν λέγεις, ὡς δὲ μετέγνωσαν οὐκ ἐνθυμῇ. καὶ ἃ μὲν οὐ δικαίως ἐψηφίσαντο κατ' ἀμφοτέρων λέγεις, ἃ δ' ὀρθῶς ἐβουλεύσαντο οὐχ ἡγῇ τοῖς μὲν προαχθεῖσιν παραίτησιν, τῷ δὲ ἀφεθέντι μεγίστην πίστιν τῆς ἀρε-
147 τῆς ἔχειν. καὶ ὡς ἔοικεν, οἱ μὲν καταγνόντες αὐτοὶ μετέγνωσαν καὶ οὐκ ἔμειναν ἐφ' ὧν ἔγνωσαν ἐξ ἀρχῆς· σὺ δὲ ὥσπερ τι κύριον ἐγκέκληκας, καὶ οὐκ ἠξίωσας ταύτῃ μιμήσασθαι τοὺς Ἀθηναίους, ἀφεὶς τὸν ἄνδρα τῆς αἰτίας, ἀλλ' ὃ μὲν ἦν χαλεπώτερον αὐτῶν ἐμιμήσω, τὸ δὲ λοιπὸν εἴασας, καὶ ταῦθ' ὃ πάντων ἀτοπώτατόν ἐστι, κατηγορῶν αὐτῶν τῶν Ἀθηναίων, καὶ τό γε κάλλιον, οὐ τὰ δεύτερα ταῦτα, ἀλλ' ἐκεῖνα ἅ τις ἂν χαίρων τῷ Κίμωνι. καὶ μηδενὸς μὲν ἂν τοιούτου συμβάντος οὐκ εἶχες ὅ τι κατηγόρεις,[37] ἐπεὶ δ' ἔλυσαν τῇ μετανοίᾳ τὸ συμβὰν καὶ τὴν αἰτίαν ἐφ' αὑτοὺς μετέθεσαν, οὐκ ἴσον τι νομίζεις εἶναι
148 ὥσπερ ἂν εἰ μηδὲν ἐξ ἀρχῆς εἰπεῖν εἴχομεν;[38] καὶ μὴν πολὺ μεῖζον καὶ κάλλιον εἰς ἀρετῆς λόγον ἐκπεσόντα

37 κατηγόρεις Reiske κατηγοροῖς U κατηγορεῖς *cett.*
38 εἶχον Keil

taught to the people in the city and to his armies on campaign.

But for heaven's sake, you may say, they ostracized him, 146
so as not to have to hear his voice for ten years![128] Yes, and they brought him back before the ten years were up, so that they could hear his voice again; that is how badly they missed him. You say that they condemned him, but do not reflect that they changed their minds. And you make the unjust measures they voted for a reproach against both sides, but do not think that the right measures they decided on constitute grounds for pardoning those who promoted them, and conclusive proof of the virtue of the man
they pardoned. It looks as if those who condemned him 147
changed their minds and did not abide by their original decision, whereas you brought your accusation as if it were something signed and sealed and did not see fit to imitate the Athenians in absolving the man from blame, but instead imitated what was roughest in their conduct while ignoring the rest. What is most extraordinary of all, it was against the Athenians themselves that you directed this accusation, and what is still more wonderful, not for that second decision of theirs, but for the first one, just as a supporter of Cimon might have done. If nothing of the kind had ever happened, you would not have had any grounds for an accusation; so seeing that they canceled out what had happened by their change of mind and shifted the blame onto themselves, do you not think it is the same
as if we had nothing to say in the first place? Indeed, in 148
reckoning up a man's virtue, it is a far greater and nobler thing to be sent into exile and then recalled than not to be

[128] *Grg*. 516d.

κατελθεῖν ἢ μὴ φυγεῖν ὅλως. τὸ μὲν γὰρ καὶ τοῖς τυχοῦσιν ὑπάρχει δήπου, τοῦτο δ' οὐ κατὰ τοὺς πολλοὺς ἄνδρας ἦν· κἀκεῖνο μὲν ἂν τῇ τύχῃ τις εἶχεν λογίζεσθαι, τοῦτο δὲ τῷ κρείττονα ἢ κατὰ τοὺς ἄλλους ὄντα γιγνώσκεσθαι. τοῦ μὲν γὰρ ἐκπεσεῖν καὶ φεύγειν φθόνος αἴτιος καὶ τάχα ἄν τι καὶ ἄλλο τοιοῦτον φανείη, τῆς δὲ πρὸ τοῦ χρόνου κλήσεως καὶ παρακλήσεως οὐδὲν ἔσθ' ἕτερον πλὴν τῆς ἀρετῆς αἰτιᾶσθαι, δι' ἣν καὶ ἀπόντα ᾐσχύνοντο καὶ παρεῖναι λυσιτελεῖν αὐτοῖς ὑπελάμβανον, καὶ τὸ μέγιστον, σφῶν αὐτῶν καταγιγνώσκειν μᾶλλον ἠξίουν ἢ ἐκείνου.

ὥστε εἰ μὲν αὐτὸν ἐφ' αὑτοῦ δεῖ σκοπεῖν, τί δεῖ λέγειν, εἴ τις εἰς ἐκεῖνον ἐξήμαρτεν; εἰ δ' ἀπὸ τῶν ἄλλων αὐτὸν δεῖ θεωρῆσαι, διαφερόντως οὗτος τιμηθεὶς φαίνεται. ἀλλὰ μήπω ταῦτα· αὐτίκα γὰρ μᾶλλον
149 ἴσως ἁρμόσει. ὃ δὲ πολλῶν καὶ μεγάλων ὄντων ὧν ἄν τις ἐπαινέσαι Κίμωνα δικαίως μέγιστον καὶ ὡσπερεὶ κεφάλαιόν ἐστιν καὶ διαφερόντως ἐκείνῳ προσῆκον, τοῦτ' εἰπεῖν ἔτι βούλομαι καὶ ἀποδοῦναι ὥσπερ ἄλλο τι τῷ ἀνδρί. σχεδὸν γὰρ ἐν ὀλίγοις τῶν πάντων, ὥς γέ μοι φαίνεται, καὶ τῶν πρότερον καὶ τῶν ὕστερον ἀντέχει τῷ λόγῳ τούτῳ καὶ οὐ συναγωνίζεται οὐδὲ δίδωσι χώραν τῇ βλασφημίᾳ, ὡς ἄρα τῶν καλῶν καὶ ἀγαθῶν ἀνδρῶν ὥσπερ εἱμαρμένον εἴη τοὺς υἱεῖς φαύλους ἀποβαίνειν καὶ ὀλίγου τινὸς ἀξίους τῆς πατρῴας ἀρετῆς, ὅστις υἱὸς ὢν Μιλτιάδου καὶ κληρο-

sent into exile at all. The latter is surely something that can happen to anyone at all, whereas the former was not within the experience of the majority of men; the latter could be set down to chance, but the former to being recognized as a superior being. It is jealousy and perhaps something else of the kind that would seem to have been responsible for Cimon's being expelled and becoming an exile, but one cannot attribute being recalled and summoned to help to anything other than the virtue that made the Athenians feel ashamed before him even in his absence and convinced that they would benefit from his presence, and most significantly of all, because of which they thought it appropriate to condemn themselves rather than him.

Thus, if we have to consider Cimon in and by himself, why is it worthy of mention if someone committed an offense against him? But if we have to look at him in comparison with the rest, it is clear that he enjoyed exceptional honor. But let us not go into that yet; it will perhaps be
more in place later on. The greatest and so to speak the 149
summation of all the many great things one might justly praise Cimon for, the one that preeminently belongs to him, still remains to tell. It is this that I now wish to bring up and give him credit for, in addition to everything else. Among very few in the human race, it seems to me, both before him and after him, he provides an exception to the principle, and offers no support or scope to the slander, that it is so to speak a rule of fate that the sons of the good and the great should turn out bad.[129] Though he was the son of Miltiades and heir to the perilous heritage of his

[129] Cf. Hom. *Od.* 2.276–77 (cited below, §359), Eurip. *Heracl.* 325–28.

νομῶν τοσούτου κινδύνου τῆς ἐκείνου δόξης οὐ κατῄσχυνεν οὐδὲν τῶν ὑπαρχόντων οὐδ' ἀποχρῆν ἡγήσατο ἐπιγράφεσθαι τοὔνομα τοῦ πατρὸς, ὥσπερ τις Ὀλυμπίασιν ἀξιῶν νικᾶν ὅτι ἐστὶν Ὀλυμπιονίκου πατρός· ἀλλ' οὕτως εὖ καὶ καλῶς ἐκεῖνον ἐμιμήσατο καὶ ὥσπερ ἰχνῶν εἴχετο τῶν ἔργων τοῦ πατρός, ὥστε εἰ μηδεὶς τῶν συγγραφέων ἐτύγχανεν εἰρηκὼς ὅτου παῖς ἦν, ἀπ' αὐτῶν εἶναι τῶν ἔργων εἰκάσαι τὸν πατέρα αὐτοῦ καὶ ὅτῳ προσῆκεν.

[*Argumentation 3: Vindication of Miltiades (150–208)*]

150 περιήκει δ' ἡμῖν ὁ λόγος εἰς αὐτὸν Μιλτιάδην, ὃν ἐγὼ μᾶλλον ἂν αἰσχυνοίμην ἐπαινῶν ἢ ψέγων· οὕτω μοι
151 δοκῶ πάντ' ἂν ἔλαττον εἰπεῖν ἢ βούλομαι. καίτοι τοσοῦτόν γ' ἂν εἴποιμι θαρρούντως· εἰ γὰρ ἀναστάς, λέγω, Πλάτων αὐτὸς ἀξιώσει κατηγορεῖν Μιλτιάδου καὶ τοῦ βελτίονος αὐτῷ τοῦτο λόγου κρινεῖ, πάνθ' ἕτοιμος ἔγωγε συγχωρεῖν καὶ μὴ πολλοῦ τινος ἄξιον τὸν ἄνδρα ἐκεῖνον ἡγεῖσθαι. ἀλλὰ οὐκ ἄν μοι δοκεῖ ῥᾳδίως, ὅς γε καὶ μνησθεὶς περὶ αὐτοῦ, Μιλτιάδην δέ, φησί, τὸν ἐν Μαραθῶνι. καίτοι τοῦτό ἐστιν ἐγγυτέρω θρήνου τινὸς ἢ μέμψεως καὶ τιμῶντος μᾶλλον ἢ κακίζοντος, ὥσπερ οὓς Σιμωνίδης εἰώθει τιμᾶν ἐν τοῖς
152 ἐπιγράμμασιν. ὅμως δὲ καὶ Μιλτιάδης μετέχει τοῦ καταλόγου καὶ περιέστηκεν αὐτῷ τὸ τῶν Πλαταιέων

glory, he brought shame on nothing he had inherited, and he refused to think it enough to have his father's name attached to his, like someone who felt entitled to win at the Olympic Games just because he was himself the son of an Olympic victor. So well and nobly did he imitate his father's example and follow in the tracks of his achievements that, even if no historian had happened to mention whose son he was, it would have been possible to guess from his own deeds who his father was and who he was related to.[130]

Argumentation 3: Vindication of Miltiades (150–208)

The argument has now brought us round to Miltiades, 150
whom I would be more ashamed about praising than about criticizing, so convinced am I that I would fall completely short of what I want to say. Yet I could at least say 151
this with confidence: if Plato himself rises from the grave and sees fit to accuse Miltiades and judges that this reflects well on him, I declare myself ready to agree entirely and to take a dim view of the man's worth; but I do not think that he could easily do so, since when he actually mentions him, it is with the words "Miltiades, the hero of Marathon."[131] This is closer to a kind of lament than to censure, and shows us someone conferring honor rather than hurling abuse, as if on the people Simonides was in the habit
of honoring in his epigrams. Yet Miltiades nevertheless 152
has a place on Plato's list and suffers the same fate as the

[130] Cf. §128 above.

[131] *Grg.* 516d.

τῶν ὑπ' αὐτοῦ τότε κοσμηθέντων. κατηγορίας γὰρ οὐδεμιᾶς αὐτοῦ προειρημένης ἐξ ἀνάγκης τρόπον τινὰ ἀγωνίζεται, διὰ τὸ ἐνεῖναι τοὔνομα ἐν τοῖς δια-
153 κόνοις αὐτοῦ. καίτοι, ὦ Πλάτων, φαίη τις ἂν τῶν δικανικῶν ἀνδρῶν, ὀρθῶς ἐποίησεν ὁ θεὶς τὸν νόμον ἀξιώσας διαρρήδην ἔχειν τάς τε δίκας καὶ τὰς γραφάς, ἔβλαψέ με ὁ δεῖνα τὸ καὶ τὸ ποιήσας, καὶ τάδε εἶπεν παράνομα· κἄν τί τις ἄλλο κατηγορῇ, τὸν αὐτὸν τρόπον φράζειν καὶ μὴ τηνάλλως φοβεῖν. σὺ δ' ὅ τι μὲν ποιῶν ἢ λέγων ἕκαστος τῶν ἀνδρῶν τούτων ἠδίκει εἰς τὴν ὑστεραίαν, ὡς ἔοικεν, ἀνεβάλου δηλώσειν, ὥσπερ ἐν ἄλλῳ τῳ διαλόγῳ, πάντας δ' αἰτιᾷ κοινῇ καὶ οὐδὲ ὃν τῶν ἄλλων διαφερόντως ἠξίωσας τιμῆσαι τὸν Περικλέα μερίσας τὰς αἰτίας αὐτῷ καὶ πλείστας ἁπάντων ἀνθείς, οὐδὲ τοῦτον ἐξήλεγξας, οὐδ' ἀπέφηνας τί λέγων ἢ τί ποιῶν ἐποίει τοιούτους, ἀλλὰ ἑνὶ τούτῳ παρὰ τοὺς ἄλλους ἐτίμησας [πλείους ποιήσας τὰς αἰτίας αὐτῷ καὶ ὡσπερεὶ σαφεστέρας, ὥστ' εἰδέναι περὶ ὧν χρὴ λέγειν].[39] ἀλλ' ἐκεῖνος μὲν οὐδὲ τοῖς παρ' ἡμῶν ἴσως ἔλαττον ἔσχηκεν, ὥστε ταύτῃ γε μηδ' ἂν πάνυ τι μέμψασθαι τῷ τὴν ἀρχὴν παρασχόντι.

154 εἶεν. Μιλτιάδην δὲ τὸν ἐν Μαραθῶνι ποῦ χοροῦ

[39] *del.* Trapp

---

132 The parallel is with the "trial" of the people of Plataea following their surrender to the Peloponnesian forces in 427 BC: Thuc. 3.52 (and 3.53–68).

Plataeans to whom he brought such distinction in days gone by: although no accusation has first been brought against him he is somehow or other forced to stand trial, because his name is included among Plato's "lackeys."[132]
Well, Plato, an expert in jurisprudence might say, it was 153
quite right of the legislator to demand that lawsuits and formal charges should be explicitly formulated so as to say "so and so has harmed me by doing such and such," or "his illegal proposition is as follows," and to specify that if anyone brings any other sort of accusation, he should phrase it in the same way and not frighten people to no purpose. But you apparently put off explaining what each of these men had said or done wrong for another day, just as you did in another dialogue,[133] and accused them all together. Pericles was the one you saw fit to single out from the others and honor with the lion's share of your accusations, but you did not subject even him to detailed scrutiny: you did not specify what he said or did to have that sort of effect on the Athenians, but honored him beyond the others in this one respect alone.[134] But Pericles at least has had the larger share of my rebuttal too, so in this respect if no other might not be entirely dissatisfied with the instigator of the whole business.

Fair enough. But when it comes to Miltiades, "the hero 154

133 *Lach.* (201b–c) or *Tht.* (210d).

134 The next words in the Greek text, bracketed opposite, look like a clumsy and inaccurate attempt to expand on "in this one respect": "namely by making the accusations against him more numerous and to some extent clearer, so as to allow people to understand what needed to be discussed."

τάξομεν ἢ τάξιν τίνα; ἢ δῆλον ὅτι τὴν πρὸ τοῦ θεάτρου καὶ οὗ πᾶσιν ἐν καλῷ τῆς θέας ἔσται; πλήν γ' ὅσον οὐκ ἀριστεροστάτης ἁνὴρ[40] *μᾶλλον ἢ τοῦ δε-*
155 *ξιοῦ τοῖς Ἕλλησι κέρως. καὶ νὴ Δί' εἴ γέ τις αὐτὸν ἐρωτῴη καὶ ἀναποδίζοι καθ' ἕκαστον ἐξ ἀρχῆς, ὥσπερ Πλάτων εἴωθεν ἐρωτᾶν, τί διδάσκων ἢ τί συμβουλεύων ἐποίει βελτίους Ἀθηναίους, ἢ πῶς ἄγων καὶ τρέφων ἐκ νέων εὐθύς, ἢ ποῖ' ἄττα ἔθη καί*[41] *ἐπιτηδεύματα εἰς τὴν πόλιν εἰσάγων, φαίημεν ἂν οὐκ ἀπορήσειν αὐτὸν μετρίας καὶ ἀληθοῦς ἀποκρίσεως, ἀλλ' ἀποκρινεῖσθαι ταυτί [καὶ παραγράψομεν τοῖς ἔπεσι Μιλτιάδου ἀποκρίσεις]·*[42]

λέξω τοίνυν τὴν ἀρχαίαν παιδείαν ὡς διέκειτο,
ὅτ' ἐγὼ τὰ δίκαια λέγων ἤνθουν καὶ σωφροσύνη
νενόμιστο.
πρῶτον μὲν ἔδει παιδὸς φωνὴν γρύξαντος μηδέν[43]
ἀκοῦσαι·
εἶτα βαδίζειν ἐν ταῖσιν ὁδοῖς εὐτάκτως ἐς
κιθαριστοῦ
τοὺς κωμήτας γυμνοὺς ἀθρόους, κεἰ κριμνώδη
καταγίφοι.

40 *ἁνήρ* Trapp *ἀνήρ* *codd.* 41 *ἔθη καί* Reiske *ἔθηκεν* *codd.* 42 *del.* Trapp
43 *μηδέν* *codd. Aristoph.* *μηδέν'* *vel* *μηδένα* *codd.*

---

135 According to the scholiast on this passage, the chorus in Athenian drama conventionally entered the *orchestra* from the west, with the audience on its left. The best *choreutai* were therefore positioned to the left, whereas the best soldiers in an army

of Marathon," where are we to place him in this chorus and what position are we to give him? Isn't it clear that we should place him out in front of the audience, where everyone can have a clear view of him? (Except that he wasn't a left-side man; where he really belonged was on
the Greek right wing.)[135] And if someone were to question 155
him and go back over every detail with him from the beginning, in Plato's habitual style, asking what lessons he taught or what advice he gave to make the Athenians better people, or how he trained and fostered them from early youth on up, or what habits and practices he introduced into the city to achieve this, we would say emphatically that he would not be lost for a measured and truthful reply, but would be able to answer in the following terms:[136]

> I will tell you, then, how the old kind of education
> was organized,
> when I spoke up for Justice in my prime and modesty
> was the norm.
> First, it was the rule for no squeak of a boy's voice to
> be heard at all.
> Secondly, the boys from any district had to walk
> through the streets to their music lesson
> all in a group with no clothes on, even if it were
> snowing thick as oatmeal.

were placed on its right wing. Cf. A. Pickard-Cambridge, J. Gould, and D. M. Lewis, *The Dramatic Festivals of Athens*, 2nd ed. (Oxford, 1968), 239–42.

136 The next words in the Greek text, bracketed opposite, look like a fussy (and confused) reader's note: "and I (we) will set Miltiades' answers alongside the verses." The lines that follow are from the speech of Right Argument in Aristophanes' *Clouds* (961–65, 967–69, 972–73), here stripped of their original irony.

εἶθ' ὑπὲρ τῆς μουσικῆς ἐρεῖ τῆς τότε ὁποία τις ἦν, ὡς οὐ τὸ παναρμόνιον οὐδὲ τὸ πρὸς ἡδονὴν αὐτῆς ἐτιμᾶτο, ἀλλὰ

ἢ Παλλάδα περσέπολιν δεινάν, ἢ τηλέπορόν τι βόαμα

ἐρεῖν ἔδει

ἐντειναμένους τὴν ἁρμονίαν ἣν οἱ πατέρες παρέδωκαν.
εἰ δέ τις αὐτῶν βωμολοχεύσαιτ' ἢ κάμψειέν τινα καμπήν,
ἐπετρίβετο τυπτόμενος πολλάς, ὡς τὰς Μούσας ἀφανίζων.
ἐν παιδοτρίβου δὲ καθίζοντας

καὶ τἄλλα δὴ καθ' ἕκαστον διεξελθὼν τελευτῶν ἐπιθήσει πρός τινας τῶν δυσχεραινόντων

ἀλλ' οὖν τάδ' ἐστὶν ἐκεῖνα,
ἐξ ὧν ἄνδρας Μαραθωνομάχους ἡμὴ παίδευσις ἔθρεψεν.

156 τοιαῦτ' ἄττα ὁ Μιλτιάδης ἀποκρινεῖται, οὔτε ἄλλως φαῦλα ἐμοὶ δοκεῖν οὔτε που ψευδῆ, ἀλλ' αὐτῷ τε προσήκοντα ταῦτα παιδεῦσαι προστάτῃ κατ' ἐκείνους τοὺς χρόνους ὄντι καὶ τοῖς Ἀθηναίοις πάλαι πεπαιδευμένοις ἥκειν ἐπὶ τὴν μάχην. οὐ γὰρ ἐνῆν, οὐκ ἐνῆν αὐθημερὸν ἄνδρας γενέσθαι κοσμίους καὶ ἀνδρείους καὶ τῶν δεινῶν κρείττονας, ἐν ῥαθυμίᾳ τραφέντας ἐξ

Then he will speak in defense of the music of those times and explain its character, how it was not the complexity of its harmony nor its ingratiating qualities that won respect, but instead people had to sing

> Either "Pallas, dread sacker of cities," or "A cry resounding from afar,"
> setting it to the mode that our fathers had handed down to us.
> And if anyone messed around or produced a fancy modulation,
> . . .
> he was put in his place with a sound beating for disfiguring the Muses.
> And when sitting in the wrestling school
> . . . ;

and going through all the rest point by point he will finish up by adding in response to any dissenters

> But just this was the basis
> on which my training raised the heroes who fought at Marathon.[137]

That is the kind of answer Miltiades will give. In my 156
opinion it is neither a trivial and pointless one nor indeed a false one, for this was the right lesson for him to teach at the time, when he was their leader, and for the Athenians to have had ingrained into them long before they came to the battle. It would have been impossible, simply impossible[138] for them to have become disciplined and brave and to have risen above their dangerous situation on

[137] *Nub*. 985–86. [138] An echo of Dem. 19.123.

ἀρχῆς καὶ φαύλως ἐν τοῖς ὅλοις ἠγμένους, ἀλλὰ ἔδει καὶ τροφῇ χρηστῇ καὶ λόγοις ἐπιεικέσιν καὶ ἔθεσιν μετρίοις καὶ δόξαις ταῖς βελτίσταις πόρρωθεν κατει-
157 λῆφθαι. οὔκουν Δολόπων γε οὐδεὶς ἐπ' ἐκείνην τὴν ἡμέραν ἀπήντησεν, οὐδὲ τῶν ἄλλων τῶν ὁμοίως ἐκείνοις ἠγμένων. οὐ τοίνυν οὐδ' ὁ τοῦ τῶν πολεμίων στρατοπέδου κύριος καὶ ἡγεμὼν Δᾶτις οὔτ' αὐτὸς ἀνὴρ ἀγαθὸς αὐθημερὸν οἷός τ' ἦν γενέσθαι οὔτε
158 ποιῆσαι τοὺς ὑφ' αὑτῷ τοσούτους ὄντας. καίτοι προείρητό γε ὑπὸ τοῦ βασιλέως αὐτῷ στέρεσθαι τῆς κεφαλῆς, εἰ μὴ Ἐρετριέας καὶ Ἀθηναίους ἀγάγοι. ἀλλ' ὅμως οὐδὲν αὐτὸν βελτίονα ἐποίησεν ὁ φόβος. ἐκεῖνα μὲν γὰρ ἦν ἐντολαὶ πρόσκαιροι παρὰ τοῦ δεσπότου, Μιλτιάδης δὲ πάλαι πεπεικὼς ἦν Ἀθηναίους μηδένα δεσπότην πλὴν τῶν νόμων ἡγεῖσθαι, μηδὲ τοῦ καλοῦ καὶ δικαίου μηδένα κρείττω νομίσαι φόβον, μηδὲ οὕτως ἀνάγκην ἰσχυρὰν δι' ἣν προσήκειν γενέσθαι
159 χείροσιν. διὰ ταῦτα εἶχεν ὅ τι χρῷτο αὐτοῖς. ἐπεὶ ναύτας γε οὐκ ἂν ἐξαίφνης οὕτως αὐτοὺς ἐποίησεν, οὐδὲ εἰ σφόδρα ἔδει ναύτας ἐκείνην τὴν ἡμέραν εἶναι, οὐδέ γε μουσικούς, οὐδέ γε ἱππικούς. οὐ τοίνυν οὐδ' ὁπλίτας ἀγαθούς, οὐδὲ συλλήβδην εἰπεῖν ἄνδρας ἀγαθοὺς καὶ λυσιτελοῦντας ἑαυτοῖς οὐκ ἂν οὕτω βραχὺς καιρὸς ἤρκεσε ποιῆσαι, ἀλλ' ὥσπερ οἱ γεωργοὶ πολλοστῷ μηνὶ τῶν σπερμάτων τὴν ἐπικαρπίαν κομί-

139 The Dolopians were a northern Greek people who contributed to Xerxes' army in 480 BC, as the scholiast in this passage

the day, if they had begun by being brought up in idleness and being badly raised in general; no, they needed to have been taken in hand long in advance by a good upbringing, virtuous principles, habits of moderation, and the best ideas. No Dolopian at any rate would have met the chal- 157
lenge of that day, nor would anyone from the peoples brought up in the same way as them.[139] Nor again would Datis, the master and leader of the enemy army, have been able either to become a hero himself or to make heroes of the great number of those under his command, in just a day. And yet he had been told in advance by his king that 158
he would lose his head if he did not make captives of the Eretrians and Athenians.[140] But even so fear did not make any the better a man of him, because those were the *ad hoc* commands of a despot, whereas Miltiades had long since convinced the Athenians to recognize no master except the laws, and to think nobility and justice mightier than any possible fear, and no compulsion strong enough to justify their going to the bad. It was thanks to this that 159
he could put them to good use—because he could not have made them sailors thus in an instant, even if there was a pressing need for sailors that day, nor good musicians, nor good horsemen, nor indeed could he have made them good hoplites. In sum, so short a time was not enough to make them brave men and men able to look after themselves. No, just as farmers harvest their crop many months after sowing and not at the same time as they

notes. Demosthenes in *De corona* (*Or.* 18) 63 mentions them scornfully as a people the Athenians would be lowering themselves by imitating.

140 A detail apparently borrowed from Pl. *Menex.* 240a.

ζονται καὶ οὐχ ἅμα τῷ καταβαλεῖν, οὕτω καὶ ἐκείνους Μιλτιάδης παλαιαῖς ὁμολογίαις κατειληφὼς εἶχεν ἐν τῷ καιρῷ χρησίμους, οὐκ ἐπὶ τῆς χρείας λαμβάνοντας τὰ μαθήματα—αἰσχρῶς γὰρ ἂν οὕτω γε ὁ χορὸς ἠγωνίσατο αὐτῷ—, ἀλλ᾽ ἐπὶ τῆς ἐξουσίας εἰς τὴν χρείαν ἠσκημένους. καὶ γάρ τοι τῆς ἀσκήσεως αὐτῶν καὶ τῆς ἐπιμελείας ἅπασα ἡ Ἑλλὰς κοινοὺς τοὺς καρποὺς ἐκομίζετο.

160 καὶ μὴν εἰ μηδὲν ἄλλο τις εἰπεῖν εἶχεν Μιλτιάδου, μηδὲ ἦν εὑρεῖν πολλὰ καὶ σεμνά, ἐξαρκεῖν ἂν ἔμοιγε δοκεῖ τὸ ψήφισμα ἀντ᾽ εἰκόνος αὐτοῦ τῆς ψυχῆς ἅπασιν εἶναι. ἢ πρὸς θεῶν τῶν μὲν ἡμετέρων λόγων καὶ συγγραμμάτων τὸ φρόνημα καὶ τὴν ῥώμην ἀξιώσομεν εὐδοκιμεῖν, κἄν τι πρὸς ἀνδρείαν ἢ δικαιοσύνην αὐτῶν ᾖ φέρον, οὐκ ἄχρηστον φήσομεν τοῖς ἐθέλουσιν χρῆσθαι, τῆς δ᾽ ἐκείνου προαιρέσεως καὶ διανοίας ὁποία τις ἦν καὶ πότερον τῶν τυχόντων ἢ τῶν ἐπιεικεστέρων μιμήσασθαι, οὐχ ἱκανὸν σημεῖον τὸ ψήφισμα, ὃ παρ᾽ αὐτοὺς τοὺς κινδύνους συνεγράψατο, μίαν γνώμην εἰς τοὺς Ἕλληνας εἰπὼν περὶ παντὸς
161 τοῦ δικαίου; καὶ μὴν εἰ προγόνους ἄξιον τιμᾶν, πῶς οὐκ ἄξιον Μιλτιάδην ὥσπερ πρόγονον κοινὸν τῶν μετ᾽ ἐκείνους τοὺς χρόνους Ἑλλήνων; ὁ γὰρ οὐ μόνον τῆς σωτηρίας αὐτῶν προστάς, ἀλλὰ καὶ δείξας ὁποίους τινὰς ἐν τοῖς περὶ τῆς ἐλευθερίας ἀγῶσιν εἶναι δεῖ

141 A reference to the speech attributed to Miltiades in Hdt.

scatter the seed, so it was that these men served Miltiades' turn at the vital moment only because he had long since bound them in a pact; they did not acquire their learning only at the time of need (if that had been the case, his band would have fought a sorry fight for him), but had already been drilled to meet that need when there was time to do so. The whole of Greece reaped a shared reward for the care with which he had trained them.

Moreover, even if there were nothing else one could 160
say of Miltiades, even if there were not a multitude of impressive points to be made, I think that his celebrated proposal would be enough to stand on its own as an image of his character for all to see.[141] For heaven's sake, are we going to expect the nobility and strength of our own speeches and writings to win renown, and are we going to say that, if there is anything in them that conduces to courage or just conduct, this will not prove useless to those who wish to apply it, and yet at the same time are we going to deny that the decree that Miltiades proposed in the very face of danger, when he delivered a single resolution to the Greeks that embraced the whole of justice, is an adequate indication of the quality of his moral temper and his resolve, and of whether it was such that just anyone, or
only the virtuous, can emulate it? If it is right to honor our 161
ancestors, how can it not be right to honor Miltiades, as the common ancestor of all the Greeks since his day? He was not only the champion who ensured their preservation, but also the man who showed them what sort of people they ought to be in their struggles for freedom, and

6.109, urging the Polemarch Callimachus to use his casting vote in favor of risking battle at Marathon.

καὶ παράδειγμα πᾶσιν εὔδηλον ἐκθεὶς οὗτός ἐστι φα-
162 νερώτατα τῶν ἄνω πάντων. εἰ τοίνυν καὶ Σόλωνα καὶ Λυκοῦργον ἐπαινοῦμεν κατὰ τοὺς νόμους οὓς ἔθηκαν, πῶς οὐ δίκαιον Μιλτιάδην ἐπαινεῖν, ὃς ἔργῳ τοῦτον ἔθηκεν τὸν νόμον, μηδένα τῶν χειρόνων θαυμάζειν μηδὲ τὸ ῥᾷστον αἱρεῖσθαι πρὸ τοῦ κρείττονος;

σκεψώμεθα γὰρ δὴ παρὰ τὸν Λυκοῦργον τὸν Μιλτιάδην ἐξετάζοντες. οὐ γὰρ δήπου κἀκεῖνον ἔστ' εἰπεῖν ὅτι ὡς τῶν διακόνων ἕν' ἔθηκεν Πλάτων· οὐκ ἔστι
163 ταῦτα οὐδ' ἐγγύς. Λυκοῦργος μὲν τοίνυν ὅτι τοὺς νόμους ἔθηκεν πρὸς ἀνδρείαν καὶ καρτερίαν βλέποντας καὶ ὅτι βελτίους ἐποίησεν τὰ τοῦ πολέμου τοὺς πολίτας, οὕτως εὐδοκιμεῖ, καθάπερ τις γυμναστὴς ἑτέρους παρασκευάσας πρὸς τὸ νικᾶν, αὐτὸς δὲ οὐδὲ ὁτιοῦν ἀποδειξάμενος τοιοῦτον. Μιλτιάδης δὲ πρὸς τῷ τὰ[44] βέλτιστα ἐθίσαι τοὺς πολίτας καὶ τῷ παρασκευάσαι μηδενὸς ὑστέρους εἶναι πρὸς τὰ τοῦ πολέμου πράγματα καὶ τοῦ μεγίστου τῶν ἔργων αὐτὸς ἡγεμὼν γεγονὼς φαίνεται. οὕτως οὐ πολλῷ τινι τοῦ Λυκούργου δεύτερος ἡμῖν φαίνεται γεγονώς, οὐδὲ παρ' ἄλλοις τισὶ μᾶλλον δίκαιος εὐδοκιμεῖν ἢ παρὰ τοῖς ἐκεί-
164 νον δικαίως ἐπαινοῦσιν. καὶ μὴν ἐν μὲν τοῖς ἄλλοις ἔργοις λέγω καὶ ἐπιτηδεύμασιν καὶ τέχναις οἱ μὲν ὡς ἄρξαντες ἐτιμήθησαν, οἱ δὲ ὡς ὑπερβαλλόμενοι· Ὅμηρον δ' ἐπαινοῦσιν, ὡς αὐτὸν ἀρξάμενόν τε καὶ
165 ἀπεργασάμενον ὡς κάλλιστα ποίησιν. Μιλτιάδης τοίνυν ἅμα τ' αὐτὸς ἦρξεν τῆς ἐλευθερίας τοῖς Ἕλλησι

it is he who most brilliantly of all our forebears set out a
clear pattern for all to follow. If we praise Solon and Ly- 162
curgus for the laws they made, how can it fail to be right
to praise Miltiades, who in his deeds laid down the law that
one should not go in awe of any of one's inferiors, or
choose the easier course in place of the better?

Let us indeed pursue our investigation by comparing
him with Lycurgus (because I am sure it cannot be said
that Plato classified Lycurgus as one of the lackeys; that
does not even come close to being possible). Lycurgus, 163
then, owes his good reputation to the fact that the laws he
made aimed at inculcating bravery and fortitude, and to
the fact that he improved the military abilities of his citizens. Like an athletic trainer he equipped others with
what they needed in order to win without showing any
such qualities at all in himself. Of Miltiades, by contrast,
it is clear that in addition to training his citizens in the best
habits and equipping them to be second-to-none in military matters, he personally led them in the greatest of their
exploits. We can thus clearly see that he does not lag far
behind Lycurgus, and that it is above all among those who
so rightly praise Lycurgus that Miltiades too deserves to
be renowned. In other areas, moreover, I mean in activi- 164
ties and professions and skills, while there are some who
have won honor for being the first to practice them, and
others for surpassing their predecessors, Homer is praised
both as the first poet and as the man who brought poetry
to perfection. Now, Miltiades at one and the same time 165
was both the first to confer freedom on the Greeks and left

---

[44] πρὸς τά Canter Reiske

καὶ οὐδενὶ τῶν Ἑλλήνων ὑπερβολὴν τῶν ἔργων τῶν ἑαυτοῦ κατέλιπεν, οὔκουν ὅσους γε ἀπὸ τῶν ἄλλων πόλεων ἔχομεν λέγειν. ὥστε δέδοικα μὴ τῶν αὐτῶν ᾖ μήτε Ὅμηρον δέχεσθαι τῇ πόλει μήτε Μιλτιάδην ἐθέλειν ἐπαινεῖν.

166 εἶτα ἐρωτᾷ Πλάτων τίνα βελτίω Μιλτιάδης ἐποίησεν ἢ τῶν πολιτῶν ἢ τῶν ξένων, ἢ δοῦλόν φησιν ἢ ἐλεύθερον, ἢ ἄνδρα ἢ γυναῖκα; τίνα μὲν οὖν, ὦ Πλάτων, χείρω Μιλτιάδης ἐποίησεν ἢ τῶν πολιτῶν ἢ τῶν ξένων, ἢ δοῦλόν φημι ἢ ἐλεύθερον, ἢ ἄνδρα ἢ γυναῖκα; ἢ τῷ τῶν πάντων εἰς ὄνειδος καὶ ζημίαν ἐτε-
167 λεύτησεν ἡ πρὸς ἐκεῖνον ὁμιλία; καὶ δή σοι λαμπρῶς ἀποκρινοῦμαι τίνα βελτίω Μιλτιάδης ἐποίησεν, καὶ οὐ κατ' ἄνδρα εἴποιμι ἄν σοι καὶ γυναῖκα, ὥσπερ οἱ περὶ μικρῶν ἔργων ἐρευνῶντες, ἀλλ' εἴ μοι δίδως εἰπεῖν, ἅπαντας Ἀθηναίους ἐκεῖνος βελτίους ἐποίησεν καὶ ὅλην βελτίω τὴν πόλιν, ὡς πόλιν εἰπεῖν λέγω καὶ ὡς δῆμον λέγω καὶ ὡς τὸ κοινὸν εἰρῆσθαι. μὴ γάρ μοι διὰ πάσης ἀκριβείας μηδὲ πρὸς ἓν μέτρον, μηδὲ ὥσπερ τὰς τοῦ Γηρυόνου κεφαλὰς ἴσους[45] δι'[46] ἁπάντων οἷον δεῖν ἐφεξῆς εἶναι, ἀλλὰ καὶ χείρους τινὰς λίπε,

ἐπεὶ οὔτοι πάντες ὁμοῖοι ἀνέρες ἐν πολέμῳ.

168 οὔκουν οὐδ' ἐν πόλει πάντες ὅμοιοι τὴν γνώμην, οὐ μᾶλλόν γε ἢ τὰ σώματα πάντες ἴσοι καὶ παραπλή-

[45] ἴσους Reiske ἴσας *codd.* [46] *add.* Reiske *ex* Σ

no subsequent Greek the possibility of surpassing his own
great deeds, at least not any of those we can name from
the other cities. I rather suspect, therefore, that it is the
same kind of people who both decline to receive Homer
into their state and refuse to praise Miltiades.[142]

So, does Plato dare ask what citizen or foreigner Mil- 166
tiades made into a better person, slave or free, as he puts
it, man or woman?[143] No, Plato, the question is rather what
citizen or foreigner Miltiades made into a worse person,
slave or free I mean, man or woman, or whether any of
them at all found his dealings with Miltiades ending in
detriment and reproaches. I will tell you now, loud and 167
clear, who Miltiades made better. I will not name you individual men and women, as if this were an inquiry into
minor matters of behavior, but if it is all right by you, I
shall say that he made all the Athenians better and the
whole city better, speaking of them as a city, that is, and as
a people, and of their communal identity. Please do not
think that absolutely all of them ought to be equal in all
respects, like Geryon's heads, when measured with utter
scrupulousness against a single yardstick, but allow for the
possibility that some of them will be worse than others,

> since by no means are all men equal in war.[144]

No more are all the inhabitants of a city equal in intelli- 168
gence, any more than they are all equal or comparable in

[142] That is, Plato, who notoriously refused Homer admission into his ideal state at *Resp.* 398a.

[143] *Grg.* 514d–15d, 516d.

[144] *Il.* 12.270–71.

σιοι· ἀλλ᾽ ὥσπερ τῶν προστατῶν αὐτῶν οἱ μὲν χείρους, οἱ δὲ βελτίους, οὕτω καὶ δῆμος οὐκ ἄν ποτε εἷς ἀκριβῶς γένοιτο, ἀλλ᾽ ἀνάγκη τοὺς μὲν χεῖρον, τοὺς δὲ βέλτιον ἔχειν πρὸς αὐτὸ τὸ πείθεσθαι τοῖς
169 προεστῶσιν. οἷου τοίνυν καὶ Μιλτιάδου προεστῶτος τοὺς μὲν ὡς πλεῖστον τῆς ἐκείνου δυνάμεως ἀπολαῦσαι, τοὺς δὲ μέσως, κἂν τῷ μέσῳ τὸ παραλλὰξ αὖ τίθει. γένοιτο δ᾽ ἄν τις ἐν πλήθει καὶ περὶ ὦτα ἀτυχέστερος. οὔτοι πάντας οὐδ᾽ ὁ ἥλιος οἷός τ᾽ ἐστὶν θερμαίνειν, ἀλλ᾽ ἤδη τις ἐν καθαρῷ τῆς μεσημβρίας ἐρρίγωσε τῆς καταβολῆς ἐπελθούσης.

170 ἂν οὕτω μετρίως καὶ πρὸς δύναμιν τῆς φύσεως ἐξετάζῃς, φανεῖταί σοι καὶ Μιλτιάδης ὅλην τὴν πόλιν εὖ πεποιηκώς. εἰ δὲ κατ᾽ ἄνδρα ζητήσεις τοὺς ἀρίστους, οὐδὲ τοὺς ἵππους τοὺς Θετταλοὺς ἐφεξῆς ἅπαντας ἀρίστους εὑρήσεις, οὐδὲ τὰς κύνας τὰς Λα-
171 καίνας, ἀλλ᾽ ὅμως σῴζεται τοῖς γένεσι τοὔνομα. οὕτω δὴ καὶ τοὺς Ἀθηναίους ἐξέταζε, τὸ πᾶν ἦθος τῆς πολιτείας ὁρῶν αὐτῶν καὶ πῶς ἔπραττον κατ᾽ ἐκείνους τοὺς χρόνους κοινῇ, ὥσπερ που καί φαμεν πόλιν εὐνομεῖσθαι, καίτοι γ᾽ οὐ δυνατὸν γενέσθαι πόλιν τοιαύτην, ἐν ᾗ μηδὲν μήτε μεῖζον μήτ᾽ ἔλαττον ἁμάρ-
172 τημα συμβαίνει μηδ᾽ ἁμαρτάνει μηδείς. καὶ μὴν καθ᾽ ὑμᾶς τοὺς σοφοὺς ἔχοι τις ἂν ὡδὶ προβιβάζειν[47] τῷ λόγῳ, ὡς ἄρ᾽ ἂν ἡ πόλις εὐνομῆται, ἀνάγκη τοὺς οἰκοῦντας αὐτὴν πάντας εὐνόμους εἶναι, καὶ ἄνδρας

[47] προβιβάζειν U προσβιβάζειν *cett.*

physique. Just as among the leaders themselves some are better and some worse, so too a people could never be entirely homogeneous, but inevitably some are worse and some better, precisely when it comes to obeying their superiors. You should therefore take it that in the case of 169
Miltiades' leadership too there were some who benefited very extensively indeed from his abilities, and some only moderately, and you should envisage some variation in that "moderately" as well. Along with everyone else in a crowd of people there could be someone who is hard of hearing; not even the sun is capable of warming everyone, and people have been known to shudder at the onset of a bout of fever under a cloudless midday sky.

If you consider the matter like this, reasonably and with 170
an eye to what is possible in nature, it will be clear to you that Miltiades really did benefit the city as a whole. If you are going to examine everybody individually in your search for the best, well, even in the case of Thessalian horses you will not find absolutely all of them of top quality, nor with Spartan hunting dogs either, and yet these breeds retain
their reputations. You should examine the Athenians in 171
the same way, looking to the whole character of their republic and how they fared communally through that period, since we surely do say that a city is law-abiding, even though it is impossible for there ever to be a city of such a kind that no offense at all, great or small, is committed
in it and no one ever puts a foot wrong. Indeed, one of you 172
philosophers might perhaps construct a chain of reasoning to the effect that if a city is law-abiding, then necessarily all its inhabitants are law-abiding, men and women alike;

καὶ γυναῖκας· εἰ δ᾽ εὐνόμους, εὐτάκτους· εἰ δ᾽ εὐτάκτους, σώφρονας· εἰ δὲ σώφρονας, καὶ φρονίμους· φρονίμων δ᾽ ὄντων ἁπάντων οὐχ οἷόν τε δήπουθεν ἁμαρτάνειν οὐδένα· ὥσθ᾽ ἕως ἂν ἡ πόλις εὐνομῆται, ἀνάγκη μηδένα μηδὲν ἁμαρτάνειν. ἀλλ᾽ οὔτε τοῦτο οἶμαι δυνατὸν οὔθ᾽ ὡς εἰ μὴ τοῦτο γενήσεται, οὐδεμίαν δοκεῖν δεῖ[48] πόλιν εὐνομεῖσθαι φαίης ποτ᾽ ἄν, ἀλλὰ τὸ κοινὸν σχῆμα τῆς πολιτείας ἐξετάζων καὶ ἅμα πρὸς τὰς ἄλλας πόλεις τὴν πόλιν κρίνων τὰ μὲν τοῖς νόμοις, οἶμαι, καὶ τοῖς ἔθεσι λογίζῃ, τὰ δὲ ταῖς
173 τῆς φύσεως ἀνάγκαις ἀποδίδως. ἐὰν οὕτω σκοπῇς καὶ τοὺς Ἀθηναίους καὶ μὴ καθ᾽ ἕκαστον ὥσπερ τοὺς θεσμοθέτας ἀνακρίνῃς, ἔχω σοι καὶ ἑτέραν προσθήκην ἔτι μείζω καὶ θαυμασιωτέραν εἰπεῖν, ὅτι Μιλτιάδης οὐ μόνον τὴν πόλιν βελτίονα ἐποίησεν, ἀλλὰ καὶ τὴν Ἑλλάδα πᾶσαν πρὸς τῇ πόλει· καὶ ὥσπερ σὺ λέγεις, τίνα τῶν πολιτῶν ἢ τῶν ξένων, οὕτως ἐγώ φημι καὶ πολίτας καὶ τοὺς ἄλλους ἅπαντας Ἕλληνας ὅτι βελτίους ἐκεῖνος ὁ ἀνὴρ ἀπειργάσατο. πᾶσι γὰρ ἡγεῖτο πρὸς τὰ κάλλιστα, ὥστε χείρω μὲν οὐδένα, βελτίους δ᾽ ἅπαντας ἐποίει τό γ᾽ αὑτοῦ μέρος.

174 σκόπει δ᾽ ἐξ ὧν αὐτὸς ὡρίσω, μηδὲν τοῖς ἐμοῖς προσέχων λόγοις, εἰ μή τι ἀπὸ τῆς ἀνάγκης συμβαίνοι. ἄλλο τι ἢ τοῦτο λέγεις παρ᾽ ὅλον τὸν λόγον, ὡς ἡ δικαιοσύνη καλὸν καὶ ὡς ὅ τι ἂν τις πράττῃ σὺν

48 δεῖ Canter Reiske δεῖν *codd.*

and if they are law-abiding, then they are also well disciplined; and if they are well disciplined, they are also self-controlled; and if they are self-controlled, they are also prudent; and if all of them are prudent, then it is evidently impossible for any of them to commit an offense; consequently, for as long as a city is law-abiding, it is necessarily true that no one commits any offense.[145] But neither, I think, can this be so, nor would you ever say that, unless it is so, no city should ever be thought of as law-abiding. Instead, examining the shared cast of the constitution and at the same time judging the city in comparison to other cities, you set down some things to the credit of its laws and the character of its people, and attribute others to
natural necessity. If you consider the Athenians too in this 173
light, and do not review them individually, as the junior archons (*thesmothetai*) do, then I can tell you another still greater and more amazing fact as well, that Miltiades made not only the city of Athens better, but also the whole of Greece into the bargain. Just as you say "what citizen or what foreigner?", so I assert that this man made both the citizens of Athens and all the other Greeks into better men. He led them all toward the highest moral standards, to such effect that he made none of them worse and all of them better as far as it depended on him.

Consider the issue in the light of your own definition 174
and do not bother with my reasoning unless logic compels you to. Do you for the whole length of your discussion say anything other than that justice is something fine, and that everything that anyone ever does should be done justly,

[145] A malicious parody of philosophical reasoning, in part inspired by *Resp.* 427e ff.

τούτῳ πρακτέον καὶ τῇ ῥητορικῇ χρηστέον πρὸς τὸ δίκαιον ἀεί; κἂν τύπτῃ μέ τις, φῄς,[49] δικαίως ἢ μή, διαφέρει, κἂν ἐξελαύνῃ τις, ἐὰν ἀδίκως, ἄθλιος, καὶ πανταχοῦ ταύταις χρῇ ταῖς προσθήκαις δικαίως ἢ ἀδίκως λέγων· καὶ τὸ μὲν δικαίως καλῶς ἀξιοῖς εἶναι, τὸ δ' ἐναντίον κακῶς· καὶ τὸ μὲν εὐδαίμονος ἀνδρὸς εἶναι, τὴν δικαιοσύνην, τὸ δὲ τοῦ ἐναντίου, τὴν ἀδικίαν· καὶ τὸ μὲν ὡς οἷόν τε διώκειν χρῆναι, τὸ δὲ φεύγειν ὡς ἕκαστος ἔχει τάχους. οὐ ταῦτ' εἰσὶν οἱ λόγοι; οὐ δικαίως μὲν ἅπαντα πραττόμενα ἐπαινεῖς, ὡς ἑτέρως δὲ ψέγεις; ἔχε δὴ καὶ σκόπει. μὴ γὰρ

175 ὥσπερ ἐν νυκτομαχίᾳ τῶν φίλων ἁπτώμεθα. ἆρ' οὐ[50] δίκαιον ἀμύνεσθαι τοὺς ἐπιόντας; δικαιότατον μὲν οὖν. τί δαί; τῶν Ἑλλήνων πλείω ποιεῖσθαι λόγον ἢ τῶν βαρβάρων οὐ δίκαιον; πᾶς τις ἂν φήσαι τόν γε Ἕλληνα δήπουθεν.

176 Μιλτιάδης τοίνυν ἐπιόντων τῶν βαρβάρων τοῖς Ἕλλησιν οὐδὲν πρότερον τῆς κοινῆς σωτηρίας ἐποιήσατο, οὐδ' ἰδίᾳ περὶ τῶν ἑαυτοῦ πραγμάτων ἐσκέψατο, οὐδ' ἀνεβάλετο εἰς ἕτερον καιρὸν τὴν ἀρετὴν

177 δεῖξαι τὴν ἑαυτοῦ. καίτοι παρῆν αὐτῷ μὴ πρὸς τὸ βέλτιστον ὁρῶντι, ἀλλὰ ταὐτὰ τοῖς τυράννοις διώκοντι, εἰ μὲν ἐβούλετο μετὰ Ἱππίου καὶ τῶν Πεισιστρατιδῶν συνεπιστρατεύειν ἐπὶ τὴν Ἑλλάδα, εἰ δὲ ἐβούλετο μετ' Ἀλευαδῶν ἐκ Θετταλίας, ἢ πρό γε

[49] φῄς Reiske φησί *codd.*
[50] οὖν Iunt. *edd.*

and that the art of oratory should always be used for just
ends? It matters, you say, whether someone hits me justly
or unjustly, and if someone banishes me, he is wretched if
he does so unjustly, and everywhere in what you say you
use these qualifiers "justly" and "unjustly"; and you claim
that to act justly is to act finely, while to act unjustly is to
act foully, and that one of the two, just action, is the mark
of the happy man, while unjust action is the mark of his
opposite; and that one should pursue the former to the
best of one's ability and flee the latter with all the speed
each of us can muster. Is this not your reasoning? Do you
not praise everything that is done justly, and reprehend
everything that is done otherwise? Wait though and
think.[146] Let us not lay into our own side, as in a night
battle.[147] Is it just to resist those who attack you? "Most 175
just indeed." And is it not right to attach more value to
Greeks than to barbarians? "Everyone would certainly say
it is, for a Greek at any rate."

Well then, when the barbarians attacked the Greeks, 176
Miltiades valued nothing more highly than their common
salvation; he did not consider his own private interests, nor
did he postpone demonstrating his own heroism to another time. And yet it would have been perfectly possible 177
for him not to look to what was best but instead to pursue
the same objectives as the tyrants: according to choice, he
could have marched against Greece with Hippias and the
Pisistratidae, or advanced from Thrace with the Aleuadae,[148] or even stolen a march on the Aleuadae. Nor do I

146 Platonizing idiom: *Grg.* 460a, *Prt.* 349e.

147 Most famously, the night battle that sealed the fate of the Athenian expedition to Sicily in 413 BC, described in Thuc. 7.44.

148 Hdt. 7.6, etc.

Ἀλευαδῶν. οἶμαι δὲ οὐδ' ἂν ἐκ Λακεδαίμονος τῶν
178 ταὐτὰ βουλομένων ἠπόρησεν. καὶ μὴν οὐδ' οἱ βάρβαροί γ' ἂν ἧττον ἐκεῖνον ἡδέως ἐδέξαντο ἢ πολλοὺς ἑτέρους. ἀλλ' ὡς ἔοικεν, οὐ πρὸς αὑτοῦ ταῦθ' ἡγεῖτο Μιλτιάδης, ἀλλὰ ταῦτα πάντα ἀφεὶς καὶ παριδὼν καὶ τοῦ μηδενὸς ἄξια κρίνας εἰς ἀρετῆς λόγον τῇ κοινῇ χρείᾳ τῆς πατρίδος καὶ τῶν Ἑλλήνων προσένειμεν
179 αὑτόν. καίτοι ταῦτα ποιῶν καὶ ταῦτα προαιρούμενος πότερον δικαιοσύνης καὶ καλοκαγαθίας, ἢ κακίας καὶ ἀδικίας δεῖγμα ἐξέφερεν; ἢ οὐδετέρου φήσομεν; ἐγὼ μὲν γὰρ εὐδαίμονα καὶ ζηλωτὸν ἀκούειν οὐδὲν κωλύειν ἐκεῖνον ἡγοῦμαι, εἴπερ ἀληθὴς ὁ Πλάτωνος λόγος ὡς τό γε δίκαιον αὐτὸ λαμπρὸν ἔπεστιν τοῖς πεπολιτευμένοις.

180 εἶεν. ἀλλ' ὑπὲρ τῆς ἀνδρείας τῆς ἐκείνου δείσομεν, ἢ μικρούς τινας καὶ φαύλους καιροὺς τοὺς δείξαντας αὐτὴν εἶναι φήσομεν; οὐ πάντες μὲν ἄνθρωποι μικροῦ δέω λέγειν τότε Πέρσαις ὑπεπεπτώκεσαν,[51] τὰ δὲ πλεῖστα ἐξ ἐντολῆς τῷ βασιλεῖ κατειργάζετο; ὅποι δ' ὁρμήσειαν, ἔχειν ὑπελάμβανον, οἵ γε καὶ ἐπὶ Σκύθας ἐλθόντες ἔδοξαν δυστυχῆσαι, ὅτι[52] οὐκ ἠδυνήθησαν εὑρεῖν αὐτούς· Αἰγύπτιοι δὲ οἱ σοφώτατοι πάντων μίαν τῶν πασῶν μηχανὴν οὐχ εὗρον, δι' ἧς ἐκφεύξονται τὸ μὴ δουλεῦσαι. Λιβύην δ' οὐδεὶς λόγος ἦν ὁ διαιρῶν ἀπὸ τῆς Ἀσίας τότε, ἀλλ' ἦν ἅπαντα μία

[51] ὑπεπεπτώκεσαν Behr ὑποπεπτώκεσαν *codd.*
[52] καὶ ὅτι *codd.* καί *del.* Reiske

think he would have been short of likeminded allies from
Sparta. The barbarians certainly would not have received 178
him any the less readily than they did many others. But
apparently Miltiades did not think these courses of action
were right for him; instead he renounced and disregarded
them all, judging that they had no value in virtue's ledger,
and devoted himself instead to the common need of his
homeland and of Greece. In doing this and making this 179
choice, was it justice and heroic virtue, or villainy and injustice that he demonstrated? Or shall we say it was neither? I certainly think there is nothing to prevent him
being called happy and admirable, if Plato is telling the
truth when he says that Justice Itself is a shining crown on
a political career.[149]

Very good. Shall we then have any fears over his brav- 180
ery, or say that the occasions that revealed it were minor
and trivial? At that time had not all men, one might almost
say, bowed down before the Persians, and was not the
majority of the world being conquered for their king in
accordance with his commands? Toward whatever objective they set out, they supposed that they already possessed it, and when they marched against the Scythians
and could not find them, it counted as a failure.[150] The
Egyptians may have been the wisest of nations, but the one
trick of all that they could not devise was the one that
would have enabled them to escape being enslaved. There
was at that time no criterion that divided Libya from Asia;
in belonging to the Persians they were just one continent.

149 "Justice Itself" is an intentional echo of Plato's terminology for the Forms, or essences of things.

150 Hdt. 4.118–42.

181 ἤπειρος ὡς Πέρσαις εἶναι. τῶν δὲ Ἑλλήνων οἱ μὲν τὴν Ἀσίαν οἰκοῦντες οἱ μὲν ἐκ τριγονίας ἐδούλευον, οἱ δ᾽ ἐκ πλείονος, αἱ νῆσοι δ᾽ οὐδὲν ἦσαν πρᾶγμα, Ἐρετριεῖς δ᾽ Εὐβοέων χεῖρας ἀνταράμενοι τριῶν ἡμερῶν ἤγοντο πανοικησίᾳ· τῶν δ᾽ ἄλλων τῶν ἐν τῇ Εὐρώπῃ οἱ μὲν τὸ ὕδωρ καὶ τὴν γῆν ἐδεδώκεσαν, οἱ δὲ τὸ μέλλον ἀπεσκόπουν, τοσοῦτον αὑτοὺς Ἐρετριέων εὐτυχεστέρους νομίζοντες, ὅσον ὕστεροι ταὐτὰ πείσεσθαι. Λακεδαιμόνιοι δέ, εἴθ᾽ ὑπὸ τοῦ πρὸς Μεσσηνίους πολέμου εἴτε καὶ τὴν πανσέληνον μένοντες,
182 οὐδὲ αὐτοὶ βοηθεῖν εἶχον. ὁ δὲ στρατὸς ἦν καὶ δὴ Μαραθῶνι κατηρκὼς ἐξ Ἐρετρίας ὡς ἐπὶ τοῖς ἴσοις. οὐ διακόνων ἐκεῖνος ὁ καιρὸς ἦν, οὐδ᾽ ὑφειμένων ἀνθρώπων, οὐδ᾽ ἐκ πολλοῦ τὸ κελευόμενον ποιεῖν εἰδότων, οὐδὲ εἰς τὸ δοκοῦν ἑτέροις βλεπόντων, οὐδ᾽ ὅπως ἀσφαλῶς βιώσονται ζητούντων, οὐδὲ τοῦθ᾽ ἡγουμένων ἀρκεῖν, ἀλλ᾽ ἐκεῖνος ὁ καιρὸς ὥσπερ κῆρυξ ἐκάλει τῶν Ἑλλήνων τὸν ἀνδρειότατον καὶ τὸν ἐκ πλείστου τοῖς ἀρίστοις λογισμοῖς ὡμιληκότα, καὶ ὅστις οἶδεν ὅπως δεῖ σῴζειν τε καὶ σῴζεσθαι.

183 οὐδ᾽ ἡμεῖς τῶν ἀνδρῶν ἐκείνων τοῦτο ἐπαινοῦμεν, λέγω τῶν ἐν ἐκείνοις τοῖς χρόνοις προστάντων, ὅτι τὴν Ἑλλάδα ἔσῳζον ὁπωσοῦν, ὥσπερ ὃν σὺ λέγεις τὸν κυβερνήτην τὸν ἐξ Αἰγίνης ἢ τοῦ Πόντου κομίζοντα· ἀλλ᾽ ὅτι ἔσῳζον καὶ πολίτας καὶ πάντας σὺν
184 καλῷ τῷ σχήματι. εἰ μὲν γὰρ τὰ ὅπλα παραδόντας ἢ

Of the Greeks who lived in Asia, some had been enslaved 181
for three generations and some for even longer; the islands posed no problem; and of the peoples of Euboea, even though the Eretrians put up some resistance, they were led off captive with their entire households within three days.[151] Of the other inhabitants of Europe, some had already handed over the earth and water, while others eyed up the inevitable outcome, convinced that they were more fortunate than the Eretrians only to the extent that they were not going to suffer the same fate quite as soon as them. Nor were the Spartans able to help, whether this was because of their war with the Messenians or because
they were waiting for the full moon.[152] There the Persian 182
army now was at Marathon, following its southward advance from Eretria, as if for a repeat performance. This was no time for lackeys or for submissive people, or those who knew from long experience how to do what they were ordered, or who looked to what others thought should be done, or were seeking a secure existence and thought this enough. No, this moment called like a herald for the bravest of the Greeks, the one who had kept company for the longest with the best calculations, and who knew how one ought to save and be saved.

What I praise in those men, meaning those who were 183
preeminent at that time, is not that they saved Greece in some manner or another, like the helmsman you mention who brings his passengers safely from Aegina or from Pontus,[153] but that they saved their fellow citizens and everybody else in such noble style. If they had thought it right 184

[151] Pl. *Menex*. 240b (Hdt. 6.101 says it took seven days).
[152] Hdt. 6.106. [153] *Grg*. 511d.

τοῖς κήρυξιν ὁμολογήσαντας, ἢ τὸν Περσῶν βασιλέα δεσπότην ἀντὶ τῶν νόμων ἑλομένους ἠξίουν σῴζεσθαι, οὐκ ἂν ἔγωγε συγχαίρειν ᾤμην δεῖν οὔτε τοῖς πείθουσι τῶν λόγων οὔτε τοῖς πεισθεῖσι τῆς σωτηρίας, ἀλλὰ ὡς ἀληθῶς διακόνους ἂν ἐκείνους εἶχον καλεῖν, καὶ τοῦ πρὸς ἡμέραν ὑπηρέτας ὥσπερ τοὺς πορθμέας, οὐ μόνον, εἰ βούλει, τοὺς κυβερνήτας. εἰ δ' ἀπ' αὐτῶν τῶν κηρύκων ἀρξάμενοι καὶ τῆς ἀποκρίσεως προηγόρευον Ἀθηναίοις ὅτι δεῖ μελετᾶν τὸν ὑπὲρ τῆς τῶν Ἑλλήνων ἐλευθερίας ἀγῶνα καὶ μὴ λιπεῖν τὴν τοῦ φρονήματος τάξιν, καὶ οὐ τὰ ὅπλα ῥίψαντας οὐδὲ τοῖς φόβοις εἴξαντας, ἀλλ' ἀναλαβόντας τὰ ὅπλα καὶ τῶν φόβων κρείττους γενομένους, μᾶλλον δ' ἕνα τοῦτον φόβον καὶ δεινὸν καὶ ἀφόρητον νομίσαντας εἶξαι τοῖς χείροσι καὶ παραχωρῆσαι τοῦ πατρίου σχήματος, εἰ ταῦτα λέγοντας καὶ οὕτω παρεσκευασμένους ἠξίουν ἀπαντᾶν ἐπὶ τὴν κρίσιν τὴν περὶ τῶν ὅλων καὶ δέχεσθαι τὸ ἐκβησόμενον ὡς ἐπ' ἀμφότερα ὁμοίως κερδανοῦντας, οὐχ ὁρῶ τίνα ταῦτ' ἔχει διακονίαν ἀγεννῆ ἢ πῶς ἔοικεν τοῖς τοῦ κυβερνήτου λογισμοῖς.

ἀλλὰ εἰ μὲν τοῦτο λέγεις ὡς τὸν αὐτὸν τρόπον ὥσπερ ἐν νηὶ μέγιστον ὁ κυβερνήτης καὶ πρὸς τοῦτον ἅπαντα καὶ τὰ τῶν ναυτῶν καὶ τὰ τῶν ἐμπλεόντων, οὕτω καὶ τότ' εἰς ἐκείνους ἧκεν τὰ τῶν Ἑλλήνων

for their people to save themselves by handing over their weapons or coming to terms with the enemy heralds, or choosing the King of Persia as their master instead of their own laws, I would certainly not have thought it proper to congratulate either the persuaders on their words or the persuaded on their salvation, but instead I would have had good cause to call them lackeys in the full sense of the word, and servants of the passing moment, like ferrymen not just, if you please, helmsmen. But if instead, beginning with the heralds and the answer given to them,[154] they proclaimed to the Athenians that they should engage themselves in the struggle for the freedom of Greece and not desert the station where their proud spirit had placed them,[155] and that instead of casting aside their weapons and giving way to their fears, they should take up their weapons and conquer their fears, or rather think that the only terrible and unbearable fear was that of yielding to their inferiors and betraying their ancestral dignity—if they had demanded that it should be with these words and with this preparation that they should face up to the decisive contest in which all would be decided, and that they should accept the outcome in the conviction that it would bring them equal benefit either way, then I cannot see what element there is in this of ignoble servility, or how it resembles the calculations of the helmsman.

If what you mean is that in the same way that in a ship the helmsman is the most important person and the safety of both passengers and crew depends entirely on him, so also at that time the affairs of Greece depended on these

[154] Hdt. 7.133. [155] "Desert the station . . . placed them" is another echo of Dem. *Or.* 13.34; cf. §§97 and 300.

πράγματα καὶ ὑπὸ τῆς ἐκείνων γνώμης ἤγετο, εἰ τοῦτο λέγεις καὶ ὅσον παραδείγματι χρῇ τῷ κυβερνήτῃ, ὥσπερ Ὅμηρος τοῖς λέουσι καὶ τοῖς κάπροις καὶ πολλοῖς τοῖς ἄλλοις οὐκ εἰσάπαξ εἰκάζων, ἀλλ' εἰς ὅσον προσήκει τῷ λόγῳ, εἰ κατὰ τοῦτο τὸ μέρος καὶ σὺ μέμνησαι τοῦ κυβερνήτου, δίδωμι καὶ συγχωρῶ· εἰ δ' ἐπὶ πᾶσι τοῖς αὐτοῖς καταχρῇ τῷ λόγῳ καὶ ταὐτὸ δίκαιον ἐπ' ἀμφοτέροις τάττεις, οὐκ οἶδα ὅστις ταῦτα ἀποδέξεται, οἶμαι δὲ οὐδὲ αὐτὸς σὺ σαυτοῦ. δύο, φής, ὀβολοὺς λαβὼν ἢ δραχμὰς ὁ κυβερνήτης ἀπήλλακται. ἀλλ' οὐ Μιλτιάδης δυοῖν ὀβολοῖν οὐδὲ δραχμαῖν, οἶμαι δὲ οὐδὲ πολλῶν χρημάτων ἐν Ἀθηναίοις ταῦτα ἐπολιτεύετο, μᾶλλον δέ, εἰ χρὴ τἀληθὲς εἰπεῖν, ἐν ἅπασι τοῖς Ἕλλησιν, ἀλλ' ἄμισθον τὴν ἀρετὴν εἰς τὸ μέσον παρείχετο τῇ Ἑλλάδι, ὥσπερ σὺ φῂς τὸν Σωκράτη τοῖς νέοις.

185 οὐδὲν βελτίους ὁ κυβερνήτης ποιεῖ τοὺς[53] ἐμβάντας
εἰς τὴν ναῦν. ὑπέρευγε, ὦ Πλάτων, καίτοι καὶ ὁ κυβερνήτης ἴσως βελτίους τοὺς ναύτας τά γε ναυτικὰ
ποιεῖ. ἀλλ' ἐῶ τοῦτο. ἔστω μηδένα μηδὲν ὁ κυβερνήτης βελτίω ποιῶν, ἀλλὰ Μιλτιάδης καὶ πρὶν εἰς τὸν
κίνδυνον ἐμβαίνειν ἅπαντας ἤσκει πρὸς τὸ βέλτιστον, καὶ ἰδιώτας ἐξαγαγὼν ὡς εἰπεῖν ἐπανήγαγεν
186 νικηφόρους. μὴ τοίνυν κατὰ τὸν κυβερνήτην θῇς
αὐτόν, ὦ χρηστέ, τὸν εἰς τὴν Ὀλυμπίαν κομίζοντα,
ἀλλὰ μᾶλλον φῶμεν αὐτὸν ἐοικέναι τῷ γυμναστῇ, ὃς
πάλαι παρασκευάσας ἐκεῖσε τὸν ἀθλητήν, εἶτα ἐξ-

[53] τούς Resike τότε *codd.* τότε τούς R^2 Barocc. 136

men and were directed by their intelligence, if this is what you mean and you are using the helmsman as an image, as Homer used lions and boars and the rest as similes not just once but as often as was appropriate to his theme, if you too speak of the helmsman in this capacity, then I grant you the point and agree with you. But if you are pressing the figure as if it were an exact analogy in every respect and stipulating that justice is the same thing in both cases, then I do not know who will accept your word on this, and indeed I think that even you yourself will not. The helmsman, you say, receives two obols or two drachmas as his fee and takes his leave. But Miltiades did not pursue this policy of his among the Athenians—or rather, if one is to tell the truth, among all the Greeks—for two obols or two drachmas, let alone for a large sum of money. No, he put his heroism at Greece's disposal for the good of all for free, just as you say that Socrates put himself at the disposal of the young.

"The helmsman does not make those who embark on 185
his ship any better." Excellently well said, Plato, although actually the helmsman may perhaps make his crew better in their nautical skills; no matter, let us take it that the helmsman does not make anyone better in anything. Miltiades, however, even before entering the danger area trained everyone to the highest moral standards; he led them out as laymen, you might say, but brought them back
as victors. So, my dear fellow, do not line him up with a 186
helmsman taking people to Olympia, but let us say instead that he is more like the athletics coach, who long in advance trains the athlete for that same venue, then leads

αγαγὼν νικῶντα ἐπανήγαγεν. εἰ δὲ δὴ προσέσται τούτῳ τὸ καὶ αὐτὸν ἀνῃρῆσθαι τὰ πρῶτα τῆς ἀγωνίας ἐπὶ τῆς αὐτῆς Ὀλυμπιάδος, Ἡράκλεις, τίς ἂν διακονίαν τοῦ τοιούτου κατηγοροίη, ἢ τίς οὐκ ἂν τῶν στεφάνων συνήδοιτο;

187 οὐκ ἔνι τῷ κυβερνήτῃ πρὸς οὐδένα τῶν ἐμπλεόντων εἰπεῖν ὅτι χρὴ τοῦ θανάτου καταφρονῆσαι, οὐδ' ὅτι ἐξεπίτηδες αὑτὸν εἰς τὴν θάλατταν ῥῖψαι, ἀλλ' ὅσον τῶν σκευῶν ἐκβαλεῖν, καὶ ταῦτα ὑπὲρ σωτηρίας τῶν σωμάτων, ἄχρι τούτου κελεύειν ὁ κυβερνήτης κύριος. τὸ δὲ σύμπαν σῴζειν προείρηται παρὰ τῆς τέχνης αὐτῷ καὶ μὴ πολυπραγμονεῖν. ἀλλ' οὐκ ἐν τοῖς Μιλτιάδου λόγοις ταῦτ' ἐνῆν ἐκ παντὸς τρόπου σῴζεσθαι, καὶ οὐδὲ τὰ ὅπλα, ἂν οὕτω τύχῃ, ῥίψαντας ὑπὲρ τούτου. πόθεν; ἀλλ' αὐτὸ τοὐναντίον, μὴ ζητεῖν ἐκ παντὸς τρόπου σωθῆναι, ἀλλ' εἰ καὶ τεθνάναι δέοι, τολμᾶν ὑπὲρ πατρίδος καὶ ἱερῶν καὶ τάφων καὶ πολιτείας· ὁρᾷς ὅσῳ καὶ τὸν κυβερνήτην παρελήλυθεν.
188 καὶ γάρ τοι ὅσοι μὲν τοῦτ' ἐπείσθησαν αὐτῷ, σεμνοὶ σεμνῶς κεῖνται, κάλλιστα δὴ πάντων Ἑλλήνων καταλύσαντες τὸν αἰῶνα, μνημεῖον τῆς ἀρετῆς τὸν τάφον κεκτημένοι καὶ ὑπὸ γῆς ὄντες τὴν γῆν φυλάττοντες αὐτήν, ἀλλ' οὐχ ὑπ' αὐτῆς ἐχόμενοι, τῆς Ἡσιόδου προσρήσεως ἐγγύτατα ἥκοντες μετέχειν, ἣν ἐκεῖνος εἰς τὴν τελευτὴν τοῦ χρυσοῦ γένους ἐποίησεν εἰπὼν

οἱ μὲν δαίμονες ἁγνοὶ ὑποχθόνιοι καλέονται,
ἐσθλοί, ἀλεξίκακοι, φύλακες θνητῶν ἀνθρώπων.

him out and brings him back victorious. And if in addition this man happens also himself to win first prize in the contest at the same Olympiad, then heavens! Who could accuse such a man as this of being a mere lackey, and who would not congratulate him on his trophy?

The helmsman is not allowed to say to any of his pas- 187
sengers that he should scorn death, or deliberately throw himself into the sea; his authority extends only so far as ordering them to throw some of the tackle overboard, and then only in the interests of the passengers' physical safety. He is professionally obliged to keep his passengers safe and not interfere any further, and that is that. But saving one's life by any available means, including (if it so chanced) throwing away one's weapons for this purpose, had no place in Miltiades' words. How on earth could it have? His exhortation was quite the reverse, not to seek to keep oneself safe at all costs, but to be bold in defense of homeland and shrines and graves and constitution, even at the cost of one's life. His superiority to the helmsman is
obvious! All those who obeyed him in this are objects of 188
reverence as they lie in honored death: having ended their lives most gloriously of all Greeks, and gained themselves a memorial to their heroism in their graves, guarding the earth that they lie beneath yet not held fast by it, they come as close as anyone can to qualifying for the designation that Hesiod created to honor the end of the Golden Race, when he said

They are called holy spirits beneath the earth,
noble, averters of evil, guardians of mortal men.[156]

[156] *Op.* 122–23, but quoted with the variants found in Plato's quotation of the same lines in *Cra.* 398a.

κἀκείνους πλὴν ὅσον οὐ δαίμονας, ἀλλὰ δαιμονίους καλῶν, θαρρούντως ἂν ἔχοις λέγειν, ὑποχθονίους τινὰς φύλακας καὶ σωτῆρας τῶν Ἑλλήνων, ἀλεξικάκους καὶ πάντα ἀγαθούς, καὶ ῥύεσθαί γε τὴν χώραν οὐ χεῖρον ἢ τὸν ἐν Κολωνῷ κείμενον Οἰδίπουν, ἢ εἴ τις ἄλλοθί που τῆς χώρας ἐν καιρῷ τοῖς ζῶσι κεῖσθαι
189 πεπίστευται. καὶ τοσούτῳ γέ μοι δοκοῦσιν τὸν Σόλωνα παρελθεῖν τὸν ἀρχηγέτην ὥσθ' ὁ μὲν ἐν τῇ Σαλαμῖνι σπαρεὶς φυλάττειν τὴν νῆσον Ἀθηναίοις δοκεῖ, οἱ δὲ ὑπὲρ ἧς ἐτάχθησαν πεσόντες διετήρησαν ἅπασαν τὴν Ἀττικήν, μᾶλλον δὲ καὶ τὴν ἄλλην Ἑλλάδα πᾶσαν, οὐ μόνον οἷς αὐτοὶ παρέσχοντο οὐδ' οἷς ἐκώλυσαν τοὺς ἐπελθόντας, ἀλλ' ὅτι καὶ τοῖς ὕστερον κατέδειξαν ὁποίους τινὰς εἶναι δεῖ καιρῶν ὁμοίων ἐπιστάντων.

190 ἀλλὰ μὴν ὅτε καὶ τοῖς τελευτήσασιν αὐτῶν οὐ χαμᾶζε ἔπεσεν τὸ κέρδος, ἀλλ' ἀπέλαυσαν τῆς διανοίας καὶ αὐτοὶ τῆς ἑαυτῶν καὶ οἱ ἄλλοι πάντες τῆς ἐκείνων, πόσον τι τοῖς γε ζῶσιν καὶ κρατήσασιν περι-
191 εγένετο; οἶμαι δ' ἔγωγε καὶ τὸν Ἡρακλέα καὶ τὸν Πᾶνα καὶ τοὺς ἐπὶ τὴν μάχην ἀπαντήσαντας καὶ συστρατηγήσαντας Μιλτιάδῃ μάρτυρας ἀξιόχρεως τῆς ἀνδρείας τῆς ἐκείνου πρὸς ἅπαντας ἀνθρώπους εἶναι καὶ φέρειν οὐκ ἐλάττω τοῦτο Μιλτιάδῃ φιλοτιμίαν εἰς ἅπασαν τὴν πολιτείαν ἢ Πινδάρῳ φασὶν εἰς τὴν μουσικὴν τὸ τὸν αὐτὸν τοῦτον θεὸν ὀρχήσασθαί τι τῶν

Although you cannot call these heroes divine spirits too,
yet you could call them divinely endowed, and have the
confidence to speak of them as subterranean guardians
and saviors of the Greeks, averters of evil and wholly good;
and you could say that they protect the country quite as
well as the Oedipus who lies buried at Colonus, and anyone who is confidently believed to lie buried anywhere
else in the country to help the living in their hour of need.
I believe that they so far surpass Solon the founder that, 189
whereas his ashes are supposed to have been scattered
over Salamis so as to guard that island for the Athenians,[157]
they by their deaths preserved the whole of Attica, in defense of which they had been stationed, or rather the
whole of the rest of Greece, not only in the deeds they
performed themselves and in their achievement in halting
the invaders, but also because they showed future generations what kind of character has to be manifested when
such a crisis impends.

Indeed, when those of them who lost their lives did not 190
see the benefit from this just fall uselessly to the ground,
but the rewards of their resolve were enjoyed both by
them and by everyone else, how great must the gain have
been for the living victors? I certainly believe that Hera- 191
cles and Pan and all those who turned up to the battle and
shared Miltiades' command provide everyone with reli-
able testimony to his bravery, and that this brings Miltiades no less distinction in his political career than was
brought to Pindar in his poetry by that same god dancing

[157] Cf. Plut. *Vit. Sol.* 32.

192 ᾀσμάτων αὐτῷ. καὶ μὴν τεχνικόν γε εἶναι περὶ λόγους Πᾶνα τὸν Ἑρμοῦ Πλάτωνος ἡ φωνή· ἀλλαχοῦ δὲ καὶ λόγον αὐτὸν εἶναι λέγει, ἤτοι λόγου γε ἀδελφόν. φαίνεται τοίνυν οὗτος οὕτως αὐτῷ χαίρων τῷ Μιλτιάδῃ, οὐκ ἄν, εἴ γε ἑώρα φαῦλον περὶ τοὺς λόγους ὄντα.

193 οὐκοῦν πάνθ᾽ ἅμα μαρτυρεῖ καὶ τὴν ῥητορικὴν τέχνην ἀλλὰ μὴ ἄτεχνον τριβὴν εἶναι, καὶ τὸν Μιλτιάδην καὶ τοῦ λέγειν τεχνίτην καὶ τὴν ἀνδρείαν ἐπὶ
194 τῶν ἔργων τοῖς λόγοις παραπλήσιον. ἆρά γε ἢ πρὸς ἀνθρώπων ἢ πρὸς θεῶν βέλτιον περὶ Μιλτιάδου τι βλασφημεῖν; ἄτοπον δ᾽ ἂν τις ἡγήσαιτο Ἀθηναίους μὲν ἐκ τούτων τῶν ἔργων ἱδρύσασθαι τῷ Πανὶ τὸν νεών, οὐ πρότερον συννοήσαντας, Πλάτωνα δὲ τῶν ἔργων τούτων ὑπαρχόντων περὶ Μιλτιάδου τολμᾶν τὰ χείρω λέγειν καὶ τοσοῦτον ἀπέχειν τοῦ τιμᾶν ὥστε καὶ τὴν ὑπάρχουσαν αὐτῷ δικαίως τιμὴν τὸ καθ᾽ αὑτὸν ἀποστερεῖν· ὅστις καὶ δέκατος αὐτὸς στρατηγήσας μόνος ὡς εἰπεῖν ὀνομάζεται, καὶ ταῦτα Ἀριστείδου τοῦ Λυσιμάχου παρόντος, ὃν οὐδὲ Πλάτων αἰτιάσασθαι μόνον τῶν πάντων ἠξίωσεν, ἀλλ᾽
195 ᾐσχύνθη. ἀλλ᾽ ὅμως ἐκεῖνος Πλαταιᾶσι μὲν ἐκφανὴς ἦν μετὰ Παυσανίου στρατηγῶν, Μαραθῶνι δὲ ἐκρύπτετο ὑπὸ τῷ Μιλτιάδῃ καὶ οὐκ ἠμφισβήτει τῶν

---

158 For the participation of Pan and Heracles at Marathon, see Paus. 1.15.4 and 1.28.4, with Hdt. 6.105; the story that Pan was seen singing one of Pindar's *Paeans* is told in the Ambrosian *Life of Pindar* (i.2.2–4 Drachmann) and alluded to by Aristides again in *Or.* 42.12.

to one of his songs.[158] Moreover, the dictum that Pan son 192
of Hermes is an expert in the art of words is Plato's, and in another place he calls him speech or at any rate the brother of speech.[159] It is therefore clear that, in Plato's view, it was on these grounds that this god was so delighted with Miltiades, and would not have been if he had seen that he was worthless as an orator.

All these considerations together bear witness to the 193
facts both that oratory is a true science and not an unscientific knack, and that Miltiades was an expert orator who moreover showed a bravery in his deeds that matched his
words. Is it then a good idea, in the eyes of either gods or 194
men, to say anything insulting about Miltiades? Anyone would think it extraordinary that although the Athenians on the strength of these deeds dedicated a temple to Pan, even though they had not previously acknowledged him, Plato in the presence of these very same deeds should make so bold as to speak disparagingly of Miltiades and should be so far from honoring him as to do his best to deprive him even of the honor that rightly belonged to him—he who although only one of ten generals is practically the only one to be remembered by name, even though Aristides the son of Lysimachus was also there. Aristides was the only one of all of them that even Plato
did not see fit to denounce, but was ashamed to;[160] but 195
even Aristides, though he distinguished himself at Plataea when sharing the command with Pausanias, was eclipsed at Marathon by Miltiades and did not lay claim to an equal

[159] *Phdr.* 263d, *Cra.* 408d.
[160] *Grg.* 526a–b.

ἴσων, δίκαιος ὤν, ὡς σὺ φῄς, καὶ ταῦτα ἀμέλει δίκαια ποιῶν. καὶ γὰρ ὁ τὴν μάχην γενέσθαι σπεύσας καὶ οὐ περιιδὼν διαφθαρέντα τὰ πράγματα ἐν τῇ τριβῇ καὶ ὁ πάντα εἰς ἑαυτὸν ἀναδεξάμενος καὶ δείξας ὃ σὺ χρησμῳδεῖς, οὐκ ἐν ἄλλοις εἰκὸς ἔχειν τὰς ἐλπίδας, ὧν ἢ εὖ ἢ κακῶς πραξάντων ἀνάγκη πλανᾶσθαι καὶ αὐτὸν καὶ τὰ αὐτοῦ τινος, ἀλλ' αὐτὸν ἐν αὑτῷ, τόν γε δὴ σώφρονα καὶ τὸν ἀνδρεῖον καὶ φρόνιμον, Μιλτιάδης εἷς ἀνήρ ἐστιν, οὐκ ἄλλος οὐδείς. διὸ δὴ καὶ προὐκρίθη μόνος ἐξ ἁπάντων, ὥς φασι, τὴν χεῖρα ἐκτετακὼς γραφῆναι, ὡς τότε ἔτυχεν τοῖς στρατιώταις παρακελευόμενος. οὕτως ἐκεῖνός γε οὐ μόνον ἐν πνυκί [τῇ ἐκκλησίᾳ],[54] ἀλλὰ καὶ Μαραθῶνι ῥήτωρ χρηστὸς ἦν καὶ τὸ τῶν λόγων ἀγαθὸν παρείχετο σῶν πανταχοῦ.

196 ἔπειτ' Ἀθηναῖοι μὲν καὶ τοὺς πεσόντας τόθ' αὑτῶν ἔθαψαν ἐν αὐτῷ τῷ χωρίῳ καὶ οὐκ ἀνέμιξαν τοῖς ἄλλοις τοῖς ἐν τοῖς δημοσίοις μνήμασι κειμένοις, ἀλλ' ἀξιοῦντες κρείττους ἢ κατὰ τοὺς ἄλλους εἶναι τὴν ἀρετὴν ἰδίας καὶ τῆς τιμῆς ἠξίωσαν· σὺ δὲ τὸν τούτων ἡγούμενον καὶ τὸν ἅπασι τοῖς Ἕλλησι τῶν ἀναγκαιοτάτων ἅμα καὶ τῶν καλλίστων κατάρξαντα, σωτηρίας, ἐλευθερίας, εὐκλείας, οὐκ ᾐσχύνθης τιθεὶς μετὰ τῶν ὀψοποιῶν, καὶ τοῖς ἐσχάτοις ὀνείδεσι δουλείας εἰ μὴ περιβαλεῖς, οὐκ ἀρκεῖν ἀξιῶν. τί λέγεις; δοῦλος Μιλτιάδης, δι' ὃν οὐκ ἐδούλευσεν ἡ Ἑλλάς; καὶ δια-

[54] *del.* Dindorf

share of the credit. As you say, he was a just man, and he certainly showed his justice in this too. For it was Miltiades alone and no one else who was keen for the battle to take place, and did not stand around watching the situation deteriorate with the delay, and took the whole burden on himself; it was he who proved the truth of what you proclaim, that it is proper not to rest one's hopes on others, since one's own fortunes must inevitably fluctuate as they fare well or badly, but to trust in oneself, as a continent and brave and prudent man.[161] It was for this reason that he alone was selected, so they say, to be painted with his arm outstretched, in the attitude in which he happened to deliver his exhortation to the troops on that day.[162] That is how true it is that he was a good orator not only on the Pnyx but also at Marathon, and in all situations upheld the values of oratory uncompromised.

Then again, the Athenians buried their dead of that day 196
in situ and did not join them to those laid to rest in the public monuments: because they judged them to be on a higher level to the others in heroism, they also judged them entitled to special honor of their own. Yet you, Plato, when it comes to the man who led them and who was responsible for bringing all the Greeks what are the most essential and at the same time the noblest of possessions, survival, freedom, and glory, you are not ashamed to rank him among the caterers, and think that nothing short of enveloping him in the most extreme reproaches of servitude will do. What on earth are you saying? Miltiades a slave, when it was thanks to him that Greece was not en-

161 *Menex.* 247e–48a. 162 In the Painted Stoa at Athens: Aeschin. 3.186; cf. Paus. 1.15.4.

κονῶν Ἀθηναίοις διεγένετο, δι᾽ ὃν οὐ διηκόνησαν Ἀθηναῖοι Πέρσαις τὰ αἴσχιστα καὶ δι᾽ ὃν οὐκ ἠδυνήθη Δᾶτις τῷ βασιλεῖ διακονῆσαι τὰ ἐπεσταλμένα; καὶ τῆς περὶ τὴν κομμωτικὴν συμμορίας ἀπογράψομεν ἄνδρα οὕτως αὐχμῶντα καὶ κεκονιμένον κάλλιον ἢ τῶν παλαισάντων καὶ τῶν γυμναστικῶν ὁστισοῦν; πολλὴν μένταν ὄφλοιμεν τὴν ἀλογίαν.

197 σκέψαι δὴ καὶ τοῦτο ὁπόσον τι τῆς ἐκείνου σωφροσύνης τεκμήριον, καὶ ὅτι εἰ χρυσῆν ἐτύγχανεν ἔχων τὴν ψυχήν, οὐκ ἂν αὐτῇ καλλίω βάσανον προσήνεγκεν. ἐκεῖνος γὰρ τοσοῦτον ἔργον ἐξεργασάμενος καὶ τοῖς Ἕλλησιν αἰτιώτατος τῆς ἐλευθερίας γενόμενος καὶ μόνον οὐ κρείττων ἢ κατ᾽ ἄνθρωπον νομισθείς, οὐκ ἔπαθεν ταὐτὸν Παυσανίᾳ τῷ τὴν Πλαταιᾶσι μάχην κατορθώσαντι, οὐδ᾽ ἐπήρθη τοῖς πεπραγμένοις, οὐδ᾽ ἐξύβρισεν, οὐδ᾽ ἐφρόνησεν μεῖζον οὐδὲν ἢ πρὸ τῆς μάχης. οὕτως εὔτακτος καὶ κόσμιος ἦν διὰ τέλους.
198 καίτοι Παυσανίας μὲν οὔτε πρῶτος δήπου τοὺς βαρβάρους ἐνενικήκει, ἀλλ᾽ εἰς παράδειγμα βλέπων τὴν Μαραθῶνι μάχην ἠγωνίζετο, οὔτε μόνους Λακεδαιμονίους ἔχων, ὥσπερ Μιλτιάδης Ἀθηναίους, ἀλλὰ καὶ αὐτῶν τῶν Ἀθηναίων παρόντων καὶ τῶν ἄλλων Ἑλλήνων, οἷς ταῦτα ἤρεσκεν· καὶ σχεδὸν τῶν γε Ἀθηναίων κἀκεῖ τὰ πλεῖστα συνεπεξεργασαμένων λέγονταί γε καὶ τὴν ἵππον τῶν βαρβάρων διαφθεῖραι καὶ τῶν Ἑλλήνων τῶν ἀντιτεταγμένων κρατῆσαι, καὶ τά

---

163 This echoes Socrates' words to Callicles at *Grg.* 486d.

slaved? A life spent in continual servitude to the Athenians, when it was thanks to him that the Athenians did not endure the foulest servitude to the Persians, and thanks to him that Datis was not able to carry out the commands of his own master, the King? Are we really to enroll in the ranks of the beauticians a man as unkempt as this, one more gloriously begrimed than any wrestler or athlete? People could call us unreasonable in the extreme if we did!

Consider also what weighty testimony to his conti- 197
nence is constituted by the following, and acknowledge that, if his soul were made of gold, he could apply no better touchstone to it than this.[163] Even though he had accomplished such a great feat and made himself principally responsible for the freedom of the Greeks and had all but been deemed superhuman, he did not react to this in the same way as Pausanias did to his victory at the battle of Plataea:[164] he was not elated by his achievements, he did not become insolent, and he did not become any more proud than he had been before the battle. So disciplined
and modest was he to the end. And yet Pausanias had not 198
been the first to defeat the barbarians, since he had the precedent of the Battle of Marathon to look to as he fought, nor did he have just the Spartans under him, as Miltiades had just the Athenians, since the Athenians were there too, along with the other Greeks who had resolved to fight. Indeed at Plataea just as at Marathon the Athenians had a hand in pretty much the majority of what was achieved; we are certainly told that they routed the barbarians' cavalry and overcame the Greeks who faced

164 Hdt. 8.3; Thuc. 1.128–35 (esp. 130).

γε τῆς τειχομαχίας ἐπ' ἐκείνους παντελῶς ἐλθεῖν.
199 ἀλλ' ὁ Μιλτιάδης οὐκ ἀνέμεινεν τοὺς Λακεδαιμονίους τότε οὐδ' ἄλλους ἀνθρώπους οὐδένας, οὐδ' ἐκοίνωσεν τὸ ἔργον, ἀλλὰ τοὺς ἀπὸ τῆς πόλεως ἔχων, ὅτι μὴ Πλαταιέων φασί τινας προσδραμεῖν, τὸν μὲν κίνδυνον αὑτοῦ, τὴν δ' ὠφέλειαν κοινὴν ἐποιήσατο ἁπάντων, πρῶτος καὶ μόνος τῶν Ἑλλήνων νικήσας ἓξ καὶ τετταράκοντα ἔθνη τὰ σύμπαντα. ὥστ' ἐκεῖνον προσῆκεν ἐπιγράφειν ὅτι στρατὸν ὤλεσε Μήδων. αὐτοῦ γὰρ ὡς εἰπεῖν ἦν τὸ ἔργον. καὶ τό γε τούτου πρότερον, τὸ Ἑλλήνων ἀρχηγὸς ἀκριβῶς ἥρμοττεν αὐτῷ·
200 πᾶσι γὰρ αὐτὸς ἦρξε τῆς ἐλευθερίας. ἀλλ' ὅμως καὶ ταῦτα πράξας ἠπίστατο σωφρονεῖν καὶ οὐδεὶς αὐτοῦ κατηγόρησεν τοιοῦτον οὐδὲν οἷα Παυσανίας πολλὰ κατηγορήθη. ἀλλὰ στάσεσιν καὶ θορύβοις ἔχοιμεν ἂν εὑρεῖν αὐτὸν προσκείμενον, ὥσπερ Λύσανδρον τὸν ἐν Αἰγὸς ποταμοῖς τὰ θαυμαστὰ δὴ πράξαντα καὶ δόξαντα μὲν καθελεῖν τὸν πόλεμον τὸν πρὸς Ἀθηναίους, τῇ δ' ἀληθείᾳ πολλῶν καὶ μεγάλων κακῶν
201 αὐτὸν τοῖς Ἕλλησιν ἄρξαντα; ἀλλὰ τοιοῦτον μὲν οὐδὲν οὔτε πράξαντα οὔτε βουλεύσαντα Μιλτιάδην, ἡττηθέντα δέ πως φιλοτιμίας καὶ τῷ τοὺς φίλους τοὺς ἑαυτοῦ συναύξειν ζητεῖν τὸ κοινῇ συμφέρον παρορῶντα ἐνίοτε, ὥσπερ Ἀγησίλαον, ὃς φιλότιμος ὢν καὶ φιλέταιρος πέρα τοῦ μετρίου παραλαβὼν τὴν πόλιν

them, and that responsibility for the siege operations de-
volved entirely upon them. But Miltiades at the time of 199
Marathon did not wait for the Spartans or for anyone else alive, and did not share the task, but with just the contingent from his own city (not counting the few Plataeans who are said to have joined him), he took the danger as his own but bestowed the benefit as a shared gift on all, and was the first and only Greek to vanquish forty-six nations all together.[165] So it is really he who should be said in the dedicatory inscription to have "destroyed the army of the Medes," because the achievement was what you might call his; and he is the one that the preceding phrase "leader of the Greeks" fits exactly, because he was the one who led
all of them to freedom.[166] Yet even though he had achieved 200
all this he still knew how to control himself and no one ever assailed him with anything like the many accusations that were brought against Pausanias. Can we see him to have been addicted to quarrels and commotion, like Lysander, the man who won an amazing victory at Aegospotami and who, though famed for bringing the war with Athens to its conclusion, in reality was himself the cause
of many great ills for Greece? Or is it that he cannot be 201
found to have done or to have planned anything of that kind, but was on occasion overcome by ambition and the desire to advance his friends, and so neglected to pursue the common good, like Agesilaus, who being ambitious and immoderately loyal to his friends did not preserve the

165 Hdt. 9.27 (an Athenian retrospective boast).

166 Aristides here claims for Miltiades the praise Pausanias bestowed on himself in his inscription on the tripod dedicated at Delphi from the Persian spoils: Thuc. 1.132.2.

τὴν Λακεδαιμονίων γῆς καὶ θαλάττης ἄρχουσαν οὐ
202 διεφύλαξεν ἐν τούτῳ τῷ σχήματι; καὶ σκόπει παρ' οὕστινας αὐτὸν ἐξετάζω· Λυκοῦργον, Πανσανίαν, Λύσανδρον, Ἀγησίλαον. ἀλλὰ ταῦτα μὲν οὐδ' ἂν εἷς αἰτιάσαιτο· ἐκρατεῖτο δὲ ὑπὸ τῶν τοῦ σώματος ἡδονῶν, ὥσπερ Θίβρωνα τὸν Σπαρτιάτην ἤδη τινὲς ᾐτιάσαντο καὶ μυρίους ἑτέρους ἔστι λέγειν καὶ Ἑλλήνων
203 καὶ βαρβάρων; ἀλλ' οἷα δὴ τὰ τῆς δημοκρατίας ἐπιχώρια, φαίνειν, ἐνδεικνύναι, δημεύειν, ὥσπερ Κλέωνα καὶ Κλεοφῶντα καὶ Ὑπέρβολον καὶ ἑτέρους ἀνθρώπους, οὐ ῥήτορας οὐδαμῶς,—οὔκουν εἴπερ γε ἦσαν τοιοῦτοι—εἴδωλον δέ τι ῥητορικῆς ἀπειληφότας, εἰ δὴ τὸ μηδαμῇ μὲν ὅμοιον, πανταχῇ δ' ἀσθενέστερον εἴδωλον χρὴ καλεῖν;

204 ἀλλ' ἐκεῖνός γε πάντων τούτων καθαρός. πῶς οὖν οὐκ ἐλυσιτέλει τοῖς Ἕλλησι τοιοῦτος ὤν; ἢ πῶς οὐκ ἐποίει βελτίους, εἴ τις προσεῖχεν αὐτῷ τὸν νοῦν; πολλῆς ταῦτα τῆς ἀνάγκης ἐστίν. εἰ δὲ μὴ σοφὸς ἦν τὰ μετέωρα ὥσπερ Ἀναξαγόρας, οὐδὲ Σωκράτης σοφὸς ἦν ταῦτά γε, καὶ ταῦτά γε,[55] ὥς φασιν, ὁμιλήσας ἐκείνῳ. ἀλλ' οὐδὲ Σωκράτης Ἀναξαγόρου φαυλότερος, οὔκουν, ὥς γε ὑμεῖς ἂν φαίητε, οὐδὲ Μιλτιάδης οὐδὲν

[55] γε *fort. secludendum*

---

[167] Spartan general convicted in 399 or 398 BC for the illicit plundering of allied cities in Asia Minor (Xen. *Hell.* 3.18).

[168] Athenian politicians remembered from Thucydides and Aristophanes as exemplars of demagogic malpractice.

Spartan state in the position of supremacy on land and sea in which he took it over? (Just look at the company in 202
which I am reviewing him: Lycurgus, Pausanias, Lysander, Agesilaus!) Or is it the case that, although no one could accuse Miltiades of any of that, he was a slave to the pleasures of the body, like Thibron the Spartiate,[167] against whom such accusations have not infrequently been made, and like the many other Greeks and barbarians one could mention? Or what about the characteristic practices of 203
a democracy, denouncing, informing, confiscating, like Cleon and Cleophon and Hyperbolus[168] and other individuals who were definitely not orators—not if that is the kind of people they were—but had hold of a kind of shadow image of oratory, if you can call an image something that is not at all similar but in all respects inferior?

No, of all of that Miltiades was entirely pure. How 204
then can he not have worked for the good of the Greek people, if that is the sort of man he was? And how could he not have improved anyone who paid attention to him? It is inevitable that he must have. If he was not an expert on celestial phenomena like Anaxagoras, well neither was Socrates, even though, they say, he was his pupil.[169] But Socrates is not worth less than Anaxagoras, so it follows (as you people might put it) that Miltiades may perhaps not be worth any less than the pundits either.[170]

169 Aristides here plays on *Ap.* 19c and 26d–e, along with *Phd.* 97b–98b, and the associated biographical clichés about Socrates.

170 "You people" = "philosophers"; Aristides here teasingly employs the logical schema "not A, therefore not (*oukoun*) B either."

205 ἴσως τῶν σοφιστῶν. οἶμαι δὲ κἂν ἐν θεῶν δικαστηρίῳ Μιλτιάδην κρινόμενον ἁπάσαις ἀποφυγεῖν, οὐχ ὥσπερ τὸν Ὀρέστην φασὶ τὰς ἡμισείας μεταλαβόντα. εἰκότως· ὁ μὲν γὰρ τὴν μητέρα ἀπέκτεινεν δικαίως, ὁ δὲ τὴν Ἑλλάδα ἔσωσεν δικαίως, καὶ τὰ τροφεῖα κάλλιστα ἀνθρώπων ἐξέτισεν οὐ μόνον τῇ πατρίδι, ἀλλὰ καὶ τῇ κοινῇ φύσει τοῦ γένους τοῦ Ἑλληνικοῦ. καὶ γάρ τοι κατὰ πόλεις μὲν ἄλλους ἄλλοι νομίζουσιν ἀρχηγέτας, κοινὸν δὲ τῆς Ἑλλάδος
206 ἀρχηγέτην ἐκεῖνον δικαίως ἄν τις ἡγοῖτο. νομίζω δ' ἔγωγε καὶ τὴν αἰτίαν ἣν ὕστερον ἔσχεν, εἰ δεῖ τι καὶ περὶ ταύτης εἰπεῖν ἤδη, μέγιστον σύμβολον εἶναι τοῦ πολλῷ τινι τῶν ἄλλων ἐκεῖνον διενεγκεῖν. ἅπαντας γὰρ ἠξίουν ἡττᾶσθαι τῆς ἀρετῆς τῆς ἐκείνου καὶ μηδὲν ἀήττητον εἶναι μηδὲ ἀνάλωτον, ὅπου Μιλτιάδης
207 παρείη. εἶτ' ἐγὼ τὸν οὕτως ἀνδρεῖον καὶ φρόνιμον καὶ σώφρονα, τὸν διὰ βίου μελετήσαντα ἀρετήν, τοῦτον κολακείας μορίῳ σχολάσαι δοκῶ; τὸν οὐδ' ὅτ' ἐκρίνετο οὐδὲν πλέον τοῖς δικασταῖς δείξαντα τοῦ τραύματος, οὐ δακρύσαντα, οὐ παιδία ἀναβιβασάμενον, ὄντος αὐτῷ Κίμωνος, τοῦτον ἐγὼ κόλακα οὑτωσὶ προσείπω μεγαλοπρεπῶς; καὶ τοῦτ' ἦν τὸ κεφάλαιον τῶν ἐκείνῳ πεπολιτευμένων καὶ βεβιωμένων, κολα-
208 κεία; καὶ πῶς οὐ δικαίως ἄν τις ἡμᾶς αἰτιῷτο αὐτοὺς κολακεύειν καὶ διακόνων ἔργον, οὐκ ἐλευθέρων ποιεῖν, εἰ τὴν ἑτέρου χάριν διώκοντες τἀληθὲς ἑκόντες δια-

I think that even if he came to trial in a court of the gods, 205
Miltiades would be acquitted unanimously, and not, as they say happened to Orestes, with just a half-share of the votes. Reasonably so: Orestes' just act was to kill his mother, while Miltiades' was to save Greece, and the repayment he made for his upbringing, the noblest repayment of all time, he made not only to his homeland but to the shared stock of the Greek race. Across the individual cities of the Greek world, different peoples do indeed acknowledge different leaders, but he is the one who might rightly be thought to be the common leader of all
Greece. Indeed, I think that the accusation that was sub- 206
sequently brought against him, if this too needs a mention at this point, is the most significant token of his immense superiority to all the rest.[171] They all expected to come second to Miltiades' heroism and believed that no enemy would go undefeated and no position uncaptured wherever he put in an appearance. Am I then to think that so 207
brave and prudent and continent a man as this, the man who practiced virtuous ways throughout his life, had any time to spare for a "subdivision of flattery"? Am I to give so magnificent a title as "flatterer" to the man who, even when he was on trial, did no more than show the jurors his wound, without weeping or bringing his children onto the witness stand, even though one of them was Cimon?[172] Was this, flattery, the summation of the policies he pursued and the life he lived? How could I myself not justly 208
be accused of flattering and of doing the work of a lackey not a free man, if I willingly corrupt the truth in the at-

[171] Hdt. 6.136, Plato *Grg.* 516d. [172] Hdt. 6.136 (given a very tendentious reading here by Aristides).

φθείροιμεν; καὶ μὴν Πλάτωνι μὲν ἂν καὶ ἄλλα πολλὰ χαριζοίμεθα, ἐκείνου δὲ εἰ ταῦτα καταψηφιούμεθα, ἄλλην τίν᾽ ἂν αὐτῷ τιμὴν ἀποδοίημεν ἔγωγε οὐχ ὁρῶ.

[*Argumentation 4: Vindication of Themistocles (209–351)*]

209 λοιπὸς τοίνυν Θεμιστοκλῆς, ἥκιστα δὴ πάντων ἄξιος ἐκ δευτερείων τὰ πρωτεῖα ἔχειν, εἰ τὰ μάλιστα καὶ τοῦτο αὐτὸ ἐκείνῳ μόνῳ τῶν πάντων ὑπάρξαν φαίνεται. ἀλλὰ μᾶλλον ὅστις ἐκείνου δεύτερος, τοῦτο ἴσως ἔργον εὑρεῖν. τοσούτῳ γὰρ ἡμῖν τὸν Μαραθῶνι, τὸν πάνυ, τὸν ὡς βούλει λέγε, τοσούτῳ δ᾽ οὖν ἐκεῖνον ὑπερεβάλετο πᾶσι τοῖς εἰς αὐτὸν ἐλθοῦσιν πῶς ἂν εἴποιμι ὁμολογουμένως, ὅσῳ Ξέρξης Δαρεῖον ταῖς παρασκευαῖς ἅπασιν δῆλός ἐστιν ὑπερβαλόμενος.
210 καὶ μὴν ὁ μὲν τοὺς ὑπάρχους τοῦ βασιλέως, ὁ δ᾽ αὐτὸν ἐνίκα βασιλέα· καὶ μετὰ μέν γε τὴν Μαραθῶνι μάχην αὖθις ἐπεστράτευσεν, μετὰ δὲ τὴν ἐν Σαλαμῖνι ναυμαχίαν φεύγων ᾤχετο. πρὸς μὲν γὰρ ἐκείνην τὴν ἧτταν παρωξύνθη, πρὸς δὲ ταύτην ἀπεῖπεν, ὥσθ᾽ ἱκανὸν κέρδος ἡγεῖτο, ἂν σωθῇ. ᾔδει γὰρ τότε μὲν πολλοστὸν μέρος τῆς πάσης ἐλθὸν δυνάμεως, νῦν δὲ σχεδὸν μετὰ πάντων ἀνθρώπων ἡττώμενος. οὔτ᾽ οὖν αὐτὸς ἐθάρρει μένειν οὔτ᾽ ἄλλον ἔπεμψεν τοῦ λοιποῦ· οὐ γὰρ ἦν ὅ τι ἐλπίσοι. ἀλλὰ καὶ ὃν κατέλιπε Μαρδόνιον θανατῶντα ὡς εἰπεῖν κατέλιπεν, καὶ ἅμα ἐμοὶ

tempt to gratify someone else? Plato to be sure I would be ready to gratify in many other matters, but if I condemn Miltiades for these offenses, that really would, I think, be taking deference to an extreme.

Argumentation 4: Vindication of Themistocles (209–351)

There now remains Themistocles, the man who least of all 209
deserved to win first prize at coming second, even if it is patent that this is exactly what happened uniquely to him.[173] The really difficult thing is perhaps to discover who comes second to him. At all events, he surpassed the victor of Marathon, the great man, the . . . describe him how you will, he surpassed him in all the circumstances of his life—how could I put this so as to command universal agreement?—by as much as Xerxes manifestly surpassed
Darius in all his preparations. Miltiades defeated the 210
King's subordinate commanders, Themistocles the King himself. After the battle at Marathon the King mounted another expedition, but after the sea battle at Salamis he ran away. The former defeat acted as a stimulus, but the latter made him give up, to the extent of thinking it enough of a gain if he could get safely away, because he knew that on the first occasion he had come with only a proportion of his whole force, but that now he had been defeated with practically all his men. So he neither had the confidence to stay put himself, nor sent anyone else after him, because he had nothing left to hope for. The man he did leave behind, Mardonius, he left behind in what you might call

[173] See §§338–40 below.

δοκεῖν ὅπως ἔχοιεν πρὸς ὃν ἀσχολοῖντο οἱ Ἕλληνες.
211 Μιλτιάδῃ μὲν οὖν εἰς ἓν κεφάλαιον ἡ τῆς ἀνδρείας ἀπόδειξις ἧκεν, εἰ καὶ τὰ μάλιστα ἐχρῆτο αὐτῇ παρὰ πᾶσαν τὴν πολιτείαν· Θεμιστοκλέα δὲ τὰ δεύτερα ἀεὶ τῶν προτέρων μείζονα ἐξεδέχετο καὶ τὸ τῆς παροιμίας αὐτῷ περιειστήκει· τὸ μὲν γὰρ ἔλιπεν αὐτὸν κῦμα, τὸ δὲ ἐγκατελάμβανεν, ἕως διεξῆλθεν διὰ τῶν
212 τρικυμιῶν νικῶν. καὶ Μιλτιάδῃ μὲν σχεδὸν ἀνδρείας μᾶλλον ἢ σοφίας ἔδει πρὸς τὰ παρόντα, Θεμιστοκλεῖ δὲ ἀνδρείας μὲν οὐχ ἧττον, εἰ μὴ καὶ μᾶλλον, ὅσῳ καὶ μείζους οἱ φόβοι· πρὸς δὲ τούτῳ καὶ ἄλλων πολλῶν καὶ οὐδὲν ἀτιμοτέρων ὑπεύθυνος ἦν ἐκ τῶν περιεστηκότων, συνέσεως, μαντικῆς μὲν οὖν ὡς εἰπεῖν, μεγαλοψυχίας, δεινότητος, πραότητος, καρτερίας, εὐαρμοστίας πρὸς τοὺς καιρούς, πρὸς τὰ πράγματα, πρὸς τοὺς ἄνδρας τοὺς ἀπὸ τῆς πόλεως, τοὺς ἀπὸ τῆς Ἑλλάδος, τοὺς πολεμίους. καί μοι δοκεῖ τὸ μὲν Μιλτιάδου στρατηγίᾳ μᾶλλον ἐοικὸς συμβῆναι πρὸς τοὺς βαρβάρους, τὸ δὲ τοῦ Θεμιστοκλέους ἀκριβῶς πολιτείᾳ γενέσθαι ἐν ἅπασι τοῖς Ἕλλησιν ἐξεταζομένη.
213 τοσαῦτ᾽ ἦν τὰ πραττόμενα καὶ δημιουργούμενα, τὰ μὲν[56] ἐν τῇ γῇ, τὰ δ᾽ ἐν τῇ θαλάττῃ· περὶ ὧν ἔμοιγε

[56] *τὰ μέν* Barocc. 136 *om. cett.*

---

[174] Aristides makes the same curious assertion about Mardonius' state of mind in *Or.* 1.170.

[175] The proverb referred to here is the idea that waves of trouble/misfortune (like literal waves) come in threes, of which

a suicidal frame of mind,[174] and at the same time I think with the intention that the Greeks should have someone to keep them busy. The demonstration of Miltiades' brav- 211
ery came in one crowning moment, however true it may be that he exercised that bravery throughout the whole of his political career. With Themistocles by contrast, his next actions were always greater than what preceded them and the reverse of the proverb proved true in his case:[175] one wave left him and another picked him up, until he
emerged victorious from the triple swell. Miltiades, it is 212
more or less true to say, needed courage rather than wisdom to deal with what confronted him. Themistocles was no less in need of courage, and if anything needed it more, inasmuch as the dangers he faced were greater; but in addition to this, his circumstances ensured that other no less valuable qualities in him were put to the test—his intelligence, what you might call his prophetic ability, his magnanimity, his cunning, his imperturbability, his perseverance, and his adaptability to the moment and to the business and the men at hand (whether these were the Athenians, the Greeks, or the enemy). It seems to me that Miltiades' achievement was more like a piece of military leadership against the barbarians, whereas Themistocles' was in the true sense of the word a feat of statesmanship that had its worth tested before the eyes of the whole of Greece.

213 That is the measure of all that he did and crafted, on land and by sea. I believe that Homer himself, had he lived

the third is the most dangerous and damaging: e.g., Pl. *Resp.* 472a; Aesch. *Sept.* 758–60, *PV* 1015; Eur. *Hipp.* 1213, with W. S. Barrett's note.

δοκεῖ καὶ Ὅμηρος ἄν, εἰ περιῆν, βουληθεὶς εἰπεῖν οὐχ ἧττον καλέσαι τὰς Μούσας ἢ περὶ τοῦ πῶς ἐνεπρήσθη ναῦς μία τῶν Θετταλῶν· εἰ δὲ βούλει, τίς πρῶτος ἀντῆρεν τῷ Ἀγαμέμνονι τῶν ἐπικούρων ἢ τῶν Τρώων αὐτῶν. μᾶλλον δὲ τοῦτο μὲν οὐκ εἶχεν οἶμαι πυθέσθαι τίς ἦν ὁ πρῶτος ἀντάρας τῷ βασιλεῖ τῆς Ἀσίας, μικροῦ καὶ τῆς Εὐρώπης· ἀπὸ ποίων δέ τινων ἔργων ἢ λόγων ταῦτα ἠδυνήθη τελέσασθαι καὶ πρὸς πόσας τινὰς [τὰς][57] τῶν πολεμίων ναῦς καὶ πρὸς ποίαν τινὰ τὴν πᾶσαν παρασκευὴν καὶ ἔφοδον τοῦ βαρβάρου παρετάξατο, καὶ πῶς εἶχεν τότε τἀνθρώπεια, τοῦτ᾽ ἔμοιγ᾽ ἂν ἐρωτᾶν δοκεῖ καὶ δεῖσθαι φράζειν, εἴπερ καὶ
214 κατὰ μικρὸν ἔμελλεν τῆς ἀξίας ἐφάψεσθαι. τί οὖν κωλύει καὶ νῦν ἡμᾶς, ἀρχὴ δὲ ἡμῖν ἐκ θεῶν, ἐξετάσαι πάλιν πῶς εἶχε τὰ τῶν καιρῶν, τὸν αὐτὸν τρόπον ὅνπερ ἀρτίως ἐξητάσαμεν, καὶ δεῖξαι διὰ βραχέων ἐν ποίοις τισὶ πράγμασιν ποῖός τις ἦν ὁ Θεμιστοκλῆς;
215 καίτοι τοῦτό γε οὐδὲν ἴσως προὔργου. ἃ γὰρ οὐκ ἔστιν ἐνδείξασθαι τῷ λόγῳ, πῶς ἄν τις ἐκ τούτων ἐκεῖνον θεωρήσειεν; πλὴν εἰ τοῦτό γε αὐτὸ ἐνθυμηθείς, ὅτι ὑπὲρ ὧν οὐδ᾽ εἰπεῖν ὡς βούλεταί τις ἐγχωρεῖ, ταῦτ᾽ ἐκεῖνος μετεχείρισεν ὡς ἐβούλετο.

δέκα μὲν γὰρ ἑξῆς ἔτη ὤδινεν ἅπασα ἡ ἤπειρος, φιλονεικοῦντες ἅπαντες ἄνθρωποι δίκην τῆς Μαραθῶνι μάχης λαβεῖν, ἡτοιμάζετο δὲ ἐκ πάσης γῆς καὶ
216 θαλάττης πάντα. Αἰγύπτου δὲ ἀποστάσης ἐν τῷ διὰ

[57] *om.* Barocc. 136 *del.* Dindorf

to see it and wished to speak of it, would have been no less keen to invoke the Muses than he was when telling how one of the Thessalian ships was set on fire, or if you prefer, when asking which of the allies or of the Trojans themselves was the first to stand against Agamemnon.[176] Or rather, I do not think that the question he would have wanted to ask was who was the first to stand against the king of Asia, and very nearly of Europe too; in my view, what he would have asked and entreated the Muses to tell him, if he was to come anywhere near doing justice to the subject, was what words and deeds enabled the accomplishment of such feats, and how many enemy ships, and what kind of overall resources and onslaught on the part of the barbarians confronted him, and what the state of
human affairs was at that time. Why then should not I too 214
now, since I have my god-given starting point, examine once more how matters then stood, in the same way as I did just now, and show briefly what sort of man Themistocles was and in what circumstances? Yet perhaps this will 215
not get us anywhere: for when there are things that are beyond human powers of expression, what basis do they provide for a review of this man? Unless, that is, on the strength of the reflection that he was someone who could deal as he wanted with things of which we cannot even speak as we want.

The whole continent of Asia was in labor for ten years as all its inhabitants vied with each other to take revenge for the Battle of Marathon; comprehensive resources were
being made ready from every land and every sea. When 216
Egypt rebelled in the meantime, it took no serious effort

[176] *Il.* 16.112–13 and 11.218–20, respectively.

μέσου βασιλεὺς οὐδὲν σπουδάσας αὖθις ἦν ἐν τοῖς αὐτοῖς· οὕτω ῥᾳδίως ἐκείνην παρεστήσατο. δεκάτῳ δὲ ἔτει συνῆλθον ἐσχατιαὶ πᾶσαι καὶ γένη πάντα ὥσπερ μετανισταμένης ἑτέρωσε τῆς οἰκουμένης· καὶ βασιλεὺς ἀπῄει δεδοικὼς μὴ οὐ δέξαιτο τὸ πλῆθος ἡ Ἑλλάς, † ὥσπερ ἀρχὴ γῆς πάσης τοῦ στρατοπέδου γιγνόμενος †[58] *καθ' ὃ βούλοιτ' ἀεί. χρυσὸς δὲ καὶ ἄργυρος καὶ χαλκὸς καὶ σίδηρος, πάντα ὁμότιμα ἤγετο, ὁμοίως ἐγγείοις ὀχήμασιν καὶ ναυτικοῖς. ὡς δ' εἰς ταυτὸν ἀπήντησαν αἱ δυνάμεις, οἱ μὲν πεζοὶ τὴν*
217 *παραλίαν, αἱ δὲ νῆες τὴν θάλατταν ἀπέκρυψαν· εἰς δὲ τοὺς Ἕλληνας ἠγγέλλετο ἄξιον μὲν τῶν ἐπιόντων κακῶν οὐδέν, ὅμως δὲ πολλὰ καὶ παντοῖα καὶ οἷα οὔπω πρότερον· καὶ οὐ τοσοῦτόν γ' ἂν αὐτοὺς ἡ τοῦ ἡλίου συμβᾶσα ἔκλειψις ἐξέπληττεν, ὅσον ἡ τῆς γῆς καὶ θαλάττης ἔκλειψις γιγνομένη, πρὸς τὴν τοῦ βασιλέως ἐμοὶ δοκεῖν ἐπιθυμίαν μᾶλλον ἢ χρείαν. ἐδόκει γὰρ μόνος ὡς ἀληθῶς γῆς καὶ θαλάττης εἶναι κύριος, καὶ ποιεῖν καὶ διαφθείρειν· ᾧ γε ὁ μὲν Ἄθως τὰς ναῦς, ὁ*
218 *δὲ Ἑλλήσποντος τὸ πεζὸν ἐδέξατο. πρὸς δὲ τούτοις τείχη μὲν ᾠκοδομεῖτο ὅπως ἀριθμοίη κατὰ μυρίους. ὁ δὲ ἥλιος συνεκρύπτετο τοῖς τοξεύμασιν· ἦν δὲ πλήρης ἡ μὲν θάλαττα νεῶν, ἡ δὲ γῆ πεζῶν, ὁ δ' ἀὴρ βελῶν. παρεῖναι δὲ καὶ μέλλειν ἴσον ἦν, ὥστ' ἔχεσθαι πάν-*

[58] *locus desperatus: alius aliter, nemo adhuc satis*

on the King's part to regain the *status quo*; that is how easy it was for him to bring her to heel. In the tenth year all the farthest-flung regions and all the nations assembled, as if the whole world were moving elsewhere, and the King ended up afraid that Greece would not have room for such a host . . . . . according to what he might want at any given moment.[177] Gold, silver, bronze and iron, all were conveyed as cargo of equal value, on land and sea transport alike. And when his forces all met together in the same spot, his infantry hid the shores and his navy the sea. Noth- 217
ing that was reported to the Greeks in any way did justice to the monstrosity of what was advancing upon them, but nonetheless they heard a great deal about all kinds of unprecedented developments. Had there been an eclipse of the sun, it would not have frightened them so much as the eclipse of the land and sea that was actually taking place, it seems to me to satisfy the King's whim rather than from any real need. With Mount Athos giving passage to his ships and the Hellespont his army, he appeared as the sole true ruler of land and sea, to make and break them as he wished. What is more, walls were built so that he could 218
count his forces in tens of thousands.[178] The sun was concealed by the arrows fired by his archers;[179] the sea was full of ships, the land of foot soldiers, and the air of missiles. Present realities and future prospects were as one, so that all were caught up; the world was shaking as if at

[177] The Greek text in the middle of this sentence is clearly corrupt, but no convincing emendation has yet been proposed. Fortunately the main sense—that the Persian army threatened to be too large for Greece to contain it—remains intact.

[178] Hdt. 7.60. [179] Hdt. 7.226.

τας· πάντα δ' ὥσπερ τοῦ Ποσειδῶνος κατιόντος ἐσείετο. πολλὰ δὲ τῶν ἐθνῶν ἐξανηλίσκετο εἰς δεῖπνον τῷ βασιλεῖ. ἀπειλαὶ δὲ κηρύκων οὐ διέλιπον πάντοσε φοιτώντων, αἰτούντων γῆν καὶ ὕδωρ ὅστις βούλεται σῶς εἶναι. τὸ δὲ μαντεῖον φωνὰς ἠφίει δεινὰς καὶ χαλεπὰς ἅπασι τοῖς Ἕλλησιν. ἐδόκουν δὲ οὔτε τῶν νεῶν τὴν εἰρεσίαν ἀνέξεσθαι οὔτε τῶν ἵππων τὸν κτύπον. εἶχον δὲ οὔτε ἱεροῖς οὔτε συμμάχοις θαρρεῖν, οὐδ'
219 εὑρεῖν οἵτινες ἀνθρώπων γένωνται. πρὸς δὲ τούτοις Γέλων μὲν καλούμενος οὐχ ὑπήκουεν, Ἀργεῖοι δὲ ἐκποδὼν ἦσαν, Κερκυραῖοι δὲ σοφώτερα ἢ δικαιότερα ἐβουλεύοντο, Θετταλοὶ δὲ ὑπ' ἀνάγκης μέν, ὅμως δὲ ἐμήδιζον, Βοιωτοὶ δὲ οὐδὲν βέλτιον Θετταλῶν ἐπεπράγεσαν, Δελφοὶ δὲ οὐκ εἶχον ὅ τι χρήσωνται, ὀλίγον δὲ ἦν τὸ ὑγιαῖνον τῆς Ἑλλάδος, καὶ τοῦτο εἰς δύο πόλεις ἀνήρτητο, μᾶλλον δὲ εἰς ἕνα ἄνδρα, ὅ τι φρονήσειεν ἢ συμβουλεύσειεν Θεμιστοκλῆς.

220 ἐν τοῖς τοιούτοις μέντοι καιροῖς καὶ τοιαύτῃ πραγμάτων ἀωρίᾳ καὶ συγχύσει τῶν πάντων ἀνὴρ ἐκεῖνος ἑστηκὼς οὐκ ἠπόρησεν, οὐδ' ἐξεπλάγη, οὐδ' ηὔξατο αὑτῷ χανεῖν τὴν γῆν, οὐδ' εὐδαιμόνισεν τοὺς πάλαι κειμένους, οὐδ' ἔπαθεν ταὐτὸ τοῖς πολλοῖς, ἀλλὰ κατέστη τοῖς Ἕλλησιν ἀντ' ἀγαθοῦ του[59] δαίμονος. πάντα γὰρ εἰς αὑτὸν ἀναδεξάμενος καὶ τὴν αὑτοῦ γνώμην ὑποθεὶς ἀντ' ἄλλου του φυλακτηρίου, καὶ μόνος ὀρθοῖς τοῖς ὀφθαλμοῖς ἀντισχὼν ἅπασι καὶ τοῖς

[59] του Reiske τοῦ *codd. om.* Barocc. 136

Poseidon's descent from the summit.[180] Many nations were consumed simply to provide dinner for the King. There were threats without cease as heralds traveled in every direction, demanding earth and water from anyone who wished to remain unharmed. The Oracle spoke in tones harsh and terrible to all Greeks. They thought that they would not be able to bear either the beat of the ships' oars or the pounding of the horses' hooves. They could take no confidence either from their holy places or from their allies, nor discover what was to become of them. In 219
addition to all this, Gelon did not answer when he was called, the Argives kept themselves out of the way, the Corcyreans were making plans more clever than morally responsible, the Thessalians had gone over to the enemy, albeit under compulsion, the Boeotians had fared no better than the Thessalians, the Delphians did not know what to do. Little in Greece was sound, and that little depended on two cities, or rather on one man, on the plans and counsels of Themistocles.

It was in such desperate times as these and such a dire 220
state of affairs and amid such universal turmoil that this man took his stand: unaffected by the emotions that afflicted the majority, he was neither baffled nor terrified, nor did he pray for the earth to swallow him up or bless the long dead for their good fortune, but took on the role of the guardian spirit of the Greek people. Taking everything upon himself and relying on his own intelligence in place of any other safeguard, alone confronting both present realities and future prospects with a steady gaze and

[180] That is, an earthquake, as in *Il.* 13.17–19 (I owe this reference to Lucarini, 212).

παροῦσι καὶ τοῖς ἐπιοῦσι πράγμασιν, καὶ οὐκ ἀποστραφεὶς ὥσπερ οἱ πρὸς τὸν ἥλιον βλέποντες, ὃ πᾶσι μικροῦ δεῖν συνέβη τοῖς τότε, οὐκ ἂν εἴποιμι ὡς οὐκ ἔψευσε τῆς ἐλπίδος τοὺς Ἕλληνας, ἀλλὰ καὶ πολὺ τὴν προσδοκίαν ἐνήλλαξεν αὐτοῖς. οὐδὲν γὰρ τῶν ἐσχάτων ὅ τι οὐ πείσεσθαι τῶν πολλῶν νομιζόντων, καὶ βλεπόντων εἰς αἰσχρὰς μηχανὰς καὶ ἀπόρους καταφυγάς, τοσοῦτον μετέστησεν τὰ πράγματα ὥστε, εἴ τις ὕστερον αὐτοὺς ἀπελθόντων τῶν βαρβάρων ἤρετο εἰ ἐβούλοντ' ἂν μήτ' ἐκείνους ἐπιστρατεῦσαι μήτε σφίσιν ταῦτα πεπρᾶχθαι μήτε τοὺς κινδύνους σφίσιν μηδὲ τὰς πράξεις γεγενῆσθαι, τεθνάναι πάντας ἂν εἰπεῖν ἐθέλειν μᾶλλον ἢ ταῦτα ἄπρακτα αὑτοῖς εἶναι. οὕτως οὐ μόνον τὰς ἐλπίδας ὅσοι γε καὶ τὰ μήκιστα ἤλπισαν αὐτῶν, ἀλλὰ καὶ τὰς εὐχὰς τῶν πλείστων ὑπερεβάλετο.

221 καὶ ἔγωγε ἡδέως ἄν, εἴ πως ἐνῆν, ἠρόμην Πλάτωνα, πρὸς θεῶν τῶν Ἑλληνίων, τί χρῆν ποιεῖν τὸν Θεμιστοκλέα κατ' ἐκείνους τοὺς χρόνους, ἢ τί λέγειν κάλλιον ὧν εἶπεν; ἢ τί γράφειν βέλτιον ὧν ἔγραψεν; ἢ τίνα ὁδὸν τῶν πραγμάτων ἐλθεῖν; ἢ ποίαν ἡγήσασθαι τοῖς Ἀθηναίοις; ἢ τίσι κρείττοσι χρήσασθαι λογισμοῖς; εἰπὲ γὰρ ὦ πρὸς θεῶν, εἰ δὲ μή, ἄλλος τις κληρονομείτω τοῦ λόγου, λεγέτω, δεικνύτω τί χρῆν πράττειν τὸν Θεμιστοκλέα τότε καὶ πῶς χρήσασθαι τοῖς παροῦσιν. πότερ' εἰς τὴν πνύκα συλλέξαντ' Ἀθηναίους περὶ τῶν ἰδεῶν αὐτοῖς διαλέγεσθαι καὶ διδά-

not, as happened to almost everyone else at that time, turning away like people who look at the sun, I would not say that he did not disappoint the Greeks in their hopes of him, so much as that he hugely changed their expectations. When the majority were convinced that there was no extremity that they would not suffer, and were eyeing shameful measures and last resorts that were doomed to fail, he brought about such a change in their fortunes that, if someone had asked them later, after the barbarians had departed, if they would have preferred it if they had not invaded and they themselves had not achieved this success, and that neither their perils nor their achievements had ever been, they would all have replied that they would prefer to die sooner than for these deeds of theirs not to have been done. To such an extent was it that he exceeded not only the most modest hopes that some few of them may have entertained, but the prayers of the vast majority.

If there were any way to do this, I would gladly ask 221
Plato what, by the gods of Greece, Themistocles ought to have done at that time, or to have said that was more admirable than what he actually did say? What decrees could he have drafted better than those he did draft? What path ought he to have traced in his actions, or led the Athenians down? What better reasoning ought he to have employed? Tell me, in heaven's name, or if you cannot, then let someone else inherit the argument,[181] and speak, and explain what Themistocles ought to have done then and how he ought to have dealt with the situation. Ought he to have assembled the Athenians on the Pnyx and discoursed to them about "the Forms," and taught them what "essential

[181] The phrase "inherit the argument" glances at *Resp.* 331d.

σκειν τί αὐτοδίκαιον καὶ τί αὐτοκαλόν, καὶ τί τὸ ὂν μὲν ἀεί, γένεσιν δὲ οὐκ ἔχον; ταχέως μέντἂν αὐτοὺς καὶ γένεσις καὶ τὸ εἶναι καὶ πάντα ἐπέλιπεν. ἀλλ' ὅθεν ἀνδρεία τὸ πρῶτον ἐκλήθη καὶ ὅθεν δειλία ζητεῖν, καὶ πότερον ῥεῖ τὰ πάντα ἢ οὔ; ἔγνωσαν μέντἂν κακῶς ῥέοντα τὰ πάντα αὐτοῖς. ἀλλὰ τί μὴν ὅλως ἔδει λέγειν ἢ ποιεῖν; τρίτον γὰρ ἤδη τὸ ἐρώτημα ὥσπερ
222 σύνθημα περιήκει. πόθεν ἐξετάσομεν τὸν Θεμιστοκλέα πότερον τῷ ὄντι σύμβουλος καὶ προστάτης καὶ ἡγεμὼν ἦν, ἢ τί καὶ ἄλλο πρέπον ἀκοῦσαι; καὶ μὴν δεῖ γε δυοῖν θάτερον, ἢ τὰ πραχθέντα ὑπ' αὐτοῦ μέμψασθαί τινα ἔχειν, ἢ δεῖξαι τί δέον πρᾶξαι παρέλιπεν,
223 τὸ ῥᾷον καὶ ἥδιον ἀντὶ τοῦ καλοῦ προελόμενος. καίτοι τήν γε ὕστερον τῶν πραγμάτων σοφίαν καὶ τοὺς ἐπὶ τῆς ἀδείας ἐλέγχους οὐδὲν ἔχειν φασὶν λαμπρὸν οὐδε ὑπερήφανον· ἐγὼ δ' οὖν καὶ τοῦτο συγχωρῶ κἄν τις ἀμείνω τινὰ πρᾶξιν, ἢ λόγους βελτίους, ἢ προαίρεσιν δικαιοτέραν ἢ τοῖς πᾶσι βελτίω δείξῃ τότε ἐγχωροῦσαν παρ' ἣν ἐκεῖνος ἐνεστήσατο, ἕτοιμος αὐτὸς τῆς αἰτίας κληρονομεῖν. εἰ δὲ μήθ' ὧν ἐπολιτεύσατο μηδὲν ἔστι καταιτιάσασθαι μήθ' ὧν ἄν τις φήσαι χρῆναι πεποιηκέναι μηδὲν ἔστ' εἰπεῖν ὡς οὐκ ἐποίησεν, ἐπαινοῦσι μᾶλλον ἐκεῖνον ἡμῖν αὐτοῖς συνηδώμεθα ἢ ζητοῦσιν ὅπως εἴποιμεν κακῶς.

224 οὑτωσὶ δὲ σκοπῶμεν, ἐπαναγαγόντες ἡμᾶς αὐτοὺς ἐπ' αὐτὰ τὰ πράγματα. ἦσαν τῶν Ἑλλήνων μερίδες τρεῖς, ἡ μὲν ἔξω πραγμάτων, ὥσπερ Ἀργεῖοι καὶ Κερ-

Justice" and "essential Beauty" are, and what that which "is" eternally and does not admit of "becoming" is? In that case, becoming and being and indeed everything would rapidly have failed them for sure! Or should he have investigated whence bravery and cowardice originally derived their names, and whether everything is in flux or not? They would for sure have realized that everything was in flux for the worse for them! I ask you, what ought he have said or done all in all? The question now comes
round for a third time, like a password. On what basis shall 222
we investigate whether Themistocles was truly a counselor and a president and a leader, or what else besides he ought to be called? At all events, one or the other of two things has to be done: either someone has to fault his achievements, or he has to demonstrate what he neglected to do that ought to have been done, by choosing the easier and
pleasanter course in place of the noble one. They say that 223
wisdom after the event and investigations conducted from a position of immunity are nothing special and nothing to be proud of. I agree about this, but I am also prepared to inherit my share of the blame, if anyone can show that a better line of action, or better words, or a more just and generally better choice of policy besides that which Themistocles actually adopted, was available to him at that time. But if it is not possible to attack any of his policy choices, nor to say that he failed to do any of the things one might say he ought to have done, then let us congratulate ourselves for praising him rather than for looking for ways of speaking ill of him.

Let us then recall ourselves to our real subject matter 224
and examine it as follows: there were three categories of Greeks. The first consisted of those who were uninvolved,

κυραῖοι καὶ Σικελιῶται καὶ Ἰταλιῶται μικροῦ πάντες, καὶ Κρῆτες δὴ καὶ ἕτεροι λέγονται· οἱ δὲ καὶ συνεπεστράτευον μετὰ τῶν βαρβάρων ἐπὶ τὴν Ἑλλάδα, ὥσπερ οἱ Θετταλοὶ καὶ πάντες οἱ μέχρι τῆς Ἀττικῆς, πλὴν Θεσπιέων καὶ Πλαταιέων ὁπόσων δή τινων ὄντων· τρίτον δ' ἦν λοιπὸν Ἀθηναῖοι καὶ Λακεδαι-
225 μόνιοι καὶ ὅσοι παρὰ τούτους κατέφυγον. ἀλλὰ μήπω τοῦτο ὅτι Ἀθηναῖοι, μηδ' ὅτι καὶ τοὺς ἄλλους οὗτοι παρεσκεύασαν. ἀλλὰ διῄρητο μὲν εἰς τοσαῦτα μέρη τὸ Ἑλληνικὸν πᾶν καὶ προὔκειτο τριῶν τούτων αἵρεσις ἐν μέσῳ πᾶσιν, ἔδει δὲ καὶ πόλιν καὶ ἰδιώτην πρὸς ταῦτα βουλεύεσθαι, τὸ διάφορον δ' οὐ μικρὸν ἦν, ἢ τῷ βαρβάρῳ προσθεμένους ἀκολουθεῖν ἐπὶ τοὺς ἀντιτείνοντας, ἢ τὴν ἡσυχίαν ἄγειν αὐτοῖς ἐξεῖναι δεηθέντας, μὴ τί τοῖς ἄλλοις συμβήσεται ζητεῖν, ἀλλ' εἰ μηδὲν αὐτοὶ πείσονται κέρδος ἡγεῖσθαι· ἢ τρίτον γ' ἤδη κατελείπετο, φάσκοντας τοῦ καλοῦ καὶ τοῦ δικαίου φροντίζειν, καὶ πυρὶ καὶ σιδήρῳ καὶ πᾶσι πράγμασιν ἀνταγωνίζεσθαι, καὶ μήτ' ἀκούοντας ἀκούειν τὰ δεινὰ μήθ' ὁρῶντας ὁρᾶν, ἀλλὰ πάντων ὡσπερεὶ φλυαρίαν καταγνόντας παρ' αὐτὸν τὸν θάνατον ἐσκηνῶσθαι, ἔσχατα τοῦ βίου ταῦτ' εἶναι προκρίναντας ἑαυτοῖς μᾶλλον ἢ παρ' ἀξίαν τι συγχωρῆσαι.
226 εἶεν. τί δὴ προσῆκεν ἑλέσθαι τότε τοὺς Ἀθηναίους, ἢ τί τὸν σύμβουλον παραινεῖν αὐτοῖς; ἐνταῦθά μοι σκέψαι τὰ τοῦ Θεμιστοκλέους δόγματα

like the Argives, the Corcyreans, the Siceliots and almost
all the Italians, and the Cretans and some others whom
they say also belong to this category. The second group
marched with the barbarians against Greece, like the
Thessalians and all the peoples as far as Attica, except for
however many Thespians and Plataeans it was. The third
and last category consisted of the Athenians and the Spartans and all those who had taken refuge with them. But 225
for the time being let us not dwell on the point that the
Athenians were part of this last group, or that they had
trained up the others too. These were the three groups
into which the whole of Greece was divided, and the
choice between the three of them was freely open to all.
Cities and individuals had to decide on this basis—and the
difference between the options was not a small one—either to side with the barbarians and accompany them
against those who still resisted, or to beg to be allowed to
remain neutral and not to ask what would happen to the
others but instead count it a gain if nothing happened to
them, or in the third and final case to assert their concern
for what was good and right, and to fight back with fire and
iron and all means at their disposal, and pay no heed to
either the sound or the sight of danger, but instead to
scorn the world as worthless foolery and to encamp by the
side of death itself, preferring this to be the end of their
lives sooner than collude in any unworthy action.

What then was the appropriate choice for the Athe- 226
nians to make, or for their counselor to advise them?
Please consider the decisions Themistocles made

ἔνθ᾽ ὅ τε δειλὸς ἀνὴρ ὅς τ᾽ ἄλκιμος ἐξεφαάνθη,

οὐκ εἰς λόχον συγκαθημένων ἡμῶν, ἀλλ᾽ ἐπ᾽ αὐτοῦ τοῦ ξυροῦ τῆς ἀκμῆς ἑστηκότος εἶναι τὴν Ἑλλάδα ἢ μή. αὕτη πρώτη Θεμιστοκλέους ἐξέτασις καὶ κρίσις.
227 ἐντεῦθεν ὅρα τὸν ἄνδρα ἀπὸ γραμμῆς ἀρξάμενος· καὶ μή μοι λόγῳ τὸν χρυσόν, ἀλλὰ τὴν βάσανον προσάγων σκόπει· τῆς γὰρ εἰκόνος μέμνησο τῆς σαυτοῦ. ἔδει τῶν ὑπὲρ τῆς κοινῆς ἐλευθερίας ἀγωνιζομένων Ἀθηναίους εἶναι, ἢ δυοῖν τοῖν ὑπολοίποιν θάτερον
228 ποιεῖν; ἔδει τῶν ἀγωνιζομένων εἶναι. τί οὖν; συνεβούλευεν ταῦτα Θεμιστοκλῆς, ἢ διεκώλυεν; οὔκ, ἀλλ᾽ ἐκεῖνος ἦν ὁ ταῦτα συμβουλεύων. οὔκουν[60] ταῦτα ἔδει πράττειν καὶ ταῦτα συμβουλεύειν; ταῦτα ἔπραττον μὲν Ἀθηναῖοι, συνεβούλευεν δὲ Θεμιστοκλῆς.

229 μέχρι μὲν δὴ τούτων τὰ μέγιστα συνεβούλευεν καὶ οὐδὲν ἔχει Πλάτων αἰτιάσασθαι, οὐ μὲν οὖν, εἰ μὴ λαμπρῶς ἐπαινοίη, ὅπως οὐκ ἂν αἰσχύνοιτο οὐκ ἂν ἔχειν μοι δοκεῖ. οὐ γὰρ μόνους τοὺς Ἀθηναίους ἐπὶ ταῦτ᾽ ἀγαγὼν καὶ τάξας ἐνταυθοῖ γνώμης φαίνεται, ἀλλὰ καὶ τοὺς ἄλλους Ἕλληνας, ὅσον μετέσχον τῶν πραγμάτων, εἷς ἀνὴρ οὗτος μάλιστα ἐπιρρώσας καὶ παροξύνας, καὶ τοὺς μὲν ἑκόντας, τοὺς δὲ ἄκοντας αὑτῶν πείσας γενέσθαι χρηστοὺς καὶ λυσιτελοῦντας ἑαυτοῖς· ὅς γε καὶ τοῖς κήρυξιν τοῖς παρὰ τοῦ βασι-

[60] οὔκουν Behr οὐκοῦν *codd.*

---

[182] Hom. *Il.* 13.278. [183] *Grg.* 486d.

Where the cowardly man and whosoever is brave are clearly seen[182]

—not, that is, when we were hunched down together in ambush, but when the existence or nonexistence of Greece itself teetered on a knife edge. This is the first test and
point of judgment for Themistocles. This is where you 227
should assess him, right at the starting line. And please, Plato, do not test this gold in word alone, but apply the touchstone to it—remember your own image.[183] Was it incumbent on the Athenians to belong to the party fighting for the common freedom of Greece, or to follow one or the other of the two remaining courses? They had to belong to the party putting up a fight. Well, then, did The- 228
mistocles advise them to do this, or did he try to prevent them? No, he did not try to prevent them; he was the one who advised them to take this course. Is that not then what needed to be done, and is that not the advice that needed to be given? Yes, and that is exactly what the Athenians did, and Themistocles advised.

Thus far, then, he gave them the weightiest possible 229
advice and Plato has no grounds for accusation against him, indeed, I do not see how he could avoid being ashamed if he did not praise him lavishly. For it is clear that it was not only the Athenians who he led toward this course of action and set in this resolve, but the rest of the Greek people as well, or as many of them as shared in the venture. This one man above all gave them strength and whetted their spirit, persuading some of them willingly and some of them in spite of themselves to turn heroes and be their own best helpers, since it was he who gave the kind of answer to the ambassadors who had come from

λέως ἐλθοῦσι περὶ τῆς γῆς καὶ τοῦ ὕδατος τοιαύτας
ἔδωκεν τὰς ἀποκρίσεις, ὥσθ᾽ ἅπασι τοῖς Ἕλλησιν
ὑπάρχειν μαθεῖν ὁποῖα ἄττα ἀποκρίνασθαι χρὴ τοῖς
ἐπὶ ταῦθ᾽ ἥκουσι τῶν βαρβάρων. καὶ οὐκ ἐνταῦθα
ἔστη τῆς ἐλευθερίας, ἀλλὰ καὶ τὸν ἑρμηνεύσαντα
ἀπέκτεινεν, κατηγορῶν ὅτι τὴν φωνὴν ὥσπερ ἄλλο τι
230 τῷ Πέρσῃ κατὰ τῶν Ἑλλήνων ἔχρησεν. καίτοι τί
τοῦτο δεινὸν ἦν τοῖς Ἀθηναίοις μαθεῖν ὅ τί ἐστι τὰ
λεγόμενα, μαθόντας δὲ βουλεύσασθαι; οὐ γὰρ αὐτός
γ᾽ εἰσηγεῖτο οὐδ᾽ ἐπηνάγκαζεν. ἀλλὰ ὅμως οὐδ᾽ ἄχρι
τούτου διακονεῖν ἠξίου, οὐδὲ γὰρ προσήκειν ἀκούειν
τὰ τοιαῦτα. ταχύ γ᾽ ἂν αὐτὸς διηκόνησεν ὁ τοῖς δια-
κόνοις οὕτω χρώμενος, ἢ παρ᾽ ἃ βέλτιστα ἐνόμιζεν
ἐδημηγόρησεν, ὁ μηδ᾽ ἑρμηνεύειν ἐῶν περὶ ὧν οὐ βέλτιον λέγειν.

231 τὰ μὲν δὴ προοίμια τοιαῦτα τῆς Θεμιστοκλέους
πολιτείας καὶ τοῦ περὶ τῆς ἐλευθερίας ἀγῶνος, οὐδὲν
τοῖς Μέλητος ἐοικότα τοῦ κιθαρῳδοῦ, οὐδ᾽ οἷς ἐκεῖνον
ᾄδειν φησὶ Πλάτων, ἀλλ᾽ ἀπεναντίον μᾶλλον. τό τε
γὰρ βέλτιστον ἔνεστιν καὶ τὸ ἥδιστον πρόσεστιν
ἀκοῦσαι παντὶ γενναίῳ καὶ ἐλευθέρῳ. ὥστ᾽ ἔμοιγε δοκεῖ τῆς Τερπάνδρου μᾶλλον ἂν εἶναι μουσικῆς εἰκάσαι, πλήν γ᾽ ὅτι καὶ παρελήλυθεν. ὁ μέν γε μίαν
πόλιν τὴν Λακεδαιμονίων εἰς ταὐτὸν ἤγαγεν, ὁ δὲ τὴν

184 *Grg.* 502a: Plato makes Socrates say that Meles was an even worse composer and performer than his son Cinesias and could not even give his audience pleasure, let alone improve them.

the King about earth and water that allowed all Greeks to learn how barbarians coming on such a mission ought to be answered. Nor did he limit himself to just that demonstration of freedom, but also had the translator put to death, on the accusation that he had casually loaned his voice to the Persian against the Greeks. Yet what would 230
have been so terrible about the Athenians learning what the ambassadors had to say, and then having learned it holding their council of war? Themistocles was not the one introducing this business or putting them under any compulsion. But all the same, he did not see fit to play the lackey even to this extent, because he did not think it was right for them even to hear the message. The man who treated the King's lackeys in this manner would scarcely have played the lackey himself, or spoken in favor of something other than what he thought was best, when he would not even allow to be translated something that was better not spoken about at all.

Such were the strains that formed the prelude to The- 231
mistocles' statesmanship and to his struggle for freedom; they bore no resemblance whatsoever to those of Meles the citharode, or to what Plato said he sang,[184] but were instead their complete opposite. Their theme is the highest good, and in addition they make the pleasantest possible sound for the virtuous and the free to hear. I think therefore that it would be more appropriate to compare them to Terpander's poetry, except that they excel it. Terpander brought together just the one city, Sparta,[185]

[185] According to ancient biographical tradition, the seventh-century lyric poet Terpander was summoned from Lesbos to Sparta at a time of civil unrest: Suda μ 701 (3.370 Adler).

Ἑλλάδα πᾶσαν ἥρμοσε καὶ συνέστησεν·—λέγω γὰρ οὖν Ἑλλάδα τοὺς τῇ Ἑλλάδι πάσῃ βοηθῆσαι δυνηθέντας—τοσούτῳ μείζονος καὶ κοινοτέρας καὶ ἐπὶ
232 πλεῖον φερούσης ὁμονοίας ἡγεμὼν ἐγένετο. πρῶτον μέν γε τοὺς πολέμους τοὺς συνεστῶτας τότε ἐν τῇ Ἑλλάδι καὶ τὰς πρὸς ἀλλήλους διαφορὰς καὶ στάσεις ἔπαυσεν ἁπάντων, καὶ ἕνα μὲν πόλεμον τὸν πρὸς τοὺς βαρβάρους, αὐτοὺς δὲ φίλους καὶ συγγενεῖς, ἔπεισεν ἡγήσασθαι. ἔπειθ᾽ ὅσοι τῶν πολιτῶν μεθειστήκεσαν, τούτους καταγαγεῖν συνεβούλευσεν Ἀθηναίοις, ἐν οἷς καὶ τῶν διαφόρων τινὲς ἦσαν αὐτῷ, τὴν αὐτὴν γνώμην ἔν τε τοῖς Ἑλληνικοῖς καὶ τοῖς κατὰ τὴν πόλιν σῴζων· αὕτη δ᾽ ἦν τὸ κοινῇ βέλτιστον σκοπεῖν ἅπασαν μικροψυχίαν ἀνελόντας.

233 παραλαβὼν τοίνυν τὰ πράγματα καὶ προστάτης τοῦ παντὸς κινδύνου γενόμενος ποῖόν τινα ἑαυτὸν παρέσχεν καὶ συνεῖναι τὰ δέοντα καὶ πρᾶξαι διὰ τέλους; τοιοῦτον οἷον, εἴ τις ἔροιθ᾽ ὁντινοῦν τί τὸ σῶσαν τὰ πράγματα τῶν Ἑλλήνων ἐγένετο, μὴ λελοιπέναι ζήτησιν, ἀλλὰ πᾶσιν εὐθὺς ὑπάρχειν εἰπεῖν ὅτι θεοὶ μὲν πρῶτον, ἔπειθ᾽, ὅσον εἰς ἀνθρώπους ἧκεν, μία μὲν πόλις ἡ τῶν Ἀθηναίων, γνώμη δὲ ἑνὸς ἀνδρὸς ἡ Θεμιστοκλέους. ὁρῶν γὰρ ὡς εἰ μή τις τῷ ναυτικῷ κρατήσει τῶν βαρβάρων, οἰχήσεται κατὰ πόλεις ἡ Ἑλλάς, προσβαλλόντων ἐν μέρει πᾶσιν καὶ πορθούντων, καὶ πρὸς τούτῳ κἀκεῖνο εἰδὼς ὅτι τἀν τῇ γῇ πολὺ πλείους καὶ δεινοτέρας ἔχει τὰς ἀπορίας καὶ πολὺ πλείοσιν ἢ κατὰ θάλατταν μαχοῦνται καὶ ἀπορω-

whereas Themistocles harmonized and unified the whole of Greece (by Greece I mean those able to come to the assistance of the whole of Greece), so much greater was the scale and the shared interest and the scope of the concord that he brought about. In the first place, he put a 232
stop to the wars that were then being waged in Greece, and to all their internecine quarrels and discord, persuading them to think that there was just the one war to be fought, against the barbarians, and to regard themselves as friends and kin. Then he advised the Athenians to restore any of their fellow citizens they had banished, among whom there were some of his own personal enemies; he thus maintained a consistent policy in both Greek and local Athenian affairs, namely that they should look to what was best for the common good and suppress all meanness of spirit.

Once he had taken over management of affairs and had 233
become leader of the whole perilous venture, what sort of man did he show himself to be, in respect of understanding what needed to be done, and seeing it through in action? Such a one as to leave no room for head-scratching, if we were to ask anyone at all what it was that saved the situation for the Greeks, but for everyone immediately to be able to say that it was first of all the gods, and then, as far as human efforts were concerned, the one city of Athens, and the judgment of the one individual, Themistocles. Seeing that, if no one defeated the barbarians with their fleet, Greece would go under city by city, as they attacked and sacked each in turn, and in addition to this knowing also that land campaigning involved more and more fearsome difficulties, and that on land they would be fighting with far larger numbers of more difficult adversar-

τέροις προσφέρεσθαι, εἵλετο πρῶτον μὲν τὴν ἐλάττονα ὑπερβολὴν ἀντὶ τῆς μείζονος, ἔπειτα οὗ πρὸς καιρὸν τῇ τόλμῃ χρήσεται. καὶ ταῦτα ἐπεψήφιζεν ὁ
234 θεὸς ὁ ἐν Δελφοῖς. ὅμως δὲ καὶ τῆς μαντείας ἐλθούσης ἦν ἀπορία τοῖς πολλοῖς τί ποτε εἴη τὸ ξύλινον τεῖχος τοῦτο. ὡς οἱ μὲν πρεσβῦται τῆς ἀκροπόλεως ἔχεσθαι παρῄνουν, οὕτω παρελήρουν, πεφράχθαι γὰρ αὐτὴν ῥάχῳ τὸ ἀρχαῖον καὶ τὸν χρησμὸν εἰς τοῦτο φέρειν. χρησμολόγοι δὲ πάντ᾽ ᾖδον, πλὴν ἓν τῶν πάντων οὐκ ᾖδον, ὡς δεῖ ναυμαχεῖν. ἀλλὰ καὶ φυλάττεσθαι παρῄνουν τὴν Σαλαμῖνα παντὸς μᾶλλον—οἵ δέ γε αὐτοί ποτε οὗτοι τὸν εἰς Σικελίαν πλοῦν ἐπέσπευδον· τοὺς γὰρ αὐτοὺς ταυτὸν ἔθνος λέγω, πλήν γε δὴ οἱ μὲν Ἀλκιβιάδῃ συναγορεύοντες, οἱ ὕστερον, οἱ δὲ τότε ἀντέλεγον τῷ Θεμιστοκλεῖ—τό τε σύμπαν ἠξίουν ἄλλο τι ζητεῖν, καὶ φυγόντας ἔξω τῆς Ἑλλάδος ἄλ-
235 λην χώραν οἰκίζειν. τέλος δ᾽ ἔδοξεν Ἀθηναίοις τοὺς μὲν δὴ χρησμῳδοὺς χαίρειν ἐᾶν, Θεμιστοκλεῖ δὲ μᾶλλον πιστεῦσαι, ξύλινον μὲν εἶναι τεῖχος τὰς τριήρεις ἐξηγουμένῳ, ἀποκεῖσθαι δέ τι χρηστὸν ἐν τῇ Σαλαμῖνι, διὸ δὴ καὶ θείαν αὐτὴν ὑπὸ τοῦ θεοῦ προσειρῆσθαι· ἐπεὶ κακοῦ γέ του μέλλοντος καταλήψεσθαι τοὺς Ἕλληνας ἐν αὐτῇ, σχετλίαν καὶ οὐ θείαν τὸ πρόσρημα ἂν αὐτῆς εἶναι. ἀλλὰ γὰρ εἰς τοὺς βαρβάρους εἰρῆσθαι τὸ πολλοὺς ἀπολεῖσθαι. δεῖν οὖν ναυμαχεῖν.

ies, he first of all chose the smaller disparity in size in preference to the greater, and then a place where he could exercise his daring when the right moment came. The god
in Delphi endorsed his decision. But even so when the 234
oracle was reported, most people were at a loss to know what this "wooden wall" could be. The old men—this was the kind of nonsense they spouted—advised them to hold fast to the Acropolis, because in olden times it had been fortified with wattle, and this was what the oracle was referring to.[186] The soothsayers chanted every possible piece of advice except for just the one that they neglected to give, that they should fight at sea. Instead they advised them before all else to beware of Salamis—these being the same people as were subsequently so keen on the Sicilian expedition, meaning by "the same people" the same class of person, except that its later representatives spoke in support of Alcibiades, whereas it was against Themistocles that the earlier group spoke on this occasion—and all in all demanded that they should look for some other solution, take flight beyond the boundaries of Greece and
settle in another country. In the end the Athenians de- 235
cided to turn their backs on the soothsayers and to trust Themistocles instead when he interpreted the wooden wall to mean their triremes and told them that something good lay in store for them at Salamis, which was why the god had called it "holy," since if some misfortune was going to descend on the Greeks there, its epithet would have been "wretched" and not "holy": the prediction of many deaths referred to the barbarians, therefore they ought to fight at sea.

[186] Hdt. 7.142.

236 καὶ ταῦτα εἰκότως οἱ μὲν ἄλλοι χαλεπῶς εἶχον συμβαλεῖν, Θεμιστοκλῆς δὲ ῥᾳδίως ἐξευρεῖν. οὐ γὰρ ὅτε ἦλθον τὰ λόγια, οὐ τότε πρῶτον ταύτην ἔσχε τὴν γνώμην, οὐδ' αὐτοσχεδιάζων, οὐδ' ἐπὶ τοῦ καιροῦ σοφὸς ταύτην τὴν σοφίαν ὥσπερ οἱ θεομάντεις γενόμενος, ἀλλὰ καὶ πρὶν πέμπειν Ἀθηναίους εἰς Δελφοὺς καὶ πρὶν τὸν βάρβαρον κινηθῆναι, πάλαι καὶ πόρρωθεν ἐκεῖνος ταῦτα ἐσκέψατο καὶ συνεῖδεν, καὶ ὅπως ἐπὶ τοῦ καιροῦ καὶ τῆς χρείας μὴ ἀπορήσῃ προὐνοήθη. περιγενομένων γὰρ τῇ πόλει χρημάτων συχνῶν ἀπὸ τῶν ἔργων τῶν ἀργυρείων, καὶ ταῦτα μελλόντων εἰκῇ νέμεσθαι, μόνος τῶν πάντων ἐτόλμησεν ἀντειπεῖν, οὐ διακόνου πρᾶγμα πράττων, οὐδ' ὑπηρετοῦντος ταῖς ἐπιθυμίαις, οὐδ' ἀποπιμπλάντος τὰς ἡδονάς, ἀλλὰ μᾶλλον, ὥς γέ μοι φαίνεται, συμβούλου καὶ διδασκάλου, καὶ τὸ μὲν ἥδιστον ἑκόντος ὑπερβαίνοντος, τὸ δὲ βέλτιστον προορωμένου καὶ πράττοντος, κἂν δέῃ λυπῆσαι, καὶ τὸν ἰατρὸν ἀλλ' οὐ τὸν ὀψοποιὸν μιμουμένου, μᾶλλον δὲ καὶ τὸν γυμναστήν, ὡς ἂν σὺ φαίης, εἴπερ πρὸ τοῦ κινδύνου καὶ τῶν δυσχερῶν ἔπραττε τὸ συμφέρον καὶ ὅπως μὴ
237 ὑποδώσει τοῖς Ἕλλησι τὰ πράγματα. ἐκέλευε τοίνυν Ἀθηναίους τῆς μὲν διαδόσεως ὑπεριδεῖν, ναῦς δὲ ποιήσασθαι ἐκ τῶν χρημάτων, πρόφασιν μὲν ὡς ἐπὶ τὸν πόλεμον τὸν πρὸς Αἰγινήτας, οὗτος γὰρ ἐνειστήκει τότε, τῇ δ' ἀληθείᾳ τὰ μέλλοντα ἔσεσθαι προορῶν καὶ

The others understandably found this conclusion hard to arrive at, but Themistocles reached it with ease, because it was not only when the oracle arrived that he first formed this opinion. He did not improvise, or acquire mastery of this kind of wisdom on the spur of the moment, like the soothsayers, but even before the Athenians had sent to Delphi and the barbarians had started out, he had long since thought all this through well in advance and understood it, and made plans so as not to be helpless when the hour of need came. When the city had amassed large sums of money from the silver-workings and they were going to be distributed randomly, he was the only one among them all to speak out against this; in so doing he did not act like a lackey, or someone ministering to people's desires and satisfying their urge to pleasure, but rather—it seems to me at least—like a counselor and teacher, that is someone who voluntarily passes over what is pleasantest and thinks forward to and puts into practice what is best, in imitation not of the caterer but of the doctor, or rather, as you might say,[187] of the athletics trainer, given that he did what needed to be done in advance of the hour of danger and difficulty and took steps to ensure that the Greek cause would not fail. He told the Athenians, then, to spurn a general distribution of largesse and to use the money to build ships, ostensibly for the war against the people of Aegina, which was under way at the time, but in reality because he could foresee what was 236 237

[187] In the division of skilled activities set out by Socrates in *Grg.* 464b–c (cf. 520b), gymnastics promotes health in the body by sustained training, whereas medicine intervenes only to rectify matters when something has gone wrong.

νομίζων τὴν Μαραθῶνι μάχην ὡσπερεὶ προοίμιον γεγενῆσθαι τοῖς Ἀθηναίοις, εἶναι δ' οὐ πέρας τοῦ πολέμου τοῦ παντὸς οὐδὲ τελευτήν, ἀλλ' ἀρχὴν μᾶλλον
238 καὶ παρασκευὴν ἑτέρων ἀγώνων μειζόνων. καὶ ταῦτα κατ' ἀρχάς τε λέγων ἔπειθεν καὶ αἱ τριήρεις ἐποιήθησαν, καὶ τότ' ἔπεισεν ὡς δεῖ ταῖς τριήρεσι χρήσασθαι καὶ τῇ θαλάττῃ προσέχειν, ὡς οὐκ ὂν αὐτοῖς κάλλιον ὁρμητήριον τοῦ πρὸς τοὺς βαρβάρους πολέμου. καὶ πρῶτον μὲν ἐπ' Ἀρτεμίσιον πλεύσας δυοῖν ναυμαχίαιν δύο ἵστησι τρόπαια, οὔτε λόγους ἀσχήμονας εἰπὼν οἶμαι πρὸς τοὺς ἐμπλέοντας Ἀθηναίων ἢ τῶν Ἑλλήνων οὔτε ἔργα φαῦλα ἀποδειξάμενος, ἀλλ', ὥς φησι Πίνδαρος, κρηπῖδα τῆς ἐλευθερίας τοῖς Ἕλλησι βαλόμενος. ἔπειτα γράφει τὸ ψήφισμα τοῦτο, οὗ θαυμαστότερον οὐδ' ἐλευθεριώτερον οὐδείς πω μέμνηται γραφέν.

239 ἔοικα δ' ὑπερβαίνειν πολλὰ τῶν ἐν μέσῳ· βέλτιον οὖν ἴσως ἐπανελθεῖν. οὕτω γὰρ ὡς ἀληθῶς ἐκεῖνος θείᾳ τινὶ μοίρᾳ καὶ ὑπὲρ τῆς Ἑλλάδος πάσης ἔφυ καὶ οὐδὲν βέλτιον ἑώρα[61] τοῦ κοινῇ συμφέροντος, ὥστε ἐπειδὴ συνελέγησαν εἰς ταυτὸν οἱ Ἕλληνες, ὑπερέβαλον μὲν Ἀθηναῖοι τῷ πλήθει τῶν νεῶν σχεδὸν πάντας, ὡρμημένων δὲ τῶν Ἑλλήνων μᾶλλον πρὸς τοὺς Λακεδαιμονίους κἀκείνους ἐθελόντων προΐστασθαι, συνιδὼν ὁ πάντα ἄριστος ἐκεῖνος ὡς, εἰ τὸ δίκαιον ἀκριβῶς ἐξετάζοι καὶ στάσις ἐγγένοιτο ὑπὲρ τῆς ἡγε-

[61] *ita* Reiske ἑώρα πλέον *codd.*

going to happen, and considered that the Battle of Marathon had been only a kind of prelude for the Athenians and was not the limit or end of the whole war but rather the beginning and a preparation for other greater struggles. With these words he had persuaded them in the first 238
instance, and the triremes had been built, and now he persuaded them that they should use their triremes and keep to the sea, on the understanding that they had no finer basis for operations in their war against the barbarians. First of all, he sailed to Artemisium and won two victories in two naval encounters. The words he spoke here to the Athenian and Greek crews were I think no unseemly ones, and the deeds he did were no mean ones; to quote Pindar, he laid the foundation stone of Greek freedom.[188] He then drafted the decree that is more astonishing and more instinct with freedom than any other in human memory.

But I think I have jumped over much intervening mat- 239
ter, so it is perhaps better to go back on my tracks. So truly was this man born thanks to some divine dispensation and for the benefit of the whole of Greece, and so true was it that he counted nothing higher than the common good, that when the Greeks all gathered together in the same place and, although the Athenians outstripped practically everybody in the number of their ships, they inclined more to the Spartans and wanted them to be in command, this utter paragon realized that, if he were to be too pedantic in his assessment of what was fair, and a quarrel should arise among them over the leadership, their entire

[188] Fr. 77 Sn-M.

μονίας, ἅπαντ᾽ ἀπολεῖται κακῶς, καὶ οὐχ ἕξουσιν ὅ τι χρήσονται, πείθει τοὺς Ἀθηναίους ὑφίεσθαι καὶ συγχωρῆσαι τοῖς Λακεδαιμονίοις ἐν τῷ τότε τὴν ἡγεμονίαν ὑποσχόμενος παρ᾽ ἑκόντων αὐτοῖς τῶν Ἑλλήνων
240 αὐτὴν ἀνακτήσεσθαι. καὶ οὐκ ἐψεύσατο, σχεδὸν δέ τι καὶ τοὔνομα τῆς ἡγεμονίας, ἀλλὰ οὐκ αὐτὴν ἔπεισε παρεῖναι, ἐπεὶ τό γ᾽ ἀληθὲς εἰπεῖν αὐτοῖς μὲν τὴν ἡγεμονίαν, ἐκείνοις δὲ τὴν ἐπωνυμίαν ἀνέθεσαν, καὶ περιεγένετο αὐτοῖς ἄνευ τῆς σωτηρίας τῆς κοινῆς καὶ τὸ τῶν μὲν πολεμίων ἀνδρείᾳ, τῶν δὲ συμμάχων πραότητι κρατῆσαι, καὶ τὸ σχῆμα τῷ παντὶ κάλλιον καὶ σεμνότερον· ἡγεμόνων γὰρ ἡγεμόνες κατέστησαν.
241 καὶ εἰ φῄς, ὦ Πλάτων, ὅτι οὐ τριήρων οὐδὲ νεωρίων αἱ πόλεις δέονται, ἀλλ᾽ εὐβουλίας καὶ σωφροσύνης, ὁ Θεμιστοκλῆς οὐ μόνον τὰς τριήρεις τοῖς Ἀθηναίοις ἐξεῦρεν οὐδ᾽, ὃ τούτου μεῖζόν ἐστιν, ὑπὲρ τῶν κοινῶν δικαίων καὶ εἰς τὸ δέον πᾶσι τοῖς Ἕλλησιν ἐχρήσατο αὐταῖς, ἀλλὰ καὶ τὴν ὁμόνοιαν τὴν ἀγαθὴν αὐτὸς ταῖς πόλεσι προσεισηνέγκατο καὶ κατέπραξεν, ὃ τῶν νεῶν αὐτῶν οὐχ ἧττον ἔσωσε τὴν Ἑλλάδα· μᾶλλον δὲ καὶ ταῖς ναυσὶν αὐταῖς ἐποίησε χρήσασθαι.

242 καὶ ὃ μικρῷ πρόσθεν ἔφην, ἐνταῦθα καλῶς ἀναφαίνεται, ὅσῳ τοῦ Τερπάνδρου κρείττων ἁνὴρ[62] τὴν μουσικήν. ὁ μὲν γὰρ ἐφ᾽ ἑαυτῶν τοὺς Λακεδαιμονίους ὁμονοεῖν ἐποίησεν, ὁ δ᾽ Ἀθηναίους καὶ Λακεδαιμονίους τότε ταὐτὸν ἔπεισε φρονῆσαι, μᾶλλον δ᾽ ἅπαν-

62 ἁνήρ Dindorf ἀνήρ *codd.*

cause would come to an evil end and they would be left helpless, and he persuaded the Athenians to give way and to concede the leadership to the Spartans for the time being, with the promise that he would recover it for them from the Greeks with the latter's full consent. He was as 240
good as his word, and what he persuaded them to hand over was pretty much leadership in name only rather than the thing itself, since to tell the truth, they assigned the leadership to themselves and its name alone to the Spartans, and they won for themselves, apart from the salvation of their common cause and victories scored over the enemy in bravery and over their allies in imperturbability, a glory utterly finer and more impressive, since they were the leaders' leaders. And if you say, Plato, that cities do not 241
need triremes and docks, but wise planning and self-control,[189] Themistocles not only came up with the idea of the triremes for the Athenians in the first place and, a still greater achievement, used them in defense of shared rights and in time of need for the whole of Greece; he was also personally responsible for initiating and completing the virtuous concord that prevailed among their cities, which saved Greece no less than the ships themselves did, or rather, he put them in a position to make good use of those ships for themselves.

As I was saying a little earlier, it is here that it becomes 242
beautifully clear how superior this man was to Terpander in his music making. Terpander brought the Spartans into concord among themselves, but Themistocles made the Athenians and the Spartans think as one, or rather made

[189] *Grg.* 518e–19a.

τας τοὺς Ἕλληνας μιᾶς γενέσθαι γνώμης· οὕτως εὖ καὶ καλῶς τὴν Ἑλλάδα ἡρμόσατο, καὶ αὐτός τε ἀπέστη τῆς ναυαρχίας καὶ ἐκείνους ἔπεισε τῆς ἡγεμονίας, οὕτω πολὺ νικῶντας καὶ μόνους ὄντας εἰς ἐλπίδα

243 τοῖς πράγμασιν. καίτοι τοσοῦτον δεῖγμα σωφροσύνης καὶ καρτερίας τίς πώποτε ἐξήνεγκε τῶν ἐν τοῖς τρίβωσι κατασαπέντων; οὐ τοίνυν ὥσπερ τοῦ σχήματος, οὕτω καὶ τῆς προνοίας τῆς περὶ τῶν πραγμάτων ὅπερ εἶπον ἐξέστη, οὐδ' ὑπεχώρησεν οὔτε πόλει οὔτ' ἀνθρώπων οὐδενί, ἀλλ' αὐτός τε ἅπαντα συνεβούλευσεν, ὥσπερ ἂν εἰ μόνος ἦν τῶν πάντων ἡγεμών, καὶ τὸν τῶν Λακεδαιμονίων ναύαρχον τὸν Εὐρυβιάδην ὥσπερ παῖδα κοσμῶν καὶ περιστέλλων καὶ προδιδάσκων διεγένετο, ὥσπερ οἱ τοὺς νεῖν ἀδυνάτους ἀνέχοντες ταῖς ἑαυτῶν χερσίν, οὐκ ἐξελέγχων, ἀλλ' οἷον ὑποκοριζόμενος τῷ τῆς ναυαρχίας ὀνόματι, ἐπεὶ ὅτι γε αὐτός τε ναύαρχος καὶ[63] κύριος ἦν τῶν ἁπάντων, πρώτου δ' αὐτοῦ τοῦ ναυάρχου στρέφειν ὅποι βούλοιτο, παρὰ πᾶσαν ἔδειξε τὴν ἀρχήν, καὶ δὴ καὶ τότε εὐθύς. ἐκπλαγέντος γὰρ τοῦ Εὐρυβιάδου πρὸς τὸ πλῆθος τῶν τριήρων τῶν βαρβαρικῶν, ὧν[64] τὰς μὲν ἑώρα καταντικρὺ προσφερομένας, τὰς δ' ἤκουεν περιπλεῖν, καὶ διανοουμένου τὸν ἀγῶνα καταλιπεῖν οὐκ ἐπ' ἐλπίδι βελτίονι, ἀλλ' ὅπερ ἐν τοῖς τοιούτοις συμβαίνει τὸ παρὸν διακρούσασθαι κέρδος ἡγεῖσθαι,

[63] *αὐτός τε ναύαρχος καί* Monac. 432 Dindorf *αὐτός τε ναύαρχος αὐτός cett. αὐτός τε ναύαρχος καὶ αὐτός* Behr

all the Greeks of one mind. That is how well and how
nobly he unified Greece, both standing aside himself
from command of the navy and persuading the Athenians
to forgo their hegemony, even though they were so very
superior and offered the only real hope in the circumstances. Which of those who fester in their cheap philoso- 243
phers' cloaks has ever produced such a demonstration of
endurance and self-control? Although he relinquished the
rank, he did not, as I have already remarked, similarly
relinquish his forethought over events, nor did he defer to
any city or to anyone among men, but himself offered
advice on all matters, as if he were sole leader of all, and
throughout he steered and fostered and instructed the
Spartan admiral Eurybiades as if he were a child, like
people who with their own hands support those unable to
swim, not showing him up, but as it were humoring him
with the undeserved name of admiral, since throughout
the whole period of his command, and indeed right at the
outset, he demonstrated that he himself was the admiral
and in control of everything, beginning with his ability to
turn the "admiral" himself in whatever direction he might
wish. When Eurybiades was panic-stricken in the face of
the number of the barbarian triremes, seeing some of
them bearing down on him head-on and hearing that others were sailing around to encircle him, and was minded
to abandon the struggle not on the strength of any hope
for something better, but because, as happens in such
situations, he thought it a gain to stave off the present
reality—when Eurybiades was in the grip of these feelings

64 ὧν Reiske ὡς *codd.*

τοιοῦτον πάθος παθόντος καὶ πρὸς τὴν Πελοπόννησον βλέποντος, αὐτὸς ὥσπερ θεός τις τῶν ἀπὸ μηχανῆς χεῖρα ὑπερέσχεν καὶ διεκώλυσεν διαφθαρῆναι τὰ πράγματα ἀπ' αἰσχρᾶς οὕτω τῆς ἀρχῆς ἀρξάμενα· καὶ τὸν Εὐρυβιάδην ὡς οὐκ ἔπειθεν λέγων, ἐπρίατο, οὐχ ὡς ἄν τις διάκονος ἀξιῶν τινος εἶναι, ἀλλ' ἐκείνῳ μᾶλλον ὡς διακόνῳ χρησάμενος· καὶ τήν τε Εὔβοιαν περιεποίησεν καὶ τὰ πράγματα τῶν Ἑλλήνων ἔστησεν μὴ παντελῶς ἄπορα εἶναι, παρασχὼν πειραθεῖσιν πιστεῦσαι.

244 ἀγγελθέντος δὲ τοῦ περὶ τὰς Πύλας πάθους καὶ τῆς κοινῆς, εἰ θέμις εἰπεῖν, τοῦ τε Ἀπόλλωνος τοῦ Πυθίου καὶ Θεμιστοκλέους μαντείας δεύτερον ἤδη φανερᾶς γεγονυίας, ὅτι πάντα ἐν ταῖς ναυσὶν ἄρ' ἦν—οἵ τε γὰρ εἰς τὴν Θετταλίαν εἰσελθόντες ὡς τὰ Τέμπη φυλάξοντες προδοθέντες ὑφ' ὅτων δή ποτε ἀνεχώρησαν, οἵ τε εἰς Πύλας ἀπαντήσαντες κατεχώσθησαν ὑπὸ τῶν βαρβάρων· καὶ οὐ τοσοῦτόν γ' ἔστι μόνον εἰπεῖν περὶ αὐτῶν, ἀλλ' ὅτι καὶ Λακεδαιμόνιοι δοκοῦσίν μοι ταῦτα γνόντες ἐξ ἀρχῆς ὥσπερ ἀφοσιούμενοι πρὸς τοὺς Ἕλληνας ἀποστεῖλαι τοσούτους ὁπόσων ἠδύναντο ἐνεγκεῖν στερηθέντες, ὡς τοῦ γε ἀποτυχεῖν ὑπάρχοντος—οὕτω δὴ τούτων κεχωρηκότων καὶ τῶν ἐν ταῖς ναυσὶ κατὰ κράτος ἤδη φευγόντων εἰς τὸ εἴσω τῆς Ἑλλάδος, καὶ τὴν Πελοπόννησον σχεδὸν Ἑλλάδα ποιουμένων, τὰ δ' ἄλλα παρεικότων, ἔσχατος μὲν ἀνεχώρει μετὰ ἐσχάτων Ἀθηναίων, οὐ τὴν αὐτὴν τάξιν φυλάττων ἥνπερ ὅτε ἐκπλεῖν ἔδει· τότε μὲν γὰρ

and looking toward the Peloponnese, Themistocles himself like some *deus ex machina* held out a protecting hand and prevented matters from going utterly to ruin after such a shameful beginning. And when he could not persuade Eurybiades with words, he bought him, thereby acting not like one who sees fit to be someone else's lackey, but rather using someone else as his own; he secured Euboea and stabilized the situation for the Greeks, so as to prevent it from becoming entirely desperate, and thus gave them grounds for confidence based on their own direct experience.

When the news came of the disaster at Thermopylae 244
and the oracle jointly issued—if it is permissible to put it like this—by Pythian Apollo and Themistocles had made it clear for a second time now that everything indeed depended on the ships—someone had betrayed the force that had gone into Thessaly to guard Tempe and it had retreated, and those who had made their stand at Thermopylae had been overwhelmed by the barbarians (nor is that all that can be said about them: it can be added, in my view, that the Spartans realized how things stood from the start and were so to speak making a token gesture toward discharging their obligations to the Greeks when they sent only as many men as they could endure losing, since they saw failure as a foregone conclusion)—with events having reached this point, and the naval contingent having been forced to retreat to the Greek heartlands, more or less making the Peloponnese into Greece and abandoning the rest, Themistocles was the last to withdraw along with the last of the Athenians, occupying a very different station to that which he occupied when the time came for aggressive

245 πρῶτος ἦν ἐν πρώτοις. εἰ δ' αὖ βούλει κἀνταῦθα τὸ τῆς ὁδοῦ πάρεργον,[65] ὃ πρὸς τοὺς Ἴωνας ἐπολιτεύσατο, οὐκ ἀπὸ τοῦ βήματος, οὐδ' ὁρώμενος αὐτοῖς, ἀλλ' ἀπὸ τῶν πετρῶν καὶ τῶν τόπων τῶν ναυλόχων, οἷς ἤλπιζεν αὐτοὺς προσμίξειν, ποῖος Μίνως Ὁμηρικὸς ταῦτα μέμψαιτ' ἄν, ἢ τίς Αἰακὸς ἄρας τὰς χεῖρας ὑπὲρ τῶν Ἑλλήνων τῷ Διί;

246 ἐνταῦθα δὴ πολὺ μείζων καὶ καλλίων ἡ τρίτη πεῖρα ἐπεγένετο ὡς αἱ τριήρεις τὸ πᾶν ἔφερον, τὰ δὲ ἄλλα μάταιον καὶ προσδοκᾶν ἦν. ἀναχωρησάντων γὰρ ἀπ' Ἀρτεμισίου τῶν Ἑλλήνων Ἀθηναῖοι μὲν καὶ οὕτως αὐτοί τε παρεσκευάζοντο καὶ τοὺς ἄλλους ἐκέλευον ἀπαντᾶν εἰς τὴν Βοιωτίαν καὶ προκινδυνεύειν τῆς λοιπῆς Ἑλλάδος· οἱ δ' εἰς τοῦτο κατέστησαν τῆς ἀπορίας, οὐ γὰρ ἄξιον λέγειν προδοσίαν, ὥστε ἐξιέναι μὲν οὐκ ἐθάρρουν, διαλαβόντες δὲ τὸν Ἰσθμὸν ἐτείχιζον, ἐκ θαλάττης εἰς θάλατταν, παραπλήσιον δρῶντες ὥσπερ ἂν εἰ συγκαλυψάμενοι σφᾶς αὐτοὺς παρεδίδοσαν. ὅπου γὰρ ἐξῆν τοῖς βαρβάροις περιπλεύσασιν κατὰ πόλεις ἑλεῖν αὐτούς, τί πλέον τοῦ τείχους ἦν, εἰ καὶ σεμνότερον τοῦ τῶν Βαβυλωνίων ἐστάθη καὶ πάσης
247 κρεῖττον μηχανῆς; οὐκοῦν τῶν μὲν Ἀθηναίων μονωθέν-

65 "*in hac regione deest* ὅρα *vel* σκόπει, *nisi gravius vulnus subest*" Reiske

---

190 A reference to the inscriptions left on Themistocles' orders, in the hopes that Ionian crews in the Persian navy might

action, when he was first in the front rank. And if you like, 245
think also at this point of the incidental measure that he directed toward the Ionians along the way, delivered not from the speaker's platform or even within sight of them, but from the rocks and havens that he hoped they would put in at:[190] what sort of Minos from Homer could fault it, or what Aeacus raising his hands in prayer to Zeus on behalf of the Greeks?[191]

Now came the third trial of strength, far greater and 246
nobler because everything now rested with the triremes and it was futile even to look toward anything else. When the Greeks had retreated from Artemisium, the Athenians prepared themselves as I have described and told the others to meet them in Boeotia and face the danger in defense of the rest of Greece. But they had reached such a depth of despair—it would be unworthy to say "betrayal"—that they lacked the confidence for an expedition and instead shut off the Isthmus with a wall from sea to sea, thus doing the same as if they had covered up their heads and surrendered.[192] Because given that the barbarians could sail around and pick them off city by city, what use was the wall, even if it were more imposing than the walls of Babylon and too strong for any siege engine? Thus, with the 247

read them: Hdt. 8.22. The text at the beginning of this sentence is uncertain: the translation follows the spirit of Reiske's suggestion. [191] Aeacus is the Underworld judge said by Socrates in the *Gorgias* to decide the fates of the dead from Europe, with Minos as the arbiter in cases of uncertainty: *Grg.* 524a and 526c–d (with a reference to *Od.* 11.569).

[192] Hdt. 8.40 and 74; covering the head is a gesture of embarrassment (e.g., Pl. *Phdr.* 237a and 243b).

των, τῶν δ' Ἑλλήνων ἀνόνητα πονούντων, λοιπὸν ἦν ἅπαντα ἔχεσθαι σιωπῇ καὶ κατὰ γῆν καὶ κατὰ θάλατταν. ἃ Θεμιστοκλῆς πόρρωθεν προορώμενος οὐκ ἐξεπλάγη τότε, ἀλλ' εἰσχεομένων ἀμφοτέρωθεν ἤδη τῶν βαρβάρων, καὶ τῶν τε νεῶν κοινῷ στόλῳ προσαγουσῶν καὶ τοῦ πεζοῦ κατὰ τὴν Βοιωτίαν εἰσβαλόντος, καὶ τοῦ πυρὸς πάντα ἐπιφλέγοντος καὶ δηλοῦντος ἀντὶ φρυκτῶν προσάγειν βασιλέα, γράφει τὸ ψήφισμα τοῦτο, τὴν μὲν πόλιν παρακαταθέσθαι Ἀθηνᾷ, Ἀθηνῶν μεδεούσῃ, παῖδας δὲ καὶ γυναῖκας εἰς Τροιζῆνα ὑπεκθέσθαι, τοὺς δὲ πρεσβύτας εἰς Σαλαμῖνα, τοὺς δ' ἄλλους ἐμβάντας εἰς τὰς τριήρεις ὑπὲρ τῆς ἐλευθερίας ἀγωνίζεσθαι.

248 ὦ μεγάλης μὲν τῆς ἐπινοίας καὶ ὑπερφυοῦς, θαυμαστῆς δὲ τῆς ῥώμης, ὅστις ταῦτα πρῶτος πείσειν ἤλπισεν καὶ οὐκ ἀπέγνω πρᾶγμα τοσοῦτον· θαυμαστῆς δὲ καὶ τῆς τῶν πεισθέντων ἀρετῆς τε καὶ παιδείας, ἣν ἐπεπαίδευντο ὑπ' ἐκείνῳ πάντα ἀνέχεσθαι καὶ καρτερεῖν, ὅσ' ἂν διδῷ μὲν ὁ δαίμων, συμβουλεύῃ
249 δὲ Θεμιστοκλῆς. τοῦτο τὸ ψήφισμα τῶν ὑφ' ἡλίῳ μαρτύριον κάλλιστον καὶ λαμπρότατον καὶ τελεώτατον εἰς ἀρετῆς λόγον, πάντων ἀπόδειξιν τῶν ἀρίστων ἑξῆς ἔχον, τοῦ θαρρεῖν τοῖς θεοῖς, τοῦ φρονεῖν ἐφ' ἑαυτοῖς, τοῦ παθεῖν ὁτιοῦν ἐθέλειν, πρίν τινος αἰσχροῦ πεῖραν λαβεῖν, ἔτι πρὸς τούτοις τοῦ φυλάττειν τὰ δόξαντα ἐξ ἀρχῆς, τοῦ μὴ μνησικακεῖν τοῖς ὁμοίοις, μηδ' ἂν ἀνομοίων ἔργα δοκῶσιν προῃρῆσθαι.
250 τοῦτο τὸ ψήφισμα οὐ κόλαξ ἐμοὶ δοκεῖν ἄνθρωπος

Athenians now on their own and the Greeks engaged in pointless labor, it only remained for all to fall silent on land and sea. Themistocles, however, because he had long since foreseen this, did not panic at this juncture, but instead, as the barbarians now poured in on two fronts, with their ships approaching in a single consolidated force and their infantry invading via Boeotia, and fire consuming all in its path and serving in place of beacons to reveal the King's advance, he drafted his famous decree, for the city to be handed over for safe keeping to its patron goddess Athena, the women and children to be removed to Troezen and the old men to Salamis, while the rest embarked on their triremes and fought for their freedom.[193]

What a great and extraordinary plan to come up with, 248
and what amazing fortitude, for someone to hope to persuade others into this course of action in the first place, and not to give up in the face of so huge a task! And what amazing heroism and good training in those who were persuaded, schooled by him to endure and persevere in whatever the heavens might grant and Themistocles might
advise! This decree is the finest testimony under the sun, 249
the most brilliant and the most conclusive for any reckoning of virtue, and contains a demonstration of all the best qualities one after the other: confidence in the gods, pride in themselves, willingness to endure anything sooner than to have any experience of disgrace, and on top of this constancy in their original decisions, and a refusal to bear a grudge against their equals, even if these later on might
seem to have chosen to act like their inferiors. In my view 250
it was no flatterer who uttered this decree, no man with

193 Hdt. 8.41 (but not attributed directly to Themistocles).

οὐδὲ κάτω βλέπων, οὐδ' ὑποπεπτωκὼς τοῖς ἀκούουσιν, ἀλλὰ θεῶν τις διὰ τῆς Θεμιστοκλέους γλώττης ἐφθέγξατο. ἢ πού σοι Μίθαικος ὁ τὴν Σικελικὴν ὀψοποιίαν συγγεγραφώς, ἢ Σάραμβος ὁ κάπηλος—νῦν γὰρ ἀνεμνήσθην τοὔνομα—ταῦτα συγγράψασθαι δοκεῖ; φέρε μοι δὴ παρὰ τοῦτο τὸ ψήφισμα τὰ τῶν σοφιστῶν, εἰ βούλει, συγγράμματα καὶ τοὺς νόμους, ὀνομαστὶ γὰρ οὐδὲν δέομαι λέγειν. οἶμαι δὲ οὐ πολλῶν ἂν αὐτὸ ἀτιμότερον φανῆναι.

251 καίτοι διακόνου μὲν ἦν καὶ τὴν ἐν τῷ παραχρῆμα χάριν διώκοντος, μάλιστα μὲν ἃ προσέταττον οἱ πολλοί, ταῦτα ὑπηρετεῖν· εἰ δὲ μή, στοχαζόμενον τῆς ἐκείνων διανοίας ἃ νομίζει καθ' ἡδονὴν αὐτοῖς ἔσεσθαι, ταῦτα καὶ λέγειν καὶ πράττειν, ἢ μικρὸν γοῦν τι παραλλάξαι τῆς ἐπιθυμίας. Θεμιστοκλῆς δὲ τοσοῦτον ἀφειστήκει τοῦ πρὸς τὴν τῶν πολλῶν ἐπιθυμίαν τε καὶ ἡδονὴν ταῦτα πράττειν καὶ πολιτεύεσθαι, ὥστε ὁρῶν μὲν αὐτοὺς δακρύοντας, ἀκούων δὲ παίδων καὶ γυναικῶν ποτνιωμένων, ἔτι δὲ ὑπολειπομένων τινῶν ἀναγκαίως, παραπλησίου δὲ μάλιστά πως ὄντος ὥσπερ ἂν εἰ ἑαλωκυίας τῆς πόλεως κατὰ κράτος, εἰκότως· τὸ μὲν γὰρ μέλλον ἅπασιν ἦν ἐν ἀφανεῖ, λεπτὴν καὶ ἄπιστον ἔχον τὴν ἐλπίδα, τὰ δὲ παρόντα στέρησις πόλεως καὶ κτημάτων καὶ διαίτης ἁπάσης τῆς πρότερον καὶ μηδὲ τὴν αὐτὴν πορεύεσθαι, μηδ' ἐν ταυτῷ μετοικεῖν, ἀλλ' ἀπεζεῦχθαι γονέας καὶ παῖδας καὶ γυναῖκας καὶ ἄνδρας, καὶ πάντα ἦν τὰ φρι-

downcast gaze kowtowing to his audience, but some god speaking with the tongue of Themistocles. Do you really think that it was Mithaecus, the author of the Sicilian cookbook, or Sarambus the grocer (his name comes back to me now)[194] who composed it? If you like, do please compare this decree with the treatises and indeed the laws authored by the experts (there is no need for me to mention them by name).[195] I do not think there are many of them it will look inferior to.

It would indeed have been the action of a lackey and 251
of someone aiming for the gratification of the moment, in the first instance to be subservient to the commands of the majority, or failing that to guess at their state of mind and say and do what he thought they would find pleasing, or at any rate only to diverge slightly from their desires. But Themistocles was so far from acting and framing his policies in the light of what the majority desired or enjoyed that when he saw them weeping and heard the piteous entreaties of the women and children, and indeed when some were of necessity being left behind and the situation was in its way very similar to what it would have been if the city had been taken by force (a reasonable comparison, because the future was completely unclear and offered room for only tenuous and untrustworthy hopes, while the present reality was the loss of their city and possessions and whole previous way of life and neither traveling the same road nor living in the same place, but being separated from parents and children and wives and husbands,

[194] *Grg.* 518b (cf. §127 above). [195] With the sneering "experts" (*sophistai*) Aristides means philosophers in general, and particularly Plato, not Sophists in Plato's sense.

κωδέστατα ἀκοῦσαι, μὴ ὅτι ὑπομεῖναι· οὗ γε καὶ τῶν κυνῶν φασι τῶν χειροήθων ὠρυομένων πρὸς τὴν ἀπόλειψιν καὶ τῶν ἄλλων θρεμμάτων ἐφεπομένων ἄχρι τῆς θαλάττης πολλὴν τὴν σύγχυσιν εἶναι· ταῦτα πάντα ὁρῶν καὶ ἀκούων ὁ πάντων[66] καρτερώτατος ἠνείχετο—ἃ ποῖος Ὀδυσσεὺς ἀδακρυτὶ τὴν γυναῖκα ὁρῶν ῥᾳδίως ἂν ἤνεγκεν;—καὶ παραλαβὼν αὐτοὺς ὥσπερ παῖδας ἐξῆγεν ἀτρεμιζούσῃ τῇ ψυχῇ καὶ τοῖς λογισμοῖς ἑστῶσιν, οὐ μόνον τοῖς ὀφθαλμοῖς, ὥσπερ εἰς πομπήν τινα αὐτοὺς ἐξάγων, ἢ κληρούχους, ἀλλ'
252 οὐκ ἄγων εἰς Σαλαμῖνα. οἱ δ' ἐπείθοντο, καὶ καταλιπόντες ἱερὰ καὶ τάφους καὶ γῆν εἰς ἕνα ἑώρων Θεμιστοκλέα, παίδων καὶ γονέων καὶ τῶν τῆς φύσεως ἀναγκαίων ἐκεῖνον προκρίναντες, καὶ ὥσπερ τῆς ἱερᾶς ἀγκύρας τῆς ἐκείνου φωνῆς ἐχόμενοι. οὐκ ἂν τότε γ' αὐτοὺς οὐδ' Ὀρφεὺς ὡς ἑαυτὸν μετέστησεν.

253 ἀλλὰ μὴν ἅ γ' ἐν τῇ Σαλαμῖνι καὶ λέγων καὶ πράττων διετέλεσεν ἐν ἅπασιν ἤδη τοῖς Ἕλλησιν πολιτευόμενος, καὶ ὅσας καὶ οἵας ἀφῆκεν φωνὰς ὑπὲρ τοῦ καλοῦ καὶ τοῦ δικαίου καὶ ὁπόσους τινὰς ἄθλους διήνεγκεν καὶ πράγμασιν οἵοις συνέσχετο, ὁπότε καὶ πείσειεν ἐξ ἀρχῆς, αὖθις αὖ περὶ τῶν αὐτῶν ἀγωνιζόμενος, καὶ τὴν συνουσίαν ἣν συνεγένετο Ἀριστείδῃ τῷ κατ' ἐπωνυμίαν ἀρίστῳ τῶν Ἑλλήνων καὶ δικαιοτάτῳ, καὶ ὡς ἐφάμιλλα ὡμίλησαν, καὶ οὐ πολὺ δὲ

66 πάντα Iunt.

and the whole situation was utterly terrifying even to hear about, let alone to have to undergo—they say that at this time great chaos was occasioned by the domestic dogs howling at their abandonment, and their other livestock following them down to the shore),[196] seeing and hearing all this, this most stalwart of men held firm—what Odysseus, who could look on his wife with dry eyes,[197] could have endured such sights?—and taking charge of them as if they were children led them out with unwavering soul and steady thoughts as well as steady gaze, as if he were taking them out for a religious procession or as colonists, rather than leading them to Salamis. They obeyed and, 252
leaving behind their holy places and tombs and land, looked to Themistocles alone, preferring him to children and parents and the ties of nature, and holding fast to his voice as if to the proverbial "holy anchor."[198] At that juncture, not even Orpheus could have induced them to transfer their allegiance to himself.

It would take for ever to describe what Themistocles 253
went on to say and do at Salamis, by this stage exercising his statesmanship among all the Greeks, and the nature of all the many speeches he made in support of virtue and justice, and all the trials he endured and all the trouble he became entangled in when persuading people all over again from the beginning and refighting the same battles once more, and to describe his encounter with Aristides, surnamed the best and most just of the Greeks, and how they conversed as evenly-matched rivals and he was not

196 Similar details are given in Plut. *Vit. Them.* 10.

197 *Od.* 19.209–12.

198 In modern terms, the sheet anchor, i.e., the last resource: cf. Lucian *Fugit.* 13, *Iupp. trag.* 51.

ὕστερος ἦν τοῖς ἀμοιβαίοις, καὶ τὸ πάταξον μὲν, ἄκουσον δὲ ὑπὲρ πάντα Σωκράτη[67] εἰρημένον πρὸς Εὐρυβιάδην καὶ μυρί' ἕτερα ἀπέραντον ἂν εἴη λέγειν.
254 ὡς δ' ἀντέλεγεν μὲν οὐδεὶς αὐτῷ, παραμένειν δὲ οὐκ ἐτόλμων, ἀλλ' ἐξεχέοντο ὑπὸ τοῦ δέους οἱ λόγοι καὶ ὁ δρασμὸς ἐνίκα καὶ πράγματα αἴσχιστα ἔμελλεν συμβήσεσθαι, καὶ οὐχ ὅσον τὸ τῆς δουλείας, ἀλλ' ἀποδρᾶναι πρῶτον, εἶτα δουλεύειν, καὶ πρότερον δούλους κακοὺς δόξαι τοῖς βαρβάροις ἢ δούλους γενέσθαι, τότε δή, τότε ὑπὲρ πάντας ἰατροὺς πρὸς ἀνάγκην καὶ πρὸς ἀηδίαν σῴζοντας ἐπάγει τοὺς βαρβάρους αὐτοῖς, ἀμφοτέρους ἐξαπατήσας, τοὺς μὲν ὡς κατ' εὔνοιαν καλῶν, τοὺς δ' ὡς οὐδὲν εἰδὼς τοῦ πράγματος· ὥσθ' ὅ γ' Ἀριστείδης χρηστὸς ἦν προσαγγέλλων αὐτῷ· καὶ λαβὼν αὐτοὺς καὶ τὸ τρίτον καταβαλὼν μέγιστον ἁπάντων, οἶμαι, πτωμάτων καὶ τελεώτατον, φυγάδα ἐκβάλλει Ξέρξην ἐξ ἐσχάτων
255 ὅρων τῆς Ἀττικῆς, καὶ προσέτι γε φεύγειν εἰπών. ὁ δ' ὥσπερ δεσπότῃ διακονῶν ἐχρῆτο ταῖς ἐντολαῖς, καὶ διώκειν τε κελεύοντι τοὺς Ἕλληνας ὑπήκουεν καὶ φεύγειν προστάττοντος ἐπείθετο, καὶ πρὸς ᾔδει χάριν· καὶ πρότερον διδοὺς αὐτὸς τοῖς ἄλλοις κατὰ τῶν Ἑλλήνων ἐντολάς, τότ' ἀκούειν ἠναγκάζετο τῶν Ἑλλήνων ἑνός, καὶ ταῦτα τοῦ πάντων ἐχθίστου καὶ πολεμιωτάτου. τοσοῦτον, ὡς ἔοικε, Θεμιστοκλεῖ περιῆν τοῦ διακονεῖν.

67 Σωκράτη Dindorf Σωκράτην *codd.*

far inferior to him in their exchanges,[199] and that "strike me, but hear me," outdoing any Socrates, that was his riposte to Eurybiades,[200] and countless other deeds. When 254
nobody argued against him, but they nevertheless lacked the courage to stand their ground, so that his words were wasted because of their fear, and flight became the favored course and the most shameful of outcomes was about to result—not simply slavery, but running away first and then being enslaved, and letting the barbarians think of them as bad slaves before they even became slaves—then it was that, in a manner excelling all doctors who use compulsion and unpleasant means to save their patients, he brought the barbarians on to them, by deceiving both sides,[201] pretending to the one that he was summoning them as a friend and to the other that he knew nothing of the business—so Aristides did good work in passing the news on to him—and seizing the enemy and throwing them in the third and I think the greatest and most comprehensive of their falls, he not only drove Xerxes as a fugitive from the furthest boundaries of Athens, but ordered him to flee into the bargain. Xerxes for his part followed his commands as 255
if playing lackey to a master, obeying him both when he ordered him to pursue the Greeks and when he told him to run away, and was grateful to him besides. Having formerly given orders himself to the others against the Greeks, he was then compelled to give ear to just one of the Greeks, and his bitterest enemy among them all at that. Such, it seems, was the benefit that Themistocles derived from his lackey's work.

199 Hdt. 8.79–80. 200 Cf. Plut. *Vit. Them.* 11; Hdt. 8.59; and (for the reference to Socrates) *Grg.* 486c, 526d–27a.

201 Hdt. 8.75–81.

256 οὐκοῦν ἐν μὲν οἷς ἀντὶ τῆς ἡσυχίας τὸν πόλεμον προῃρεῖτο, ἀνδρείας δεῖγμα ἐξέφερεν, ἐν οἷς δὲ ὑπὲρ τῶν Ἑλλήνων πρὸς τοὺς βαρβάρους πολεμεῖν ᾑρεῖτο, ἀλλὰ μὴ πρὸς τοὺς Ἕλληνας μετὰ τῶν βαρβάρων, ἅμα ἀνδρείας καὶ δικαιοσύνης, τοὺς μὲν ἐλάττους ἀντὶ τῶν πλειόνων καὶ μειζόνων, τοὺς δ' οἰκείους ἀντὶ
257 τῶν ἀλλοφύλων αἱρούμενος. καὶ μὴν τῷ μὲν εὑρίσκειν τὰ δέοντα καὶ προορᾶν καὶ μηδαμοῦ τῶν πραγμάτων ψευσθῆναι, ἀλλ' ἄμεινον τῶν μάντεων τὸ μέλλον προλέγειν, σοφίας εἰκότως δόξαν ἠνέγκατο· τῷ δὲ μηδὲν ὧν γνοίη διαφθείρειν ὑπὸ τῶν τοῦ σώματος ἡδονῶν, ἀλλ' ἀεὶ σχολάζοντα τοῖς βελτίστοις ἑαυτὸν παρέχειν καὶ[68] προσέχειν τοῖς λογισμοῖς τοῖς περὶ τῆς ἡγεμονίας, καὶ τῷ γε[69] κατασχεῖν τοὺς Ἀθηναίους περὶ τῆς ἡγεμονίας, καὶ πᾶσι τούτοις οὐκ ἔνι δήπου σωφρονεῖν, ὅστις μὴ τὰ πρῶτα ἐκείνῳ σωφροσύνης νέμει.
258 ἆρά τις ὑμῶν τῶν ἀκινδύνως φιλοσοφούντων τοσαύτην πίστιν δεδωκὼς ἀρετῆς, ἢ διὰ τοσούτων ἐλέγχων ἀφιγμένος εἰπεῖν ἔχει; ἡγοῦμαι δὲ καὶ πρὸς ἀμφοτέρους καὶ παρ' ἀμφοτέρους ἂν εἶναι Θεμιστοκλέα, τόν τε Μιλτιάδην καὶ τὸν Κίμωνα. πρῶτός τε γὰρ φαίνεται νικήσας τοὺς βαρβάρους κατὰ θάλατταν, ὥσπερ Μιλτιάδης κατ' ἤπειρον· ὥστ' εἰκότως ἂν ἄρξαι ταύτῃ τῆς ἐλευθερίας δοκοίη. καὶ τοῖς ὑπάρχουσιν αὖ προσθεὶς φαίνεται· τῇ γὰρ πεζομαχίᾳ τὰς ναυμαχίας προσέθηκε, καὶ τρία ἀνθ' ἑνὸς ἔστησε τρό-

68 *καὶ* <*τῷ*> Behr   69 *καὶ τῷ γε codd. ἀλλ' οὖν γε* Behr

So it was that in preferring war to peace he demon- 256
strated courage, and in choosing to fight for the Greeks against the barbarians, rather than with the barbarians against the Greeks, he demonstrated both courage and justice, by choosing the fewer in number in preference to the greater and more numerous, and his own people in
preference to foreigners. Moreover, by his ability to think 257
up what was needed and to exercise foresight and never to be wrong about events, but to predict the future better than the seers, he justifiably won a reputation for wisdom. And thanks to his never spoiling any of his plans under the influence of bodily pleasure, but showing himself always to have time for the call of virtue, and concentrating his attention on calculations over the leadership, and indeed thanks to his restraining of the Athenians over the leadership—thanks to all of this, it is assuredly not possible for anyone who refuses to grant him preeminence in self-
control to be himself of sound mind. Can any of you 258
armchair philosophers speak now with the authority of comparably weighty proof of your virtue, or having come through so many tests? I think that Themistocles would bear comparison with both of the two, Miltiades and Cimon, and would surpass them both. He is manifestly the first to have defeated the barbarians at sea, as Miltiades did on land, so that he could rightly be held to have laid the foundations for freedom by this means. It is also clear that he added more to the existing stock of achievements: he added the naval battles to the land battle and won three victories in place of one, just as Cimon achieved a second

259 παια, ὥσπερ Κίμων ἐπεξῆλθεν τὰ δεύτερα. καὶ μὴν οὔτ᾽ ἐπὶ τῆς αὐτῆς ἀδείας ἐφ᾽ ἧσπερ Κίμων ὄντας ἤδη τοὺς Ἕλληνας παρέλαβεν οὔτ᾽ ἐπὶ τῶν ἴσων φόβων ὥσπερ Μιλτιάδης, ἀλλ᾽ ἔσχατα ἐσχάτων πράττοντας καὶ πρῶτα καὶ τελευταῖα κινδυνεύοντας· συνελόντι δὲ εἰπεῖν, βασιλέα γ᾽ αὐτὸν πανοικησίᾳ καὶ πρῶτος νικήσας[70] καὶ μόνος, οὐχ ὥσπερ τοὺς ὑπάρχους Μιλτιάδης πρῶτον Μαραθῶνι καὶ Παυσανίας ὕστερον Πλαταιᾶσι· <ὥστε>[71] μάχης παράδειγμά τις ἂν λέγοι τὴν Μαραθῶνι καὶ τῷ χρόνῳ πρεσβεύοι, τὰς δὲ Θεμιστοκλέους πράξεις αὐτὰς ἐφ᾽ αὑτῶν λογίζοιτο, ὡς τοῖς μὲν χρόνοις ὕστερον πραχθείσας [τῆς μάχης τῆς Μαραθῶνι],[72] τὴν δ᾽ ἀρχὴν οἴκοθεν ἐσχηκυίας ἀπὸ τῆς ἐκείνου συνέσεως καὶ πολιτείας. οὐδὲν γὰρ πρότερον παραπλήσιον τοῖς Ἕλλησι μὴ ὅτι ἐπέπρακτο,
260 ἀλλ᾽ οὐδὲ ἤλπιστο. οὕτω καὶ τὸν Μιλτιάδην καὶ τὸν Παυσανίαν καὶ τὸν Κίμωνα παρέρχεται· καὶ γίγνεται τριῶν ἀντάξιος, οὐκ ἀρτοποιοῦ καὶ μαγείρου καὶ καπήλου, ἀλλ᾽ ἀνδρῶν γενομένων τι τοῖς Ἕλλησιν. μόνος δέ τοι καὶ τὸ πεζὸν καὶ τὸ ναυτικὸν ὀρθῷ λόγῳ νενικηκὼς φαίνεται. οὔτε γὰρ αἱ νῆες ἀντέσχον καὶ βασιλεὺς ἅμα τοῖς πλείστοις φεύγων ᾤχετο.

261 καὶ ὅσῳπερ ἄν τις σεμνύνῃ τὴν ἐν Πλαταιαῖς ὕστερον νίκην, τοσούτῳ μειζόνως τὴν ἐκείνου τοῦ ἀνδρὸς σύνεσίν τε καὶ πρόνοιαν κοσμεῖ. εἰ γὰρ πολλοστημόριον τῆς κατὰ γῆν δυνάμεως ὑπολειφθὲν παρέσχεν ὅμως θόρυβον τοῖς Ἕλλησιν, καὶ ταῦτ᾽ ἤδη παρα-

success on top of his first. Moreover, the Greeks when he took over responsibility for them were not in the same state of security as they had been when Cimon inherited them, nor the same state of fear as with Miltiades, but in the direst of dire straits and with everything from first to last at risk. To sum it all up, he was manifestly the first and the only one to defeat the King of Persia himself with all his entourage, unlike Miltiades first and then subsequently Pausanias, who defeated his underlings at Marathon and Plataea respectively, so that though one might speak of the victory at Marathon as an exemplary battle and allow that it came first, one would still consider Themistocles' achievements in a category of their own, as having had their origin in his own native intelligence and policies, even if subsequent in time. Nothing similar had so much as been hoped for by the Greeks, let alone accomplished. 259

That is the measure of how far he surpasses Miltiades and 260
Pausanias and Cimon, and makes himself equal in worth to three—not a baker, a butcher, and grocer, but men who really meant something to the Greeks. He is also manifestly the only one who in the true sense of the term defeated both the land army and the fleet, in that the ships could not withstand him and the King took to his heels and fled with most of his army.

And the more one builds up the subsequent victory at 261
Plataea, the more highly one honors this man's intelligence and foresight. Because if even a small proportion of the land force left behind still caused the Greeks consterna-

[70] *fort.* φαίνεται νικήσας ("νικήσας *non habet verbum*" Reiske) [71] ὥστε Trapp γε μήν *post* μάχης Reiske
[72] *del.* Trapp

δειγμάτων αὐτοῖς καὶ κατὰ γῆν καὶ κατὰ θάλατταν ἑστηκότων, ὅσῳ κρείττοσιν εἶναι προσήκει τῶν βαρβάρων, καὶ προσέτι ὑπάρχου βασιλέως, ἀλλ' οὐκ αὐτοῦ βασιλέως ἐμμείναντος, ᾗ που τὸν πυρφόρον οὐδ' ἂν εἷς ἔγνω <περιγενησόμενον>,[73] πρὸς ἅπαντας μὲν ἀγωνιζομένων, ἀλλ' οὐ μέρος, βασιλέως δ' ἐφεστῶτος τοῖς πράγμασιν, οὐδενὸς δὲ ὥς γ' ἐν τοῖς παροῦσιν ὅτῳ θαρρήσουσιν ὑπάρχοντος, κακῶν δ' ἀπαθοῦς καὶ μετ' ἐλπίδων ἀκραιφνῶν ἐπιόντος τοῦ στρατοῦ, καὶ τῷ περὶ τὰς Πύλας ἔργῳ προεπηρμένου, καὶ μόνον οὐκ ἐν τοῖς ὀφθαλμοῖς ἔχοντος ὅτι καὶ τούτους πάντας αὐτίκα δὴ κεῖσθαι δεήσει.

262 ἀλλὰ ταῦτα πάντα ἡ Θεμιστοκλέους, ὥς φησιν Πλάτων, διακονία καὶ κολακεία, ὡς δ' ἡ κοινὴ ψῆφος τῶν Ἑλλήνων, σοφία καὶ πρόνοια διεκώλυσεν καὶ τάξιν πᾶσι τοῖς ἔργοις ἐπέθηκεν. ὥστ' οὐ μόνον ἐξ ὧν αὐτὸς ἡγούμενος κατώρθωσεν, ἀλλὰ καὶ ἐξ ὧν τοῖς ὕστερον αἴτιος τοῦ κατορθῶσαι τὰ ἐφ' αὐτοὺς ἥκοντα ἐγένετο, οἷον τῷ Παυσανίᾳ, τῷ Κίμωνι, τοῖς ἄλλοις, δικαίως ἂν τῆς παρὰ πάντων εὐφημίας τυγχάνοι. ἦ κομιδῇ γ' ἄν, ὦ Πλάτων, ἀδικοῖμεν, εἰ τὸν ἔργων φιλανθρώπων οὕτως εἰς τοὺς Ἕλληνας ὑπάρξαντα μηδὲ
263 ῥήματος τῶν ἐπιεικῶν τολμήσομεν ἀξιῶσαι. ἐμοὶ μὲν οὖν οὐδὲν φαυλότερος οὐδ' ἀτιμότερος δοκεῖ Θεμιστοκλῆς γενέσθαι στρατηγῶν Ἀθηναίων ἢ Σωκράτης

[73] περιγενησόμενον Behr (*sed post* πυρφόρον) σωθησόμενον *hic* Reiske

tion, even when they had established examples both on land and at sea to show them how superior to the barbarians they ought to be, and if besides it was a subordinate of the King and not the King himself who had stayed behind, then for sure no one at all would have been confident of the fire-bearer's survival if they had been fighting against the whole force and not just part of it,[202] and the King himself had been in charge of operations, and there was nothing in the circumstances that they could draw any confidence from, and the Persian army was advancing intact and with undamaged hopes, elated in advance by what they had achieved at Thermopylae and all but picturing to themselves the inevitability of all these men too soon lying dead before them.

It was all this that was prevented by what Plato calls Themistocles' lackey work and flattery, but the consensus of the Greeks calls his wisdom and foresight, as he brought good order to all their activities. It is therefore not only on the strength of his own successes as leader, but also on the strength of his responsibility for the achievements of his successors (such as Pausanias, Cimon, and the rest) in what fell to them, that he would rightly win the praise of all. We would be doing a complete injustice, Plato, if we could not bring ourselves to think the man who thus led the way in generous action toward the Greeks worthy of even a single seemly word. In my eyes, Themistocles leading the Athenians as general cut no meaner or less valu- 262 263

[202] A reference to Hdt. 8.6.2, where it is recorded that the advancing Persians were determined that "not even the fire bearer (to use their term) should survive," i.e., determined on the complete annihilation of the Greek army.

συστρατευόμενος ἐπὶ Δηλίῳ καὶ ἐν Ἀμφιπόλει καὶ ἐν Ποτειδαίᾳ. καίτοι σύ γ' ἐκεῖνον ἐπαινεῖς, ὅτι ἐν τῇ ἀπὸ Δηλίου φυγῇ θαρρούντως ἀπῄει, καὶ καταφανὴς ὢν ὅτι, εἴ τις ἅψοιτο αὐτοῦ, εὖ καὶ καλῶς ἀμυνεῖται.
264 οὔκουν δεινὸν ὦ γῆ καὶ θεοὶ καὶ λόγων καὶ ἔργων ἡγεμόνες, ἐξάγομαι γὰρ εἰπεῖν, Σωκράτη μὲν καὶ τῆς φυγῆς ἐπαινεῖν καὶ φάσκειν ἐκεῖνον ἀναχωρεῖν κάλλιον Λάχητος, Θεμιστοκλέα δέ, ὃς διώκων, οὐ φεύγων τοὺς πολεμίους τὴν ἀνδρείαν ἐπεδείκνυτο, καὶ οὗ τῆς ἀρετῆς ἅπασα ἀπέλαυσεν ἡ Ἑλλάς, ἃ τῆς δειλίας καὶ τῆς ἀνανδρείας ἔστ' ὀνόματα, τούτοις καλοῦντα μὴ φροντίζειν; ὃς καὶ ὅτ' ἀπ' Εὐβοίας ἀνεχώρει νενικηκώς, τοιαῦτα τἀν μέσῳ διεπράττετο, οἷα ἂν οὐδείς πω τῶν ἐπειγομένων ὁπωσοῦν ἀπελθεῖν.

265 εἶτα λέγεις ὡς οὐ πολλοῦ τινος ἄξιον ἡ σωτηρία. τί οὖν κωλύει καὶ τοῖς σωτῆρσι θεοῖς, οἳ καὶ καθ' ἕνα ἡμᾶς σῴζουσιν, καὶ τότ' ἐκεῖνα κατεργάσασθαι τοῖς Ἕλλησι παρέσχον—; ἀλλ' ἐγὼ μὲν ἐάσω τὸ βλάσφημον, ὑπονοεῖν δ' ἔστιν τό γ' ἐκ τοῦ λόγου συμβαῖνον. ἐγὼ δ' ἐκεῖνον ἂν ᾤμην ἀμείνω καὶ δικαιότερον τὸν λόγον εἶναι, κἀκείνως λέγοντά τινα οὐκ ἂν ἁμαρτάνειν ὡς θεοὶ μὲν τῷ ὄντι σωτῆρες καὶ τὴν Ἑλλάδα οἱ τότε σώσαντές εἰσιν οὗτοι, διηκόνησαν δὲ Μιλτιάδης καὶ Θεμιστοκλῆς, ἥπερ μεγίστη καὶ καλλίστη δύναμις ἀνθρώπου, διακονῆσαι τοῖς κρείττο-

able a figure than Socrates did fighting in the ranks at Delium and Amphipolis and Potidaea.[203] Yet it is the latter that you praise, because in the retreat from Delium he retreated confidently, making it abundantly clear that if anyone laid hands on him he would well and truly defend himself.[204] Is it not then monstrous, O Earth and you gods 264
who direct both words and deeds, I am moved to say, to praise Socrates even for running away and to maintain that he retreated more nobly than Laches, but although Themistocles showed his courage by pursuing the enemy rather than running away from them and the whole of Greece benefited from his heroism, not to feel concerned about calling him by all possible names for cowardice and unmanliness? Moreover, when he was withdrawing victorious from Euboea, he accomplished such things in the process as have never yet been done by people hastening to get away by any means available.

Then you say that mere salvation is not worth anything 265
very much.[205] What then is to prevent even the saving gods, who preserve each one of us individually and who enabled the Greeks to achieve what they did at that time, from . . .—but I pass over the blasphemous suggestion, although one can surmise where this line of thought leads. I would have thought it to be a better and fairer line of thought, and anyone maintaining it not to be in error, that these gods, saviors in very truth, are the ones who also saved Greece on that occasion, and that Miltiades and Themistocles worked as their lackeys, exercising that greatest and finest of human capacities, servitude to the

[203] *Ap.* 28e, *Symp.* 219e–21d. [204] *Symp.* 220e–21b.
[205] *Grg.* 511b–13a.

266 σιν. τοῦτ᾽ οὖν, ὦ θεία κεφαλή, προσήκει λέγειν, κἀγὼ φαίην ἂν ἐκείνους γενέσθαι τοὺς ἄνδρας ὑπηρέτας καὶ διακόνους, οὐ τοῦ δήμου τῶν Ἀθηναίων—πόθεν;—οὐδ᾽ ἀνθρώπων οὐδενός, εἰ μὴ τὸ προεστάναι καὶ τὸ
267 κελεύειν διακονεῖν καὶ ὑπηρετεῖν εἶναι δεῖ λέγειν. ἔτι τοίνυν οὐδὲ τοῖς γονεῦσι χάριν ἄν τις ἔχειν ἐῴη τοῖς λόγοις τούτοις, οὐδ᾽ εἰς εὐεργεσίας τιθέναι μέρος, οἳ τοῦ ζῆν καὶ σῴζεσθαι παρέσχον ἡμῖν τὰς ἀρχάς. εἰ δὲ δὴ καὶ τὸν Εὐριπίδην μάρτυρα ἐπάγοιτο λέγοντα ὅτι

ἔδει γὰρ ἡμᾶς σύλλογον ποιουμένους
τὸν φύντα θρηνεῖν εἰς ὅσ᾽ ἔρχεται κακά,

268 ἦ που σφόδρα ἄν τι δόξειεν λέγειν. ἀλλ᾽ οἶμαι τῶν μὲν πραγμάτων οἷς ἐντυγχάνομεν καὶ τοῦ χεῖρον ἢ βέλτιον βιῶναι τὸν δαίμονα καὶ τὴν τύχην αἰτιώμεθα, καὶ νὴ Δί᾽, εἰ βούλει, προστίθει τὸ καὶ ἡμᾶς αὐτοὺς δεῖν, οὐδὲν γὰρ βλάβος τῷ λόγῳ, τοῖς δ᾽ ὑπηρετήσασιν εἰς τὴν γένεσιν καὶ δι᾽ ὧν πρῶτον ἤλθομεν εἰς φῶς, τούτοις τὴν πρώτην καὶ μεγίστην χάριν ἡγούμεθα δεῖν ἔχειν μετὰ τοὺς ἔτι τούτων προτέρους θεούς.

269 εἰ τοίνυν τοῖς γονεῦσι δι᾽ αὐτὸ τὸ εἶναι μόνον τοσαύτην ἔχομεν χάριν καὶ ὁμολογοῦμεν ὀφείλειν χρέα πάντων χρεῶν πρεσβύτατα, πῶς οὐ Μιλτιάδῃ γε καὶ

---

[206] Another echo of *Phdr.* 234d. [207] Fr. 449 *TrGF*, a widely quoted passage from the *Cresphontes*.
[208] *Leg.* 717b.

Higher Powers. That then is what it is appropriate to say, 266
you fount of inspiration:[206] I too would assert that these men were servants and lackeys, just not of the Athenian people—how could this have been?—nor of any human master, unless we are to say that to lead and to give orders
is to be a lackey and a servant. On your line of argument, 267
moreover, someone could forbid us to be grateful to our parents, or to count them as our benefactors, even though they furnished us with the origins of our life and preservation, and if he were to summon Euripides as a witness, with his lines

> We should have gathered ourselves together in assembly
> and lamented the newborn for the ills he is entering onto,[207]

he would certainly give the impression of talking good
sense. But in fact I think that, whereas we blame divinity 268
and chance for the fortunes we encounter and for our having a worse or a better life to live (and indeed if you like, because it will do no damage to the argument, by all means add that we should blame ourselves for this too), we believe that we should give our first and greatest thanks—after the gods who take precedence even over them—to those people who served to bring about our birth and through whom we first saw the light of day.

If therefore we are so grateful to our parents simply for 269
our existence and confess that we owe them debts that go back before all others,[208] how can we not be obliged to think that something beneficial was done by Miltiades and

Θεμιστοκλεῖ πλέον τι πεπρᾶχθαι χρὴ δοκεῖν, οἵτινες
οὐ τοῦ ζῆν μόνον οὐδὲ τῆς σωτηρίας αἴτιοι τοῖς Ἕλλησι κατέστησαν, ἀλλὰ καὶ βελτίους ἀντὶ χειρόνων
270 ἐν αὐτοῖς οἷς ἔπραττον εἴθιζον εἶναι; ἄτοπον δέ μοι
φαίνεται, εἰ μὲν συμμάχους τινὰς ἢ φρούριον προὔ-
δοσαν, ἢ ναῦν μίαν ἢ δύο, ἢ φυγῆς αἴτιοί τισιν
ἢ θανάτου κατέστησαν, πολλοῖς ἂν καὶ πυκνοῖς
ἐλαύνειν αὐτοὺς τοῖς ῥήμασιν καὶ μετ᾽ Εὐρυβάτου
καὶ Φρυνώνδου καταλέγειν, ὥσπερ τὸν Ἀρχέλαον
κακοδαίμονα δήπου καὶ ἄθλιον προσείρηκεν, ἀποκτείναντα οὓς οὐ προσῆκεν, ἐπεὶ δ᾽ ἅπαντας μὲν ἠλευ-
θέρωσαν καὶ κατὰ γῆν καὶ κατὰ θάλατταν προκιν-
δυνεύοντες, ἔσωσαν δὲ οὐ μόνον τὰ σώματα καὶ τὰς
ψυχὰς τῶν ἑαυτοὺς παρακαταθεμένων, ἀλλὰ καὶ
πόλεις καὶ χώραν καὶ πολιτείαν καὶ ἔθη καὶ νόμους
καὶ τὴν ἐπωνυμίαν αὐτὴν τοῦ γένους, ἀνδρείας δὲ καὶ
δικαιοσύνης οὐδ᾽ ὁτιοῦν ἀπέλιπον, μείζω δὲ ἢ παρέλα-
βον παρέδοσαν τὴν Ἑλλάδα, τοῖς δὲ θεοῖς πρέποντα
χαριστήρια τούτων ἀνήγαγον,[74] διεγένοντο δ᾽ ‹ὡς›[75]
εἰπεῖν πανηγυρίζοντες καὶ ταῖς πράξεσι καὶ τοῖς πο-
λιτεύμασιν καὶ φανερὰν ἅπασι τὴν ἑαυτῶν ἀρετήν, ἣν
εἴς τε θεοὺς καὶ ἀνθρώπους εἶχον, κατέστησαν, τῆς
Μιθαίκου καὶ Θεαρίωνος μοίρας αὐτοὺς ἀξιοῦν εἶναι·
καὶ τοὺς μὲν ἰατροὺς τῶν μαγείρων φάσκειν εἶναι
βελτίους ὅτι σῴζουσι, τοὺς δὲ τῆς σωτηρίας τῶν Ἑλλήνων προστάντας μὴ τοῖς ἰατροῖς ἀπεικάζειν, ἀλλὰ

[74] ἀνήγαγον Abresch ἀπήγαγον *codd.* [75] *add.* Iunt.

Themistocles, who were not only responsible for the
Greeks' continued existence and preservation, but also in
the very course of their actions trained them to be better
rather than worse people. It seems bizarre to me that, if 270
they had betrayed some of their allies or a fortified position, or a ship or two, or had been responsible for some
people's exile or death, Plato would have pursued them
with a thick hail of names and categorized them with Eurybates and Phrynondas,[209] just as he called Archelaus ill-
starred and wretched because he killed people he should
not have killed,[210] but when they actually freed all by putting themselves at risk on land and sea on their behalf, and
saved not only the bodies and souls of those who had entrusted themselves to them, but also their cities and territory and constitutions and customs and laws and the very
name of the Greek nation, and left no proof of bravery and
justice ungiven, and handed Greece on mightier than they
had inherited her, and rendered the gods fitting thanks for
this, and as one might say celebrated a continual festival
with their deeds and their administration of affairs, and
made clear to all the virtue that they exercised in their
dealings with both gods and men, Plato said that they
deserved to belong to the same category as Mithaecus and
Thearion.[211] It is similarly bizarre that he should say that
doctors are better than butchers because they save lives,[212]
but should compare the champions of Greek freedom not

[209] *Prt.* 327d.
[210] *Grg.* 470d–71d, 479d–e.
[211] *Grg.* 517b–18b.
[212] *Grg.* 464b–e.

271 τοῖς ὀψοποιοῖς. καὶ μὴν εἰ μηδὲν βελτίους ἐποίουν, ἔσῳζον δέ, ἰατρῶν ἓν τοῦτό γ' ἐποίουν, οὐκ ὀψοποιῶν. ὥστε τῶν γ' ἰατρῶν οὐδὲν ἦσαν χείρους.

272 πῶς οὖν οὐδενὸς ἦσαν ἄξιοι τοῖς Ἕλλησιν; οὐκ ἂν ταῦτα συγχωρήσειεν Πλάτων αὐτὸς αὑτῷ. ἑτέρωθι γοῦν, οὗ μηδεμία ἐστὶν φιλονικία, λέγει ταυτί·—λέγει δὲ ὑπὲρ Σικελιωτῶν ἀνδρῶν, ἀρχήν τινα πράττων αὐτοῖς βασιλικήν, ὡς ἂν δὴ Δίων αὐτὸς ὤν—

> ὧν οἱ πρόγονοι—φησίν—τό γε μέγιστον ἔσωσαν ἀπὸ βαρβάρων τοὺς Ἕλληνας, ὥστ' ἐξεῖναι περὶ πολιτείας νῦν ποιεῖσθαι λόγους· ἔρρουσιν δὲ τότε οὔτε λόγος οὔτ' ἐλπὶς ἐλείπετο ἂν οὐδαμῇ οὐδαμῶς.

273 οὐκοῦν ἐν τούτοις ἐπαινεῖ τοὺς τῆς σωτηρίας αἰτίους τοῖς Ἕλλησι καταστάντας, καὶ χάριτάς γέ φησι δεῖν ἐκτίνειν αὐτοῖς, καὶ ταύτας οὐ φαύλας, ἀλλ' οἵας οὐδ' ἂν αὐτὸς ἄν τις ῥᾳδίως αἰτήσειεν, καὶ πρὸς τὸν δυσχεραίνοντά φησιν ὅτι τὸ μέγιστον ἔσωσαν οἱ πρόγο-
274 νοι[76] ἀπὸ βαρβάρων τοὺς Ἕλληνας. οὐκοῦν ἢ 'κεῖν' ἀπαλείφειν προσῆκεν, ἢ ταῦθ' ὑπ' ἐκείνων ἐξελήλεγκται. οὐ γὰρ ἐκεῖνό γ' ἔστιν εἰπεῖν ὡς τοῖς μὲν τοὺς ἐν Σικελίᾳ σεσωκόσι τῶν Ἑλλήνων χάριτας καὶ

[76] οἱ πρόγονοι TQ²M² *om. cett. fort. delenda*

to doctors but to caterers: even if they did not make them 271
any better people, but did save their lives, in that one respect at least they were acting like doctors not caterers, and so were at least no worse than doctors.

How then could they have been worthless in the eyes 272
of the Greeks? Plato would not even agree with himself about this. At any rate, in another place, where he is not straining to win an argument, he has this to say, when speaking in support of some Sicilians and, in the persona of Dion, negotiating a monarchical form of rule for them:

> It was your ancestors—he says—who performed the supreme feat of saving the Greeks from the barbarians, which is what allows us now to discuss forms of political organization; if they had failed then no scope for discussion and no hope at all would now remain.[213]

In these words, therefore, he praises those who were re- 273
sponsible for the preservation of Greece and says that they should be given no mean thanks, indeed such thanks as no one would find it easy to request even for himself, and his reply to anyone who bridles at this is that "your ancestors performed the supreme feat of saving the Greeks from the
barbarians."[214] Either then his first proposition ought to 274
have been expunged, or his second is refuted by it. Because it is at all events not possible to say that the men who saved the Greeks of Sicily are properly owed thanks and

213 *Ep.* 7.355d.

214 The repetition of "your ancestors" here is slightly awkward and may be due to a reader's clarification; if it is removed, Aristides says "his reply . . . is that they performed the supreme feat . . ."

δωρεὰς εἰκὸς ὑπάρχειν, τοῖς δ' ἅπασαν μὲν τὴν ἀρχαίαν Ἑλλάδα, [καὶ][77] τῆς δ' αὐτῆς ὁδοῦ τῆς πολιτείας καὶ Σικελίαν καὶ Ἰταλίαν καὶ τοὺς ὅπου δὴ γῆς καὶ θαλάττης Ἕλληνας, τούτοις οὐδὲ λόγου δεῖ μετεῖναι φιλανθρώπου, οὐδ' ὡς χρηστοί γ' ἦσαν ἀκούειν ὑπάρχειν.

275 καὶ μὴν αὐτός γε σὺ φῂς οὐ τῶν ἐν Κυρήνῃ μᾶλλον ἢ τῶν Ἀθήνησι κήδεσθαι. εἶτα σὺ τοῖς ἐκγόνοις αὐτῶν ἐφεὶς λέγειν περὶ δωρεῶν, αὐτοὺς κακῶς λέγειν ἠξίωσας, καὶ ἅμα μὲν τοὺς τυράννους ἐλέγχεις, ἅμα δὲ τοὺς τῆς ἐλευθερίας αἰτίους τοῖς Ἕλλησιν ψέγεις. κἀνταῦθα ὁ κολοφὼν τοῦ λόγου, ὡς οὐδ' ἡ ἐλευθερία πάνυ τι σεμνόν, ἀλλὰ καὶ πολλοῖς ἄμεινον ἀκούειν

276 ἑτέρων ἢ ἐλευθέροις εἶναι. καλῶς. ἆρ' οὖν καὶ τότε τοῖς Ἀθηναίοις ἄμεινον ἦν ἀκοῦσαι; καὶ μὴν οὐ πόρρωθεν, ἀλλ' ἐξ αὐτῶν ὧν ἔπραττον ἄξιοι τῆς ἐλευθερίας ὄντες ἐδείκνυσαν. ἔτι δ' οὐ Διοσκούροις, οὐδὲ Θησεῖ τῷ Ποσειδῶνος, οὐδ' Ἡρακλεῖ τῷ κοινῷ πάντων προστάτῃ, οὐδὲ τοῖς ἀρίστοις καὶ δικαιοτάτοις τῶν ἡμιθέων ὑπακοῦσαι κίνδυνος ἦν, ἀλλ' ἀνθρώποις ὕβρεων καὶ κακῶν μεστοῖς, ὑφ' ὧν ἀγαθὸν μὲν οὐδ' ὁτιοῦν ἔμελλον δήπου μαθήσεσθαι, πάντα δὲ πείσεσθαι τὰ αἴσχιστα καὶ δεινότατα. ὥστε πῶς οὐκ ἂν αἴσχιστα πραγμάτων συνέβη, εἰ πρότερον τοὺς

[77] *del.* Lenz

rewards, while those who saved the whole of old Greece, and, in the course of pursuing the same objectives, Sicily and Italy too and the Greeks in general wherever they lived on land or sea, should not benefit from so much as a kind word nor have the possibility of hearing it said of them that they were good men.

You yourself, Plato, say that you are less concerned 275
about things in Cyrene than about things in Athens.[215] Yet, while permitting their descendants to talk about benefits bestowed, you then saw fit to speak ill of these men themselves, and you simultaneously condemn tyrants and castigate the authors of Greek freedom. And then comes the finishing touch to your argument, in the form of the statement that freedom itself is nothing very imposing, and that there are many for whom it is better to be subservient to
others rather than free. Bravo! Let me ask you then, are 276
the Athenians of that time included among those for whom it was better to be subservient to others? No, they proved themselves worthy of freedom at first hand, by their own deeds! What is more, the danger they were in was not of having to obey the Dioscuri, or Theseus the son of Poseidon, or Heracles the shared champion of all alike, or the best and most just of the demigods, but rather men replete with violence and villainy, by whom they were certainly not going to be taught anything good, and would be subjected to all possible degradation and outrage. So how could it not have turned out an utter disgrace if on

215 *Tht.* 143d. Aristides' characteristically labored point is that for Plato to allow Sicilians to praise fifth-century Athenian heroes while himself, though an Athenian, condemning them, is inconsistent with this declaration that he put into Socrates' mouth.

Ἡρακλείδας εἰς ἐλευθερίαν ἀφαιρούμενοι τότ' αὐτοὶ
277 τοῖς βαρβάροις ὑπέκυψαν ἐν φαύλῳ θέμενοι; ἀλλὰ
μὴν εἰ μήτ' αὐτοὶ δουλεύειν ἄξιοι μήθ' οἱ ἐπιόντες
βελτίους ἐκείνων, ὅ τε κίνδυνος περὶ τῶν ἐσχάτων
κρατηθεῖσιν, πῶς οὐκ ἐνταῦθα εἴπερ που καιρὸς ἦν
δεῖξαι δουλείαν θανάτου μᾶλλον πεφοβημένους; ἐπι-
θήσω γὰρ τὰ Πλάτωνος αὐτοῦ ῥήματα. εἰ δὲ τοῦτο
παντὶ γνώριμον καὶ πάσῃ, <ὅτι>[78] ταῦτ' ἦν ἄριστα καὶ
σπουδαιότατα καὶ μόνα τοῦ λόγου τοῦ βελτίονος καὶ
τῆς πολιτικῆς ἀρετῆς, εἰ δεῖ τἀληθὲς εἰπεῖν, ἐπ' ἔσχατον ἥκοντα, πῶς τούς γε εἰς ταῦτα παρασχόντας ἑαυτοὺς καὶ βεβαιώσαντας ἅπασι μετὰ τῆς σωτηρίας
τὴν ἐλευθερίαν ὀλίγου τινὸς ἀξίους ἢ τοῖς πολίταις ἢ
τοῖς Ἕλλησι νομιστέον;

278 καὶ μὴν οὐδ' ἀνειμένην γε τὴν ἐλευθερίαν ἐποίησαν
αὑτοῖς· οἵ γε πρὸς μὲν τοὺς βαρβάρους οὕτως εἶχον
ὥστε μηδὲ φωνὴν ἐθέλειν ἀκούειν, πρὸς δὲ τοὺς Ἕλληνας οὕτω κοινῶς καὶ φιλανθρώπως ὥσθ' εἶξαν τῆς
ἡγεμονίας ἑκόντες Λακεδαιμονίοις, προέχοντες πλεῖστον ὁπόσον αὐτῶν. καὶ γάρ τοι παρ' ἑκόντων πάλιν
279 αὐτὴν τῶν Ἑλλήνων ἐκομίσαντο. οὕτως οὐκ ἄνευ δικαιοσύνης οὐδὲ σωφροσύνης, ὦ Πλάτων, ἐνέπλησαν
τὴν πόλιν συμμάχων καὶ φόρων καὶ φλυαριῶν, ὡς σὺ
φῄς, ἀλλ' ἀπὸ σώφρονος καὶ δικαίας καὶ θαυμαστῆς
ἀρξάμενοι τῆς ἀρχῆς, καὶ τοὺς τῆς ἐλευθερίας ὅρους
κάλλιστα ἐφύλαξαν, μέσην αὐθαδείας καὶ ταπεινότη-

[78] πάσῃ ὅτι Reiske πᾶσι *codd.*

this occasion, having in earlier times liberated the children
of Heracles, they had bowed to the barbarian yoke and
thought nothing of it? Indeed, if they themselves did not 277
deserve to be slaves, and those attacking them were not
better men than they were, and defeat would have placed
them in the ultimate danger, how can this time if any not
have been the right one to show that they were (to invoke
Plato's own words)[216] more afraid of servitude than of
death? But if it is well known to every man and woman
that theirs were the best and most virtuous of actions and,
if the truth be told, the only ones to reach the summit of
enlightened principle and political virtue, how are those
who presented themselves for this task and secured the
freedom and salvation of all to be deemed to be people of
little value to their fellow citizens or to the Greek nation?

It was moreover no degenerate freedom that they se- 278
cured for them, given that they were so disposed toward
the barbarians as not to be willing even to hear their
voices, and so public spirited and generous toward the
Greeks that they willingly surrendered the leadership to
the Spartans, even though they were enormously superior
to them. And what is more the Greeks willingly returned
it to them again. So true is it, Plato, that they did not as 279
you allege sate the city on allies and tribute and trifles
without regard for justice and self-control,[217] but based
themselves on a foundation of remarkable self-control and
justice, and guarded the frontiers of freedom most splendidly, keeping their fellow citizens on a course midway
between arrogance and humility, and ushering in not an

[216] *Resp*. 387b.
[217] *Grg*. 519a.

τος ἄγοντες τοὺς πολίτας, καὶ οὐ τὴν ἀνέδην, οὐδὲ ἣν οὑτωσί τις ἂν φήσειεν ἐλευθερίαν εἰσάγοντες, ἀλλὰ τὴν μετὰ τοῦ δικαίου καὶ τοῦ σωφρονεῖν.

280 καὶ μὴν ὅτι γε οὐκ ἄτιμον οὐδὲ τοῦ τυχόντος ἀνδρὸς ἐλευθερῶσαι πατρίδα, μὴ ὅτι γε τὴν Ἑλλάδα, αὐτὸς Πλάτων, εἰ δὲ βούλει Δίων, ὑπάρχει μάρτυς, ἐπεὶ καὶ ταῦτα τῆς ἐκείνου ῥήσεως

> ἐπὶ δὲ τούτοις ξύμπασιν ἀδόλῳ γνώμῃ καὶ ὑγιεῖ μετὰ τῶν θεῶν βασιλέα στήσασθε πρῶτον μὲν τὸν ἐμὸν υἱὸν χαρίτων ἕνεκα διττῶν, τῆς τε παρ' ἐμοῦ καὶ τῆς παρὰ τοῦ ἐμοῦ πατρός. ὁ μὲν γὰρ ἀπὸ βαρβάρων ἠλευθέρωσεν ἐν τῷ τότε χρόνῳ τὴν πόλιν, ἐγὼ δὲ ἀπὸ τυράννων νῦν δίς, ὧν αὐτοὶ μάρτυρες ὑμεῖς γεγόνατε.

281 ἆρα ὀλίγου τινὸς ἢ φαύλου τίθησι λόγου[79] Πλάτων ἐλευθέραν ποιῆσαι πόλιν, ἢ μέλλουσαν ἄλλων ἔσεσθαι κωλῦσαι; ὅτε τοίνυν καὶ βασιλείαν ἄξιον ἀντὶ τούτου διδόναι, καὶ ταῦτά γε τοῖς ἐκγόνοις, καὶ μικροῦ τῆς ἐλευθερίας αὐτοῖς παραχωρῆσαι, διότι αὐτῶν οἱ πρόγονοι τὴν ἐλευθερίαν ἐφύλαξαν, ἦ που τούς γε αὐτοὺς ἐλευθερώσαντας οὐ μόνον τοὺς πολίτας, ἀλλὰ καὶ σύμπαν τὸ τῶν Ἑλλήνων γένος ἕν τι τῶν δεινοτάτων, μηδ' αὐτοῦ τοῦ δοκεῖν ἐλευθέρους εἶναι μετέχειν ἐᾶν, ἀλλ' ἣν ἔργῳ τοῖς ἄλλοις διετήρησαν, ταύτης αὐτοὺς τὸ γιγνόμενον τῆς ἐλευθερίας ἀφαιρεῖ-

[79] *om.* T *secll. edd.*

unrestrained freedom, or one that might be described in the terms you use, but the kind that goes together with justice and the practice of self-control.

Indeed Plato himself, or if you prefer Dion, is available 280
to testify to the fact that it is no mean feat, nor one within just anybody's capacity, to liberate one's homeland, let alone the whole of Greece, since his message also includes this:

> On this set of terms, with sincere and sound intent, and with the help of the gods, appoint a king. Let the first king be my son, in recognition of the double debt that you owe to me and to my father: he freed your city from barbarians in times gone by, and I more recently have twice freed it from tyrants, as you yourselves have witnessed.[218]

Does Plato count it of little or of trivial account to make a 281
city free, or to prevent it from falling into the hands of others when it is about to do so? If it is justifiable to bestow even royal power in return for this service, and what is more on people's descendants, and almost to cede one's freedom to them because their ancestors preserved their country's freedom, then surely it ranks among the most monstrous of things, if there are men who freed not only their fellow citizens but also the whole of Greece, not to allow them some share even in the name of free men, but to deprive them of the proper rewards of the freedom that they defended for others by their deeds.

[218] *Ep.* 8.355e–56a.

282 σθαι. φέρε δὴ κἀκεῖνο σκεψώμεθα, ὅσῳ καὶ κατὰ τοῦτο Μιλτιάδης καὶ Θεμιστοκλῆς Δίωνος δικαιότεροι καὶ βελτίους τὰ πολιτικὰ καὶ τὸ ἴσον μᾶλλον φυλάττοντες, εἴ γε οἱ μὲν ἀντ᾽ ἐκείνων τῶν ἔργων οὐδὲν πλέον ᾔτησαν οὔθ᾽ αὑτοῖς οὔτε παισίν, ἀλλ᾽ ἐξαρκεῖν ὑπελάμβανον εὖ πεποιηκέναι τοὺς Ἕλληνας, Δίων δέ, ὡς σὺ φῄς, καὶ τοιούτων δωρεῶν προσεδεῖτο, ἐν αἷς ἦν ἀκούειν τῶν ἐξ ἐκείνου τοὺς ἄλλους, μὴ ἐφ᾽ ἑκάστου τῶν καιρῶν μηδ᾽ ἐπὶ τῶν πραγμάτων αὐτῶν, ὅτι βέλτιον τῶν ἄλλων φρονοῦσιν ἢ λέγουσι πειθομένους, ἀλλ᾽ εἰσάπαξ στησαμένους βασιλέας, κἂν εἴ τινες αὐτῶν βελτίους ἐνεῖεν.

283 ἆρ᾽ οὐ πανταχόθεν σαυτὸν ᾕρηκας; ὅπου γε δὴ καὶ τῆς ἰσότητος καὶ τῆς γεωμετρίας ἐκεῖνοι μὲν οὑτωσὶ μνημονεύοντες φαίνονται, Δίων δ᾽ οὐχί, οὐδ᾽ οἱ Δίωνος παῖδες, καὶ ταῦτα ὁμιλήσαντες τῷ δεινοτάτῳ γεωμετρίαν Πλάτωνι.

284 τρίτον δὲ—φησὶν ἡ ἐπιστολή—προκαλεῖσθαι χρὴ βασιλέα γίγνεσθαι Συρακουσῶν ἑκόντα ἑκούσης τῆς πόλεως τὸν νῦν τοῦ τῶν πολεμίων ἄρχοντα στρατοπέδου, Διονύσιον τὸν Διονυσίου, ἐὰν ἐθέλῃ ἑκὼν εἰς βασιλέως σχῆμα ἀπαλλάττεσθαι, δεδιὼς μὲν τὰς τύχας, ἐλεῶν δὲ πατρίδα καὶ ἱερῶν ἀθεραπευσίαν καὶ τάφους, μὴ διὰ φιλονικίαν πάντως πάντ᾽ ἀπολέσῃ βαρβάροις ἐπίχαρτος γενόμενος.

Let us also reflect by how much in this respect Miltiades and Themistocles were juster men than Dion, and better politicians and better preservers of equality, at any rate if they asked for nothing more in return for their achievements for themselves or for their children, but thought it was enough simply to have done the Greeks good, whereas Dion, in your account, asked for such considerable rewards as he did, among them that everybody else should be subjects to his descendants, not on specific occasions and on the basis of actual fact, because they were satisfied that they had better plans or better things to say than the rest, but appointing them kings once and for all, even if there were better men than they available. 282

Have you not comprehensively caught yourself out, given that these men were so evidently mindful of equality and geometry, and that neither Dion nor his sons were, even though they had kept company with the master geometer Plato?[219] 283

> The man you must invite—the letter says—to be the third king of Syracuse, with both his agreement and that of the city, is the current commander of your enemies' army, Dionysius son of Dionysius, in the hopes that he may be ready to take the position of king instead, out of a combination of fear for what chance may have in store and pity for his country and its untended shrines and its tombs, lest his ambition should cause him to lose absolutely everything and allow the barbarians to revel in his downfall.[220] 284

219 *Grg.* 508a; *Ep.* 7.327a–c.

220 *Ep.* 8.356a–b.

285 εἰ τοίνυν καὶ τῷ τοῦ τυράννου παιδὶ καὶ τοῦ τῶν[80]
πολεμίων ἄρχοντι στρατοπέδου καιρόν ἐστιν ἔχον δι-
αλλάττεσθαι, ἐὰν βούληται βασιλεὺς ἀντὶ τυράννου
γίγνεσθαι, ἐλεήσας πατρίδα καὶ ἱερῶν ἀθεραπευσίαν
καὶ τάφους, ἦ που τοῖς γε τῶν Ἑλλήνων εὐεργέταις
καὶ δι' οὓς ἱερὰ καὶ τάφοι καὶ πάντα ἐσώθη καὶ οὐκ
ἐπίχαρτος ἡ Ἑλλὰς τοῖς βαρβάροις ἐγένετο, εἰκὸς ἦν
σπείσασθαι, καὶ τήν γε βλασφημίαν αὐτοῖς ἀνεῖναι,
286 εἰ καὶ μηδὲν εἶχεν ἔργῳ νεῖμαι πλέον. φέρε γὰρ πρὸς
θεῶν εἰ ὅτε ἦν ἐκεῖνα τὰ πράγματα, ὁ Θεμιστοκλῆς
καλούντων αὐτὸν τῶν Ἀθηναίων καὶ βοηθεῖν ὅ τι ἔχοι
κελευόντων, ἄλλο μὲν οὐδὲν ᾔτησεν, μήτε τυραννίδα
μήτ' ἔννομον βασιλείαν, τοσοῦτον δὲ μή τι διάκονός
γε ὑπ' αὐτῶν κληθῆναι, μηδὲ τοιοῦτον ὄνειδος λαβεῖν,
ἐὰν καταστήσῃ τὰ πράγματα αὐτοῖς, εἰ παρὼν ἔτυχε
Πλάτων, τί ἂν τοῖς Ἀθηναίοις συνεβούλευσεν ὁ τοῖς
Συρακοσίοις ταῦτα συμβουλεύων; ἆρ' οὐ μετρίαν νομίσαι τὴν πρόκλησιν τοῦ Θεμιστοκλέους καὶ δοῦναι
τὴν χάριν; ἐμοὶ μὲν γὰρ κἂν προσηγγυῆσθαι δοκεῖ
287 ταῦτα ὑπὲρ τῆς πατρίδος. οὐκοῦν ἄτοπον μελλόντων
μὲν ἔσεσθαι τῶν ἔργων καὶ ὅπως πραχθείη <ἐν ἀφανεῖ ἔτι>[81] κειμένων[82] ταῦθ' ὑπὲρ πάντων ὑπισχνεῖσθαι,
ὄντων δὲ καὶ πεπραγμένων καὶ τῆς ἀρετῆς τῆς ἐκείνου
φανερᾶς ἅπασιν Ἕλλησι καὶ βαρβάροις γεγονυίας,
ὅμως ὑβρίζειν ἐπιχειρεῖν, καὶ μήτε ἱερὰ μήτε τάφους

[80] τοῦ τῶν U τῷ τῶν *cett.* τῷ τοῦ τῶν *edd.*
[81] ἐν ἀφανεῖ ἔτι Trapp *post* Behr (<ἐν ἀδήλῳ> *post* κειμένων)

If then it is opportune to come to an agreement even with 285
a tyrant's son and the commander of the enemy army,
provided he is willing to be a king rather than a tyrant, and
to take pity on his country and its untended shrines and
its tombs, then for sure it would have been reasonable for
Plato to be reconciled with the benefactors of Greece and
the men thanks to whom shrines, graves, and all were
saved and the barbarians were not allowed to revel in
Greece's downfall, and at least to let up on his verbal insults toward them, even if he had no more practical benefit to bestow on them. Look, for heaven's sake, if at the 286
time of those great events, when the Athenians were calling on him and enjoining him to give all the help he could,
Themistocles had asked for nothing else, not tyrannical
power nor lawful kingship, but only that they should not
call him a lackey and that he should not have to endure
such a reproach as this, provided that he should save the
day for them, if Plato had happened to be there, what
would the man who gives this advice to the Syracusans
have advised the Athenians? Would he not have advised
them to think Themistocles' proposal a reasonable one,
and to be grateful to him? In my view, he would even have
gone surety for him on his homeland's behalf. Is it not then 287
bizarre to offer these guarantees of benefit for all when
their fulfillment lies in the future and it is still unclear how
they will turn out, but once they are fulfilled and done and
Themistocles' heroism has become universally clear, to
Greek and barbarian alike, nevertheless to try to insult
him outrageously, unashamed before holy places, tombs,

---

82 κειμένων Behr καὶ μόνον *codd.*

αἰσχύνεσθαι μήτε ἐπιγράμματα, ἀλλὰ κακῶς λέγειν ὃν ἐπαινεῖν βουληθέντα τῆς ἀξίας ἔργον ἦν τυχεῖν;

288 *καὶ μὴν οὐχ ὅμοιον ἐν μέσῃ τῇ θαλάττῃ περὶ τῶν ἐν τῷ πλοίῳ λέγειν καὶ τὴν εὐψυχίαν τὴν αὑτοῦ δεικνύναι καὶ καθήμενον ἔξω τῆς ζάλης ὑπὸ τῷ τειχίῳ· ἃ Πλάτων παντὸς μᾶλλον καλῶς εἰδὼς ἑκὼν ὑπερβαίνει καὶ κατηγορεῖ Θεμιστοκλέους ἐμβιβάσαντος Ἀθηναίους εἰς τὰς τριήρεις, ἐν τούτοις μὲν οὐ τοῖς λόγοις, ἑτέρωθι δέ, φάσκων αὐτοὺς ἐθισθῆναι φεύγειν ἐκ τού-*

289 *του καὶ μὴ μάχεσθαι μένοντας. ὡς δὴ σὺ μὲν κἀγὼ πολλὰς τροπὰς ὁπλιτῶν ἐποιησάμεθα, Θεμιστοκλῆς δὲ οὐδὲν ἄλλο ἢ φεύγειν ἠπίστατο. ἐγὼ δ᾽ εἰ μὲν ἦν ἕτερον τρόπον νικῆσαι, ἢ καὶ σωθῆναι τὸ πρῶτον, τάχ᾽ ἂν τι τούτους ᾤμην εἶναι τοὺς λόγους· ὅτε δ᾽ ἦν αἵρεσις ἢ ναυμαχοῦντας κρατεῖν, ἢ κατὰ γῆν ἀπολωλέναι, πῶς ἦν ἴσον ἢ τίς ἡ θαυμαστὴ φιλοσοφία τεθνάναι μάτην, ἐξὸν μετὰ τῆς μεγίστης εὐδοξίας σωθῆναι;*

290 *ἀρχὴν δ᾽ ἔγωγε οὐκ ἐπινοῶ ποῦ διακέκριται κατὰ γῆν μὲν νικῆσαι καλὸν εἶναι, ἐν θαλάττῃ δ᾽ αἰσχρόν· ἢ τὴν μὲν κρανίαν καὶ τὴν βύρσαν πολλοῦ τινος ἀξίαν εἶναι, τὰ δὲ νήια καὶ τοὺς κωπέας τοῦ μηδενός· ὥσπερ ἂν εἴ τις τὴν θάλατταν ἐξαιροῖ τῶν ὄντων, ἢ μάτην γενέσθαι λέγοι καὶ διαγράφοι τὴν τοῦ Ποσειδῶνος ἀρχὴν δεύτερα τῶν πάντων ἔχουσαν, ὥς φησιν*

and inscriptions, and to speak ill of a man it would be a hard task to praise as he deserved even if one wanted to?

What is more, it is not the same thing to speak of ship- 288
board matters and to show off one's confidence while one is sitting safe from the swell in the shelter of one's little wall,[221] as it is to do so out on the open sea. Plato knows this truth better than anyone but willfully contravenes it and, albeit elsewhere and not in this dialogue, condemns Themistocles for embarking the Athenians on their triremes, asserting that this got them into the habit of running away, rather than standing their ground and fighting.[222] As if you and I had many times been responsible 289
for routing an infantry line, while Themistocles knew only how to run away! Had there been some other way of winning, or indeed of keeping safe in the first place, I might have thought there was something in this line of argument; but given that the actual choice was between conquering in a fight at sea and being annihilated on land, how can it have been an evenly balanced one, and what would the marvelous philosophical cleverness have been in dying in vain, when it was possible to come safely through with the greatest glory?

I simply do not have the slightest idea how the distinc- 290
tion has been made that says that it is noble to win a victory on land, but shameful to do so at sea, or that cornel wood and ox hide are worth a great deal, but ship timbers and oars nothing, as if one could remove the sea from the list of existing things, or declare that the realm of Poseidon, which Homer says is the second most important part of the world,[223] is pointless and strike it out.

221 *Resp.* 496d. 222 *Leg.* 706c. 223 *Il.* 15.189–92.

291 Ὅμηρος. τί οὖν οὐχὶ καὶ περὶ τοῦ σίτου κατηγορήσομεν αὐτῶν, ὅτι χρῶνται ἐπεισάκτῳ τῷ πλέονι καὶ προσδέονται θαλάττης, ἐξὸν τῇ χώρᾳ στέργειν ἣν γεωργοῦσιν, ὦ θειότατε ἀνδρῶν· τοῦτο μὲν ἔστ' ἀπολωλέναι λιμῷ. καὶ μὴν εἴ γε ἡ τοῦ σίτου κομιδὴ κατὰ θάλατταν αὐτοῖς ἀναγκαῖον καὶ σωτήριον, τῆς αὐτῆς ἕνεκα σωτηρίας καὶ τότε τῇ θαλάττῃ προσεχρήσαντο
292 καὶ προσῆν ἡ τοῦ καλοῦ μερὶς τῇ χρείᾳ. καὶ μὴν οὐδ' ἐκεῖνό γ' ἔστιν εἰπεῖν ὡς τὸν μὲν σῖτον ἔδει κατὰ θάλατταν αὐτοῖς φοιτᾶν, τῆς δὲ σιτοπομπίας οὐ χρῆν προϊδεῖν ὅπως ἔσονται κύριοι. οὐκοῦν ἔδει τριήρων
293 καὶ τοῦ ναυμαχεῖν ἐπίστασθαι. πῶς οὖν ὁ ταῦτα συμβουλεύων περιειργάζετο, ἢ πῶς οὐχ ἡρμόττετο πρὸς τὴν φύσιν τῆς χώρας, ἵνα καὶ τοῦτο προσθῶμεν; ὅμοιον δ' ἄν μοι δοκοῦμεν ποιεῖν εἰ ταῦτα κατηγοροῖμεν, ὥσπερ ἂν εἰ καὶ τῇ φύσει τῆς Ἀττικῆς μεμφοίμεθα, ὅτι αὐτὴν ἔχει θάλαττα κύκλῳ μικροῦ πᾶσαν.
294 τί οὖν εἰ τοῖς κρείττοσιν οὕτως ἔδοξεν; ἀλλ' ὅμως ἐῶ ταῦτα Πλάτωνος χάριν. ἔστω τὸ γειτόνημα ἁλμυρόν, ὥς φησιν. εἰ μὲν τοίνυν Θεμιστοκλῆς νίκην ἀντὶ νίκης ἠλλάττετο, ἠδίκει τοὺς ναυπηγοὺς ἀντὶ τῶν δορυξόων
295 κοσμῶν; καίτοι καὶ τὸ τῆς ναυμαχίας ἔργον εἰς τοὺς ὁπλίτας δήπου τοὺς ἐπὶ τῶν καταστρωμάτων ἀφίκετο· ὧν τοὺς πλείους εἶναι χρὴ δοκεῖν τῶν Μαραθῶνι κινδυνευσάντων. εἰ δὲ διπλοῦν ἀνθ' ἁπλοῦ τότε κίνδυνον

224 Contrast Aristides' own praise of the geography of Attica in *Or.* 1.8–11.

In that case, you most inspired of men, why shouldn't we 291
condemn them for importing the majority of their grain and needing the help of the sea, when they could rest content with the countryside they farm, that is to say die
of hunger? Indeed, if importing grain by sea is necessary 292
to them and keeps them alive, it was for that same purpose of keeping alive that they availed themselves of the assistance of the sea on that occasion too, when moreover it was a question of heroism as well as of practical need. Nor is it possible to say that, although grain had to come to them by sea, they did not also have to see to it that they were in control of its transport. They therefore needed triremes
and knowledge of naval warfare. How then can it be said 293
that the man who gave this advice was wasting his efforts, or that it was not—to add this point too—appropriate to the physical character of the country? If we brought this accusation, I think that we would be doing the same as someone who found fault with the physical character of Attica on the grounds that it is almost entirely encircled
by sea.[224] What if that is how the higher powers decided 294
that it should be? But I will not press the point, as a favor to Plato. Let it be agreed that the neighborhood is, to use his term, saline.[225] If then Themistocles exchanged one kind of victory for another, was he doing wrong by bringing glory to the shipwrights instead of to the spear makers?
Yet the work of the sea battle also of course involved the 295
hoplites on the fighting platforms, the majority of whom we must believe came from the ranks of those who braved the danger of Marathon. And if it was a double rather than

[225] *Leg.* 705a; according to the scholia, Plato was here, in his turn, quoting the lyric poet Alcman (fr. 108 *PMG*).

μετέλαβον, τὸν μὲν πρὸς τοὺς πολεμίους, τὸν δὲ κατ'
αὐτὴν τὴν θάλατταν, οὐδὲν οἶμαι ταύτῃ φαυλότεροι.

296 ἀλλ' ἔγωγε καὶ ταύτας ἀφαιρῶ τὰς προσθήκας.
ἔστω πᾶν ἁμάρτημα, εἴ τις ἄλλος πόρος ἦν τοῖς
πράγμασι σωτηρίας. εἰ δ' ἅπασα μὲν ἡ γῆ κατείληπτο, ἐπέρρει δὲ ὥσπερ θαλάττης ἐπίκλυσις ἡ στρα-
τιά, πάντα δὲ ἄρδην ἀνηρπάζετο, ἀναβλέπειν δὲ οὐκ
ἦν, ἀλλ' οἱ μὲν ἑκόντες προσετίθεντο, οἱ δὲ ἄκοντες
ἤγοντο, οἱ δ' ἔφευγον εἰς τὸ εἴσω τῆς Ἑλλάδος ἀεί,
μόνοι δ' ἔξω κατελείποντο Ἀθηναῖοι, πρὸς δὲ τούτοις
ἐκάλουν μὲν κἀνταῦθα τῶν πραγμάτων ὄντων τοὺς
ἐν τῇ συμμαχίᾳ, καὶ προκινδυνεῦσαι τῶν ὑπολοίπων
ἐκέλευον μεθ' ἑαυτῶν ἀπαντήσαντας εἰς τὴν Βοιωτίαν,
ὑπήκουεν δὲ οὐδείς, ἀλλ' ἐν τοῖς στενοῖς οὐ τῆς Πελοποννήσου μόνον, ἀλλὰ καὶ τῶν ἐλπίδων ἐκάθηντο,
ἀπέκειτο δὲ μήτε γῆς μήτε θαλάττης εἶναι μηδαμοῦ,
τί ταῦτα τοὺς Ἀχαιοὺς ἀπὸ τοῦ πύργου κρίνομεν; ἢ
297 τί τὰ μηδαμῇ συμβαίνοντα κατηγοροῦμεν; ἐγὼ μὲν
οὐ τοσαύτην αἰσχύνην ἔχειν ἡγοῦμαι τὴν ἐν Σαλαμῖνι
ναυμαχίαν, ὥσθ' αἱρετώτερον εἶναι πρὸ αὐτῆς ἀπολωλέναι, ἀλλὰ μᾶλλον τοῦ βίου καὶ τῆς σωτηρίας τῆς
εἰς ἐκεῖνον τὸν χρόνον τοῦτο φήσαιμ' ἂν ὡσπερεὶ κέρδος τοῖς τότε συμβῆναι, τὸ κατεργάσασθαι πρᾶγμα
τοσοῦτον καὶ στῆσαι τρόπαιον κοινὸν ἁπάντων ἀν-

---

226 According to Apostol. *Prov.* 16.71 and the Aristides scholia, proverbial for judging from a partial or biased vantage point; derived from the *teichoskopia* (viewing from the walls) scene in the *Iliad* (3.161–244).

a single danger that they undertook on this occasion, not only in facing the enemy, but also from the simple fact of doing so at sea, then I do not think that this cheapens them in any way.

But I will withdraw these additional comments too. Let 296
it be agreed that it would all have been a complete mistake, if there was any other means of salvation under the circumstances. But in fact the land had been occupied in its entirety, the Persian army was pouring in like a tidal wave, everything was being torn up by the roots and plundered, and it was impossible to regain confidence, but instead some were willingly going over to the enemy, some were being dragooned against their will, some were fleeing ever further into the interior of Greece, and the Athenians alone were left on the outside of all this; and in addition, with the situation having reached this point, although they were calling on the members of the alliance to meet them in Boeotia and brave the danger along with them on behalf of the rest, no one was responding, but instead they were sitting as restricted in their hopes as they were by the narrow confines of the Peloponnese, and the prospect that awaited them was total nonexistence, anywhere, land or sea. Given this state of affairs, why are we "judging the Achaeans from the wall"[226] like this? And why are we making utterly inappropriate accusations
against them? I do not think that the Battle of Salamis was 297
so shameful as to make it preferable to have died before it took place, but would instead say that what you might call the profit that the men of those times enjoyed, sooner than their lives and their immediate salvation, was this, the achievement of such a great feat, and the planting of a trophy shared, you might say, by the whole of humanity

θρώπων ὡς εἰπεῖν καὶ κατὰ παντὸς τοῦ χρόνου. δοκοῦσιν γάρ ἔμοιγε οὐ μόνον τοὺς ἀνταγωνιστὰς νικῆσαι τῇ τότε ἡμέρᾳ, οὐδὲ τοὺς παρόντας τῶν Ἑλλήνων, ἀλλὰ καὶ πάντας ἀνθρώπους μεγέθει τόλμης καὶ νίκης σεμνότητι παρελθεῖν. εἰ γὰρ ἓν ἐξ ἁπάντων εἰπεῖν δεῖ τῶν εἰς μνήμην ἡκόντων, μέγιστον ἐκεῖνό τις ἂν τὸ ἔργον λέγοι δικαίως.

298 μόνος δέ μοι δοκεῖ πάντων ἀνθρώπων ἢ κομιδῇ γε ἐν ὀλίγοις δεῖξαι Θεμιστοκλῆς ἀληθῆ τὸν λόγον ὄντα, ὃν πάλαι μὲν Ἀλκαῖος ὁ ποιητὴς εἶπεν, ὕστερον δὲ οἱ πολλοὶ παραλαβόντες ἐχρήσαντο, ὡς ἄρα οὐ λίθοι οὐδὲ ξύλα οὐδὲ τέχνη τεκτόνων αἱ πόλεις εἶεν, ἀλλ᾽ ὅπου ποτ᾽ ἂν ὦσιν ἄνδρες αὑτοὺς σῴζειν εἰδότες,
299 ἐνταῦθα καὶ τείχη καὶ πόλεις. οὔκουν τῷ γε ἀληθεστάτῳ τῶν λόγων ἐκλιπεῖν τὴν πόλιν ἡγεῖτο, ἀλλὰ μετασκευάζειν ὥσπερ ἐν σκηνῇ πρὸς τὸ παρεστός· οὐδὲ γὰρ ἐν τοῖς δράμασιν οὐδένα τῶν ἀγωνιστῶν ἀπολλύναι τὴν ἑαυτοῦ φύσιν, ἐὰν πρὸς τὸ παρὸν μεταμπίσχηται· καὶ τότε τοῖς Ἀθηναίοις ἐπιβάλλειν θαλαττίων σχῆμα προσθέσθαι καὶ δεῖξαι τὴν πόλιν
300 ἐν τούτῳ. διὰ ταῦτα τὴν μὲν χώραν καὶ τοὔδαφος τῆς πόλεως προεῖτο, τὴν δ᾽ ἀξίαν κάλλιστα ἀνθρώπων διεσώσατο, καὶ πρότερον τείχη καὶ ἑστίας καὶ νεὼς ἢ τὴν τοῦ φρονήματος τάξιν προὔλιπεν καὶ ἃ πεπεικὼς αὑτὸν ἦν. ᾔδει γὰρ ὅτι, εἰ μὲν ἐκείνων ἀντέχοιτο καὶ περὶ αὐτὰ φιλοψυχοίη, ταχέως κἀκείνων στερήσεται καὶ τοὺς ἄνδρας αὐτοὺς προσαπολεῖ καὶ πάσας εἰσ-

and for all time. For they seem to me on that day not only to have defeated their opponents, and the Greeks who were there too, but also to have surpassed all men in the magnitude of their daring and the impressiveness of their victory. If we had to specify just one event from the whole of recorded history, I think that we would be justified in calling this the greatest of all deeds.

I think that Themistocles was the only human being 298
ever, or at least one of very few indeed, to have demonstrated the truth of the saying, long ago formulated by the
poet Alcaeus and subsequently taken up and used in popular speech, that cities are not stones or beams of wood or
walls made by builders, but that wherever there may be
men who know how to work out their own salvation, there
too are walls and cities.[227] In the truest perspective, there- 299
fore, he did not think of himself as abandoning the city,
but of making it over to meet the present circumstances,
like in the theater: just as no actor in a play loses his own
identity if he temporarily changes costume, so too on this
occasion the Athenians had the experience of putting on
seafarers' costumes and representing the city in them. By 300
this means, Themistocles may have sacrificed the physical
site and foundations of the city, but he preserved its value
in the most splendid way humanly possible; he deserted
walls and hearths and temples sooner than the station of
his pride[228] and his own convictions. He knew that if he
clung to those things as if his life depended on it, he would
soon be deprived of them too, and lose the men them-

[227] Fr. 112.10 L-P. Cf. Hom. *Od.* 11.556; Callinus 1.20; Theognis 233; Aesch. *Pers.* 349; Soph. *OT* 56; Pl. *Leg.* 778d.

[228] A Demosthenic phrase: [Dem.] 13.34.

ἅπαξ τὰς ἐλπίδας ἐκβαλεῖ, εἰ δὲ τὰς ναῦς προβάλοιτο αὐτῶν καὶ τόν γε αὐτῆς τῆς κρίσεως χρόνον ἐκσταίη, καθάπερ τις ἀγωνιστὴς ἐπ' ἄθλοις ἀποδημῶν ῥᾳδίως ἤλπιζεν, ὥσπερ τότε τὴν θάλατταν ἀντὶ τῆς γῆς ᾑρεῖτο, οὕτω πάλιν ἐκ τῆς θαλάττης εὑρήσειν καὶ τὴν χώραν καὶ τὴν πόλιν καὶ οὐδὲν χείροσι χρήσεσθαι.[83]

301 ταῦτα δὲ ἐνθυμηθεὶς τοὺς δρομέας ἐμιμήσατο τοὺς ἐκ πολλοῦ τοὺς πρόσθεν αἱροῦντας· καὶ παραχωρήσας οὐ μόνον τῆς Ἀττικῆς, ἀλλὰ καὶ τῆς γῆς ἁπάσης Ξέρξῃ καὶ προλαβεῖν ἐάσας, καὶ τῆς θαλάττης τοσοῦτον ἀπολαβών, ὅσον ταῖς ναυσὶν ἤρκει, περιέτρεψεν ἁπάσας αὐτῷ τὰς ἐλπίδας, καὶ τὴν Ἑλλάδα ἐρρύσατο, οὐ ναύτας ἀνθ' ὁπλιτῶν ἐθίζων Ἀθηναίους εἶναι, οὐδὲ φυγῆς ἐφόδιον τὰς τριήρεις αὐτοῖς ἐξευρών, οὐδ' ἵνα τὸν πάντα χρόνον τὴν θάλατταν οἰκῶσιν, ὥσπερ τὸν Γλαῦκόν φασιν τὸν Ἀνθηδόνιον, ἢ τὸν Σάρωνα τὸν ἐπώνυμον τοῦ πελάγους, ἀλλὰ τοὐναντίον πᾶν, ὦ θαυμάσιε, ὅμως μηδὲν πλῆθος τῶν πολεμίων φοβῶνται μηδὲ φεύγωσιν, ἀλλὰ κἂν τὴν γῆν ἅπασαν δέῃ προλιπεῖν, κἂν τῶν σωμάτων αὐτῶν ἀποστῆναι, ῥᾳδίως ὑπομένωσιν ὑπὲρ τοῦ κρείττονος, καὶ μὴ τοῖς κτήμασι δουλεύωσιν μηδ' ἱκανὴν πρόφασιν μηδεμίαν νομίζωσιν τοῦ γενέσθαι χείρους, μὴ πλῆθος

[83] χρήσεσθαι Stephanus χρήσασθαι *codd.*

---

[229] Glaucus, a human being transformed into a sea god after eating a magic herb, is used by Plato as an example in *Resp.* 611c, though without reference to Anthedon as his birthplace. Saron

selves into the bargain, flinging all their hopes overboard once for all; but if he made the ships their defense and abandoned hearths and temples just for the period of the decisive encounter, in the manner of an athlete who is happy to travel abroad for a competition, he hoped that, just as then he had chosen sea in preference to land, so he would emerge from the sea once more to regain both territory and city, and would find them none the worse.

With these thoughts in his mind, he imitated runners 301
who catch up with the competitors in front of them from far behind. Abandoning not only Attica but the whole of Greece to Xerxes and allowing him to take possession of them, and keeping for himself only as much of the sea as was sufficient for his ships, he turned all of Xerxes' hopes on their head and saved Greece. In so doing he was not getting the Athenians into the habit of being sailors instead of heavy infantry and had not hit on the triremes as a way of enabling them to escape, nor with the intention that they should inhabit the sea forever, like Glaucus of Anthedon in the stories, or Saron who gave his name to the gulf,[229] but for a quite opposite reason, my dear fellow: so as to ensure that they should not be afraid of or run away from any enemy however numerous, but that, even if they had to abandon the whole earth and even leave their own bodies, they should find it easy to do this in the service of a greater cause, and should not be enslaved to material possessions or think that there was any good excuse for moral failing—not the number or strength of the

was the third king of Troezen, who swam out to sea in pursuit of a deer he was hunting and drowned in what was henceforward called the Saronic Gulf (Paus. 2.30.7).

πολεμίων, μὴ ἰσχύν, μὴ πάντας ἀνθρώπους δουλεύειν συγκεχωρηκότας, μὴ πάντ' ἄνω καὶ κάτω γιγνόμενα, ἀλλὰ καὶ θάλατταν οἰκειοτέραν καὶ πάντα κίνδυνον ἀνεκτότερον ἡγῶνται τοῦ ζῆν μετ' αἰσχύνης.

302 τοῦτο καὶ ὁπλίταις ἀγαθὸν παράδειγμα καὶ ἱππεῦσιν καὶ τοξόταις καὶ τριηρίταις καὶ πᾶσι πόλεως πληρώμασιν. οὐ χρή, φησί, τοῖς ἐναντίοις διδόναι τὰ νῶτα οὐδὲ αἰσχρὰν σωτηρίαν ζητεῖν, οὐδ' ἀφέντας τοὺς περὶ τῶν δικαίων λογισμοὺς ἐφεῖναι τῷ φέροντι,
303 οὐδὲ φεύγειν ὅπως τις μὴ μάχηται. οὔκουν ἔγωγε, φησίν, φεύγων ᾠχόμην εἰς Ἰταλίαν, οὐδ' ἐκεῖ πόλιν ἠξίουν οἰκίζειν, καίτοι τῶν μάντεων κελευόντων, ἀλλ' ἔμενον τὰς τριήρεις ἔχων, οὗ καιρὸς ἦν ὑπὲρ τῆς Ἑλλάδος ἀντιτάξασθαι. καὶ ἐπειδὴ τὰ ἐν τῇ γῇ κατείληπτο, ἤρκει μοι τῆς θαλάττης μικρὸν μέρος· καὶ σοί, φησίν, παραινῶ μένειν καὶ σῴζειν τὴν τάξιν, ἐάν τε ὁπλιτῶν ἀγῶνα ἀγωνίζῃ ἐάν τέ τινα ἱππέων ἐάν[84] θ' ὁντινοῦν. ἐὰν δὲ καὶ πάντων ἐξείργῃ, γενοῦ μοι θαλάττιος τοῦτον τὸν χρόνον, ἐνταῦθα ὁπλίτευσον, προβαλοῦ τὴν ἀσπίδα ἀπὸ τῆς νεώς, εἰ δ' οἷόν τε καὶ ἐξ αὐτῆς τῆς θαλάττης ὑπὲρ τοῦ ῥοθίου φέρε.

304 ταῦτα ἐδίδασκε Θεμιστοκλῆς, καὶ τοῦτο ἠδύνατο αὐτῷ τὸ εἰς τὰς τριήρεις μεταστῆσαι τὴν πόλιν· διὰ ταῦτα κενὴν ἀνθρώπων ἠξίωσεν τὴν χώραν πρότερον ποιῆσαι ἢ ληφθέντα τινὰ ἐν αὐτῇ δουλεῦσαι. τούτων οὐ γεγόνασι λογισμοὶ καλλίους οὐδὲ πράγματα ἐντι-

[84] ἐάν Reiske ἄν *codd.*

enemy, not the acquiescence of the whole of humanity in slavery, not the whole world turned upside down—but should instead think the sea more truly their home and any danger more bearable than living in shame.

This was a noble example for hoplites, cavalry, archers, 302
trireme crews, and the whole complement of the city. "You should not turn your back on the enemy in flight," he says, "nor seek safety at the cost of dishonor, nor abandon all consideration of what is just and simply go with the prevailing wind, nor run away to avoid a battle. I did not take 303
to my heels and run away to Italy, he says, and I didn't see fit to found a city there, although that was what the seers were telling me to do, but I stayed with my triremes, when the vital moment came to make a stand on behalf of Greece; and since everything on land had been captured, a small portion of the sea was enough for me. I advise you too, he says, to stand firm and remain at your post, whether it is a hoplite battle or a cavalry battle or any kind of battle at all that you are fighting. And if all of these are barred to you, then, I suggest, turn seafarer for the duration and fight your hoplite battle there, thrust your shield forward from the ship's deck, and if such a thing may be hold it up out of the sea itself over the foaming waves."

These were the lessons Themistocles taught, and this 304
is what transferring the city into its triremes meant for him; this was why he saw fit to empty the country of human inhabitants sooner than see anyone be captured in it and enslaved. There have never been nobler calculations

μότερα, οὐδὲ μᾶλλον ὁμοῦ σύνεσιν καὶ μεγαλοψυχίαν καὶ ἀνδρείαν ἔχοντα· ἐπεὶ ὅτι γε οὐ καθάπαξ αὐτοὺς ἠξίου τῆς πόλεως ὑπεριδεῖν οὐδὲ κύκλῳ φεύγειν ἐπὶ τῶν τριήρων, ἀλλὰ τοῖς παροῦσιν καιροῖς ταῦτα συμφέρειν ὑπελάμβανεν, καὶ στρατοπέδῳ τῇ Σαλαμῖνι χρησάμενος τὸν αὐτὸν τρόπον ὅνπερ οἱ πρότεροι τῷ Μαραθῶνι πάλιν τῶν ἐξ ἀρχῆς ἐμέμνητο, ἔδειξεν οὐκ εἰς μακράν. ἀπελθόντων γὰρ τῶν βαρβάρων, εἴς τε τὴν πόλιν ἦγεν εὐθὺς αὐτοὺς ἄνω καὶ συνῴκιζεν κατὰ τὰ πρότερα, καὶ μείζω γε τὸν περίβολον, ὥς φασιν οἱ ἐξηγηταί, ἐξήγαγε πανταχῇ, τειχίσαι τε δεῆσαν μό-
305 *νος ἐξ ἁπάντων εὗρεν ὅπως δυνήσονται. πῶς οὖν αὐτοὺς φεύγειν εἴθισεν, ἢ κατὰ ποίαν τύχην, ὅς γε ἐν μὲν τοῖς ἐσχάτοις κινδύνοις ὄντας αὐτοὺς διώκειν, οὐ φεύγειν εἴθισεν, νικήσαντας δὲ καὶ τὰ μέγιστα εὖ πράττοντας καὶ παρὸν ἥντινα βούλονται χώραν καὶ πόλιν αὐτοὺς λαβεῖν, εἰς τἀρχαῖα ἐπανῆγεν, καὶ οὐκ εἴα τῶν ὑπαρχόντων ἀμνημονεῖν;*

306 *πρὸς Διός, ὦ Πλάτων, εἰ δὲ δή σού τις [αὐτοῦ]*[85] *λαβόμενος κατηγόρει λέγων ὅσα διέπλεις ἐν ὁλκάσι τὴν θάλατταν καὶ πλάνην ὁπόσην πεπλάνησαι περὶ τὴν Χάρυβδιν, ὁμοῦ τοῖς ναύταις ἐσκηνωμένος καὶ δεόμενος τῆς κώπης καὶ τοῦ τροπωτῆρος, καὶ ταῦθ' οὕτω δυσχεραίνων τὰ ναυτικὰ καὶ τοῖς ὁπλίταις*

[85] *om.* U *del.* Dindorf

---

[230] Cf. Thuc. 1.93.2–3.

nor more highly honored deeds than these, nor ones that better embodied intelligence, nobility of spirit, and courage all together, since it did not take him long to show that he was not demanding that they scorn their city once and for all or take refuge on their triremes at regular intervals, but that instead he saw this as a constructive measure for the present circumstances, and having exploited Salamis as an encampment in the same way as his predecessors had Marathon, he turned his thoughts back to how things had been previously. When the barbarians had gone, he immediately led them back ashore to the city and settled them as they had been before, and as the historians tell us enlarged the circuit of the walls right round,[230] and when fortification work was needed he on his own devised a way
in which they could accomplish it. In what sense then was 305
he getting them into the habit of running away, or in what state of their fortunes, seeing that when they were in the ultimate peril it was pursuing not fleeing that he got them used to, and that when they had won and were at the height of their good fortune, and it was open to them to choose whatever territory or city they wished, he led them back to their original home and did not allow them to forget what they already had?

For goodness' sake, Plato, what if someone were to 306
seize hold of you and arraign you with an account of all the journeys you made across the sea in merchant ships, and the length of your wanderings around Charybdis, quartered with sailors and dependent on the oar and the rowlock thong, in spite of your impatience with things nautical and your partisanship for hoplites?[231] There's a line of

[231] Another reference to Plato's voyages to Sicily, as described in *Ep.* 7, with an echo of the mention of Charybdis in 345e.

προσκείμενος, ἆρ᾽ οὐκ ἐκεῖνο μὲν οὐκ ἔμελλες ἐρεῖν, ἅτε ὢν μουσικὸς καὶ πάλαι κατεγνωκὼς τοῦ ῥήματος, τὸ ποῖον δὴ λέγω, ὦ μοχθηρὲ μελαγχολᾷς, εἶπες δ᾽ ἂν οὑτωσί πως, ὦ δαιμόνιε, ἐγὼ ταῦτα ἔπραττον, οὐ τὸν τῶν ναυτῶν βίον ᾑρημένος, οὐδ᾽ ἐκείνους ἀντὶ τῶν ὁπλιτῶν κοσμῶν, οὐδ᾽ ἐν γήρᾳ ναυτίλλεσθαι μεταμανθάνων, οὐδὲ τοῖς κατ᾽ ἤπειρον πράγμασι λυμαινόμενος, ἀλλ᾽ οὐκ ἦν ἄλλως ἐλθεῖν εἰς Σικελίαν; ταῦτ᾽ ἂν εἶχες, οἶμαι, λέγειν, ὥσπερ καὶ ἡμεῖς ὑπὲρ Θεμιστοκλέους, ὅτι οὐκ ἦν ἄλλως τοῖς Ἕλλησι σωθῆναι.

307 καὶ μὴν οὐδ᾽ ἐκεῖνό τις ἂν φήσειεν ὡς ὑπὲρ μὲν τῶν Δίωνος πραγμάτων ἔδει πλεῖν εἰς Σικελίαν καὶ μήτε γῆρας μήτε κίνδυνον μήτε τὸ πολλάκις ἐξηπατῆσθαι μήτε ἄλλο μηδὲν ὑπολογίζεσθαι πρὸς τὸ δίκαιον καὶ τὴν ἐκείνου χρείαν, ὑπὲρ δὲ τῆς Ἑλλάδος καὶ τοσούτων πραγμάτων οὐκ ἄρ᾽ ἔδει ταῖς ναυσὶν χρήσασθαι, ἀλλ᾽ ἀναίνεσθαι τὴν θάλατταν. οὐδ᾽ ἂν εἷς

308 ταῦτα φήσειεν. ὁ δέ γε Βελλεροφόντης, ὦ ἄριστε, ὥς φασιν οἱ ποιηταί, τὴν Χίμαιραν ἐχειρώσατο οὐκ εἰς τὴν θάλατταν ἐμβάς, ἀλλ᾽ εἰς τὸν ἀέρα ἀναβὰς ἐπὶ τοῦ Πηγάσου, καὶ ὅμως οὐκ ἔδοξε δειλὸς εἶναι, ὅς γε καὶ λόχους ὅλους διαφθείρειν ἐδόκει δύνασθαι. ἀλλ᾽

309 οἶμαι πρὸς τὸ πῦρ οὐκ ἦν χαμόθεν ἀντισχεῖν. οἶδα δὲ ὑπὲρ Θεμιστοκλέους ὅτι κἂν εἰ τὸν Δαίδαλον οἷός τ᾽ ἦν μιμήσασθαι καὶ πτερώσας ἑαυτὸν ὑπὲρ τῶν Ἑλλήνων ἐπιθέσθαι τῷ βαρβάρῳ, οὐδὲ τοῦτο ἂν ὤκνη-

yours that you wouldn't have been likely to use, being a cultivated individual and having long since renounced it—which one do I mean? "you wretch, you're off your head"[232]—but you might have said something like this, mightn't you: "My dear fellow, I did this not because I had positively chosen a sailor's life, nor because I was promoting them in preference to hoplites, nor because I had had a change of heart and was learning to sail in my old age, but simply because there was no other way of getting to Sicily"? I think you could have said that, just as I can say in defense of Themistocles that there was no other way for the Greeks to be brought safely through.

Nor could anyone say that, whereas in defense of Di- 307
on's interests it was necessary to sail to Sicily with no
thought for age or danger, or for the many deceits endured, or anything else given the demands of justice and
that man's need, it was in fact not necessary in defense of
Greece and of such high stakes to use the ships, but that
they should instead have spurned the sea. Not one single
person would say as much. Bellerophon, my dear fellow, 308
so the poets tell us,[233] subdued the Chimera not by embarking and taking to the sea, but by ascending into the
air on Pegasus, and yet he did not acquire a name for
cowardice, seeing that he was reputed to be able to destroy
whole regiments. The point was, I take it, that he couldn't
have stood up to the Chimera's fire from ground level. On 309
Themistocles' account, I know both that if he had been
able to imitate Daedalus and give himself wings for the
Greeks' sake in order to attack the barbarians, he would

[232] *Phdr.* 268e.

[233] For example, Hom. *Il.* 6.156–202; Pind. *Ol.* 13.84–91.

σεν, ἢ κἂν εἰ μάχην πεζὴν μέλλων συνάψειν ἐκ τῶν ὑψηλοτέρων ἐπῄει, δειλίαν ὀφλήσειν ἔμελλεν. Λακεδαιμονίους δέ γε αὐτὸς σὺ φῂς τὴν ἐν Πλαταιαῖς μάχην μαχομένους οὐκ ἐθέλειν μένειν, ἀλλ' ὑπάγειν τοὺς Πέρσας πρὸς τὸ συμφέρον αὑτοῖς. ἐῶ γὰρ Σκύθας ὅσα δὴ φεύγοντες νενικήκασιν. ὅπου τις πλέον ἕξειν ἡγεῖται, ἐνταῦθα ἀμυνέσθω τοὺς πολεμίους, ἄλλως τε κἂν μηδὲν τῶν μειζόνων παραβαίνῃ δικαίων.

310 εἰ μὲν τοίνυν αὑτοῦ γνώμῃ μόνον περὶ τούτων ἐκέχρητο Θεμιστοκλῆς, ἐκείνου τις ἂν εἶπεν αὐτὸν τὴν κατηγορίαν πεποιῆσθαι, ἐπεὶ δὲ καὶ θεὸς ταῦτ' ἀνελὼν φαίνεται, ἐγὼ μὲν ὀκνῶ λέγειν, πᾶς δ' ἄν τις συνίοι τὸ λοιπόν.

311 ὁ δ' οὖν Θεμιστοκλῆς λαμπρῶς ἀποφεύγει τὴν αἰτίαν. ἢ πρὸς τῶν θεῶν αὐτῶν, ὅταν μὲν δέῃ Σωκράτη σοφώτατον εἶναι δοκεῖν, εἰς ἀξιόχρεων μάρτυρα ἀνοίσομεν τὸν θεὸν τὸν ἐν Δελφοῖς καὶ τοῖς λογίοις ἰσχυριούμεθα, ἃ Χαιρεφῶν καὶ ὀλίγοι τινὲς ᾔδεσαν, οἷς ἔμελε Σωκράτους, ὧν δ' οἱ Ἕλληνες ἅπαντες μάρτυρες καὶ ἃ τῶν πώποτε κοινότατα ἐφθέγξατο ἡ Πυθία καὶ οἷς ἅπαντα τὰ μέλλοντα ἠκολούθησεν, ταῦτα δὲ οὐδαμοῦ θήσομεν εἰς λόγον, οὐδὲ τῇ Θεμιστοκλέους σοφίᾳ μέγιστα εἶναι μαρτύρια συγχωρησόμεθα; ὅπου γὰρ ταὐτὰ ἔδοξεν ἐκείνῳ καὶ τῷ θεῷ περὶ σωτηρίας τῶν ὅλων, τί χρὴ λέγειν ἄλλο;

not have hesitated to do so, and that even if, on the point of beginning an infantry engagement, he had attacked from a superior height, he would not have incurred a charge of cowardice. You yourself say that the Spartans at the Battle of Plataea did not want to stand their ground, but instead led the Persians on to the terrain that suited them,[234] not to speak of the many victories the Scythians won by turning tail. Let everyone fight his enemies where he thinks he will have the advantage, especially if he transgresses none of the weightier principles of justice. If The- 310
mistocles had relied on his own judgment alone in this matter, one would say that it is against him that Plato has brought his accusation; but since it is clear that the god too gave this answer, though I hesitate to put the consequence into words, anyone can see what it is.

311 At all events, Themistocles is manifestly acquitted of the charge. Or, in heaven's name, is it the case that, when it is a question of upholding Socrates' reputation as the wisest of all men, we refer to the god of Delphi as a credible witness and confirm the point with the oracle that was known only to Chaerephon and a few other of his partisans,[235] but that when it comes to things that the whole of Greece witnessed, the most public pronouncements the Pythia ever made, and the basis from which all subsequent events followed, we take no account of them at all and refuse to admit that they are the greatest testimony to Themistocles' wisdom? When he and the god took the same view about the preservation of the world, what more is there to be said?

[234] *Lach.* 191b–c.
[235] *Ap.* 21a.

312 τίν᾽ οὖν ἦν τὰ χρησθέντα; ἄρχεται μὲν ἄνωθέν ποθεν, ἔπειτά ἐστι τοῦτο ὃ πάντες θρυλοῦσιν

τεῖχος Τριτογενεῖ ξύλινον διδοῖ εὐρύοπα Ζεύς.

ἆρά γε καὶ μόνον τοῦτο εἴρηκεν ὁ χρησμός; οὔκ, ἀλλ᾽ ὥσπερ ἐπισφραγίζεται τὴν γνώμην τῇ προσθήκῃ. τίς οὖν ἔσθ᾽ αὕτη;

μοῦνον ἀπόρθητον τελέθειν·

ἵνα μὴ † τοῦτο οὕτω λέγων ἀρτίως †[86] αἵρεσιν εἶναι δοκῶσιν αὐτοῖς Ἀθηναῖοι ἢ κατὰ γῆν νικῆσαι ἢ κατὰ θάλατταν, μηδὲ τρυφῶσιν, ἀλλ᾽ εἰδῶσιν ὅτι ἐν ταῖς ναυσὶν ἅπαντα τὰ πράγματα ἕστηκεν καὶ ἄλλως οὐκ
313 ἔνεστι σῴζεσθαι. ἔτι δὲ αὐτὸ μειζόνως ηὔξησεν ἐν τοῖς ἐφεξῆς, ἅτ᾽ ὢν μουσηγέτης ὁ θεὸς καὶ λέγειν ἄριστος δήπου. προσέθηκε γὰρ

τὸ σὲ τέκνα τ᾽ ὀνήσει,

τί τοῦτο λέγων τὸ σὲ τέκνα τ᾽ ὀνήσει; οὐ τοὺς[87] παῖδας οὓς εἰς Τροιζῆνα ὑπεξέθεντο ἐμοὶ δοκεῖν, ἀλλὰ καὶ τοὺς ὕστερον μέλλοντας ἔσεσθαι. οὕτω συνεκληρώθησαν τῇ τύχῃ τῆς πόλεως αἱ τριήρεις. εἴ ποτε γὰρ εὖ πράττοιεν, κατὰ ταύτας εὖ πράττειν αὐτοῖς περιῆν
314 ὅλως. καὶ οὐδ᾽ ἐνταῦθ᾽ ἔστη τῆς δημηγορίας, ἀλλ᾽

86 *locus desperatus* λεγόντων UR[2] Monac. 432 Barocc. 136 λέγων *cett.* τούτων οὕτως λεγομένων Lenz
87 διὰ τούς UPh[M3] τούς *cett.*

So what was it that the oracle said? There are some opening lines of some sort or another, and then comes the one that is on everybody's lips:[236] 312

Far-seeing Zeus grants a wooden wall to
Tritogeneia . . .

Is this all that the oracle said? No, there is an addition, with which it so to speak sets the seal on its declaration. What is this?

. . . For it alone to remain unsacked;

—added just to prevent the Athenians supposing . . .[237]
that they had the luxury of a choice between winning on land and winning on the sea, and to make sure they realized that their fortunes rested entirely with their ships and
that they had no other possible means of salvation. The 313
god expanded on the point still more amply in the sequel, as you might expect from one who is Leader of the Muses and, surely, an extremely accomplished orator. He added

This will benefit both you and your children.

But what did he mean by the words "this will benefit both you and your children"? Not in my view the children they removed from danger to Troezen, but those still to be born in the future. That is how firmly the fortunes of the city were bound up with the triremes. If ever they did well, their good fortune came to them entirely through these
vessels. Nor was that the end of the god's harangue, but as 314

236 Hdt. 7.141.

237 The Greek text is partly unintelligible at this point, although the overall sense is clear.

ὥσπερ προκαταλαμβάνων καὶ [ὥσπερ][88] ὑποτεμνόμενος τὰς Πλάτωνος ἐπιτιμήσεις ἔγκειται πάσας φωνὰς ἀφιεὶς καὶ λέγων ἐκ τοῦ εὐθέος ἤδη

μηδὲ σύ γ' ἱπποσύνην τε μένειν καὶ πεζὸν ἰόντα
πολλὸν ἀπ' ἠπείρου στρατὸν ἥσυχος, ἀλλ' ἀναχωρεῖν.

εἶτ' ἐστὶν ἀκροτελεύτιον

ἔτι τοί ποτε κἀντίος ἔσσῃ.

315 καὶ ἔγωγε ἡδέως ἂν ἐροίμην τοὺς τὰς βαθείας ὑπήνας ἕλκοντας, ἔφη τις τῶν κωμικῶν, καὶ μέχρι τούτου τὸν Πλάτωνα σεμνύνοντας, εἰ κατ' ἐκείνους τοὺς χρόνους ἦν ἡμῖν Πλάτων, καὶ αὐτῷ τὰ πράγματα ἐπετέτραπτο, εἶθ' ἧκεν ὁ χρησμός, τίνας ἂν λόγους λέγειν ᾤετο δεῖν, ἢ τί πράττειν ἠξίου τοὺς Ἀθηναίους. ἢ νὴ Δία, εἰ μὴ στρατηγῶν αὐτὸς ἐτύγχανεν, τῷ γε Θεμιστοκλεῖ τί που ἂν συνεβούλευεν; πότερον ταῦθ' ἅπερ αἱ μαντεῖαι, ἢ τἀναντία τούτων; εἰ μὲν γὰρ οὐκ ἔμελλεν εἴσεσθαι τὸν νοῦν τῶν χρησμῶν, οὐ σοφοῦ πρᾶγμα ἔμελλε πείσεσθαι· εἰ δὲ γιγνώσκων καὶ συνιεὶς ἀντιλέγειν ἐπεχείρει, παντὸς μᾶλλον ἔργον διεπράττετο ἢ Πλάτωνος. δυοῖν γὰρ τοῖν ἐσχάτοιν ἀπόδειξις ἦν, ἀσεβείας εἰς τὸν θεὸν καὶ προδοσίας τῆς σωτηρίας οὐ μόνον τῆς πόλεως, ἀλλὰ καὶ τῶν Ἑλλήνων ἁπάντων. εἰ δὲ δὴ τὰ μάλιστα ἕτερα μὲν ὁ

[88] *del.* Reiske

if anticipating and cutting the ground from under Plato's reproaches he now unleashed all his vocal resources to press the point home and declared straight out

> Do not remain still and await the cavalry and the
> great army
> advancing from the mainland, but withdraw.

And then there is a leftover half-line:

> Still one day he will meet you face-to-face.

I would happily ask the men with the long trailing 315
beards, to quote the comic poet,[238] who venerate Plato to this extreme, if Plato had been alive at that time and had been in charge of affairs, and if then the oracle had come, what words would he have thought ought to be spoken, or what would he have required the Athenians to do? Or indeed, if it so happened that he was not general himself, what advice would he have given to Themistocles? The same as the prophecies, or the opposite to them? If he was not going to understand the meaning of the oracular responses, then his would not have been a wise man's contribution either; but if he had recognized and understood it, and then tried to speak against it, then he would have been behaving like anyone sooner than Plato. It would have been a demonstration of the two most extreme of all failings, impiety toward the god and betrayal of the safety not of the city of Athens alone but of the whole of Greece. But if in fact it had been precisely the case that the god

[238] Ar. *Lys.* 1072.

θεὸς προσέταττεν, ἑτέραν δὲ ἦγεν Πλάτων, ποτέρῳ τὸν Θεμιστοκλέα πεισθῆναι προσῆκεν, ἢ ποτέρῳ μᾶλλον προσέχων ὀρθῶς ἂν ἔδοξε φρονεῖν; τουτὶ γὰρ ἔν μοι τῆς ἀπορίας διαλύσαντες σταθήτωσαν παρὰ τὸν τρίποδα τὸν ἐν Δελφοῖς, ὃν Ἕλληνες ἀπὸ τῶν βαρβάρων ἀνέστησαν. ἀλλὰ μὴν οὐκ ἦν πρὸς δαίμονα φωτὶ μάχεσθαι.

316 καὶ μὴν οὐδ᾽ ἐκεῖνό γ᾽ ἔχει λόγον τῶν μὲν ἐν τῇ Πλάτωνος πόλει καὶ πολιτείᾳ τελευτώντων τῇ Πυθίᾳ τὰς τιμὰς ἐπιτρέπειν αὐτὸν Πλάτωνα καὶ ταῦτα τίθεσθαι κύρια ἅττ᾽ ἂν ἐκείνῃ δοκῇ, ἃ δ᾽ ὑπὲρ τῆς τῶν ζώντων σωτηρίας καὶ φυλακῆς τῆς πάσης Ἑλλάδος ἡ Πυθία προσέταξεν, ταῦτα τῷ πεισθέντι καὶ διοικήσαντι μέμφεσθαι. τρισὶ γὰρ τοῖς μεγίστοις φαίνεται σχεδὸν εἰς τὸν Θεμιστοκλέα μόνον ἐλθοῦσα τῶν Ἑλλήνων ἅπασα ἡ σωτηρία, τῷ τε κατ᾽ ἀρχὰς συμβουλεῦσαι ποιήσασθαι τὰς τριήρεις, πρὶν καὶ προσδοκᾶν τινα τῶν πολλῶν ἥξειν τοὺς βαρβάρους, καὶ τῷ παρόντος τοῦ πολέμου πεῖσαι ναυμαχεῖν καὶ τῷ ποῦ τῆς θαλάττης συνοίσει προϊδεῖν. εἴτε γὰρ μὴ ἐποιήθησαν ἐξ ἀρχῆς αἱ τριήρεις, οὐδὲν ἂν ἦν ἄξιον τοῖς Ἕλλησι λόγου ναυτικόν, οὐδ᾽ ᾧ θαρρήσαντες ἔμελλον οἱ λοιποὶ συστήσεσθαι· ὥστε τῶν μὲν κατὰ γῆν ἀπόρων ὄντων, ἐν δὲ τῇ θαλάττῃ δυνάμεως οὐχ ὑπαρχούσης ἀπώλλυντ᾽ ἂν ἀκονιτὶ πάντα τὰ πράγματα· εἰ δὲ αἱ μὲν

239 An echo of *Phdr.* 236b. 240 Hom. *Il.* 17.98.
241 *Resp.* 427b, 540b–c; *Leg.* 947d.

ordered one thing and Plato pursued another, which of them would it have been it right for Themistocles to obey, and which of them would he have been thought to have shown greater good sense in taking his orders from? If they can solve just this one part of the puzzle for me, then let them be honored with statues beside the tripod at Delphi that the Greeks dedicated from barbarian spoils![239] But in actual fact it was not possible "to fight a man against the wishes of a god."[240]

Nor does it make any sense that, in the case of those 316
who die in Plato's state and under his constitution, Plato himself should entrust their honors to the Pythia and take as authoritative whatever it is she says,[241] but in the case of the Pythia's orders on behalf of the salvation of the living and the preservation of the whole of Greece, he should blame the man who obeyed them and saw to their execution. In the three most important respects it is clear that the whole safety of Greece depended pretty well solely on Themistocles: in his original advice to have the triremes built, before anyone from the majority of the population even expected that the barbarians would come; in his persuading them to fight at sea when the war did arrive; and in his foreseeing where at sea it would be advantageous to fight. If the triremes had never been built in the first place, the Greeks would have had no navy worth speaking of, nor anything round which the rest could confidently assemble, so that with the situation on land being desperate and there being no force by sea, everything would have been lost without a struggle. If they had had the ships, but had

νῆες ὑπῆρχον, ἄλλον δέ τινα αὐτοῖς ἔδοξεν τρόπον τὸν πόλεμον διαφέρειν, οὐδ' οὕτω πλέον οὐδὲν ἦν. ‹. . . . .›[89] καὶ μὴν ἥ γε φύσις τῆς θαλάττης ἄχρηστον τὸ πλῆθος τῶν νεῶν τοῖς βαρβάροις ἐποίησεν. τοῦτο δ' ἦν ὁ δεινὸς ἀγὼν Θεμιστοκλέους καὶ ὁ προαγὼν[90] ἐν τοῖς Ἕλλησιν αὐτοῦ μεῖναι καὶ παύσασθαι πρὸς
317 τὸν Ἰσθμὸν βλέποντας. λέγουσι δέ τινες καὶ τέταρτον ὑπὲρ Θεμιστοκλέους ὡς πρὸς τῷ τόπῳ καὶ τὸν καιρὸν ἐξεῦρεν, στησάμενος τὴν ναυμαχίαν κατιόντος τοῦ πνεύματος. ὃ δὴ καὶ Φορμίων ὕστερον, ὡς ἔοικεν, μιμησάμενος Λακεδαιμονίους περὶ Ναύπακτον κατεναυμάχησεν. οὕτω πολλοῦ δεῖ Θεμιστοκλῆς ἐθίσαι φεύγειν Ἀθηναίους ἢ διαφθεῖραι τὰ φρονήματα.

318 ἀλλ' ἐπάνειμι πρὸς τὰ λοιπὰ τοῦ χρησμοῦ. εἶεν. τίνα δὴ τἀπὶ τούτοις ἐφθέγξατο ὁ θεὸς καὶ πῶς κατεκόσμησε τὴν συμβουλήν;

ὦ θεία Σαλαμὶς ἀπολεῖς δὲ σὺ τέκνα γυναικῶν.

319 ὁ μὲν τοίνυν θεὸς θείαν τὴν Σαλαμῖνα προσεῖπεν, ὡς ἐν αὐτῇ μελλόντων ἔργων ἔσεσθαι κρειττόνων ἢ κατὰ πάντα τἀνθρώπινα. Πλάτων δὲ τὸν ταῦτα κατειργασμένον καὶ τὸν κομίσαντα αὐτοὺς εἰς τὴν Σαλαμῖνα λυμήνασθαί φησι τοῖς πράγμασι καὶ τῶν πρὸς ἡδονὴν ὑπηρετούντων οὐδὲν γενέσθαι βελτίω.
320 καὶ ὁ μὲν Ἴακχος ἐξεφοίτησεν καὶ μετέσχεν τῶν δρω-

[89] *lac. stat.* Behr (*sed inter* διαφέρειν *et* οὐδ')
[90] προαγών Reiske προάγων *codd.*

decided to conduct the war in some other manner, they would not have gotten any further either. <. . . . .>[242] It was the physical character of the sea that made the numerical superiority of the barbarians' ships useless to them, and Themistocles' awful struggle, the preliminary contest that he had to win on the Greek side, was to get them to stay where they were and to stop looking toward the Isthmus.
Some people also have a fourth point to make on Themis- 317
tocles' behalf, that he hit on the moment as well as the place, in starting the naval battle when the wind came up, a maneuver that was, it seems, subsequently imitated by Phormio in his defeat of the Spartans at Naupactus.[243] That is how far Themistocles was from making the Athenians accustomed to running away or corrupting their fighting spirit.

But I shall return to the remainder of the oracle. So, 318
what did the god say after that, and how did he marshal his advice?

O divine Salamis, you will destroy the sons of women.

The god, then, called Salamis "divine," on the understand- 319
ing that deeds were going to be done there that surpassed every possibility of human nature; yet Plato says that the man who achieved this and brought the Greeks to Salamis did damage to their interests and was no better than servants who minister to their masters' pleasures. Dionysus 320
sallied forth and took part in the rituals being performed;

[242] Something seems to have fallen out of the text here: a third conditional, saying something like, "If they had decided to fight at sea, but picked a different place to join battle, that too would have been disastrous."

[243] Thuc. 2.84.

μένων καὶ νέφη παρὰ ταῖν θεαῖν εἰς τὴν ναυμαχίαν ἐγκατέσκηψεν καὶ θεοὶ καὶ ἥρωες οἱ κοινοὶ τῶν Ἑλλήνων σύμμαχοι συνηγωνίζοντο, καὶ συνεναυμάχουν τιμῶντες ἔργῳ Θεμιστοκλέα, καὶ ἡ προσηγορία τῇ Σαλαμῖνι πανταχόθεν ἠκριβοῦτο καὶ κατέστη θεία
321 τοῖς ἅπασιν. καίτοι ὅτε ἡ Σαλαμὶς τοῦτ' ἤκουσεν, ἡ ναυμαχία δήπου τοῦτο ἤκουσεν· οὐ γὰρ ἄλλης γέ τινος χώρας Σαλαμὶς <. . .>[91] τὸν πρὸ τοῦ χρόνου ἦν, ἀλλ' ὁ θεὸς [τὴν ναυμαχίαν][92] θείαν δι' ἐκείνης προσεῖπεν· Πλάτων δέ, ὡς ἔοικεν, ἀναίνεται τὴν νίκην καὶ θάνατον τῶν ταῦτα πραξάντων καταψηφίζεται καὶ προκρίνει σεμνῶς ἀπολωλέναι μᾶλλον ἢ νικᾶν
322 μετὰ τῶν θεῶν. Ὅμηρος δὲ εἰ περιῆν, κἂν Διὶ μῆτιν ἀτάλαντον προσεῖπεν τὸν ταῦτα συμβουλεύσαντα καὶ πράξαντα πολλῷ μᾶλλον ἐμοὶ δοκεῖν ἢ τὸν τῶν Κεφαλλήνων στρατηγὸν τὸν ἐπαλείψαντα τῇ μίλτῳ τὰς ναῦς. εἰ γὰρ ὁ μὲν Ζεὺς ἐδίδου τῇ Ἀθηνᾷ δωρεὰν τὰς ναῦς, ὁ δ' Ἀπόλλων ταῦτα ἔφραζεν, ὁ δὲ ἐξ ἀρχῆς πρὸς ταῦτα ἥρμοστο κἀν τοῖς παροῦσι μόνος ταὐτὰ τοῖς θεοῖς ἐγίγνωσκεν, πῶς οὐκ ἔμελλε τοῦτο τὸ πρόσρημα οἴσεσθαι; ἀλλ' οὐ Πλάτων οὕτως, ἀλλ' ἀντὶ τοῦ Διὶ τὴν γνώμην ὅμοιον καὶ θεῖον προσειπεῖν Σαράμβῳ καὶ τοῖς καπήλοις εἰκάζει πᾶσιν.

[91] *lac. stat.* Reiske (*sed post* χώρας) <τιμιωτέρα ἢ> Behr <θειοτέρα ἢ> Lucarini

[92] *del.* Behr, *qui et* <αὐτήν> *ante* θείαν

a cloud from the twin goddesses descended on the battle at sea;[244] the gods and heroes, the allies that all the Greeks hold in common, joined their efforts to theirs and fought alongside them, in a practical demonstration of honor to Themistocles;[245] the epithet bestowed on Salamis was confirmed to the letter on all hands and the place established as divine in all respects. But when Salamis received 321
this name, then surely the sea battle received this name as well: Salamis had not previously been any more distinguished than any other place, and it was because of the battle that the god called it "divine."[246] But Plato, apparently, scorns the victory and passes a death sentence on those who achieved it and haughtily declares death preferable to victory in the company of the gods. If Homer had 322
still been alive, he would I think have been far readier to address the man who gave this advice and brought it to achievement as "equal to Zeus in cunning wit" than he would even the leader of the Cephallenians with his ocher-smeared ships.[247] If Zeus gave Athena the ships as a gift, and Apollo declared it, and Themistocles was attuned to this from the start and in the prevailing circumstances was the only one to think the same as the gods, how was he not in line to be the bearer of this epithet? But that was not how Plato told it: instead of calling him "like Zeus in intellect" and "divine," he compared him to Sarambus and the

244 Hdt. 8.65. 245 Cf. Plut. *Vit. Them.* 15, embroidering on Hdt. 8.64–65. Neither Plutarch nor Herodotus, however, mentions Dionysus in connection with Salamis.

246 The precise wording here is uncertain, but the overall sense is not in doubt.

247 *Il.* 2.636–37 (Odysseus).

πῶς ἄν τις μᾶλλον μεγαλοπρεπείᾳ παρὰ καιρὸν ἐχρήσατο;

323 φέρε δὴ κἀκεῖνο σκεψώμεθα, εἰ ὥσπερ τινὲς ἤδη λέγονται τῶν ἡρώων ἐν θεοῖς δικασταῖς κριθῆναι, οὕτω καὶ Θεμιστοκλῆς περὶ ὧν συνεβούλευσεν ἐκρίνετο ἐν τῷ Ἀπόλλωνι τῷ Πυθίῳ, ποτέραν ἂν ἤνεγκε τὴν ψῆφον ὁ θεὸς περὶ αὐτοῦ. πότερον τὴν καταγιγνώσκουσαν; ἀλλ᾽ ἄτοπον προειπεῖν μὲν αὐτὸν ταῦτα καὶ χρῆσαι, τοῦ δὲ ὑπακούσαντος καταψηφίζεσθαι. ὅπου γὰρ καὶ τὸν Ὀρέστην ἀφεθῆναι λόγος ἐν τοῖς ἄλλοις θεοῖς κρινόμενον εἰς τὸν Ἀπόλλω τὸ ἔργον ἀνενεγκόντα, ἦ που τόν γε παρ᾽ αὐτῷ τῷ Ἀπόλλωνι φεύγοντα ὑπὲρ ὧν μετ᾽ ἐκείνου κατέπραξεν οὐδεὶς λόγος ἦν ἁλῶναι. εἶθ᾽ ὃν οὐκ ἦν ἑλεῖν παρὰ τῷ θεῷ

324 κριτῇ, τούτου Πλάτων ἠξίωσε κατηγορεῖν; καὶ εἰ μὲν Ἀθήνησιν ἐκρίνετο μηδεμιᾶς τοιαύτης λέγω μαντείας προϋπαρχούσης, ἔπειτ᾽ ἔδοξεν ἐκείνοις ἐπιτρέψαι τῷ θεῷ καθάπερ πρότερόν φασιν τὸ περὶ τῶν φυλῶν, εἰ καλῶς αὐτῷ βεβουλεῦσθαι ἀνεῖλεν, ἀφεῖσθαι λοιπὸν ἔδει, καὶ μηδενὶ μηδὲν ἐξεῖναι παρὰ ταῦθ᾽ ἕτερον λέγειν· ἐπεὶ δ᾽ ἔφθη πρὸ τῆς αἰτίας αὐτὸν ἀφεὶς ὁ θεὸς καὶ πρότερον τὰς πράξεις ἐπῄνεσεν, πρίν τινα ἀνθρώπων εἰδέναι εἰ πραχθήσονται, καὶ μόνον οὐ συνεῖπεν αὐτῷ περὶ ἁπάντων ἐξ ἀρχῆς καὶ τὴν γνώμην ἣν εἶ-

---

248 A rhetorical generalization: examples apart from Orestes are in fact hard to come by.

whole class of grocers. Could there be any more unseasonable demonstration of hauteur than this?

Let us also consider the following. If, just as some of 323
the heroes are said to have been tried in the past before a jury of gods,[248] so too Themistocles had been tried in the court of Pythian Apollo, what verdict would the god have passed on him? A condemnation? But it would be bizarre to predict and to give his oracular response as he did, and then to condemn the man who listened to him. Given that even Orestes, when he was on trial before the other gods, is said to have been acquitted when he placed the responsibility for his deed on Apollo, there is certainly no good reason for the man on trial before Apollo himself for the actions he took in concert with him to be convicted. Did Plato then think it proper to prosecute the man who could
not be convicted before the god as his judge? Again, if 324
Themistocles had been tried at Athens, I mean without any such prophecy already on the record, and they had then decided to defer to the god over the issue, as it is said they did previously with the issue of the tribes,[249] and if the god replied that his actions had been well advised, then they would have had to acquit him, and nobody could have been allowed to dissent from this in any way. But when in actual fact the god acquitted him before the charge had even been brought and praised his deeds before anyone on earth knew whether they would be accomplished, and all but said the same as him about everything from the start and articulated his resolve in advance, even

249 According to [Arist.] *Ath. Pol.* 21.6, the oracle was asked to select ten names from a list of a hundred heroes to be the eponyms of the ten tribes freshly constituted by Cleisthenes.

χεν προεξήνεγκεν, ὅμως οὐκ ἀπέσχηται Πλάτων, ἀλλ' ἐναντία τῷ χρησμῷ πεφιλοσόφηκεν καὶ κατηγόρηκε τῶν πεπραγμένων, ἃ πρὶν γενέσθαι τῶν κρειττόνων τις ἐπῄνεσεν.

325 τί οὖν οὐ καὶ τοὺς Ἡρακλείδας, ὦ βέλτιστε, ᾐτιάσω,
διότι οὐ κατὰ γῆν εἰς Πελοπόννησον εἰσῆλθον, ἀλλ'
ἀπὸ τοῦ Ῥίου πρὸς τὸ Ῥίον περαιωθέντες; ἀλλ' οἶμαι
κἀκείνοις ταὐτὸν ἦν, ὅπερ τοῖς Ἕλλησι τοῖς περὶ Θε-
μιστοκλέα· κατὰ γῆν μὲν γὰρ ἔδει κρατεῖσθαι, κατὰ
θάλατταν δὲ ὑπῆρξεν καὶ σῴζεσθαι καὶ κρατεῖν. μέγα
δὲ σημεῖον· ἕως μὲν γὰρ δι' Ἰσθμοῦ τῆς εἰσβολῆς
ἐπειρῶντο, ἠτύχουν, ἐλθόντες δὲ ἐπὶ τὸν πόρον τὸν
Ἀχαϊκόν, εὗρον αὐτὸν πόρον ὄντα τῆς σωτηρίας αὐτοῖς. διόπερ ἐκείνοις ὁ θεὸς διὰ τῶν στενῶν τούτων
ἐπιχειρεῖν προὔλεγεν· οἱ δὲ ἀγνοήσαντες καὶ τὴν
326 ἑτέραν τραπόμενοι μικροῦ καθάπαξ ἀπώλοντο. τὸ δὲ
αὐτὸ καὶ τοῖς Ἕλλησι περιειστήκει τότε. οἱ μὲν γὰρ
ἐν Πύλαις ἀπωλώλεσαν αὐτῶν, οἱ δ' ἐν ταῖς ναυσὶν
ἐνίκων πανταχοῦ. στενὰ δ' ἦν, ὡς ἔοικεν, ἀμφοτέρωθι·
ὧν τὰ[93] μὲν φυλάξασθαι προσῆκεν, τοῖς δὲ χρήσασθαι. διὸ καὶ τότε οἶμαι Θεμιστοκλῆς τὸν Ἰσθμὸν
παντὸς μᾶλλον φεύγειν ἠξίου, ὥσπερ ἄλλο τι ἀρχαῖον κακὸν φυλαττόμενος, καὶ τὴν Σαλαμῖνα προὐ-
327 βάλλετο. καὶ μὴν οὐδέν γε ἀτιμότερον οὐδ' ἀδοξότε-
ρον τὴν Πελοπόννησον ἐκεῖνοι τότε ἔσχον παρὰ τὰς

[93] τά Canter Reiske τό *codd.*

so Plato could not hold back, but pitted his philosophy against the oracle and condemned the deeds that one of the higher powers had praised even before they happened.

Why did you not also bring a charge against the chil- 325
dren of Heracles, sir, for not entering the Peloponnese by land, but by crossing from Rhium to Rhium?[250] But I think the situation was the same for them as it was for Themistocles and the Greeks under his command: on land they were bound to be defeated, whereas at sea they had the prospect of both salvation and victory. A significant proof of this is that for as long as they attempted to invade via the Isthmus, they had no luck, but when they came to the Achaean Channel, they found in it a channel to their salvation. That was why the god told them in advance to make their attempt via these narrows; but they not knowing this and taking the other route were nearly destroyed once and
for all. The same reversal of fortunes happened to the 326
Greeks on this occasion too. Some of them perished at Thermopylae, while those in the ships were everywhere victorious. There were narrows, as it seems, in both cases, the one set of which it was appropriate to avoid, and the other to exploit. That is, I think, why then too Themistocles thought that they should avoid the Isthmus at all costs, and was as wary of it as he would be of any other ancient
curse, and why he thrust Salamis forward. Assuredly the 327
occupation of the Peloponnese by the children of Heracles was a no less honorable and glorious achievement because

[250] Two capes at the entrance to the Gulf of Corinth, one of them also called Antirrhium ("Opposite Rhium"), offering a narrow crossing point (Paus. 8.5.6).

ναῦς, ἀλλὰ πολλῶν κἀγαθῶν ὁπλιτῶν πρόγονοι κατέστησαν καὶ οὓς οὐδ' ὁ Πλάτων οὐδαμοῦ πώποτε
ἐμέμψατο τῶν εἰς τοὺς πολέμους ἕνεκα, καὶ πλείω
τοὺς ἐκγόνους αὐτῶν ἢ τὴν ἄλλην δόξαν <. . .>.[94]
[αὐτὸς γὰρ Πλάτων ὑμνεῖ τὸ Δωρικὸν τοῦτο στρατό-
328 πεδον.][95] τούτου τοίνυν οὐχ ἧττον ἐν καιρῷ τοῖς Ἕλλησι τὸ Θεμιστοκλέους τοῦτο στρατόπεδον φαίνεται
γενόμενον. ὅτι τοίνυν οὐδὲ χείρους ἐγένοντο ἐκ τούτων
Ἀθηναῖοι τὰ κατ' ἤπειρον ἔδειξε μὲν ἡ Πλαταιᾶσι
μάχη, ἐν ᾗ μόνους Λακεδαιμονίους ἐφαμίλλους ἔσχον·
ἔδειξεν δ' ἡ ἐν Μυκάλῃ, ἐν ᾗ μόνοι προὐκρίθησαν·
ἔδειξεν δ' ἡ ἐν Οἰνοφύτοις ὕστερον, ἐξ ἧς τὴν Βοιω-
329 τίαν ἔσχον καὶ Λοκροὺς καὶ Φωκέας. εἰ δέ ποθ' ὕστερον καὶ προσέπταισαν, οὐδ' ἐν ταῖς ναυσὶν ἐνίκων ἀεὶ
νικήσαντες τότε, ἀλλ' οὐ Θεμιστοκλῆς γε οὐδετέρου
τῶν πταισμάτων τούτων αἴτιος οὐδαμοῦ, οὗ γε καὶ
ζῶντος καὶ μετὰ τὴν τελευτὴν οὐκ ὀλίγον χρόνον τοσοῦτον ἴσχυον ἀμφότερα.

330 τὰ μὲν δὴ μέχρι τῆς ναυμαχίας καὶ τῆς φυγῆς τῆς
βασιλέως Θεμιστοκλέους ἔργα καὶ πολιτεύματα τοιαῦτα, οἷα προσῆκεν ἀνδρὸς εἶναι τὸ μὲν κολακεύειν,
ὡς ἐγὼ νομίζω, πλεῖστον ἀνθρώπων ἀποφυγόντος,
συνέσεως δὲ καὶ τόλμης ἐπὶ πλεῖστον ἥκοντος μετὰ
σωφροσύνης καὶ δικαιοσύνης ἁπάσης.

[94] *lac. stat.* Trapp *post* Reiske *fort.* <ἀπεφήνατο> *vel sim.*
[95] *del.* Trapp

they used ships; they became the ancestors of many brave
hoplites, of a quality that not even Plato could ever fault
in any way as far as their martial prowess was concerned,[251]
and he ‹counted›[252] their progeny as a greater glory than
anything else they were famed for.[253] This armada of The- 328
mistocles', then, was clearly a no less timely development
for the Greeks than that one had been. And that the Athenians did not thereby become any worse at land campaigning is shown by the Battle of Plataea, at which the Spartans
were their only rivals, and the Battle of Mycale, at which
they were the only ones to distinguish themselves. It was
also subsequently shown by the Battle of Oenophyta, as a
result of which they acquired Boeotia and Locri and Pho-
cis. If at any later time they did meet with failure, and in 329
spite of their victory on that occasion were not always
victorious at sea, Themistocles at least is not in any way to
blame for either kind of failure, seeing that both during
his lifetime and for a considerable time after his death they
were so strong in both theaters of operation.

Themistocles' actions and policies up to the sea battle 330
and the flight of the Persian king were such as befitted a
man who, in my opinion, shunned flattery more than anyone and attained the highest measure of intelligence and
daring combined with complete self-control and justice.

[251] *Leg.* 685b–e. [252] A word or more is missing from the Greek text at this point, and something like "reckoned" or "counted" is a plausible but by no means certain supplement.

[253] Perhaps based on *Leg.* 684a–e and 736c? The following sentence in the Greek text (bracketed opposite) looks like a reader's addition: "For Plato himself sings the praises of this Dorian army."

331 τὰ δ' ὕστερον ποῖ' ἄττα, ὡς ἐν βραχέσι διελεῖν; Μαρδόνιος μὲν ὑπὲρ βασιλέως ἐπεκηρυκεύετο Ἀθηναίοις, ἔργῳ πεῖραν εἰληφὼς ὅτι ἐν ἐκείνοις ἐστὶ τῶν πραγμάτων ἡ ῥοπή, καὶ ὁποτέροις ἂν πρόσθωνται,[96] τούτους ἀνάγκη κρατεῖν. ὁ δὲ πρεσβεύων ἦν Ἀλέξανδρος Μακεδόνων βασιλεύς. Ἀθηναῖοι δὲ ἀκούσαντες μὲν ὡς ἀνοικιεῖ τὴν πόλιν αὐτοῖς καὶ τὴν χώραν ἀποδώσει, ἀκούοντες δὲ ἑτέρας φιλανθρωπίας καὶ φιλίαν καὶ συμμαχίαν τὸν ἀεὶ χρόνον, οὐδενὶ τούτων ἐπήρθησαν, οὐδὲ κατῄσχυναν τῶν προϋπηργμένων οὐδέν, ἀλλὰ τὸν μὲν κίνδυνον τὸν ὑπὲρ τῶν Ἑλλήνων ἀντὶ τῶν κατὰ τῶν Ἑλλήνων δωρεῶν ἐδέξαντο, τῷ δὲ πρεσβευτῇ τὸ μὴ ταὐτὰ τοῖς προτέροις ἀγγέλοις παθεῖν διὰ τὸ σχῆμα τῆς προξενίας ἀφεῖσαν, προσέταξαν δ' ἐκποδὼν εἶναι παραχρῆμα καὶ τοῦ λοιποῦ τοιαύτας ἀγγελίας μὴ φέρειν. τοιαῦτα τῆς Θεμιστοκλέους πο-
332 λιτείας καὶ στρατηγίας ἀπέλαυσαν. εἰς τοῦτο δ' ἅπαντας προήγαγεν ἀνδρείας καὶ μεγαλοψυχίας καὶ τοῦ μισεῖν ἅπασαν ἀγεννῆ διακονίαν, ὥσθ' ἑαλωκότος μὲν δεύτερον αὐτοῖς τοῦ ἄστεος, πέμποντος δὲ πάλιν Μαρδονίου τοὺς λόγους, ἐν Σαλαμῖνι τῆς βουλῆς οὔσης καὶ τοῦ κήρυκος Ἀθήνηθεν ἥκοντος, ἐπειδή τις εἶπεν ἐν τῇ βουλῇ δέχεσθαι, συλλεγέντες πάντες κατέλευσαν, αὐτοὶ μὲν αὐτόν, αἱ δὲ γυναῖκες τὴν γυναῖκα αὐτοῦ, οὐδὲν ἀτιμότερον δήπουθεν, ὦ Πλάτων,

[96] πρόσθωνται *edd.* προσθοῖντο *codd. plerique*

What were his subsequent actions like, in a brief characterization? Mardonius had sent proposals to the Athenians on the King's behalf, having discovered from practical experience that it was with them that the decisive influence over events lay and that victory would necessarily go to whichever side they adhered to. The envoy was Alexander King of Macedon. The Athenians, on hearing that he would reestablish their city for them and give them back their territory, and also of further generous gestures and of perpetual friendship and alliance, were not moved by any of these inducements and did not disgrace any of their previous actions, but instead accepted the danger incurred in the defense of Greece in preference to the bribes they were being offered against the Greeks, and as for the envoy, although letting him off the same fate as had befallen the previous emissaries because of the respect owed to his status as *proxenos*, none the less told him to remove himself immediately and not to bring such messages in future.[254] That was the benefit they derived from Themistocles' statesmanship and military leadership. He brought them all on to such a pitch of courage and greatheartedness and hatred for all ignoble servitude that, when their city had been captured for a second time and Mardonius again sent his proposals, with the Council now sitting in Salamis and the envoy coming to them from Athens, when someone said in the Council that they should be received, they all gathered together and the men stoned him, while the women stoned his wife,[255] in a

331 acterization? … (margin)

254 For this episode see also *Or.* 1.172–75 and Hdt. 8.136–44.

255 See also *Or.* 1.157–58, along with Hdt. 9.5 and Dem. 18.204.

ἔργον ἐργασάμεναι οὐδ' ἐλάττονος ἄξιον εὐφημίας
τῶν ἐν τῇ σῇ πόλει τρεφομένων γυναικῶν, ἃς σὺ κε-
λεύεις μετὰ τῶν ἀνδρῶν συστρατεύεσθαι τὰ καὶ τὰ
333 ποιούσας. ἆρά σοι διακονεῖν ὁ Θεμιστοκλῆς λέγων
φαίνεται, ἢ ταῦτα παιδεύων τοὺς παρ' αὐτὸν συλλε-
γομένους; ἐλθόντων τοίνυν Λακεδαιμονίων ὑπὸ τοὺς
αὐτοὺς χρόνους Ἀλεξάνδρῳ καὶ παρακαλούντων ὑπὲρ
τῶν Ἑλλήνων, καὶ ὑπισχνουμένων παῖδας καὶ γυναῖκας αὐτοῖς καὶ τοὺς ἔξω τῆς ἡλικίας θρέψειν, ἕως
ἂν ὁ πόλεμος ᾖ, τοσοῦτον ἀπέσχεν τοῦ ταῦτά γε
θελῆσαι δέξασθαι ὥστε συγγνώμης αὐτοὺς ἀξιώσας
ἀπέστειλεν, ὡς οὐκ εἰδότας παρ' οὕστινας πρεσβεύ-
ονται.

334 τοῦ δ' αὐτοῦ φρονήματός ἐστιν καὶ ἡ στήλη, ἣν
ὕστερον τούτων ἔστησαν λέγουσαν τάδε, Ἄρθμιον
τὸν Πυθώνακτος τὸν Ζελείτην ἄτιμον καὶ πολέμιον
εἶναι τοῦ δήμου τῶν Ἀθηναίων αὐτὸν καὶ γένος, ὅτι
τὸν ἐκ Μήδων χρυσὸν εἰς Πελοπόννησον ἤγαγεν.
335 ἐγὼ μὲν οὐκ οἶδα ὅ τι τούτου ψήφισμα Πλάτων ἂν
ἔγραψεν κάλλιον ἢ σεμνότερον περὶ τοῦ αὐτοῦ πράγματος. σκοπῶ δὲ κἀκεῖνο ὅτι τῆς αὐτῆς φιλοσοφίας
ἐστὶν ἄμφω τὼ δόγματε· ὁ μὲν γὰρ τοῖς φύλαξιν
ἀπεῖπεν μὴ κτᾶσθαι χρυσίον, ὁ δὲ τὸν κομίσαντα τὸ
ἐκ Μήδων χρυσίον πολέμιον τῆς πόλεως ἀνέγραψεν,
336 κἂν τις ἀποκτείνῃ, μὴ εἶναι δίκας. οὐκοῦν ἣν Πλάτων
τῆς ἄριστ' οἰκουμένης πόλεως φυλακὴν ὑπελάμβανεν,

---

[256] *Resp.* 457a, 466e. [257] Hdt. 8.144.

deed deserving no less praise than do the women brought up in your Republic, whom you order to serve in the army alongside the men in one capacity or another.[256] Do you 333
think that Themistocles was playing the lackey when he spoke, or when he taught these lessons to those assembled around him? When the Spartans came at around the same time as Alexander and exhorted them on the Greeks' behalf, and promised that they would look after their children and wives and old people for the duration of the war, he was so far from being willing to accept this offer that he sent them away, in the belief that they deserved to be pardoned because they did not know what sort of people they were approaching with their embassy.[257]

The same proud spirit is also responsible for the stele 334
that they set up subsequently to these events with the following inscription: "Arthmius son of Pythonax of Zelea is stripped of his civic rights and deemed an enemy of the people of Athens, both himself and his family, because he took the Medes' gold to the Peloponnese."[258] I do not 335
know what nobler or more impressive decree than this one Plato could have composed on the same subject. But I do see that both their doctrines spring from the same philosophy: Plato on the one hand forbade his Guardians to own money,[259] Themistocles placed it on public record that the man who conveyed the money from the Medes was an enemy of the state and that if anyone should kill him, he should not face trial. Thus what Plato supposed to 336
be a safeguard for the best administered state Themisto-

[258] Also cited in *Or*. 1.369; cf. Dem. 9.42–43, 19.271; Aeschin. 3.258; Din. 2.24–25.

[259] *Resp*. 416e.

ταύτην ἐκεῖνος τῆς Ἑλλάδος ἠξίου ποιεῖσθαι, καὶ ταύτην τὴν στήλην καθιέρωσαν Ἀθηναῖοι τῇ θεῷ παραστήσαντες τῷ ἀγάλματι τῷ Μαραθωνόθεν, νομίζοντες οὐδὲν ἀτιμοτέραν οὐδὲ ἀχρηστοτέραν εἶναι τῶν ἄλλων ἀναθημάτων ἐν ᾗ τοῖς διαφθείρειν ἐπιχειροῦ-
337 σιν τοὺς Ἕλληνας ὅπως δεῖ χρῆσθαι γέγραπται. ἀμφοτέροις δέ μοι δοκεῖ τοῖς ἔθνεσι προσήκειν ἅπασαν ὑπὲρ Θεμιστοκλέους ψῆφον φέρειν ἀγαθήν. ὅσοι τε γὰρ τὴν σωτηρίαν οἰκειότατον καὶ πρῶτον νομίζουσι, Θεμιστοκλῆς ἐστιν ὁ βεβαιώσας αὐτὴν ἅπασι τοῖς Ἕλλησιν, ὅσοι τε φρονήματι κρίνουσι τὰ πράγματα καὶ τοὺς ὑπὲρ τῶν καλῶν κινδύνους καὶ τὴν εὐδοξίαν τοῦ ζῆν ἀσφαλῶς ἐντιμότερον ἡγοῦνται, οὐκ ἔχουσι τῶν ἐκείνου καλλίω παραδείγματα. ὥστ' ἀμφοτέροις ἂν τοῖς κριταῖς νικῴη δικαίως.

338 καὶ γάρ τοι μετὰ τὴν ναυμαχίαν συλλεγέντων εἰς τὸν Ἰσθμὸν ἁπάντων καὶ φερόντων τὴν ψῆφον ἀπὸ τοῦ βωμοῦ τοῦ Ποσειδῶνος περὶ τῶν ἀριστείων, ἔξεστι μέν τι καὶ ἄγνωμον ἐνταῦθα κατηγορῆσαι τῶν Ἑλλήνων, ἔξεστι δὲ τὸ λοιπὸν τῆς εὐγνωμοσύνης ἐπαινέσαι καὶ λαβεῖν ὑπὲρ Θεμιστοκλέους. ἕκαστος γὰρ ἑαυτὸν πρῶτον φέρων, δεύτερον συνεξέπιπτον
339 ἅπαντες φέροντες Θεμιστοκλέα. ἡ μὲν οὖν τοῦ πρωτείου ψῆφος, οἶμαι, τοῦ φύσει πᾶσιν ἀνθρώποις συμβεβηκότος ἦν, τοῦτο δ' ἐστὶν μηδένα ἑαυτοῦ μᾶλλον φιλεῖν· ὥστ' οὔτ' ἰσχυρὸν εἶχεν οὐδὲν οὔτε συγγνώμης ἀπήλλακτο· ἡ δὲ ὑπὲρ τῶν δευτέρων σαφῶς ἤδη σύμ-

cles engineered for the whole of Greece, and in dedicating this stele to the god the Athenians situated it next to the statue made with the spoils of Marathon, thinking it in no degree less worthy of honor or less useful than the other dedications, since it had inscribed on it a lesson in how to treat those who attempted to destroy Greece. It seems to 337
me that it is appropriate for both of two constituencies to vote unanimously in Themistocles' favor. For all who think that preservation is the primary consideration and the one that affects everyone most intimately, Themistocles is the man who secured it for the whole of Greece; those who judge matters by the criterion of pride and think that dangers in pursuit of noble ends and good repute are more honorable than living in safety have no finer examples to look to than those he set. It would therefore be only just for him to win in the eyes of both sets of judges.

Indeed, when everyone assembled at the Isthmus after 338
the naval encounter and they were casting their votes for the prize for heroism at the altar of Poseidon, the Greeks can be accused of an element of ingratitude at this point, but it is also possible in the main to praise them for their gratitude and to take it as a compliment to Themistocles.[260] For although each person awarded first place to himself, all the votes coincided in awarding second place to Themistocles. The vote for first place therefore, I think, 339
followed the natural pattern for the whole of mankind, namely to love no one more than oneself; it thus carried no weight and was entirely understandable. But the vote for second place really was a clear indication of the truth, and of their inability to vote otherwise. If therefore it had

[260] Hdt. 8.123–24; cf. §209 above.

βολον ἦν τῆς ἀληθείας, καὶ ὅτι οὐκ εἶχον ἑτέρως θέσθαι. ὥστ᾽ εἰ προείρητο ἐξ ἀρχῆς μηδένα ἑαυτὸν φέρειν, ἀλλ᾽ ἕτερον, Θεμιστοκλέα πάντες οἴσειν ἔμελλον, ὅν γε καὶ παντὸς ἄλλου πᾶς τις προὔκρινεν αὐτῶν, καὶ ὁμοίως ἂν πρῶτος ἐγίγνετο ὥσπερ τότε δεύτερος. οὕτω καὶ νῦν δεύτερον εἶναι ψηφισάμενοι προσόμοιον ἐποίουν ὥσπερ ἂν εἰ πρῶτον ἐψηφίσαντο.
340 οὐ μὴν οὐδ᾽ οὕτως ἔλαττον ἔχων ἀπῆλθεν, ἀλλὰ ἀμφοτέροις ἐνίκησεν. τὰ μὲν γὰρ πρῶτα καὶ παρὰ τῆς ἀληθείας καὶ παρ᾽ αὐτοῦ λαβὼν εἶχεν· τὸ γὰρ αὐτὸ τοῖς ἄλλοις ἐποίησεν μόνος τῶν ἄλλων δικαίως· τὰ δὲ δεύτερα ἤδη συνεκεχωρήκει· ὥστ᾽ ἐξ ἁπάντων πρῶτος ἦν.

341 ἀναχωρησάντων δὲ τῶν Ἑλλήνων καὶ διαλυόντων τὸν σύλλογον, ὡς εἶδον τὸ συμβαῖνον, κἀνταῦθα δὴ καλῶς αὐτοὺς ἐξελεγξάντων ὡς οὐχ ἁπλῶς οὐδὲ πολιτικῶς ἔχουσιν, οὐδὲ ἐκεῖνα ἐπὶ πᾶσιν δικαίοις ἐψηφίσαντο, ἀλλ᾽ ὑπ᾽ ἐσχάτης ἀνάγκης τῶν πραγμάτων ἀγχόμενοι καὶ οὐ πρὸς χάριν οὐδὲ πρὸς εὔνοιαν, τοσοῦτον ἁπάντων κατεγέλασεν ὥστ᾽ ἐν μὲν τῷ παραχρῆμα οὐδ᾽ ὁτιοῦν ἐφρόντισεν, καταστάντων δὲ τῶν πραγμάτων ἦλθεν εἰς Λακεδαίμονα ὥσπερ ἐπίτηδες. οὕτω φαῦλός τις ἦν τοὺς τρόπους καὶ αὐτόχρημα δι-
342 άκονος. Λακεδαιμόνιοι δὲ οὐ κατέσχον <αὐτοὺς>[97] πρὸς τὴν ἐπιδημίαν αὐτοῦ, ἀλλὰ καὶ παρόντα ἐτίμη-

[97] *add.* Keil (*sed plura deesse susp.* Reiske)

been prescribed from the start that everyone should vote not for himself but for someone else, they would all have been bound to vote for Themistocles, since every one of them preferred him to anyone else, and he would have come first in the same sort of way as on that occasion he came second. That is how true it is that, in voting for him as they actually did to be second, they were doing much
the same as if they had voted him first place.[261] In fact even 340
as things actually were he did not go away defeated, but won on both counts: first place he held because both the truth and he himself had awarded it to him (since he had done the same as the others, but was the only one to be justified in doing so), second place had already been conceded to him, so on all counts he came first.

When the Greeks drew back and, on seeing how things 341
had turned out, made to dissolve the conference, thereby neatly convicting themselves of not acting in an honest or civil manner, and of not having had full justification for voting as they did, but of having done so under the pressure of the utmost compulsion of circumstances and without any considerations of gratitude or goodwill, he was so scornful of them that he did not let it bother him at all in the immediate aftermath; but when things had settled down again he went to Sparta as if this was exactly how he had planned it. That is how commonplace a character he
had and how perfect a lackey he was. The Spartans did not 342
hold back <. . . . .>[262] in the face of his visit, but both hon-

[261] This sentence, which somewhat clumsily repeats what Aristides has just in effect said more allusively, may be a reader's addition.

[262] At least one word ("themselves") has dropped out of the text here, perhaps more (e.g., "their enthusiasm"). The episode is taken from Hdt. 8.124.

σαν ὡς οὐδένα τῶν παρ' αὐτοῖς βασιλέων, καὶ ὡς ἀπῄει, προέπεμψαν τριακοσίοις λογάσι τῶν νέων ἄχρι τῶν ὅρων τῆς Λακωνικῆς, μόνον Ἑλλήνων καὶ βαρβάρων καὶ τῶν πρότερον καὶ τῶν ὕστερον. τοσοῦτον αὐτοῖς ἔδοξεν ὑπὲρ ἅπαντας ἀνθρώπους Θεμι-
343 στοκλῆς εἶναι. καίτοι ὅτε τῶν Ἑλλήνων οἱ κράτιστοι τὰ κατ' ἤπειρον οὐκ ᾐσχύνοντο προπέμποντες ἐκεῖνον μέχρι τῶν ὁρίων τῆς χώρας τῆς ἑαυτῶν, πῶς ἔνεσθ' ἡμῖν τῶν ὁπλιτῶν ἕνεκα ψέγειν; ἢ πῶς μὴ ἐθέλειν ἐπαινεῖν, ὃν οἱ ἀντίπαλοι δοκοῦντες εἶναι καὶ ἄκοντες ἐτίμων ἃ μηδένα τῶν πώποτε;

344 τριῶν τοίνυν ὄντων καιρῶν ἀφ' ὧν τις ἐξετάσειεν Θεμιστοκλέα, κατὰ πάντας ἀνὴρ ἄριστος καὶ πρῶτος φανήσεται. πρὶν μὲν γὰρ ἥκειν τοὺς βαρβάρους, τάς τε πόλεις διήλλαξεν καὶ τοῖς ἀπὸ τῆς πόλεως πολίταις ἀνῆκεν τὰ ἐγκλήματα· συμβάντων δὲ τῶν ἀγώνων, Λακεδαιμονίοις μὲν οὐ διηνέχθη, τοὺς πολεμίους δ' ἐξέωσε μόνος· καταστάντων δὲ τῶν πραγμάτων καὶ Λακεδαιμονίων ἐθελόντων ἐκσπόνδους τὰς πόλεις ποιεῖν, ὅσαι μετὰ τῶν ἐναντίων ἐγένοντο, ἀντεῖπεν καὶ διεκώλυσεν, νομίζων ὅμοιόν τι συμβήσεσθαι τῷ τὴν Ἑλλάδα ἔκσπονδον αὐτὴν ὑφ' αὑτῆς ἀποφανθῆναι. πλέον γὰρ ἢ τριάκοντα πόλεις ἔδει τῇ συμφορᾷ ταύτῃ περιπεσεῖν. οὔκουν ἡγεῖτο προσήκειν εὐτυχηκυῖαν τὴν Ἑλλάδα λαμπρῶς οὕτως καὶ τῶν ἐχθρῶν κρείττω γεγονυῖαν τοσοῦτον ἐλάττονα ἢ πρότερον γενέσθαι. πῶς ἂν κρείττων ἀνὴρ ἐγένετο, ἢ πῶς δεξιώτερος τὰ πολιτικά;

ored him while he was there with them as they did none of their own kings, and when he went away again escorted him to the frontiers of Laconia with three hundred picked young men, a privilege extended to him alone among Greeks and barbarians both before and since. That is how far above all other men they thought Themistocles to be.
But if the people of the mightiest land power in Greece 343
were not ashamed to escort him as far as the frontiers of their own country, how can we criticize him for not using his heavy infantry? And how can we refuse to praise the man whom those reputed to be his enemies honored even against their will like no one in history?

There are then three crucial moments which might 344
allow us to assess Themistocles' quality, and in all of them he emerges clearly as the best and foremost of men. Before the barbarians came he reconciled the cities and remitted the charges against the Athenians who had been banished from Athens; when the conflict broke out, he avoided a quarrel with the Spartans and repelled the enemy single handedly; and when things settled down again and the Spartans wanted to remove from the protection of the treaty all those cities that had sided with the enemy, he spoke up against this and prevented it, considering that this would be comparable to Greece declaring herself removed from the protection of the treaty, because more than thirty cities would necessarily be caught up in this catastrophe.[263] He did not think it was proper for Greece, when she had succeeded so brilliantly and defeated her enemies, to be made so much smaller than she had been before. How could there have been a greater man, or one more politically astute?

[263] Cf. Plut. *Vit. Them.* 20.

345 *ἔχων δὲ λέγειν καὶ περὶ τῶν ὕστερον αὐτοῦ συμφορῶν, καὶ ὅπως [ἂν][98] ἅπαν τὸ πρᾶγμα συνεσκευάσθη, καὶ ὁποῖόν τινα κἀν τούτοις παρέσχεν ἑαυτόν, ἐβουλόμην μὲν ἂν ἐν τούτῳ χρείας εἶναι τὸν λόγον ὥστε καὶ περὶ τούτων ἐπείγειν διελθεῖν· οἶμαι γὰρ οὐδὲν[99] φαυλότερα οὐδ' ἐλάττω εἰπεῖν ἂν τῶν εἰρημένων ἤδη περὶ αὐτοῦ. ἐπεὶ δ' ἅμα τ' ἔξω τῆς ὑποθέσεώς ἐστιν καὶ μῆκος ἐπεισέρχεται τοῖς λόγοις, παραλείψω ταῦτα, τοσοῦτον ἐπιφθεγξάμενος καὶ περὶ τούτου τοῦ μέρους, ὅτι ἐπειδὴ ἔδει στρατεύειν ἐπὶ τὴν Ἑλλάδα, προὔκρινεν τελευτᾶν, ἔργῳ μὲν ἅπασαν λύσας αἰτίαν, δείξας δ' ὁπόσου τιμᾶται τὰς πρότερον πράξεις καὶ τὰ πολιτεύματα, καὶ ὅτι οὐδέποτε ἑκὼν εἶναι τοῦ καλοῦ καὶ τοῦ προσήκοντος οὐδὲν πρότερον ποιήσεται, οὐ πλοῦτον, οὐ παῖδας, οὐκ ἐλπίδας, οὐ*
346 *τὴν σωτηρίαν αὐτήν. εἶθ' ὧν ἵνα μηδὲν ἀνάξιον πράξειεν τεθνάναι δεῖν ᾤετο, ταῦθ' ἡμεῖς αὐτοῦ διαβαλοῦμεν; καὶ διάκονον προσεροῦμεν ὃς οὔτε Ἀθηναίοις οὐδὲν πώποτε ὑπηρέτησεν οὔτε τῷ βασιλεῖ πώποτε ἠξίωσεν, ἀλλ' ἀντὶ τούτου ταῦτ' ἐβουλεύσατο; καὶ πῶς οὐκ αἰσχρὸν ἂν εἴη καὶ ὑπερφυές, εἰ μήτε τὸν βίον μήτε τὸν θάνατον αἰσχυνθέντες αὐτοῦ ῥᾳδίως*
347 *οὑτωσὶ βλασφημήσομεν; ἐγὼ μὲν οἶμαι καὶ ἱερέας καὶ ἱερείας καὶ ὅστις ἄλλος Ἀθήνησιν εὔχεται δημοσίᾳ, τοῦτ' ἂν εἰκότως καθ' ἕκαστον ἔτος πρὸς ἅπασι τοῖς ἄλλοις προσεύχεσθαι, κατὰ γοῦν ἐκείνους τοὺς*

98 *om.* P.Ant. *del.* Dindorf   99 *οὐδέν* Ph^{AM} *οὐδέ cett.*

Since there are things that I could say about his subse- 345
quent misfortunes too, about how that whole business worked out and what sort of person he showed himself to be in these circumstances as well, I could have wished that the needs of this speech were such as to urge an account of them as well, because I think what I said would be in no way less creditable or substantial than what has already been said about him. But since this is extraneous to my main purpose and my discussion is becoming a long one, I will leave these matters to one side, saying only this by way of epilogue about this portion of his career, that when the need came to mount a campaign against Greece he preferred to die, thus absolving himself from all blame by practical action, and at the same time demonstrating how high a value he set on his earlier actions and political aims, and showing that he would never willingly place anything before virtue and duty—neither wealth nor children nor
hopes nor even survival. Are we then going to reproach 346
him for the very deeds about which he thought that he ought to die so as to avoid doing anything unworthy of them? And are we going to call a lackey the man who was never subservient to the Athenians in any way and never thought it right to serve the King of Persia either, but instead of that planned as he actually did? How could it fail to be a monstrous disgrace for us to reproach him as casually as this without feeling any shame before either his life
or his death? I for my part think that both priests and 347
priestesses, and anyone else who offers public prayers in Athens, could with every justification, along with all their other annual prayers, also pray—at any rate, in those

χρόνους καὶ ἕως ἐξῆν, φῦναί τινα αὐτοῖς ἄνδρα ὅμοιον Θεμιστοκλεῖ, καὶ μετὰ τῆς ἄλλης φορᾶς καὶ τοῦτο ἐνεγκεῖν τὴν γῆν τἀγαθόν. οὔκουν ἐλάττω γ᾽ ἂν ὄνασθαί μοι δοκοῦσιν ἢ εἰ πάντα εἰς ἑκατὸν καὶ ἔτι πλείω τῆς χώρας αὐτοῖς ἐξενεγκούσης.

348 ἄλλως μὲν τοίνυν ᾐσχυνόμην ἔγωγε ἐπὶ τοσούτοις καὶ τοιούτοις τοῖς εἰρημένοις μάρτυσιν προσχρώμενος· ἔστιν δέ τι προὔργου μιᾶς μαρτυρίας, ἣν δεῖ παρασχέσθαι. σκεψώμεθα δὴ ποῖ᾽ ἄττα λέγει περὶ Θεμιστοκλέους ἡμῖν Αἰσχίνης ὁ Σωκράτους μὲν ἑταῖρος, Πλάτωνος δὲ συμφοιτητής·

> ἐπειδὴ τοίνυν τοῦ Θεμιστοκλέους βίου ἐπιλαμβάνεσθαι ἐτόλμησας, σκέψαι οἵῳ ἀνδρὶ ἐπιτιμᾶν ἠξίωσας. ἐνθυμήθητι γὰρ ὁπόθεν ὁ ἥλιος ἀνίσχει καὶ ὅπου δύεται.—ἀλλ᾽ οὐδὲν, ἔφη, χαλεπόν, ὦ Σώκρατες, τὰ τοιαῦτα εἰδέναι.—ἤδη οὖν σοι πώποτ᾽ ἐμέλησεν ὅτι τῆς χώρας τοσαύτης οὔσης ὅσην ὁ ἥλιος πορεύεται, ἣ καλεῖται Ἀσία, εἷς ἀνὴρ ἄρχει;—πάνυ μὲν οὖν, ἔφη, ὁ μέγας βασιλεύς.—οἶσθα οὖν ὅτι ἐκεῖνος ἐστράτευσεν δεῦρο καὶ ἐπὶ Λακεδαιμονίους, ἡγούμενος εἰ τούτω τὼ πόλεε καταστρέψαιτο, ῥᾳδίως τούς γε ἄλλους Ἕλληνας ὑπηκόους αὐτῷ ἔσεσθαι· καὶ οὕτως εἰς φόβον Ἀθηναίους κατέστησεν ὥστ᾽ ἐκλιπόντες τὴν χώραν εἰς Σαλαμῖνα ἔφυγον, ἑλόμενοι Θεμιστοκλέα στρατηγόν, καὶ ἐπέτρεψαν ὅ τι βούλοιτο τοῖς ἑαυτῶν πράγμα-

olden times and while there was the scope for it[264]—for the birth of another man like Themistocles, and for the earth to bear this blessing too along with everything else that it yields. I think that this would be no less a benefit for them than if their land were to bear everything a hundredfold or even more.

In all other respects I would be ashamed to call wit- 348
nesses in support as well when so much has been said and in such a vein as this; but there is some gain to be had from one particular testimony, which ought to be presented. Let us then consider what we are told about Themistocles by the Aeschines who was Socrates' companion and Plato's fellow pupil:

> Since then you have been so bold as to attack the life of Themistocles, consider what sort of a man it is you have seen fit to criticize. Think of where the sun rises and where it sets.—But there's nothing difficult about knowing that, Socrates, he said.—Then has it ever yet crossed your mind that this whole territory, which is as broad as the course of the sun, is ruled by just one man?—Yes, of course, he said, the Great King.—You know then that he marched against us and against the Spartans, thinking that if he subdued these two cities, the rest of the Greeks would easily be subjected to him; and he so frightened the Athenians that they left their country and fled to Salamis, electing Themistocles general, and they entrusted it to him to manage

264 That is, the Roman Empire leaves no room any more for great, independent Greek statesmen.

σιν χρήσασθαι. καὶ δὴ αὗται μέγισται ἐλπίδες ἦσαν Ἀθηναίοις τῆς σωτηρίας, ἅττα ἂν ἐκεῖνος ὑπὲρ αὐτῶν βουλεύσαιτο. καὶ οὐ τούτου γʼ ἕνεκα Θεμιστοκλῆς τοῖς παροῦσιν ἠθύμησεν, ὅτι πλήθει νεῶν τε καὶ πεζῶν καὶ χρημάτων τὰ τῶν Ἑλλήνων πράγματα πολὺ ἐλείπετο, τὰ δὲ βασιλέως προεῖχεν, ἀλλʼ ᾔδει ὅτι εἰ μὴ αὐτοῦ[100] τῷ[101] βουλεύεσθαι ἐκεῖνος[102] περιέσται, τά γε ἄλλα αὐτὸν τοσαῦτα ὄντα τὸ μέγεθος οὐδὲν μέγα ὠφελήσει· καὶ τοῦτο ἐγνώκει ὅτι ὁποτέρων ἂν οἱ ἐφεστῶτες τοῖς πράγμασιν σπουδαιότεροι ἐν ἀρετῇ ἄνθρωποι ὦσιν, τούτων καὶ αὐτῶν τὰ πράγματα κρείττω εἴωθε γίγνεσθαι. καὶ τότε ἄρα βασιλεὺς ᾔσθετο τὰ ἑαυτοῦ πράγματα ἀσθενέστερα ὄντα, ᾗ ἡμέρᾳ ἀνδρὶ ἑαυτοῦ σπουδαιοτέρῳ ἐνέτυχεν. ὁ δὲ οὕτω ῥᾳδίως τηλικαῦτα ὄντα τὰ ἐκείνου μετεχειρίσατο ὥστʼ ἐπειδὴ αὐτὸν κατεναυμάχησεν, λῦσαι τὴν σχεδίαν ἣν ἔζευξεν βασιλεὺς πεῖσαι Ἀθηναίους ἐβουλήθη. ἐπειδὴ δὲ οὐκ ἠδύνατο, βασιλεῖ ἔπεμψε τἀναντία τοῖς ὑπὸ τῆς πόλεως δεδογμένοις, ὅτι κελευόντων Ἀθηναίων λῦσαι τὴν σχεδίαν αὐτὸς ἠναντιοῦτο, σῶσαι βασιλέα καὶ τοὺς μετʼ ἐκείνου πειρώμενος· ὥστʼ οὐ μόνον ἡμεῖς οὐδʼ οἱ ἄλλοι Ἕλληνες αἴτιον τῆς σωτηρίας Θεμιστοκλέα ἡγούμεθα εἶναι, ἀλλὰ καὶ αὐτὸς ὁ βασιλεὺς ὁ καταπολεμηθεὶς ὑπʼ αὐτοῦ ὑπὸ μόνου ἀνθρώπων ἐκείνου ᾤετο σεσῶσθαι. τοσοῦτον

their affairs as he wished. Indeed, the Athenians' best hopes of salvation lay in whatever plans he might make on their behalf. Themistocles did not despair of the situation simply because the Greeks' condition lagged far behind in the quantity of ships, infantry, and supplies they had and because the King's position was superior, but knew that unless the King was going to excel him in his ability to plan, all the rest of his resources, for all their magnitude, would not do him much good. He also knew that the side that had the more morally virtuous men in charge of its affairs was also the side that normally came out on top. And it was indeed only on the day when he encountered a man more virtuous than himself that the King realized that his was the weaker cause. But Themistocles found it so easy to master his forces for all their great size that, when he had defeated him at sea, he wanted to persuade the Athenians to destroy the pontoon bridge that he had yoked together. And when he failed in this, he sent a message to the King telling him the opposite of what the city had decided, that the Athenians had ordered the destruction of the bridge of boats and he had opposed it, in an attempt to save the King and his entourage. Thus not only do we and the other Greeks hold Themistocles responsible for our salvation; the King himself, who was defeated by him in war, also thinks that he owes his salvation uniquely to him. That is how much cleverer than the

---

100 αὑτοῦ Krauss αὐτοῦ *codd.* 101 τῷ QEU τό *cett.*
102 ἐκεῖνος E P.Oxy. ἐκεῖνοι UR² ἐκείνοις *cett.*

αὐτοῦ ἐκεῖνος τῷ φρονεῖν περιεγένετο. τοιγάρτοι φυγάδι ποτὲ αὐτῷ τῆς πόλεως γενομένῳ, ὡς σεσωσμένος ὑπ᾽ αὐτοῦ χάριν ἀπέδωκεν, καὶ ἄλλα τε δῶρα πολλὰ ἐδωρήσατο καὶ Μαγνησίας ὅλης ἀρχὴν ἔδωκεν, ὥστε καὶ φεύγοντος αὐτοῦ τὰ πράγματα μείζω ἦν ἢ πολλῶν Ἀθηναίων καὶ καλῶν καὶ ἀγαθῶν δοκούντων εἶναι οἴκοι μενόντων. τίς ἂν οὖν ἐκείνῳ τῷ χρόνῳ δικαίως αἰτίαν ἔχοι μέγιστον δύνασθαι ἄλλος ἢ Θεμιστοκλῆς, ὃς τὸν τῶν ἀφ᾽ ἡλίου ἀνίσχοντος μέχρις ἡλίου δυομένου βασιλεύοντα στρατηγήσας τῶν Ἑλλήνων κατεστρέψατο; ἐνθυμοῦ οὖν, ἔφην ἐγώ, ὦ Ἀλκιβιάδη, ὅτι ἐκείνῳ τοιούτῳ ὄντι οὐχ ἱκανὴ ἡ ἐπιστήμη τοσαύτη οὖσα ἐγένετο ὥστε φυλάξασθαι μὴ ἐκπεσεῖν μηδὲ ἀτίμῳ ὑπὸ τῆς πόλεως γενέσθαι, ἀλλ᾽ ἐνεδέησεν. τί οὖν οἴει τοῖς τε φαύλοις τῶν ἀνθρώπων καὶ ἐν μηδεμιᾷ ἐπιμελείᾳ ἑαυτῶν οὖσιν; οὐ θαυμαστὸν εἰ καὶ τὰ μικρὰ δύνανται κατορθοῦν; καὶ μηδέν γ᾽ ἐμοῦ, ἦν δ᾽ ἐγώ, ὦ Ἀλκιβιάδη, καταγνῷς ὡς πρὸς τὰς τύχας καὶ τὰ θεῖα πράγματα ἀλλοκότως καὶ ἀθέως ἔχοντος, εἰ προστίθημι ἐκείνῳ ἐπιστήμην πάντων ὧν ἔπραττεν καὶ μηδεμίαν οἴομαι τύχην αἰτίαν τούτων τῶν ἔργων γεγενῆσθαι. πολὺ γὰρ ἂν ἐγώ σοι μᾶλλον ἔχοιμι ἀποδεῖξαι τοὺς τἀναντία ἐμοὶ δοξάζοντας ἀθέως ἔχοντας ἢ ἐκεῖνοι ἐμέ, οἵτινες ἐξ ἴσου οἴονται τοῖς τε πονηροῖς καὶ τοῖς χρηστοῖς τὰς τύχας γίγνεσθαι, ἀλλὰ μὴ

King Themistocles was. Moreover when on one occasion he was exiled from Athens, the King thanked him as the one to whom he owed his life and bestowed many gifts on him, including in particular the kingship of the whole of Magnesia, with the result that even when he was in exile his circumstances were better than those of many highly reputable members of the Athenian élite who had stayed at home. Who therefore at that time could rightly be thought to wield the greatest power other than Themistocles, who as general of the Greeks subdued the man who ruled everything from sunrise to sunset? Take it to heart, then, Alcibiades, I said, that even such a man as this found that even such deep understanding as he possessed was not sufficient to protect him from being exiled and having his civic rights taken away by his city, but fell short. How then do you think things stand for commonplace humanity and those who take no care for themselves? Is it not amazing if they have the ability to score even small successes? And do not convict me, Alcibiades, I said, of having a strange, godless attitude to fortune and the divine, if I credit him with knowledge of everything he did and think that fortune was not in any way responsible for these achievements. It would be far easier for me to demonstrate that those who hold the opposite opinions to me are godless than for them to demonstrate it of me, since they think that fortune works out the

τοῖς καλοῖς κἀγαθοῖς εὐσεβεστέροις γε οὖσιν ἀμείνω τὰ παρὰ τῶν θεῶν ὑπάρχειν.

349 οὐκοῦν <ὁ>[103] αὐτὸς μέν ἐστι Σωκράτης ὁ λέγων κἀνταῦθα κἀκεῖ, φαίνεται δὲ ἐν μὲν τοῖς Πλάτωνος λόγοις διάκονον καὶ ὑπηρέτην ὀνομάζων καὶ μετὰ τῶν κολάκων τιθεὶς αὐτόν· ἐν οἷς δὲ νυνὶ παρεσχόμεθα, ἄριστον τῶν Ἑλλήνων ἡγεῖσθαι κελεύων καὶ προστιθεὶς ἐπιστήμην αὐτῷ τῶν πραγμάτων ἁπάντων, καὶ μηδεμίαν τύχην ἀξιῶν αἰτίαν γεγενῆσθαι, ἀλλὰ πάντ'
350 εἶναι τῆς ἐκείνου γνώμης. ἐγὼ τοίνυν τὸ μὲν τῆς προσθήκης τοῦτο οὐ δέχομαι, ἀλλ' ἀξιῶ τὴν γ' ἀγαθὴν τύχην ἁπάντων τῶν καλῶν ἡγεῖσθαι· ὅτι δὲ οὐχ ὁμολογεῖ ταῦτα ἐκείνοις ἐλέγχω. εἰ μὲν γὰρ ἅπαντα ταῦτά ἐστι λόγος ἀμφοτέρωθεν λεγόμενος καὶ πρὸς τὴν ὑπόθεσιν ἣν ἄν τις ἐνστήσηται δεῖ τὸ λοιπὸν ἅπαν περαίνειν, ὁμολογείσθω τοῦτο, καὶ οὐδὲν πλέον ζητοῦμεν· πάντως καὶ οὕτως ἀναίτιον τό γ' ἡμέτερον. εἰ δ' ἀπὸ σπουδῆς δικαίας λέγεται καὶ κρίσιν τῆς ἀληθείας ἔχει, ποτέροις χρὴ πιστεύειν, ὅταν ταῦτ'
351 ἐκείνοις ἐναντίως ἔχοντα φαίνηται; καὶ μὴν ἐξ ἴσου μὲν ἔγωγ' οὐδέποτ' ἂν θείην Αἰσχίνην Πλάτωνι, μήποθ' οὕτω φιλονικήσαιμι, ἀλλ' ἀφείσθω τοῖς ἀτόποις τῶν σοφιστῶν ἡ κρίσις αὕτη· φημὶ δὲ ὅσῳ μείζων καὶ τελεώτερος Πλάτων εἰς λόγους, τοσούτῳ μᾶλλον ὑπέρ γε Θεμιστοκλέους ἐκεῖνα προσήκειν[104] δέχεσθαι. τὸν

[103] *add.* Dindorf
[104] προσήκειν *edd.* προσήκει *codd.*

same for wicked and good alike, and that the noble and virtuous are not better rewarded by the gods because they are more pious.[265]

It is the same Socrates who speaks in both places: in 349
Plato's dialogue he clearly calls Themistocles a lackey and a servant and places him among the flatterers; but in the passage I have just adduced, he clearly tells us to think of him as the best of the Greeks, crediting him with knowledge of all his actions and asserting that chance played no part in bringing them about, and that they were all the
result of his intelligence. Now, I do not accept this addi- 350
tional comment, since I hold that fortune guides all good things; but I do detect an inconsistency between the first set of statements and the second. If all of this is an exercise in arguing for and against a proposition, and one has to complete the whole of the rest of one's case in line with whatever position one adopts to start with, then let this be agreed to and we will inquire no further; at all events, my position is entirely blameless even on this supposition. But if our discussion is being conducted with all due sincerity and involves a judgment about what is actually true, which side is one to believe, when it is clear that they contradict
each other? I would never, indeed, place Aeschines on the 351
same level as Plato—may I never be that eager to win an argument, and let us leave that particular judgment to sophistic paradox-mongers—but I do say that the greater and more perfect Plato is as a writer, the more ready we should be to accept what the other says in Themistocles'

265 Aeschin. *Alcibiades* fr. 8 Dittmar = 50 [fr. 9] Giannantoni.

μὲν γὰρ ἃ ἤκουσεν εἰκὸς λέγειν, ἢ ὅτι ἐγγυτάτω ἐκείνων, ὁ δὲ τῆς φύσεως οἶμαι κέχρηται τῇ περιουσίᾳ, ὥσπερ καὶ ἄλλα μυρία δήπου διεξέρχεται ἐπὶ τῷ Σωκράτους ὀνόματι, περὶ ὧν ὁμολογεῖται μηδὲν ἐκεῖνον πραγματεύεσθαι, δίκαια μὲν οἶμαι ποιῶν κατ' αὐτό γε τοῦτο καὶ ἀνδρὸς ἀρίστου, τὸ τὸν διδάσκαλον ἀξιοῦν κοσμεῖν, πλήν γε ὅτι καὶ τὸ μηδ' ἄλλους τῶν οὐκ ἀξίων καταισχύνειν ἐθέλειν προσεῖναι προσήκει.

[*Argumentation 5: Collective Vindication of the Four (352–510) (i) Unsustainability of the Charge of Corruption (352–460)*]

352 ἃ μὲν τοίνυν περὶ τῶν ἀνδρῶν εἰκὸς ἦν εἰπεῖν μήτε τῶν ἀναγκαίων εἰρῆσθαι μηδὲν παριέντας μήτε πάντα ἐφεξῆς οἰομένους δεῖν λέγειν, ὡς ἂν μή τῳ δοκοίημεν ἀπειροκάλως ἔχειν, ταῦτά ἐστιν. ἰσχυρίζεται δὲ οἷς προσέπταισαν πρὸς τὸ δημόσιον, ὥσπερ εἴ τινες χεῖρον ἔγνωσαν περὶ αὐτῶν, αὐτοὺς χείρους ἡγεῖσθαι προσῆκον, ἢ τῷ καὶ ἄλλους τινὰς εἰς αὐτοὺς ἐξαμαρτεῖν οὐδ' ἡμᾶς τοῦ προπηλακίζειν ἀπέχεσθαι δέον.
353 ἐγὼ δὲ οὐδ' ἄλλον τινὰ ἠξίουν ἂν ταῦτα ὀνειδίζειν, μή τί γε δὴ Πλάτωνα, ἀλλὰ μεμνῆσθαι τοῦ τί δὲ χείρων ἐγώ, ἂν ὁ δεῖνα ἐπὶ κόρρης ἀδίκως πατάξῃ με; τοῦ

[266] Aristides returns to this point about Plato's fictionalizing tendencies and their basis in §§ 577–87 below.

favor. For it is probable that the one says what he had heard, or something very close to it, whereas the other in my view has given rein to his superior natural talent, in the same way as he certainly relates thousands of other things in Socrates' name which it is agreed that Socrates had nothing to do with.[266] I think this was justifiable behavior and that of an excellent man, insofar as he saw fit to honor his teacher, except that he ought also to have wanted to avoid saying discreditable things about others who did not deserve it.

Argumentation 5: Collective Vindication of the Four (352–510) (i) Unsustainability of the Charge of Corruption (352–460)

So much then for what it was reasonable for me to say 352
about the Four, if I was to avoid both leaving out anything that absolutely had to be said, and thinking that I needed to mention absolutely everything point by point, so as not to give anyone the impression that I was deficient in finer feelings. Plato however lays emphasis on the reverses they encountered in their dealings with the demos,[267] as if it were appropriate for us to think worse of them if others have shown worse sense in judging them, or as if other people's mistakes toward them meant that we too should
not hold back from slinging mud. I for my part would not 353
have thought that anyone should revile them in this way, let alone Plato, but should instead remember his question "How am I a worse person, if someone or other wrongfully

[267] *Grg.* 515e–16e.

μὲν γὰρ ἢ φυγεῖν, ἢ χρήμασιν ἢ θανάτῳ ζημιωθῆναι, ἢ ἄλλ' ὁτιοῦν τοιοῦτον παθεῖν ἡ τύχη κυρία δήπου, τοὺς δὲ λόγους καὶ τὴν πολιτείαν αὐτῶν ἀφ' ὧν προείλοντο δίκαιον σκοπεῖν, ὧν ἐγὼ μὲν ὅπως ἂν ἐμαυτῷ συγγνοίην ἀξιοῦντι κατηγορεῖν οὐκ ἔχω.

354 οὐ γὰρ εἰκός, φησίν, παιδευθέντας ὑπ' αὐτῶν εἰς αὐτοὺς ἐξαμαρτεῖν, οὐδ' ἐξ ὧν βελτίους ἐγένοντο, ἐκ τούτων ἄδικόν τι ψηφίζεσθαι. ἐγὼ δὲ οὐχ ᾧ βελτίους ἐγένοντο φήσαιμι ἂν ἁμαρτεῖν αὐτούς, ἀλλ' ὅτι μὴ πάντ' ἐκείνοις ἠδυνήθησαν ὅμοιοι γενέσθαι. τούτου δὲ πολλὴν συγγνώμην οὖσαν ἀμφοτέροις εὑρίσκω. οὔτε γὰρ μὴ πάντ' ἀναμαρτήτους γενέσθαι, καὶ ταῦτα ὄντας δῆμον, οὔτε μὴ πάντας ἀναμαρτήτους δυνηθῆναι ποιῆσαι μεγάλης ἄν τις τῆς κατηγορίας ἄγοι. ὅπου γὰρ οὐδὲ ἄνδρα ἰδίᾳ καθάπαξ αἰτίαν ἐκφεύγειν ῥᾴδιον, ἴσως δ' οὐδ' ἐν δυνατῷ, ἦ που πόλιν γε τοσαύτην οἴεσθαι προσήκει. ἀλλὰ μὴν ὅπου γε καὶ τοῖς ἁμαρτοῦσιν αὐτοῖς εἰκὸς εἶναι συγγνώμην, ἦ που τοῖς γε ἄγουσιν αὐτοὺς πρὸς τὸ βέλτιστον καὶ οἷς ὅθ' ἡμάρτανον οὐκ ἐπείθοντο, δεινὸν εἰ μὴ φήσομεν.

355 Πλάτων τοίνυν ὧν[105] μὲν ἐκείνοις χρώμενοι κατώρθουν οὐδὲν ἐᾷ σκοπεῖν, ἃ δ' εἰς αὐτοὺς [ἐκείνους][106] ἐξήμαρτον, τοσοῦτον ἀπεῖχον τοῦ δοκοῦντά γ' ἐκεί-

[105] ὧν Trapp ὡς *codd.* [106] *del.* Trapp

---

[268] A question implied by *Grg.* 508d and 527c, though not formulated there in so many words.

[269] *Grg.* 516a–17a, 519b–d.

strikes me in the face?"[268] It is chance, surely, that was responsible for their being exiled, or being punished with a fine or with the death penalty, or having anything of that sort happen to them; but when it comes to their words and their political aims, it is only right to consider them on the basis of the choices they themselves made, and I for one cannot see how I could forgive myself if I saw fit to condemn them.

It is not likely, Plato says, that the people educated by 354
the Four should offend against them, or that the same things that were responsible for a moral improvement in these people should also be responsible for their voting for an unjust measure.[269] But I would say that their people went wrong not in virtue of their moral improvement, but because they were unable to become completely like their leaders. And I find that both sides have every excuse for this, because one would not think that either the failure to become completely free from error, especially for a whole people, or the inability to make everybody error free, was the grounds for a serious accusation. If it is not easy even for a single individual in isolation entirely to escape blame, and perhaps not even in the realm of the possible, then one should certainly think the same about a city the size of Athens. Moreover, if it is reasonable for the people making the mistake themselves to be forgiven, then it is surely monstrous if we are not going to say the same about those leading them for the best, whom they failed to follow when they were making their mistake.

Plato forbids us to consider any of the successes the 355
Athenians scored by following their advice, but the errors they committed against them (so far were they from doing

νοις ποιεῖν, ταῦτα[107] κατηγορεῖ.[108] καὶ ἃ μὲν τῆς παιδείας αὐτῶν ἀπέλαυσαν ὑπερβαίνει, ἃ δʼ οὐχ ὧν ἐπαιδεύθησαν ἦν, ἀλλὰ τῆς ἀνθρωπείας φύσεως ἐμμεμενηκότα, ταῦτʼ ἐπʼ ἐκείνους ἄγει τοὺς ὅπως μηδὲν ἁμαρτήσονται πᾶν ὅσον ἦν ἐν αὑτοῖς πράττοντας, ὥσπερ ἂν εἴ τις τοὺς γραμματιστὰς τοὺς παραδείξαντας τοῖς παισὶ τὰ γράμματα καὶ δείξαντας γράφειν ἐκ τῶν δυνατῶν αἰτίους εἶναι φάσκοι τῶν περὶ ταῦτα ἁμαρτημάτων, εἴ τι μὴ καλῶς ὕστερον μηδὲ ὡς χρὴ
356 γράφοιεν ἐφʼ αὑτῶν. ἀλλʼ οὐ ταῦτά γʼ ἐστὶν ὧν προϋπέδειξεν αὐτοῖς ὁ διδάσκαλος οὐδʼ ὧν ἐπαιδεύοντο, ἀλλʼ ἐκεῖνος μὲν ὅπως ὀρθῶς γράφωσιν εἰσηγεῖτο, καὶ ἅ γε σῴζουσι, τῶν ἐκείνου μαθημάτων σῴζουσιν, ταῦτα δὲ αὐτῶν ἐστιν ἁμαρτήματα, εἴτʼ ἐνδείᾳ μαθήσεως εἴτε ῥᾳθυμίᾳ εἴθʼ ὅπως δή ποτε ἐπακολουθήσαντα, πλὴν οὐ διʼ ἐκεῖνόν γε οὐδὲ τὴν παρʼ ἐκείνου συντέλειαν, οὐ μᾶλλόν γʼ ἢ καὶ οἱ τῶν τροφῶν ἀποροῦντες διὰ τοὺς πορίσαντας καὶ διδόντας αὐτοῖς ἀποροῦσιν. ἀλλʼ οἶμαι τῆς ἐνδείας ἐστὶν ἅπαντα ταῦτα, οὐχ ὧν τις μετέσχεν οὐδʼ ὧν ὅσον οἷόν τʼ ἦν
357 ἐκαρπώσατο. εἰ μὲν οὖν τι χεῖρον Ἀθηναίους ἐκεῖνοι προὐδίδαξαν, λεγέσθω τοῦτο κατʼ αὐτῶν, οὐδεὶς λόγος αὐτοὺς παραιτήσεται τὸ μὴ οὐ φαύλους εἶναι· εἰ δὲ μὴ πάντας ἐπαίδευσαν μηδʼ ὡς οἷόν τε ἀκριβέστατα μηδʼ ὡς μάλιστα ἐβουλήθησαν, τί τό γε

107 ταῦτα UR^2Ph^{M3} ὡς ταῦτα *cett.*
108 κατηγορεῖ UR^2Ph^{M3} κατηγορεῖν *cett.*

what those men thought was right) he denounces. And he overlooks the benefits the Athenians derived from their instruction, while attributing the blame for what belonged not to the lessons they had learned from them, but to the residue of their human nature, to men who in fact did everything in their power to ensure that they should not make any mistakes. This is like asserting that primary school teachers who teach children their letters and show them how to write to the best of their ability are to blame for their mistakes in this area, if subsequently left to themselves they were to write something badly or improp-
erly.[270] But these mistakes are not part of what their 356
teacher showed them previously or what they were educated in: he explained to them how to write correctly, and what they retain, they retain from his teaching, but the mistakes are their own. They may follow from faulty learning or laziness or whatever other cause, but they do not come about through the teacher or through his contribution to the process, any more than people who lack subsistence lack it because of those who supply them with it and donate to them. No, their mistakes are entirely a symptom of their lack, and have nothing to do with what any of them
did pick up or profit from as far as he was able. If there 357
was something defective in these men's instruction of the Athenians, then let it be set down to their discredit and no argument will excuse them from being called worthless. But if they did not educate all of them, and did not educate them in every possible detail and exactly as they wanted,

[270] The comparison with primary-school teachers (*grammatistai*) is picked up by Aristides from Pl. *Prt.* 326d; cf. §111 above.

ἐκπεφευγὸς τῆς ἐκείνων προστασίας ἄν τις τιθείη; οὐ γὰρ τῆς ἐκείνων ὁμιλίας τοῦτο ἀπώναντο, ἀλλ' οὐκ
358 ἀπώναντο ἐκείνων ἔτι τοῦτό γε. οὔκουν ἐξ ὧν προσεῖχον αὐτοῖς, ἐκ τούτων ἥμαρτον, ἀλλ' ἐξ ὧν οὐ προσεῖχον ἐπλημμέλησαν. οὕτως ἅ γ' ἐπείθοντο σαφῶς ἄρ' οἱ πείθοντες ἔπειθον καλῶς.

359 ἔπειτα μουσικὴν μὲν καὶ γεωμετρίαν καὶ τὰς ἄλλας τέχνας λέγω καὶ τὰς πάνυ φαύλας οὐ πάντες οἱ φοιτήσαντες παρὰ τοὺς διδασκάλους λαμβάνουσιν, ἀλλ' ἐκ τῶν πολλῶν ὀλίγοι κομιδῇ τινες· καὶ οὐδ' ἐν τούτοις οὐδεὶς ἐπαναγκάζει τοὺς διδασκάλους αὐτοὺς ὑπευθύνους εἶναι τοῦ διὰ παντὸς ἀκριβοῦς, οὐδ' ἂν ὁ μαθὼν μὴ πάντα κατορθοῖ, μηδ' ὅμοιος ᾖ τῷ διδάξαντι, οὐδεὶς τοῦτ' ἀναμφισβήτητον κατ' ἐκείνου τίθησιν, οὔθ' ὡς οὐδὲν ἐπισταμένου τῆς τέχνης οὔθ' ὡς ἑκόντος ὑποστειλαμένου οὔθ' ὡς τὸ σύμπαν εἰπεῖν ἀδικοῦντος. ἀλλ' ἴσμεν τὸν τοῦ Ὁμήρου λόγον ὃν περὶ τῶν παίδων ἔφη κἀπὶ τῶν τοιούτων ἰσχύοντα·

> παῦροι γὰρ (φησὶν) παῖδες ὁμοῖοι πατρὶ
> πέλονται,
> οἱ πλέονες κακίους, παῦροι δέ τε πατρὸς ἀρείους.

καὶ διδασκάλῳ τὸν μὲν ὅμοιον συνέβη γενέσθαι, τὸν δὲ οὔ, καὶ ὁ μέν γε χείρων, ὁ δὲ βελτίων ἐγένετο.

360 οὕτω ταῦτ' ἔχοντα σύνισμεν καὶ ἐν γένεσιν καὶ ἐν τέχναις· τὴν δὲ πολιτικὴν εἰ μὴ πάντας ἐπαίδευσαν

how then should we categorize the element that escaped their supervision? This was not a benefit the Athenians derived from associating with them but rather one respect in which they still failed to benefit from them. Equally, it 358
was not as a result of the attention they paid to their leaders that they went wrong, but rather their error resulted from the extent to which they did not pay attention to them. That is how clear it is that in fact, in the respects in which the Athenians did follow their advice, their persuaders did well in persuading them.

Or again, take the case of music and geometry and all 359
the other arts and crafts including the entirely trivial ones. Not all of those who go for regular lessons with their teachers pick these skills up, but only a very few out of the many, and not even in those cases does anyone compel the teachers themselves to be responsible for perfection in every detail: even if the learner does not get everything right and fails to resemble his teacher, no one sets this down unambiguously to the teacher's discredit or takes it to show that he knows nothing about his craft or is holding back on purpose, or in a word is doing anything wrong at all. We all know that Homer's declaration about children holds good in this sort of case too:

> For few children—he says—are like their father:
> most are worse and few are better than their sire.[271]

Similarly, some turn out like their teacher and some not, and one is worse and another better.

We are well aware that this is how things are both in 360
families and in the arts and crafts. So are we then to say,

[271] *Od.* 2.276–77 (cf. §149 above).

Ἀθηναίους Θεμιστοκλῆς καὶ Περικλῆς καὶ Μιλτιάδης καὶ Κίμων, μηδ' ἅπαντας ἐφεξῆς βελτίους ἐποίησαν κατὰ φυλὰς καὶ κατὰ ἄνδρα ὥσπερ θεωρικὸν τὴν ἐπιστήμην διανέμοντες, εἶθ' ὑπερφυές τι φήσομεν κατ' αὐτῶν εὑρηκέναι, ὡς οὐδ' αὐτοὶ βελτίους οὐδενὸς ἦσαν εἰς ταῦτα; καὶ τοῦ μὲν χυτρέως οὐ κατηγορεῖς ὅτι μὴ πάντας ἐφεξῆς πλάττειν ἐδίδαξεν, τῶν δ' ἄκρων ἐν τοῖς Ἕλλησιν κατηγορεῖς ὅτι μὴ πάντας
361 ἑαυτοῖς προσομοίους ἐποίησαν; καὶ οὐκ ἀγαπᾷς τὸ τοῦ σοῦ Πρωταγόρου, εἰ καὶ καθ' ὁσονοῦν [τὸ κατὰ μικρὸν][109] προὐβίβασαν τοὺς πολλοὺς εἰς τὸ βέλτιον, ἀλλ' εἰ μὴ πάντα ἀνεγκλήτως ὁ δῆμος καὶ ὥσπερ ἂν εἷς ἀνὴρ μετεχείρισεν, τοῦτ' ἤδη κατὰ τῶν προστατῶν ἐστίν σοι.

362 καὶ μὴν ὁρῶ μέν γε καὶ τοὺς ἰατροὺς καὶ τοὺς πάνυ χρηστοὺς εἶναι δοκοῦντας οὐ καθάπαξ οὕτως ἐξαιροῦντας τὰ νοσήματα ὥστε μηδὲ ἴχνος ἐμμεῖναι τῷ σώματι, ἀλλὰ καὶ τῶν ἀρχαίων πολλάκις ἐγκαταλιπόντας καὶ τὸ πραῦναι χάριν ἀρκοῦσαν τιθεμένους, καὶ ταῖς παντελέσι θεραπείαις τήν γε φύσιν οὐχ οἵους τε ὄντας ὑπερβῆναι, ἀλλὰ ταύτης μὲν ἀπήλλαξαν τῆς νόσου, ἑτέραν δ' οὐδὲν ἐκώλυσαν ἐπελθεῖν ὕστερον. οὐ γάρ ἐσθ' ἡ τέχνη διὰ τέλους ἀξιόχρεως,

[109] *om.* Monac. 432 Ph^{AM} *del.* Dindorf

---

[272] The fund established in Athens (probably in the fourth rather than the fifth century) to subsidize citizens' attendance at the dramatic festivals.

if Themistocles and Pericles and Miltiades and Cimon did not educate all the Athenians in political skills and did not make all of them better, one after the other, tribe by tribe and man by man, doling out understanding like money from the theoric fund,[272] that we have made some immense discovery to their discredit, and established that they themselves were not any better at these skills either? Can you decline to charge the potter with not teaching absolutely everyone pottery,[273] but still charge the foremost of the Greeks with not making everyone like themselves? Do you refuse to be satisfied if, in the words of your 361
Protagoras,[274] they induced even a slight moral improvement in the majority of the citizen body, but instead count it a black mark against the leaders if the people did not manage all its business irreproachably and as a single individual would have done?

I observe that doctors too, even those reputed to be 362
very good ones, do not remove diseases once for all in that sort of way, so that not even a trace of them remains in the body, but often leave something of the former condition behind in it and consider that in palliating it they have done service enough; even with all their therapeutic resources they are not able to overcome nature, but while ridding the body of one disease they have done nothing to prevent another coming on subsequently. For medical science is not completely adequate to the task, and it is na-

273 Aristides' challenge to Plato here seems to depend on a general truth about what it is reasonable to expect of craftsmen, rather than on any explicit declaration in the dialogues (neither *Resp.* 421d–e nor *Resp.* 467a exactly fits).

274 *Prt.* 328a.

363 ἀλλ' ἡ φύσις νικᾷ.[110] τί οὖν θαυμαστὸν εἰ κἀκεῖνοι πολλὰ καὶ χρηστὰ συμβουλεύσαντες Ἀθηναίοις καὶ πολλὰ τῶν δυσχερῶν κωλύσαντες μὴ διὰ τέλους αὐτοὺς ἠδυνήθησαν κατασχεῖν μηδ' ἀθάνατα ἰάσαντο, ἀλλ' ἡττήθησαν τῆς δήμου φύσεως, εἴτε καὶ τῆς κοινῆς ἀνθρώπων δεῖ λέγειν, καὶ μὴ ἠδυνήθησαν καθάπαξ ἐκ τῆς πόλεως ἐξελεῖν ἀδικίαν, ὥσπερ γεωργοὶ τὰ λυμαινόμενα τῇ χώρᾳ καθ' ἕκαστον ἐνιαυτὸν ἐκκόπτοντες, εἶτ' οὐκ ἐφικνούμενοι διὰ παντὸς τοῦ
364 σπέρματος. εἰ τοῦτον τὸν τρόπον κἀκείνους ἐθέλοντας καθαίρειν τὴν πόλιν ἐξέφυγε καὶ ἐνέμεινεν σπέρμα ἀναγκαῖον ἀδικίας καὶ ἀγνωμοσύνης, καὶ οὐ πάνθ' ὑπήκουσεν αὐτοῖς, ἀλλ' ἔσθ' ἃ καὶ καθ' αὑτὸν ὁ δῆμος ἐβουλεύσατο, τίνα ταῦτ' ἔχει τοῖς ἀνδράσι φαυλότητα, ἢ τί δεῖ τὰ ἑτέρων ἐκείνοις λογίζεσθαι, ὥσπερ ἂν εἰ καὶ στάσεως οὔσης ἐν τῇ πόλει καὶ τούτων τῆς ἑτέρας ἡγουμένων τῆς τῶν ἐπιεικῶν, εἶτα τὰ τῶν ἑτέρων ἁμαρτήματα καὶ τῶν εἰς τούτους πλημμελούντων αὐτοῖς τούτοις τις προσετίθει; καὶ τίν' ἔχει φύσιν, οἳ μήτ' ἔδρων ταῦτα καὶ προσέτι κωλύειν ἠξίουν; ἀλλ' ἴσως οὐκ αὐτοῖς ἐγκαλεῖν, ἀλλ' ὑπὲρ αὐτῶν ἄξιον ἐγκαλεῖν.

365 καὶ δῆτ' ἔγωγ' ἐνεθυμήθην ὡς λυσιτελούντως αὐτῷ Πλάτωνι τὰς αἰτίας ἀπολύομαι καὶ ὁποίας τινὰς αὐτὸς καθ' αὑτοῦ δίδωσι τὰς λαβὰς ἐκ τῶν ἐγκλημάτων τούτων, εἴ τις αὐτὸν βούλοιτο μιμήσασθαι.

[110] *οὐ γάρ—νικᾷ fort. secludenda*

ture that triumphs.[275] Why then should anyone be amazed 363
if these men too, although giving the Athenians much good advice and preventing many of their difficulties, could not restrain them completely and failed to cure the ineradicable, but were defeated by the people's nature—or should one say by common human nature?—and were not able to rid the city once and for all of injustice, like farmers who each year cut down and remove the growths that are damaging their land, but then do not deal comprehensively with the seeds from which they grow? If in 364
the same way, although these men wanted to purge the city, some inevitable germ of injustice and ingratitude escaped them and remained there, and instead of obeying them in every respect, the people took some decisions by themselves as well, what defect on their part does this involve, and why should other people's actions be put down to their account, for all the world as if there were civil strife in the city and they were the leaders of one side, the good party, and then someone were to blame them for the other party's mistake and the crimes the other party had committed against them? How can this be natural, when they did not commit these actions and what is more thought that they ought to be stopped? Perhaps the right thing is not in fact to accuse them, but instead to bring an accusation on their behalf.

It occurs to me, indeed, to reflect how much in Plato's 365
own interest it is that I should be refuting these charges, given the sort of handles against himself he offers by making his accusations, should anyone want to follow his ex-

[275] This sentence clumsily repeats Aristides' point, and should perhaps be expelled as a reader's note.

φέρε γὰρ πρὸς θεῶν, εἰ καθάπερ τὸν Πρωτεσίλαόν φασι παραιτησάμενον τοὺς κάτω γεγενῆσθαι μετὰ τῶν ζώντων, ἢ καὶ ὥσπερ τῶν κωμικῶν τις ἐποίησεν τέτταρας τῶν προστατῶν ἀνεστῶτας, ἐν οἷς δύο τούτων ἔνεισιν, οὕτως οἱ τέτταρες ἡμῖν οὗτοι, περὶ ὧν ἡ νυνὶ διαδικασία, ἀνάστασιν εὕροντο, ὥστε συγγενέσθαι Πλάτωνι μίαν μόνην ἡμέραν ἐπὶ τοῖς λόγοις τούτοις, ἔπειτα ἔλεγον τὸν Περικλέα προστησάμενοι, εἰ δὲ βούλει τὸν Θεμιστοκλέα, οἵπερ ἡμῖν ἐπὶ κέρως[111] *τῶν ῥητόρων—καὶ ὅπως μηδεὶς ἐμοὶ τὸ τραχὺ τῆς ἀποκρίσεως λογιεῖται· μάλιστα μὲν γὰρ οὐδ᾽ ἔσται τοιοῦτον οὐδέν, ἀλλ᾽ εἰς ὅσον οἷόν τε ἐπανήσομεν, ἔπειτ᾽ αὐτῶν ἐκείνων οἴεσθαι χρὴ τοὺς λόγους εἶναι καὶ οὐκ ἐμούς. τὸν ξύοντα δ᾽ ἀντιξύειν καὶ τοῖς ὄνοις ἡ παροιμία δήπου δίδωσι. Περικλέα δὲ κἂν τοῖς λέουσι μᾶλλον ἢ τοῖς ὄνοις εἰκάζειν φαῖεν ἂν Ὁμηρίδαι. ὥστε τοσοῦτόν γ᾽ ἐξέσται μεταδοῦναι παρρησίας αὐτῷ, ὅσον εἰ μηδεὶς ἀξιοῖ Πλάτωνος καταψηφίζεσθαι,* [*εἰ*][112] *μηδ᾽ ἐκεῖνον ἐκ τῶν αὐτῶν τούτων ἐνεῖ-*
366 *ναι*[113] †*κεκωλύσθαι διδάσκειν. εἰ δέ τις ἀχθεσθήσεται*

[111] *ἐπὶ κέρως* V² *ἐπικαίρως cett.*
[112] *del.* Reiske [113] *ἐνεῖναι* Trapp *ἐνείη μή codd.*

---

[276] For example, Apollod. *Epit.* 3.29–30. [277] Eupolis in his *Demes* had depicted the reanimation of Miltiades, Aristides, Solon, and Pericles (frr. 99–146 Kassel-Austin). [278] Diogenian *Prov.* 8.48, also used by Aristides in *Or.* 2.337 and explained in the Suda (*τ* 767, 4.570 Adler) and the Aristides scholia.

ample. Because come on, let us imagine what would happen if, just as we are told that Protesilaus gained permission from the powers below and moved again among the living,[276] or just as one of the comic poets portrayed four of the leaders of Athens, including two of our set, coming back to life,[277] so too these four men of ours, who are the subject of the present dispute, were to find a way of coming back to life, so as to keep company with Plato for just one day to debate this matter, and then they chose Pericles as their spokesman, or Themistocles if you prefer (they are the stars among our orators), and said—and please, everyone, be careful not to hold me responsible for the harshness of their response: because first and foremost it will not have any such character, and I will as far as possible soften it, but secondly because you must understand the words as theirs not mine. The proverb certainly allows even donkeys to scratch back at the one who scratches them,[278] and it is to lions rather than to donkeys that the epicists would say they liken Pericles.[279] So it will be permissible to allow him at least the freedom he needs to prove that, if no one thinks it right to condemn Plato, it would on the same grounds not have been possible for him to be . . . . . either.[280] And if anyone objects to this on 366

[279] "Epicists" here translates Aristides' "*Homeridai*" (sons/descendants of Homer); the reference is to the frequency of lion similes in Homeric epic to describe the demeanor and actions of its heroes, but cf. also §97 above.

[280] The Greek text is very uncertain at this point: a word meaning something like "criticized," "abused," or "condemned" seems to be needed in place of the transmitted *κεκωλύσθαι*, and other surgery is also needed.

τούτοις ὑπὲρ Πλάτωνος, αὐτόχρημα τἀναντία οἷς βούλεται ποιήσει. οἷς γὰρ τὸν Πλάτωνα συκοφαντεῖσθαι φήσει, τούτοις ὅπως <οὐχ ὡς>[114] συκοφαντεῖ βεβαιώσει; ἀλλὰ μὴν εἴ γε μηδὲ κακῶς ἀκούσασιν καλῶς ἔχειν οἰήσεται ταῖς αὐταῖς χρήσασθαι λαβαῖς, καὶ ταύταις μὴ ἐπὶ τῷ κακῶς ἀντειπεῖν, ἀλλ᾽ ἐπὶ τῷ διὰ τῶν ἐκείνου τὰ ἑαυτῶν ἀπολύσασθαι, πῶς εἰρηκέναι γ᾽ αὐτὸν πρότερον κακῶς ἃ μηδεὶς ἐπηνάγκαζεν καὶ δι᾽ ὧν χείρους ᾤετο ἐκείνους ἀποφαίνειν δεξιόν τι νομίζειν κελεύσει;

367 ἐροῦσι τοίνυν, ὡς ἐγὼ νομίζω, ταυτί, μᾶλλον δ᾽ εἶπον ἄν, "ἡμεῖς, ὦ Πλάτων, πολλὰ καὶ βλάσφημα ἀκούσαντες ὑπὸ σοῦ οὐ τοῖς ἴσοις ἀμυνούμεθά σε οὐδ᾽ ἐροῦμεν κακῶς, ἀλλὰ καὶ ἄνδρα ἐν τοῖς πρώτοις καὶ ἄριστον τῶν Ἑλλήνων ἡγούμεθα, καὶ τῇ πόλει συγχαίρομεν, οὐ σοὶ μόνῳ, τῆς σῆς φύσεως. πάντως δ᾽ ἐξ ἀρχῆς ἕρμαιον ἡμῶν αὐτῶν ἐποιησάμεθα ὅ τι ἡ πόλις ἡμῶν κερδαίνοι. κάλλιστον δὲ πάντων κερδῶν ἡ τῶν ἀγαθῶν ἀνδρῶν φορά· ὧν καὶ ἡμεῖς ποτε ᾠό-
368 μεθα εἶναι, σὺ δὲ οὐ δίδως. ἐπειδὴ δὲ καὶ Μιθαίκῳ προσεικάζεις ἡμᾶς τῷ τὴν Σικελικὴν ὀψοποιίαν συγγεγραφότι, εἰκὸς μέν σέ γ᾽ ἄμεινον ἡμῶν ταῦτ᾽ ἐπίστασθαι. οὐ γὰρ ἡμεῖς γ᾽ ἴσμεν περὶ τοιούτων συγγραμμάτων οὐδέν, οὐ γὰρ πυκνὰ ἐπεμίξαμεν τῇ Σικελίᾳ. ἀλλ᾽ ὥσπερ σὺ πρὸς τὰ πολιτικὰ ἀσχόλως ἔσχες ὑπὸ τῶν λόγων τῶν ἐν φιλοσοφίᾳ, οὕτως ἡμῖν

[114] οὐχ ὡς Keil

Plato's behalf, he will automatically be doing the opposite to what he wants; because precisely in claiming that Plato is being maliciously accused, he cannot—can he?—avoid confirming that Plato's own accusations are themselves malicious. Moreover, if he is going to think that it is not all right even for those who are being slandered to use the same wrestling holds, even when they are doing so not in order to return the slander but in order to use their opponent's actions to absolve their own, how can he possibly tell us to think it was a clever move for Plato to have taken the lead in hurling insults that no one was forcing him to utter and that he thought were going to show the Four in a worse light?

They will, then, in my opinion, speak, or rather would 367
have spoken, as follows: "Plato, although we have been on the receiving end of many insults from you, we will not repay you in kind or speak ill of you; rather, we think you an outstanding individual and the best of the Greeks, and we congratulate not just you but also the city of Athens on your genius. We have certainly from the very start counted any profit our city might derive from us as a piece of luck for us too. The finest of all profits is a crop of good men. We once counted ourselves as part of this crop, but you
refuse to grant this. Since you compare us to Mithaecus, 368
the author of the book on Sicilian cuisine,[281] it is likely that you understand these matters better than we do; we know nothing about that sort of treatise because we did not have frequent dealings with Sicily. Just as you had no free time for political activity because of your philosophical debates,

[281] *Grg.* 518b.

ὑπὸ τῶν λόγων τῶν πολιτικῶν οὐχ ὑπῆρχεν σχολὴ τῶν ἐκεῖ μαθεῖν οὐδέν. ἀλλὰ σέ γ' οὐκ ἀπεικὸς προστυχεῖν τοιούτοις ἀνθρώποις καὶ συγγράμμασιν, εἰ καὶ μὴ ἑκόντα, ἀλλὰ καὶ ἄκοντα, ὥσπερ που καὶ ἄλλων πολλῶν καὶ ἑκουσίων καὶ ἀκουσίων πεῖραν λαβεῖν, ἅτε πολλάκις διὰ τοῦ Σικελικοῦ πελάγους κομισθέντα.
369 φέρε δὴ πρὸς αὐτῆς τῆς ἐν Σικελίᾳ τραπέζης, εἴτε Μίθαικος αὐτὴν εἴτε καὶ ὁστισοῦν παρετίθει, τί σοι τεκμήριόν ἐστι τῆς ἡμετέρας φαυλότητος; ὅτι νὴ Δί' οὐ πάντας Ἀθηναίους δικαίους ἐποιήσαμεν. σὺ δ' ἐποίησας βελτίω τί Διονύσιον, εἰ μὲν βούλει τὸν Ἑρμοκράτους, εἰ δὲ βούλει τὸν Διονυσίου; συνεγένου μὲν γὰρ ἀμφοτέροις. οἱ δὲ τί σοῦ καὶ τῆς σῆς συνουσίας ἀπώναντο; καίτοι διελέγου δήπου πρὸς αὐτοὺς περὶ τοῦ δικαίου καὶ νόμου καὶ πολιτείας, καὶ τὴν ἰσότητα τὴν ἐν γεωμετρίᾳ καὶ πρὸς ἐκείνους ἐπῄνεις, καὶ οὕτω φιληκόως εἶχον ὥστε καὶ μετεπέμποντό σε, καὶ σὺ προθυμίας ἐνέλιπες οὐδέν, ὅπως ἀγαθόν τι πράξωσι
370 δι' ἐκείνων αἱ πόλεις. ἐλελήθεις δὲ ἄρα σαυτὸν ἁπάσαις ταῖς παροιμίαις ἐνεχόμενος, εἰς πῦρ ξαίνων καὶ λίθον ἕψων καὶ σπείρων τὰς πέτρας. τί γὰρ τῶν σῶν

[282] Plato's three visits to Sicily, described in the probably spurious Platonic *Epp.* 7 and 8, on which Aristides has already traded in *Or.* 2 (see §§279–90, with n. 144) and to which he now gleefully returns.

[283] Dionysius I and II of Syracuse.

[284] As at *Grg.* 508a.

so we had no free time to learn anything about how things
were there because of our political deliberations. But it is
not unnatural that you should have encountered individuals and writings of that kind, at least against your will even
if not of your own free choice, just as we suppose you
voluntarily or involuntarily had experience of many other
things, both freely chosen and forced on you, in the course
of your frequent journeyings over the Sicilian sea.[282] But 369
tell us, in the name of that same Sicilian table, whether it
was Mithaecus or whoever else that set it for you, what
proof do you have of our worthlessness? That we did not
make all Athenians just, of course, you will say. But did
you make Dionysius any better, whether Dionysius the son
of Hermocrates, or if you prefer Dionysius the son of
Dionysius (because you kept company with both)?[283]
What benefit did they derive from you and from your
company? Yet you surely conversed with them about justice and law and politics, and you praised geometrical
equality to them too,[284] and they were so fond of listening
to you that they actually sent for you,[285] and you yourself
showed all possible keenness to ensure that the cities of
men should be somehow advantaged through their agency.
But it turns out that without realizing it you have fallen 370
foul of all the proverbs: you have been carding wool into
the fire, cooking a stone, and sowing on rocks.[286] What

[285] According to *Ep.* 7, in fact true only of Dionysius II (327d, 338b).

[286] A trio of proverbs for wasted effort: Zen. *Prov.* 5.27; Leutsch-Schneidewin, *Corp. Paroem. Gr.* 1, Appendix 1.67; [Lucian] *Am.* 20. Aristides' jibe is all the more pointed in that all three are used by Plato himself: *Leg.* 780c and 838e, and *Eryx.* 405b.

νουθεσιῶν καὶ λόγων ἀπέλαυσαν ἐκεῖνοι; τί τῶν θείων ἢ τῶν ἀνθρωπείων ἄμεινον μετεχειρίσαντο μετ' ἐκείνην τὴν ἡμέραν, ἐν ᾗ σοὶ τὰ ὦτα ὑπέσχον; τίς αὐτοὺς μετάνοια τῶν πρόσθεν ἡμαρτημένων εἰσῆλθεν; τίς ἔρως φιλοσοφῆσαι πάντα τὰ ἄλλα ὑπερβάντας; τί βέλτιον ἢ τῶν κατ' αὐτὴν τὴν πόλιν ἔσχεν ἢ τῶν ἔξω; τίς Γελώων ἢ Λεοντίνων ἢ τῶν ἄλλων Ἑλλήνων [ἢ][115] τῶν ἐν Σικελίᾳ χρηστῶν καὶ δικαίων ἐκείνων ἔτυχε διὰ σὲ καὶ τοὺς σοὺς λόγους; εἰ δὲ μὴ τῶν Ἑλλήνων, τίνι[116] τῶν βαρβάρων [τίνι][117] τῶν ἐν Σικελίᾳ ὄντων
371 ἐνεδείξαντο ὡς βελτίους γεγόνασιν; εἶεν. ἀλλὰ τῶν μὲν Σικελίαν οἰκούντων οὐδενί, τῶν δ' ἐν Ἰταλίᾳ βαρβάρων ἢ Ἑλλήνων τίσιν εἰπέ μοι κάλλιον ἢ πρὸ τοῦ προσηνέχθησαν; εἰς τί καὶ πρὸς τίνας ἀνθρώπους ἐποίησε βελτίους αὐτοὺς ἡ σὴ πολιτεία; τίνι Καρχηδονίων, εἰ μὴ τῶν Ἑλλήνων ἔχεις εἰπεῖν, ἢ τίνι τῶν ἄλλων τῶν ἐν τῇ Λιβύῃ βαρβάρων ἀρετὴν ἀσκῶν ἐπεδείξατο ὁ τύραννος, ἀφ' οὗ τῶν Πλάτωνος δογμάτων ἠκροάσατο, εἴτ' οὖν ὁ πρεσβύτερος λέγω εἴθ'
372 ὁ νεώτερος; καὶ μὴν εἰ μὲν τοῖς συμβούλοις ἀνατιθέναι χρὴ τὰ τῶν ἐν ταῖς ἐξουσίαις ἁμαρτήματα, τί μᾶλλον ἡμῶν ἢ σαυτοῦ," φήσουσι, "κατηγορεῖς; ἐπειδή γε καὶ κατὰ σοῦ τὰ ἐκείνων ὑπάρχει λέγειν. εἰ δ' οὐδὲν ἂν εἶναι ταῦτα φαίης πρὸς σέ, τοῖς αὐτοῖς τούτοις καὶ ἡμᾶς ἀπολύεις, εἴ τι καὶ ὁ Ἀθηναίων δῆμος ἔξω τι τῶν ἡμῖν δοκούντων ἔπραξεν."

[115] *eras.* U *del.* Reiske [116] τίνι UR^2 τίσι *cett.*

good did the Dionysiuses get from your advice and teaching? What in the realm of divine or of human affairs did they handle better after that day when first they lent ear to you? What repentance overcame them for their previous misdeeds? What passion to leave all else aside and philosophize? What went better in the life of the city itself or in its external dealings? What inhabitant of Gela or Leontini, or from among the other Greeks in Sicily, found them good and just because of you and your teaching? And if not any of the Greeks, to which of the barbarians who live in Sicily did they demonstrate that they had become
better people? Alright, perhaps none of the inhabitants of 371
Sicily; but tell me, which of the barbarians or Greeks in Italy did they behave more nobly toward than previously? In what and toward which people did your political thinking make them better? To which Carthaginian, if you cannot name a Greek, or which representative of the other barbarian nations in Libya, did the tyrant demonstrate himself to be a practitioner of virtue once he had become a pupil of Plato's doctrines, whether it is the older tyrant
or the younger one that I mean? Furthermore," they will 372
say, "if the errors of those in power are to be attributed to their advisers, why are you accusing us rather than yourself, since their doings can be used to discredit you too? And if you were to say that all this is nothing to you, by this very assertion you absolve us as well, for anything that the Athenian people did beyond what we thought ought to be done."

---

[117] *om.* EV[2]

373 οἶμαι τοίνυν οὐκ ἀρκέσειν τοῖς ἀνδράσι ταῦτα, ἀλλ' ἐκεῖνο ἥδιστ' ἂν αὐτοὺς ἤδη προσθεῖναι, τὸ ποῖον; τὸ "ἐπειδὴ τοίνυν ἐν ἀμφοτέροις ἔνεστιν μὴ πάνθ' ὡς ἐδόκει τῷ συμβούλῳ πεπρᾶχθαι, πότεροι βελτίονι καὶ δικαιοτέρῳ πράγματι τὴν ἀρχὴν ἐπέθεντο ἡμῶν; πότερον ὁ τὸν τύραννον παιδεύειν ἀξιῶν καὶ πλέων ἔξω τῆς πατρίδος τοσοῦτον, ἢ οἱ τοῖς πολίταις τοῖς ἑαυτῶν τὰ βέλτιστα ἐθελήσαντες συμβουλεῦσαι, καὶ τούτοις ἐκ τῶν δυνατῶν ἀμείνω τὰ πράγματα ποιεῖν;
374 τί φῄς, ὦ Πλάτων, πρὸς ταῦτ'," ἐροῦσι, "καὶ ὅτε γε καθάπαξ οὐκ ἐκρατήσαμεν, πότεροι μᾶλλον τῆς γνώμης τῆς ἐξ ἀρχῆς ἐφικόμεθα; καὶ πότεροι πλέον προὐβιβάσαμεν; πότερ' ἡμεῖς βελτίους Ἀθηναίους ἀπεφή-
375 ναμεν, ἢ σὺ τοὺς τυράννους; καὶ μὴν ἐκείνοις μὲν πλὴν ἴσως ὀλίγων ἅπανθ' ἡμάρτηται, τοῖς δὲ μεθ' ἡμῶν ἅπαντα κάλλιον πλὴν ὀλίγων ἢ κατὰ πάντας ἀνθρώπους πεποίηται. τοσοῦτον ἡμεῖς ἀμείνους τοὺς ἡμῖν χρωμένους ἀπεδείξαμεν ἢ σὺ τοὺς σοί. εἰ δ' ἐρεῖς ὅτι βελτίους οὗτοι τὴν φύσιν, καὶ ταύτῃ φρονιμωτέρους ἡμᾶς ἀποδεικνύεις, εἴ τινας ἐν τούτοις ἔσχομεν ἐλπίδας, οὐχ ὥσπερ σὺ τοῦ παντὸς διήμαρτες, ἐκείνοις διαλέγεσθαι προὔργου τι δόξας εἶναι.
376 ἔπειτα ὥσπερ ἐν οἷς βελτίους ἑτέρων γεγόνασι τὴν φύσιν αἰτιᾷ, οὕτως εἴ τι καὶ προπετέστερον εἰργάσθαι σοι δοκοῦσιν, τῆς φύσεως αὐτὸ θὲς τῆς αὐτῆς καὶ μὴ λάμβαν' ἐφ' ἡμᾶς, μηδ' ἃ μὲν ἡμῶν ἡγουμένων κατέπραξαν, ἀποστέρει τοὺς συμβουλεύσαντας καὶ τοὺς

I think in fact this would not be enough for our men, 373
but they would at this point very much like to add—well,
what? This: "Since then it is a feature of both our two cases
that not everything was done as the one giving the advice
thought it ought to be, which of the two of us was it that
initiated the better and more righteous course of action?
Was it the one who thought it right to educate the tyrant
and sailed so far away from his homeland, or the ones who
wanted to give the best advice to their own fellow citizens,
and make things better for them as far as they were able?
What is your answer to this, Plato," they will say, "and 374
given that we neither of us scored an out and out victory,
which of us came closer to achieving our original aim?
Which of us made the more progress? Did we make the
Athenians better than you did the tyrants? Certainly your 375
tyrants except perhaps in a few cases did everything
wrong, whereas our people with a few exceptions acted
more nobly in everything than any people anywhere could.
That is how much better we made those who availed themselves of our services than you did those who availed
themselves of yours! And if you say that these people were
better in natural endowment, this too is a way of showing
that we are the more prudent, in resting some hope on
them, unlike you who missed your target completely in
supposing that there was anything to be gained by talking
with your tyrants. Again, just as in those respects in which 376
they have proved better than others you give the credit to
their natural endowment, so too if you think they have also
acted rashly to some extent, you should put the blame on
that same natural endowment and not take it out on us;
you should not on the one hand, in respect of what they
achieved under our leadership, deprive us who advised

συγκατεργασαμένους ἡμᾶς τὸ[118] δοκεῖν τὰ βέλτιστα παραινέσαι, ἃ δ' ἐπὶ σφῶν αὐτῶν ἐξήμαρτον εἰς ἡμᾶς, ταῦθ' ὡς ἡμεῖς ἀδικοῦμεν λέγε. ἐκείνων μὲν γὰρ καὶ ἡμεῖς αἴτιοι τὸ μέρος, τούτων δὲ οὐδὲ μικρόν. ἀλλὰ ταῦθ', ὡς ἔφη Σοφοκλῆς, πεπονθότα ἐστὶ μᾶλλον ἢ δεδρακότα.

377 "καὶ μὴν εἴ γε τὸ προσκροῦσαι καὶ χρήσασθαί τινι συμφορᾷ κακίας ἔλεγχός ἐστιν καὶ μέμψιν δικαίαν ἔχει τῷ πεπονθότι, σκόπει πρὸς τὰ ἡμέτερα καὶ τὰ σαυτοῦ. ποῖα ἄττ' ἀπέλαυσας τῶν τυράννων οὓς παιδεύειν προῃροῦ; μὴ ἄρ' οὐ Πολυκράτης τὴν ἔξωθεν τύχην οὐδ' αὐτὸς ἡμῖν ἦσθα. οὕτω μὲν ἐξ ἀρχῆς εἰρχθεὶς ἐτρέφου παρ' ἐλπίδα καὶ παρ' ἀξίαν ἅπασαν σεαυτοῦ, καὶ εἰ μή σε ἀνὴρ Ἰταλιώτης ἐξῃτήσατο τῶν Πυθαγορείων, ὥσπερ σὺ φῂς τὸν πρύτανιν, ὅτι ἡμῶν ἕνα μέλλοντα εἰς τὸ βάραθρον ἐμπεσεῖσθαι διεκώλυσεν, κἂν αὐτὸς ἴσως εἰς τὰς λιθοτομίας ἐνέπεσες, ἢ δή τοι τό γε δεύτερον οὐκ ἂν ὑπεξέφυγες 'Στυγὸς ὕδατος αἰπὰ ῥέεθρα' τοῦ πορθμοῦ, ἀλλ' ἐτεθνήκεις ἂν αὐτοῦ ἐν Σικελίᾳ. νῦν δὲ Ἀρχύτας ἦν ὁ κωλύσας καὶ Διονύσιος Ἀρχύταν μὲν ἐπιστέλλοντα ᾐσχύνθη καὶ ἔδωκε τὴν χάριν, Πλάτωνα δὲ οὐκ ᾐσχύνετο, ᾧ συνῆν

[118] τό E (Reiske) τῷ *cett.*

---

[287] *OC* 267. [288] The comparison is apparently between the treatment of Plato by Dionysius II (cf. *Ep.* 7.329d–30b, 347e–50b), and the arrest and murder of the unsuspecting Polycrates, tyrant of Samos, when on a visit to the Persian satrap Oroetes

them and acted with them of our repute for having given the best possible advice, while on the other hand, in respect of the misdeeds they committed against us on their own initiative, saying that these are our wrongdoings. We are in part responsible for the former, but not in the slightest for the latter, which in Sophocles' phrase are things that we had done to us rather than things that we did.[287]

“Indeed, if suffering a reverse and meeting with disas- 377
ter is damning proof of wickedness and fair grounds for reproaching the person it happens to, look at our case and at yours. What rewards did you reap from the tyrants whom you set yourself to educate? Perhaps we will find after all that circumstances made a kind of Polycrates of you.[288] That is certainly suggested by the fact that, right at the start, entirely against your hopes and against all that you deserved, you were put in prison and kept there; and if an individual from Italy, one of the Pythagoreans, had not interceded on your behalf, just as you say that the Chair of the Council prevented it when one of us was about to be thrown into the execution pit,[289] you yourself would perhaps have been thrown into the stone quarries, and would not for a second time have escaped 'the fast-flowing Stygian streams' of the crossing,[290] but would have died there in Sicily. As things actually worked out, it was Archytas who prevented this. It was out of respect for Archytas when he wrote to him that Dionysius granted the favor; he had no respect for Plato, with whom he had kept

(Hdt. 3.120–25). §385 below, however, suggests some confusion in Aristides' mind between the respective contributions of the two Dionysii to Plato's persecution.

289 Miltiades: *Grg.* 516d–e.

290 Hom. *Il.* 8.369.

καὶ οὗ τοὺς καλοὺς ἐκείνους καὶ σεμνοὺς λόγους ἤκουσεν, ἀλλὰ τοσοῦτον ἔδει τιμᾶν ἢ πείθεσθαι λέγοντι ὥσθ', ἵνα σου τῆς φωνῆς μὴ ἀκούοι, καθείρξας
378 εἶχεν 'ὥς εἴ τιν'[119] ἀτίμητον μετανάστην.' καὶ περιειστήκει σοι τὸ τοῦ Κίμωνος, ὃ σὺ φῂς πρὸς αὐτὸν τοὺς Ἀθηναίους οὐκ ἐθέλειν αὐτοῦ τῆς φωνῆς ἀκούειν, οὐδὲ σοῦ τότε ἠξίου Διονύσιος, πλὴν ὅσον οὐκ ἐν τοῖς ἴσοις ἦσθα. ἐκεῖνον μὲν γὰρ Ἀθηναῖοι μετέστησαν ὅπως αὐτοῦ δέκα ἐτῶν μὴ ἀκροάσαιντο, σοὶ δὲ οὐδ' αὐτὸ τοῦτο ἐξῆν μεταστῆναι καὶ πάνυ δήπου βουλομένῳ τε καὶ ζητοῦντι, νοῦν ἔχοντι, ὡς ἐγώ φημι. ἀλλὰ τοῦτ' ἦν ἡ δεινὴ συμφορὰ τὸ μὴ ἐξεῖναι ἀπελθεῖν, ἀλλὰ μένειν πρὸς βίαν καὶ μόνον οὐ προσηλῶσθαι.

379 "καὶ παραδίδωσι δή σε μετὰ ταῦθ' ὁ φίλτατος ἀνδρὶ Σπαρτιάτῃ Πόλλιδι, καὶ οὐδ' ἐνταῦθ' ἔστη τῆς ὕβρεως, ἀλλ' ἀποδόσθαι προσέταξεν, ἀποδόσθαι τὸν ἄριστον οἴμοι τῶν Ἑλλήνων, ὥσπερ ἀνδράποδον τῶν ἐπ' ἐξαγωγῇ. οὐκ ἂν ἡμῶν γε ζώντων καὶ τῶν τριήρων οὐσῶν τοῦθ' ὕβρισεν ὁ θεοῖς ἐχθρὸς ἐκεῖνος. ὅμως δ' ἐπέταξεν καὶ Πλάτων ἐξήγετο ἐκ Σικελίας ὑπὸ Πόλλιδος καὶ ὁ Πόλλις αὖ πάλιν παραλαβὼν Διονύσιον μὲν καὶ ἀπόντα ᾐσχύνετο καὶ ὧν ἐπέσκηψεν ἐμέμνητο, σὲ δ' ὁρῶν καὶ συνὼν παρ' οὐδὲν ἐποιεῖτο, ἀλλ' ἡ θαυμαστή σου δύναμις καὶ πειθὼ κατὰ τοὺς

[119] ὥς εἴ τιν' U ὡσεί τινα Q ὡς εἴ τινα *cett.*

company and whose famously noble and impressive teaching he had been exposed to, but was so far from honoring you or acting on your words that in order not to hear your voice he kept you imprisoned 'like some dishonored vagabond.'[291] The same thing happened to you as did to Cimon, 378
in that, as you say in your attack on him, the Athenians did not want to hear his voice, and on that occasion Dionysius did not see fit to hear you either. Not that you were in exactly the same position: the Athenians displaced Cimon so that they would not have to listen to him for ten years, whereas changing your location was exactly what you could not do, even though—very sensibly, I would say—you very much wanted to and were trying to. What was so terrible about your situation was precisely that you could not leave but were being compelled to remain and were all but nailed to the spot.

"After this your dear friend handed you over to the 379
Spartiate Pollis and, not limiting his outrageous behavior to just that, told him to sell you into the bargain, to sell—oh!—the best of the Greeks, like a slave for export![292] The impious wretch would not have committed this outrage if we had been alive and had our triremes! Nevertheless, he gave his orders and Plato was removed from Sicily by Pollis, and Pollis in his turn took control of you. Dionysius he respected, even though he was not there, and he remembered his orders, but he thought nothing of you, even though he could see you and had you with him: your amazing power and persuasiveness with words were trounced

[291] Hom. *Il.* 9.648. [292] The Spartan naval commander Pollis does not feature in *Ep.* 7 or 8, but his role in the story is reported by Plut. *Vit. Dion.* 5, and Diog. Laert. 3.19–20.

380 λόγους ἡττᾶτο τῶν ἐντολῶν τοῦ Διονυσίου. καὶ Πόλλις ἐκείνῳ μὲν συνεβάλλετο, καὶ ταῦτα τοιαῦτα ἐπιτάξαντι, σοὶ δὲ οὐδέν· προσθῶμεν δὲ ὅτι καὶ Σπαρτιάτης ὢν καὶ τεθραμμένος ἐν νόμοις καὶ πολιτείᾳ δεύτερα τῶν πασῶν ἐχούσῃ παρὰ σοὶ κριτῇ, μᾶλλον δὲ πρῶτα τῶν οὐσῶν. καί σοι μάτην, ὡς ἔοικεν, τὰ πολλὰ ἐκεῖνα εἰς τὴν τῶν Λακεδαιμονίων πόλιν ὕμνητο. ὁ γοῦν τῶν Λακεδαιμονίων ποτὲ ναύαρχος τοσοῦτον διήμαρτεν τῆς σῆς ἀξίας, ὅσον οὐδ᾽ ἂν εἷς Περσῶν ἢ Σκυθῶν, οἷς οὐκ ἦν συνεῖναι τῆς σῆς
381 φωνῆς τὸ παράπαν. καίτοι γε εἰ μὲν ἠξίους αὐτὸν ἀμείνω γενέσθαι Διονυσίου περὶ σὲ καὶ βουλεύσασθαί τι βέλτιον, ὁ δὲ οὐ προσεῖχέ σοι τὸν νοῦν, ἀλλὰ τοῦ μὴ παρόντος ἦν καὶ τοῦ τὰ αἴσχιστα ἐντειλαμένου, πῶς οὐχ ἡττῶ πάμπολυ τοῦ τυράννου καὶ ποῦ δίκαιος εἶ προφέρειν εἴ τίς τινα πείθειν ἐγχειρῶν ἀπέτυχεν; εἰ δὲ σὺ μὲν στέργειν ἠξίους τοῖς παροῦσιν, ὁ δὲ οὐκ ᾐδεῖτό σου τὴν σιωπὴν οὐδ᾽ ἁπάντων λόγων ἡγεῖτο ἱκανωτέραν εἶναι τοὺς προσήκοντας αὐτῷ λογισμοὺς περὶ σοῦ παραστῆσαι, πῶς τῶν εἰκότων ἐτύγχανες, ἢ πῶς τὰ πρέποντα ἀπέλαυες τῆς φύσεως τῆς σεαυτοῦ; νὴ Δία ἀλλ᾽ οὐδὲν σὺ χείρων, εἰ παρέπαιεν Πόλλις καὶ Διονύσιος. οὐδέ γ᾽ ἡμεῖς, ὦ μακάριε, εἴ τις περὶ ἡμᾶς φαῦλος Ἀθηναίων ἐγένετο.

---

293 This diagnosis of Plato's political opinions is based on the combination of *Resp.* 544c (timarchy, as represented by Sparta

by the commands of Dionysius. Pollis sided with him, even 380
given the character of those orders of his, and not at all with you, even though, let us add, he was a Spartiate and had been raised in the surroundings of the laws and the constitution which in your judgment are the second best of all, or rather the best of those that actually exist.[293] It looks as if all that praise of yours for the Spartan state went in vain. At any rate, the man who once commanded the Spartan navy mistook your worth more completely than any of the Persians or Scythians, who didn't understand
your language at all. If, in spite of your thinking that Pollis 381
ought to behave better toward you than Dionysius and be more enlightened in his decision making, he nevertheless took no notice of you, but sided with the absent party from whom these most disgraceful orders had emanated, how can it be that you were not utterly worsted by the tyrant, and how can you be justified in making it matter for reproach if a person fails in his attempt to persuade someone else? If on the other hand you saw fit to acquiesce in your situation, but he was not impressed by your silence and did not find it more effective than any words could be in inspiring him to the appropriate reflections on your case, how could you be said to have received your just deserts, or reaped the appropriate reward of your genius? For heaven's sake, you will say, it does not make you a worse person if Pollis and Dionysius were madmen. Nor does it make us worse people, my dear fellow, if any Athenian treated us badly.

and Crete, as the next best form of government after that of the philosopher kings) and the complimentary treatment of Sparta and Crete in the opening books of the *Laws*.

382 "εἰς τοίνυν τοῦθ' ἧκεν ὁ Πόλλις ὑπερβολῆς καὶ οὕτω σφόδρα ἐσπούδασεν, κύριος καταστὰς βουλεύσασθαι περὶ ἀνδρὸς οἷου μηδ' ὄναρ ἤλπισεν, εἶτα φανῆναί τι παμμέγεθες βεβουλευμένος καὶ ὑπερβάλλον φιλανθρωπίᾳ τε καὶ παιδείᾳ, ὥστε κομίσας εἰς Αἴγιναν, ἐν ᾗ θάνατος προείρητο εἴ τις Ἀθηναίων ἐπι-
383 βαίνων ληφθείη, ἐνταῦθα ἐκβιβάζει σε. κἀνταῦθα αὖ τὸ τοῦ Θεμιστοκλέους ἠτύχεις, μᾶλλον δὲ καὶ ηὐτύχεις. ἐκεῖνός τε γὰρ εἰς Μολοττοὺς ὡς Ἄδμητον ἐχθρὸν ὄντα αὐτῷ παραγίγνεται καὶ δι' ἐκείνου σῴζεται καὶ σοὶ παρὰ τοῖς ἐχθροῖς τοῖς κοινοῖς τῆς πατρίδος τῆς σαυτοῦ συνέβαινεν ἐξετάζεσθαι. καὶ εἰ μὴ ἐκεῖνοι βελτίους ἐγένοντο τοῦ τυράννου καὶ τοῦ διακόνου, [καὶ οὗτοί γε καλῶς ποιοῦντες τὴν Πλάτωνος φιλοσοφίαν καὶ δόξαν ᾐσχύνθησαν][120] ἐτεθνήκεις ἂν αὐτόθι νῆσον ἀντὶ νήσου μεταλαβών, ἐν προθύροις τῆς πατρίδος, οὐκ ἐν Σικελίᾳ· τοσοῦτον ἔμελλες κερ-
384 δαίνειν. ὁ δὲ χρηστὸς σύμπλους ὁ Σπαρτιάτης οὐδ' ὣς ἐπελάθετο ὧν ἤκουσε παρὰ τοῦ Διονυσίου, ἀλλ' ἐπώλησε 'τὴν ἱερὰν κεφαλήν·' καὶ πωλοῦντος Πόλλιδος Ἑλλήνων μὲν οὐδεὶς ὠνεῖτό σε—οὕτω πάντες κατείχοντο ὑπὸ τῶν σῶν λόγων—Λίβυς δ' ἄνθρωπος Ἀννίκερις ὄνομα, ὃν οὐδ' ἠπίστατο ἀνθρώπων οὐδείς,

[120] *del.* Trapp *ut parenthesim distinx.* Reiske

---

[294] Thuc. 1.136; Plut. *Vit. Them.* 24.

[295] Following these words, the transmitted text adds "and these men at least did well in respecting Plato's reputation and

"Well then, Pollis, given the authority to decide the fate 382
of a greater man than he had ever even dreamed of, and
on the strength of this having planned for the commission
of some great deed of superabundant generosity and culture, reached such a pitch of extravagance and such an
intensity of enthusiasm that he took you to Aegina, where
the prescribed penalty for any Athenian caught landing
was death, and put you ashore there. Here once again 383
you experienced the same ill fortune as Themistocles, or
rather the same good fortune.[294] He turned up among the
Molossians at the court of Admetus, although Admetus
was his enemy, and was saved by his agency, and you too
had the experience of presenting yourself among the common foes of your homeland; and if they had not been
better men than the tyrant and his lackey,[295] you would
have died there having merely exchanged one island for
another, with the only advantage that you stood to gain
from this being that it was happening on the threshold of
your own country rather than in Sicily. But your excellent 384
traveling companion the Spartiate did not even so forget
his instructions from Dionysius and sold your 'dear sacred
person.'[296] And when Pollis sold you, it was no Greek who
bought you—so heavily under the spell of your words were
they all—but a Libyan by the name of Anniceris, whom no
one at all would ever have heard of if he had not taken

his philosophy." This clumsy expansion of Aristides' point looks like a reader's annotation and has accordingly been bracketed in the Greek text opposite.

296 An echo of Platonic idiom: *Phdr.* 234d; cf. 264a, *Grg.* 513e, *Ion* 531d, *Euthyd.* 293e.

εἰ μὴ ταῖς σαῖς συμφοραῖς ἀπεχρήσατο. νῦν δ' οὐ Πλάτωνα ἐπρίατο, ἀλλὰ δόξαν αὐτῷ καὶ τὸ γιγνώσκεσθαι. καὶ τότε ἤδη Δίων τὰ θαυμαστὰ ἐφιλανθρωπεύετο πέμπων τὰ λύτρα τῷ Λίβυϊ. ἀλλ' οὐδ' ἐκεῖνός γ' ἡττήθη τοῦ Δίωνος, ἀλλ' ἀφῆκέ σε προῖκα, ὁ μηδεπώποτ' ἰδὼν πρότερον μηδ' ὁμιλήσας μηδαμοῦ μήτε νήσων μήτ' ἠπείρου.

385 "ἐλθὼν τοίνυν οἴκαδε καὶ διαφυγὼν ὥσπερ τις Ὀδυσσεὺς οὐ θανάτους μόνον, ἀλλὰ καὶ δουλείαν, καὶ οὑτωσὶ σαφῶς ἐπὶ τῇ ἑτέρων κακίᾳ καὶ φιλανθρωπίᾳ γενόμενος χρόνον μέν τινα ἡσυχάσας· ὡς δὲ τελευτήσαντος τοῦ προτέρου Διονυσίου παραλαβὼν τὴν ἀρχὴν ὁ ἐξ ἐκείνου Διονύσιος μετεπέμπετο αὖθίς σε εἰς τὴν πολυΰμνητον Σικελίαν, ὥσπερ μετὰ τῶν ἄλλων ὧν παρὰ τοῦ πατρὸς παρειλήφει καὶ τὴν εἰς σὲ ὕβριν παρειληφώς, καὶ κληρονομῶν καὶ τοῦ σοι προστάττειν, ὥσπερ Συρακοσίοις ἢ τοῖς ἄλλοις τοῖς ἐν Σι-
386 κελίᾳ, ᾤχου δὴ πλέων. καὶ ποίων τινῶν ἀπέλαυσας πάλιν αὐτὸς οἶσθα, ὡς οὔθ' ὧν ἀπῆρας χάριν διεπράξω ἠνέσχου τε πολλὰ καὶ παντοῖα, καὶ παντὸς μᾶλλον ἢ σαυτοῦ, τοσοῦτον εὐτυχήσας μόνον, εἰρήσεται γάρ, ὅσον οὐ μετέσχες τῆς Φιλοξένου τοῦ διθυραμβοποιοῦ τύχης, καίτοι πράττων μάλιστά πως

297 Like Pollis', Anniceris' role in the story is not mentioned in *Ep.* 7, but it is noted in Diog. Laert. 3.20; his connection with Plato features also in Ael. *VH* 2.27.

advantage of your misfortune.[297] In the event, what he bought was not Plato, but fame and recognition for himself. It was at this point at long last that Dion performed his amazing act of generosity by sending the Libyan the price of your freedom. The latter however was not to be outdone by Dion and set you free for nothing—a man who had never seen you before and had not kept company with you anywhere on islands or mainland.

"Having returned home, then, and like some Odysseus 385
escaped not just death but also enslavement,[298] and having
thus clearly been at the mercy of other people's malice and
generosity, you rested for a while. But when the first Dionysius died and his son Dionysius succeeded to the throne
and summoned you once more to the Sicily of which we
hear so much,[299] as if along with the rest of his inheritance
from his father he had also inherited his outrageous behavior toward you, and was heir to the right to order you
about, just like the Syracusans and the other Sicilians, off
you sailed. What sort of reward you received this time, you 386
yourself know only too well: how you did not accomplish
what you had set out to do, and had to endure all manner
of tribulations of a kind appropriate to anyone sooner than
you, and—be it said—were fortunate only to the extent
that you did not share the fate of the dithyrambic poet
Philoxenus, even though your deeds and his were in pretty

298 The comparison echoes Plato's own in *Ep.* 7.345e.

299 "Of which we hear so much" (*polyhymnetos*) is ambiguous between "so well known in poetry" and "so much talked of in connection with you (Plato)."

387 ἀντίπαλα ἐκείνῳ. μή τοι νομίσῃς ἡμᾶς ἀγνοεῖν τοὺς σοὺς λόγους ἢ μὴ συγχωρεῖν ἀληθεῖς εἶναι, ὡς οὐ θέμις ἀνδρὶ βελτίονι ὑπὸ χείρονος οὔθ' ὑβρίζεσθαι οὔτε βλάπτεσθαι. σύνισμεν ταῦτα καὶ μαρτυροῦμεν ὡς ἀληθῆ λέγεις, ὅμως δέ γε ὁ θαυμαστὸς ἐκεῖνος ἐραστής σου οὐδ' ὁτιοῦν ὕβρεως καὶ ἀσελγείας ἀπέλιπεν. καὶ σὺ μὲν ἴσως οὐδὲν ὑβρίσθης, ὁ δ' οἷς ἡγεῖτο ὑβρίζειν, πλείω ταῦτ' ἔπραττεν ἢ δι' ὧν ᾔδει τιμήσων.

388 "καὶ οὐδ' οὕτω κατέλυσας τὴν πρὸς ἐκεῖνον ὁμιλίαν καὶ τὸ πλεῖν, ἀλλ' οὕτω παρ' ἐλπίδα καὶ παρ' ἀξίαν ἀπαλλάξας καὶ ἀγαπητῶς ἀποσωθεὶς πάλιν οἴκαδε τοσοῦτον ἀπέσχες τοῦ ἑτέροις τι δύνασθαι συμβουλεῦσαι ὥστ' οὐδὲ σαυτῷ συνεβούλευσας, ὅπερ λοιπὸν ἦν. ἀλλ' ἡ μὲν παροιμία καὶ Ὅμηρός φησιν,

ῥεχθὲν δέ τε νήπιος ἔγνω·

σὺ δ' ὁ τῶν Ἑλλήνων σοφώτατος οὐδ' οὕτως ἐπαιδεύθης, ἀλλὰ πάλιν σε χειροῦται Διονύσιος, ἐλπίδας φιλανθρώπους ὑποτείνας, καὶ πάλιν αὖ τῶν τῆς τυραννίδος κακῶν ἐπειρῶ, τὸ τρίτον πλεύσας ὥσπερ οἱ παλαισταὶ παλαίουσιν, δὶς μὲν πρὸς τὸν αὐτὸν προσπταίσας, τρίτον δ' ὅλως πρὸς τύραννον καὶ τυραννικὴν οἰκίαν. οὕτως οὐδ' αὐτὸς ἐξ οὐρίας τὰ πάντα

300 Philoxenus of Cythera (ca. 435–380 BC; *PMG* 814–35) attempted to seduce Dionysius I's mistress and was sent by him to the stone quarries; either there or subsequently, after his es-

close correspondence.[300] Do not suppose that we do not know or do not concede the truth of your declaration that it is not in accord with divine law for a better man to be outraged or harmed by a worse.[301] We are well aware of that and testify to the truth of what you say, yet even so that amazing lover of yours left no outrageous or insolent action undone. You perhaps did not suffer any outrage, but he certainly did more that he thought would inflict outrage on you than he knew would do you honor. 387

"Even this did not persuade you to put an end to your voyaging and to your dealings with him: although you escaped as you did in such an unexpected and undignified way and had the joy of reaching home again safely, you were so far from being able to give others good advice that you did not even advise yourself well over what still remained to happen. Homer and the proverb both say 388

> the fool realizes only when the deed is done,[302]

but you, the wisest of the Greeks, lacked even this modicum of learning; instead, Dionysius got the better of you one more time with a devious appeal to your hopes of helping your fellow men, and you yet again experienced the evil of tyranny, sailing off for a third time like a wrestler coming back for the third round. It was your second debacle with the same man, and your third overall with a tyrant and his household. That is the extent to which you failed to set everything fair even in your own case.

cape, he wrote his poem *Cyclops*, satirizing the affair (Ath. *Deipn.* 1.6e–7a; *schol.* Ar. *Plut.* 290).

301 *Ap.* 30c–d.

302 *Il.* 17.32, 20.198; cf. Hes. *Op.* 218; Pl. *Symp.* 222b.

389 ἔθεις. τί οὖν ἡμῖν τὴν τύχην προφέρεις αὐτὸς τοιαύτης πεπειραμένος; ὥσπερ ἂν εἰ Ὀδυσσεὺς τῷ Μενέλεῳ τὴν πλάνην ὠνείδιζεν, 'ὦ οὗτος, ἧκον μὲν οὐδ' αὐτὸς μετὰ πάντων, μετὰ πλειόνων δὲ ἢ σὺ καὶ θᾶττον ἢ σύ, καὶ πλεύσας οὐκ ἴσα· καὶ πρός γε οὐ περιεργασάμενος, ὥσπερ σὺ καθήμενος ἐν Σικελίᾳ παρὰ τῷ
390 Κύκλωπι.' ἀλλ' ὦ πάντων θαυμάσιε Πλάτων, μὴ δι' ἀμφοῖν ὤθει, καὶ ταῦτ' οὐ διὰ τῶν φίλων ἑνὸς καὶ τῶν ἐχθρῶν, ἀλλὰ διὰ σαυτοῦ τε καὶ τούτων, οὓς φίλους εἰκὸς ἦν μᾶλλον ἡγεῖσθαι, εἰ δὲ μή, σκόπει μὴ ὅ τι ἐγκαλέσεις, ἀλλ' ὅ τι ἀπολογήσει πρότερον· τοσαῦτ' ἐστὶν καὶ τὰ σά.

391 "καίτοι σὺ καὶ τῶν διθυραμβοποιῶν ἀξιοῖς καταγελᾶν ὡς πρὸς τὴν ἡδονὴν καὶ τὸ χαρίζεσθαι μόνον ὡρμημένων. φαίνεται δὲ Φιλόξενον μὲν τὸν Κυθήριον οὐ δυνηθεὶς αὖθις ὑφ' αὑτῷ λαβεῖν Διονύσιος, ἀλλ' οἰμώζειν ἐκεῖνος ἐλευθέρως γράφων αὐτῷ, σοῦ δέ γε δεύτερον καὶ τρὶς ἐγκρατὴς γενόμενος μετὰ τὰς
392 πρώτας ἐκείνας διατριβάς. φήσεις καλὴν εἶναί σοι τὴν πρόφασιν· ὑπὲρ γὰρ τῶν Δίωνος πραγμάτων ἅπαντα ταῦτα ποιεῖν καὶ λέγειν· καλῶς γε σὺ καὶ λέγων καὶ ποιῶν. σκόπει δὴ καὶ τὴν ἡμετέραν πρόφασιν, κἂν εὕρῃς ἀτιμοτέραν, ἢ μικρῶν ἕνεκα ἡμᾶς πολυπραγμονήσαντας, στίξον λαβὼν καὶ γενοῦ Διονύ-

---

303 An allusion to the story of the deposition of the Magi by Darius and his coconspirators, told in Hdt. 3.76–78.

Why then do you reproach us with our fortunes when this 389
was the kind of thing you experienced in your own? It is
as if Odysseus had reproached Menelaus for his wanderings! 'Look, I did not reach home with many companions
either, but I had more than you, and I came home sooner,
and I did not sail as far as you; what is more I did not waste
time on extra adventures, as you did sitting on Sicily in the
Cyclops' cave.' Most admirable Plato, do not thrust your 390
blade through both together, all the more as it is not a
question of skewering one of your friends along with the
enemy,[303] but of skewering yourself along with us, who it
would be more reasonable to think of as your friends.
Otherwise, think first not of what charge to bring but of
what defense to offer; your case is the same as ours.

"Again, you think it is right to deride dithyrambic po- 391
ets, as one more set of people who aim only at pleasure
and gratification.[304] Yet it is quite clear that while Dionysius was unable to get Philoxenus of Cythera into his hands
a second time—Philoxenus wrote him a free-spirited letter telling him to go to hell[305]—he got you into his power
a second and even a third time after that first encounter.
You will say that you had a noble pretext, since you were 392
doing and saying what you did in defense of Dion's interests, and it was indeed noble of you to do it and say it. So
look at our pretext too, and if you find that it was less respectable, or that we were wasting our efforts over trivi-
alities, take us and brand us and be a Dionysius toward us

[304] *Grg.* 502a.

[305] Unless this is a reference to the satirical content of Philoxenus' *Cyclops* (see n. 300 above): "showed his free spirit by telling him to go to hell in his writing."

σιος ἀντὶ Πλάτωνος εἰς ἡμᾶς. εἰ δ' ὥσπερ σὺ Δίωνος χάριν καὶ τῆς ἐκείνου ξενίας καὶ ἑταιρίας ἅπαντα ταῦθ' ὑπέμεινας, οὕτως ἡμεῖς ὑπὲρ τῆς ἑστίας τῆς κοινῆς πατρίδος καὶ ὑπὲρ τῶν κοινῶν σπονδῶν καὶ δικαίων οἱ μὲν [ὑπὲρ][121] τῆς πόλεως, οἱ δὲ καὶ τῶν Ἑλλήνων, ὁτιοῦν καὶ λέγειν καὶ πράττειν καὶ πάσχειν ὑπέστημεν, αἰσχυνθέντες μὲν ἁπάσας τὰς τοῦ Διὸς ἐπωνυμίας, αἰσχυνθέντες δὲ τὰς τῶν ἄλλων ἁπάντων θεῶν ἐπωνυμίας τε καὶ τιμάς, ἔτι δ' ἥρωας καὶ προγόνους τοὺς κοινούς, καὶ τὴν τοῦ παρελθόντος χρόνου μνείαν καὶ τὸν τοῦ μέλλοντος αἰῶνος λόγον, καὶ πάνθ' ὅσαπερ μέγιστα νομίζεται παρὰ πᾶσιν καὶ Ἕλλησι καὶ βαρβάροις, εἰ δέ τι καὶ παρὰ γνώμην ἐκ τούτων ἀπήντησεν, τί τὰ μὴ σὰ κατηγορεῖς;

"καὶ μὴν εἰ δεῖ καὶ τοῦτο προσθεῖναι, ἡμεῖς μὲν εἴ τι καὶ προσεπταίσαμεν, ἀλλ' οὖν πράξαντές γε ὑπὲρ ὧν ἐσπουδάζομεν οὕτω προσεπταίσαμεν, σὺ δ' εὐθὺς
393 ἐξ ἀρχῆς. οὐκοῦν εἰ μὲν τὸ χρήσασθαί τισι δυσκόλοις ὄνειδός ἐστι τῷ συμβούλῳ καὶ μέμψις, οὐδὲν ἐλάττοσιν ἡμῶν κέχρησαι. καὶ πρόσεστι τὸ μηδὲν ὧν ἐβούλου κατορθῶσαι. εἰ δ' αὐτὴν ἐφ' αὑτῆς δεῖ τὴν προαίρεσιν ἐξετάζειν, ἀναίτιον μὲν τὸ σὸν εἰκότως, ἀναίτιον δ' ἐκ τῶν αὐτῶν καὶ τὸ ἡμέτερον. καὶ πρόσεστιν τὸ κρατῆσαι τῶν πραγμάτων καὶ τὸ μείζω ταῦτ' εἶναι τῶν θ' ὑπὸ σοῦ σπουδαζομένων ὧν τ' αὐτοὶ
394 προσεκρούσαμεν. σὺ μὲν τοίνυν ἐλέγχειν ἡμᾶς ἀξιῶν καὶ κατὰ σαυτοῦ λέγεις, ἡμεῖς δ' ὑπὲρ ἡμῶν αὐτῶν

rather than a Plato. But if, just as you endured all that you endured for Dion and for his hospitality and comradeship, so we undertook to do and say and suffer whatever we had to in defense of the common hearth of our homeland and in defense of common treaties and rights—some of us those of Athens, some those of all Greece—out of respect for all the titles of Zeus and the titles and privileges of all the other gods, and in addition for the heroes and our common ancestors, and the memory of the past and future renown, and everything that is universally regarded as most important among Greeks and barbarians alike, and if as a result we encountered something out of line with our intentions, why do you tax us with accusations that are not yours to make?

"Moreover (if this too must be added) if we did indeed meet with reverses, it was at least only when we had achieved what we were striving for that we did so, whereas
you encountered them right at the outset. So if it is a cause 393
for blame and reproach for an adviser to encounter difficulties, then you encountered no fewer than we did, and what is more you did not succeed in any of your objectives; but if on the other hand it is intentions, in and of themselves, that one ought to scrutinize, then it is reasonable to say that your case is blameless, but so is ours on the same grounds. There is also the fact that we succeeded in our undertakings, and that they were more significant both than what you were striving for and than our own
failures. The upshot is that, in seeing fit to expose us, you 394
are also speaking against yourself, whereas we in defend-

---

121 *del.* Reiske

λέγοντες καὶ τὸ σὸν θεραπεύομεν. μᾶλλον δὲ τῆς μὲν σῆς ἀπολογίας καὶ ἡμεῖς μετέσχομεν, σοὶ δ' οὐχ ὅσον ἡμῖν ὑπάρχει. ὥστ' εἰ μὲν ἡμῶν τις φείσεται, ἄδηλον εἰ καὶ σοῦ· εἰ δὲ σοῦ τις καταγνοίη, τάχ' ἂν ἡμῖν γε συγγνοίη· εἰ δ' αὖ μηδ' ἡμῶν φείσεται, σοῦ γε σχολῇ. οὕτω τὸ νικᾶν ἡμᾶς ὑπὲρ σοῦ γίγνεται.

395 "'πρὸς ταῦτα σκόπει μὴ τοὐμόν, ἀλλὰ καὶ τὸ σόν,' Τεῦκρος ἔφη τινί, καὶ μὴ βούλου πάντα ἀκριβῶς ἐξετάζειν, μηδὲ τριῶν ὄντων εἰς ἅ τις ἂν βλέψειεν, τῆς γνώμης, τῶν ἔργων, τῆς τύχης, ἀφεὶς τὼ δύο, τοῦ τρίτου λαμβάνου, καὶ ταῦτα καὶ τούτου τοῦ πλείστου μέρους μεθ' ἡμῶν ὄντος. εἰ γὰρ ἡμᾶς ἔδει ταῦτα προειδότας ἐξ ἀρχῆς ἐξεπίτηδες ὑπὲρ τῆς Ἑλλάδος ἡμᾶς αὐτοὺς ἐπιδοῦναι, οὐκ ἂν ὠκνήσαμεν οὐδὲ ἡττήθημεν τοῦ Κόδρου τοσοῦτον, καὶ σύ γ' ἂν οἶμαι ταῦτα συν-
396 εβούλευσας. ἐπεὶ φέρε πρὸς φιλίου, πότερ' ἂν μᾶλλον ἐβουλήθης, μήτε τὰ πραχθέντα δι' ἡμῶν πεπρᾶχθαι τῇ πόλει μήτ' εἰς ἡμᾶς μηδένα τῶν πολιτῶν ἐξαμαρτεῖν—οὐκοῦν ἕτεροι καὶ εἰς ἡμᾶς καὶ εἰς ἐκείνους ἔμελλον—ἢ ἐκείνων γε ἕνεκα ὥστε πραχθῆναι, καὶ
397 ταῦτ' εἰ δέοι συμβῆναι; ἐγὼ μὲν οἶμαι ταῦτα. οὐκοῦν ὅτ' ἀμφότερ' ἂν φαίης ἐθέλειν μᾶλλον ἢ μηδέτερα ὁμολογεῖς, καὶ τοῖς πεπολιτευμένοις ἡμῖν ἅπαντα ἃ

---

306 Soph. *Aj*. 1313 (Teucer to Agamemnon).

307 An early (in some accounts the last) king of Athens, who sacrificed his life to frustrate a Peloponnesian invasion: Lycurgus, *Leoc*. 84–87. Cf. *Or*. 1.87.

ing ourselves are simultaneously looking after your cause. Or to put it another way, we too are entitled to a share of your defense, but you do not have as much to draw on as we do. Consequently, if someone is going to absolve us, it is unclear if he will absolve you too, and if someone were to condemn you, he might perhaps still pardon us; but if on the other hand he is not going to absolve even us, then he is hardly going to absolve you either. That is how definitely our victory helps your cause.

"Therefore, as Teucer once said to somebody, 'do not 395
consider my case but your own as well';[306] do not be so keen to scrutinize everything meticulously, and do not, when there are three things that one might look to—intention, results, and luck—put two of them to one side and latch onto the third, especially when this too for the most part went our way. Because if we had had to sacrifice ourselves deliberately for Greece, in full foreknowledge from the outset, we would not have hesitated to do so, and would not have lagged so very far behind Codrus,[307] and
I think you would have advised us to act in this way. For 396
tell us, in the name of the god of Friendship, which would you have preferred, that the things we achieved had not been achieved for Athens and that no citizen had offended against us either—then others would have, both against us and against them—or that in order for the former to be achieved the latter should also happen if it had to? I think
you would have preferred the latter option. Given then 397
that you would say that you wanted both sooner than neither, you thereby concede both that our political management had everything that it ought to have had, and that

προσήκει προσεῖναι καὶ μείζω[122] τὰ πρὸς εὐδοξίαν τῇ
398 πόλει τῆς αἰτίας εἶναι. πῶς οὖν οὐ δίκαιος ἦσθα μᾶλλον ἐπαινεῖν ἢ ψέγειν; εἰ γὰρ αὐτοῖς τοῖς ἡμαρτηκόσιν εἰς ἡμᾶς τὰ καλῶς βουλευθέντα καὶ πραχθέντα πλείονός ἐστι λόγου, καί τις ἂν οὐκ ἀλόγως ταῦτα ἐκείνοις παρείη, πῶς οὐχ ἡμᾶς γε δίκαιον ἀφεῖσθαι πάσης αἰτίας, οἷς τῶν μὲν ἐγκλημάτων οὐδ' ὁτιοῦν δήπου μέτεστιν, τῶν δὲ εἰς ἔπαινον ἡκόντων, ἂν τἀληθῆ λέγειν ἐθέλῃς, τὸ πλεῖστον;

399 "ἡμεῖς τοίνυν πόλλ' ἂν ἔχοντες ἡμᾶς αὐτοὺς σεμνῦναι παραλείπομεν. ἀλλ' ἵνα εἰδῇς ὅσον ἡμῖν ἐπιεικείας περίεστιν καὶ ὅσον πανταχῇ τοῦ πλεονεκτεῖν ἐθέλειν ἀπέχομεν, ἔστω τὸ πᾶν κοινόν, ἀφαίρει πάσας, εἰ βούλει, τὰς ἄνω προσθήκας, ἐπὶ τοῖς ἴσοις καταλυώμεθα—πάντως δ' οὐκ ἄπειροι συνθηκῶν ἡμεῖς—μήτε σὺ μέμνησο πρὸς ἡμᾶς περὶ συμφορῶν οὔθ' ἡμεῖς πρὸς σὲ τούτῳ χρησόμεθα. ὡς οὐκ ἔστι μέσον οὐδέν, ἀλλ' ἢ καὶ ἡμᾶς μετὰ σοῦ τούτοις ἑαλωκέναι δεῖ ἢ καὶ σὲ καὶ ἡμᾶς ἀθῴους ἀφιέναι καὶ ἀποχρῆν ἅ τινες τῶν ἄλλων ἐξήμαρτον εἰς ἡμᾶς."

400 ταῦτ' εἰπόντας ἂν αὐτοὺς οἶμαι ῥᾳδίως πάλιν πορεύεσθαι παρὰ τοὺς πλείονας, εἰ δὴ δεῖ κἀκείνους μετὰ τῶν πλειόνων κεῖσθαι δοκεῖν ὥσπερ ἔγωγε οὐκ οἶμαι. ἐγὼ μὲν οὖν ἥδιστα ἂν ἀμφοτέρων ἀποψηφιζοίμην· εἰ δέ τις ἄλλως γιγνώσκει, θρασυκάρδιον ἄν τινα αὐτὸν φαῖεν οἱ ποιηταί.

[122] μείζω Reiske μειζόνως *codd.*

the factors tending to enhance the glory of Athens out-
weighed any blame. How then can it not have been right
for you to praise rather than to blame? Because if even in 398
the eyes of those who offended against us our successes in
planning and action carry more weight, and it would not
be irrational for someone to allow the latter to compensate
for the former, how can it not be right to absolve us of all
guilt, given that we are clearly not liable to even the least
share of the blame, but are entitled, if you want to tell the
truth, to the lion's share of the praise?

"There is then much that we could boast of, but we will 399
leave it to one side. To let you see how abundantly decent
we are and how far we are in every way from wanting to
seize an advantage, let it all be common ground, cancel
out if you wish all the qualifications we made just now, and
let us make peace on equal terms (we are certainly no
strangers to agreements ourselves): you forgo any mention
to us of our catastrophes and we will not use this line of
attack against you. There is no third way: either we too
must be convicted along with you on these charges, or you
and we both must be discharged without penalty, and the
offenses that some others committed against us must suffice."

With these words I think our heroes would happily go 400
back to rejoin the great majority, if indeed we have to
believe—as I for one think we do not—that it is there that
they lie. I then would be very happy to acquit both sides,
and if anyone thinks differently, he is the sort of person
the poets would call "bold-hearted."[308]

[308] For example, *Il.* 10.41, 13.343; [Hes.] *Sc.* 448; Bacchyl. 13.73.

401 *φέρε δὴ καὶ τὰ παραδείγματα αὐτοῦ σκεψώμεθα.*

> *οὔκουν οἵ γε ἀγαθοί—φησίν—ἡνίοχοι κατ' ἀρχὰς μὲν οὐκ ἐκπίπτουσι τῶν ζευγῶν, ἐπειδὰν δὲ θεραπεύσωσιν τοὺς ἵππους καὶ αὐτοὶ γένωνται ἀμείνους ἡνίοχοι, τότ' ἐκπίπτουσιν.*

καὶ ἔτι ἄνω που τῶν εἰς τὸν Περικλέα

> *ὄνων γοῦν—φησίν—ἐπιμελητὴς καὶ ἵππων καὶ βοῶν τοιοῦτος ὢν κακὸς ἂν ἐδόκει εἶναι, εἰ παραλαβὼν μὴ λακτίζοντας αὐτὸν μηδὲ κυρίττοντας μηδὲ δάκνοντας ἀπέδειξε*[123] *ταῦτα ποιοῦντας δι' ἀγριότητα.*

402 *ἀλλ' ὄνους μὲν ὦ τᾶν καὶ ἵππους καὶ βοῦς τοὺς αὐτοὺς ἑκάστους λέγεις,* Ἀθηναίων *δὲ οὐ τῶν αὐτῶν ἅπαντες οἶμαι προὔστησαν, οἷον δὴ λέγω,* Σόλων *καὶ* Κλεισθένης *καὶ* Μιλτιάδης *καὶ* Περικλῆς *καὶ ὅστις ἕκαστος. ἀλλ' ἡ μὲν πόλις μία καὶ ἡ προσηγορία, οἱ*
403 *δ' ἄνδρες ἄλλοι καὶ ἄλλοι παρὰ τοὺς χρόνους. τί οὖν θαυμαστὸν τοὺς μὲν πρᾳοτέροις καὶ ῥᾴοσι χρησαμένους τυχεῖν, τοὺς δ' αὖ τραχυτέροις καὶ θυμοειδέσι μᾶλλον, ὥσπερ καὶ ἄλλα μυρία δήπου μεταβάλλει κατὰ τοὺς χρόνους. οὔκουν οὐδὲ τοὺς ἐκ τῆς γῆς καρποὺς παραπλησίους καθ' ἕκαστον ἐνιαυτὸν κομιζόμεθα, οὔτε τὸ πλῆθος οὔτε τὴν ἀρετὴν λέγω. ἀλλ' ἔτους ἰσχὺς οὐκ ἔλαττον ἢ χώρας εἶναι δοκεῖ. ὥστ' εἰ*

[123] ἀπέδειξε Reiske *cum codd. Plat.* ἐπέδειξε *codd.*

Moving on, let us turn our attention now to Plato's comparisons. 401

> It is therefore not the case—he says—that good charioteers are not initially thrown from their chariots, but when they tend their horses and themselves become better charioteers, then they are.[309]

And earlier on too, somewhere in the discussion of Pericles, he says

> Someone in charge of donkeys and horses and oxen would have a bad reputation if he were this sort of person—if when he took them over they did not kick him or butt him or bite him, but he then turned them into wild creatures that did just this.[310]

Now, Plato, when you speak of donkeys and horses and 402
oxen, you are speaking of creatures that are all the same
as each other, but I do not think that the Athenians led by
our men—I mean for instance Solon and Cleisthenes and
Miltiades and Pericles and whoever else one might specify—were the same for all of them. The city and its name
remained one and the same, but its inhabitants varied over
time. What then is so surprising about some of them hav- 403
ing the luck to have tamer and easier charges to deal with, while others for their part had rougher and more spirited ones, just as, surely, countless other things also vary over time? The produce that we harvest from the earth is not the same year in year out either, either in quantity, that is, or in quality; the year seems to be no less influential a factor than the terrain. If, therefore, even though previously

[309] *Grg.* 516e. [310] *Grg.* 516a.

τὸν ἔμπροσθεν χρόνον εὐκολώτεροι τὰς φύσεις ὄντες κατ' ἐκείνους ἤδη χαλεποὶ κατέχειν ἦσαν, οὐκ ἔξω τῆς ὅλης φύσεως τὸ πάθημ' ἂν εἴη, ὥσπερ γε καὶ προϊόντος οἶμαι τοῦ χρόνου τὸ φρόνημ' ἀνῆσαν[124] κατὰ <τὰς>[125] συμφοράς.

404 ἔτι τοίνυν οὐδ' ἡνίοχοι τοὺς ἵππους οὕτω διαφθείρουσιν, ἂν τοὺς μὲν παιδεύωσι, τοὺς δὲ μὴ δυνηθῶσιν αὐτῶν, ἀλλ' ἐὰν οὓς πρότερον χρηστοὺς καὶ ἀναμαρτήτους εἶχον, τούτους χείρους ἀποφήνωσιν· Μιλτιάδης δὲ καὶ οἱ εἰς ἐκεῖνον οὐ τοὺς αὐτοὺς εἶχον διὰ τέλους, ἀλλ' οἱ μὲν ἐπεγίγνοντο δήπουθεν, οἱ δὲ
405 ἀπεγίγνοντο, οἱ δὲ καὶ ἀπεφοίτων παρ' αὐτῶν. πῶς οὖν πρὸς τοὺς ἡνιόχους εἰσὶ κρίνεσθαι δίκαιοι, ἢ πῶς ὡς τῶν αὐτῶν ἵππων μενόντων αὐτοῖς οὕτω δεῖ διδόναι τὸν λόγον; ὥσπερ ἂν εἴ τις τοὺς Μολιονίδας ἠξίου καὶ τῶν Διομήδους τοῦ Θρᾳκὸς οὕτως ἄρχειν, ὥσπερ
406 ὧν εἶχον ἐξ ἀρχῆς. καὶ μὴν οἱ μὲν ἡνίοχοι καθ' αὑτοὺς ἕκαστοι τῶν ζευγῶν ἄρχουσι καὶ οὐδεὶς παραλυπεῖ, τὸ δ' αὐτὸ τοῦτο λέγω καὶ περὶ τῶν ἐπὶ τοῖς ὄνοις τε καὶ βουσίν· ὥστε εἴ τι πλημμελοῖτο, βέβαιον τὴν αἰτίαν ἔχοιεν ἂν εἰκότως. ἀλλ' οὐ Περικλῆς γε καὶ Θεμιστοκλῆς, οὐδ' ἐκείνων τῶν ἀνδρῶν οὐδεὶς καθ' αὑτὸν Ἀθηναίων ἦρξεν, οὐδὲ τοῦ τι πράττειν ἐναντίον

[124] ἀνῆσαν a² ἂν ἦσαν *codd.* [125] *add.* Reiske

---

[311] The two Moliones (sons of Poseidon and Molione, also known as the Actoriones after their stepfather Actor), were

the Athenians had been more tractable in nature, they had by this time become hard to restrain, this would not be a phenomenon completely outside the bounds of nature, just as I think subsequently disaster brought about a relaxation in the intensity of their pride.

Again, in the case of charioteers, it is not if they can 404
train some of their horses but not others that they count as corrupting them, but if they make worse those in their possession that were previously good and blameless. Miltiades and his associates, on the other hand, did not have the same people throughout; some were added, some subtracted, and some indeed absconded from them. How 405
then can it be fair to judge them in comparison to charioteers, and why on earth should they have to account for themselves on the assumption that they had the same horses in their possession throughout? That would be like expecting the sons of Molione to control the horses of Diomedes of Thrace just as well as those they had had in their possession from the start.[311] What is more, in the case 406
of charioteers, each one of them manages his own team for himself, and no one else interferes, and I would point out that the same goes for the supervisors of donkeys and oxen too, so that if anything goes wrong it is quite reasonable that the blame should be securely theirs. But neither Pericles and Themistocles, nor anyone of those men, led the Athenians on his own, or free from people attempting

skilled charioteers (and in some accounts conjoined twins): See Hom. *Il.* 11.706–52, 23.638–42. The mares of Diomedes, king of Thrace, were the flesh-eating horses captured by Heracles as one of his Labors.

ἐγχειρήσαντος ἀπηλλαγμένος, ἀλλὰ καὶ ἕτεροι πολλοὶ δήπου μετ' αὐτῶν ἔπραττον τὰ πολιτικά, οὔτε φύσεις τὰς αὐτὰς οὔτε γνώμας ἔχοντες, ὥστ' ἔτι μᾶλλον τούτοις ἢ ἐκείνοις ἄξιον προστιθέναι τὰ ἁμαρτήματα. ἐγὼ μὲν γὰρ τοσούτῳ μᾶλλον ἂν φαίην ἐκείνοις, ὅσῳπερ εἰς τούτους ἦν τὰ ἁμαρτανόμενα. ὡς δ' ἁπλῶς εἰπεῖν ποῦ δίκαιον μόνους ἀπαιτεῖν εὐθύνας τοὺς οὐ μόνους τῶν πραγμάτων αἰτίους;

407 οὔκουν τούς γ' ἡνιόχους αἰτιώμεθα τοὺς ἐξ ἀρχῆς, ἂν ἕτερος τοὺς αὐτοὺς ἵππους παραλαβὼν κακίους ἀποδείξῃ· ἀλλὰ καὶ ἡνίοχοι καὶ διδάσκαλοι μειζόνως εὐδοκιμοῦσιν, ὅταν τῶν αὐτῶν ἕτεροι κύριοι καθεστῶτες μὴ τῶν ἴσων ἄξιοι γένωνται. καὶ νὴ Δί' ἄν γε καὶ κατὰ τοὺς αὐτοὺς χρόνους [οἷον τῆς αὐτῆς ἡμέρας][126] ἕτερος παραλαβὼν τὸ ἅρμα ἀναβαίνῃ, οὐκέτι τοῦ παντὸς ὑπεύθυνος ὁ χρηστὸς ἡνίοχος οὐδ' ὁ ἔνδοξος, ἀλλ' ἐὰν καθάπαξ πρὸς αὐτὸν ἡ ἐπιμέλεια καταστῇ, οὕτω καὶ ταῦτα κρίνεται, τῶν δὲ ἑτέρου κακῶν οὐδεὶς κληρονομεῖ. ἀλλὰ καὶ τοῦτ' αὐτὸ φαύλων ἐστὶ κατηγόρημα, ὅτι τὸν βελτίω καὶ τὸν οὐ καθ' αὑτοὺς οὐκ εἴων χρῆσθαι τῇ τέχνῃ, ἀλλ' ὑπεσκέλιζον ὥσπερ οἱ τοὺς ἐν τοῖς δρόμοις.

408 οὕτω τοίνυν καὶ περὶ τῆς ἐκείνων πολιτείας, ἕως ἂν μὴ δείξῃς ὅτι βασιλευόντων τῶν φιλοσόφων καὶ μόνων ἐφεστηκότων τοῖς πράγμασι ταῦθ' ἡμαρτήθη—

[126] *del.* Dindorf

to act in opposition to them in some way; there were clearly many other people engaging in politics along with them, differing from them in both character and aims, so that it is these latter who deserve to bear the responsibility for the offenses that were committed rather than our men. Indeed, I would say that these latter deserve it all the more because it was against our men that the offenses were committed. Simply stated, how can it be justifiable to hold solely to account those who were not solely responsible for what happened?

With charioteers, it is not the original ones we blame, 407
if another man takes over the same horses and makes them worse; rather, the reputations of charioteers and teachers both increase whenever other people, taking over control of the same charges, do not prove worthy of the same esteem. For that matter, if another takes over the chariot during the same period and mounts it,[312] the good and reputable charioteer is no longer completely responsible, but only if the responsibility for looking after it rests wholly with him; that is how these matters are judged, and no one inherits someone else's defects. It is indeed precisely a charge that is brought against deficient practitioners, that they did not allow their better, who was on a different level to them, to practice his art, but tripped him up, like people who trip up runners in races.

So it is also with these men's political records: as long 408
as you cannot show that these mistakes were made when the philosophers were on the throne and in sole charge of

312 The words bracketed in the Greek text opposite—"say for example on the same day" following "during the same period"—look like a reader's note and should be discounted.

λέγω τοῦ Μιλτιάδου, τοῦ Θεμιστοκλέους, τοῦ Περικλέους, τοῦ Κίμωνος—μηδαμῶς τήν γε φιλοσοφίαν αὐτὴν αἰτιῶ. ἀλλ᾽ εἰ μὲν αὐτοὺς καθ᾽ αὐτοὺς ἐλέγχειν οἷός τ᾽ εἶ, χρῶ τούτῳ καὶ δείκνυ θἀμαρτήματα· εἰ δὲ μή, τῶν ὄνων μᾶλλον ἢ τῶν ἐπιστατῶν κατηγορεῖς. εἰ μὲν γὰρ οὐκ ἦν ἁμαρτήματα, πρὶν ἐκείνους Ἀθήνησι πολιτεύεσθαι, ἀλλὰ ταῦτα πάντα ἀπὸ Μιλτιάδου καὶ Θεμιστοκλέους κἀπ᾽ ἐκείνων ἤρξατο, ἄλλος ἂν εἴη λόγος· οὐδ᾽ εἴ τινες ἄλλοι κατὰ ταυτὸν ἐκείνοις ἐπολιτεύοντο εἴποιμι ἄν, ἀλλὰ δίδωμι πάντων ἐκείνους ὑπευθύνους μόνους εἶναι. εἰ δὲ εἰκὸς ἦν τι καὶ ἄλλο ἡμαρτῆσθαι πρότερον, "τί ταῦτα τοὺς Λάκωνας αἰτιώμεθα;" προσπαίζειν γὰρ ἔξεστιν δήπου σέ γε, ἐπεὶ καὶ αὐτὸ τοῦτο τὸ τῶν συμφορῶν ὅτι μὲν παλαιόν ἐστιν καὶ ὡς σύ που φῂς ἀπὸ Θησέως ἀρξάμενον, ἴσως δὲ καὶ ἔτι ἄνωθεν, καὶ οὐχ οὗτοι πρῶτοι προσέπταισαν
409 ἐάσω. καίτοι ὁ Θησεὺς φυγών τε καὶ διαφθαρεὶς ἐν τῇ Σκύρῳ τελευτῶν οὐκ ἄτιμος ἔμεινεν παρὰ τῷ θεῷ, ἀλλ᾽ ἐπέταξεν Ἀθηναίοις μετενεγκεῖν αὐτοῦ τὰ ὀστᾶ, πολλοῖς ὕστερον χρόνοις, ὥς φασιν. ἀλλ᾽ ὅμως ἐάσω ταῦτα.

---

313 Pointedly phrased, so as to underline both that in Aristides' eyes the Four are as significant as leaders as the philosopher kings were to Plato and that Plato would be outraged if others brought against his philosopher kings the kind of charges he has made against the Four.

affairs—it is Miltiades, Themistocles, Pericles, and Cimon I am referring to—do not accuse philosophy itself.[313] If you are able to catch them out individually, then exploit this and reveal their errors; otherwise it is against the donkeys rather than their supervisors that you are bringing your charges. If there were no errors before these men were in politics in Athens, but all this started with Miltiades and Themistocles and under their influence, it would be another story; even if there were others engaged in politics at the same time as them, I would not make a point of it, but freely grant that they were solely responsible for everything. But if it is probable that mistakes were made earlier too, then "why do we bring these charges against the Spartans?"[314] A dig at you is certainly permissible here, seeing that I am in fact going to pass over this very point, that the experience of catastrophe is an ancient one, going all the way back to Theseus, as I think you maintain,[315] and maybe even further, and these men were not the first to stumble. And yet Theseus, although he was killed in exile 409
on Scyros, did not go unhonored by the god in death, but instead the god ordered the Athenians to bring back his bones many years afterward, as the story goes.[316] Even so I will pass over this point.

314 Ar. *Ach.* 514.

315 A reference to the expulsion of Theseus from Athens thanks to the machinations of Menestheus, as described in Plut. *Vit. Thes.* 32–35; Aristides is wrong to suggest that Plato mentions this (unless in fact what he has in mind is Theseus' trouble with Hippolytus, which is mentioned at *Leg.* 687d–e and 931b).

316 Cf. Plut. *Vit. Thes.* 36.

410 ἀλλ᾽ οἴχεταί σοι διαφθαρεὶς ὁ λόγος περὶ αὐτῶν· οἷς γὰρ ἁπάντων ταὐτὰ κατηγόρηκας, τούτοις ὃ δοκεῖς ἰσχυρὸν ἔχειν ἀνῄρηκας. διὰ τί; ὅτι Μιλτιάδου μὲν ἴσως ἂν εἴη τι τοῦτο κατηγόρημα, Θεμιστοκλέους δὲ οὐκ ἂν ἔτι· εἰ δέ τοι καὶ Μιλτιάδου καὶ Θεμιστοκλέους, ἀλλ᾽ οὐ Κίμωνός γε· εἰ δὲ καὶ Μιλτιάδου καὶ Θεμιστοκλέους καὶ Κίμωνος, ἀλλ᾽ οὐ δή τοι καὶ Περικλέους, ἀλλὰ τούτου καὶ πάντων ἥκιστα. Θεμιστοκλῆς μὲν γὰρ αὐτοὺς παρὰ Μιλτιάδου παρέλαβεν κυρίττοντας, Κίμων δὲ παρὰ Μιλτιάδου καὶ Θεμιστοκλέους, Περικλῆς δὲ παρὰ Μιλτιάδου καὶ Θεμιστοκλέους καὶ Κίμωνος. οὕτω πάντων ἥκιστα ὅ γε Περικλῆς ὑπεύθυνος ἦν, ὃν σὺ μάλιστα πάντων ᾐτιάσω καὶ τοῖς κακοῖς ἐπιμεληταῖς τῶν ὄνων τε καὶ βοῶν ἰδίᾳ τῶν ἄλλων εἴκασας.

411 ἐνθυμηθῶμεν τοίνυν καὶ περὶ ὧν ἀρτίως ἐλέγομεν, τῆς πρὸς τὸν Διονύσιον αὐτοῦ Πλάτωνος ὁμιλίας. εἰ γὰρ αὕτη μία ἐστὶ καὶ ἀληθὴς καὶ δικαία καὶ ἀποχρῶσα μόνη πασῶν ἀπολογία καὶ παραίτησις ὑπὲρ Πλάτωνος, περὶ ὧν ὁ τύραννος ἐπλημμέλει, καὶ συνὼν ἐκείνῳ καὶ πάλιν καθ᾽ αὑτὸν γενόμενος, ὅτι καὶ πρὶν ἰδεῖν Πλάτωνα καὶ τῶν ἐκείνου λόγων ἀκοῦσαι πολλὰ καὶ παντοῖα ἐδεδράκει, τί κωλύει καὶ ὑπὲρ ἐκείνων τὸ μὲν ἐξ ἴσου τὰ τοῦ δήμου τοῖς τῶν τυράννων εἶναι, μὴ λέγειν, ἀλλὰ καὶ τὰ πρὸ τῆς ἐκείνων πολιτείας ἐλάττω τῶν ὑπὸ τῶν τυράννων ἐξ ἀρχῆς ἡμαρτημένων εἶναι, καὶ τὰ παρ᾽ αὐτὴν τὴν πολιτείαν μὴ τῆς ἴσης ἄξια μέμψεως, ὅσησπερ τὰ τοῖς τυράννοις, ἀφ᾽

3. IN DEFENSE OF THE FOUR

Actually your argument against these men has gone to pieces, because in bringing the same charge against all of them you have in fact done away with what you thought to be the strong point in your case. Why so? Because while there might be some substance in it as a charge against Miltiades, it ceases to be one against Themistocles; and even if it has some purchase against Miltiades and Themistocles, it does not against Cimon; and even if cuts against Miltiades and Themistocles and Cimon, it certainly does not against Pericles as well, in fact against him least of all of them. Themistocles inherited the Athenians from Miltiades prone to butt, Cimon from Miltiades and Themistocles, and Pericles from Miltiades, Themistocles, and Cimon. Thus Pericles, whom you blamed more than all of them and singled out from the others in comparing to bad overseers of donkeys and oxen, was in fact the least responsible of all of them. 410

Let us also reflect on what we were talking about just now, Plato's own association with Dionysius. If the one true and justified defense and excuse for Plato and the only one out of all of them that suffices, with respect to the crimes the tyrant committed both when he kept company with him and when he was again on his own, is that his actions had been many and various even before he saw Plato and listened to his teaching, what is to prevent us in defense of these men too saying—not indeed that what the Athenian people did was comparable to what the tyrants did, since their actions before the Four came to power were less serious than the initial crimes of the tyrants, and during the actual period of these men's administration their actions were not equally blameworthy with those of the tyrants from the time they started listening to Plato— 411

οὗ Πλάτωνα προσίεντο· αὐτὸ δὲ τοῦτ᾽ ἐξεῖναι κοινὸν εἰπεῖν, ὅτι καὶ πρὶν ἐκείνους ἐγχειρεῖν λέγειν, ἦν Ἀθήνησιν ἁμαρτήματα, εἰ δ᾽ ἐλάττω τῶν Διονυσίου, οὐδὲ τὰ ὕστερον δήπου τοῖς ἐκείνου παραπλήσια, ἀλλ᾽ εἰς ὅσον εἰκὸς ἁμαρτεῖν ὄντας ἀνθρώπους.

412 φέρε δὴ καὶ περὶ τῶν συμβεβηκότων αὐτῶν τοῖς ἀνδράσιν σκεψώμεθα καὶ διέλθωμεν. οὐ γὰρ ἁπάντων ὁ δῆμος οὑτωσὶ κατεψηφίσατο, οὐδ᾽ ἀπὸ κοινοῦ δόγματος ταῦτ᾽ ἔπαθον, ἀρχὴν δὲ οὐδὲ ταὐτὰ πάντες.
413 πόθεν; ἀλλὰ Θεμιστοκλῆς μὲν καὶ Κίμων ἐξωστρακίσθησαν. τοῦτο δ᾽ ἦν οὐ μῖσος οὐδ᾽ ἀλλοτρίωσις τοῦ δήμου πρὸς αὐτούς, ἀλλ᾽ ἦν νόμος αὐτοῖς περὶ ταῦτα, ἔχων μὲν ὁπωσδήποτε—ἐῶ γὰρ εἰ μὴ σφόδρ᾽ ἄν τις ἐπαινέσαι τὸν νόμον—τὸ δ᾽ οὖν ἁμάρτημα οὐκ ἀπαραίτητον αὐτῶν, ἀλλ᾽ ἔχον ὡς ἐν τούτοις εὐπρέπειαν, νόμῳ γάρ, ὥσπερ εἶπον, ἐγίγνετο. ἦν δ᾽ οὗτος ὁ νόμος· ἐκόλουον τοὺς ὑπερέχοντας μεθιστάντες ἔτη δέκα, ἄλλο δ᾽ οὐδὲν ἔγκλημα προσῆν, οὐδὲ ὡς ἐπ᾽
414 ἐλέγχῳ πραγμάτων ὀργή. καίτοι πῶς οὐ δεινόν, εἰ οὓς οὐδ᾽ αὐτοὶ οἱ μεθιστάντες εἶχον αἰτιάσασθαι, τούτους αἰτιασόμεθ᾽ ἡμεῖς διὰ τοὺς μεταστήσαντας; ὥσπερ οἱ βέβαιον μὲν οὐδ᾽ ὁτιοῦν ἐπιστάμενοι, ἀκοὴν δέ τινα κατηγοροῦντες, καὶ ταῦτ᾽ οὐδ᾽ αὐτὴν σαφῆ τὴν ἀκοήν.

415 ἀλλ᾽ ἐκεῖσε ἐπάνειμι, ὅτι ὑπὲρ τοῦ τὰ φρονήματα ἐπισχεῖν τοῦτο τὸ εἶδος τῆς φυγῆς ἐνόμισαν. οὐκοῦν

but what can be said about all of them in common is that there were mistakes at Athens before these men set themselves to speak, and if these mistakes were less weighty than those of Dionysius, their subsequent actions were surely not comparable to his either, but kept within the limits of reasonable human error.

Moving on, let us look also at what actually happened 412
to these men and work our way through it. The people of Athens did not simply condemn all of them, nor did this happen to them as a result of a single decision, and in fact
they did not all suffer the same fate in the first place. How 413
could they have? No, Themistocles and Cimon, to begin with them, were both ostracized. This was not a question of hatred or of an estrangement of the people from them; Athens had a convention covering such cases, and whatever the merits of that custom—I will pass over this in case someone is not so very keen to praise it—it is at all events the case that their offense was not an unpardonable one but had in the circumstances a certain dignity, because as I have said it was conducted according to customary practice. The custom was this: they used to rein in their leading citizens by sending them into exile for ten years, but there was no other charge on top of this, nor any of the anger
consequent on conviction for misdeeds. So how can it not 414
be monstrous if the people who not even those who exiled them could bring charges against are charged by us because of those who exiled them? We would be like people who know nothing at all for certain and bring an accusation on hearsay, without actually having heard the rumors clearly either.

But I return to the point that the Athenians practiced 415
this kind of banishment in the interests of containing

τούτῳ μεγίστῳ δῆλόν ἐστιν ὅσον κολακείας οἱ ἄνδρες ἀπεῖχον, οὓς γε ὅπως ὑφεῖντο τοῦ φρονήματος, διὰ τοῦτο μεθίστασαν, οὐδενὸς ἄλλου τῶν πάντων ἕνεκα. ὥστε τοῦτό γε οὐ κατ᾽ αὐτῶν, ἀλλ᾽ ὑπὲρ αὐτῶν ἔλαθες εἰρηκώς, ὦ[127] δεινὸς σὺ τηρεῖν τὰ λεγόμενα καὶ τοὺς ἄλλους ἐλέγχειν. δοκοῦσι γάρ μοι τὰς συμφορὰς ἐνθυμούμενοι τὰς ἐπὶ τῶν Πεισιστρατιδῶν γενομένας ἑαυτοῖς μηδένα βούλεσθαι μεῖζον ἐὰν τῶν πολλῶν
416 φρονεῖν, ἀλλ᾽ ἐξ ἴσου εἰς δύναμιν εἶναι. δίκαια ἄρα ἐποίουν ἐλαύνοντες Κίμωνα καὶ Θεμιστοκλέα; οὐ λέγω ταῦτα. ἀλλ᾽ οὐδ᾽ ἀναίσχυντά γε παντελῶς, ἀλλὰ καὶ αὐτοῖς ἔχοντα παραίτησιν κἀκείνοις οὐκ ἀσχήμονα
417 τὴν συμφοράν. εἰ δ᾽ οὖν καὶ τοῖς δεδρακόσιν οὐκ ἀποχρῶσα ἡ πρόφασις, τοῖς γε πεπονθόσιν ἐξαρκεῖ τοῦτ᾽ αὐτὸ δήπου μὴ φαύλοις νομίζεσθαι, ἢ μείζω γ᾽ ἡμεῖς τῶν ἐκβαλόντων ἀδικήσαιμεν ἄν. εἰ γὰρ ἐκεῖνοι μὲν τοῦτό γ᾽ αὐτοῖς συνεχώρησαν καὶ παρεῖσαν τὸ μηδ᾽ ὁτιοῦν ἀδικεῖν τὴν πόλιν, ἡμεῖς δὲ καὶ τοῦτ᾽ ἀφαιρησόμεθα καὶ τῇ δυστυχίᾳ τὴν βλασφημίαν προσθήσομεν, πῶς οὐ χαλεπώτεροι τῆς φυγῆς αὐτοῖς ἐσόμεθα, ἢ πῶς οὐ μείζω τῶν ἐξ ἀρχῆς εἰς αὐτοὺς ἁμαρτανόντων ἀδικήσομεν;

418 οὕτω τοίνυν καὶ διὰ ταῦτα μεταστήσαντες Κίμωνα μὲν καὶ οὕτω κατήγαγον ἐντὸς τοῦ χρόνου τοῦ νενο-

127 ὦ Trapp ὡς *codd.* ὥς Keil

---

317 Manuscript U (Vat. Urbin. gr. 123) has a marginal note at

pride. It is this more than anything else that makes it clear how far our men were from being flatterers, since they were sent into exile to make them shed some of their pride, and for absolutely no other reason. In saying what you did, therefore, you were without realizing it speaking not against them but against yourself, you genius at watching out for what people say and showing up the mistakes of others![317] Because in my view, it was with the disasters Athens suffered under the Pisistratidae in mind that they did not want anyone to give themselves airs over the mass of the people, but for them to be on a level as far as possible.
416 Did the Athenians then act justly in expelling Cimon and Themistocles? I do not say that, but it was not a completely shameless action either, rather one that was excusable on their part and not a disgrace and a disaster for our two.
417 But even if the perpetrators did not have sufficient excuse, these same circumstances are surely enough for the victims not to be thought of as villains, or otherwise we would be doing them a greater wrong than those who exiled them. Because if these latter agreed and conceded that our two did not do the city any wrong whatsoever, but we on our account are actually going to deprive them of this concession and add insult to injury, surely we will be treating them more harshly than the sentence of exile, and wronging them more severely than those who originally offended against them.

418 Now, although the Athenians had exiled them in this way and for these reasons, even so they recalled Cimon

this point, suggesting that the last clause of this sentence is actually a reader's note, exclaiming at *Aristides'* cleverness, which has wrongly been interpolated into the text.

μισμένου, Θεμιστοκλέα δὲ ἐκωλύθησαν ἐμοὶ δοκεῖν ὑπὸ Λακεδαιμονίων. συμβάντων γὰρ τῶν περὶ τὸν Παυσανίαν, ἅμα μὲν εἰς ἀθυμίαν ἐμπεσόντες καὶ βουλόμενοι συνεπισπᾶσθαι τοὺς Ἀθηναίους, ἵνα δὴ μὴ μόνοι τῆς αἰσχύνης συναπολαύοιεν, ἅμα δὲ εἰ καταλείποιτ᾽ ἐκεῖνος Ἀθήνησιν, δεδοικότες μὴ πρὸς ἅπαντ᾽ ἔχοιεν δύσμαχον ἀνταγωνιστήν, καὶ πρὸς τούτοις ὧν περὶ τὸν τειχισμὸν ἐξηπάτηντο μνησικακοῦντες, ἀπόντος κατηγοροῦντες, διώκειν μετὰ σφῶν ἐκέλευον, τεκμηρίῳ τῇ Παυσανίου μοχθηρίᾳ κατ᾽ ἐκείνου χρώ-
419 μενοι. Θεμιστοκλῆς δὲ τῶν μὲν τὴν ἐπιβουλήν, τῶν δὲ τὴν προπέτειαν ἐφόδιον λαβών, σοφισάμενος ὥσπερ εἰώθει τὸν βασιλέα, τῆς καθόδου μὲν ἀπεστερήθη, αὐτῷ δὲ ἀρκῶν ἔδειξεν πρὸς ἅπασαν τύχην.

420 καὶ τὰ μὲν δὴ Θεμιστοκλέους καὶ Κίμωνος ταῦτα. Περικλέα δὲ καὶ Μιλτιάδην ὁ μὲν δῆμος οὐδὲν οὔτε μεῖζον οὔτε ἔλαττον ἔδρασεν κακόν, δικασταὶ δ᾽ ἑκατέρῳ καθήμενοι χρήμασιν ἐζημίωσαν πολλοστὸν δή-
421 που μέρος ὄντες τῶν πάντων Ἀθηναίων. πάλιν τοίνυν καὶ τούτων οὕτω συμβάντων Περικλέα μὲν ὁ δῆμος ἅπας οὐδ᾽ ὁτιοῦν ἧττον στρατηγὸν εἵλοντο, καὶ πάντ᾽ ἐπέτρεψαν, ὡς ὁ αὐτὸς[128] μάρτυς δηλοῖ ὅνπερ ἀρτίως περὶ αὐτοῦ παρειχόμεθα· Μιλτιάδης δ᾽ ἔφθη τελευτήσας, οὐ τῶν δικαστῶν θάνατον καταγνόντων αὐτοῦ, οὐδ᾽ ὡς σὺ φῂς κἂν εἰς τὸ βάραθρον ἐμπεσών, εἰ μὴ

[128] ὁ αὐτός Reiske αὐτὸς ὁ *codd.*

sooner than the customary time, and in my view were only prevented from recalling Themistocles too by the Spartans. Because, in the aftermath of the events centering on Pausanias, the Spartans had experienced a collapse in their morale and wanted to drag the Athenians down with them, so that they should not be the only ones to feel the effects of the disgrace, and were at the same time afraid that, if Themistocles were left in Athens, they would have an intractable opponent in every confrontation, and in addition bore a grudge over the way they had been deceived about the fortifications, they accused him in his absence and told the Athenians to join them in hounding him, citing the base behavior of Pausanias as evidence
against him. For his part Themistocles, turning the plots 419
of the one people and the hastiness of the other to his own advantage, and tricking the King in his usual way, may have been deprived of the possibility of returning home, but still showed that he could look after himself in the face of any turn of fortune.

So much then for Themistocles and Cimon. As for 420
Pericles and Miltiades, the people of Athens did them no harm great or small; it was a set of jurors, representing only a small proportion of the whole citizen body of Athens, who sat on each of their cases and punished them with
fines. And when it had all passed off in this way, with 421
Pericles the whole people were not in the slightest degree the less prepared to elect him general and entrust everything to him, as is shown by the same witness as we produced in his case earlier.[318] Miltiades for his part forestalled matters by dying, not when a jury had condemned

[318] Thuc. 2.65.4; cf. §§20–24 above.

διὰ τὸν πρύτανιν, ἀλλὰ τοῦ τραύματος αὐτῷ σφακελίσαντος. καὶ τούτων πολλοί, μᾶλλον δ' ἅπαντες μάρ-
422 τυρες. δῆλον τοίνυν ἐστὶν ἐξ ὧν τῷ Περικλεῖ διηλλάγησαν καὶ τὴν πόλιν καθάπαξ ἐπέτρεψαν μετὰ τὴν τῆς κλοπῆς, ὡς σὺ φῄς, καταδίκην, ὅτι κἂν πρὸς τὸν Μιλτιάδην αὐτὸ τοῦτ' ἐποίησαν, εἰ μὴ τὰ τῆς τύχης ἐκώλυσεν.

423 ἐν οἷς τοίνυν καιροῖς τοῦ Περικλέους κατεψηφίσαντο οἱ καταψηφισάμενοι σκέψαι, ἐπειδὴ καὶ ἔφης ὅτι ἐπὶ τελευτῇ τοῦ βίου τοῦ Περικλέους κατέγνωσαν κλοπήν. ἐκεῖνος γὰρ ἕως μὲν εἰρήνην ἡ πόλις ἦγεν, οὐδεμίαν οὔτε μείζω οὔτε ἐλάττω παρ' αὐτοῖς αἰτίαν ἔσχεν, ἀλλ' ἐξ ἴσου τοῖς θεοῖς ἐθαυμάζετο· καὶ ἔτι πρότερον στρατιὰς πολλὰς ἐξαγαγὼν [Ἀθηναίους][129] ἐπὶ τοὺς οὐκ ἐθέλοντας τοῖς δικαίοις ἐμμένειν, οὐκ ἄμεμπτος μόνον, ἀλλὰ καὶ πολλῷ τινι πρῶτος ἦν. ἐπεὶ δ' ἅμα τῆς τε χώρας ἠναγκάζοντο στέρεσθαι καὶ ὁ λοιμὸς ἅπαντα φθείρων ἐπέκειτο καὶ κακῶν ἀνάπαυσις οὐκ ἦν, οὕτω δὴ τῶν συμφορῶν ἡττηθέντες ἐτραχύνθησαν πρὸς αὐτόν.

424 καί μοι τοῦ παραδείγματος ἐνταῦθ' ἀναμνήσθητι τοῦ τῶν ἡνιόχων. τάχ' ἂν γὰρ ἁλοίης τοῖς ἅρμασιν τοῖς σαυτοῦ καὶ οὐ τοῖς πτεροῖς. ὁ γοῦν Νέστωρ ἱππικώτατος ἦν, ὡς λέγεται, τῶν ἐφ' αὐτοῦ. καὶ Ὅμηρος

[129] *del.* Keil Ἀθηναίων U

---

[319] *Grg.* 516e. [320] Hdt. 6.136. [321] *Grg.* 516a.

him to death, nor when as you would have it he would even have been flung into the execution pit had it not been for the Chair of the Council,[319] but when his wound became gangrenous. Many people, everyone indeed, can testify to the truth of this.[320] It is therefore clear from the way the 422 Athenians were reconciled with Pericles and entrusted the city absolutely to his care after what you call his conviction for embezzlement, that they would have done exactly the same with Miltiades too had not the hand of chance prevented it.

Now consider the timing with which those who con- 423 demned Pericles condemned him, when you say that it was "at the end of Pericles' life" that they found him guilty of embezzlement.[321] Because for as long as the city was at peace, they did not hold him liable to any degree of blame, great or small, but admired him equally with the gods; and even before that, when he led them on many campaigns against those unwilling to limit themselves to their proper entitlement, he not only went without blame but was by a long way first among them. But when they were forced to do without their land and the all-destroying plague bore down on them and their sufferings were without respite, then indeed they were overcome by their sorry circumstances and their attitude toward him became harsher.

At this point I should like you to remember your char- 424 ioteer comparison—because perhaps you may come to grief thanks to your own chariot rather than your own feathers.[322] Nestor anyway is said to have been the most

[322] Another allusion (cf. *Or*. 2.55) to the Aesopic fable of the eagle shot with an arrow fletched with its own feathers (273 Hausrath), also employed by Aeschylus (*Myrmidons*, fr. 139 *TrGF*).

ἱππότην αὐτὸν μετ᾽ ὀλίγων ἐν τοῖς ἔπεσιν καλεῖ. ὥστε κἀν τοῖς ἄθλοις τοῖς ἐπὶ Πατρόκλῳ τῷ Ἀντιλόχῳ μέλλοντι τὸ ἅρμα καθιέναι προσελθών τε καὶ ὑπειπὼν ὅτι αὐτὸν ὁ Ζεύς τε καὶ ὁ Ποσειδῶν πᾶσαν διδάξειαν τὴν ἱππικὴν εὐθὺς ἐκ παιδός, καὶ οὐ πάνυ τι δέον αὐτὸν διδάσκειν ὅμως ὑποτίθεται καὶ παραδείκνυσιν αὐτῷ τινὰ τῶν εἰς τὸν δρόμον καὶ ὅπως διαθήσεται τὸν
425 ἀγῶνα. τοσοῦτον αὐτῷ περιῆν τῆς ἐπιστήμης. οὗτος μέντοι φυγῆς ποτε γιγνομένης τῶν Ἀχαιῶν ἔμεινεν μόνος,

> οὔ τι ἑκών, ἀλλ᾽ ἵππος ἐτείρετο, τὸν βάλεν ἰῷ
> δῖος Ἀλέξανδρος, Ἑλένης πόσις ἠϋκόμοιο,
> ἄκρην κὰκ κορυφήν, ὅθι τε πρῶται τρίχες ἵππων
> κρανίῳ ἐμπεφύασι, μάλιστα δὲ καίριόν ἐστιν.
> ἀλγήσας δ᾽ ἀνέπαλτο, βέλος δ᾽ εἰς ἐγκέφαλον δῦ,
> σὺν δ᾽ ἵππους ἐτάραξε κυλινδόμενος περὶ χαλκῷ.

426 καὶ οὔτε ὁ ἵππος ἔτι ἠδύνατο ὑπὸ τοῦ κακοῦ καὶ τοῦ τραύματος πείθεσθαι, πάντα τὸν ἔμπροσθεν χρόνον παρέχων ἑαυτὸν εὐπειθῆ οὔθ᾽ ὁ Νέστωρ εἶχεν ὅ τι χρήσαιτο μὴ ὅτι ἐκείνῳ, ἀλλ᾽ οὐδὲ τοῖς ἄλλοις ἵπποις τεταραγμένοις ὑπὸ τοῦ πάθους. ἀλλ᾽ οὐδ᾽ ἀπολῦσαι τὸν ῥυτῆρα ἐν τῷ θορύβῳ ῥᾳδίως ἠδύνατο, ἀλλ᾽ ὥσπερ ἐπὶ χαλκοῦ ζεύγους εἱστήκει μένων, ὅσα μὴ

---

[323] For example, *Il.* 2.336, 2.601, 4.317; Phyleus, Tydeus, Oineus, and Peleus (all heroes of an older generation, not present at Troy) are the other characters given this epithet.

[324] *Il.* 23.304–50.

[325] *Il.* 8.81–86.

expert equestrian of his times; Homer gives him the epithet "horseman" along with only a few others in his poetry.[323] Accordingly, in the funeral games for Patroclus he
goes up to Antilochus when he is about to enter his chariot
in the race and says by way of preamble that Zeus and
Poseidon taught him all the skills of horsemanship already
when he was a boy; and even though there is no great need
to instruct Antilochus, he nevertheless makes suggestions
and passes on advice bearing on the race and about how
to manage the contest, out of a superabundance of expert
knowledge.[324] Yet on another occasion, when there was a 425
rout, this same man alone of the Greeks remained where
he was,

> not at all willingly, but his horse was hard-pressed, hit by an arrow
> from glorious Alexander, husband of lovely-haired Helen,
> on the top of its head, where the first hairs of a horse's mane
> grow on the skull, and there is a most vulnerable point.
> It reared up in pain, as the arrow sank into its brain,
> and it stampeded the horses as it writhed about the bronze.[325]

The horse was no longer able to obey its master's com- 426
mands because of the pain of its wound, consistently obe-
dient though it had proved to be previously, and Nestor
was at a loss to control not only this one, but all the other
horses as well that had been panicked by what had happened to it. In fact he could not even easily untie the reins
in the confusion, but remained standing there as if on a
chariot of bronze, except without the unruffled calm. That

ἀπῆν τό γε ἀτρεμεῖν. οὕτως ἠπόρησεν ὑπὸ τοῦ καιροῦ καὶ τῆς συμφορᾶς, ἄριστος ὢν τά γε τῆς τέχνης.

427 τὸν αὐτὸν δὴ τρόπον οἶμαι καὶ Περικλῆς, ἕως μὲν οὐδὲν ἀνήκεστον ἦν, κατεῖχεν τοὺς ἵππους, καὶ μάλα ῥᾳδίως ἤκουον αὐτοῦ καὶ τοῦ Νέστορος οὐδὲν χείρω τὴν φωνὴν ἐνόμιζον, καίτοι πολλά γε καὶ παντοῖα ἐχρήσατο αὐτοῖς καὶ εἰρήνης καὶ πολέμων ἐχόμενα. ἐπεὶ δ᾽ ὅ τε χιλὸς αὐτοῖς ἔξω διεφθείρετο καὶ οἴκοι τε πονήρως ἐπεπράγεσαν καὶ οὐδ᾽ ἀναστραφῆναι περιῆν, ἀλλ᾽ ἐνέκειντο αἱ ταλαιπωρίαι δειναὶ καὶ συνεχεῖς, καὶ τοῦτο μὲν ἡ κεφαλὴ καὶ τὰ ἐντὸς ἐκάετο, τοῦτο δ᾽ οἱ νεκροὶ πολλοὶ νύκτα καὶ ἡμέραν ἑωρῶντο, πάντα δ᾽ ἦν μεστὰ κυλινδομένων καὶ πιπτόντων καὶ ἀπορουμένων, ἐλπίδος δ᾽ οὐδ᾽ ὁτιοῦν ἐσῴζετο χρηστῆς, οὕτως ἤδη πανταχόθεν κατακλεισθέντες καὶ κρατηθέντες ὑπὸ τῆς ἀηθείας καὶ τῆς ὑπερβολῆς τῶν παρόντων κακῶν ἀπεσείσαντο τὸν ἡνίοχον. ἀποσεισάμενοι δὲ οὕτως εὖ καὶ καλῶς ἤχθησαν ὑπ᾽ αὐτοῦ τὸν ἄνω χρόνον ὥστ᾽ ἔγνωσάν τε ὃ ἔδρασαν καὶ μετέγνωσαν καὶ ὑποκύψαντες ἐξ ἀρχῆς παρεῖσαν ἄρχειν
428 καὶ ἄγειν ὅποι βούλοιτο ἑαυτούς. οὕτω τὰ μὲν τῆς ἱππικῆς οὐκ οἶδα, τοὺς δὲ λόγους οὐ πολλῷ τινι χείρων ἦν τοῦ Νέστορος.

ὥστ᾽ εἴ σοι θαυμαστὸν φαίνεται ὅτι ἐπὶ τελευτῇ κατεψηφίσαντο αὐτοῦ, πρῶτον μὲν αὐτὸ τοῦτο τὸ τοῦ

---

[326] Besides "horseman," Nestor's other regular epithet in the *Iliad* is "clear-voiced orator" (λιγὺς . . . ἀγορητής; e.g., 1.248,

is how helpless the untoward turn of events at that crucial moment had made him, supremely expert horseman though he was.

In the same way I think that, as long as nothing irreme- 427
diable had happened, Pericles too could keep his horses in check and they made no trouble at all about obeying him and thought him Nestor's equal in eloquence,[326] even though he took them into many varied adventures of both peaceable and warlike character. But when their fodder abroad was being destroyed and they were in dire straits at home and there was no scope for turning back, and awful sufferings were crowding in on them, when heads and innards were on fire and there were corpses to be seen in great numbers night and day, and people reeling, falling, and hopelessly afflicted on all hands,[327] and not the slightest glimmer of hope remained, then indeed shut in on all sides and overwhelmed by the unfamiliarity and the excessive scale of their present sufferings, they shook off their charioteer. But once they had shaken him off they had been so well and nobly led by him previously that they realized what they had done and repented of it; they submitted to his yoke all over again and allowed him to command them and lead them wherever he desired. I do not 428
know how his horsemanship compares, but that is how little short of Nestor he fell in his oratory.

Thus, if you find it amazing that they condemned him at the end, for a start this very comparison with the chari-

4.293), and for rhetorical theorists he was a paradigm of the smooth or middle, Isocratean, style of oratory (e.g., Cic. *Brut.* 40; Quint. *Inst.* 12.10.64); see also §623 below. [327] A reference to the plague at Athens, as described in Thuc. 2.49–52.

ἡνιόχου παράδειγμα ἀφίησι τῆς αἰτίας αὐτόν. [φαί-
νονται][130] [ὥστ᾽ ἐγγυτέρω τῆς τελευτῆς αὐτοῦ γίγνεται τοῦ Περικλέους, καὶ πρός γε τῇ τελευτῇ τιμήσαν-
429 τες αὐτόν, οὐκ ἀτιμάσαντες φαίνονται.][131] ἀλλὰ μὴν
ὅτε καὶ τὸν ἔμπροσθεν χρόνον εὐδοκίμει πόλλ᾽ ἐξῆς
ἔτη καὶ μετὰ τὴν καταδίκην μέγιστος πάλιν ἦν τῶν
πολιτῶν, πῶς οὐκ ἀμφοτέρων ἕνεκα ζηλωτός ἐστιν,
καὶ τῆς ἀρχῆς καὶ τοῦ τέλους; οὐ γὰρ τὸ προσκροῦσαι τοῖς ἔμπροσθεν ἐπεσκότησεν, ἀλλὰ τὸ τιμᾶσθαι
μετὰ τοῦτο πᾶσαν παρεγράψατο τὴν συμφοράν. οὐ
γὰρ τὸ μέσον κύριον ἀμφοτέρων ἐστὶ τῶν καιρῶν,
ἀλλὰ κρατεῖ τὸ συναμφότερον τοῦ μέσου. εἴτε γὰρ
τοῖς πρώτοις δεῖ διδόναι τὴν ψῆφον, ἐτιμᾶτ᾽ ἐξ ἀρχῆς,
εἴτε τοῖς ὕστερον, οὐκ ἐν οἷς κατέγνωσαν ἔστησαν,
430 ἀλλὰ προσεῖχον πάλιν ὡς αὐτῶν κρείττονι. καὶ μὴν
οὐχ ὅσον δύο ἀνθ᾽ ἑνός ἐστιν, ἀλλ᾽ ὅτι καὶ τὸ πλῆθος
ἑκάστου τοῦ χρόνου οὐκ ἴσον οὐδ᾽ ἐγγύς, ἀλλὰ καὶ τὸ
τῆς εὐδοξίας θαυμαστὸν ὅσον κρατεῖ. ὥστε καὶ τὸ
μέσον τοῦ χρόνου τοῦ παντὸς οὐκ εἰς συμφορὰν ἔρχεται, ἀλλ᾽ ἐπὶ λαμπρᾶς τῆς τιμῆς ἐστιν αὐτῷ. τὸ μὲν
γὰρ ἡμέρας ἀτύχημα ἐγένετο, τὸ δὲ πρωτεῖον ἀναμφισβήτητον ἦν κατὰ παντὸς τοῦ χρόνου. ὥστ᾽ εἰ καὶ
τὴν γνώμην ἀφέντας τὴν τύχην ἐξετάζειν δεῖ, τοσοῦτον τῆς ἀγαθῆς τύχης αὐτῷ περίεστιν.
431 καὶ μὴν τὸ μὲν ὀργῇ συνέβη, τὸ δ᾽ ἐκ τῆς δικαιο-

[130] *φαίνονται codd. nonnulli del. edd.*
[131] *del.* Trapp

oteer absolves him of blame.[328] Moreover, given that Pericles had both enjoyed an uninterruptedly good reputation for many years previously, and after his condemnation was again the greatest of the citizens, how can he fail to be admirable on both counts, for his beginning and for his end? His reverse did not cast a shadow over his earlier achievements, but instead the subsequent honor he enjoyed erased all trace of his misfortune: the stage in between does not prevail over both the other periods, but rather the two other periods combined prevail over the stage in between. If the vote has to go to the first period, he was honored in the beginning; if it has to go to the last, the Athenians did not stay with their condemnation, but heeded him again as their superior. Moreover, this is not 429
430
simply a matter of two against one; it is also the case that the duration of each of the periods of time is not anywhere near the same, but the period of his good reputation is astonishingly more substantial. Thus the midpoint of the whole span of his career does not bring us to an episode of disaster, but falls at what was a time of glory and honor for him. The one episode was the misfortune of a day, whereas his primacy at Athens was undisputed for all time. Such, then, even if we have to pass over his intellect and scrutinize only his luck, was the magnitude of his superabundant good fortune.

What is more, Pericles' misfortune came about through 431

[328] The next sentence in the manuscripts, bracketed opposite, looks like a reader's note rather than part of Aristides' text: "Therefore it happens rather close to the death of Pericles, and actually at the time of his death it is clear that they honored him rather than dishonoring him."

τάτης κρίσεως ὑπῆρχεν αὐτῷ, καὶ τὸ μὲν ἐξ ὀλίγων, τὸ δ' ἐξ ἁπάντων ὁμοίως. πῶς οὖν ταῦτ' ἐκείνοις ἴσα;
432 καὶ μὴν οὐδὲ τοὺς λαχόντας ἅπαντας οἴεσθαι χρὴ καταγνῶναι τὴν γραφὴν αὐτοῦ, ἀλλ' εἶναί τινας, οἳ καὶ τῷ Περικλεῖ καλῶς ποιοῦντες ἔθεντο. οὐκοῦν τούτους γε βελτίους τε καὶ βελτίστους ἦν πεποιηκώς. οὕτω καὶ τοὺς πολλούς, ὡς ἔοικε, καὶ τοὺς ὀλίγους καλῶς ηὔχει, ὥστ' εἰ μὲν τοῖς πολλοῖς δεῖ τίθεσθαι μάρτυσιν, ὁ δῆμος ὁ τιμῶν αὐτὸν ἦν, εἰ δὲ τοῖς βελ-
433 τίστοις, ἀφείθη τό γε τούτων μέρος. εἰ δὲ μὴ πάντας ἐφεξῆς ἐπαίδευσεν μηδὲ πάντας ὁμοίους ἀπέδειξεν, ἀλλ' εἰσὶν οἳ καὶ ἐξέφυγον τὴν ἐκείνου βούλησίν τε καὶ δύναμιν, τί θαυμαστόν, ἢ πῶς ἄν τις νεμεσῴη
434 δικαίως; οὔτοι[132] πάντας γε οὐδ' ὁ Σωκράτης ἐπαίδευσε τοὺς συγγενομένους αὐτῷ, ἀλλὰ κατηγοροῦσι μὲν Κριτίου τοῦ Καλλαίσχρου, κατηγοροῦσι δὲ Ἀλκιβιάδου τοῦ Κλεινίου τῇ τε πόλει τὰ αἴσχιστα βουλεύσασθαι καὶ τὸν ἄλλον βίον ἥκιστα βιῶναι [ἢ][133]
435 κατὰ Σωκράτη. ἆρ' οὖν τούτου γε ἕνεκα ἠδίκει Σωκράτης, ἢ διὰ τὴν ἐκείνου κακίαν κακὸς αὐτὸς ἦν; ἐγὼ μὲν οὐκ οἶμαι. ἀλλ' ἠδίκουν ἐκεῖνοι μὴ παρέχοντες αὑτοὺς ὁμοίους Σωκράτει μηδὲ τοῖς ἐκείνου πειθόμενοι λόγοις. εἰ μὲν γὰρ ἐν οἷς ἐπείθοντο ἡμάρτανον, Σωκράτους τὸ ἔγκλημα, εἰ δ' ἐν οἷς ἠπείθουν, ἐκείνων.
436 σὺ τοίνυν δι' ὧν αὐτοὺς φῂς οὐκ ἐθέλειν πείθεσθαι

132 οὔτοι Stephanus οὕτω *codd.*
133 *del.* Reiske

anger and derived from only a few, whereas his primacy
was the result of the most fully justified of judgments, and
it came from all alike. How then can there be any parity
between the two? Moreover, we should not think that ev- 432
eryone on the jury panel found him guilty of the charge,
but should realize that there were also those who voted in
his favor and did well to do so—these ones at least he had
made better and indeed as good as they could be! He
could thus, it seems, fairly boast of the favor of both the
many and the few: if one has to decide the issue on the
evidence of the many, it was the people that honored him,
and if on the evidence of the elite, he was acquitted as far
as depended on them. And if he did not educate absolutely 433
everybody and did not make them all the same, but there
were some who escaped his wishes and capacity, what is
so amazing about that, and how could anyone justly resent
it? Socrates did not educate all those who associated with 434
him either, and both Critias son of Callaeschrus and Alcibiades son of Cleinias stand accused of plotting the most
disgraceful fate for their city and in other ways leading
lives utterly unworthy of Socrates.[329] Was Socrates then 435
guilty of wrongdoing thanks to the one of them, or was he
a bad man himself because of the villainy of the other? I
for one do not think so. Rather, in doing wrong they
showed themselves unlike Socrates and disobeyed his
teaching: if their wrong actions were among those they
committed in obedience to him, it is Socrates who stands
accused, whereas if their actions were instances of disobe-
dience, it is they.

It is then through the actions in which you say the 436

[329] As reported in Xen. *Mem*. 1.2.12–47.

Περικλεῖ, διὰ τούτων ἀξιοῖς ἐλέγχειν Περικλέα. καὶ τίς ἂν μεῖζον ὑπὲρ Μιλτιάδου καὶ Θεμιστοκλέους καὶ Περικλέους[134] ἀπολογήσαιτο ἢ ὅτι πειθόμενοι μὲν ἐκείνοις Ἀθηναῖοι τὰ βέλτιστα ἔπραττον, ὅτε δὲ οὐκ ἤθελον τοῦτο ποιεῖν, τηνικαῦτα ἐξήμαρτον; οὕτως ἐκεῖνοι τὰ βέλτιστα ἔπειθον, Ἀθηναῖοί τε ἀεὶ τὰ βέλτιστα ἂν ἔπραττον, εἰ διὰ τέλους ἐκείνοις ἐπείθοντο.
437 καίτοι Σωκράτει μὲν οἱ βουλόμενοι χρῆσθαι συνῆσαν ὁσημέραι, Περικλεῖ δὲ καὶ τοῖς ἄλλοις ῥήτορσι τρεῖς ἡμέρας ἑκάστου μηνὸς συνῆσαν Ἀθηναῖοι ὡς ἔπος εἰπεῖν δημοσίᾳ. καὶ μὴν ὅτι γε ῥᾷον καὶ δύο καὶ τρεῖς ἢ τοσούτους ὁμοῦ κατέχειν καὶ νέους γ᾽ ἔτι παιδεύειν ὁτιοῦν ἢ προήκοντας καὶ πᾶσαν ἐφεξῆς ἡλικίαν, τίς οὐκ οἶδε τῶν πάντων; ἔτι δὲ Σωκράτης μὲν οὐδὲν ὀχληρὸν δήπου τοῖς ὁμιλοῦσιν αὐτῷ προσέταττεν ἀλλ᾽ ἢ τοσοῦτον ὅσον σωφρονεῖν, Θεμιστοκλῆς δὲ καὶ Περικλῆς καὶ Μιλτιάδης καὶ Κίμων καὶ τῆς πόλεως ἀπεῖναι καὶ τοῖς σώμασι κινδυνεύειν, καὶ πολλὰ δὴ καὶ ταλαιπωρίαν ἔχοντα ἐπέταττον· ἐν οἷς οὐκ εἰ μὴ καθάπαξ διεγένοντο θαυμαστόν ἐστιν, ἀλλ᾽ εἰ τοσοῦτον διήρκεσαν. εἶτα Σωκράτη ἀφεὶς τῆς ἐπ᾽ ἐκείνοις αἰτίας, τούτους ἀφ᾽ ὧν ἥμαρτόν τινες ἐξετά-
438 ζεις; καὶ μὴν τὰ μὲν ἄλλ᾽ ὁποῖ᾽ ἄττ᾽ ἀπέβη τῶν ἀνδρῶν ἐκείνων, λέγω Κριτίου καὶ Ἀλκιβιάδου, καὶ ὁπό-

[134] post Περικλέους <καὶ Κίμωνος> Canter

Athenians refused to do as Pericles said that you think Pericles should be shown up. But what more powerful defense of Miltiades and Themistocles and Pericles[330] could anyone make than that when the Athenians did what they said, they pursued the best courses of action, but that when they refused to do this, it was then that they went wrong? So true is it that those men habitually urged the best courses of action, and that the Athenians would always have followed such courses if they had done as those men said from start to finish. In the case of Socrates, those 437
who wanted to benefit from him kept company with him every day, whereas with Pericles and the other orators, roughly speaking, the Athenians enjoyed their company for just three days a month, and in public. And who on earth does not know that it is easier to keep two or three in check than so many all at once, and to educate people in anything while they are still young than when they have grown up and are at any and every stage of life? Moreover, Socrates did not instruct his associates in anything burdensome, except to the extent that he taught them self-control, whereas Themistocles and Pericles and Miltiades and Cimon taught theirs to spend time away from the city and to run physical risks, and gave them many orders that entailed hard toil. The wonder is not that they did not abide by this instruction to the finish, but that they lasted as long as they did. Can you then criticize our Four on the strength of some people's misdeeds, when you have absolved Socrates of any blame in those individuals' case?
The historians certainly tell us about the nature of all the 438
other things that resulted from those individuals—Critias

[330] Canter suggests adding here "and Cimon."

σων τινῶν αἴτιοι πραγμάτων καὶ τῇ πόλει καὶ τοῖς ἄλλοις Ἕλλησιν κατέστησαν καὶ ποίαν τινὰ τὴν παιδείαν ἐπεδείξαντο τὴν ἑαυτῶν οἱ συγγραφεῖς λέγουσιν· ἀλλ' εἰ τοῦτο δοκεῖ Πλάτων ἰσχυρόν τι λέγειν τὸ εἰς αὐτὸν Μιλτιάδην ἐξαμαρτεῖν Ἀθηναίων τινάς, καὶ Κριτίας αὖ τῷ[135] Σωκράτει ζημίαν ἐπέθηκεν, καὶ ταύτην οὐ φαύλην, ἀλλ' ἣν ἥκιστα ἐκεῖνος ἐδέξατο.
439 ἀπεῖπε γὰρ αὐτῷ μὴ διαλέγεσθαι τοῖς νέοις. καίτοι τοῦτο τί ἐστὶν ἀλλ' ἢ ἀτιμία λαμπρά; καὶ ταύτης τῆς ἀγνωμοσύνης ἔπεισε καὶ τοὺς ἄλλους μετασχεῖν, ὅσοι μετ' αὐτοῦ τότ' εἶχον τὴν πόλιν. προσθῶμεν τοίνυν ὅτι καὶ Περικλέα μὲν οὐδεὶς τῶν ὁμιλητῶν, οὐδὲ τῶν ἐκ τοῦ δήμου τὴν γραφὴν ἐκείνην ἐγράψατο, ἀλλ' εἷς τῶν ἀντιστασιωτῶν, μᾶλλον δὲ οὐδὲ εἰδὼς εὖ καὶ καλῶς ἐκεῖνον ἄνθρωπος, Σωκράτει δὲ ὁ τῶν νέων ἀπέχεσθαι καὶ σιωπᾶν ἐπιτάξας οὐ τῶν σοφιστῶν ἦν οὐδεὶς οὐδὲ τῶν ἀντιτέχνων, ἀλλ' εἷς τῶν ὅτ' ἦν νέος φοιτώντων παρ' αὐτῷ. τοσοῦτον, ὡς ἔοικεν, ἀπώνατο τῆς συνουσίας αὐτοῦ. ταῦτ' οὖν ἡμεῖς ἐπὶ Σωκράτη οἴσομεν; ἀλλ' οὐχὶ δίκαια ποιήσομεν ἴσως.

440 δοκεῖ δέ μοι καὶ Πλάτωνα δίκῃ μετελθεῖν τοῦ λόγου καὶ τῆς ἐπιτιμήσεως. παραιτοῦμαι δ' εὐμενῆ καὶ ἵλεων εἶναι τοῖς λεγομένοις, εἴ τίς ἐστιν αἴσθησις. καὶ οὐκ ἐρῶ Διονύσιον οὔτε τὸν Ἑρμοκράτους οὔτε τὸν Διο-

[135] αὖ τῷ Dindorf αὐτῷ *codd.*

and Alcibiades, I mean—and about the volume of the troubles they caused for Athens and the rest of Greece, and what kind of education they showed that they themselves had received; but if Plato thinks that he has a strong point to make in the fact that some Athenians offended against Miltiades himself, well Critias too on his own account imposed a punishment on Socrates, and no trivial one either, but one that he least welcomed: he forbade him to converse with the young.[331] What is this if not a blatant 439
example of public shaming? He also persuaded the others who controlled the city along with him at that time to share in this act of ingratitude. Let us add that it was not one of Pericles' associates or anyone from the mass of the people that mounted the prosecution against him, but a member of an opposing faction, or rather an individual who did not even know him well and properly,[332] whereas the man who ordered Socrates to keep away from the young and to hold his tongue was not one of the sophists or his professional rivals, but one of those who went to school with him when he was young. That, apparently, is how much he benefited from his company. Are we then going to put this down to Socrates? That would perhaps not be fair of us.

I believe that Plato was in fact duly punished for his 440
argument and his censure. (I beg for his kindly and propitious indulgence toward what I am saying, if he has any consciousness of it.) I am not going to talk about Dionysius—either the son of Hermocrates or the son of Diony-

[331] Xen. *Mem.* 1.2.31, 1.2.33. [332] Cleon, Simmias, or Lacratides, according to different sources: Plut. *Per.* 35. §448 below shows Aristides opting for Cleon.

νυσίου οὔτε τῶν ἐν Σικελίᾳ μετ᾽ ἐκείνου συνδιατριψάντων οὐδένα, ἀλλ᾽ εἰσὶν οἳ λέγουσιν, ἕτεροι δ᾽ αὖ φασιν ἀληθῆ λέγειν τούτους ὡς ὅτε τὴν τρίτην ἀποδημίαν εἰς Σικελίαν ἀπεδήμησεν, τότε τῶν ἑταίρων τινὲς αὐτοῦ καὶ τῶν εἰς τὰ μάλιστα ὡμιληκότων ὑπολειφθέντες οἴκοι νεώτερα ἐβουλεύσαντο, καὶ τοὺς Ἀθηναίους ἐμιμήσαντο, μᾶλλον δὲ οὐ τοὺς Ἀθηναίους, ἀλλὰ τοὺς Ἀθηναίων ὑπηκόους λέγω τοὺς ἀφ-
441 ισταμένους. καίτοι τό γ᾽ ἐκείνων ἐπαναστάσει προσεοικὸς ἦν, οἳ δὲ διατριβάς τε ἀντικατασκευάζειν αὐτοῖς[136] ἠξίουν πλησίον τῆς ἐκείνου καὶ ᾠκοδόμουν ἐπὶ τῇ Ἀκαδημίᾳ, τό τε σύμπαν ὑπερφρονεῖν ἐκέλευον ὅτου δὴ—οὐ γὰρ ἔγωγ᾽ ἂν ἐφεξῆς οὑτωσὶ προσθείην τοὔνομα—φάσκοντες γέροντά τε εἶναι πολλοῦ καὶ
442 παραφρονεῖν ἤδη. ὥστε, ὦ φίλε Πλάτων, ἀτεχνῶς τὸ τοῦ Περικλέους συνέβη σοι. καὶ ὥσπερ ἀρτίως Μιλτιάδου καὶ Θεμιστοκλέους καὶ Κίμωνος, ἑκάστου τε τῆς τύχης ἐφαίνου μετέχων, οὕτω σοι καὶ ὁ τέταρτος λοιπὸς ἐνταῦθα ἀπήντηκεν. σαφῶς γὰρ οὑτωσὶ τῷ Περικλεῖ ταυτὸν ἔπαθες ἐπὶ τελευτῇ τοῦ βίου, καὶ προσέτι ἐν τῷ γήρᾳ σύ γε, καὶ πολλῷ πρεσβύτερος τῆς ἐκείνου τόθ᾽ ἡλικίας τοιαῦθ᾽ ὑβρισθείς, εἰ θέμις

[136] αὑτοῖς Lenz

---

[333] That is, Dionysius I or Dionysius II.

[334] Aristides' ultimate source here is Aristoxenus' *Life of Plato* (frr. 64–65 Wehrli, Euseb. *Praep. evang.* 15.2), filtered through

sius[333]—or any of those who associated with Plato on Sicily, but a different episode. There are those who say, and others who say that they are telling the truth, that when he made his third visit to Sicily, it was just then that some of his companions, indeed some of those who had associated with him most intimately, who had been left behind at home, plotted revolution and imitated the example of the Athenians, or rather, I mean not their example but that of the subjects who revolted from them. At any rate, while 441
the action of those Athenian subjects did indeed resemble an insurrection, these individuals decided to set up a rival school for themselves near to his and built it right by the Academy, and in fine told people to despise whoever it was—I would not want to go on and add his name just like that—insisting that he was very old and had now become senile. Thus, my dear Plato, precisely what happened to Pericles happened to you.[334] And just as it became clear 442
just now with Miltiades, Themistocles, and Cimon that you and each of them shared the same fortunes, so now the fourth and last of them has come to meet you too. Because this example makes it clear that the same thing happened to you as did to Pericles at the end of your life, and what is more in your old age, so that you were subjected to this outrageous treatment when you were much older than he was at the time, if it is permissible to say so.

however many intermediates; the rival establishment was there identified as the Lyceum. According to Eusebius, some did and some did not believe that the "companions" involved were Aristotle and his supporters.

443 εἰπεῖν. καὶ εἰ μὴ Χαβρίας καὶ Ἰφικράτης, ἄνδρες τῆς Περικλέους καὶ Θεμιστοκλέους ἰδέας καὶ τάξεως εἰς ὅσον ἐστὶ τούτους ἐκείνοις εἰκάσαι, αἰσθόμενοι τὰ γιγνόμενα ἠγανάκτησαν καὶ τὸ ἐπιτείχισμα διέσπασαν καὶ τοῦ λοιποῦ προσέταξαν σωφρονεῖν αὐτοῖς, πάντ' ἂν ἐκεῖνα μεστὰ τραγῳδίας ἦν.

444 καίτοι τί φήσομεν, ὦ τῶν Ἑλλήνων ἄριστε, πότερον δικαίως εἰς σὲ ταῦτ' ἐκείνους τότε τολμᾶν, ἢ σὲ τῆς ἐκείνων μανίας ὑπεύθυνον εἶναι; ἐγὼ μὲν γὰρ οὐδέτερον ἂν φαίην. καὶ μὴν ἔχοι γ' ἄν τις τοὺς σοὺς λόγους ἀμυνόμενος διπλᾶ στρέφειν κατὰ σοῦ καὶ κατὰ Σωκράτους, ὡς εἰ καὶ τὰ μάλιστ' ἀδίκως ταῦθ' ὑμῖν συνέβαινεν, τρόπον γέ τινα τὰ προσήκοντα ἐπάσχετε, εἴπερ γε τοιούτους ἀπεδείκνυτε οὓς ἐπαιδεύετε· καὶ τῷ τῶν σοφιστῶν παραδείγματι, ᾧ σὺ κέχρησαι κατὰ τῶν δημαγωγῶν, πολὺ μᾶλλον ἂν καθ' ὑμῶν χρῷτό <τις>[137] δικαίως, ὅσῳπερ ἐγγυτέρω τῶν τοῖς σοφισταῖς ὁμιλησάντων εἰκάσαι οἱ σοὶ καὶ Σωκράτει συνδιατρίψαντες γίγνοιντο ἄν, ἢ οἱ τῷ Περικλεῖ καὶ

445 τοῖς μετ' ἐκείνου χρώμενοι. οὐκοῦν εἰ μὲν τὰ τῶν ὁμιλητῶν ἁμαρτήματα τῶν προεστηκότων ἐστὶν κατηγορήματα, σαυτοῦ καὶ τοῦ ἑταίρου μᾶλλον κατηγόρηκας ἢ Περικλέους τε καὶ ὧν οἴει, καὶ νὴ Δί', εἰ βούλει, τὸ μᾶλλον ἀφίημί σοι, ὅτι δ' οὐχ ἧττον, ἀρκεῖ. εἰ δ'

[137] *add. edd.* τις χρῷτο Q^2 R^2

---

335 Distinguished Athenian military commanders of the first

And if Chabrias and Iphicrates,[335] who were men of the stamp and rank of Pericles and Themistocles, to the extent that it is possible to compare the one duo with the other, had not realized what was happening and been angered by it and torn down their fortification and told them to behave themselves in future, the whole business would have been an utter tragedy. 443

So what are we to say, best of the Greeks? That this bold move of theirs against you at that time was justified, or that it was a piece of folly on their part and that you were responsible for it? I would say that neither of these was the case. But certainly, someone could in the course of rebutting your arguments turn these episodes back doubly on you and on Socrates both, with the claim that even if it was completely unjust for this to happen to the pair of you, in a certain sense what you experienced was only what you deserved, if you made your pupils into these sorts of person. And the comparison with sophists, which you misuse against politicians,[336] could with much more justice be used against the two of you, inasmuch as yours and Socrates' companions would be much more closely comparable to the associates of the sophists than those who associated with Pericles and his circle. Thus if leaders can be charged on the strength of their associates' errors, then you have charged yourself and your friend sooner than Pericles and the people you think you have charged—or indeed, if you like, I will remit you that "sooner"; "every bit as much" is 444

445

half of the fourth century BC. Chabrias is also connected to Plato in Plut. *Mor.* 1126c and Diog. Laert. 3.23–24; Iphicrates is anecdotally linked to Socrates in Diog. Laert. 2.30.

336 *Grg.* 464b–66d, 519c.

ὑμεῖς ἀθῷοι, κἀκείνους ἐκ τῶν αὐτῶν εἰκός ἐστιν εἶναι, εἴπερ γε τοῦ ἴσου μέμνησαι καὶ μὴ ὑπερβαίνεις τὴν γεωμετρίαν ἑκών.

446 καὶ μὴν καὶ ὁ Σωκράτης ἐν γήρᾳ φαίνεται τὴν γραφὴν τῆς ἀσεβείας ἁλούς, καὶ οὐ μόνον ἐπὶ τελευτῇ τοῦ βίου, ἀλλὰ καὶ ταύτης αὐτῆς[138] τυχὼν τῆς
447 τελευτῆς. θανάτου γὰρ ἐτίμησαν αὐτῷ. ἆρ᾽ οὖν οὐκ ἄτοπον τὸν μὲν ἄλλον χρόνον τοσοῦτον ὄντα τὸ πλῆθος διαλέγεσθαι καὶ παιδεύειν τοὺς ἐντυγχάνοντας, καὶ μήτε τῶν πολιτικῶν μηδένα δυσμεναίνειν μήτε τῶν περὶ τοὺς ποιητὰς ἐσπουδακότων, ἀλλὰ καὶ κωμῳδίαν τινὰ συνθέντα εἰς αὐτὸν ἡττηθέντ᾽ ἀπελθεῖν, καὶ εἴ τινα καὶ ἤρεσεν, μηδὲν πλέον τοῦ γέλωτος τότε συμβῆναι, τοσούτῳ δ᾽ ὕστερον χρόνῳ καὶ ὅτ᾽ ἐκ τοσούτων κακῶν ἡ πόλις αὐτὴν ἀνελάμβανεν, καὶ ἡνίκα τοῖς ἠδικηκόσι μὴ μνησικακήσειν ὠμωμόκεσαν, τηνικαῦτα δυσχερᾶναι τοὺς λόγους αὐτοῦ; ἀλλὰ ταῦτ᾽ ἴσως μὲν εἰκότα, ἴσως δ᾽ οὔ, ἔσχεν δ᾽ ὅμως οὑτωσί.

448 ὅμως δὲ οὐδὲν χείρων ὅ γε Σωκράτης· ἡμεῖς δὲ καὶ τὰ εἰκότα ὑπὲρ τοῦ Περικλέους ἀπεδώκαμεν, οἷς οὐδὲν ἄγνωμον καὶ Πλάτωνα συγχωρεῖν, εἴπερ γε, ὃ μικρῷ πρόσθεν ἔφην, τοῦ δικαίου φροντίζει. καὶ γὰρ αὖ καὶ τοῦτο εἴ τις ἤρετο τὸν Πλάτωνα, εἰ δικαστὴς αὐτὸς τῷ Περικλεῖ καθῆστο, ὅτ᾽ ἔφευγε τῆς κλοπῆς, πότερον

[138] ταύτῃ αὐτῇ Behr

quite sufficient. But if you are innocent, then it is reasonable that they should count as innocent on the same grounds, as long as you keep equality in mind and do not of your own free will break the rules of geometry.[337]

Another point. It was obviously in old age that Socrates 446
was convicted on the charge of impiety; not only did this come toward the end of his life, it was actually with this very event that the end came, since they condemned him
to death. Is it not then extraordinary that for the whole of 447
the rest of his lifetime, which was so extended in duration, he should have conversed with and educated everyone he met, and no politician and no enthusiast for the poets should have born him any ill will, but even when someone wrote a comedy satirizing him he went away defeated,[338] and even if it did actually appeal to anyone, nothing more than laughter resulted at the time, but that so many years later, when the city had recovered from its deep misfortunes, and they had sworn to maintain an amnesty toward the guilty parties, they should then take offense at his teaching? This is perhaps reasonable and perhaps not, but that is how it was.

At all events, it did not make Socrates any the worse a 448
person; and I have also given Pericles his due, with which it would be entirely sensible for Plato too to agree, if indeed, as I said a few moments ago, he cares about justice. Indeed, if someone had asked Plato this further question, whether, if he himself had been sitting as one of Pericles' jurors when he was on trial for embezzlement, he would

337 Another reference to *Grg.* 508a; cf. §§38 and 369 above.

338 Aristophanes with *Clouds*, which came in last at the City Dionysia of 424/3.

τῶν καταψηφιζομένων ἂν ἦν, καὶ πλείονος ἀξίους τοὺς Κλέωνος λόγους τῶν Περικλέους ἡγεῖτο—ὅταν δὲ τοῦτ᾽ εἴπω, λέγω τῆς ἀληθείας—ἣ κἂν ἠρυθρία τοῖς γιγνομένοις, ὥσπερ ἔγωγ᾽ ἂν διισχυρισαίμην ὑπὲρ Πλάτωνος, ἀδύνατον δήπου φῆσαι ὡς ὅμοιος ἂν
449 ἦν Κλέωνι. εἶθ᾽ ὃν αὐτὸς ἀφῆκας ἂν τῆς αἰτίας, τοῦτον διαβάλλεις ἐκ τῆς αὐτῆς ταύτης αἰτίας; καὶ πῶς οὐκ ἄτοπον ἄλλῳ μὲν ἂν λέγοντι μὴ πιστεύειν, αὐτὸν δὲ κατηγορεῖν; καὶ δι᾽ ἃ τὸν λέγοντα ἂν ἡγοῦ χείρω, διὰ ταῦτα Περικλέα ἀξιοῦν φαῦλον νομίζεσθαι; καὶ τοὺς καταψηφισαμένους αἰτιώμενον ἡμᾶς πείθειν συγκαταγιγνώσκειν, ὥσπερ χρηστοῦ τινος πράγματος μεθέξειν μέλλοντας, ἀλλ᾽ οὐχ ὃ μηδ᾽ ἐκείνοις καλῶς εἶχε ποιῆσαι; κἀκεῖνοι μὲν αὐτοὶ τὴν ἑαυτῶν καταδίκην οὐχ ὑπελογίσαντο, ἀλλ᾽ ἐτίμων πάλιν ὡς χρηστὸν καὶ δίκαιον, ἡμεῖς δὲ οὗ μηδὲν ἄλλο κατηγορεῖν ἔχομεν, τοῦτον ἀτιμάσομεν διὰ τὴν δίκην, καὶ τῶν αὐτῶν ἀνδρῶν ὃ μὲν ἥμαρτον ἰσχυρὸν ποιησόμεθα, ἃ δ᾽ εὖ φρονοῦντες ἔπραττον ἐν οὐδενὸς μοίρᾳ θήσομεν, καὶ ταῦθ᾽ ὁμολογοῦντες ὡς ἥμαρτον, μᾶλλον δὲ κατηγοροῦντες;

450 καὶ τίνα ταῦτ᾽ εἶχε λόγον ἐγὼ μὲν οὐκ ἐπινοῶ. τῷ γὰρ οὐκ ἂν ὅρος καὶ πέρας εἶναι δόξειεν τῆς ὑπὲρ αὐτῶν ἀπολογίας ἃ Πλάτων ἐγκαλεῖ; οἷον εἰ τῆς κατηγορίας τῶν ἀνδρῶν γεγονυίας καὶ τοῦ κακίζοντος αὐτοὺς τούτοις καταχρησαμένου τοῖς λόγοις, ὡς παρ᾽ αὐτοῖς Ἀθηναίοις ἑάλωσαν καὶ δίκην ἔδωκαν[139] ὡς

[139] ἔδωκαν *edd.* ἔδοσαν *codd.*

have been one of those voting for his condemnation, and would have thought more highly of Cleon's words than of Pericles'—and when I say this, I mean "than of the truth"—or whether, as I would insist on his behalf, he would have blushed at what was going on, it is surely impossible to say that he would have sided with Cleon. Can 449
you then really slander someone on the very same charge on which you yourself would have acquitted him? And how is it not absurd to bring the charge yourself when you would not have believed someone else if he had made it? And to think it proper to consider Pericles a villain on the same grounds as would have made you think the worse of the man who alleged them? And while accusing those who voted for his condemnation to persuade us to condemn him too, as if we were going to be participants in some good deed, rather than one which was not a noble action for them to perform either? When the Athenians themselves did not take their own condemnation seriously, but honored Pericles once more as a good and just man, are we going to dishonor a man against whom we have no other charge to bring simply on the strength of this trial, and are we going in the case of the same people to lay stress on their mistakes, but count their well-advised actions as unimportant, even as we concede that they made mistakes, or rather accuse them of doing so?

I for one cannot see what sense there would be in this. 450
Who after all would not think that Plato's accusations in fact constitute the very definition and contours of our politicians' defense? That is to say, if when the accusation of these men had been delivered and their detractor had made his misuse of the argument that they had been convicted in Athens itself and punished as guilty men, he had

ἀδικοῦντες, εἶτ᾽ ἐπέδειξεν ὅτι ἀλλ᾽ οὐκ ὀρθῶς γε οὐδ᾽ ἐπὶ πᾶσι δικαίοις ταῦτ᾽ ἐγένετο, ἀλλὰ γνώμῃ διήμαρτον οἱ καταψηφισάμενοι, ἢ καὶ δι᾽ ἄλλο τι ταῦτ᾽ ἐψηφίσαντο, ἀλλ᾽ οὐκ ἀδικεῖν αὐτοὺς καταγνόντες, πᾶσιν ἂν δήπου ταῦτ᾽ ἐξήρκει καὶ λελύσθαι τὰ τῆς αἰτίας
451 ἱκανῶς ἂν ᾤοντο. Πλάτων τοίνυν αὐτὸς[140] αἰτιώμενος τὰ συμβεβηκότα καὶ λέγων ὡς ἁμαρτήματα τῶν πολλῶν, ὅμως ἐν ἐλέγχῳ κατ᾽ ἐκείνων λαμβάνει, καὶ τὴν συμφορὰν ὡς ἀδίκημα κατηγόρηκεν, τὴν μὲν τύχην ἀντὶ γνώμης ἐξετάζων, τὴν δ᾽ ἑτέρων ἁμαρτίαν ὡς
452 ἐκείνων οὖσαν τιθείς. ἡδέως δ᾽ ἂν ἐροίμην τοὺς προσκειμένους αὐτῷ τί ποτ᾽ ἂν λέγειν ἠξίουν κατὰ τῶν ἀνδρῶν, ἢ τίνα γνώμην ἔχειν ἡμᾶς ἔπειθον, εἰ τοῦτ᾽ εἶχον δεικνύειν ὡς ἐν παντὶ δικαίῳ μετ᾽ οὐδεμιᾶς φαύλης προφάσεως Ἀθηναῖοι κατεψηφίσαντο αὐτῶν, ὁπότ᾽ αὐτὸς φάσκων αὐτοὺς παρανενομῆσθαι καὶ τοῖς ἵπποις τοῖς λακτίζουσιν ἀπεικάζων τοὺς καταψηφισαμένους ἰσχυρόν τι λέγειν κατ᾽ ἐκείνων οἴεται. ταχύ γ᾽ ἂν εἰ τοῖς δώδεκα θεοῖς ἔσχεν εἰκάσαι τοὺς καταγνόντας, ἀπέσχετ᾽ ἂν τῶν ἁλόντων τὸ μὴ οὐ κακῶς εἰπεῖν.

453 ἔπειθ᾽ ὡς οὐ κατ᾽ ἀρχὰς ταῦτ᾽ ἔδρων αὐτοὺς λέγει, ὥσπερ τὸν Κριτίαν καὶ τοὺς ἄλλους τοὺς εἰς αὐτὸν ἁμαρτάνοντας, εὐθὺς ἐν ἀρχῇ ταῦτα ποιοῦντας, ἀλλ᾽ οὐ πολλοῖς ὕστερον [ἔτεσι καὶ][141] χρόνοις κυρίττειν

140 *αὐτός* EaA²R² *αὐτῶν* TU *αὐτόν* QVA¹R¹
141 *del.* Dindorf *ἔστιν καί* VA¹

then gone on to demonstrate that in fact it had not been right for this to happen and it was not fully justified, but that those who had voted for condemnation had been mistaken in their judgment, or had voted as they did for some other reason and not because they thought them guilty of wrongdoing, that would surely have been enough for everybody, and they would have thought that the charges
had been adequately dispelled. Yet Plato, while himself 451
reprehending what happened and speaking of it as an error on the part of the people, nevertheless takes it as damning evidence against the Four and has condemned their misfortune as if it were a crime on their part, making their luck rather than their intentions the object of his scrutiny and setting down other people's error as if it were
theirs. I would gladly ask his supporters what on earth they 452
would think they ought to say against these men, and what view they would try to persuade us to take, if they were able to show that the Athenians condemned them with full justification and without any flaws in their reasons for doing so, when he himself thinks he can make a valid case against them by asserting that they were the victims of wrongdoing and by comparing those who condemned them to horses that kick. How readily, if he could have compared those who delivered the guilty verdict to the Twelve Gods, would he have held back from speaking ill of the condemned parties!

Plato also says that the Athenians did not act as they 453
did toward the Four at the outset, unlike Critias and the others who offended against Socrates, who did so right at the beginning, rather than beginning to butt only a long

ἀρξαμένους ἢ παρ' ἐκείνους ἐφοίτησαν. ἀλλ' εἰ καὶ μὴ ἐποίουν ταῦτ' ἐξ ἀρχῆς, εἶχόν γ' ἐν τῇ φύσει δήπουθεν καὶ τὸ κωλῦσαι κρείττονος παντελῶς ἢ κατ' ἄν-
454 θρωπον ἦν. εἰ δ' ἐπ' ἀμφότερα αἰτιάσεται Πλάτων τοὺς ἄνδρας ὥσπερ σοφοῦ τινος εἰλημμένος, τί κωλύει τινὰ τὰς ὁμοίας ἀνταποδιδόντα ἐπ' ἀμφότερ' αὖ φιλονείκως ὑπολαμβάνοντα διαλύειν ὡδὶ τὸν λόγον, ὅτι εἰ μὲν καλῶς καὶ τὰ δίκαια αὐτῶν Ἀθηναῖοι κατέγνωσαν, οὐκ ἦσαν ὑπ' αὐτῶν διεφθαρμένοι· τὰ γὰρ δίκαια ἐποίουν. οὐκοῦν οὐδ' ἐκεῖνοι διεφθάρκεσαν. ὥστ' εἰ δικαίως ἑάλωσαν, οὐδὲν ταύτῃ γε χείρους ἦσαν, εἰ δ' ἀδίκως αὐτῶν ἐκεῖνοι κατεψηφίσαντο, ἠδικῆσθαι τοῖς ἀνδράσι περίεστιν, ἀδικεῖν δὲ οὐδαμῶς· τοῖς δ' ἀδικηθεῖσιν βοηθεῖν, οὐκ ἐγκαλεῖν εἰκός ἐστιν· εἰ δέ τοι καὶ μὴ δυνατὸν βοηθεῖν, ἀλλ' οὐχὶ δίκαιόν γε ἐγκαλεῖν.

455 ἐγὼ δὲ ταῦτα μὲν τοῖς κομψοτέροις παρίημι· αὐτὸς δὲ τί φημι καὶ πῶς δέχομαι τὸν λόγον; οὐκ ἔστιν δίκαιον ἅμ' ἀμφοῖν κατηγορεῖν, καὶ τοῦ δήμου κἀκείνων· ἢ σαφῶς τοὺς ἑτέρους συκοφαντήσομεν. εἰ μὲν γὰρ ὀρθῶς ἐκεῖνα κατεγνώσθη, ἠδίκουν μέν, ὡς ἔοικεν, ἐκεῖνοι, τῷ δήμῳ δ' ἃ προσήκει πέπρακται. ὥστε
456 οὐχὶ δίκαιον ταῦτά γε δήπου κατηγορεῖν αὐτοῦ. πῶς οὖν τοῖς ἀγριαίνουσι τῶν ζῴων αὐτὸν ἀπεικάζοντες ὀρθῶς φήσομεν ποιεῖν; εἰ δ' ἥμαρτεν ὁ δῆμος, ἅμα τ'

time after they had attended their school. But even if they did not behave like this in the beginning, they surely had it in their natures and the task of putting a stop to it was
one utterly beyond human capacity. And if Plato, as if he 454
has hit on a really clever strategy, is going to accuse our men either way, then what is to prevent someone else paying him back in the same coin and responding competitively in his turn with an each-way argument, so as to settle the issue as follows: if the Athenians acted properly in condemning the Four and were in the right, then they had not been corrupted by them, because they were acting justly; therefore our men did not exert a corrupting influence either, so that if they were justly convicted they were not in that respect any the worse men. But if on the other hand the Athenians condemned the Four unjustly, it follows that our men were the victims of injustice, and in no way responsible for any unjust action themselves; and the proper course is to help victims of injustice rather than to prosecute them. And if in fact it is not possible to help them, that certainly does not mean there is any justification for prosecuting them.

I leave all this to cleverer people than me. But what do 455
I say myself, and how do I understand the argument? It is not fair simultaneously to charge both parties, both the people of Athens and the Four; if we do, our accusation against either one or the other will be a malicious one. Because if on the one hand the condemnation was rightly delivered, it would appear that the Four were indeed guilty of wrongdoing, and that the people of Athens acted appropriately, in which case it is manifestly not just to
prosecute them on this score. So how can we claim to be 456
acting correctly if we compare them to animals gone wild?

ἐκείνῳ ἡμάρτηται καὶ τοῖς ἀνδράσι τοὔνειδος λέλυται. αὐτὸ γὰρ τοῦτό φαμεν δήπουθεν ἁμαρτεῖν Ἀθηναίους, τιμήσαντας ἐκείνοις φυγῆς, ἢ χρημάτων, ἢ ὁτουδήποτ' ἐτίμησαν ἑκάστῳ. οὗτος δὲ ὁ λόγος τί λέγει; μη-
457 δενὸς τούτων ἐκείνους ἀξίους εἶναι. καὶ μὴν εἴ γε ἠδίκουν, ἄξιοι τούτων ἦσαν. ὅτε δὲ οὐ τούτων ἄξιοι, σαφὲς ὡς οὐκ ἠδίκουν. τοὺς δ' οὐκ ἀδικοῦντας κακῶς λέγειν καὶ συκοφαντεῖν οὐχὶ δίκαια ποιεῖν οὐδαμῶς ἐστιν.

458 ἡμεῖς τοίνυν ἀντὶ τοῦ κατηγορεῖν ἀμφοτέρων ὑπὲρ ἀμφοτέρων τὰ πρέποντ' ἀπολογούμεθα, οὔτε τοῦ δήμου τὴν αἰτίαν παντὸς εἶναι φάσκοντες οὔτ' ἐκείνους προσήκειν εἴ τι[142] προσέπταισαν χείρους νομίζεσθαι. δείκνυμεν δὲ ὅτι τεττάρων ὄντων τοῖν δυοῖν μὲν οὐδὲ προσήψατο ὁ δῆμος, ὧν δ' ἔδοξαν καταψηφίζεσθαι δυοῖν, οὐδὲ τούτων ἀδικεῖν κατεψηφίσαντο, ἀλλ' ὥσπερ παῖδες διδάσκαλον αὐτοῖς ἠξίωσαν ὑποχωρῆσαι.

459 πάλιν τοίνυν ἐφ' ἑκατέρας τῆς συζυγίας ἅτερος εὑρίσκεται τῆς δικαιοτάτης τυχὼν παρὰ τοῦ δήμου φιλανθρωπίας, ὁ μὲν ἐντὸς τοῦ χρόνου κατελθών, ὁ δὲ στρατηγῶν πρὶν ἐκτῖσαι, καὶ κύριος ὢν τῶν ἁπάντων, καὶ τῶν καταψηφισαμένων αὐτῶν. πῶς ἄν τις κάλλιον ὑπὲρ ἀμφοῖν ἀπολογήσαιτο, εἴ τι δεῖ τῶν
460 ὄντων καὶ περὶ τῶν αὐτοῦ λόγων εἰπεῖν; εἰ τοίνυν ἁπάντων μὲν ὁ δῆμος κατεγνώκει, μηδὲν δὲ ὕστερον

142 εἴ τι Reiske εἰ ὅτι *codd.*

If on the other hand the people made a mistake, then Plato
is also guilty of an error and the Four are absolved from
blame. And we surely do say precisely that the Athenians
went wrong in sentencing them to exile, or a fine, or whatever it was that they sentenced each of them to. What then
does this line of argument show? That they did not deserve
any of these things. If they had done wrong, they would 457
have deserved them; but given that they did not deserve
them, it is clear that they were not guilty of wrongdoing
either. To speak ill of those who have committed no offense and to bring malicious prosecutions against them is
in no way a just course of action.

Rather, then, than accusing both sides, I offer the ap- 458
propriate defense for both of them, asserting neither that
the blame belongs to the whole of the Athenian people,
nor that it is appropriate to think the worse of our men if
they stumbled in some respect. I demonstrate that, of the
Four, the people did not even lay a hand on two of them,
and that even the two whom they were supposed to have
condemned, they did not condemn for wrongdoing, but
rather thought, as pupils do of their teacher, that they
ought to show some deference to them.

Again, in each pair one of the two can be found to have 459
enjoyed the most just of generous treatment from the
people, in the one case returning from exile within the
appointed period, and in the other before even paying his
fine being appointed general and put in charge of everything, including even the people who had voted for his
condemnation. How could anyone offer a finer defense of
both of them, if we must tell the truth about Plato's argument too? Even if the people had condemned all of them, 460

πρὸς μηδέν' αὐτῶν ἐφιλανθρωπεύσατο, οὐδ' οὕτω δίκαιον ἦν ἃ μὲν τοῖς ἑτέροις ἡμάρτητο κατ' ἀμφοτέρων λέγειν, ἃ δ' ἀμφοτέροις ὑπῆρχεν εἰς εὐφημίαν μηδετέροις ἀξιοῦν ἀποδοῦναι. εἰ μὲν γὰρ ἐκ τούτων μόνον οἵ τε Ἀθηναῖοι κοινῇ καὶ οἱ προστάντες αὐτῶν ἐγιγνώσκοντο, καλῶς εἶχε ταῦτ' ὀνειδίζειν· εἰ δ' ἔσθ' ἕτερα ἀμείνω καὶ πλείω τούτων, καὶ σύ γ' αὐτὸς κάλλιστα ὡμολόγηκας—ὀψὲ γάρ ποτε ἔφης αὐτοὺς εἰς ταῦτ' ἐμπεσεῖν, ὡς τόν γε ἄνω χρόνον πάντα κἀκείνους ὡς ἐβούλοντο πράττοντας καὶ τὸν δῆμον παρέχοντα αὑτὸν οἷον χρή—πῶς οὐκ ὀρθῶς εἶχε μιμήσασθαι τὸ τῶν Περσῶν; ἐκείνοις γάρ φασιν εἶναι νόμον, ἄν τις αὐτῶν σχῇ τινα φαύλην αἰτίαν, μὴ πρότερον καταγιγνώσκειν, μηδ' ἂν ἐλέγχηται, πρὶν ἂν παρ' ἄλληλα ἐξετάσαντες ἅ τε εὖ καὶ ἃ κακῶς ἐποίησεν εὕρωσι τὰ χείρω νικῶντα· ὅταν δὲ τὰ τῶν εὐεργεσιῶν ἔμπροσθεν ᾖ, καὶ τοῖς φανερῶς ἀδικοῦσιν ἀφεῖσθαι τάττειν τὸν νόμον.

[*(ii) The Four Not to Blame for the Vagaries of Fortune (461–98)*]

461 *εἶτ' ἐν μὲν τοῖς βαρβάροις οὕτως, Πλάτων δ' ὁ τῶν Ἑλλήνων ἄριστος καὶ ὁ τῶν ἀνθρωπίνων πραγμάτων ἐπιστήμων, προσθήσω δὲ καὶ τῶν θείων, πῶς ἀξιώσει συλλήβδην πάντα κατορθοῦν καὶ πάντων κρατεῖν ὄντα ἄνθρωπον, καὶ ταῦτα μὴ μόνον ὧν ἡ γνώμη κυ-*

and had not shown any generosity to any of them subsequently, it would even so not be fair to use the mistakes of the one party against both, and not see fit to allow either of them the grounds for praise that are available to both. If it was from these events only that the Athenians collectively and their leaders were known, it would be fine to reproach them on these grounds; but if there are other better episodes that outnumber them, as you yourself have very nobly conceded—because you said that it was only late on that they stumbled into this situation, since previously the Four had operated as they wished and the people had behaved itself—how would it not be right to follow the Persian practice? It is said to be a custom of theirs, if one of them is accused of some kind of vile action, not to condemn him, even if he is found guilty, before they have conducted a comparative examination of the good and bad that he has done and found the bad to predominate; and in cases where someone's good deeds preponderate, the custom prescribes that even the manifestly guilty should be let off.[339]

(ii) The Four Not to Blame for the Vagaries of Fortune (461–98)

If that is how things are done among the barbarians, how 461
then can Plato, the best of the Greeks and an expert in human affairs (and divine affairs too, I might add) demand that a mere human should be universally successful in all his doings and in control of everything, not only what hu-

[339] Hdt. 1.137.

ρία, ἀλλὰ καὶ ὅσα πρὸς τὴν τύχην ἐστίν, ἢ τοῦ μηδενὸς ἄξιον εἶναι τὸν καὶ μικρόν τι προσπταίσαντα; οὐκ ἄρα ἐκείνων μόνον κατηγορεῖν δόξομεν, ἀλλὰ καὶ
462 τῆς φύσεως τῆς ἀνθρωπείας ἁπάσης. βλέψον δέ, εἰ βούλει, πρὸς τὰ σαυτοῦ πάλιν αὖ παραδείγματα. εὑρήσεις γὰρ οὔτε τοὺς ἡνιόχους τοὺς ἀγαθοὺς ἅπαντα νικῶντας ἐφεξῆς οὔτε ταῦτ' ἐπαγγελλομένους, οὔτε τοὺς ἵππους αὐτοὺς ὥσπερ ἐπὶ ῥητοῖς θέοντας, ἀλλὰ καὶ τὰς τοῦ Μιλτιάδου καὶ τὰς τοῦ Κίμωνος ἵππους ἀρίστας γενέσθαι δοκούσας οὐχ ἅπαντας τοὺς ἀγῶνας ἀνῃρημένας, οὐδὲ ἅπαντα ὃν ἔζων συνεχῶς νικώσας χρόνον. οὐδ' αὖ τοὺς κυβερνήτας λέγω τοὺς ἀρίστους ἀεὶ καὶ πάντας ἐκ τοῦ θανάτου σῴζοντας, ἀλλ' ἤδη τινὰ καὶ σκηπτοῦ καὶ χειμῶνος ἡττηθέντα καὶ χρησάμενον τύχῃ τῆς τέχνης κρείττονι, πάντως δ' ἅπαντας παραχωροῦντας τῷ Ποσειδῶνι, κἀν ταῖς συγγραφαῖς οὕτω γραφόμενον, σωθείσης τῆς νεὼς τὸ καὶ τὸ ποιήσειν. ὅτι δ' ἡ ναῦς σωθήσεται
463 οὐδείς πω κατεπηγγείλατο. ταῦτ' ἐστὶ πρὸς ἃ καὶ Ὅμηρος βλέπων ἔφη

ξυνὸς Ἐνυάλιος καί τε κτανέοντα κατέκτα.

ᾔδει γὰρ τῆς ἀνθρωπίνης φύσεως τὴν ἀσθένειαν καὶ τούτου τοῦ λόγου παράδειγμα ἱκανὸν καὶ ἅμα αὐτόθεν. τῶν μὲν γὰρ Ἑλλήνων κράτιστος Ἀχιλλεὺς αὐτῷ δή-

man intellect has power over but also everything that falls into the domain of chance into the bargain, and that the man who instead encounters even a small setback should count as worthless? In that case people will think we are bringing our accusation not only against the Four, but
against human nature in general! If you please, take an- 462
other look at your own comparisons. Because you will find that even good charioteers do not win absolutely every competition or promise that they will either, and that the horses themselves do not run as if according to prearranged conditions, but that even Miltiades' and Cimon's horses, which were reputed to be the best of all, did not carry off the prizes in all their competitions, or remain victorious for the whole of their lives without interruption. Nor again will you find that helmsmen, even the best ones, can always save everybody from death, but there are many on record who have been defeated by thunderbolt and storm, and have encountered bad luck that overwhelmed their skill, and in any case all of them defer to Poseidon, and the clause "if the ship comes safely to port, they will do such and such" is written into their contracts. But nobody has ever categorically guaranteed that the ship will
indeed come safely to port. This is what Homer had his 463
eye on when he wrote

> The War god is impartial, and ever kills the intending
> killer.[340]

He knew the weakness of human nature, and sufficient illustration of this proposition is immediately to hand in his work. The mightiest of the Greeks in his poem, by a

340 *Il.* 18.309.

που πεποίηται, καὶ ταῦτά γε πολλῷ τινι· τῶν δ' αὖ βαρβάρων ὁ Πάρις πάντων σχεδὸν μαλακώτατος, ὥστε καὶ ὁ Ἕκτωρ πολλάκις αὐτῷ προφέρει τὴν δειλίαν, ἀδελφὸς ὢν καὶ ταῦτα, καὶ Δύσπαριν μετὰ προσθήκης καλεῖ. ἀλλ' ὅμως Ἀχιλλεὺς μὲν τήν τε ἄλλην ἅπασαν τῶν Τρώων στρατιὰν εἰς τὸ τεῖχος κατέκλεισεν καὶ τὸν Ἕκτορα πρὸς ταῖς πύλαις ῥᾳδίως ἀπέκτεινεν. ὁ δ' αὖ Πάρις ἢ Δύσπαρις, ὁ τοσοῦτον χείρων τοῦ Ἕκτορος, αὐτὸν τὸν Ἀχιλλέα πρὸς ταῖς αὐταῖς ταύταις πύλαις ἀποκτείνας ᾄδεται. ὥστ' ἀπὸ τῶν ἐσχάτων ὅρων ἑκατέρωθεν, τῆς τε ἀνδρείας λέγω καὶ τῆς ἀνανδρείας, τὸ ἔπος βεβαιοῦται·

464 οἶμαι δ' οὐ μόνον ξυνὸς Ἐνυάλιος, ἀλλὰ καὶ Ἑρμῆς ἂν κοινὸς ἀκούοι δικαίως. καὶ εἰ μὲν τοῦτο καὶ ἡ παροιμία βούλεται δηλοῦν ἢ περιλαμβάνει γε, ἔστω καὶ αὕτη μαρτυροῦσα· εἰ δ' ἐπ' ἄλλῳ τῳ γεγένηται, ἡμεῖς γε τοσοῦτον προσθῶμεν ὅτι καὶ ταύτῃ δικαίως ἂν ὁ θεὸς τὴν ἐπωνυμίαν φέροιτο, ἐπείπερ ἔστ' ἐναγώνιος. ἐπεὶ καὶ τὰ τῶν στεφανιτῶν οἶμαι παραπλησίως ἔχει τοῖς τῶν πολέμων· οὐδεὶς κρατεῖ τοσοῦτον ὅσον βούλεται, οὐδ' ὥστε καὶ προειπεῖν ἔχειν
465 ὅτι νικῶν ἄπεισι. δηλοῖ δ' ἔτι καὶ νῦν ἡ τῶν Ὀλυμπίων θεωρία, πλεῖστον ἀεὶ τὸ παράδοξον φέρουσα,

---

[341] *Il*. 3.38–57.

[342] *Il*. 22.359–60, in Hector's dying prophecy.

long way, is of course Achilles; of the barbarians Paris is just about the softest of the lot, so that even Hector frequently reproaches him for his cowardice, even though he is his brother, and adds a syllable to his name so as to make him "Ill-Paris."[341] But even so, although Achilles shut the whole of the rest of the Trojan army up inside their walls and made easy work of killing Hector by the gates, it was Paris or "Ill-Paris," the one who was so deeply inferior to Hector, who is said in the poem to have been the one to kill Achilles himself by those very same gates.[342] Thus Homer's line is borne out from the two opposite ends of the scale, namely bravery and cowardice.

I think that it is not only the War god who is impartial, 464
but that Hermes too could justifiably be called "shared in common." If this is indeed what the proverbial phrase means to show, or at any rate allows for,[343] then let it too serve as evidence; but if it came into being for a different purpose, I can add on my own initiative that there is a further reason why the god deserves the epithet, if he is indeed the patron deity of athletic competition. Because I think that things stand with the world of athletic competition more or less as they do with the world of war: no one dominates as comprehensively as he wishes, nor to the extent of being able to predict that he will emerge victorious.This is demonstrated even in our time by visits to 465
the Olympics, which always bring enormous surprises, for

343 "*Koinos Hermes*" ("Hermes in common," "Finders sharers") was the conventional cry used to claim a share in a chance find of something valuable (a *hermaion*): Theophr. *Char.* 30.9, Men. *Epit.* 283–85. Aristides suggests stretching the meaning of *koinos* in this phrase beyond its normal application.

οἷον ἀμέλει καὶ τὸ τοῦ Πολυδάμαντός ποτέ φασι συμβῆναι. ἐκεῖνος γὰρ τὰ μὲν ἅρματα ἵστη τρέχοντα, Ὀλυμπίασι δ' ἡττήθη μικροῦ τινος ἀνταγωνιστοῦ. ἀλλ' οὔ τί γε τοῖς ὅλοις οἶμαι Πολυδάμας ἐκείνου χείρων, οὐδὲ τῆς πάσης δόξης παρὰ τοῦτο στέροιτ'
466 ἂν δικαίως. καὶ οὐκ ἐπὶ μὲν τῶν ἀθλητῶν οὕτως συμβαίνει, τὰ δὲ τῆς μουσικῆς ἑστηκυῖαν ἔχει τὴν νίκην τοῖς κρείττοσιν, ἀλλὰ κἀνταῦθα τὸ τοῦ Πινδάρου κρατεῖ. πάνυ γὰρ μετ' ἀληθείας τοῦτ' ἐκεῖνος ὕμνησεν·

ἐν ἔργμασι δὲ νικᾷ τύχα,
οὐ σθένος.

Σοφοκλῆς Φιλοκλέους ἡττᾶτο ἐν Ἀθηναίοις τὸν Οἰδίπουν, ὦ Ζεῦ καὶ θεοί, πρὸς ὃν οὐδ' Αἰσχύλος εἶχε λέξαι τι. ἆρ' οὖν διὰ τοῦτο χείρων Σοφοκλῆς Φιλοκλέους; αἰσχύνη μὲν οὖν αὐτῷ τοσοῦτον ἀκοῦσαι, ὅτι βελτίων Φιλοκλέους.

467 ἄλλα μυρία ἄν τις ἔχοι λέγειν, ἀλλ' Ὅμηρος πῶς ἐξαγγέλλει τὸν ἀγῶνα τὸν ἐπὶ Πατρόκλῳ γενέσθαι; οὐχ αἱ μὲν ἄρισται τῶν ἵππων αἱ Θετταλαί,

---

344 The wrestler Polydamas of Scotussa in Thessaly won the *pankration* at the Olympic Games of 408 BC but lost his title four years later to Promachus of Pellene: Paus. 7.27.6. The story about his stopping a chariot at full tilt was one of several told about his extraordinary strength: Paus. 6.5.4–9.

example what they say once happened in the case of Polydamas.[344] Polydamas could stop racing chariots in their tracks, but at Olympia he was beaten by a small opponent. But I definitely do not think that overall Polydamas was this man's inferior, or that it would be justifiable for him to lose his whole reputation on this account. Nor is it the 466
case that that is how things happen with athletes, but that in the field of music victory belongs unshakably to the superior performers; no, here too Pindar's principle prevails. He had the truth entirely on his side when he sang,

> in deeds it is chance that conquers,
> not strength.[345]

Sophocles lost to Philocles in Athens with his *Oedipus*, for heaven's sake, and he was the poet of whom not even Aeschylus had anything bad to say.[346] Was Sophocles then inferior to Philocles because of this? No, it would even be a source of shame to him to have it said that he was superior to Philocles!

There are thousands of other instances one might men- 467
tion. How does Homer report that the funeral games in honor of Patroclus passed off? Didn't the best of the horses, the Thessalians,

345 Fr. 38 Sn-M, also cited in *Or.* 2.112.

346 Philocles, Aeschylus' nephew and a prolific tragic poet, notoriously won the dramatic competition in which Sophocles came in second with *Oedipus Tyrannos*: Dicaearchus (fr. 80 Wehrli), cited in *OT* Hypoth. II (*TrGF* 1.24 T3). Aristides' assertion that even Aeschylus admired Sophocles is apparently based, with a little license, on Ar. *Frogs* 1515–19.

τὰς Εὔμηλος ἔλαυνε ποδώκεας, ὄρνιθας ὥς,

ὕσταται πάντων ἐγένοντο ἐν τῷ τότε, καὶ ὁ Εὔμηλος αὐτὸς ἐκπίπτει τοῦ ἅρματος, οὔπω πρόσθεν παθὼν αὐτό, ἀλλ' ἔποχος μένων, καὶ ταῦτά γε ὡς ἐπ' ὀρνίθων τῶν ἵππων ὀχούμενος, ὃ μηδενί πω τῶν ἄλλων ἦν ῥᾴδιον. ὥστε καὶ ἰδὼν αὐτὸν Ἀχιλλεὺς ᾤκτειρέ τε καὶ λέγει

λοῖσθος ἀνὴρ ὥριστος ἐλαύνει μώνυχας ἵππους.

468 ἆρ' οὖν οὐ παράδοξον ἑξῆς οὑτωσὶ θεῖναι παρ' ἄλληλα καὶ τὸν αὐτὸν λοῖσθόν τε καὶ ἄριστον προσειπεῖν; ἀλλ' ὅμως τοιαῦτά φησι τἀνθρώπεια—τοῦτο γάρ μοι δοκεῖ τῶν ῥημάτων τὸ βούλημα εἶναι—ὁ αὐτὸς ἄριστός τε ἀνὴρ καὶ ἔσχατος, ὅπερ περὶ τοῦ δακτύλου φασί ποτ' εἰπεῖν Ὀρόντην τὸν Πέρσην ὡς ὁ αὐτὸς[143] ὢν τῇ θέσει ποτὲ μὲν τὰ μύρια σημαίνει, ποτὲ δὲ οὐ πλέον ἢ ἕν. ὥστ' ἐμοὶ μὲν ἄντικρυς εἰς τὸ Πλάτωνος παράδειγμα ὁ Εὔμηλος τείνειν δοκεῖ κατά τε τἄλλα καὶ ὅτι[144] οὐχ ὅσον τῆς νίκης ἐστερήθη, ἀλλὰ καὶ

ἀγκῶνάς τε περιδρύφθη στόμα τε ῥῖνάς τε

143 ὁ αὐτός Ph^s Wyttenbach αὐτός *codd.*
144 *add.* Reiske

---

347 *Il.* 2.764. 348 *Il.* 23.536.

349 Another version of Orontes' observation is given in Plut. *Mor.* 174b, and the circumstances are given in Diod. Sic. 15.10–

> the swift-footed mares that Eumelus drove, as fast as birds,[347]

come in last of all on that occasion, and wasn't Eumelus himself thrown from his chariot, although that had never happened to him before, but he had always remained in his car, even when he was driving horses like birds, which none of the others ever found easy? As a result, didn't Achilles take pity on him and say

> the last man to drive up his solid-hoofed horses is the best?[348]

Isn't it surprising that he puts the two things side by side 468
like this and calls the same man both last and best? But all the same, that is what he says human life is like—this is what it seems to me his words are getting at—the same man can be both the best and the hindmost. It's like what they say Orontes the Persian once said about the finger: it is the same finger, but according to its positioning it sometimes signifies ten thousand and sometimes no more than one.[349] It therefore seems to me that Eumelus is directly relevant to Plato's comparison in a number of ways, in particular in that he was not only cheated of victory, but that

> the skin was torn from his elbows and mouth and nose[350]

11; Orontes was son-in-law and general to Artaxerxes II of Persia (405/4–359/8 BC), disgraced for bringing a false accusation. On ancient systems of finger reckoning, see K. A. Wirth, "Fingerzahlen," in the *Reallexikon zur Deutschen Kunstgeschichte* VIII (1986), 1225–1309, online at http://www.rdklabor.de/wiki/Fingerzahlen. [350] *Il*. 23.395.

ὑπὸ τῶν ἵππων τῶν ἀρίστων καὶ ὑφ' ὧν οὐδεπώποτ' ἐσφάλη, ἄγων δ' αὐτὰς ὅποι βούλοιτ' ἀεὶ καὶ παρὰ πάντας ἐθαυμάζετο.

469 ὁ δέ γε Αἴας νὴ Δί' ὁ τάχιστος τῶν Ἑλλήνων θεῖν καὶ πλείστους ἐν ταῖς φυγαῖς αἱρῶν, ἐφ' οὗ τοῦτ' εἴρητο

οὐ γάρ οἵ τις ὁμοῖος ἐπισπέσθαι ποσὶν ἦεν
ἀνδρῶν τρεσσάντων ὅτε τε Ζεὺς ἐν φόβον ὄρσῃ·

καὶ οὗτος τοιαῦθ' ἕτερα ἀπέλαυσεν τοῦ δρόμου, γυμνός τε καὶ πολεμίων καθαρὸς τρέχων, ἀπῆλθεν τῆς τε νίκης στερηθεὶς καὶ τῆς ὄνθου προσέτι ἐμπεπλησμένος. "βλάψεν γὰρ Ἀθήνη," φησὶν ὁ ποιητής· τὴν δ' αὐτὴν ταύτην καὶ τὸν Εὔμηλον ἐκ τοῦ ἅρματος ἐκβαλεῖν. τί τοῦτο λέγων; τὴν τύχην διὰ τῆς Ἀθηνᾶς, ὥς γ' ἐμοὶ δοκεῖ, δηλῶν, ὅτι τὰ ἀνθρώπεια ὅπῃ βούλεται στρέφει, καὶ οὐ πάντῃ τῶν προεχόντων τὰ ἆθλα.

470 ὁ δέ γ' ἕτερος νὴ Δία Αἴας, ὁ τοῦ Τελαμῶνος, τὸ μέγα ἕρκος τῶν Ἀχαιῶν καὶ ὃς ἦν ἀντὶ τείχους τοῖς Ἕλλησιν οὐ μόνον αὐτός, ἀλλὰ καὶ ἡ ἀσπὶς αὐτοῦ, οὗτος περὶ μὲν τὸν δίσκον ὡς ἔπραξεν ἔλαττον ἂν ἴσως εἴη λέγειν, καίτοι δόρυ γ' εἰωθὼς ἔχειν ἐν ταῖν χεροῖν

κολλητὸν βλήτροισι, δυωκαιεικοσίπηχυ,

---

351 *Il.* 14.521–22. 352 *Il.* 23.777.
353 *Il.* 23.774 and 391–93.

as well, by the best horses and the ones he had never before been thrown by, but had always driven where he wanted amid universal admiration.

And look at Ajax, the fastest of the Greeks at running, 469
who had caught hundreds as they took to their heels, and of whom it was said

> no one was his equal in pursuing on foot when men fled
> in panic, after Zeus had stirred up the rout among them.[351]

He too got the same sort of reward from his race: though running unarmed and with no enemies in his path, he ended up cheated of victory and stuffed full of dung into the bargain.[352] "Athena tripped him," says the poet; and it was the selfsame goddess who he says also caused Eumelus to be thrown from his chariot.[353] What did he mean by this? As I see it at any rate, he was using Athena to show that chance twists and turns human affairs as it wishes, and that the prizes do not always go to the foremost.

As for the other Ajax, the son of Telamon, the great 470
"bulwark of the Achaeans"[354] and the man who, along with his shield, served the Greeks in place of a wall–well, it might perhaps be less significant to say how he fared in the discus throwing, even though someone who was in the habit of having in his hands a spear

> firmly jointed with dowels, and twenty-two cubits long,[355]

354 For example, *Il*. 3.229.
355 *Il*. 15.678.

καὶ πάντας τοὺς Τρῶας ἐκείνῳ σοβῶν καὶ ἀπείργων ἀπὸ τῶν νεῶν, ἦ που ῥᾳδίως τόν γε δίσκον ἔμελλεν μεταχειριεῖσθαι καὶ παῖδας τόν τε δὴ Πολυποίτην καὶ τοὺς ἄλλους ἀποφανεῖν, τοῦ γ᾽ εἰκότος νικῶντος. ἀλλὰ δῶμεν τοῦτο ἑτέρας τινὸς ἕξεως δεῖσθαι· ἀλλὰ πῶς ἔπραξεν περὶ τὴν πάλην; εἰ δὲ καὶ τοῦτ᾽ ἔλαττον, ἀλλ᾽ ἀναλαβών γε τὰ ὅπλα, οὗ μέγιστος καὶ κάλλιστος ἦν αὐτὸς αὑτοῦ καὶ ἰσχυρότατος καὶ ῥωμαλεώτατος, πολὺν θόρυβον παρέσχε τοῖς Ἕλλησι. καὶ τὰ μὲν ἄλλα ἐῶ· ἔδεισαν δὲ περὶ ἐκείνου μᾶλλον ἢ τοῦ Διομήδους.
471 οὕτως ἔπραξε κἀνταῦθα. καίτοι ὅ γε κήρυξ ἀνεῖπεν οὑτωσὶ γιγνομένης ποτὲ τῶν Ἀχαιῶν ἁπάντων ἐξετάσεως

> ἀνδρῶν αὖ μέγ᾽ ἄριστος ἔην Τελαμώνιος Αἴας.

καὶ οὐχ ἅπαξ γε οὐδὲ τοσοῦτον μόνον εἰπὼν ἀπηλλάγη, ἀλλ᾽ ὥσπερ ἐξεπίτηδες πανταχοῦ διατελεῖ κηρύττων καὶ διαμαρτυρόμενος,

> Αἴαντός θ᾽, ὃς ἄριστος ἔην εἶδός τε δέμας τε
> τῶν ἄλλων Δαναῶν μετ᾽ ἀμύμονα Πηλείωνα.

καὶ

> Αἴας, ὃς πέρι μὲν εἶδος, πέρι δ᾽ ἔργ᾽ ἐτέτυκο.

---

356 *Il*. 23.826–49.

357 *Il*. 23.700–739 (a draw with Odysseus).

358 *Il*. 23.798–825 (the duel between Ajax and Diomedes for the arms of Sarpedon).

and who used to beat back all the Trojans with it and keep them from the ships, was certainly going to find it easy to handle the discus and show Polypoetes and the others up as children,[356] if the likely outcome prevailed. But let us grant that this requires a different kind of conditioning. How did he do in the wrestling, however?[357] And even if that too is a minor matter, the fact remains that when he armed himself again, for the event in which he was at his greatest and noblest and strongest and most forceful, he still caused great consternation among the Greeks. Without going into any other details, they were more alarmed for him than they were for Diomedes.[358] That is how he did in this instance too. And yet this is how the herald 471
proclaimed him once when a muster of all the Achaeans was being called:

> of men, by far the best was Ajax, son of Telamon.[359]

And Homer did not leave off once he had said only this much, or say it just the once, but as if on purpose he continues to proclaim and testify to his worth all over the place:

> and Ajax, who was the best in form and body
> of the other Greeks after the excellent son of
> Peleus;[360]

and

> Ajax, who was wrought surpassing in form and
> surpassing in deeds;[361]

[359] *Il*. 2.768. [360] *Od*. 11.469–70.
[361] *Il*. 17.279.

καὶ

ἀνδρὶ δ᾽ οὐκ εἴξειε μέγας Τελαμώνιος Αἴας,

καὶ ἄλλα τοιαῦτα, ὥσπερ προκαταλαμβάνων ἡμῶν τὰς γνώμας, ὅπως μὴ ἐπὶ τοῦ ἀγῶνος ταραχθείημεν μηδ᾽ εἴ τινος ἄλλου χεῖρον ἠγωνίσατο, ταύτῃ φαυλότερον αὐτὸν ἡγοίμεθα, μηδὲ χείρω μηδενὸς ἄλλου
472 τῶν Ἀχαιῶν ἀλλ᾽ ἢ τοῦ Ἀχιλλέως. καὶ μὴν καὶ ὁ ἀδελφὸς μετεῖχεν αὐτῷ τῆς τύχης ἐπιθήκην, ὁ Τεῦκρος, περὶ τὴν τοξικήν, ὅς γε τῆς μηρίνθου μὲν ἔτυχεν, τὴν δὲ περιστερὰν αὐτὴν παρῆκεν ἑτέρῳ λαβεῖν,[145] καὶ οὗτος ἑαυτοῦ χείρονι.

473 ταῦτα πάντα ἐφεξῆς οὕτως ἔχοντα τί χρὴ νομίζειν εἶναι; ἆρ᾽ οὐ χρησμούς τινας εἰς ἅπαντα ἡγεῖσθαι τἀνθρώπεια; ὥστε οὔτ᾽ εἴ τις ῥώμῃ σώματος ἢ μεγέθει προφέρειν δοκεῖ οὔτ᾽ εἴ τις ἵππους ἀρίστους κέκτηται οὔτ᾽ εἰ ταχὺς αὐτὸς ἢ καλός, οὐδὲν αὐτῷ τούτων κύριον, ἂν μὴ δοκῇ τοῖς κρείττοσιν. εἰ φίλοις ἰσχύεις, εἰ χρήμασιν, εἰ δόξαν ἔχεις ἐν τῇ πόλει, μηδενὶ τούτων ἐπαρθῇς, μηδὲ μεῖζον φρονήσῃς τῆς ἐξουσίας. εἰ πάντων κρατήσεις, ἡττήσῃ τῆς τύχης. ταῦτ᾽ ἐστὶν ὁ ἀγὼν οὗτος, ταῦθ᾽ Ὅμηρος λέγει. οὐδὲν τῶν ἀνθρωπείων ἀσφαλὲς οὐδ᾽ ὁμαλὸν οὐδ᾽ αὔταρκες, ἀλλ᾽ ἡττήσεται μὲν ὁ ἰσχυρὸς τοῦ ἀσθενοῦς, ὅταν καιρὸς ᾖ τούτου, ἁλώσεται δὲ Βαβυλὼν αὐτοῖς τείχεσιν, πάλιν

[145] βαλεῖν Lucarini

and

> great Ajax, son of Telamon, would not yield to any
> man,[362]

and other such declarations, as if forestalling our judgment and working so as to prevent us becoming upset over the games and thinking more cheaply of Ajax if he came off worse than someone else in the contest, or ranking him below any of the Greeks with the exception of Achilles.
Moreover, as a kind of supplement to this, his brother 472
Teucer shared his bad luck, in the archery competition: he too lost out to an inferior, when he hit the cord but left the dove itself for someone else to take.[363]

What ought we to think is the meaning of all these in- 473
stances working out like this one after another? Should we not take them as oracles bearing on the human condition in general? Thus even if someone has a reputation for excelling in physical strength or size, or has horses of the highest quality, or is himself fast or handsome, none of this is decisive for him unless the higher powers sanction it. If you have many friends or a lot of money, if you enjoy a high reputation in your city, do not be carried away by any of this, and do not conceive a higher opinion of yourself than your actual power warrants. Even if you control all, you will be undone by chance. That is what this contest turns on, that is what Homer is talking about. Nothing in human life is secure or consistent or sufficient in itself, but the strong is defeated by the weak when the time comes, and Babylon will be captured walls and all, and others in

362 *Il.* 13.321.
363 *Il.* 23.850–83 (Meriones).

δὲ τοὺς Πέρσας πορθήσουσιν ἕτεροι. πάντα ταῦτ' ἐναλλὰξ περιέρχεται.

474 οὕτω καὶ τὸ σὸν, ὦ Πλάτων, σῴζεται, τὸ ἄνθρωπον
εἶναι θεοῦ παίγνιον. ὅταν ἐκπίπτῃ μὲν τοῦ ἅρματος ὁ
ἡνίοχος, ἐν ᾧ πρόσθεν εἱστήκει βεβαίως, ἀπορῇ δὲ ὁ
κυβερνήτης ὅπως χρὴ σῴζειν τὴν ναῦν πολλάκις ἤδη
σεσωκώς, ἰλιγγιᾷ δὲ ὁ κρείττων ὑπὸ τοῦ χείρονος,
"κιχάνῃ δὲ βραδὺς ὠκύν," πάντα δ' ἄνω καὶ κάτω
περιχωρῇ, τότ' ἄν τις ἴδοι τὸν σὸν λόγον, τόθ' ὡς
ἀληθῶς προφήτου τινὸς εἶναι δόξειεν ἂν, ὡς θεὸς μὲν
καὶ τύχη πάντ' ἄγουσιν, τὸ δ' ἡμέτερον πᾶν ἦν ἄρα
475 παιδιά. εἰ δ' ἔσῳζον μὲν οἱ κυβερνῆται πάντες ἅπαντας τοὺς ἐμπλέοντας, ἔσῳζον δ' οἱ ἰατροὶ πάντες
ἅπαντας τοὺς κάμνοντας, ἐνίκων δ' οἱ κρείττονες,
ἐνίκων δ' οἱ μείζονες, τὸ δ' ἀεὶ τούτοις πᾶσι προσῆν,
μηδεὶς δὲ ἐσφάλλετο τῶν ἀρξαμένων κατορθοῦν, εὐχὴ
δὲ καὶ δύναμις μηδὲν διέφερεν, ἀθάνατ' ἂν πάντ' ἦν
τὰ τῶν ἀνθρώπων πράγματα καὶ οὐδὲν ἂν εὐχῆς ἴσως
προσέδει, οὐδ' ἂν κακτέκλυζεν ἡμᾶς τῶν πίθων ἅτε-
476 ρος ὥσπερ νῦν. νῦν δ' οἱ ποιηταὶ πολλὰ χρήσιμοι
κἀνταῦθα πρόσκεινται καὶ παρακολουθοῦσιν ἡμῖν,
ὑπομιμνήσκοντες ἀεὶ τῆς φύσεως, ἐφημέρους τε κα-
λοῦντες καὶ χαμαὶ ἐρχομένους, καὶ πάντα τρόπον
τὴν ἀλαζονείαν καθαιροῦντες, ὅπως μηδ' εἴ τις εὖ

364 *Leg.* 803c. 365 *Od.* 8.329. 366 *Leg.* 709b.

367 A reference to Achilles' image in *Il.* 24.527–33 of the two jars from which Zeus distributes human fortunes, picked up by Plato in *Resp.* 379d.

their turn will plunder the Persians—all such fates come circling round in alternation.

This also means, Plato, that your assertion, that the human is the plaything of the divine, is upheld.[364] Whenever the charioteer is thrown from the chariot in which he had previously stood securely, and the helmsman is at a loss how to bring his ship safely to port even though he has done so many times before, and the superior is made to reel by his inferior, and "the slow catches up with the swift,"[365] and everything is turned upside down, then we may see your principle at work; then indeed it may seem to be the utterance of some oracular spokesman, that god and chance govern all,[366] and that all of our efforts were after all only childish play. If all helmsmen brought all their passengers safely to land, and all doctors saved the lives of all their patients, and victory went to the superior and the greater, and what is more all these things always happened, and no one failed successfully to complete what he had started, and there was no difference between wish and ability, then the whole of the human world would be immortal and there would perhaps be no need for prayer, and we would not be overwhelmed as we are now by the flow from the other jar.[367] But as things actually are, the poets who are useful in so many ways here too stand close beside us and accompany us, reminding us constantly of our true nature, calling us "creatures of a day" and "walkers on the earth" and humbling our boastfulness by all means at their disposal,[368] so as to prevent anyone who may seem to prosper from being brash on that ac-

474

475

476

[368] "Creatures of a day": Pind. *Pyth.* 8.95, Semon. 1.3, Aesch. *Pers.* 83, etc; "walkers on the earth": Hom. *Il.* 5.442.

πράττειν δοκοίη, τούτῳ θρασύνοιτο, μηδ' ἑτέρῳ πταίσαντί που προφέροι τὴν τύχην ῥᾳδίως.

477 καὶ τί δεῖ τἄλλα λέγειν ὡς ἔχει; ἀλλὰ τὰ τῶν δικῶν πῶς εἶχεν ἐξ ἀρχῆς; ἔλθωμεν γὰρ ἐπ' αὐτὸ τὸ κυριώτατον ἤδη. ὁ Παλαμήδης σοφώτατος ὢν τῶν Ἀχαιῶν ἑάλω τὴν δίκην τῆς προδοσίας. καὶ οὐκ ἐρεῖς ὡς ἐκείνου γε Ἀθηναῖοι κατεψηφίσαντο. ἀλλὰ πᾶσα μὲν ἡ Ἑλλὰς συνεληλύθει, ἐγένετο δὲ ἡ κρίσις ἐν μέσῳ, καὶ ἀδικεῖν ἔδοξεν, ὅτι δὲ οὐχὶ δικαίως ἔδοξεν αὐτὸς σὺ
478 λέγεις ἐν Σωκράτους ἀπολογίᾳ. καίτοι τίς οὐκ ἂν φήσειεν οὑτωσὶ πολλὴν εἶναι τὴν ἀλογίαν, ὄντα μὲν αὐτὸν κυριώτερον τοῦ Ὀδυσσέως εἰς σοφίας λόγον, ὡς ἔφη Πίνδαρος, εἶθ' ἡττηθῆναι τοῦ χείρονος, καὶ ταῦτ' οὐκ εἰς χειρῶν κρίσιν οὐδ' εἰς ἄλλο τι τοιοῦτον ἐλθόντος τοῦ πράγματος, ἀλλ' εἰς αὐτὸ τοῦτο ἐν ᾧ κρείττων ἦν; αὖθις δ' αὖ τοὺς Ἀχαιοὺς οὕτω πολλὰ καὶ μεγάλα ὑπ' αὐτοῦ πεπονθότας εὖ, δι' ἃ καὶ φιλεῖν καὶ θαυμάζειν αὐτὸν προσῆκεν, εἶθ' οὕτως ἀγνώμονα καὶ ἀνόμοιον ἀποδοῦναι τὴν χάριν, ὅς γε καὶ σπουδαίων καὶ τῶν εἰς ψυχαγωγίαν ἡγεμὼν αὐτοῖς ἐγεγό-
479 νει σχεδὸν ἁπάντων; ἓν δὲ μέγιστον καὶ τελεώτατον καὶ πλείστης ἄξιον τιμῆς ἐξεῦρεν τὰ τακτικά, ὑφ' ὧν ἅμα σῴζεσθαι καὶ τῶν ἐναντίων κρείττοσιν εἶναι περιῆν αὐτοῖς. ὡς μὲν γὰρ ἡ τραγῳδία φησίν, οὐδὲ τῶν βοσκημάτων οὐδὲν διέφερον πρὶν ἐκείνῳ συγγενέσθαι. οἱ δὲ τοσοῦτον ἀπεῖχον τοῦ σύμπαντας ἂν

369 *Ap.* 41b. 370 Fr. 260.7 Sn-M.

count, and from being too ready to tax another with his misfortune should he ever suffer a reverse.

But let us turn now to the real heart of the matter. No 477
need to say how it is with everything else: how was it with lawsuits, right from the start? Palamedes the cleverest of the Achaeans was put on trial for treason and found guilty, and you cannot say that he was condemned just by the Athenians. No, the whole of Greece had assembled, and the trial took place in public, and it was decided that he was guilty, though you yourself say in Socrates' defense
speech that the decision was not a just one.[369] Yet who 478
would not say that it is completely nonsensical for it to have turned out like this: that when, as Pindar says,[370] Palamedes had a greater mastery than Odysseus in intellectual matters, he should then be defeated by his inferior, even when the whole issue came down not to a trial of physical strength or anything like that, but to the very abilities in which his superiority lay? Or again that the Achaeans, when they had received so many and such substantial good services from him, should make such an ungrateful and ill-matched return of thanks to someone who had been their leader in practically all of both their serious
business and their entertainments? One of his inventions 479
in particular was of the greatest magnitude and perfection, and deserved the highest honor: the arts of strategy, through which the Greeks succeeded simultaneously in keeping themselves safe and prevailing over their enemies. As the tragedy says, they were not even any better than cattle before they met him.[371] So far were they from being able to count how many they were in all, or how

371 Aesch. *Palam.* fr. 182 *TrGF*; cf. Fr. Adesp. 40a.

αὐτοὺς ἀριθμῆσαι, ἢ τὰς ναῦς ὁπόσαι τινὲς ἦσαν ἃς ἦγον, ὥστ᾽ οὐδ᾽ ὁπόσοι τινὲς αὐτοῖς εἰσὶν οἱ βασιλεῖς ὅ τε Ἀγαμέμνων καὶ ὁ Μενέλαος ἔμελλον εὑρήσειν, οὐδέ γε, ὡς ἔοικεν, ἐκεῖνοι τοὺς αὑτῶν πόδας ἢ καὶ τὰς χεῖρας ἑκάτερος, μὴ ὅτι τὴν στρατιάν.

480 ἀλλὰ ταῦτα μὲν Πλάτων τε ἡμῖν προσπαίζει τοὺς
τραγικοὺς καὶ ἡμεῖς συνεπαίξαμεν. τὸ δ᾽ οὖν πολλῶν
καὶ μεγάλων ὀφείλοντας τῷ Παλαμήδει χάριν καὶ δικαίως ἂν καὶ ἐπὶ μειζόνων ἐκτίνοντας, μηδ᾽ εἰς αὐτὴν
τὴν σωτηρίαν ἀπομνημονεῦσαι, πῶς οὐ πολλῆς ἄν τις
φήσαι τῆς ἀτοπίας εἶναι, καὶ τό γ᾽ αὐτὸν ἐκεῖνον τὰ
μὲν ἄλλα σοφίζεσθαι, τῶν δ᾽ εἰς τὴν ἀπολογίαν
ἀπορῆσαι, καὶ ταῦθ᾽ οὕτω ῥᾳδίαν οὖσαν καὶ τῶν
πραγμάτων αὐτῶν βοηθούντων; ἀλλ᾽ ὑπὲρ μὲν τῶν
ἄλλων σοφὸς ἦν, αὑτὸν δ᾽ ὠφελεῖν οὐκ εἶχεν, καὶ
ταῦτα τὸν περὶ τῆς ψυχῆς τρέχων, ὃν χρῆν, εἰ καὶ ἐν
τοῖς Τρωσὶν ἐκρίνετο συλληφθείς, ὑπὸ τῆς σοφίας
ἔχειν ἑαυτὸν ἂν σῶσαι. ὁ δὲ τῶν φίλων καὶ τῶν συμμάχων καὶ ὧν εὐεργέτης ἦν χαλεπωτέρων ἢ τῶν πολεμίων ἀπῄει τυχών, καὶ πάσας τὰς ἄλλας εὑρίσκων
481 μηχανὰς μίαν οὐχ εὗρεν ὅπως σωθήσεται. ἀλλ᾽
ἐπειδὴ κατεψηφίσαντο ἀδικεῖν αὐτοῦ, οὐ ταυτὸν τοῖς
Ἀθηναίοις ἐποίησαν· οὐ γὰρ χρημάτων ἐτίμησαν
οὐδὲ φυγῆς οὐδ᾽ ὅσον δέκα ἔτη μετέστησαν, ἀλλ᾽ ἄρδην ἀπέκτειναν. οὕτω μέχρι μὲν τοῦ μὴ κατὰ νοῦν
ἀγωνίζεσθαι καὶ τοῦ τῶν συκοφαντῶν ἔλαττον ἔχειν
κοινωνεῖ τῷ Παλαμήδει τῆς τύχης ἡμῖν ἡ τοῦ Περι-

many ships they had brought with them, that they were not even in a position to discover how many kings they had in Agamemnon and Menelaus, nor indeed, apparently, were those kings in a position to count how many hands and feet they each had, let alone the size of their army.

That is what we find Plato teasing the tragedians 480
with;[372] all I have done is join in the fun. But all the same how could one avoid saying that it is completely absurd that the Greeks, when they owed Palamedes thanks for many great services and could even justifiably have paid him interest on the debt, should not even have had the gratitude to spare his life, and that the man himself, though so ingenious in everything else, should have been short of things to say in his own defense, even when his defense was such an easy one, and the facts themselves were on his side? No, this man who ought to have been able to save himself through his intellect even if he had been captured and was being tried among the Trojans was clever on other people's behalf but unable to help himself, even when the race he ran was for his very life. In the event he found his friends and allies and beneficiaries harsher than his enemies; and after all the other devices he had invented, the one thing he could not invent was a
means to save his own life. When the Greeks had found 481
him guilty of wrongdoing, they did not act in the same way as the Athenians; they did not punish him with a fine or exile, or send him away for only ten years, but killed him outright. We can thus see that, to the extent that they didn't achieve the result they wanted in their trials and were worsted by their false accusers, Pericles and his tribe

[372] *Resp.* 522d.

κλέους φατρία, τὰ δ᾽ ἐφεξῆς καὶ διαφέρει, καὶ οἵ τε Ἀθηναῖοι συμπάντων τῶν Ἑλλήνων ἡμερώτεροι πολλῷ τινι φαίνονται καὶ οἱ ῥήτορες αὖ τοῦ ῥητόρος[146] πρᾳότερον ἐπταικότες, καὶ ταύτῃ γε σοφώτεροι τοῦ Παλαμήδους ὄντες, τοσοῦτον, εἰ μή τι ἄλλο, πεῖσαι δυνηθέντες, ὡς οὐ θανάτου γ᾽ ἄξιοι τοῖς Ἀθηναίοις εἶεν, οὐχ ὥσπερ ἐκεῖνος οὐδ᾽ εἰς τὸ τίμημα χρήσιμος οὐδὲν ἦν αὐτῷ.

482 ἀλλ᾽ οἶμαι καὶ Παλαμήδει καὶ Μιλτιάδῃ καὶ Περικλεῖ καὶ πᾶσιν ἀνθρώποις μέτεστι τῆς κοινῆς ἀπολογίας ἣν αὐτὸς Πλάτων ἐνδίδωσιν, ἧς ἀρτίως ἐμνήσθην, ὡς τύχαι καὶ καιροὶ τὰ τῶν ἀνθρώπων ἄγουσι πράγματα, ἐπεὶ καὶ ὃ προσδιωρθώσατο καὶ προσέθηκεν πρὸς τῷ θεῷ καὶ τῇ τύχῃ καὶ τὴν τέχνην τρίτον ὡρίσατο, εὖ φρονῶν. φησὶ γοῦν οὕτως

> ἡμερώτερον μέντοι τρίτον συγχωρῆσαι τούτοις δεῖν ἕπεσθαι τὴν τέχνην.

483 ἄριστά γε καὶ θειότατα, ὦ Πλάτων, ὡς ἀληθῶς. εἰ τοίνυν καὶ τῇ τάξει καὶ τῇ δυνάμει τρίτον ἡ τέχνη, πῶς ἀποχρῶν ἂν εἴη καθάπαξ; ἢ πῶς ἄν τις τὸ ἐλάχιστον καὶ τὸ φαυλότατον τῶν πλειόνων καὶ τῶν μειζόνων ἀξιοίη κρατεῖν; οὐκ ἔστιν ὅπως δικαίως.

484 μὴ τοίνυν θαυμάσῃς, εἰ Περικλῆς ἔχων ἐπιστήμην καὶ τέχνην τοῦ θεοῦ καὶ τῆς τύχης ἡττᾶτο, μηδ᾽ ἀμνημόνει τῶν καιρῶν, οὓς αὐτὸς φῂς οὐκ ὀλίγον δύ-

[146] τοῦ ῥητόρος Reiske τῶν ῥητόρων *codd.*

shared the same fate as Palamedes, but that the sequel turned out differently. It is quite clear that the Athenians were far gentler than the army of all the Greeks and that for their part the speakers in the one case had a softer fall than the speaker in the other; they were moreover cleverer than Palamedes to the extent that they were able to persuade their audiences, even if nothing more, at least that they did not deserve the death penalty from the Athenians, unlike him, who was no use to himself even in the fixing of the penalty.

But in fact I think that Palamedes, Miltiades, Pericles, 482
and the whole of mankind can all avail themselves of the shared defense that Plato himself allows and that I mentioned a moment ago, that chance and opportunity control the course of human affairs, since as an extra correction and an addition to god and chance he also specified human skill as a third factor, and was well advised to do so. At any rate he says

> A gentler way of putting it is to acknowledge that a third factor, human skill, must accompany these.[373]

Truly an excellent and divinely inspired addition, Plato! If 483
then skill comes third in both position and effectiveness, how could it be sufficient on its own? And how could anyone expect the least and meanest factor to triumph over the greater and more numerous ones? It is impossible to do so with any justification.

Do not therefore be surprised that Pericles, although 484
he possessed knowledge and skill, was defeated by god and chance, and do not forget the times, which you your-

373 *Leg.* 709b.

νασθαι, οἷς οὐ πραοτάτοις ἐκεῖνος τότε χρησάμενος
φαίνεται. πολλὰ καὶ παράδοξα κατ᾽ ἀνθρώπους καὶ
γέγονεν καὶ γενήσεται. ὧν ἐστι καὶ τὰ τούτοις τοῖς
485 ἀνδράσι συμβάντα. τίς δ᾽ οὐκ ἂν φαίη; ἀλλ᾽ οὔπω
ταῦτ᾽ ἐστὶν ἔλεγχος κατ᾽ αὐτῶν ὡς οὔτε ἠπίσταντο
χρηστὸν οὐδὲν οὔτ᾽ ἠδύναντο βελτίους ποιεῖν, ἀλλ᾽
ἐξῆν αὐτοῖς τήν τε[147] τέχνην ἔχειν δήπουθεν καὶ τὸ
χρηστοὺς εἶναι, εἰ καὶ τῶν μειζόνων ἐπικουριῶν ἔν γε
τῷ τότε ἐστέρηντο· μηδέ γ᾽ ἐλάττους φῶμεν αὐτοὺς
τῶν ἀντιπάλων γενέσθαι, μὴ δῆτα ἡμεῖς γε, ἀλλ᾽
ὥσπερ ὀλισθεῖν κρείττους ὄντας τοῖς ὅλοις.

486 ἐκράτει Κλέων Περικλέους. ὁ δέ γε αὐτὸς οὗτος καὶ
Λακεδαιμονίων ποτέ, ὡς ᾤετο, καὶ δεδεμένους γε ἤγαγεν ἐν πέδαις Ἀθήναζε, καὶ ὃ τούτου μεῖζον εἶναι δοκεῖ, καὶ χρόνον προειπὼν ἡνίκ᾽ ἐξῄει, καὶ τοῦτον οὐ
πλεῖστον, ἀλλ᾽ ὅσον εἴκοσιν ἡμερῶν· ἀλλ᾽ ὅτι γ᾽ οὐ
πάνυ κρείττων ἦν τῶν Λακεδαιμονίων ἔδειξεν Ἀμφί-
πολις, πρὸς ἣν μαχόμενος οὐ πολὺ τῷ Βρασίδᾳ παρέσχε τὸ ἔργον. ἀλλὰ κἀκείνου τεθνεῶτος ἤρκεσεν
πελταστὴς Μυρκίνιος φεύγοντα βαλὼν ἀποκτεῖναι,
ὥς φησιν ὁ μηνυτής. ὁ δέ γε αὐτὸς οὗτος λέγει καὶ
περὶ τῶν ἑκατέρωθεν νεκρῶν ὡς οὐκ ὀλίγον τὸ διάφορον συνέβη γενέσθαι. ἑπτὰ γὰρ οἶμαι πρὸς ἑξακο-
487 σίους ἀντιλογίζεται. οὕτω τοίνυν κἂν τῇ δίκῃ οὐ τῶν
Περικλέους λόγων οὐδὲ τῆς ἐπιστήμης ἐκράτησεν,

[147] τε Reiske γε *codd.*

self say exert no little influence and which clearly for him then were not of the most untroubled. Many surprising things have happened in the world of men and will happen in future, and that includes what happened to these men. Who could deny it? But this is not enough to constitute 485
damning proof that they were ignorant of anything good and unable to make people better; no, it was perfectly possible for them to possess a skill and to be good men, even if at that particular time they had to do without the support of the more important factors. And let us not be the ones to say that they were worsted by their opponents, but instead let us say that in a sense they slipped up, even though in general superior to them.

Cleon defeated Pericles. This same man also once, in 486
his own estimation, defeated the Spartans too, and what is more brought them as prisoners in chains to Athens, and in what seems a still greater feat than this had predicted how long it would take on his departure (not a very long time too, only twenty days).[374] But that he was not entirely superior to the Spartans was shown by Amphipolis, his attack on which did not set Brasidas a very demanding task. On the contrary, even with Brasidas dead a skirmisher from Myrcinus was all it took to shoot him as he fled and kill him, as our informant tells us. And this same source also tells us that the difference between the casualties on each side was not a small one: I think he calculates
it as seven against six hundred.[375] In the same way in the 487
court case too Cleon did not defeat Pericles' oratory or his knowledge, nor did he get the better of him as if he were

[374] Thuc. 4.27.3–4.39 (the Athenian victory at Pylos).
[375] Thuc. 5.2–11 (with the casualty figures at 5.11.2).

οὐδέ γε ὡς ἀνεπιστήμονος περιεγένετο, ἀλλ᾽ ἀπέλαυσε τοῦ καιροῦ, ὥσπερ κἂν τῇ Πύλῳ τῇ τύχῃ καὶ τῷ καιρῷ προσεχρήσατο· ἐπεὶ Περικλῆς γε καὶ τεθνεὼς ἐκράτει Κλέωνος, εἰ δεῖ τἀληθὲς εἰπεῖν. μέγα δὲ σημεῖον· τὸν μὲν γὰρ οὐδεὶς ἦν ὅστις οὐκ ἂν εὔξαιτο ἀναστῆναι, ὥστε κἂν τοῖς δράμασιν ὡς ἀνεστῶτα ὁρῶντες εὐφραίνοντο, τὸν δ᾽ οὐκ ἔστιν ὅστις οὐκ ἂν ἐβούλετο ἀντ᾽ ἐκείνου κεῖσθαι. τοσούτῳ κρείττων ἦν τεθνεὼς Περικλῆς ἐκείνου ζῶντος.

488 πάρες οὖν τοῖς συκοφάνταις ταῦτα, αὐτὸς δὲ πάλιν σαυτοῦ τι μνημόνευσον. ὅτι γὰρ οὐδὲν οὔτε τῶν ἀδυνάτων οὔτε τῶν ἀπεικότων καὶ τὰ βέλτιστα λέγοντας ὑπὲρ τοῦ δήμου τῷ δήμῳ προσκροῦσαι, ἀλλὰ καὶ τοῦτ᾽ αὐτὸ τῶν συμφορῶν ἐπιεικῶς αἴτιον γίγνεται, τὸ μὴ βούλεσθαι τῆς ὀρθοτάτης ἀφεῖσθαι γνώμης, οὐ τῶν μάντεων ἀκούσαντα δεῖ γνῶναι, ἀλλ᾽ ὁ πολλῶν δήμων καὶ πόλεων ἀντάξιος Πλάτων ὁ τοῦ Ἀρίστωνος διαμαρτύρεται διαρρήδην οὑτωσὶ λέγων, καὶ ταῦτ᾽ ἐν αὐτοῖς οἷς Σωκράτης ἐκινδύνευσεν οὐχὶ δικαίως αὐτῷ.
489 τίνα οὖν ἐστι τὰ ῥήματα;

> οὐ γὰρ ἔστιν ὅστις ἀνθρώπων σωθήσεται οὔθ᾽ ὑμῖν οὔτ᾽ ἄλλῳ τινὶ πλήθει οὐδενὶ γνησίως ἐναντιούμενος καὶ διακωλύων πόλλ᾽ ἄδικα καὶ παράνομα ἐν τῇ πόλει γενέσθαι, ἀλλ᾽ ἀναγκαῖόν ἐστι τὸν τῷ ὄντι μαχούμενον ὑπὲρ τοῦ δικαίου, καὶ εἰ μέλλει ὀλίγον χρόνον σωθήσεσθαι, ἰδιωτεύειν, ἀλλὰ μὴ δημοσιεύειν.

some ignoramus, but simply exploited the moment, just as at Pylos too he took advantage of chance and opportunity; because if the truth be known even in death Pericles defeated Cleon. A substantial proof of this proposition is that whereas everyone would have prayed for the resurrection of Pericles, so that they were glad to see him alive again even on the stage,[376] there is no one who would not have liked to see Cleon dead in his place. That is the measure of the superiority of the dead Pericles over the living Cleon.

488 So, Plato, leave all that to the professional prosecutors, and remind yourself once more of something you yourself say. That there is nothing impossible or implausible in falling foul of the people even when uttering the best possible sentiments on the people's behalf, but that unwillingness to let go of the most correct view is itself a probable cause of disaster, is not something that one needs to discover by listening to soothsayers: Plato the son of Ariston, who on his own is worth as much as many peoples and states, testifies explicitly to this effect, and what is more he does so in the very work in which he shows us Socrates
unjustly on trial. What then are his exact words? 489

> There is no one on earth who will be safe if he genuinely opposes you or any other popular assembly and tries to prevent many injustices and illegalities from taking place in his state; it is essential for the man who is in truth fighting for what is just, if he is going to keep himself safe even for a short time, to operate as a private citizen rather than in a public capacity.[377]

376 In Eupolis' *Demes* (cf. §365 above).

377 *Ap.* 31e–32a.

490 εἶεν, ὦ φιλότης. εἶτα ἔτι θαυμάζεις εἰ Μιλτιάδης καὶ
Θεμιστοκλῆς καὶ Περικλῆς καὶ Κίμων προσέκρουσαν
Ἀθηναίοις, τὰ βέλτιστα λέγοντες αὐτοῖς καὶ φεύγοντες τὰ πρὸς ἡδονήν; ἀλλὰ μὴν αὐτός γ' ἔφης ἐντεῦθεν
ὡρμῆσθαι τοὺς κινδύνους, καὶ οὐδ' ὀλίγον χρόνον
491 ἐγχωρεῖν διαφεύγειν. πότερον οὖν εἰ προσέκρουσαν
θαύμαστόν ἐστι καὶ τοῦτ' ἄξιον αὐτῶν κατηγορεῖν, ἢ
ἐκεῖνο πολλῷ μᾶλλον ἄξιον αὐτῶν θαυμάσαι, ὅτι τόν
γε τοσοῦτον χρόνον διεγένοντο, καὶ μήτε θᾶττον τοῦτ'
ἔπαθον μήθ' ὅτε καὶ προσέκρουσαν θανάτῳ γ' ἐζη-
μιώθησαν, ἀλλὰ μέσην τινὰ ὁ δῆμος ἐχώρησεν, καὶ
τῇ μὲν ὡς εὖ καὶ καλῶς ὑπ' αὐτῶν ἀχθεὶς ᾐσχύνθη
καί τινα πραότητος τύπον διεσώσατο, τῇ δὲ οὐκ ἠδυνήθη τὴν τοῦ πράγματος φύσιν διαφυγεῖν, ἀλλ' ὧν
δήμῳ προσῆκεν ἁμαρτεῖν, μέρος γοῦν τι μετέσχεν;
492 ἡδέως δ' ἂν ἐροίμην, ὅστις βούλεται δέξασθαι τὸ
ἐρώτημα ὑπὲρ Πλάτωνος, αὐτὸς δὲ δὴ τί μαθὼν ἡμῖν
ὁ Πλάτων οὐκ ἐπολιτεύσατο; ἆρ' ἄλλο τι φήσειεν ἂν
ὁστισοῦν ἢ τὸ αὐτὸ τοῦτο ὅπερ καὶ Σωκράτης λέγων
ἐκείνῳ φαίνεται; τί μὴν ἕτερον; εἶθ' ἃ φοβηθεὶς μὴ
πάθῃς οὐκ ἐδημηγόρεις, ταῦτ' εἴ τις ἐκείνων πέπονθεν,
493 ὡς οὐ τὰ βέλτιστα συνεβούλευεν ἰσχυρίζῃ; καὶ μὴν
εἰ μὲν οὐδεὶς ἐπῆν κίνδυνος, τοῦ χάριν οὐδὲν ὤνησας
τὴν πατρίδα; εἰ δ' ἕτοιμον ἦν ἀπολωλέναι, τί θαυμάζεις εἴ τις ἐκείνων ἐχρήσατο συμφορᾷ καὶ τῷ τὰ βέλτιστα λέγειν τιθεὶς αὐτὸς ἕπεσθαι τὸ κινδυνεύειν,
ἐκείνους ἐξ ὧν ἠτύχησαν ἀποστερεῖς τὸ λέγειν τὰ
βέλτιστα;

Well, then, my friend: can you still be amazed that Miltia- 490
des, Themistocles, Pericles, and Cimon all fell foul of the
people by recommending the most virtuous courses of
action and shunning what would merely give pleasure?
You yourself said that this was the prime source of danger,
and that it could not be avoided for long. So is it surprising 491
that they stumbled and is it fair to make this the grounds
of an accusation against them? Or is the thing that we really ought to find surprising about them that they survived
for such a long time and neither suffered what they did
sooner, nor when they did stumble were punished with
death, but that instead the people took a middle path, to
some extent ashamed and preserving a semblance of docility because they had been well and nobly led by these
men, but in other way unable to escape the essential nature of the matter and at least to a degree party to the kind
of errors that it was characteristic of a people to make?

I would gladly ask whoever is willing to take up the 492
question on Plato's behalf what it was that we think made
Plato abstain from politics. Would anyone at all say anything other than exactly what his Socrates so clearly says?
But why ask someone else? Plato, if any of these men suffered exactly what you were afraid of when you were de-
terred from a career as a public speaker, are you insisting
that he did not recommend the most virtuous course of
action? Again, if there was no attendant danger, why did 493
you not do good for your homeland? But if there was a real
risk of death, why are you surprised that any of them met
with disaster? Why, having posited yourself that danger
attends speaking up for the most virtuous course of action,
do you use their misfortunes to deny them the achievement of speaking up for the most virtuous course of
action?

494 φέρε δὴ κἀκεῖνο σκεψώμεθα· ὁπότ' ἦν ἐν τῷ τὰ
δίκαια πράττειν προαιρεῖσθαι τοιοῦτόν τι λαβεῖν παρ'
αὐτῶν, πότεροι πρὸς θεῶν πῶς ἂν εὐπρεπῶς εἴποιμι
κοινότεροι τὴν γνώμην, καὶ εἰ μὴ τὸ ὅλον βελτίους,
τῇ γε πόλει χρησιμώτεροι, πότερ' οἵτινες προορώμε-
νοι τὸν προσόντα[148] κίνδυνον εἶτ' ἐκποδὼν ἔστησαν, ἢ
οἵτινες εἰδότες οὐκ ἀπώκνησαν; ἐμοὶ μὲν γὰρ δοκεῖ τὸ
μὲν μηδὲν εἰπεῖν αἰσχρὸν κοινὸν ἀμφοῖν εἶναι, τὸ δ'
ἐγχειρῆσαι τὰ βέλτιστα εἰπεῖν <ἀντὶ>[149] τοῦ μηδ'
ὅλως εἰπεῖν οὐ τῶν φαυλοτέρων ὂν ἐκείνοις ὑπάρχειν.
εἰ γάρ τι καὶ διήμαρτον, οἷς γε προείλοντο φήσει τις
495 αὐτοὺς νικᾶν. εἰ τοίνυν μὴ μόνον προείλοντο, ἀλλὰ
καὶ κατώρθωσαν πολλὰ καὶ καλὰ καὶ δίκαια καὶ
κοινῇ συμφέροντα, μὴ πρὸς ἐλαττώματος αὐτοῖς γέ-
νηται. τοῦτο γὰρ ἔξεστι δήπουθεν αὐτοῖς εἰπεῖν.

496 εἰ δὲ καὶ τοῦτ' ἔξεστιν ἐρωτῆσαι, πότεροι τῷ Σωκράτους αὐτοῦ καὶ Πλάτωνος λόγῳ μᾶλλον συμβαίνοντα καὶ βεβούλευνται καὶ πεποιήκασιν; τῷ ποίῳ δὴ
λέγω τούτῳ λόγῳ; ὅσπερ ἐστὶν ἁπάντων λόγων οἶμαι
κάλλιστος. τίς οὗτος;

> οὐ καλῶς—φησίν—λέγεις, ὦ ἄνθρωπε, εἰ οἴει δεῖν κίνδυνον ὑπολογίζεσθαι τοῦ ζῆν ἢ τεθνάναι ἄνδρα ὅτου τι καὶ σμικρὸν ὄφελός ἐστιν, ἀλλ' οὐκ ἐκεῖνο μόνον σκοπεῖν, ὅταν πράττῃ, πότερον δίκαια ἢ ἄδικα πράττει καὶ ἀνδρὸς ἀγαθοῦ ἔργα ἢ κακοῦ.

148 *an* προσιόντα?
149 *add.* Keil

Let us also consider the following. Given that the possibility of receiving some such return from the people of Athens was inherent in the choice of just action, which of the two for heaven's sake were—how can I put this decently?—more public-spirited in their intentions and, if not wholly better, at least more useful to the city: the ones who foresaw the attendant danger and then got themselves out of the way, or the ones who knew about it but did not flinch? In my view at least, the avoidance of saying anything shameful is common to both parties, but the attempt to articulate the best course of action rather than not to speak at all, which is not among the meanest of achievements, belongs to the latter. Even if they did make some mistakes, everyone will say that that they were superior in their aims. And if moreover, besides making 495 them their objectives, they actually succeeded with many just and noble measures in the public interest, let this not count to their detriment. This surely they are entitled to say.

494 (at "Let us also consider the following")

If this too is a permissible question, which of the two 496 groups planned and executed actions more in tune with the principle of Socrates himself and of Plato? What principle do I mean by this? The one that in my view is the finest of them all. Which is this?

> Your suggestion is dishonorable, sir—he says,—if you think that any man who is of the slightest use should take account of the risk of life or death, rather than in anything he does considering just this, whether his actions are just or unjust, and those of a good man or a bad.[378]

[378] *Ap.* 28b.

497 οὐκοῦν ὅτ᾽ ἐκεῖνοι φαίνονται μηδὲν τῶν μελλόντων αὐτοῖς ἔσεσθαι δυσχερῶν ὑπολογισάμενοι πρὸς τὸ δίκαιον, ἀλλ᾽ ἀφειδῶς καὶ ἁπλῶς δόντες αὑτοὺς ὑπὲρ τοῦ κοινῇ βελτίστου τῷ Σωκράτους κέχρηνται λόγῳ. ὥστ᾽ ἢ δεικτέον ἐστὶν ὡς οὔτε δίκαια οὔτε ἀγαθῶν ἀνδρῶν ἦν ἔργα ἃ προείλοντο καὶ οἷς ἐνεχείρησαν, ἢ συγχωρητέον χρηστοὺς εἶναι τοὺς ἄνδρας, εἰ καὶ ὁτιοῦν ἀπήντησεν, καὶ τοσούτῳ μᾶλλον καὶ μειζόνως, ὅσῳ τὴν δυσκολίαν τοῦ πράγματος οὐκ ἔδεισαν.

> φαῦλοι γὰρ ἂν τῷ γε σῷ λόγῳ εἶεν—λέγω δὲ ἤδη τὰ Πλάτωνος αὐτοῦ—τῶν ἡμιθέων ὅσοι ἐν Τροίᾳ τετελευτήκασιν, οἵ τε ἄλλοι καὶ ὁ τῆς Θέτιδος υἱός, ὃς τοσοῦτον τοῦ κινδύνου κατεφρόνησεν παρὰ τὸ μὴ αἰσχρόν τι ὑπομεῖναι ὥστ᾽ ἐπειδὴ εἶπεν ἡ μήτηρ αὐτῷ,

498 καὶ πάντα δὴ λέγω τἀπὶ τούτοις. οὐ γὰρ δήπου τοὺς μὲν εἰς Τροίαν τῶν Ἑλλήνων ἐλθόντας ἐπαινεσόμεθα, ὅτι εἵλοντο καλῶς ἀποθανεῖν, τοὺς δ᾽ εἴ τι πείσονται δυσχερὲς ἐκ τῆς πολιτείας οὐ προτιμήσαντας οὐδὲ παρέντας τῷ φόβῳ τὸ βέλτιστον, τούτους ἀπὸ τῶν συμβάντων κρινοῦμεν· οὐδὲ τοὺς μὲν ὑπὲρ μιᾶς γυναικὸς ὑβρισθείσης ἀγανακτήσαντας ἀνδρῶν ἀγαθῶν λογισμῷ χρῆσθαι φήσομεν, τοὺς δ᾽ ἁπάσης τῆς Ἑλλάδος προστάντας, ἡνίχ᾽ ὑπὲρ παίδων ὁμοῦ καὶ γυναικῶν καὶ ἱερῶν καὶ τάφων καὶ πάντων τῶν ὄντων

---

379 *Ap.* 28b–c.

So when these men attached no importance to the difficulties they were going to encounter in comparison to just action, but sacrificed themselves unsparingly and unconditionally for what was in the best interests of the community, they were applying Socrates' principle. Therefore it must either be shown that the deeds which they chose as their objectives and set themselves to perform were neither just nor those of good men, or it must be conceded that they were indeed good men, whatever they may have met with, and all the more and in greater measure in that they were unafraid of the difficulty of the thing. 497

> All the demigods who died at Troy would be of little worth—I am now quoting Plato's own words—on your principle, including even the son of Thetis, whose contempt for danger was such, when compared with the avoidance of all dishonor, that when his mother said to him . . .[379]

and everything that follows this, let it be understood. Because we are surely not going to praise the Greeks who went to Troy for choosing a noble death, and yet when it comes to those who did not attach special importance to any odium they might suffer as a result of their policies or abandon what was for the best out of fear, judge them on the strength of what became of them. Nor will we say that those who had taken umbrage on behalf of one violated woman were applying the reasoning of good men, while ranking among the caterers and declining to judge comparable to the demigods those who championed the whole of Greece, when the risks they ran were on behalf of children together with wives and shrines and graves and in- 498

ἐκινδύνευον, τούτους μετὰ τῶν ὀψοποιῶν καταλέξομεν, πρὸς τοὺς ἡμιθέους ἀφέντες κρίνειν· οὐδ' εἰ μέν τις φίλῳ τιμωρῶν ὑπέμεινε τελευτᾶν, εἰς μακάρων νήσους πέμψομεν, εἰ δέ τινες τῇ τε πόλει πάσῃ καὶ τοῖς τῶν Ἑλλήνων πράγμασιν ἀντὶ πάντων τῶν ἄλλων κατέστησαν, τούτοις εἴ τί ποθ' ὕστερον συνέβη, τὸ κακῶς ἀκούειν προσθήσομεν. οὐχ ἕως γ' ἂν τοὺς περὶ τῶν δικαίων λόγους φυλάττωμεν. ἀφαιρεῖν γὰρ τοῖς χρηστοῖς τῶν συμφορῶν εἰκὸς ἦν, εἴ πως ἐνῆν, μᾶλλον ἢ τοῦτο οὐκ ἔχοντας ἐπεμβαίνειν, ὃ δὴ λέγεται, κειμένοις.

[*(iii) Plato's Criticism and Demosthenes' Praise (499–510)*]

499 βούλομαι τοίνυν καὶ Δημοσθένους τοῦ Παιανιέως μνησθῆναι βραχύ τι· οὐδὲν γὰρ ἦν χεῖρον, ἄλλως τε καὶ περὶ ῥητόρων ὄντος τοῦ λόγου, μνησθήσομαι δ'
500 ὅσον εἰς τούτους ἀνήκει. πῶς οὖν ἐκεῖνος περὶ τῶν αὐτῶν τούτων διείλεκται, κατηγορηκότος μὲν Αἰσχίνου ὡς ἀνάξιος εἴη τοῦ στεφάνου, παρεξετάσαντος δὲ αὐτὸν πρὸς τοὺς πρότερον καὶ μόνον οὐκ ἀνάγκην προσθέντος ὥστ' ἐξαχθῆναι καὶ παρὰ γνώμην εἰπεῖν, καὶ φιλονεικῆσαι πρὸς τοὺς ἄνδρας ἕνεκα τῆς ἐκείνου βλασφημίας; ὁ δέ πως μάλα πράως καὶ σωφρόνως καὶ ἀξίως ἑαυτοῦ τὴν μὲν δεινότητα εἰς τὸν Αἰσχίνην

380 Achilles: Pind. *Ol.* 2.70–80, Apollod. *Epit.* 5.

deed everything that they had. Nor will we send someone to the Isles of the Blessed if he dies avenging a friend,[380] but if there are people who were more valuable than anybody else to their city and to the whole of Greece, visit them with a bad reputation if some misfortune subsequently befell them. Not at least for as long as we uphold the principles of justice. It would have made sense to free the good from their misfortune, if there had been any way of doing this, rather than, on proving unable to do so, trampling on them once they were dead, as the saying goes.[381]

(iii) Plato's Criticism and Demosthenes' Praise (499–510)

I should like now briefly to mention Demosthenes of Pae- 499
ania—no bad idea, especially when it is orators that we are discussing, though I shall confine my reference to him to
what is relevant to these men. What then are the terms in 500
which he discussed them? This was when Aeschines had accused him of not being worthy of the crown, comparing him to the politicians of the past and thereby all but placing him under compulsion to digress and speak off his topic, and to enter into a competition with these men because of his detractor's calumnies. In a very calm and self-controlled manner, and one entirely worthy of him, he turned the full intensity of his oratory on Aeschines, while

381 As reprehended in Hom. *Od.* 22.412; Archil. fr. 134 *IEG*; Cratinus fr. 102 Kassel-Austin; and Chilon *ap*. Diog. Laert. 1.70.

ἔτρεψε, τοῖς δ' ἀνδράσι τὴν εὐφημίαν ἐτήρησεν. λέγει γάρ, ὡς ἐγᾦμαι, ταυτὶ

> εἶτα τῶν πρότερον γεγενημένων ἀνδρῶν ἀγαθῶν μέμνησαι· καὶ καλῶς ποιεῖς.

501 πρῶτον μὲν δὴ τοῦτο τὸ μικρὸν τὸ τῆς προσθήκης πῶς οὐ φιλάνθρωπον ἅμα καὶ γενναῖον, τὸ καὶ καλῶς ποιεῖς; οὐχ ὥσπερ Πλάτων φησὶν ὅτι

> οὐ καλῶς ποιεῖς, Καλλίκλεις, μεμνημένος τῶν ἀνδρῶν τούτων ὡς ἀγαθῶν· οὐ γὰρ ἦσαν τοιοῦτοι.

502 ἔπειτα τοσούτου ἐδέησε τῆς ὑπαρχούσης ἐκείνοις δόξης ἀφελεῖν ἐπιχειρεῖν, ἵνα δὴ μείζων αὐτὸς φανείη, ὥστε τὴν αὑτοῦ πολιτείαν εἰς τὴν ἐκείνων ἀνενήνοχεν, φάσκων ταὐτὰ βουλομένην εἶναι. λέγει γὰρ οὕτως, ὅσον ἐγὼ μέμνημαι

> καὶ μὴν εἰ καὶ τοῦτ' ἄρα εἰπεῖν δεῖ, ἡ μὲν ἐμὴ πολιτεία καὶ προαίρεσις, ἐάν τις ὀρθῶς σκοπῇ, ταῖς τῶν τότε ἐπαινουμένων ἀνδρῶν ὁμοία καὶ ταὐτὰ βουλομένη φανήσεται, ἡ δὲ σὴ ταῖς τῶν τότε τοὺς τοιούτους συκοφαντούντων.

503 καίτοι τρία γ' εἰς ὑπερβολὴν ὑπῆρχεν εἰπεῖν αὐτῷ

at the same time upholding these men's good name. This is what he says, I think:

> Then you bring in the heroes of the past, and you do well to do so.[382]

That little extra comment, to begin with, that "and you do 501
well to do so," surely combines generosity and nobility of spirit, unlike Plato, with his

> you are wrong, Callicles, to speak of these men as if they were good people, because they were not of that sort.[383]

In the sequel Demosthenes fell so far short of trying to 502
deprive these heroes of the good reputation that they had, in order to make himself look better, that he traced his own policies back to theirs, insisting that they had the same aims. As far as I remember, what he says is this:

> If I must deal with this matter too, I say that, if my policy and my principles are properly considered, they will be found to resemble in spirit and purpose those of the venerated individuals of that period, whereas yours are like those of the men who then maligned them.[384]

And yet there were three hugely important things that 503
he had justification and to spare for saying about his own

382 Dem. *De cor.* (18) 314, responding to Aeschin. *In Ctes.* (*Or.* 3, comparing Demosthenes to the politicians of the past in 181–87).

383 A summary of Socrates' contention against Callicles in the *Gorgias* rather than a direct quotation.

384 Dem. *De cor.* (18) 317.

τὰ μέγισθ' ὑπὲρ τῆς αὑτοῦ πολιτείας· πρῶτον μὲν ὅτι
οὐχ ὁμοίως εἶχεν τὰ τῶν καιρῶν οὔτε τοῖς Ἀθηναίοις
οὔτε τοῖς ἄλλοις Ἕλλησι τότε καὶ καθ' αὑτόν, ἀλλ' οἱ
μὲν ἐν εὐθενοῦσι τοῖς πράγμασι τὴν αὑτῶν ἀρετὴν
ἔδειξαν, οὗτος δὲ νοσούντων καὶ μόνον οὐκ ἀπολω-
λότων ἤδη πάντων ἐπὶ τὴν προστασίαν τῶν κοινῶν
παρῆλθεν. ἔπειθ' ὅτι οὐδὲ τὰ τῶν ἀντιπάλων παραπλήσια, ἀλλὰ πρὸς ἄνδρας ὀξεῖς καὶ δεινοὺς καὶ συγ-
κεκροτημένους καὶ τούτους ὁμόρους καὶ προσοικοῦν-
τας, καὶ ἅμα τῷ κηρυκείῳ καὶ τῷ σιδήρῳ χρωμένους,
καὶ τὰ πλεῖστα τῶν πραγμάτων ἐξ ἀφανοῦς ἀφαι-
ρουμένους, αὐτός θ' ἑαυτὸν ἔταξεν ἀγωνίζεσθαι καὶ
τὴν πόλιν ἠξίου καὶ ἃ μηδὲ τοῖς μάντεσιν ἦν προϊδέ-
σθαι μηδὲ προειπεῖν, ταῦθ' ὁμοῦ προλέγειν καὶ δια-
κωλύειν ἠναγκάζετο. τρίτον δ' ἐπὶ τούτοις ὅτι καὶ
μόνος ὡς ἔπος εἰπεῖν ἀντετάξατο τῇ κατὰ τῶν Ἑλλήνων τύχῃ, τῶν μὲν ταὐτὰ προῃρημένων καὶ συνερ-
γούντων πολλῆς τινος ἐνδείας οὔσης, τῶν δ' ὑπὲρ τῶν
ἐναντίων λεγόντων καὶ πραττόντων ἀφθονίας θαυμαστῆς, ὧν κρατῆσαι πολὺ μεῖζον ἦν ἢ τῶν ἔξω καὶ
504 φανερῶν πολεμίων. ἀλλ' ὅμως ἐκ τοσούτων καὶ τοιούτων ἐλαττωμάτων κατάλογόν τινα ποιεῖται συμμάχων καὶ πόρων καὶ δυνάμεων, ὧν συνήγαγεν αὐτοῖς
ἐκ τοῦ δικαιοτάτου, ἰδίᾳ που τοῦ λόγου λέγων ταῦτα
καὶ πρὶν τῶν ἀνδρῶν τούτων μνησθῆναι. μνησθεὶς δὲ
τούτων οὐδὲν ἔτι τοιοῦτον, ἀλλ' ἔχων ἃς εἶπον ὑπερ-
βολὰς οὐκ ἐλύπησεν, ἀλλ' ἀποχρῆν ἡγήσατο ὁμοίαν

political career. First, that the situation was not the same either for the Athenians or for the rest of Greece at that time as it was in his own day, but that whereas they displayed their heroism in flourishing circumstances, he had made his way to preeminence in public life when the situation was already ailing and all but lost. Secondly, that the nature of the adversaries involved was not comparable, but that he had set himself, and expected his city, to wrestle with sharp, cunning, and highly disciplined people, near neighbors into the bargain, who worked with herald's staff and sword in tandem and achieved the majority of their successes by secrecy and subterfuge, and that he was under the obligation of simultaneously predicting and preventing what not even the soothsayers could foresee or foretell. Thirdly and finally, that he also stood virtually alone in combating the sorry fortunes of Greece, with a serious shortage of likeminded allies to share his work and an extraordinary abundance of opponents speaking and acting against him, overcoming whom was a far greater task than overcoming his open and external foes. But in 504
spite of such numerous and serious disadvantages, he can nevertheless draw up a list of the allies, resources, and forces that he had with perfect legitimacy assembled for them. He includes this elsewhere in his speech in a section to itself, before mentioning these men.[385] But once he had mentioned them, he made no further reference to any such thing. Even though he surpassed them in the ways I have detailed, he did not make a nuisance of himself but

[385] Dem. *De cor.* (18) 237.

505 τὴν ἑαυτοῦ πολιτείαν τῇ ἐκείνων προσειπεῖν. καὶ πρός γ' ἔτι τὴν ὑπερβολὴν ἐκείνοις ἀπέδωκεν εἰπὼν οὑτωσὶ

> κἀκεῖνο λογίζου καὶ σκόπει. πότερον κάλλιον καὶ ἄμεινον τῇ πόλει διὰ τὰς τῶν προτέρων εὐεργεσίας οὔσας ὑπερμεγέθεις, οὐ μὲν οὖν εἴποι τις ἂν ἡλίκας, τὰς ἐπὶ τὸν παρόντα βίον γιγνομένας εἰς ἀχαριστίαν καὶ προπηλακισμὸν ἄγειν, ἢ πᾶσιν ὅσοι τι μετ' εὐνοίας πράττουσι τῆς παρὰ τούτων τιμῆς καὶ φιλανθρωπίας μετεῖναι;

506 κἀνταῦθα μὲν οὕτως· ἑτέρωθι δ' αὖ πολλοῖς πρότερον χρόνοις δημηγορῶν ἐν τοῖς Ἀθηναίοις καὶ παρρησιαζόμενος, πείθων αὐτοὺς τὰ βέλτιστ' ἀντὶ τῶν ἡδέων αἱρεῖσθαι, ἐξὸν αὐτῷ καὶ χωρὶς τοῦ μνησθῆναι τῶν ἄνω ῥητόρων περαίνειν τὰ τῆς ὑποθέσεως, ὥσπερ ἐπεισόδιον χρηστὸν ἐπεισήγαγεν, καὶ τοῦ τε Περικλέους αὐτοὺς ὑπεμίμνησκεν καὶ ἄλλων ὡδὶ λέγων

> ἀλλὰ δικαίου πολίτου κρίνω τὴν τῶν πραγμάτων σωτηρίαν ἀντὶ τῆς ἐν τῷ λέγειν χάριτος αἱρεῖσθαι. καὶ γὰρ τοὺς ἐπὶ τῶν προγόνων ἡμῶν λέγοντας ἀκούω, ὥσπερ ἴσως καὶ ὑμεῖς, οὓς ἐπαινοῦσι μὲν οἱ παριόντες ἅπαντες, μιμοῦνται δ' οὐ πάνυ, τούτῳ τῷ ἔθει καὶ τῷ τρόπῳ τῆς πολιτείας χρῆσθαι, τὸν Ἀριστείδην ἐκεῖνον, τὸν Νικίαν, τὸν ὁμώνυμον τὸν ἐμαυτοῦ, τὸν Περικλέα.

was content to describe his own policies as similar to theirs. What is more he even granted their superiority, in 505
the following words:

> Register this question too and think it over: is it nobler and better for the city that on account of the services rendered by men of old, enormous as they were, indeed inexpressibly great, the services that are now being rendered to the present age should be treated with ingratitude and vituperation, or that instead all who act in a spirit of loyalty should receive some share of the respect and consideration of their fellow citizens?[386]

That is what he says in this particular passage. Else- 506
where, on a much earlier occasion, addressing the Athenians in public and speaking his mind, in an attempt to persuade them to choose the best course rather than the pleasant one, even though he could have completed the essentials of what he had set out to say without mentioning the politicians of the past, he brought them in like a useful extra scene in a play, and reminded his hearers of Pericles and the rest with the following words:

> But I consider it the part of a right-minded citizen to set the safe conduct of our affairs above popularity as an orator. Indeed I understand—as perhaps you do too—that the orators of past generations, always praised but not always imitated by those who address you, adopted this very habit and manner in their statesmanship. I refer to the famous Aristides, to Nicias, to my own namesake, and to Pericles.[387]

[386] Dem. *De cor.* (18) 316.

[387] Dem. 3.21 (*Olynthiac* 3).

507 δύο τοίνυν ταῦτ᾽ ἄν τις τῶν λόγων τούτων ἐπισημαίνοιτο· ἓν μὲν ὅτι οὐ κατ᾽ ἀνάγκην, ἀλλ᾽ ἐκ περιουσίας καὶ γνώμης ἐπιεικείᾳ τὴν μνήμην τῶν ἀνδρῶν καὶ τὸν ἔπαινον τούτων ἐποιήσατο, ἕτερον δὲ ὅτι καὶ αὐτὰ τὰ ἐναντιώτατα αὐτοῖς ἀπέδωκεν ὧν κατηγόρηκεν ὁ Πλάτων. ὁ μὲν γὰρ κολακείας καὶ δουλείας καὶ τῆς ἡδονῆς θεραπευτάς, καὶ μηδὲν πλέον τούτου σκοπεῖν αὐτούς, ὁ δ᾽ ὡς παρρησίᾳ τῇ δικαιοτάτῃ χρωμένους καὶ τὸ χαρίζεσθαι μηδαμοῦ τιθέντας πρὸς τὸ βέλτιστον, οὕτως ἐπαινῶν φαίνεται, τὴν αὐτὴν τῷ Θουκυδίδῃ φωνὴν ἀφιείς, ἐπεὶ κἀκεῖνος, ὥσπερ ἐν τοῖς ἄνω λόγοις ἐπεδείκνυμεν, θαυμαστὸν ὅσον φησὶν περιεῖναι τῷ Περικλεῖ τῆς ἐλευθερίας καὶ παρρησίας, οὐ γὰρ ἄγεσθαι μᾶλλον ἢ ἄγειν τὸν δῆμον, καὶ μὴ τί λέγων χαριεῖται σκοπεῖν, ἀλλ᾽ ὅ τι βέλτιστον αὐτοῖς ἡγοῖτο, τοῦτο συμβουλεύειν. ἐπαινεῖ δέ που καὶ τὸν Νικίαν διὰ τὸ πᾶσαν ἀρετὴν ἐπιτηδεύειν. οὕτω καὶ ἔντιμα καὶ ὁμολογούμενα ὑπὲρ τῶν ἀνδρῶν εἴρηκεν ὁ Δημοσθένης.

508 φέρε δὴ σκεψώμεθα τἀπὶ τούτοις μετὰ πάσης εὐμενείας, ὥσπερ ἐν κοινῷ τινι τῶν Ἑλλήνων συλλόγῳ. πάντως δὲ ἄκρω μὲν ἀμφοτέρω τὼ ἄνδρε, ὑπὲρ μεγάλων δὲ καὶ οἱ λόγοι. ἀλλὰ μὴν τό γε τοῦ λέγοντος αὐτοῦ ὅπως τις βούλεται τιθέναι, οὕτως ἐχέτω τὰ νῦν. ἀλλ᾽ ὅ γ᾽ ἐβουλόμην εἰπεῖν, πότερος καὶ τὴν ὅλην γνώμην φιλανθρωπότερος καὶ περὶ αὐτοὺς τοὺς λό-

388 Thuc. 2.65.5–11 (cf. §§20–25 above).

There are two things in these words that one might particularly applaud. The first is that he mentioned and praised these men not because he was forced to, but as an aside and out of the goodness of his heart, and the second is that he credited them with the exact opposite of Plato's accusations. Plato accuses them of being flatterers and lackeys and ministers to pleasure, and says that they have no further aim than this, whereas Demosthenes manifestly praises them as men who spoke with the most fully justified frankness and placed the gratification of their audience nowhere in comparison to what was for the best. In this he was agreeing with Thucydides, since that author too, as I have shown in my earlier remarks,[388] credits Pericles with an extraordinarily high degree of independence and frankness, because he led the people rather than being led by them, and did not ask himself what he could say to curry favor, but advised them to follow whatever course of action he believed to be best for them. He also somewhere praises Nicias for embodying every kind of virtue.[389] Such was the honor that Demosthenes paid to these men, which all would agree to be justified. 507

Let us in all goodwill consider what follows from this with complete benevolence, as if in some great Panhellenic assembly. Certainly both of the two—Plato and Demosthenes—were men of extreme distinction, and they were speaking about weighty matters. But for now let the status of the speaker himself be as anyone wishes to determine it. What I wanted to ask is this: which of them in this particular connection was the more generous in his overall intentions and the more accomplished in his use of words? 508

389 Thuc. 7.86.5.

γους δεξιώτερος κατὰ τοῦτο τὸ μέρος, πότερ' ὅστις
αὐτῷ μηδεμιᾶς ἀνάγκης ὑπαρχούσης κακῶς λέγειν
εἵλετο τοὺς ἄνδρας, ἢ ὅστις ὄντος μὲν τοῦ παροξύνον-
τος οὐ προήχθη οὐδ' ἠξίωσεν αὐτὸν σεμνύνειν, ἐν
οἷς ἑτέρους ἔμελλεν κακῶς ἐρεῖν, πάλιν δὲ μηδεμιᾶς
ἀνάγκης ὑπαρχούσης ἐπὶ τοῖς βελτίστοις αὐτῶν
509 ἐμνημόνευσεν ἐξεπίτηδες; †μή[150] τῳ φαυλοτέρα τῆς
διαλεκτικῆς ἡ ῥητορικὴ φαίνεται. καίτοι ἔγωγε ᾤμην
οὐ πάνυ ταῦτ' ἀλλήλων κεχωρίσθαι, ἀλλ' εἶναι τὴν
διαλεκτικὴν μέρος τι τῆς ῥητορικῆς, ὥσπερ τὴν
ἐρώτησιν τοῦ παντὸς λόγου, καὶ τὸν αὐτὸν τρόπον
ὅνπερ τοῖς δρομεῦσι μέτεστι τοῦ βαδίζειν, οὐ μὴν
τοῖς βαδίζουσιν ἅπασι τὸ θεῖν οἷόν τε, οὕτω καὶ τοὺς
510 ῥητορικοὺς πρὸς τοὺς διαλεκτικοὺς ἔχειν. Πλάτωνα δὲ
ἐξαιρῶ λόγου, ἱκανὸς γὰρ καὶ ἀμφότερα. ἀλλ' οὔ τί
γε τοῖς περὶ τῶν ἀνδρῶν τούτων λόγοις ἄγων ἡμᾶς
οἰχήσεται, ἐπεὶ ὅτι γε οὐκ ἀλόγως οὐδ' ἀπεικότως
συνήγαγον τὰς δυνάμεις Πλάτων ἐστὶ σύμψηφος,
οὐδὲ γὰρ τοῦτο ἴσως ἔξω τοῦ πράγματος. ὅταν γὰρ
περὶ τῆς τῶν ὀνομάτων ὀρθότητος διαλεγόμενος τοὺς
ἥρωας ῥήτορας εἶναι λέγῃ, καὶ πάλιν διαλεκτικούς,
τότ' ἄμφω δήπου μαρτυρεῖ, καὶ τὴν ῥητορικὴν οὐ κολάκων ἔργον, ἀλλ' ἡρώων τινῶν εἶναι, ὥστε μὴ τοῖς
μαγείροις γε προσήκειν ἀπεικάζειν τοὺς ἐπιτηδεύον-
τας αὐτήν, ἀλλὰ τοῖς ἥρωσι μᾶλλον, καὶ τὴν διαλεκτικὴν αὖ τῇ ῥητορικῇ προσήκειν. ὅταν γὰρ διὰ

[150] εἰ μή Reiske

Was it the one who chose to speak ill of our men when there was no compulsion on him to do so, or was it the one who, when under provocation from someone else, was not moved, and did not think it right, to cry himself up when this was going to involve speaking ill of others, and who also, when there was no compulsion on him to do so, deliberately mentioned them in the most complimentary of terms? . . . . . oratory is inferior in value to dialectic.[390] I 509
myself would certainly have thought that the two are not entirely separate from each other, but rather that dialectic is a subdivision of oratory, just as the question is a subdivision of speech in general, and that just as people running can also be said to walk, while not all who walk are able to run, so things also stand between orators and dialecticians.
Plato I except from this generalization, since he is in fact 510
equally good at both.[391] But he will not run away with our helpless consent to his words about those men, since on the point that it was not irrational or implausible of me to associate the two faculties, Plato himself agrees with me, and this is perhaps not an irrelevant consideration either. Because when in discussing correct naming he says that the heroes were orators, and again dialecticians,[392] he surely testifies to both points, both that oratory is the work not of flatterers but of heroes of a kind, so that it is appropriate not to compare its practitioners with cooks but rather with the heroes, and that dialectic is in its turn re-

390 Something is amiss with the text here; Reiske's conjecture ("—unless anyone thinks that oratory is . . .") indicates the problem without providing an entirely satisfactory solution.

391 Aristides here echoes Eryximachus' words about Socrates at *Symp.* 176c.

392 *Cra.* 398d.

μέσου τοῦ τῶν ῥητόρων ὀνόματος τοὺς διαλεκτικοὺς τοῖς ἥρωσι συνάπτῃ, πῶς οὐχ ὃ λέγω μαρτυρεῖ;

[Argumentation 6: A Counterattack on Plato (511–662) (i) Plato's Self-Contradictions, Omissions, and Ineptitude (511–76)]

511 ἀλλ᾽ ὑπὲρ μὲν τούτων οὐ διαφέρομαι· ὅτι δ᾽ οὐ μόνον ἐξ ὧν Δημοσθένης καὶ Θουκυδίδης καὶ Αἰσχίνης μαρτυροῦσιν, ἀλλὰ καὶ ἀφ᾽ ὧν αὐτὸς Πλάτων ὡμολόγησεν ἐν αὐτοῖς τούτοις τοῖς διαλόγοις, καὶ νὴ Δί᾽ ἐν αὐτῷ γε τούτῳ τῷ μέρει τῶν λόγων ἐν ᾧ περὶ τῶν ἀνδρῶν διείλεκται, καὶ μάτην ἅπαντα εἰρῆσθαι καὶ ψευδεῖς εἶναι τὰς βλασφημίας συμβαίνει, τοῦτ᾽ ἤδη βούλομαι δεῖξαι, εἰ μή τῳ δοκῶ πολυπραγμονεῖν λίαν
512 ἀκριβῶς ἅπαντ᾽ ἐξετάζων. ὅμως δὲ τοσοῦτον προειπεῖν βούλομαι· εἰ γὰρ ἁλοίην ψευδόμενος, δίδωμι καὶ πάντα ἐξαλεῖψαι τῷ βουλομένῳ, καὶ χάριν προσείσομαι· εἰ δ᾽ ἀλήθειαν λέγων οὐχ ἥδιστα ἐρῶ πᾶσιν,
513 ἄλλος ἂν εἴη λόγος. τὴν γοῦν ἀλήθειαν, ὡς χρὴ τιμᾶν πολλοὶ μὲν εἰρήκασιν, οὐ μὴν ἔσθ᾽ ὅστις πλείονος ἄξιος ἢ Πλάτων. πάρεστιν δ᾽ ὃ λέγω σκοπεῖν ἤδη.

ὡρμήθη μὲν γὰρ ἅπας αὐτῷ δήπουθεν ὁ περὶ τῶν ἀνδρῶν λόγος ἐκ τούτου, δύο τούτων παρασκευῶν οὐσῶν, τῆς μὲν πρὸς ἡδονὴν ὁμιλεῖν, τῆς δὲ πρὸς τὸ βέλτιστον, τοὺς ῥήτορας εἶναι τούτων ἄρα τῶν πρὸς

lated to oratory. For when by using name "orators" as his middle term he connects dialecticians with heroes, how can he not be testifying to the truth of what I say?

Argumentation 6:
A Counterattack on Plato (511–662)
(i) Plato's Self-Contradictions, Omissions, and Ineptitude (511–76)

But I do not want to argue over that. What I do want to 511
show, unless someone thinks that I am wasting my efforts by examining everything too closely, is this: that not only from the evidence of Demosthenes, Thucydides, and Aeschines, but also from the concessions of Plato himself in this very dialogue, and indeed in the very part of the discussion in which he is talking about our men, it emerges
that it is all nonsense and that the calumnies are false. I 512
do however want to say this much by way of preface. If I am caught out peddling falsehoods, I grant anyone who wants it the right to erase the lot, and I will be grateful as well; but if I am telling the truth, and not everyone is
delighted to hear it, that would be another story. At all 513
events, the obligation to respect the truth has often been articulated, but never by anyone who carries more weight than Plato. The task now at hand, however, is to consider what I have to say.

The basis of Plato's whole discussion of our men is this, that given the existence of two practices, one interacting with people with a view to giving pleasure and the other with a view to what is best, orators belong to the group

τὸ χαρίζεσθαι βλεπόντων, καὶ δημηγορεῖν οὕτω τοῦ ἰδίου ἕνεκα τοῦ ἑαυτῶν, ἄλλο δὲ μηδὲν βλέπειν. μνησθεὶς δὲ καὶ τούτων τῶν ἀνδρῶν, διὰ τὸ τὸν Καλλικλέα δὴ τούτους γε ὑπεξελέσθαι, βουλόμενος δεῖξαι παραπλησίως τοῖς ἄλλοις ἔχοντας καὶ οὐδὲν βελτίους ὄντας, ἀλλὰ καὶ αὐτοὺς διακόνους καὶ τοιούτους οἵους τὰς ἐπιθυμίας ἐμπιμπλάναι, κατηγορήσας ἃ ἐβούλετο καὶ τὰς συμφορὰς ὀνειδίσας αὐτοῖς, εἶθ' ὥσπερ τῶν πρώτων ἐπιλαθόμενος, μᾶλλον δὲ καὶ τῆς ὑποθέσεως ὅλης, ἐπέθηκεν ἐπὶ τελευτῆς

> ὥστ' εἰ τοιοῦτοι ῥήτορες ἦσαν, οὔτε τῇ ἀληθινῇ ῥητορικῇ ἐχρῶντο, οὐ γὰρ ἂν ἐξέπεσον, οὔτε τῇ κολακικῇ.

514 ἔχε δὴ πρὸς θεῶν. πῶς ἄν τις μᾶλλον ἁλοίη τἀναντία λέγων αὐτὸς αὑτῷ, ὅστις λέγων μὲν ὡς ἦσαν κόλακες καὶ τοῦτ' ἀγωνιζόμενος, εἶτ' αὐτὸς αὖ φησιν ὡς οὐκ ἐχρῶντο τῇ κολακικῇ, πάλιν δὲ ὧν ἀφῆκεν αὐτούς, ταῦτα κατηγορεῖ, καὶ δι' ὧν μὲν ἐλέγχειν προὐθυμεῖτο, διὰ τούτων ἀφεῖναι ἠναγκάσθη, διὰ δ' ὧν ἀφῆκεν οὓς ᾐτιάσατο τῆς κολακείας, διὰ τούτων ῥητορικὴν ὡς κολακείαν ἐλέγχειν ἀξιοῖ, καὶ ἅμα μέν φησιν ἐξ ἴσου τοῖς ἄλλοις εἶναι τούτους, ἅμα δ' οὐ χρήσασθαι τῇ κολακείᾳ, τοῖς ἄλλοις κολακείαν ἐγκα-
515 λῶν; καὶ μὴν εἰ μὲν τῆς τῶν διακόνων καὶ τῆς τῶν κολάκων ἐπωνυμίας εἰσὶ δίκαιοι τυγχάνειν, τί τοῦτο

aiming at the gratification of their audience and make their speeches on this basis, to further their own private advantage, with no other end in view.[393] Bringing the Four into his discussion, and wanting because Callicles had cited them as exceptions to the rule to show that they were in fact in just the same state as the rest and no better than them, that they too were lackeys and the kind of people to glut their audience's desires, he denounced them as he pleased and used their ill fortune to discredit them. But then, as if forgetting his starting point, or rather his whole case, he rounded off his discussion as follows:

> Thus if such men as these were orators, they practiced neither the true form of oratory (because they would not have been exiled) nor the arts of flattery.[394]

Hold on, for heaven's sake! How could anyone be caught 514
out in a more flagrant self-contradiction? Having said that
they were flatterers and argued this point strenuously, he
turns around and says that they did not employ the arts of
flattery, but then accuses them all over again of the things
he has acquitted them of; he is forced to acquit them on
the very grounds that he had been keen to prove them
guilty, and thinks to show up oratory as flattery by the very
means he had used to acquit those whom he had accused
of it; he simultaneously says both that these men are on a
level with the rest, and that they did not employ the arts
of flattery that he accuses the rest of using. If they deserve 515
to have the labels "lackey" and "flatterer" attached to
them, what do you mean when you say that they did not

393 *Grg.* 463e–66a, resumed in 502d ff.

394 *Grg.* 517a.

λέγεις, ὡς οὐκ ἐχρῶντο τῇ κολακικῇ; εἰ δ᾽ αὖ μηδὲν μετῆν αὐτοῖς τῆς κολακικῆς, πῶς μετὰ τῶν κολάκων αὐτοὺς τίθης; ὅρα μὴ οὐχ ὁμολογῇ ταῦτα ἀλλήλοις, ἀλλ᾽ ὡς ἀληθῶς ἔχῃ τὴν τοῦ Ἀμφίονος ἀνταποδοῦναι ῥῆσιν ὁ Καλλικλῆς, ὅτι ἄρα οὐ συμφωνεῖ Πλάτων αὐτὸς αὐτῷ κατὰ ταῦτά γε.

516 καίτοι ποτέροις τῶν λόγων χρὴ πιστεῦσαι, πότερον
τοῖς αἰτιωμένοις τοὺς ἄνδρας καὶ διαβάλλουσιν, ἢ
τοῖς ἀφιεῖσιν; ἤρξατο μὲν γὰρ ὡς κατήγορος, ἔληξεν
517 δὲ ὡς ἄν τις μάρτυς ἥκων αὐτοῖς. καὶ μὴν εἰ μὲν ἔμελλεν, τοῦτο γάρ ἐστιν ἤδη τὸ ἰσχυρότατον, κόλακας
τρόπον τιν᾽ αὐτοὺς ἐκ τῶν αἰτιῶν δόξειν ἀποφαίνειν,
κἀνταῦθα στήσεσθαι τοῦ λόγου, τάχ᾽ ἂν εἰ καὶ τὰ μὴ
ὄντα κατηγόρησεν, ἀλλ᾽ οὖν ἐδόκει γ᾽ ἄν τι προὔργου
τῶν λόγων εἶναι· ὅτε δ᾽ εἰπὼν ἅπανθ᾽ ὅσ᾽ ἔχειν ἡγεῖτο
κατ᾽ αὐτῶν, εἶθ᾽ ὥσπερ δικαστὴς ἑτέρου λέγοντος
ἀκηκοὼς ἀφῆκεν τῆς αἰτίας αὐτούς, τίς ἔσθ᾽ ἡ χρεία
τῶν λόγων; ἢ πῶς οὐχ ἅμα τε ψευδῆ καὶ μάτην ἅπαντ᾽
εἴρηται; μὴ γὰρ μελλόντων φανεῖσθαι τοιούτων ὁποίους τινὰς αὐτοὺς ὄντας ἐβούλετο δεικνύναι, τί τηνάλλως ἔδει βλασφημεῖν; ὅπου γὰρ εἰ καὶ τὰ μάλιστα
ἠλέγχοντο, ὑπέρ γε πάσης τῆς ῥητορικῆς λόγος κατελείπετο, ὡς οὐ τοιοῦτον εἴη, πῶς εἰκὸς ἔκ γε τῶν
518 ἀφειμένων αὐτὴν δοκεῖν ἐλέγχεσθαι; τὸ δὲ δὴ λέγειν
ὡς οὐδὲ τῇ ἀληθινῇ ῥητορικῇ ἐχρῶντο, οὐ γὰρ ἄν

employ the arts of flattery? But if on the other hand they had nothing to do with the arts of flattery, how can you rank them among the flatterers? Watch out that there is not a contradiction between these two propositions, and that Callicles may not really and truly be able to repay you with Amphion's speech and say that Plato is after all out of harmony with himself, in this matter at least.[395]

Which of the arguments should one believe, the one 516
that accuses and slanders our men, or the one that acquits them? Because Plato began as prosecutor and ended up as if he had come to testify in their defense. Certainly— 517
this is the strongest point we are coming to now—if he had meant to give the impression of demonstrating on the strength of his accusations that they were in some sense flatterers, and to stop at that point in his argument, then even if his accusations were unfounded, it would perhaps have seemed that his case had gotten at least somewhere. But since in fact, having said everything he thought he could to their discredit, he then like a juror who had listened to the other side too acquitted them of the charge, what use is his argument? How can the whole thing not have been both false and pointless? Because if they were not going to be made to seem the kind of people he wanted to show them to be, what need was there to indulge in pointless slander? Given that, even if they had been shown to be utterly guilty, it would still have been possible to argue that oratory as a whole was not of that character, how could oratory reasonably have been thought to be convicted on the strength of what secured their acquittal?
How can it fail to be monstrous to say that they did not 518

395 Alluding to *Grg.* 506b (as also in *Or.* 2.394) and 482b.

ποτ᾽ ἐξέπεσον, πῶς οὐχ ὑπερφυὲς ἤδη καὶ παρ᾽ ἐκεῖνον αὖ τὸν λόγον, ὃν μικρῷ πρόσθεν ἐδείκνυμεν αὐτῷ, ὡς οὐκ ἔστιν ὑπὲρ τῶν δικαίων λέγοντα πρὸς δῆμον σωθῆναι;

519 πάλιν δὲ μνημονεύσωμεν τῶν ῥημάτων καὶ παρ᾽ ἄλληλα θεασώμεθα ἅ τ᾽ ἐκεῖ λέγει καὶ ἅ φησιν ἐνταῦθα.

> οὐ γὰρ ἔστιν ὅστις ἀνθρώπων σωθήσεται οὔθ᾽ ὑμῖν οὔτ᾽ ἄλλῳ πλήθει οὐδενὶ γνησίως ἐναντιούμενος καὶ διακωλύων πόλλ᾽ ἄδικα καὶ παράνομ᾽ ἐν τῇ πόλει γίγνεσθαι, ἀλλ᾽ ἀναγκαῖόν ἐστι τὸν τῷ ὄντι μαχούμενον ὑπὲρ τοῦ δικαίου, καὶ εἰ μέλλει ὀλίγον χρόνον σωθήσεσθαι, ἰδιωτεύειν, ἀλλὰ μὴ δημοσιεύειν.

520 φέρε δὴ τί αὖ φησιν ἐνταῦθα;

> προστάτης γὰρ πόλεως οὐδ᾽ ἂν εἷς ποτε ἀδίκως ἀπόλοιτο ὑπ᾽ αὐτῆς ταύτης τῆς πόλεως ἧς προστατεῖ.

ταῦτ᾽, ὦ πρὸς Διός, πῶς τις εἶναι φῇ τῆς αὐτῆς γνώμης ἢ πρὸς τὸ αὐτὸ τελευτᾶν, ἅμα μὲν τὸν τῷ δικαίῳ βοηθοῦντα ἀναγκαίως ἔχειν ἀπολέσθαι ὑπὸ τῆς πόλεως ἧς προστατεῖ, ἅμα δ᾽ ἂν ἀπόληται, οὐκ ἄν ποτε τοῦτ᾽ ἀδίκως παθεῖν ὑπὸ τῆς πόλεως ἧς προστατεῖ; ποῦ ταῦτ᾽ ἐστὶν ἐοικότα, ἢ πῶς εἰς ταυτὸν τελεῖ;

practice the art of true oratory either, because otherwise they would never have been sent into exile, and how can it fail to be in contradiction with that other proposition of his, which I pointed to just now, that it is not possible for anyone who champions justice in his public speeches to escape with his life?

Let us recall his actual words again and compare side 519
by side what he says in each place.

> There is no one on earth who will be safe if he genuinely opposes you or any other popular assembly and tries to prevent many injustices and illegalities from taking place in his state; it is essential for the man who is in truth fighting for what is just, if he is going to keep himself safe even for a short time, to operate as a private citizen rather than in a public capacity.[396]

And what does he say here in our *Gorgias* passage? 520

> For no leader of a city could ever unjustly be put to death by the same city as he leads.[397]

For heaven's sake, how can anyone say that it belongs to the same line of thought or leads to the same conclusion to say at one and the same time both that the man who supports the cause of justice must inevitably be put to death by the city he leads, and that if he is put to death this could never happen to him unjustly at the hands of the city he leads? What plausibility do these statements have, and how can they be said to point to the same conclusion?

[396] *Ap.* 31e–32a. [397] *Grg.* 519b–c.

521 εἰ δὲ δὴ καὶ τὰ μάλιστα μήτε τῇ ἀληθινῇ ῥητορικῇ ἐχρῶντο μήτε τῇ κολακικῇ, δῶμεν γάρ, κακῶς λέγειν αὐτοὺς οὐδ᾽ οὕτως οἶμαι προσῆκεν. τί γὰρ μᾶλλον κόλακας καὶ φαύλους ὑποληπτέον αὐτούς, εἰ μὴ τῇ ἀληθινῇ ῥητορικῇ ἐχρῶντο, ἢ σπουδαίους τε καὶ χρηστούς, ὅτι οὐκ ἐχρῶντο τῇ κολακικῇ; εἰ γὰρ μεταξὺ τούτων ἦσαν οἱ λόγοι καὶ αἱ προαιρέσεις αὐτῶν, οὐ
522 κολάκων γε ἦσαν οὐδὲ φαύλων ἀνθρώπων. σὺ γοῦν αὐτὸς τὰ μεταξὺ τῶν ἀγαθῶν καὶ τῶν κακῶν οὐδὲν μᾶλλον κακὰ δήπου καλεῖς. πῶς γὰρ ἂν καὶ αὐτὸ τοῦτ᾽ ἔτι λείποιτο αὐτοῖς τὸ μεταξὺ τούτων ἀμφοτέρων εἶναι, εἰ τοῖς γ᾽ ἑτέροις ἐνέχοιντο; ὥστε τί μᾶλλον ψέγειν αὐτοὺς ἢ ἐπαινεῖν προσῆκεν, εἰ μηδετέρου γε μετεῖχον, μήτε τοῦ καλοῦ μήτε τοῦ φαύλου;

523 θαυμάζω δὲ τί ἄν ποτ᾽ ἐποίησεν, ἢ τίνος ἂν μετέδωκεν αὐτοῖς εὐφημίας, εἰ τὴν κολακείαν ἐλέγχειν ἔμελλεν, ὁπότ᾽ αὐτοῦ τοῦ λόγου πρὸς τοῦτ᾽ ἐκφέροντος ὡς οὐχ οἷόν τε μετεῖναι τούτου τοῦ πράγματος αὐτοῖς, ὅμως οὐκ ὤκνησεν τὰ μηδαμῇ συμβαίνοντα
524 κατηγορεῖν. ἀλλὰ μὴν ὅτε γ᾽ αὐτὸς δύο ταῦτα διείλου, καὶ τὴν μὲν ἀληθινὴν προσεῖπες ῥητορικήν, τὴν δὲ κολακικήν, πῶς ῥητορικῆς καθάπαξ ὡς κολακείας κατηγορεῖς, καὶ ὅπου τοὺς ἄνδρας ἀφῆκας οὓς ᾐτιάσω, πῶς ἐλέγχεις ῥητορικὴν ἣν αὐτὸς καὶ χρηστὴν προσείρηκας;

525 εἶεν. τίνι μὴν καὶ τὸ λοιπὸν ἐχρῶντο τῷ τύπῳ τῶν

---

398 *Grg.* 468a.

Again, even if it is absolutely the case that the Four employed neither the arts of true oratory nor those of the flatterer (let us grant that for the sake of argument) even in that case I do not think it is proper to speak ill of them. Because why should we be any the more ready to suppose them worthless flatterers if they did not employ the arts of true oratory, or virtuous and good because they did not employ the arts of the flatterer? If their words and their purposes fell in between these two, then they were at least not flatterers or worthless characters. At any rate, you yourself are certainly not inclined to call something bad if it falls between good and bad[398]—how could this very possibility, of being intermediate between the two, still be open to it if it was stuck fast in one or the other of them? So why would it be any the more appropriate to censure our men than to praise them, if they had a stake in neither, neither nobility nor villainy? 521 522

I am puzzled to know what on earth he would have done, or what share of praise he would have granted them, if he had been going to convict them of flattery, given that when the argument itself led him to the conclusion that it was impossible for them to have anything to do with this activity, he nevertheless did not hesitate to subject them to completely incompatible accusations. Again, given that you yourself, Plato, distinguished between these two things, and called the one of them the true art of oratory and the other the art of the flatterer, how can you flatly accuse the true art of oratory of being a kind of flattery? And given that you have absolved the men you accused, how can you convict the art of oratory that you yourself called good? 523 524

Very well. It remains to ask what form of oratory they 525

λόγων, ἢ τίν' ἐρητόρευον τρόπον; εἰ γὰρ μήθ' ὡς ἄν τινες κηδόμενοι μήθ' ὡς ἄν τινες χαριζόμενοι, ἄλλος γέ τις αὐτοῖς τρόπος κατελείπετο. εἰ γὰρ αὖ καὶ τρίτος τίς ἐστι παρὰ τούτους, οὐ σύ γ' ἐμνήσθης αὐτοῦ, ἀλλὰ δύ' εἶναι ταύτας παρασκευὰς διωρίσω, τὴν μὲν πρὸς ἡδονὴν ὁμιλεῖν, τὴν δὲ πρὸς τὸ βέλτιστον. ὥσθ' ὅτε μήτε πρὸς ἡδονὴν ὡμίλουν μήτε πρὸς τὸ βέλτιστον, πρὸς τί λοιπὸν ὡμίλουν; ἢ πῶς οὐ τούς γε σοὺς ὅρους ἐκπεφεύγασιν, οὓς ἔστησας αὐτοῖς ὡς
526 ἀφύκτως καὶ βεβαίως αἱρήσων; ἀλλὰ μή τις αὖ τῶν ἐκείνοις τοῖς ἀνδράσιν εὐμενῶν εἰς ὑμᾶς μᾶλλον τοῦθ' ὑπολάβῃ τοὺς σοφούς, ὡς ἄρα παντὸς μᾶλλον οὔτε τῇ ἀληθινῇ ῥητορικῇ ἐχρήσασθε πρὸς τὸν δῆμον οὔτε τῇ κολακικῇ. τοῦτο γὰρ ἦν δήπουθεν ἐν τῷ τὴν
527 ἡσυχίαν ἄγειν. καίτοι ὅθ' ὑμεῖς οὐδετέρᾳ τούτων φαίνεσθε κεχρημένοι, τί δεινὸν ἐκείνοις πεποίηται, εἰ καὶ δημηγοροῦντες μηδετέρᾳ τούτων ἐχρήσαντο; ἀλλ' ἴσως ἀναγκαῖον ἦν τῇ γε ἑτέρᾳ χρήσασθαι, ἐπειδὴ ὅλως ἐφθέγγοντο καὶ οὐχ οἷόν τε ἀμφοτέρων αὐτοὺς ἐκπεσεῖν.

528 ὅτι μὲν τοίνυν διακονεῖν ὥρμηντο Πλάτων εἴρηκεν μόνος, ὡς δ' οὐ τοιοῦτον τὸ ἐκείνων πρᾶγμα πάντες τε λέγουσι καὶ προσέτι αὐτὸς Πλάτων προσωμολόγηκεν, ὥσθ' ἣν ἐπήνεγκεν μόνος αἰτίαν, εἰ φαίνεται λύων αὐτός, λείπεται τὴν ἐξ ἀρχῆς δόξαν κρατεῖν, ὡς

[399] As articulated in *Ap.* 31e–32a, just cited, but also in such famous passages as *Resp.* 496d and *Tht.* 176a–b.

actually employed and how they delivered their speeches. Because if they did so neither as people who cared for their audience nor as people who sought to curry favor with them, then it would follow that they had some other mode of speaking. And if there is indeed a third mode besides these ones, then you at any rate did not mention it, but instead said that there were two distinct practices, of addressing people with a view to giving them pleasure and of addressing them with a view to what was best. So if they addressed their audiences with a view neither to giving pleasure nor to what was best, what were they aiming at when they addressed them? How can they not have evaded the confines of your definitions, which you established with the intention of catching them firmly and inescapably? Watch out that one of these men's supporters 526
does not in his turn make this supposition about you philosophers, that in fact it was you more than anyone who employed neither the art of true oratory toward the people nor the art of the flatterer. That is surely what was involved in your quietism.[399] Yet, if it is clear that you employed 527
neither of these two arts, what terrible crime have the Four committed if they did not employ either of them in their public speaking either? But perhaps they must necessarily have employed one or the other of them, since they were at all events speaking and it was not possible for them to fall outside both.

Now, it is Plato alone who has said that they set out to 528
be lackeys; everyone else says that that was not what they were about, and what is more Plato himself has agreed with them. Thus if he himself manifestly absolves them of the charge that he is the only person to have brought, then the conclusion must be that the original view triumphs,

ἀγαθοί τ' ἦσαν πολῖται καὶ τὰ βέλτιστ' ἐδημηγόρουν.
529 ἐγὼ μὲν οὖν οὕτως ἂν μᾶλλον φαίην, ἢ ῥήτορας ὄντας αὐτοὺς μηδετέρᾳ χρήσασθαι τῇ ῥητορικῇ. σκοπῶ δὲ κἀκεῖνο, ὡς εἰ μέν ἐστιν ἡ ῥητορικὴ κολακεία, καθάπαξ δεῖ τῇ κολακείᾳ χρωμένους αὐτοὺς φαίνεσθαι, ἐπειδή γε ἦσαν ῥήτορες. ὥστε πῶς ἢ ἐκείνους ἀπολύει τῆς αἰτίας, ἢ ῥητορικὴν προσείρηκέν τινα ἀληθινήν; εἰ δ' αὖ χρηστὸν ἡ σπουδαῖον ἡ ῥητορική, δεῖ τοῦ βελτίστου δοκεῖν μέλειν αὐτοῖς. ὥστε πῶς ἢ ἐκείνους μὴ πρὸς τὸ βέλτιστον λέγειν αἰτιᾶται, ἢ τὴν ῥητορικὴν κολακείαν καλεῖ; εἰ δ' αὖ διπλοῦν τι τὸ τῆς ῥητορικῆς ἐστιν, καὶ τὸ μὲν αὐτοῦ κολακεία τε καὶ αἰσχρὰ δημηγορία, τὸ δ' ἕτερον προστασία τοῦ δικαίου, ἀναγκαῖον ἐκείνοις τοῦ γ' ἑτέρου μετεῖναι σαφῶς γε οὑτωσί. πῶς οὖν ἀμφοτέρων ἀποστερεῖς
530 αὐτούς; καὶ μὴν εἴ γε καὶ δικαίως ἀποστερεῖς ἀμφοτέρων, τρίτη τις ἂν εἴη παρ' ἀμφοτέρας ταύτας ῥητορικὴ πάλιν. ὥστ' οὐδὲ διπλοῦν ἔτι τούτῳ τῷ λόγῳ τὸ τῆς ῥητορικῆς, οὐδ' ἔδειξε δήπου Πλάτων ἥτις ἔσθ' ἡ
531 τρίτη. καὶ μὴν εἰ μέσον τι τούτων ἐστὶ τοῦ τε πρὸς ἡδονὴν λέγειν καὶ τοῦ πρὸς τὸ βέλτιστον, οὐδ' οὕτως ἐκείνους γε προσῆκεν ἀκούειν κακῶς. καὶ γὰρ εἰ μὴ τὰ βέλτιστα ἐδημηγόρουν, οὐκ ἐδημηγόρουν γε πρὸς ἡδονήν.

532 οὐ τοίνυν μόνον ἐξ ὧν αὐτοὺς ἀφῆκε τῆς τοῦ κολακεύειν αἰτίας δείκνυται μάτην τὰς βλασφημίας τὰς

that they were good citizens and spoke with an eye to what
is best. I would rather put it like that, than say that al- 529
though they were orators, they employed neither kind of oratorical art. Reflect also that, if the art of oratory is a form of flattery, then it is absolutely inevitable that they should be seen to be employing flattery, since they were orators. How then is it that he absolves them of blame, or that he has spoken of a true version of the art of oratory? But if on the other hand the art of oratory is something serious and good, then necessarily they must be thought of as concerned for what is best. How then can he accuse them of not speaking with a view to what is best, or call the art of oratory a kind of flattery? Or if again the art of oratory is something double, with one form of it being a kind of flattery and of base demagoguery, while the other is a championing of what is just, then necessarily on this line of argument they must participate in at least one of the two. How then can you deny them both together?
Again, if you are right to deny them both together, then 530
we would be back with the conclusion that there is a third version of the art of oratory besides these two. On this line of argument, therefore, the art of oratory is no longer a twofold phenomenon, and Plato has apparently not shown
what the third kind is either. Moreover, if there is indeed 531
some third term in between speaking with a view to giving pleasure and speaking with a view to what is best, it is not appropriate for our men to be ill spoken of on this understanding either, because even if they did not advise the best course in their speeches, they certainly did not make their speeches with a view to giving pleasure.

It is moreover not only because he absolved them of 532
the charge of flattery that Plato is shown to have launched

κατ' αὐτῶν πεποιημένος, ἀλλὰ καὶ ἐξ ὧν τὸν Ἀριστείδην ἐπῄνεσεν λαμπρῶς οὕτως μετ' ἐκείνους. εἰ μὲν γὰρ μηδένα μηδαμῶς εἶχεν ἐπαινέσαι, μηδ' ἦν εὑρεῖν ὅστις ῥήτωρ δίκαιος καὶ χρηστὸς γεγένηται, τάχ' ἄν τις ἔφησεν ὡς ἐκ περιουσίας ἐπὶ τοῦθ' ἧκε τὸ μέρος, τὸ ἐλέγχειν τοὺς ἄνδρας, ἵνα πανταχόθεν τὸν κατὰ τῆς ῥητορικῆς λόγον βεβαιώσηται· μέλλοντι δ' ἐπαινέσεσθαι καὶ ὁντινοῦν τί κέρδος ἦν τούτους κακῶς εἰπεῖν; οὐ γὰρ τίς ἄριστος τῶν πολιτευσαμένων προὔκειτο λέγειν, οὐδ' εἰ βελτίων τούτων Ἀριστείδης, ἀλλ' εἰ ἔνεστι τῇ ῥητορικῇ τὸ ὑπὲρ τοῦ δικαίου λέγειν. ὥσθ' ὅτε καὶ ὁστισοῦν εὑρέθη τοιοῦτος, παραπλήσιον ἂν ἦν ὥσπερ ἂν εἰ καὶ τούτων ὁστισοῦν τοιοῦτος
533 εὕρητο. τὸ δὲ δὴ καὶ ἄλλους γεγενῆσθαι φάσκοντα καὶ Ἀθήνησι καὶ ἑτέρωθι, καὶ νὴ Δία προσθέντα γε καὶ ἔσεσθαι, ὅμως εἰς τοσοῦτον φιλονικίας πρὸς τούτους ἐλθεῖν τίν' ἔχει λόγον; ἐκεῖνο μὲν γὰρ ἦν ὑπὲρ τοῦ πράγματος δοκεῖν σπουδάζειν, τοῦτο δὲ ἰδίᾳ τινὰς κακῶς εἰπεῖν βεβουλῆσθαι. ὥστε δικαίως μὲν αὐτῶν ἐγκεκλημένων οὐδὲν πλέον εἰς τοὺς κατὰ τῆς ῥητορικῆς λόγους, ἀκηκοότων δ' ἃ μὴ προσῆκεν
534 μάταιος ἐξ ἀμφοῖν ἡ βλασφημία. ἀλλ' οἶμαι ἅμα μὲν τοῖς εἰρημένοις κατ' ἐκείνων λόγοις αἰσχυνθείς, ἅμα δ' ἡττηθεὶς τῆς ἀληθείας, οὐ κακῷ τὸ κακόν, οὐ μὴν καλῶς γ' ἰάσατο, μᾶλλον δ' ἀγαθῷ τὸ κακὸν ἐξήλεγ-

[400] *Grg.* 526b (cf. *Or.* 2.346–61).

his calumnies against them in vain, but also because he went on to praise Aristides as highly as he did.[400] Because if he had had no praise to bestow on anyone at all, and had found it impossible to identify anyone as having been a just and good orator, then perhaps someone would have said that he came to this part of things, showing these men up, as an extra item, in order to reinforce the case against the art of oratory from every possible direction; but if there was anyone at all that he was going to praise, what good did it do him to speak ill of these men? The task in hand was not to say who was the best of the politicians or whether Aristides was better than them, but whether it is inherent in the art of oratory to speak in the cause of justice. So when anyone at all was discovered to have been of this kind, it was the same as if any one of these men had been found to be such. What sense does it make to assert 533
that there have been others too in Athens and elsewhere, and indeed to add that there will be in future, and still be so intent on doing these men down? To do the former was to give the impression of concentrating on the substantive issue; to do the latter, of wanting to speak ill of them on personal grounds. Thus if they were justly arraigned it added nothing to the case against the art of oratory; and if they did not deserve what was said about them, the defamation was doubly pointless. But I think that in fact Plato 534
simultaneously was ashamed of the case he had made against them and had to bow to the truth and so, rather than confuting ill with ill, since that would not have been a good way of healing things,[401] he confuted ill with good,

[401] Aristides here plays on a proverbial formula: cf. Soph. *Aj.* 362–63 and fr. 77 *TrGF*; Hdt. 3.53; Thuc. 5.65.2.

535 ξεν, τῷ γ' Ἀριστείδῃ τὰ πρέποντ' ἀποδούς. καίτοι εἰ μὲν μηδεὶς ῥήτωρ ἐπιεικής, τί τοῦτον κοσμεῖς; εἰ δ' οὗτός γε σαφῶς δίκαιος, τί σοι πλέον τῆς ἐκείνων κακίας; οὐδὲ γὰρ ἂν ἐλέγχῃς, ὃ βούλει ποιεῖς. οὐδὲν γὰρ μᾶλλον ἡ ῥητορικὴ φαῦλον τοῖς ὅλοις.

536 πόθεν οὖν εἰς ταῦθ' ὑπήχθη; καὶ πῶς ταῦτα ἅμα τε καὶ ἐκεῖνα λέγων φαίνεται; ὅθεν ἐρώτημ' ἐκεῖνο[151]

> πότερόν σοι δοκοῦσιν πρὸς τὸ βέλτιστον ἀεὶ λέγειν οἱ ῥήτορες, τούτου στοχαζόμενοι ὅπως οἱ πολῖται ὡς βέλτιστοι ἔσονται διὰ τοὺς αὐτῶν λόγους, ἢ καὶ οὗτοι πρὸς τὸ χαρίζεσθαι τοῖς πολίταις ὡρμημένοι καὶ ἕνεκα τοῦ ἰδίου τοῦ ἑαυτῶν ὀλιγωροῦντες τοῦ κοινοῦ ὥσπερ παισὶ προσομιλοῦσι τοῖς δήμοις, χαρίζεσθαι αὐτοῖς πειρώμενοι μόνον, εἰ δέ γε βελτίους ἔσονται ἢ χείρους διὰ ταῦτα οὐδὲν φροντίζουσιν;

ἐχρῆν γὰρ αὐτὸν εἰ τὰ μάλιστ' ἐβούλετο τὴν ῥητορικὴν κακῶς λέγειν, τό γ' ἐρώτημα φυγεῖν, διπλοῦν ὂν τῷ μέλλοντι ὑπολήψεσθαι, καὶ καθάπερ τὰ παραδείγματα ἁπλῶς οὑτωσὶ περαίνειν· λέγω τὸ τοῦ κυβερνήτου καὶ τοῦ μηχανοποιοῦ καὶ τἄλλα. νῦν δ' οὔτ' ἐκ τῶν ἑτέρων ἀναγκαίας οὔσης τῆς ἀποκρίσεως οὔτε

[151] ὅθεν ἐρώτημ' ἐκεῖνο <. . . . .> Reiske ὅθεν ἠρώτησε τὸ ἐρώτημ' ἐκεῖνο UR^2

by giving Aristides at least his due. And yet, if no orator is 535
a good one, why do you compliment this man? But if he
at least is clearly a just man, what good does the villainy of
the Four do you? Because even if you expose them, you
are not doing what you want: the art of oratory overall is
not thereby cheapened at all.

How was he drawn into doing this? What was his start- 536
ing point, and how does it become clear that he says both
things simultaneously? It all starts with that fatal question:[402]

> Do you think that orators always speak with a view to what is best, with the aim that their fellow citizens should be as good as they can be made through their words? Or do they too, because they have set out to gratify their fellow citizens, and because they scorn the common good in pursuit of their own private interest, deal with whole peoples as if with children, trying only to gratify them, and do they care nothing about whether this will make them better or worse?[403]

However badly Plato wanted to abuse the art of oratory, he ought to have avoided this question, which in the eyes of its respondent called for a twofold answer, and ought to have completed his case simply and directly, just as he did with his comparisons. (I mean the steersman example and the engineer example and the rest.)[404] But as it is, when there was no logical necessity for the answer to be given in favor of either one of the two possibilities, and it could

[402] The Greek text at this point may be faulty, but the general sense is not in doubt. [403] *Grg.* 502e. [404] *Grg.* 511d–12c.

κατ' ἀμφότερα ἁλωσίμου, σχίζει τὴν ὑπόθεσιν καὶ δίδωσι τὰ δεύτερα τῷ Καλλικλεῖ ἀμέλει καὶ λέγει

> οὐχ ἁπλοῦν ἔτι τοῦτ' ἐρωτᾷς. εἰσὶ μὲν γὰρ οἳ κηδόμενοι τῶν πολιτῶν λέγουσιν ἃ λέγουσιν, εἰσὶ δὲ καὶ οἵους σὺ λέγεις.

537 νὴ Δί', εἴποι τις ἄν, αὐτὸ γὰρ τοῦτο προθυμῇ, τὸ δεῖξαι καὶ διελέσθαι διττὸν εἶναι τὴν ῥητορικήν, τὴν μὲν ὑπὲρ τοῦ βελτίστου, τὴν δὲ πρὸς ἡδονήν. ἐγὼ δ' εἰ μέν ἐστι διπλοῦν ἡ ῥητορικὴ ἢ μὴ τότε δεῖν οἰήσομαι ζητεῖν, ὅταν καὶ τὴν φιλοσοφίαν εἰ διπλοῦν ἐστιν ἐπισκοπώμεθα καὶ τήν γε ἰατρικὴν καὶ τὴν κυβερνητικήν, διὰ τοὺς ἐφ' ἑκάστῃ τῶν ἐπιστημῶν τοῦ δέοντος ἁμαρτάνοντας.

538 πολλὰ δ' ἂν φαίην, πρῶτον μὲν ὅτι οὐχ οὕτως ἐλέγετο ἐν τοῖς λόγοις τοῖς πρὸς Πῶλον, ἀλλ' ἁπλῶς οὑτωσὶ πολιτικῆς μορίου εἴδωλον ἤκουεν ἡ ῥητορική· ἔπειθ' ὅτι εἰ τὰ μάλιστα διπλοῦν ὑπελάμβανεν τὴν ῥητορικήν, οὐκ ἐν οἷς γε λόγοις κακῶς αὐτὴν λέγειν προῄρητο, ἐν τούτοις προσῆκεν ἐπαινοῦντα φαίνεσθαι, οὐδ' ἐξ ὧν ἤλεγχεν ἀφιέναι. χωρὶς γάρ ἐστι διπλοῦν εἶναι φάσκειν καὶ πειρώμενον καθάπαξ φαῦλον ὂν δεῖξαι μὴ δύνασθαι. πῶς γὰρ οὐκ ἄτοπον, εἰ μὲν ἤλεγξεν ὡς ἔστιν κολακεία τοῦτ' ἂν ἰσχυρὸν μέ-

405 *Grg.* 503a.
406 *Grg.* 463d.

not have been faulted if given in favor of both, he divides the material in two, giving the role of respondent to Callicles of course, and writes:

> What you are now asking doesn't have a simple answer. Some of them say what they say out of a true concern for their fellow citizens, others are as you describe.[405]

But, somebody might object, this is exactly what you are striving to do, to draw a distinction and show that the art of oratory is twofold, with one form championing what is best and the other aiming at pleasure. I think however that the question whether the art of oratory is twofold or not should only be asked when we are also ready to consider whether philosophy and medicine and navigation are twofold as well, on account of those who miss their proper targets in each of these sciences. 537

There is much that I might say on this score. For a start, Plato did not speak in these terms in the discussion with Polus, but instead the art of oratory was unequivocally called a shadow image of a part of the art of politics.[406] Then, secondly, however firmly Plato believed the art of oratory to be twofold, it would still not have been appropriate for him to be seen clearly praising it in the discussion in which he had set out to denigrate it, nor to absolve it on the strength of the crimes he had convicted it of. Saying that it is twofold, and trying to demonstrate that it is flatly worthless are two different things. Surely it is bizarre that, if on the one hand he had succeeded in showing oratory to be a form of flattery, this conclusion would have held firm, but that on the other he should, on proving 538

νειν, ἐπεὶ δ' οὐδαμοῦ τοῦτο διδάξαι δεδύνηται, καταφεύγειν εἰς τὸ διπλοῦν εἶναι λέγειν;

τὸ δὲ δὴ πάντων μέγιστον, εἰ γὰρ ᾤετο χρῆναι τοὺς μὲν ἐπαινεῖν τῶν ῥητόρων, τοὺς δὲ κακῶς λέγειν, τί δή ποθ' ὁ Σωκράτης, αὐτὰ δὴ ταῦθ' ὑπολαβὼν

> ἐξαρκεῖ· εἰ γὰρ καὶ τοῦτ' ἐστὶ διπλοῦν, τὸ μὲν ἕτερον τούτου κολακεία ἂν εἴη καὶ αἰσχρὰ δημηγορία, τὸ δ' ἕτερον καλόν, τὸ παρασκευάζειν ὅπως ὡς βέλτισται ἔσονται τῶν πολιτῶν αἱ ψυχαί, καὶ διαμάχεσθαι λέγοντα τὰ βέλτιστα, εἴτε ἡδίω εἴτε ἀηδέστερ' ἐστὶ τοῖς ἀκούουσιν·

οὕτω θεὶς καὶ διελόμενος πάλιν πρὸς θάτερον φιλονίκως ἀπέκλινεν ἐπειπὼν ὅτι

> ἀλλ' οὐ πώποτε σὺ ταύτην εἶδες τὴν ῥητορικήν· ἢ εἴ τιν' ἔχεις τῶν ῥητόρων τοιοῦτον εἰπεῖν, τί οὐ καὶ ἐμοὶ αὐτὸν ἔφρασας ὅστις ἐστί;

539 μὴ γὰρ ὅτι οὑτωσὶ λέγει τῷ ῥήματι, "οὐ πώποτε εἶδες·" μάλιστα μὲν γὰρ τί σοι τοῦτο διαφέρει, εἰ καὶ μὴ εἶδον, ἔχω δ' εἰπεῖν; ἔπειτ' οὐδὲ οὓς ἐλέγχει δὴ τούτους, τῶν τότε ὄντας ἐλέγχει ῥητόρων, οὐδ' οὓς εἶδεν ὁ Καλλικλῆς, ἀλλ' οὓς ἀκούειν αὐτὸν εἰκὸς εἶναί
540 φησιν. οὐκοῦν ὅτε τούτους ἐλέγχειν πειρᾶται, κατὰ πάντων ἐθέλει λέγειν. οὕτω κατηγορῶν μὲν ὡς ἁπλῶς κακοῦ τῆς ῥητορικῆς ἠναγκάσθη διπλοῦν αὐτὸ θέ-

407 *Grg.* 503a. 408 *Grg.* 503b. 409 *Grg.* 503c, 515e.

completely unable to establish the point, then take refuge in saying that it is twofold?

Most importantly of all, if he thought that it was incumbent to praise some orators and speak ill of others, what on earth was Socrates doing responding in the following terms:

> That is all I need. Even if this is a twofold phenomenon, then presumably in one of its two aspects it would be a form of flattery and shameful demagoguery, though in the other it is something good, namely trying to make the souls of the citizens as good as possible and striving to say what is best, whether your audience enjoys hearing it or not,[407]

but then, once he had posited this and made his distinction, once more showing his avid partisanship for one of the two propositions, with the comment,

> but you have never yet seen this form of the art of oratory—or if you can say that one of the orators was of this kind, why don't you tell me too who he is?[408]

This is, moreover, to say nothing of the fact that he says in 539
so many words "you have never yet seen"—just what difference does it make to you if I have indeed not seen them,
but can name them?—but then convicts as representatives
of contemporary oratory neither these principal objects of
his criticism, nor those whom Callicles had seen, but the
ones he says he is likely to have heard of.[409] So, when he 540
attempts to convict these individuals, he means to denounce the whole class. Thus in denouncing the art of
oratory as an unequivocal evil, he was forced to stipulate

σθαι, θέμενος δὲ διπλοῦν αὖθις αὖ τοῦτ' ἀναιρεῖν πειρᾶται τῷ κατὰ πάντων ἐθέλειν λέγειν. δῆλον δὲ καὶ τοῖς ἀμοιβαίοις. ἔχει γὰρ οὑτωσὶ

> ἀλλὰ μὰ τὸν Δί' οὐκ ἔχω σοι εἰπεῖν τῶν νῦν ῥητόρων οὐδένα.—τί δαί; τῶν παλαιῶν ἔχεις τιν' εἰπεῖν;

δῆλον ὅτι ὡς οὐδ' ἐκείνων οὐδενὸς χρηστοῦ γεγενημένου. τί γὰρ ἂν βουλόμενος ἢ τούτους ἔψεγεν τῶν παλαιῶν ὄντας, ἢ ἐκεῖνον ὅλως εἴ τινα τῶν πάντων
541 εἰπεῖν ἔχει προὐκαλεῖτο; καίτοι πῶς οὐκ ἐναντίον περιφανῶς λέγειν μὲν ὡς οὔπω ταύτην εἶδε τὴν ῥητορικήν, ὅπερ αὐτῷ βούλεται μηδένα πω τοιοῦτον γεγενῆσθαι ῥήτορα, πάλιν δ' ἀποφαίνειν ὡς Ἀριστείδης τοιοῦτος εἴη γεγονώς; τούτων γὰρ ἀνάγκη δήπου θάτερον ψεῦδος εἶναι. καὶ πρὸς τοσοῦτον ἧκεν τοῦ διαφωνεῖν αὐτὸς αὑτῷ ὥσθ' ἅμα μὲν λέγειν ὡς οὐδεὶς Ἀθήνησιν πολίτης εἴη ἀγαθὸς γεγενημένος, ἅμα δ' ὡς καὶ ἄλλοθι τοιοῦτοι γεγόνασι μαρτυρεῖν, καὶ προσμαντεύεσθαί γε ὅτι καὶ γενήσονται.

542 ἴσως δ' ἄν τις κἀκεῖνο θαυμάσειεν, ὅτι τέτταρας μὲν ἐφεξῆς εἶπεν κακῶς, καὶ ταῦτα τῶν Ἑλλήνων οὐ τοὺς φαυλοτάτους, ἑνὸς δὲ πρὸς εὐφημίαν ἐμνήσθη μόνου, καὶ παρῆλθεν μὲν Νικίαν τὸν Νικηράτου, καὶ

that it was twofold; but having stipulated that it was twofold he then once more attempts to cancel this out with his desire to condemn them all. This is clear too from the exchange between the interlocutors, which goes like this:

> I really can't name any present-day orator to you in this capacity—Well, then, can you name one from previous generations?[410]

—clearly on the assumption that none of them had been a good man either. What else could he have had in mind either in censuring those representatives of previous generations, or in challenging his interlocutor to say if he could name any one at all out of the whole collection? But 541
how can it fail to be manifestly contradictory on the one hand to say that he had never yet seen that form of the art of oratory, meaning that an orator of that kind had never yet existed, but then to go back on that and declare that Aristides had been that sort of orator? One or the other of these propositions definitely has to be false.[411] He even reached such an extreme of self-contradiction as simultaneously to assert that no one at Athens had ever been a good citizen, and to testify that there had already been such people elsewhere, and indeed predict that there would be in the future too.

We might perhaps also be surprised by the fact that 542
Plato spoke ill of four men one after the other, men who were moreover not the most worthless of the Greeks, but mentioned one only for praise, thus passing over Nicias

[410] *Grg.* 503b.

[411] This sentence may be a reader's addition: Aristides' focus here is on the contradictoriness of what Plato says, not its falsehood.

ταῦτα τῶν ἐφ' αὑτοῦ ῥητόρων ὄντα, ὅτι μὴ καὶ τούτου πρὸς διαβολὴν μᾶλλον ἐμνημόνευσεν ἐν ᾧ γ' ἐμνημόνευσε μέρει τοῦ λόγου. οὐ γὰρ τῆς γε πολιτείας
543 αὐτοῦ λόγον οὐδένα ἐποιήσατο. καίτοι Νικίας οὕτως ἦν πόρρω τοῦ πρὸς ἡδονὴν τοῖς πολίταις δημηγορεῖν καὶ τοῦ τὰς ἐπιθυμίας συναύξειν αὐτοῖς, ὥστε κρατοῦντας μὲν τῷ προτέρῳ πολέμῳ Λακεδαιμονίων τοσοῦτον ἔπεισεν εἰρήνην ποιήσασθαι καὶ μηδὲν πλέον ζητεῖν, πάλιν δὲ τινῶν τῶν Σωκράτους μὲν ἀκηκοότων πολλὰ δὴ καὶ πολλάκις περὶ τούτων, πειθομένων δ' οὐ πάνυ τοῖς ἐκείνου λόγοις, ἐναγόντων Ἀθηναίους πλεῖν εἰς Σικελίαν καὶ πράγμαθ' αἱρεῖσθαι πρὸς ἅπαντας ἀνθρώπους, ἁπάσας ἠφίει φωνάς, ἀντιλέγων ὑπὲρ τοῦ βελτίστου καὶ διαμαχόμενος ὡς οἷά τις ἂν τῶν ἐπ' ἔσχατον ἡκόντων φιλοσοφίας. εἰ δὲ τοὺς μὲν ὡς τῷ δήμῳ προσκειμένους κόλακας προσεροῦμεν, τοῖς δ' ὡς ὀλιγαρχικοῖς ἐπιτιμήσομεν οὑτωσὶ δι' ἀπορρήτων, καὶ τὰ μὲν οὐκ ὄντα ἐλέγχειν πειρασόμεθα, δι' ὧν δ' ἐλεγχόμεθα ἑκόντες παραλείψομεν, οὐκ ἔστιν ὅπως οὐ λαβήν τινι τῶν ῥητόρων δώσομεν.
544 χρῆν μὲν οὖν ἴσως καὶ Νικίαν εἶναί τι συγχωρῆσαι, κἂν εἰ μὴ ἐπαινεῖν αὐτὸν ἐβούλετο, οὑτωσὶ μεμνημένον, αἰσχυνθῆναί τε παρ' αὐτῷ καὶ τὴν πολιτείαν

---

[412] *Grg.* 472a.

[413] A reference to the so-called Peace of Nicias of 421 BC, concluded in fact following Athenian as well as Spartan reverses: Thuc. 5.13–24.

son of Niceratus, even though he was one of the orators of his time—except that he did mention him, though in the part of the speech where he did so, it was for slander rather than for praise, since he did not have a high opinion of his political achievements.[412] And yet Nicias was so far 543
from addressing his fellow citizens with a view to giving them pleasure, and from stoking up their desires, that when they were so spectacularly victorious over the Spartans in the earlier part of the war, he persuaded them to make peace and to seek no advantage from it,[413] and when subsequently some of Socrates' pupils, who had heard him speak often and at length about these matters, but were not entirely convinced by what he had to say, were trying to induce the Athenians to sail against Sicily and take on the whole world, he unleashed the full force of his eloquence, speaking up against them in favor of the best course and exerting himself in a manner worthy of the greatest of philosophers.[414] If we are going to call the one group flatterers on the grounds that they side with the people, and stigmatize the others in this cryptic manner as oligarchs, and try to convince them of nonexistent crimes while knowingly passing over what proves that we are the ones who are in the wrong, then we will inevitably lay ourselves open to attack by one of the orators. Plato should 544
then perhaps have conceded that Nicias too had some worth, and even if he did not want to praise him, he should have felt some shame at having mentioned him as he did, and should have acknowledged that his political career

414 Thuc. 6.8–14; Aristides' generalizing plural "some of Socrates' pupils" is in fact a reference to Alcibiades (Thuc. 6.8 and 15–18).

αὑτοῦ νομίσαι τοῖς κατὰ πάντων λόγοις ἐμποδὼν εἶναι. εἴτε γὰρ καὶ τοῦτον ἃ τοὺς ἄλλους ἔψεγεν οὐκ
ἀληθῆ λέγων ἂν ἐφαίνετο εἴτ' οὐδὲν ἔχων τοῦτον
αἰτιάσασθαι πάντας ὁμοίως ἔλεγεν κακῶς, οὐδ' οὕτως
545 ἀληθὴς ὁ λόγος. καὶ μὴν ὅτι καὶ τοῦτον κακῶς εἴρηκεν δῆλον. ἔστιν γὰρ εἷς τῶν ἐπ' ἐκείνου ῥητόρων,
τούτους δ' ἅπαντας εἴρηκε δήπου κακῶς.
546 εἰ δ' ἄρα καὶ τὸν Νικίαν εὐκαταφρόνητον ἡγεῖτο,
ἀλλ' οὐχ ὅ γε δήπου Σόλων ἐλάνθανεν αὐτὸν ὅσου[152]
τινὸς ἄξιος γένοιτο ἐπὶ τῶν προτέρων τῇ πόλει. οὐ
γὰρ καὶ περὶ ἐκείνου γ' ἔμελλεν ἐρήσεσθαι τίνα βελτίω τῶν δούλων ἢ τῶν ἐλευθέρων ἐποίησεν, οὐδ' ὡς
ἄνευ τάξεως καὶ κοσμιότητος τὴν πόλιν φόρων καὶ
φλυαριῶν ἐνέπλησεν ὀνειδιεῖν. ἀλλ' εἰ μὴ ἐκεῖνος αὐτοὺς νομίμους καὶ κοσμίους ἐκ τῶν δυνατῶν ἐποίη-
547 σεν, ἄλλος γέ τις ἂν δόξειεν. ἐκεῖνος μέντοι παρὸν
αὐτῷ στασιαζούσης τῆς πόλεως ὁποτέρων βούλοιτο
προστάντι τυραννεῖν, ἀπεχθάνεσθαι μᾶλλον ἀμφοτέροις εἵλετο ὑπὲρ τοῦ δικαίου· καὶ τῶν μὲν πλουσίων
ὅσον καλῶς εἶχεν ἀφεῖλεν, τῷ δήμῳ δ' οὐκ ἔδωκεν
ὅσον ἐβούλετο, ἔστη δ' ἐν μεθορίῳ πάντων ἀν-
δρειότατα καὶ δικαιότατα, ὥσπερ τινὰς ὡς ἀληθῶς ἐκ
γεωμετρίας περιγραπτοὺς φυλάττων ὅρους· καὶ οὔτε

[152] ὅσου Reiske ὡς οὐ *codd.*

posed some obstacle to his condemnation of all orators.
Because if on the one hand he had criticized Nicias on the
same grounds as the others he would clearly have been
telling untruths, and if on the other he had spoken ill of
all of them alike without having anything to charge Nicias
with, his argument would have been false on those terms
too. And it is clear that he did speak ill of Nicias too: he is 545
one of the orators of Plato's time, and Plato undeniably
spoke ill of all of these.

But if he did indeed think Nicias as contemptible as the 546
rest, he was at any rate not unaware how valuable Solon
was to Athens in earlier times. He was certainly not going
to ask in his case what slave or free man he made into a
better person, or to reproach him for abandoning all discipline and good order and filling the city with tribute
money and rubbish.[415] If this man did not make the Athenians as law-abiding and disciplined as could possibly have
been done, then for sure someone else could have claimed
the distinction! Now Solon, although civic strife at Athens 547
offered him the opportunity of putting himself at the head
of whichever of the two factions he wished and wielding
tyrannical power, chose instead to incur the hatred of both
sides in defense of what was just; he took from the rich as
much as it was decent to take and refused to give the
people as much as they wanted, standing in the no man's
land between them with greater courage and justice than
all of them, as if guarding boundary lines drawn in the
truest sense in conformity with the laws of geometry.[416]

[415] *Grg.* 519a, 508a.

[416] Aristides' description of Solon's policy blends allusions to Solon's own words in his frr. 5, 33–34, and 36–37 *IEG* with a nod to *Grg.* 508a.

φόβος τῶν ἰσχυροτέρων οὔτε τιμὴ παρὰ τῶν πολλῶν οὔτ᾽ ἄλλο τοιοῦτον οὐδὲν προηγάγετο αὐτόν, οὐδ᾽ ἐξέστησεν, οὐδ᾽ ἐπῆρεν παρ᾽ ἃ βέλτιστα ἡγεῖτο πρᾶξαί τι. οὕτως οὔτ᾽ αὐτὸς ᾤετο δεῖν τοῦ ἰδίου ἕνεκα τοῦ αὑτοῦ δημηγορεῖν καὶ τοῦ τοῖς ἄλλοις ἀποπιμπλάναι
548 τὰς ἐπιθυμίας παμπληθὲς ἀπεῖχεν. καίτοι τί φησιν Πλάτων; εἰς τοὺς ποιητὰς αὐτὸν τιθέναι. νὴ Δία τῶν τριμέτρων ἕνεκα καὶ τῶν ἐλεγείων. ἔστω ταῦτα. σὺ τοίνυν αὐτὸς φῂς ὅτι εἴ τις τῆς ποιήσεως περιέλοι τὸ μέτρον καὶ τὸν ῥυθμόν, δημηγορία δὴ τὸ λειπόμενόν ἐστιν. ὥστ᾽ εἰ καὶ μηδεπώποτ᾽ ἐφθέγξατο ἐπὶ τοῦ βήματος, τὰ δὲ ποιήματα ᾖδεν μόνα, κατά γε σὲ καὶ τὴν σὴν ψῆφον ἐδημηγόρει. ἢ πρὸς θεῶν ἂν μέν τι δέῃ κακῶς εἰπεῖν ἐκ ποιητικῆς ῥητορικήν, ἕν τι καὶ ταυτὸν εἶναι φήσομεν, ἢ μικρόν τι διαλλάττειν, ὅταν δ᾽ ὡς ἀληθῶς οἱ ποιηταὶ ῥητορεύωσι καὶ τὰ βέλτιστα καὶ τὰ χρησιμώτατα ἀκούειν λέγωσιν, ἄλλο τι τοῦτ᾽ ἤδη φήσομεν εἶναι καὶ διαφέρειν πολλῷ τινι; οὔκουν δίκαιόν γε οὐδ᾽ εἰκός.

549 καίτοι Σόλων τὰ μὲν εἰς Μεγαρέας ἔχοντα ᾆσαι λέγεται, τοὺς δὲ νόμους οὐκ ᾖδεν περιιών, οὐδὲ τοὺς λόγους τοὺς ὑπὲρ τῶν εὐπόρων πρὸς τὸν δῆμον, οὐδὲ τοὺς ὑπὲρ τῶν πολλῶν πρὸς τοὺς πλουσίους οὐκ ᾖδεν, οὐδ᾽ ὅσα ἄλλα ἐπολιτεύετο, οὐκ ᾄδων οὐδ᾽ ἐν μέτροις ἐπολιτεύετο, ἀλλὰ τῷ τῆς ῥητορικῆς τύπῳ καθαρῶς χρώμενος, ἐν οἷς ἅπασι κάλλιστα ἐπέδειξεν ὅτι τῷ γε ὀρθοτάτῳ τῶν λόγων αὐτὸς ἂν εἴη ῥήτωρ καὶ σοφός,

Neither fear of those stronger than him nor popular honor nor anything else of the kind moved him or clouded his wits or induced him to act in any way against what he believed to be for the best. So firmly did he believe that he himself should not speak so as to further his own private interests, and so completely did he abstain from satiating the desires of others. Yet what does Plato say? That 548
he ranks him among the poets.[417] Yes indeed, because of his trimeters and elegiacs! Agreed! But you yourself say that if one were to strip poetry of its meter and rhythm, what remained would be a form of public speaking.[418] Therefore even if Solon never uttered a word from the speaker's platform, and only ever recited his poems, according to you and on your verdict, he would have been a public speaker. Or for heaven's sake, is it the case that, if the need arises to use poetry to denigrate the art of oratory, we are going to say that they are one and the same, or differ only a little, but that when poets truly make speeches and say what is best and most useful to hear, we are now going to say that this is another matter and that the two are very different? That would be both unjust and implausible!

Solon however, though he is said to have delivered his 549
comments on the Megarian situation in verse,[419] did not go around articulating his laws in verse, and did not put all his other political measures into meter and verse either, but instead used oratorical form and oratorical form alone. In all of this he made it beautifully clear that in the strictest possible definition he himself would count as an orator

[417] *Ti.* 21b–c. [418] *Grg.* 502c.
[419] Solon fr. 1 *IEG*; cf. Plut. *Vit. Sol.* 8.1–3.

ἀμφοτέρας γοῦν ἔσχε τὰς ἐπωνυμίας τε καὶ δυνάμεις,
καὶ ὅτι γε ἡ ῥητορικὴ καὶ ἡ νομοθετικὴ τῆς αὐτῆς
εἰσι φύσεως. ἀλλ' οὐ μὰ Δί' οὐχ ἡ ῥητορικὴ τοσούτῳ
χείρων τῆς νομοθετικῆς ὥστε τοῦ δευτέρου καὶ χείρο-
550 νος εἴδωλον εἶναι κατεψευσμένον. καὶ μὴν εἰ τῶν ἄλλων μηδεὶς μηδένα τῶν ἐφ' αὑτοῦ βελτίω ποιήσας
φαίνεται, Σόλων γε καὶ τοὺς μέλλοντας Ἀθηναίων
ἔσεσθαι φαίνεται βελτίους εἰς ὅσον ἐξῆν πεποιηκώς,
καὶ ταῦτά γε ἃ μάλιστα Πλάτων σπουδάζει. νομίμους
γὰρ καὶ δικαίους καὶ τάξιν σῴζοντας ἠξίωσε ποιῆσαι
τὸ καθ' αὑτόν. οἶμαι δ' οὐκ Ἀθηναίους μόνον, ἀλλὰ
καὶ πολλοὺς ἄλλους τῶν Ἑλλήνων, οἳ τοῖς ἐκείνου
551 χρῆσθαι νόμοις ἔγνωσαν. εἶτα τούτου μὲν οὐ μέμνηται Πλάτων, ἑτέρους δ' ἐξετάζει τινάς. καὶ τὸν μὲν
Ἀριστείδην ἐπαινέσας, "γεγόνασιν," ἔφη, "καὶ ἄλλοι,"
καὶ τοσοῦτον ἀρκεῖν ἡγήσατο προσθεῖναι· ἐπ' ἐκείνων
δ' οὐ ταυτὸν τοῦτ' ἐποίησεν, οὐδ' εἰ μηδ' οἷός τ' ἦν
κατασχεῖν ἑαυτόν, ἕνα τιν' αὐτῶν κακῶς εἰπὼν ἀπηλ-
552 λάγη, ἀλλὰ πάντων ἐφεξῆς κατέδραμεν. καίτοι τί τὸ
κωλῦον ἦν ὥσπερ ἐνταῦθα ἑνὸς μνησθεὶς τοὺς ἄλλους
παρῆλθεν, οὕτω κἀκεῖ μὴ πάντας κακῶς λέγειν ὀνομαστί; νῦν δ' ὥσπερ ὡς ἀληθῶς τέταρτον μόριον τῇ
πολιτικῇ νέμων παρὰ τὴν κολακείαν ἑνὸς μὲν ἐπ' εὐφημίᾳ, τεττάρων δ' ἐπὶ τοῖς ἑτέροις ἐμνημόνευσεν.

---

[420] *Grg.* 463d (cf. 464b–66a).
[421] *Grg.* 526a.

and a sage—at all events he bore both names and had both
sets of abilities—and that the art of oratory and the art of
legislation have one and the same essential nature. What
is emphatically not true is that the art of oratory is so inferior to the art of legislation as to be the counterfeit
shadow-image of the second and inferior constituent.[420]
Even if it is not clear that any of the others made any of 550
his contemporaries a better person, it is clear that Solon
for one made future generations of Athenians better people too, as far as could be done, and moreover did so in
the respects that Plato was most keen on. And not only
Athenians, I think, but many other Greeks as well, who
decided to live by his laws. Yet Plato makes no mention of 551
him, but turns his attention to others instead. Once he had
praised Aristides, moreover, he said only "there have been
others too" and thought it was enough to add that little;[421]
but in the case of the Four he did not do the same, nor did
he, if unable to restrain himself, speak ill of just one of
them and have done with it, but ran them all down one
after the other. But what was there to prevent him refrain- 552
ing from abusing them all by name, just as in the other
case he mentioned one and passed over the others? As it
was, however, as if all too truly granting a quarter share to
the science of politics in the comparison with flattery, he
mentioned one man for praise and four for the other kind
of treatment.[422]

422 A very strained point: in *Grg.* 464b–66a, "politics" is the name Plato gives to half the field of science (the half concerned with the soul as opposed to the body), not a quarter (the quarters being "legislation" and "justice"); and in any case, a ratio of 4:1 is not the same as 3:1.

553 ὅτι τοίνυν οὐδ' ὃν ἐπῄνεσεν οὐδαμῶς ἐν καιρῷ τοῖς λόγοις ἐπῄνεσεν τοῖς ἑαυτοῦ, ἀλλὰ κἀνταῦθα οὗ ἥκιστα αὐτῷ συνέφερεν ἐμνημόνευσεν, ὑπερβολὴ μὲν εἶναι δόξει τις, ὅμως δ' ἔγωγε καὶ τοῦτο οὐ χαλεπῶς οἴομαι δείξειν. κατηγόρηκεν γὰρ τοῦ Μιλτιάδου καὶ Κίμωνος καὶ Θεμιστοκλέους δὴ καὶ Περικλέους, ὅτι τῷ δήμῳ προσέκρουσαν, καὶ μέγιστον τοῦτο σύμβολον πεποίηται τοῦ μηδὲν βελτίους ὑπ' αὐτῶν Ἀθηναίους γεγονέναι, προσῆκον, εἴπερ γε ἦσαν αὐτοὶ δίκαιοι καὶ δικαίους ἐποίουν. τὸν δὲ Ἀριστείδην ἐπῄ-
554 νεκεν ὡς καλὸν κἀγαθὸν καὶ δίκαιον. φαίνεται δὲ καὶ οὗτος οὐδὲν πραοτέρων τῶν Ἀθηναίων τυχὼν εἰς αὐτόν, ἀλλὰ καὶ αὐτὸς ἐξοστρακισθεὶς εὖ καὶ καλῶς, καὶ νὴ Δί', ὡς ἐγᾦμαι, πρότερος μὲν τοῦ Κίμωνος, πρότερος δὲ καὶ τοῦ Θεμιστοκλέους. ἑλοῦ δὴ κἀν-
555 ταῦθα ὁπότερον βούλει δυοῖν. εἰ μὲν γὰρ ἐκ τῶν συμφορῶν δεῖ τοὺς ἄνδρας θεωρεῖν, κἂν ὁ δῆμός του καταψηφίσηται, φαῦλον εὐθέως ἡγεῖσθαι, οὐδὲν βελτίων ἐκείνων οὗτος· οὐδὲ γὰρ αὐτὸς ἀθῷος φαίνεται διαφυγών, ἀλλὰ ταὐτὰ παθὼν ἐκείνων ἐνίοις· εἰ δ' αὖ μηδὲν κωλύει τὸν Ἀριστείδην χρηστὸν νομίζεσθαι, μηδ' εἰ πολλάκις ἐξωστρακίσθη, τί λέγεις κατ' ἐκείνων ὡς ἰσχυρὸν τὸ προσκροῦσαι; τὸ γὰρ αὐτὸ δίκαιον ἐπ' ἀμφοῖν, καὶ οὐδὲ αὐτὸς ἐκεῖνος ἄλλως ἄν, εἰ περιῆν, ἔφη, δίκαιός γε ὤν, ὡς σὺ φῄς. ἢ τοίνυν καὶ τοῦτον ψέγειν ἢ μηδ' ἐκείνους αἰτιᾶσθαι προσῆκον ἐκ τῶν αὐτῶν δείκνυται.

It will look as if I am going too far, but all the same I 553
think it will not be difficult to show also that even in the
case of the one he praised, Plato did not deliver his praise
opportunely for his own argument, but in this case as well
brought in what it was least advantageous for him to mention. He arraigned Miltiades, Cimon, Themistocles and
Pericles on the grounds that they fell foul of the people,
and made this his weightiest proof of the failure of the
Athenians to become better people under their influence,
as should have happened if they themselves really were
just men and made others just; but Aristides he praised as
virtuous and just. But Aristides too found the Athenians 554
not a whit gentler to him than they were to the others: he
too was ostracized in good and proper form, and indeed,
I think, before Cimon, and before Themistocles too. Here 555
you can again choose whichever you wish of two alterna-
tives. If we have to assess our men on the strength of the
disasters they endured, and must if the people condemn
someone immediately think him worthless, then Aristides
is no better than the others, since it is clear that he did not
emerge unscathed either, but suffered the same fate as
some of them. But if on the other hand there is nothing to
prevent Aristides being thought a good man, even if he
was ostracized many times, why do you bring up these
men's collision with the people against them as if it was a
strong point in your case? The rights and wrongs were the
same in both instances, and not even Aristides himself
would say otherwise if he were still alive, at least not if he
was the just man you say he was.[423] One and the same set
of considerations shows that the proper course is either to
criticize him too, or not to accuse them either.

[423] *Grg.* 526b.

556 ὡς τοίνυν καὶ πάντας ἐπαινεῖ λαμπρῶς καὶ οὐ μόνον ἐξ ὧν τῆς αἰτίας ἀφῆκεν αὐτοὺς ἣν ᾐτιάσατο, οὐδ' ἐξ ὧν τῷ γε Ἀριστείδῃ τὴν πρέπουσαν εὐφημίαν ἀπέδωκεν, οὐδὲν κύριόν ἐστι τῶν βλασφημιῶν, ἀλλὰ καὶ ἐξ ὧν ἄντικρυς ταὐτὰ ἐμοὶ φθέγγεται, περὶ τούτων βραχὺς ἀρκέσει μοι λόγος. ὁ γὰρ τοὺς Μαραθῶνι προκινδυνεύσαντας ἐπαινῶν εἰς ἀρετὴν καὶ φάσκων πατέρας τῆς ἐλευθερίας τοῖς Ἕλλησιν εἶναι, καὶ προσέτι γε τῇ ἠπείρῳ πάσῃ, καὶ πάλιν τοὺς τὰ δεύτερα ἐκδεξαμένους ἐγκωμιάζων, τοὺς ἐπ' Ἀρτεμισίῳ καὶ Σαλαμῖνι ναυμαχήσαντας, καὶ τούς γε εἰς Κύπρον καὶ Παμφυλίαν πλεύσαντας, καὶ βεβαίους τῆς ἐλευθερίας τοῖς Ἕλλησι στήσαντας τοὺς ὅρους, καὶ τοὺς Ἕλληνας αὖ τῆς ἀγνωμοσύνης αἰτιασάμενος τοὺς ἐπὶ τὴν γῆν ἐκείνων στρατεύσαντας, καὶ τοὺς ἑλόντας τοὺς ἡγουμένους αὐτῶν ἐπαινῶν τὰ πρέποντα, καὶ λόγον πανηγυρικὸν διεξιὼν αὐτοκέλευστος ἐπ' αὐτοῖς, τί ἄλλο οὗτος ἢ τὸν Μιλτιάδην καὶ τὸν Θεμιστοκλέα καὶ τὸν Κίμωνα καὶ τὸν Περικλέα κοσμεῖ τοῖς λόγοις τούτοις; ὅταν γὰρ τὰ πολιτεύματ' αὐτῶν ἐπαινῇ, πῶς οὐκ αὐτοὺς ἐπαινεῖ; οὐ γὰρ ἐκεῖνό γ' ἔστιν εἰπεῖν, ὡς ἃ τοῖς πεισθεῖσιν ἀρετῆς ἔχει δείγματα, ταῦτ' ἐν κακίᾳ χρὴ κατὰ τῶν πεισάντων λαμβάνειν, οὐδ' ὡς τοὺς μὲν διακονήσαντας ὡς ἀγαθοὺς ἄνδρας ἐπαινεῖν, τοὺς δ' εἰσηγησαμένους ταῦτα καὶ συμβουλεύσαντας διακόνους πειρᾶσθαι τῷ λόγῳ ποιεῖν· οὐδ' ὧν αἱ προαιρέσεις τῆς ἐλευθερίας τοῖς Ἑλ-

Now to show that Plato did indeed praise them all in glowing terms, and that it follows not only from the fact that he absolved them of the charges he brought against them and the fact that he gave Aristides at least the praise due to him, but also from the fact that he says exactly the same as me, that none of his calumnies bears any authority. A few words will suffice for this, for if a man praises those who once risked their lives at Marathon for their heroism and asserts that they are the fathers of Greek freedom, and moreover the freedom of the whole continent, and also lauds the men who took up the second challenge, the men who fought at sea at Artemisium and Salamis, and indeed the men who sailed on the expeditions to Cyprus and Pamphylia and set the frontiers of Greek liberty firmly in place, and again accuses the other Greeks of ingratitude in marching against their country, and gives all due praise to those who captured their leaders, and of his own accord delivers a panegyric on them,[424] what else is he doing but glorifying Miltiades, Themistocles, Cimon, and Pericles with these words of his? Because when he praises their political achievements, how can he not be praising them too? It certainly cannot be said that what counts as a sign of virtue in those who have been persuaded into a course of action has to be taken as a proof of vice in those who did the persuading and used to discredit them; nor that one should praise the underlings as good men, but try by one's words to make those who themselves led and advised them in this into underlings; nor yet that one should say that those whose choices of policy 556

[424] In the speech of Aspasia in *Menex.* 240c–46a.

λησιν ἦρξαν, τούτους ὡς ταῖς τῶν πολιτῶν ἐπιθυμίαις ἐδούλευον λέγειν.

557 εἰ μὲν γὰρ ἄλλως ταῦτ' ἐστὶν λόγου χάρις τε καὶ ἡδονή, τί τῆς ῥητορικῆς ταῦτα κατηγορεῖ; καὶ τί τῶν κολάκων εἷς γίγνεται λέγων τὰ ἡδίω πρὸ τῶν ὄντων, καὶ ταῦτα μηδεμιᾶς ἀνάγκης ἐπούσης; εἰ δ' ἐφ' ἅπασι δικαίοις καὶ μετὰ τῆς ἀληθείας εἴρηται, τίνι χρὴ μείζονι λῦσαι τὰς βλασφημίας; ἢ τίνα καλλίω ποιήσασθαι μάρτυρα αὐτοῦ Πλάτωνος, ὅταν ἐνταυθοῖ μὲν καὶ παραχρῆμα ἀφιεὶς φαίνηται τῆς αἰτίας αὐτούς, ἑτέρωθι δὲ καὶ καθάπαξ ἐγκωμιάζων καὶ τὸν Στησίχορον μιμούμενος τῇ παλινῳδίᾳ;

558 καὶ μὴν καὶ τοὺς νόμους γε τιθεὶς [τῶν Μηδικῶν][153] ἄλλα τε δὴ <. . . . .>[154] περὶ τῆς πολιτείας τῆς κατ' ἐκείνους τοὺς ῥήτορας ἥκιστα τοῖς τῆς κολακείας ἐγκλήμασι συμβαίνοντα καὶ ὅτι εἰ μὴ τὸ Ἀθηναίων καὶ Λακεδαιμονίων διανόημα ἔσωσε τοὺς Ἕλληνας, τῆς γε ἄλλης Ἑλλάδος οὐδαμῶς ἄν τις εὐσχήμονα
559 κατηγοροίη, δίκαια λέγων καὶ τὰ ὄντα. οὐκοῦν τοῖς γε Ἀθηναίοις εὐσχημόνως ταῦτα ἐπράττετο· εἰ δὲ εὐσχημόνως, καὶ τεταγμένως· εἰ δὲ τεταγμένως, καὶ κοσμίως. κοσμίως ἄρα ἦγον αὐτοὺς οἱ κεκοσμηκότες καὶ οὔτε αὐτοὶ ᾤοντο δεῖν λέγειν εἰκῇ οὔτ' ἐκείνους πράττοντας ὅ τι τύχοιεν περιορᾶν. οὐκ ἄρα χωρὶς σω-

[153] *del.* Reiske
[154] *lac. stat.* Reiske (e.g. διεξέρχεται)

were responsible for the freedom of Greece were themselves the slaves of their fellow citizens' desires.

If all this was simply idle verbal entertainment and 557
self-indulgence, then why did he attack oratory as he did? And why does he turn himself into one of the flatterers by saying what will give pleasure rather than what is true, when there is no pressing necessity to do so too? But if it was said truthfully and with full justification, what more powerful argument is needed to refute his slanders? Who better to take as our witness than Plato, given that it is evident—immediately evident, indeed—that in this context he absolves our men of blame, and that elsewhere, in imitation of Stesichorus in his *Palinode*,[425] he straightforwardly praises them?

When he is making his laws, moreover, he says a num- 558
ber of things about political arrangements in the time of those orators that consort very badly with the charge of flattery,[426] and in particular observes that if the Athenians' and Spartans' resolve had not saved the Greeks, it would have been impossible to say anything creditable about the rest of Greece, which it is only fair and realistic of him to
do.[427] It was thus creditable of the Athenians to act in this 559
way; if it was creditable, it was also disciplined; and if it was disciplined, it was also orderly. Therefore those who marshaled them led them in an orderly manner, in the belief that they themselves should never say anything without a definite purpose and that they should not passively allow the people to act haphazardly either. They did

425 Stesichorus fr. 192 *PMG*, cited by Plato in *Phdr.* 243a.

426 The translation here follows Reiske's emendations of an obviously faulty MS text.

427 *Leg.* 692e–93a.

φροσύνης φόρων καὶ συμμάχων καὶ τῶν τοιούτων ἐνέπλησαν τὴν πόλιν, εἴπερ δεῖ τοῖς Πλάτωνος πείθεσθαι λόγοις καὶ νόμοις.

560 ἔτι δ' αὐτὸ δείξω σαφέστερον καὶ κατὰ ῥῆμα ἐπεξιών· ἔστι γὰρ οὕτως ἔχοντα

> ἡμῖν γὰρ κατ' ἐκεῖνον τὸν χρόνον, ὅτε ἡ Περσῶν ἐπίθεσις τοῖς Ἕλλησιν, ἴσως δὲ σχεδὸν ἅπασι τοῖς τὴν Εὐρώπην οἰκοῦσιν ἐγίγνετο, πολιτεία τε ἦν παλαιὰ καὶ ἐκ τιμημάτων ἀρχαί τινες τεττάρων, καὶ δεσπότις ἐνῆν τις αἰδώς, δι' ἣν δουλεύοντες τοῖς τότε νόμοις ζῆν ἠθέλομεν.

561 οὐκοῦν ὅταν αἰδουμένους μοι διδῷς αὐτούς, ἐπιεικεῖς ἄνδρας εἶναι δίδως.

> καὶ πρὸς τούτοις δὴ τὸ μέγεθος τοῦ στόλου κατά τε γῆν καὶ κατὰ θάλατταν γενόμενον φόβον ἄπορον ἐμβαλὸν δουλείαν ἔτι μείζονα ἐποίησεν ἡμᾶς τοῖς τε ἄρχουσι καὶ τοῖς νόμοις δουλεῦσαι.

εὖ γε, ὦ φίλτατε Ἑλλήνων. τόν τε γὰρ δῆμον οἷς μάλιστα προσήκει δουλεῦσαι λέγεις ἄρχουσι καὶ νόμοις, τούς τε προεστηκότας αὐτῶν ἄρχειν καὶ κρατεῖν, οὐ κολακεύειν οὐδὲ ἄρχεσθαι.

> καὶ διὰ ταῦτα πάνθ' ἡμῖν ξυνέπεσεν πρὸς ἡμᾶς αὐτοὺς σφοδρὰ φιλία.

not therefore intemperately fill the city with tribute money and allies and suchlike,[428] if we are to believe Plato's arguments in the *Laws*.

I will prove the point still more clearly by quoting his 560
exact words. This is how they go:

> In those days, at the time of the Persian onslaught on Greece, and you might say on pretty well the whole population of Europe, we Athenians had an ancient constitution and magistracies based on four property classes; this arrangement was marked by a dominating reverence, which caused us to live as willing slaves to the laws then in existence.[429]

So when you grant me that they showed reverence, you 561
grant that they were decent men.

> Moreover, the vast size of the Persian land and sea force filled us with a helpless dread and made us still more firmly subservient to our magistrates and our laws.[430]

Well said, dearest of the Greeks! Because what you are saying is that the people were subservient to the very things it was most proper for them to be subservient to, their magistrates and their laws, and that those who led them ruled them and exercised power over them, rather than flattering them and being ruled by them.

> And because of all of this, a tight bond of reciprocal friendship developed among us.[431]

428 *Grg.* 519a. 429 *Leg.* 698b. 430 *Leg.* 698b–c.
431 *Leg.* 698c.

ταῦτα πάνθ᾽ ὡς ἀληθῶς εὐφημίας μεστὰ καὶ κατὰ τοῦ
562 δήμου καὶ κατὰ τῶν προεστηκότων. ἔπειτα προελθὼν

> ἐπὶ δὲ τῆς ἐλπίδος—φησίν—ὀχούμενοι ταύτης εὕρισκον καταφυγὴν αὐτοῖς εἰς αὐτοὺς μόνους εἶναι καὶ τοὺς θεούς.

οὐκοῦν ἐσωφρόνουν πάντες γε, ὡς ἔγωγε οἶμαι, μᾶλλον.

> ταῦτ᾽ οὖν αὐτοῖς πάντα φιλίαν ἀλλήλων ἐποίει, ὁ φόβος ὁ τότε[155] παρὼν ὅ τ᾽ ἐκ τῶν νόμων τῶν ἔμπροσθεν γεγονώς, ὃν[156] δουλεύοντες τοῖς πρόσθεν[157] νόμοις ἐκέκτηντο, ἣν αἰδῶ πολλάκις ἐν τοῖς ἄνω λόγοις εἴπομεν, καὶ ᾗ δουλεύειν ἔφαμεν δεῖν τοὺς μέλλοντας ἀγαθοὺς ἔσεσθαι.

ἀπήλλαξας ἅπασαν ἀμφισβήτησιν, ἀγαθοὺς προσειπὼν τοὺς ἄνδρας, καὶ ταῦτα οὐ μόνον αὐτούς, ἀλλὰ
563 καὶ τοὺς προσέχοντας αὐτοῖς. πῶς οὖν ἢ ᾽κείνους ὡς διεφθαρμένους, ἢ τούτους ὡς διεφθαρκότας αἰτιᾷ; ἢ πῶς ἔνεστιν μὴ ἀγαθοὺς εἶναι οἷς τὸ δουλεύειν ἀγαθὸν εἶναι τίθης;[158]

564 εἶεν. κοινῇ μὲν δὴ τοὺς ἄνδρας οὕτως ἐπῄνεκεν ἡμῖν λέγων τοὺς τότε προστάντας, πανηγυρίζων τε καὶ νομοθετῶν, ἰδίᾳ δ᾽ αὖ τὸν Περικλέα ποῦ καὶ πῶς, ὃν

[155] τότε Iunt. *cum codd. Plat.* ὅ τε *codd.*
[156] ὅν *codd. Plat.* ᾧ *codd.*
[157] πρόσθεν *codd. Plat.* ἔμπροσθεν *codd.*
[158] τίθης Reiske τίθησιν *codd.*

This is all truly replete with praise both for the people and
for their leaders. Then further on he says 562

> Buoyed up by this hope, they discovered that their only refuge lay in themselves and the gods.[432]

All the more true then is it, in my view at any rate, that they were all of them exercising the virtue of temperance.

> All of this then created a reciprocal friendship among them—the combination of the fear that then possessed them with that engendered by the laws they had beforehand, acquired through their subservience to those earlier laws, a fear that we referred to repeatedly above as reverence and which we said those who were going to be good people had to be in thrall to.[433]

With this he abandons all ambiguity and calls the men
good, and what is more not only them but also those who
looked to them. How then can you fault either the latter 563
as corrupted or the former as having corrupted them? And
how is it possible for those for whom you say it was a good
thing to be subservient not to be good people?

Very well then. We have thus established that Plato has 564
praised our men as a group, referring to them as those who
led the people at that time, in both his panegyric oration
and in his work of legislation; but where and how was it
that he did the same for Pericles individually, when he has

[432] *Leg.* 699b.
[433] *Leg.* 699c.

ἐνταῦθα προθυμότατα εἴρηκεν κακῶς; τὸ μὲν τοίνυν ὅπου τί δεῖ λέγειν; τὸ δὲ ὅπως εἰρήσεται.

προσπεσὼν γάρ, οἶμαι, τοιούτῳ ὄντι Ἀναξαγόρᾳ μετεωρολογίας ἐμπλησθεὶς καὶ ἐπὶ φύσιν νοῦ τε καὶ διανοίας ἀφικόμενος, ὧν γε δὴ πέρι τὸν πολὺν λόγον ἐποιεῖτο Ἀναξαγόρας, ἐντεῦθεν εἵλκυσεν ἐπὶ τὴν τῶν λόγων τέχνην τὸ πρόσφορον αὐτῇ.

565 οὐκοῦν ἐνταυθοῖ δύο μαρτυρεῖ, καὶ τὴν ῥητορικὴν οὐκ ἄτεχνον τριβὴν εἶναι, ἀλλὰ τέχνην περὶ λόγους, καὶ τὸν Περικλέα κράτιστον ἐν αὐτῇ, καὶ τὴν αἰτίαν προστίθησιν. τοσοῦτον ἀπέχει τοῦ κολακείαν ἢ δια-
566 κονίαν ὀνειδίζειν. οὐκοῦν οὐχ ἡ ῥητορικὴ φαῦλον ἐκ τῆς τοῦ Περικλέους πολιτείας φαίνεται, ἀλλ' ὁ Περικλῆς ἄριστος τὴν ῥητορικὴν ἐν τουτοισὶ τοῖς λόγοις ἐγγέγραπται.

567 φαίνεται τοίνυν αἰτιασάμενος μὲν κοινῇ τοὺς ἄνδρας ὡς διακόνους καὶ κόλακας, πάλιν δὲ τῆς αἰτίας ἀφιεὶς αὐτούς, τούτου δ' ἕνεκ' αἰτιασάμενος, τοῦ μηδένα δόξαι ῥήτορα χρηστὸν Ἀθήνησι γεγονέναι, πάλιν δ' αὖ τῶν ῥητόρων ἕνα τῶν Ἀθήνησιν ἐπαινῶν, καὶ ταῦτα τοῖς αὐτοῖς ἐνεχόμενον οἷσπερ οὗτοι, τὸν Ἀριστείδην λέγω, καὶ δυοῖν θάτερον, ἢ μὴ προσήκοντα ἐπαινούμενον, ἢ ἐκείνους δεικνύντα ἃ μὴ προσῆκεν ἀκηκοότας, ἔτι δ' οὐ τοῦτον μόνον, ἀλλὰ

so very enthusiastically abused him here in the *Gorgias*? As for the "where," is there really any need to say? But I will explain how.

> This was, I believe, because he fell in with Anaxagoras, who was just such a man, and this filled him with elevated lore and brought him to an understanding of the nature of mind and purpose, which were topics on which Anaxagoras had much to say, and drawing from this he applied to the art of speaking what was appropriate to it.[434]

In this passage, then, he testifies to two things, that the art 565
of oratory is not some unscientific knack, but a true science of words, and that Pericles was supreme in it, and he supplies the explanation too. That is how far he is from
uttering any reproaches of flattery or servility. In this way, 566
rather than the art of oratory being shown up as something worthless on the strength of Pericles' political career, Pericles is recorded in these words as the best practitioner of the art of oratory.

It is thus clear that, having accused the Four jointly as 567
lackeys and flatterers, Plato then absolved them again of the charge, and having accused them on the grounds that there seemed never to have been a good orator at Athens, he then turned around and praised one of the orators at Athens, one who moreover was enmeshed in the same troubles as they were, namely Aristides. This means one of two things, either that he was praising someone who did not deserve it, or that he was demonstrating that the Four were being undeservedly abused. Moreover, in another

434 *Phdr.* 270a.

καὶ πάντας ἐφεξῆς αὐτοὺς ἐπῃνεκὼς ἑτέρωθι, ἡνίκ' οὐδεμιᾶς ἐστι φιλονικίας, καὶ πάλιν γ' ἰδίᾳ τὸν Περικλέα φάσκων τελεώτατον εἰς τὴν ῥητορικὴν γεγονέ-
568 ναι. πῶς οὖν ἄν τις νεμεσῴη δικαίως ἡμῖν, ὅταν αὐτὸς Πλάτων ὡς ἀληθῆ λέγομεν ἐπιψηφίζῃ; ἃ μὲν γὰρ οὗτος αἰτιᾶται τοὺς ἄνδρας παρ' ἡμῶν οὐχ ὁμολογεῖται, ἃ δ' ἡμεῖς ἐπαινοῦμεν, τούτοις ἐστὶν αὐτὸς σύμψηφος. ὥστε τὸ νικᾶν ἡμᾶς παρ' ἀμφοῖν ὁμολογεῖται, τὸ δ' ἐκεῖνον οὐδὲ παρ' αὐτοῦ συμβαίνει.

569 εἰς τοσοῦτον δ' ἥκει τοῦ τἀναντία τῶν ὄντων λέγειν ὥστε φησὶν ὡς Περικλῆς παραλαβὼν Ἀθηναίους ἡμερωτέρους ἀγριωτέρους καὶ χαλεπωτέρους ἀπέδει-
570 ξεν, καὶ ταῦτα εἰς αὐτὸν ὃν ἥκιστα ἐβούλετο. πῶς, ὦ μακάριε; εἰ γάρ ἐστιν ἀληθὴς ὁ σὸς λόγος ὡς Μιλτιάδην γε μικροῦ εἰς τὸ βάραθρον ἐνέβαλον, πᾶν τοὐναντίον ἤδη φαίνεται, ὁ μὲν Θεμιστοκλῆς ἀγριωτάτους παραλαβὼν ἡμερωτέρους ποιήσας, τὸ γοῦν ἐξοστρακισθῆναι, καὶ πρός γε, εἰ βούλει, φυγῇ ζημιωθῆναι, κέρδος παρ' ἐκείνην τὴν συμφοράν. πάλιν δ' ὁ Κίμων ἐξωστρακίσθη μέν, φυγῇ δὲ οὐ προσεζημιώθη, ἀλλὰ καὶ κατῆλθε πρὸ τοῦ χρόνου. οὕτως ἔτι πραοτέροις οὗτος ἐχρήσατο· ὁ δ' αὖ Περικλῆς ἔτι τούτου μετριώτερα δυστυχήσας, ὅστις χρήματα ἐζημιώθη μόνον καὶ πάλιν ὁ[159] αὐτὸς ἦν τῇ τάξει καὶ ταῖς τιμαῖς. οὕτως ἐκ τραχυτέρων καὶ χαλεπωτέρων ἀεὶ πραότεροι καὶ ῥᾴους φαίνονται γεγενημένοι, καὶ σχε-

[159] *add.* Dindorf

work, where there was no question of any competitiveness, he praised not that man alone but all of them together, and again Pericles individually with the assertion that he was supremely accomplished in the art of oratory.[435] How then could it be justifiable for anyone to bear 568
me any ill will, when Plato himself endorses the truth of what I say? His accusations against these men do not meet with my agreement, whereas my praise for them is supported by him. Thus both of us agree that I am the winner, but not even he agrees that he is.

So comprehensively does he assert the opposite of the 569
truth that he says that Pericles, having inherited the Athenians in a milder state, made them more savage and harsher, and what is more toward the one he least desired.[436] How so, my dear fellow? If what you say is true 570
and they nearly threw Miltiades into the execution pit,[437] then the complete reverse can be seen to be the case. Themistocles for a start evidently inherited the Athenians in a more savage state and made them milder, at least if being ostracized and also, if you wish to add this, being punished with exile, is a gain compared to that other fate. Then Cimon, though ostracized, was not also punished with exile, and even returned before the stipulated time, thus finding them calmer still. Pericles in his turn experienced a still more moderate degree of misfortune, since he was only punished with a fine and was restored to the same rank and privileges as before. That is how clear it is that from being relatively harsher and harder to manage they grew ever calmer and more tractable; Pericles found

435 *Phdr.* 269e.
436 *Grg.* 515e–16c.
437 *Grg.* 516d–e.

δὸν πάντων ἐπιεικεστάτοις αὐτοῖς ὁ Περικλῆς χρησάμενος καὶ ἀποδείξας ἡμερωτέρους ἢ παρέλαβεν. πρὸς ταῦτ᾽ ἔστων οἱ δίκαιοι καὶ ἥμεροι, καὶ Ὅμηρος μαρ-
571 τυρείτω, προστίθει γάρ. εἰκότως ἄρα καὶ ζῶντα ἐτίμων αὐτὸν καὶ τεθνεῶτα ἐπόθουν καὶ προαχθέντες[160] μετέγνωσαν.

572 ὃ τοίνυν ἄξιον μετὰ τῶν ἄλλων ἐπισημήνασθαι, οὕτω γὰρ καὶ σαφῶς τὰ δίκαια ἐπαινέσας τὸν Περικλέα δι᾽ ὧν ἐπεδείξαμεν ἀρτίως πάλιν ἀλλαχοῦ φαυλίζων φαίνεται. αἰτιασάμενος γὰρ τὸν Ἀλκιβιάδην ἀμαθίᾳ συνοικεῖν καὶ φήσας οὐ μόνον αὐτὸν τοῦτο πεπονθέναι, ἀλλὰ καὶ τοὺς πολλοὺς τῶν τὰ τῆς πόλεως πραττόντων, κατασκευάσας κἀνταῦθα ὁδόν τινα αὑτῷ κατὰ τοῦ Περικλέους, πειρᾶται κἀκείνῳ τὴν αὐτὴν αἰτίαν περιάπτειν, οὐδὲν προκαλυπτόμενος, ἀλλ᾽ ὡς τὸ λεγόμενον δὴ τοῦτο, οὔτε γράμματα οὔτε νεῖν
573 εἰδότα ἐλέγχειν ἀξιῶν. καίτοι χωρὶς τοῦ μὴ ὁμολογεῖν ταῦτα ἐκείνοις, πότερον κρεῖττον ἦν, εἴπερ καὶ τἀναντία ἔδει λέγειν περὶ τοῦ ἀνδρός, πρὸς μὲν τὸν Φαῖδρον τὸν Μυρρινούσιον καὶ μηδὲν προσήκοντα τὰ δυσχερέστατα εἰπεῖν, πρὸς δὲ τὸν Ἀλκιβιάδην ἐκεῖνα τὰ ἐπιεικέστερα, ἢ πρὸς τὸν Φαῖδρον ἐπαινέσαντα κακῶς λέγειν πρὸς ἐκεῖνον; ἐγὼ μὲν ἐκεῖνο οἶμαι. ἐλέγχειν μὲν γὰρ δήπου καὶ τοῦτον κἀκεῖνον βουλε-

160 προσαχθεσθέντες TQ^2U^2γρ. προαχθέντες *cett.*

438 Apparently, a reference to the Homeric formula "savage and not just" (*Od.* 6.120, etc), following *Grg.* 516c.

them more or less the most reasonable people on earth, and made them tamer than he had inherited them. In the light of this let it be granted that "the just are also gentle" and let Homer be our witness (please add him too).[438] It 571
was then entirely plausible that they should have honored Pericles in life and longed for him when he died and repented when induced to do so.[439]

572 Along with everything else it deserves to be emphasized that, having thus clearly praised Pericles as he deserved in the terms I demonstrated just now, there is another place where he once more clearly belittles him.[440] Accusing Alcibiades of living a life of ignorance and asserting that this experience was not unique to him but shared by the majority of those responsible for the conduct of the city's affairs, here too he furnishes himself with a means of attacking Pericles and he tries to hang the same charge on him as well, without any attempt to veil the point, but as if he thought himself to be showing him up as unable, as the saying goes, either to read and write or to swim. Yet, 573
quite apart from the issue of inconsistency between the two passages, would it have been a better idea, if he really had to say contradictory things about the man, to say the most unpleasant of them to Phaedrus, who came from Myrrhine and had no connection to him,[441] and the more reasonable ones to Alcibiades, or to praise him to Phaedrus but speak ill of him to the latter? I for one would think the former. Without doubt, he wants to show that both of them are in the wrong, and it cannot be said that he wants

439 Behr here accepts an alternative manuscript reading giving the sense "repented of their discontent toward him."

440 *Alc. I* 118b–19a.

441 *Phdr.* 244a, 270a.

ται καὶ οὐκ ἔνεστ᾽ εἰπεῖν ὡς τὸν Ἀλκιβιάδην μέν, τὸν
Φαῖδρον δὲ οὔ. ὥστ᾽ εἰ πρὸς τοῦτον διὰ τοῦτο κατη-
574 γόρηκε τοῦ Περικλέους, εἰκὸς ἦν καὶ πρὸς ἐκεῖνον. τὸ
διάφορον δὲ οὐ μικρόν. πρῶτον μὲν γὰρ περὶ συγγε-
νοῦς πρὸς τοῦτον ἐβλασφήμει καὶ ἐπιτρόπου, καίτοι
ὥσπερ οὐκ ἦν εἰκὸς τὸν πατέρα αὐτοῦ πρὸς αὐτὸν
ψέγειν, οὐδ᾽ εἰ φαυλότατος τῶν πολιτῶν ἦν, οὕτως
οὐδὲ τὸν θεῖον κακίζειν, οὐδ᾽ εἰ συνῄδει τι τοιοῦτον,
εἰς καιρὸν ἐγίγνετο. οὐ γὰρ ὁμοίως ἐκείνῳ τε κακῶς
ἀκούειν καὶ τούτῳ τῶν κατ᾽ ἐκείνου λόγων ἀκούειν
575 προσῆκεν. ἔπειτα πρὸς ἄνθρωπον ἐγίγνονθ᾽ οἱ λόγοι
μὴ ὅτι Περικλέους ῥᾳδίως ἂν ὑπερφρονήσαντα, ἀλλὰ
τοιοῦτον ὥσθ᾽ ὅ γ᾽ Αἰσχίνης φησὶν περὶ αὐτοῦ ὅτι
κἂν τοῖς δώδεκα θεοῖς ἥδιστα ἐπετίμησεν. τοσοῦτον
αὐτῷ φρονήματος περιῆν καὶ τοῦ μηδένα μηδενὸς
ἄξιον εἶναι νομίζειν. διόπερ καὶ ὅ γ᾽ ἐκείνου Σωκράτης
οὐ τὴν αὐτὴν ἐτράπετο. ἀλλὰ τί φησίν;

> γνοὺς οὖν αὐτὸν ἐγὼ ζηλοτύπως ἔχοντα πρὸς Θεμιστοκλέα,

ἔπειτ᾽ ἐστὶν ὁ τοῦ Θεμιστοκλέους ἔπαινος, δυοῖν ἕνεκεν ὀρθῶς ἔχων οἶμαι, τῆς τε ἀληθείας καὶ τοῦ καιρὸν
576 ἔχειν τῷ μειρακίῳ τοὺς λόγους. καὶ οὐ κακῶς λέγει
τὸν Θεμιστοκλέα παρόντος ἐκείνου, ὅπως μὴ ἔτι μᾶλλον ἀκούων διαφθείροιτο, οὐδέ γε εἰς παραμυθίας
μέρος αὐτῷ κατατίθεται τὸ μὴ μόνον αὐτὸν τῇ ἀμαθίᾳ

442 Aeschin. *Alcibiades* fr. 5 Dittmar = 46 [fr. 5] Giannantoni.

to do this to Alcibiades but not to Phaedrus. So if he has
accused Pericles on these grounds to the one, it would be
reasonable to do so also to the other. The difference be- 574
tween the two cases is however not a small one. In the first
place, to Alcibiades he was slandering a kinsman and a
legal guardian, even though, just as it would not have been
reasonable behavior to criticize his father to him even if
he was the most worthless citizen of them all, so it was
inappropriate to abuse his uncle too, even if he knew
something of the kind to be true of him. It was equally
inappropriate for the one to be ill spoken of and for the
other to hear what was being said to his discredit. Sec- 575
ondly, these words were being delivered to a man who
would not only have found it easy to despise Pericles but
was also the kind of person who (so Aeschines at any rate
can say of him) would have been delighted to censure the
Twelve Gods.[442] Such was the excessive degree of his conceit and of his belief in the worthlessness of everybody else. That is why Aeschines' Socrates does not take the same tack with him. What does he say instead?

> So since I realized that he was jealous of Themistocles, . . .[443]

after which comes the praise of Themistocles, justified in
my view for two reasons, both because it is true and because the words are the right ones for the lad to hear. He 576
does not speak ill of Themistocles to his face, so as to avoid
his being still further corrupted by hearing it, nor yet does
he offer him the consoling thought that he is not alone in

443 Aeschin. *Alcibiades* fr. 7 Dittmar = 49 [fr. 8] Giannantoni, (cf. §348 above).

συνοικεῖν, ἀλλὰ καὶ πάντας εἶναι τοιούτους ὅσοι τὰ τῆς πόλεως πράττουσιν· οὐδαμῶς· ἀλλ' ἀναγκάζει κλάειν θέντα τὴν κεφαλὴν ἐπὶ τὰ γόνατα ἀθυμήσαντα, ὡς οὐδ' ἐγγὺς ὄντα τῷ Θεμιστοκλεῖ τὴν παρασκευήν· καὶ προσέτι συμμέτρως ἐπέτεινεν τὸν λόγον. εἶπε γάρ που μεταξὺ λέγων ὡς οὐδ' ἐκείνῳ ἡ ἐπιστήμη τοσαύτη οὖσα ἤρκεσεν, ἀλλ' ἐνεδέησεν, ὥστε τὴν μὲν βλασφημίαν περιῃρῆσθαι, ὃ δ' ἦν χρήσιμον εἰς τὸ προτρέψαι, παρ' ἀμφοῖν ἐνεῖναι, καὶ παρὰ τῆς εὐφημίας καὶ παρὰ τοῦ μηδὲ ταῦτα ἀρκέσαι φῆσαι τῷ γε Θεμιστοκλεῖ.

[*(ii) Plato's Lofty Indifference to Chronological and Factual Accuracy (577–87)*]

577 οὕτω καίτοι τοῖς ἄλλοις Αἰσχίνης λειπόμενος Πλάτωνος, τοῦτό γε ἄμεινόν πως διεχείρισεν. ἀλλὰ γὰρ ὡς μὲν οὐκ[161] ἄριστος τῶν Ἑλλήνων Πλάτων κάκιστος ἂν εἴη καὶ Ἑλλήνων καὶ βαρβάρων ὅστις οὐκ ἐθέλει λέγειν. ἔοικεν δέ τι καὶ τῆς φύσεως ἀπολαύειν, ὥσπερ οἱ βασιλεῖς τῆς ἐξουσίας, οἷον καὶ περὶ αὐτὴν τὴν λέξιν ἔστιν οὗ φανήσεται ποιῶν, ἀδείᾳ λόγων πλείονι χρώμενος, καὶ περί γε αὐτὰς τὰς ὑποθέσεις, οἷόν ἐστιν ἐν τῷ λόγῳ οὗ μικρῷ πρόσθεν ἐμεμνήμεθα.

[161] οὐκ *abesse vult* Reiske

living a life of ignorance, but that all those conducting the city's affairs are in the same condition. Not a bit of it! Instead he makes him put his head on his knees and weep in despair at the thought that he is not even close to Themistocles in his state of readiness.[444] What is more, he gave his argument just the right degree of intensity, saying along the way that even Themistocles' great expertise was not enough but fell short, so as to remove any insult but at the same time ensure that his words contained what was useful for protreptic purposes, both in the element of praise, and in the insistence that not even those qualities sufficed in Themistocles' case at least.

(ii) Plato's Lofty Indifference to Chronological and Factual Accuracy (577–87)

Thus even though inferior to Plato in all other respects, 577
Aeschines handled this matter at least rather better. Yet anyone who is prepared to deny that Plato is the best of the Greeks would himself be the worst of any, Greek or barbarian. Plato does seem, however, to take a kind of advantage of his own natural genius, as kings do of their regal power: as will become clear, he does so on occasion both in his diction, where he indulges in considerable freedom in his phrasing, and in his content.[445] A good example of the latter comes in the dialogue I mentioned

444 Also from Aeschin. *Alcibiades*: fr. 9 Dittmar = 51 [fr. 10] Giannantoni.

445 For similar verdicts on Plato's style and ethos, see *De sublim.* 32.7; Dion. Hal. *Dem.* 5–7; Dio Chrys. 36.27; Max. Tyr. 18.4 (and cf. §351 above).

ὑπόκειται μὲν γὰρ αὐτῷ δήπου Σωκράτης τὸν ἐπιτάφιον διεξιών, μέμνηται δὲ τῶν ἐν Κορίνθῳ τετελευτηκότων καὶ τῶν ἐν Λεχαίῳ καὶ τῆς εἰρήνης τῆς ἐπὶ
578 *Ἀνταλκίδου κληθείσης. καίτοι ἐτελεύτησε μὲν Σωκράτης ἐπὶ Λάχητος ἄρχοντος, τῆς δ' ἐν Κορίνθῳ μάχης καὶ τῆς ἐν Λεχαίῳ μέσος ἄρχων Εὐβουλίδης. ἀπὸ δὲ Λάχητος εἰς Εὐβουλίδην ἕβδομος ἄρχων Εὐβουλίδης αὐτός, ἀπὸ δὲ Εὐβουλίδου πάλιν ἄρχων ὄγδοος Θεόδοτος, ἐφ' οὗ ἡ εἰρήνη ἐγένετο. ὁμοῦ τετταρεσκαίδεκα οἱ σύμπαντες ἄρχοντες εἰς τὴν εἰρήνην ἀπὸ Λάχητος ἄρχοντος. ὥστε οὐ μόνον Σωκράτης οὐδὲν ἑοράκει τούτων, ἀλλ' οὐδ' ἠπίστατο δήπουθεν εἰ γενήσεται· οὐδ' ἂν τὸ δαιμόνιον προὔλεγεν αὐτῷ περὶ τῶν τοσοῦτον μετ' αὐτόν.*

579 *ἕτερον τοίνυν. ἐν γὰρ τῷ Συμποσίῳ συνάγει μὲν εἰς ταυτὸν Ἀριστοφάνη καὶ Σωκράτη καὶ Ἀγάθωνα, ἔτι μειράκιον ὄντα, ὥς φησι, προάγει δὲ εἰς τοσοῦτον τοὺς χρόνους, ὥστε λέγων ὁ Ἀριστοφάνης, ἐπειδὴ τῆς λυγγὸς ἐπαύσατο, τὸν προβληθέντα λόγον μέμνηται καὶ οὗτος αὖ πάλιν Ἀρκάδων ὑπὸ Λακεδαιμονίων δι-*

---

446 The discussion of Plato's anachronisms that now follows is closely comparable to that in Ath. *Deipn.* 217c ff. and may well be drawing on the same sources.

447 *Menex.* 245b and e; the Battle of Lechaeum took place in 391 BC, and the Peace of Antalcidas (also known as the King's Peace) was concluded in 387/6.

448 Laches was eponymous archon in Athens in 400/399 BC, Euboulides in 394/3, and Theodotus in 387/6.

shortly beforehand.[446] His subject matter there is of course Socrates giving an account of the funeral oration, and mentioning the dead at Corinth and at Lechaeum, and the so-called Peace of Antalcidas.[447] But Socrates died in 578
the archonship of Laches, and in between the battles at Corinth and Lechaeum came the archonship of Euboulides. Counting from Laches, Euboulides is the seventh archon; and counting on from Euboulides, Theodotus, in whose archonship the Peace was made, comes eighth.[448] All in all, starting from Laches' archonship, that makes fourteen archons up to the Peace. So Socrates not only did not witness any of these events, he did not even know if they were going to happen; nor would his *daimonion*[449] have forewarned him of things so long after his time either.

Here is another example. In the *Symposium* Plato 579
brings together in the same place Aristophanes, Socrates, and a still young Agathon (as he describes him),[450] and stretches the chronology to such an extent that Aristophanes too in his turn, giving the speech they have all been challenged to give (once he has got over his hiccups),[451] returns to the same territory with his reference to the dispersal of the Arcadians by the Spartans.[452] But the

449 The divine sign ("a kind of voice"), which in Plato's account only ever intervened to prevent an action on Socrates' part (e.g., *Ap.* 31d, 40a–b, *Phdr.* 242b–c), but which in later imagination (e.g., Max. Tyr. 8.1) exercised a prophetic function.

450 *Symp.* 175e, 198a.

451 *Symp.* 185c, 188e–89a.

452 *Symp.* 193a; Aristides can say "returns to the same territory" because the dissolution of Mantinea in Arcadia into its twelve original villages in 385/4 BC was one of the events consequent on the Peace of Antalcidas.

ᾠκισμένων. διῳκίσθησαν δὲ Μαντινεῖς ὑπὸ Λακεδαιμονίων ἤδη τῆς εἰρήνης ὀμωμοσμένης. οὕτως ἐστὶ
580 ταῦτ᾽ ἐκείνων ἔτι νεώτερα. πῶς οὖν ἢ Ἀριστοφάνης ἂν
εἴη λέγων ταῦτα, ἢ Σωκράτης ἀκούων ἢ Ἀγάθων ἔτι
μειράκιον περὶ τούτους τοὺς χρόνους; πῶς δ᾽ ἂν καὶ
Ἀλκιβιάδης κωμάζοι παρ᾽ αὐτούς, καὶ οὗτος νέος τε[162]
ὢν ἔτι καὶ καλός, ὃς πρότερος τοῦ Σωκράτους ἐτεθνήκει, βιοὺς τόσα καὶ τόσα ἔτη τὰ σύμπαντα; εἰ μὴ
ἄρα ἐν τῷ Ἠλυσίῳ πεδίῳ τὸ συμπόσιον συνεκροτεῖτο.
581 τίς δὲ καὶ ἡ λὺγξ ἡ τοῦ Ἀριστοφάνους; καὶ ποῦ σὺ
τοῦτ᾽ ἐτήρησας; ἀλλ᾽ οἶμαι λύζειν αὐτὸν ἔδει, ἵνα εἰς
582 ἀπληστίαν σκωφθῇ. εἰ δέ τις τῇ Πλάτωνος δόξῃ περὶ
πάντων ἰσχυρίζοιτο, καὶ φάσκοι μὲν ζῆν Σωκράτη,
ὅτε ὁ τῶν ἐν Κορίνθῳ καὶ Λεχαίῳ τε τελευτηκότων
ἐλέγετο ἐπιτάφιος, πίνειν δ᾽ ἐν Ἀγάθωνος μετὰ τὴν
εἰρήνην, λύζειν δ᾽ Ἀριστοφάνη ἐν τῷ συμποσίῳ, κω-
μάζειν δὲ Ἀλκιβιάδην, μειράκια δ᾽ εἶναι τηνικαῦτα
Ἀγάθωνα καὶ Ἀλκιβιάδην, ὁμοῦ δ᾽ εἶναι πάντα χρήματα, πῶς οὐχὶ ληρήσει μὴ προσεξετάζων, εἴ τι καὶ
κατ᾽ ἐξουσίαν ἁνὴρ[163] λέγοι, ἀλλ᾽ ὥσπερ παῖς ἔμ-
βραχυ τοῦτ᾽ ἀρκεῖν ὑπολαμβάνων ὅ τι φαίη Πλάτων;
583 ἢ εἴ τις αὖ πείθοιτο τὸν Αἰγύπτιον δαίμονα τὸν
Θεῦθ, οὕτω γὰρ αὐτὸς εἴρηκνε τοὔνομα αὐτοῦ, τοῦτον
περὶ Ναύκρατιν τῆς Αἰγύπτου γενέσθαι, καὶ μὴ
ἐθέλοι συγχωρεῖν ὅτι ἐστὶν μὲν Ἑλλήνων Ἑρμῆς

162 τε Reiske γε *codd.*
163 ἁνήρ Dindorf ἀνήρ *codd.*

Mantineans were dispersed by the Spartans only after the
peace treaty had been concluded—that is how much more
recent the one event is than the other. How then could 580
Aristophanes have said this, or Socrates have heard it, or
Agathon still have been a lad around this time? And how
could Alcibiades have visited them with his band of revelers,[453] he too still young and handsome, when actually he
died before Socrates did, after a life of so-and-so many
years in all? Unless of course the symposium was being got
together in the Elysian Fields! And what about Aristoph- 581
anes' hiccup? Where did you observe that? No, I think he
had to have hiccups so that he could be satirized for his
gluttony. Imagine someone firmly trusting Plato's views 582
about everything, and insisting that Socrates was still alive
when the funeral oration for the dead at Corinth and
Lechaeum was pronounced, and drank at Agathon's after
the Peace, and that Aristophanes had hiccups at the symposium, and Alcibiades showed up with a band of revelers, and that Agathon and Alcibiades were both young lads at the time, and "everything was mixed up together."[454] How can it not be crazy of them not to go on to ask whether the man was in some respects taking liberties in what he says, but instead childishly to suppose absolutely that whatever Plato says is good enough?

Or again, imagine someone believing him when he says 583
that the Egyptian god Theuth—that is the form in which
he gives his name—lived in the vicinity of Naucratis in
Egypt,[455] and refusing to concede that his name in Greek

[453] *Symp.* 212c ff.

[454] An allusion to the famous first sentence of Anaxagoras' treatise *On Nature*, 59 B1 DK (also quoted by Plato in *Grg.* 465d).

[455] *Phdr.* 274c.

φωνή, ἀπὸ δὲ Ναυκράτιδος εἰς τὴν ἐπώνυμον πόλιν
αὐτοῦ καὶ οὗ πάντες αὐτὸν ὁμολογοῦσιν Αἰγύπτιοι
584 γενέσθαι ἀνάπλους ἡμερῶν ἐστιν οὐκ ὀλίγων; οὐ τοίνυν εἰ Πλάτων πολὺ πρῶτος τῶν Ἑλλήνων, ταὐτόν
ἐστι Ναύκρατίς τε καὶ Ἑρμοῦ πόλις, οὐδ᾽ αὖ περὶ
Ναύκρατιν, ἀλλ᾽ οὐκ ἐν τῇ ἑαυτοῦ πόλει δεῖ δὴ τὸν
585 Ἑρμῆν γεγενῆσθαι δοκεῖν. [οὐδέ γε Εὐριπίδου φήσομεν οἶμαι τὸ ἰαμβεῖον εἶναι τὸ

σοφοὶ τύραννοι τῶν σοφῶν συνουσίᾳ,

οὐδ᾽ εἴ τις οὕτω τῶν σοφῶν εἴρηκεν· ἔστιν γὰρ ἐξ
Αἴαντος Σοφοκλέους, Αἴαντος τοῦ Λοκροῦ.][164]

586 ἀλλ᾽ ἐστὶν ταῦτα ἀπὸ τῆς τῶν διαλόγων ἐξουσίας
καὶ συνηθείας ὡρμημένα. τῷ γὰρ ἅπαντας αὐτοὺς
ἐπιεικῶς εἶναι πλάσματα καὶ πλέκειν ἐξεῖναι δι᾽ ὧν ἄν
τις βούληται, ἔνεστίν τι κἀν τοῖς λόγοις αὐτοῖς οὐ
σφόδρα τηροῦν τὴν ἀλήθειαν. καὶ ἅμα μοι δοκεῖν
ἐφέλκεταί τι τῆς ἐλευθερίας καὶ τῆς μεγαλοπρεπείας,
καὶ οὐ παντάπασιν ἀκριβολογεῖται, ἀλλ᾽, ὥσπερ
587 ἔφην, συγχωρεῖ τῇ φύσει. ἔπειτα ταῦθ᾽ ἡμεῖς ἁπλῶς
οὕτως παραδεξόμεθα; οὐκ ἄρ᾽ εἰδέναι τἀκείνου δόξομεν. οὐδέ γε τῶν Πλάτωνος "σύγγραμμά ἐστι Πλάτωνος οὐδὲν οὐδὲ ἔσται·" πόθεν; ἀλλὰ ταῦτ᾽ "ἐστὶ Σωκράτους νέου καὶ καλοῦ γεγονότος." εἶθ᾽ ὁ μὲν γράψας
οὔ,[165] <ὁ δὲ οὔ,>[166] γέγραφεν.

164 *del.* Lenz 165 οὔ Behr οὐ *codd.*
166 *add.* Trapp *post* Reiske *et* Behr

is Hermes, and that from Naucratis to the city named after him, where all Egyptians agree in locating him, is a good
few days' voyage up river? It certainly does not follow from 584
the fact that Plato is by far the greatest of the Greeks that Naucratis and Hermopolis are the same place, nor yet that we have to believe that Hermes lived in the vicinity of Naucratis rather than in his own city.[456]

These are things that owe their origin to the character- 586
istic literary license of the dialogues: because they are all pretty much fictions and can be woven together from whatever elements one may want, there is even in their actual wording a less than pressing concern for the truth. And at the same time, as it seems to me, Plato assumes a degree of freedom and grandiloquence and is not altogether meticulous in what he says, but as I was saying, he
gives way to his natural talent. Are we then going to take 587
all this just at face value? It won't look as if we understand what he is like if so. Indeed, in Plato's work "there is no piece of writing by Plato, nor will there be"—how can this be?—but instead these "are the works of a Socrates grown young and handsome."[457] So the man who wrote them didn't, while the man who didn't write them did!

[456] The next sentence in the Greek text, bracketed opposite, is rightly expelled by Lenz as a reader's addition in the margin of Aristides' text: "[585] Nor do I think we will say that the iambic line 'Despots are wise through the company of the wise' is by Euripides, even if a philosopher says so; it comes from Sophocles' *Ajax, Ajax the Locrian*." Plato cites this line (Soph. fr. 14 *TrGF*) as by Euripides in *Resp.* 568a, and the attribution is repeated in [Pl.] *Theag.* 125b.

[457] [Pl.] *Ep.* 2.314c.

[(iii) Plato's Arbitrary Construction and Use of Categories (588–604)]

588 λοιπὸν οὖν αὐτῷ καὶ τοὔνομα ἐξαρνουμένῳ πείθειν οὐχ ἡμᾶς γε, ἐὰν σωφρονῶμεν, ἀλλ' εἰσόμεθα αὐτοῦ τὰς παιδιάς—εἰρήσθω γὰρ ὃ κἂν αὐτὸς εἶπεν περὶ αὐτοῦ—οἷα κἀν τούτοις ἀμέλει τοῖς λόγοις, ἵνα μὴ τὰ πόρρω λέγωμεν, ἡ[167] περὶ γυμναστικῆς καὶ ἰατρικῆς ἔνεστι θέσις, ὡς ῥᾳδίως καὶ ἁπλῶς ἔχουσα, τὸ[168] βελ-
589 τίω γυμναστικὴν ἰατρικῆς εἶναι. καίτοι γε ἤδη ἔγωγέ τινος ἤκουσα λέγοντος τῶν ἰατρῶν ὅτι ἡ μὲν γυμναστικὴ τοῖς ἀθληταῖς ἐπίπαν διαλέγεται καὶ περὶ τοῦτό ἐστιν, ἡ δ' ἰατρικὴ συλλήβδην ἅπασιν ἐπιστατεῖ, καὶ πολὺ τοὐμμέσῳ. ὅπου γὰρ οὐδ' αὐτοῖς τοῖς ἀθληταῖς οἷόν τε τῇ ῥώμῃ χρήσασθαι, μὴ τοῦ ὑγιαίνειν ὑπάρχοντος, πῶς οἷόν τε ἡττᾶσθαι τὴν ἅπασι τοῦτο παρασκευάζουσαν τέχνην τῆς τοῖς ὀλίγοις ἐκεῖνο ὃ μηδέποτ' ἔστιν χωρὶς τούτου λαβεῖν; τό τε σύμπαν οὐ συνεχώρει τοσοῦτον εἶναι τὴν ἰατρικήν, ὅσον τοὺς κάμνοντας ἐπισκοπεῖν, ἀλλ' εἶναι διττόν. δεῖν γὰρ τὸν ἰατρὸν τὴν μὲν ὑπάρχουσαν ὑγίειαν διασῴζειν, τὴν δ' οὔπω παροῦσαν ἐμποιεῖν, ὥσπερ τὸν γυμναστὴν τὴν μὲν ὑπάρχουσαν ῥώμην διασῴζειν, τὴν δ' οὔπω παροῦσαν ἐμποιεῖν. οὐ γὰρ ἄλλου μέν ἐστι τοὺς ὄντας ἀθλητὰς δήπου γυμνάσαι, ἑτέρου δὲ τοὺς μέλλον-

167 ἡ EU ἥ QVA^{1}R^{1} ἤ TA^{2}R^{2}
168 τό Canter τῷ *codd.* τῷ <παντί> Reiske

(iii) Plato's Arbitrary Construction and Use of Categories (588–604)

It follows then that, if we have any sense, we certainly 588
should not believe this man, who can even abjure his own name, but will recognize his playfulness for what it is (let us make no bones about saying only what he too would have said about himself).[458] So for instance in precisely this dialogue of ours (so as not to invoke any more distant example) we find the proposition about gymnastics and medicine, given as a simple and unambiguous truth, that
gymnastics is the better of the two.[459] Yet I for one have 589
certainly before now heard a doctor say that there is a great difference between the two, in that gymnastics deals exclusively with athletes and is concentrated on this, whereas medicine supervises everyone collectively. Because given that not even athletes can use their physical strength if they are not first healthy, how can the science that furnishes health to everybody be inferior to the one that furnishes only the few with what can never be acquired without it? My doctor also completely disagreed that medicine is limited to looking after the sick, but said instead that it is twofold: the doctor must both preserve the health that already exists, and create the health that is not yet there, just as the gymnastic trainer must preserve the strength that already exists, and create the strength that is not yet there. It is obviously not one man's job to train those who are already athletes and another's to pre-

[458] A reference to the dismissal of all written texts as "childish play" in *Phdr.* 275c–78a.

[459] *Grg.* 520b, referring back to 464b–68a.

τας ἔσεσθαι παρασκευάσαι, ἀλλ' ἑνὸς ἀνδρὸς καὶ τῆς
590 *αὐτῆς τέχνης. εἰ δὲ τοῦθ' οὕτως ἔχει, ῥᾴδιον ἤδη κατα-*
μαθεῖν ὅτι δευτέρα τῆς ἰατρικῆς ἡ γυμναστικὴ καὶ
παντελῶς ὑπ' αὐτὴν γίγνεται. καὶ γὰρ αὐτὸ τὸ γνῶναι
τίνι δεῖ γυμνασίων καὶ πότε καὶ πόσων καὶ ποίων
τινῶν ἑκάστῳ, λέγω τῶν ἰδιωτῶν, τῆς τοῦ ἰατροῦ
σοφίας ἤδη γίγνεται, καὶ οὗτός ἐστιν ὁ πέμπων παρὰ
τὸν γυμναστήν, ἂν δέῃ. παραλαβὼν δὲ ἐκεῖνος τὸ τοῦ
διακόνου πράξει, καὶ οὐ φιλοτιμήσεται πρὸς τὸν ἰα-
τρόν, ἀλλ' ἐν τῇ τοῦ ἡνιόχου τάξει μενεῖ. καὶ γὰρ
ἐκεῖνος παραλαβὼν παρὰ τοῦ ἰατροῦ τὸν μέλλοντα
αἰωρήσεσθαι παρέχει τὴν διακονίαν καὶ γυμνάζει τὸν
αὑτοῦ τρόπον. εἰ δ' αἰωρεῖσθαι βέλτιον ἢ μή, τὸν ἰα-
591 *τρὸν ἤδη δεῖ τοῦτο ἐσκέφθαι. καὶ νὴ Δί' ὁ μὲν ναύτης*
εἰς τὸ πλοῖον ἐνθέμενος κομιεῖ παρὰ τὰς ἀκτὰς ἢ καὶ
μέσον πόρον, εἰ βούλοιτο, καὶ κινήσει διὰ τῆς εἰρε-
σίας ἄνω καὶ κάτω περιάγων, ἢ καὶ τοῖς ἱστίοις
προσχρώμενος, καὶ καθεδεῖται, καθάπερ τις αὐτο-
κράτωρ ποιῶν ὅ τι βούλεται. εἰ δ' ἄμεινόν τῳ πλεῦσαι
τὸ παράπαν καὶ ὑγιεινότερον αὐτὸν τοῦτο ποιήσει,
τῆς ἰατρικῆς τοῦτο τέχνης ἴδιον ἦν, ἀλλ' οὐ τῆς ναυ-
592 *τικῆς. καὶ μὴν ὅτι καὶ πολλοὺς ἤδη καὶ τὰ τοιαῦτα*
ὤνησεν καὶ οὐδὲν ἔλαττον ἢ τὰ ἐν ταῖς παλαίστραις

---

460 Passive exercise: Aetius of Amida 16.67 (Byz.); Antyllus in Oribasius 6.23; Sor. *Gyn* 1.49.4; Vestricius Spurinna described at Plin. *Ep.* 3.1.5; cf. M. Gleason, *Making Men* (Princeton, 1995),

pare those who are going to be; both tasks belong to the same man and the same art. And if that is how things are, 590
it is easy to grasp that gymnastics comes second to medicine and is entirely under her supervision. Even knowing who needs gymnastic training, I mean in the case of an individual from the general public, and when and how much and what sort, already falls within the scope of the doctor's expertise, and it is the doctor who sends people to the gymnastic trainer if it is necessary. The gymnastic trainer will then take them on and do the underling's job; he will not enter into competition with the doctor, but will keep to the same station as the coachman—because just like him the coachman will take over from the doctor the patient who is to be given passive exercise and then deliver his subordinate service, by exercising the patient in his own particular way.[460] But whether it is better for the patient to be treated by passive exercise or not, is something
that the doctor must already have considered. Or come to 591
that the sailor will put the patient into his vessel and transport him along the coast or across a stretch of open sea, if he should so wish, and will move him by oar stroke as he takes him around this way and that, or will use the sails as well, and he will sit there like some absolute ruler on his throne doing just as he pleases. But it would be the province of medical science, not the science of navigation, to say whether it is better for someone to sail in the first
place, and whether this will make him healthier. That such 592
measures are on record as having done many people good, no less than gymnasium exercises, we are so to speak all

87 with n. 32; V. Nutton, *Ancient Medicine* (London, 2004), 173 n. 87.

γυμνάσια πάντες ὡς ἔπος εἰπεῖν σύνισμεν, ἀλλ᾽ οὐ
διὰ τοῦτο οἱ ἡνίοχοι τοῖς ἰατροῖς ἀμφισβητοῦσιν,
οὐδὲ οἱ ναῦται λέγουσιν ὡς αὐτοὶ μὲν φύλακες τῆς
ὑγιείας θαυμαστοί τινες εἶεν καὶ γυμνάζοιεν ἅπαντας
τοὺς βουλομένους, ἐκεῖνοι δ᾽ οὐδὲν ἄρα εἰδεῖεν πλὴν
593 καθείρξαντες ἀπολλύναι. καίτοι εἰ βελτίων ἡ γυμναστικὴ τῆς ἰατρικῆς, τί κωλύει καὶ τούτους ἐκ τῶν
αὐτῶν ἀμείνους εἶναι τῶν ἰατρῶν, ἐπειδή γε καὶ αὐτοῖς
μέτεστιν ἀμηγέπῃ τῆς γυμναστικῆς; ἢ κατὰ πασῶν
τούτων τῶν τεχνῶν ἓν τοῦτο[169] ἰσχυρὸν[170] ὑπάρξει λέγειν, ὅτι εἰ μὴ αὕτη ἦν, οὐδ᾽ ἂν τούτων οὐδεμία ἦν
χρησίμη, ἀλλὰ καὶ αὐτὸ τὸ τούτων τινὶ χρήσασθαι
καὶ πάλιν μὴ δεῖν ἐπ᾽ αὐτὴν ἔρχεται; ὥσπερ οἶμαι κἂν
τοῖς σιτίοις· κρίνει μὲν τὰ δέοντα ὁ ἰατρός, παρασκευ-
άζει δὲ ὁ μάγειρος, ἀλλ᾽ οὐκ ἀμφισβητήσει γε τῷ
ἰατρῷ τῆς ἡγεμονίας, οὐ μᾶλλόν γε ἢ καὶ τῷ δε-
594 σπότῃ. τοιοῦτόν τι καὶ τὸ τῆς γυμναστικῆς φαίη τις
ἂν εἶναι πρὸς τὴν ἰατρικήν, δεύτερον καὶ ὑπακοῦον
καὶ πάντα μᾶλλον ὡς ἔπος εἰπεῖν ἢ κρεῖττον. ἀλλ᾽
ὑπὲρ μὲν τούτων τοῖς ἰατροῖς ὑπέρ τε[171] σφῶν αὐτῶν
ὅ τι γιγνώσκουσίν τε καὶ βούλονται παρείσθω λέγειν.

169 ἓν τοῦτο Behr *post* Iunt. ἓν τούτοις Ua^{2} ἐν τούτοις *cett.*

170 ἰσχυρὸν τῆς ἰατρικῆς καὶ τὸ τῆς Αἰσώπου κυνὸς ἕξει (ἑξῆ) ὑπάρξει Q (Vat. gr. 76) ἰσχυρὸν τῆς ἰατρικῆς καὶ τὸ τῆς Αἰσώπου κυνὸς ἑξῆς ὑπάρξει Barocc. 136 ἰσχυρὸν τὸ τῆς ἰατρικῆς ὑπάρξει καὶ τὸ τῆς Αἰσώπου κυνὸς ἕξει Laur. 60.9$^{p.c.}$ Ph^{M3} καὶ τὸ τῆς Αἰσώπου κυνὸς ἕξει ὑπάρξει E

171 τε Reiske δέ *codd.* *del.* U

of us well aware, but coachmen do not for this reason compete with doctors, and sailors do not say that they are wonderful protectors of people's health and give gymnastic training to all who want, whereas doctors do not know how to do anything except imprison people and kill them. Yet if gymnastics is better than medicine, what is to pre- 593
vent these people on the same grounds being better than doctors, since they too in some sense have a stake in gymnastics? Or is the one secure point that can be made about all these skills that if medicine did not exist none of them would have any usefulness either, and that the very question of employing any of them, or again of the need not to employ them, is her responsibility?[461] So too I think in the case of foodstuffs: the doctor decides what is needed and the chef prepares it, but the chef does not compete with the doctor to direct things, any more than he does with his master. The relationship of gymnastics to medicine is, 594
one might say, of this general kind: secondary, subordinate, and in a word anything but superior. But on these matters, where they speak on their own behalf, let it be left to the doctors themselves to say what they know and want to say.

[461] Some manuscripts give a different, longer version of this question: "Or in the case of all these skills is the one secure point that provided by medicine, and will it be possible to use the line about Aesop's dog, that if she did not exist, none of them would have any usefulness either, and that the very question of employing any of them, or again of the need not to employ them, is her responsibility?" This looks like the result of incorporating a reader's marginal note. For the fable (Perry 356), see Babrius 128 and Xen. *Mem.* 2.7.13–14.

595 ἀξιοῖ δὲ καὶ τῆς δικαιοσύνης κρεῖττον εἶναι τὴν νομοθετικήν. καίτοι πότερον κρεῖττον ἡ νομοθετικὴ τῆς δικαιοσύνης, ἢ μέρος; ἐγὼ γὰρ οἶμαι πάντας ἂν ὡς ἔπος εἰπεῖν συμφῆσαι ὅτι καὶ νόμους θεῖναι καὶ ψήφους ἐνεγκεῖν καὶ συνειπεῖν τὰ δίκαια καὶ συμβουλεῦσαι καὶ χειροτονῆσαι, καὶ νὴ Δία περὶ αὐτοὺς τοὺς θεοὺς ἃ χρὴ πράττειν καὶ πάντα τὰ τοιαῦτα εἰς ἓν κεφάλαιον κοινὸν τὴν δικαιοσύνην ἀναφέρει. ὁ δὲ τοῦ μείζονος τοὔλαττον καὶ τοῦ παντὸς τὸ μέρος πρότερον
596 καὶ κρεῖττον εἶναί φησιν. καὶ εἰ μέν γε τὴν εὐσέβειαν τῆς δικαιοσύνης ἔφασκεν εἶναι κρεῖττον, ἐξῆν ἂν ἐπαινεῖν, ὡς δυοῖν μὲν τῆς δικαιοσύνης μερῶν ὄντων τῶν ἀνωτάτω, πρεσβυτέρου δὲ καὶ κρείττονος τοῦ περὶ τοὺς θεούς· νῦν δ' οὐ τοιοῦτόν ἐστιν, ἀλλ' ἁπλῶς καὶ καθάπερ νόμον ὡς ἀληθῶς τιθεὶς ἀνεξέταστον
597 γνώμην ἀποφαίνεται. ἔπειτα τίθησι δύο μὲν τὰς τοῦ σώματος εἶναι θεραπείας, τὴν γυμναστικὴν καὶ τὴν ἰατρικήν, δύο δ' αὖ τὰς ἐπὶ τῆς ψυχῆς, τήν τε νομοθετικὴν καὶ τὴν δικαιοσύνην. αὐτὴ δ' ἡ φρόνησις ἡμῖν ποῦ πρὸς θεῶν; ποῦ δ' ἡ σωφροσύνη; ποῦ δ' ἡ ἀνδρεία; ταυτὶ γὰρ δήπου τέτταρα μέρη τῆς ἀρετῆς ἔστιν ἀκούειν ἀεὶ θρυλούντων, τὴν φρόνησιν, τὴν σωφροσύνην, τὴν δικαιοσύνην, τὴν ἀνδρείαν· ὧν ἓν μὲν τίθησι διπλοῦν, τὴν δικαιοσύνην, μέρος αὐτοῦ προσλαβὼν τὴν νομοθετικήν, τὰ δὲ λοιπὰ πάντα παρῆκεν.
598 πῶς οὖν ὀρθῶς ἢ δικαίως ταῦτα ὑπόκειται κατ' αὐτὸν τὸν περὶ τῆς δικαιοσύνης λόγον; εἶτα καὶ ποῦ παραπλήσιον; ἡ μὲν γὰρ γυμναστικὴ καὶ ἰατρικὴ οὐκ ἀρε-

Plato also claims that legislation is superior to jus- 595
tice.[462] But is legislation superior to justice, or a constituent part of it? I ask because I believe that just about
everyone would agree that making laws, casting votes,
advocating the just cause, giving advice, voting, and indeed acting properly in relation to the gods, and all such
things, all relate to one single common category, justice.
But Plato says that the lesser is prior and superior to the
greater, and the part to the whole. If he had said that piety 596
was superior to justice, it would have been possible to applaud him, on the grounds that, justice having two primary
categories, the one of them relating to the gods is the senior and superior. But in actual fact the situation is different: he simply asserts an unexamined opinion as if he really were making a law.[463] Then he posits that there are 597
two ways of looking after the body, gymnastics and medicine, and again two dealing with the soul, legislation and
justice.[464] What becomes of wisdom, for heaven's sake? Or
self-control? Or courage? Because the four parts of virtue
that one can hear people always going on about are surely
these four—wisdom, self-control, justice, and courage.[465]
Plato makes one of these four, justice, twofold, drafting in
legislation to be one of its constituents, and passes over all
the rest. How, on the principles of justice itself, can it be 598
correct or just for all this to be presupposed? Moreover,
where is the comparability? Gymnastics and medicine are

[462] *Grg.* 520b, again looking back to 464b–66a.

[463] "Unexamined" echoes Socrates' celebrated declaration that "the unexamined life is no life for a human being" in *Ap.* 38a.

[464] *Grg.* 464b–c.

[465] Including Plato of course: *Resp.* 427e–28a.

ταὶ δήπου τοῦ σώματός εἰσιν, ἀλλ᾽ ἐπιστῆμαι περὶ
τὴν τοῦ σώματος χρείαν, ἡ δὲ δικαιοσύνη τῆς περὶ
599 τὴν ψυχὴν ἀρετῆς ἄντικρυς μόριόν ἐστιν. οὐδὲν οὖν
ἄλλο ἢ σοφίζεται κατ᾽ ἐπωνυμίαν ὥσπερ παῖδα Σωκράτης τὸν Πῶλον.

600 καὶ οὔπω ταῦτ᾽ ἐστὶ τὰ κάλλιστα, ἀλλ᾽ ὅτι καὶ τὴν
σοφιστικὴν τῆς ῥητορικῆς ἀμείνονα λέγει, ὥσπερ τὴν
γυμναστικὴν τῆς ἰατρικῆς καὶ τὴν νομοθετικὴν τῆς
δικαιοσύνης, φυλάττων μὲν οἶμαι τὸν αὐτὸν ἐφ᾽ ἅπασι
λόγον, τὸ δ᾽ αὐτὸ πταίων περὶ ἅπαντα, ὥσπερ οἱ τὸ
πρῶτον σφαλέντες ἐν τοῖς διαγράμμασιν, χρῶμαι δ᾽
αὐτοῦ Πλάτωνος τῷ παραδείγματι· καὶ τοτὲ μέν γέ
φησι "ταυτόν ἐστιν, ὦ μακάριε, ῥήτωρ καὶ σοφι-
στής," τοτὲ δ᾽ αὖ τὴν σοφιστικὴν κρεῖττον εἶναι τῆς
ῥητορικῆς καὶ διαφέρειν. ἀλλ᾽ ἵνα μὴ πάντα ἀκριβο-
λογεῖσθαι δοκῶ, συγχωρήσωμεν τὸ αὐτὸ λέγειν αὐτὸν
601 ἀεί, κρεῖττον τὴν σοφιστικὴν εἶναι. σκεψώμεθα δὴ
πρὸς τί ποθ᾽ ἡμᾶς οὗτος ὁ λόγος προάγει. φανήσεται
γὰρ ἐνταῦθα δὴ καὶ καθαρῶς πᾶσα ἡ ὕβρις, εἰ οἷόν
602 τε εἰπεῖν. οὐκοῦν σοφισταὶ μὲν Πρωταγόρας καὶ Ἱππίας καὶ Πρόδικος καὶ οἱ περὶ τούτους, ῥήτορες δ᾽ αὖ
Μιλτιάδης καὶ Κίμων καὶ Περικλῆς καὶ Θεμιστοκλῆς.
φαίνεται δ᾽ αὖ τοὺς σοφιστὰς κατὰ τοὺς ἐν Ἅιδου
κολαζομένους τιθεὶς καὶ καταλέγων, "καὶ μὴν Τάνταλον εἰσεῖδον" καὶ "τὸν δὲ μετ᾽ εἰσενόησα" τοῖς ἐκ
Νεκυίας αὐτοὺς κόσμοις τιμῶν, Πρόδικον μὲν ὡς

clearly not excellences of the body, but kinds of knowledge
about the treatment of the body, while justice is straightforwardly a subcategory of excellence of soul. Socrates is 599
thus simply hoodwinking Polus with clever talk as if he
were a child, just as his name suggests.[466]

Even this however is not yet the best of it. Plato ac- 600
tually says that the art of sophistry is better than the art of
oratory, just as gymnastics is better than medicine and
legislation is better than justice.[467] In so doing I think he
upholds the same principle in all cases, but also succumbs
to the same error in all cases, like people who make an
initial slip in drawing their diagrams (to use his own comparison).[468] (At one moment, moreover, he can say "my
dear fellow, the orator and the sophist are the same
thing,"[469] and then at another he says that the art of the
sophist is superior to that of the orator and different to it;
but to avoid my giving the impression of splitting hairs
over everything, let us concede that he says the same thing
throughout, that the art of the sophist is superior.) Let us 601
consider where this argument takes us, because here
certainly the full extent of his insolence, if one may call it
that, will be seen in sharp relief. Protagoras, then, and 602
Hippias and Prodicus and their accomplices were sophists, while Miltiades, Cimon, Pericles, and Themistocles
on the other hand were orators. Plato clearly categorizes
the sophists with the sinners being punished in Hades
when he says as he lists them "And I spied Tantalus" and
"After him I noticed," thus honoring them with compliments drawn from Book 11, Prodicus as if he were Tanta-

[466] As a common noun, *pôlos* means "colt"; cf. *Grg.* 461c–d, 463e. [467] *Grg.* 520b. [468] *Cra.* 436c–d. [469] *Grg.* 520a.

Τάνταλον ὄντα, Ἱππίαν δὲ ὡς τὸ εἴδωλον τοῦ Ἡρα-
603 κλέους. Πρωταγόρας δ' αὖ μετὰ τούτων διαιτᾶται, μέρος τι τῆς οἰκίας κατειληφὼς καὶ τούτοις ἐνδείκνυσθαι βούλεται, καὶ ἔστι θαυμαστὸς καὶ οὗτος τὴν φρόνησιν. ἐρωτᾷ δὲ Σωκράτης Ἀπολλόδωρον[172] εἰ οὐκ αἰσχύνοιτο σοφιστὴν ἐθέλων παρέχειν ἑαυτὸν εἰς τοὺς Ἕλληνας. καὶ τί ἄν τις ἀγωνίζοιτο; ῥᾴδιον γὰρ καὶ τῷ τυχόντι γνῶναι τοῦτό γε, ὁπόσον τι Πλάτων ἀεὶ τῶν σοφιστῶν καταγελᾷ καὶ ὁπόσου τινὸς ἀξίους
604 αὐτοὺς ἡγεῖται. ὅτε τοίνυν κρείττων μὲν ἡ σοφιστικὴ τῆς ῥητορικῆς, σοφισταὶ δὲ οὓς εἶπον οὗτοί εἰσι κατὰ τὸν Τάνταλον, καὶ τὸ γενέσθαι τούτων ἕνα καὶ τὸ λαβεῖν τὴν τούτων προσηγορίαν αἰσχύνη σαφής, ποῖ ποτε ἐκπίπτει τῆς ῥητορικῆς τὰ πράγματα, ἢ τί τῷ Μιλτιάδῃ καὶ τῷ Κίμωνι καὶ τῷ Περικλεῖ καὶ τῷ Θεμιστοκλεῖ καταλείπεται; ἆρα ἄλλο τι ἢ τῷ ὄντι ὥσπερ εἴδωλον ᾆττον[173] φέρεσθαι, καὶ τίς ταῦτα ἀνέξεται;

[*(iv) Plato's Gratuitously Ungenerous Attitude to the Glories of Hellenism (605–26)*]

605 καίτοι ὅταν οἱ μὲν σοφισταὶ μηδὲν τῶν ἐν Ἅιδου κολαζομένων διαφέρωσιν, οἱ δὲ ῥήτορες χείρους ἔτι τούτων ὦσιν, καὶ μηδὲν αὖ τῶν μαγείρων οὗτοι σε-

172 *an* ‹τὸν› Ἀπολλοδώρου?
173 ᾆττον Reiske ἔλαττον *codd.*

lus and Hippias as if he were the ghost of Heracles.[470] As 603
for Protagoras, he has occupied part of the house and
keeps them company; he wants to put on a performance
for them, and he too is amazingly wise.[471] Socrates asks
Apollodorus if he is not ashamed at wanting to present
himself to the Greeks as a sophist.[472] Why labor the point?
It is easy for even the casual observer to grasp how con-
temptuously Plato always derides the sophists, and what
he thinks they are worth. If then the art of the sophist is 604
superior to that of the orator, and sophists are these people
I have just mentioned, like Tantalus, and becoming one of
them and acquiring this name is manifestly shameful,
where on earth will the case of oratory end up, and what
fate will be left for Miltiades, Cimon, Pericles, and Themistocles? Can it be other than to flit about as if they really
were ghosts,[473] and who will tolerate that?

(iv) Plato's Gratuitously Ungenerous Attitude to the Glories of Hellenism (605–26)

But when sophists are no different from sinners being 605
punished in Hades, and orators are even worse than they
are, and they moreover are no more impressive than

[470] *Prt.* 315b–d; the quoted words are from *Od.* 11.582 and 601. [471] *Prt.* 314e–15b, 317c. [472] It is in fact Hippocrates, *son* of Apollodorus whom Socrates asks in *Prt.* 311e–12a; Aristides' credit could be saved by emending the Greek text, but he has probably just made a mistake. [473] *Od.* 10.495.

μνότεροι, κωμῳδίαν δὲ καὶ τραγῳδίαν μὴ οὐδὲ διδάσκειν δέῃ τὸ παράπαν, ἀλλ᾽ ἐκκηρύττειν ἐκ τῆς ἀγαθῆς πόλεως, ὁ δὲ διθύραμβος κολακεία τις ᾖ, φαῦλον δ᾽ οἱ χοροί, κἂν παιᾶνας ᾄδωσιν, Ὅμηρον δὲ εἰσαλείψαντες ἐκπέμπωμεν ὡς οὐκ ἐπιτήδειον συνεῖναι τοῖς νέοις, ἀλλὰ ὄντα γόητα καὶ τοῦ πρὸς ἡδονὴν θηρευτήν, πάντες δ᾽ ὦσιν τοῦ μηδενὸς ἄξιοι, οὐ φροῦδα τὰ τῶν Ἑλλήνων πράγματα; [ἢ πῶς οὐκ εἰς πονηρὸν κάτεισι τοῖς Ἕλλησι τὰ πράγματα;][174] ἢ τοῦ ποτε λοιπὸν ἡμῖν ὁ Σωκράτης ἔσται βελτίων, εἰ πάντας ἐφεξῆς οὑτωσὶ διαγράψομεν καὶ ξενηλασίαν τοσαύτην τῶν Ἑλλήνων ποιησόμεθα, ὅσην οὐδ᾽ ἐν Λακε-
606 δαίμονί πω συμβᾶσαν ἀκούομεν; οὐ πρὸς ἡμέρων ταῦτα καὶ δικαίων, ὥς φασιν οἱ πρῶτοι τῶν Ἑλλήνων Ὅμηρος καὶ Πλάτων. καὶ ταῦτ᾽ οὐχὶ Πλάτωνος
607 λέγω καθαπτόμενος. πόθεν; μὴ μὲν οὖν ἔμοιγε κατ᾽ Αἰσχύλον μήτε παρασπιστὴς μήτ᾽ ἐγγὺς εἴη ὅστις μὴ φίλος τῷ ἀνδρὶ τούτῳ μηδὲ τιμᾷ τὰ πρέποντα· ἀλλ᾽ ὥσπερ ἔφη Λυσίας κοινὸν ἑαυτὸν εἶναι φίλον τῆς πόλεως, οὕτως καὶ περὶ ἡμῶν χρὴ διανοεῖσθαι κοινούς τινας εἶναι τοῖς Ἕλλησι φίλους, καὶ νῦν ὑπὲρ
608 τῶν κοινῶν δικαίων ἀγωνίζεσθαι. οὔτοι φιλαθηναίου γέ ἐστιν τὴν Ἀκαδημίαν μόνην ἀσπάζεσθαι τῆς Ἀττι-

174 *del.* Trapp

474 *Grg.* 518b. 475 *Resp.* 394b–d. 476 *Grg.* 501e–2a. 477 *Grg.* 501e. 478 *Resp.* 398a.

chefs,[474] and one must not only not produce comedies and tragedies at all,[475] but also banish them from the good city, and the dithyramb is a kind of flattery,[476] and choruses are vile even if they perform paeans,[477] and we anoint Homer and send him away as unsuitable to associate with our young,[478] but instead a charlatan and a hunter out of what gives pleasure, and all of them are without value, are not the fortunes of Greece lost and gone?[479] Who on earth will we be able to say Socrates is better than, if we rule out everybody in this way one after another and perpetrate an expulsion of Hellenes on a scale that exceeds anything we
are told ever happened in Sparta?[480] In the words of the 606
first of the Hellenes, Homer and Plato, these are not the actions of "mild and just" people![481] And I do not say this
as an attack on Plato. How could I? To quote Aeschylus, 607
may he who is not a friend to this man and does not honor him as he deserves "not be comrade in arms or anywhere near" to me.[482] No, just as Lysias said of himself that he was a friend to the whole city of Athens,[483] so too it should be understood of me that I am a friend to all Hellenes alike
and am now fighting for their common rights. It is for sure 608
not the mark of a lover of Athens to cherish the Academy

479 The next sentence in the Greek text, bracketed opposite, looks like a reader's explanatory paraphrase of the preceding: "Or will not the fortunes of the Greeks inevitably decline and be ruined?"

480 A reference to the Spartan custom of *xenêlasia* ("expulsion of foreigners": Xen. *Lac.* 14.4; Plut. *Vit. Lyc.* 27.3–4).

481 Cf. §570 above.

482 Fr. 303 *TrGF*.

483 Fr. 296 Baiter-Sauppe (but not categorized as a fragment by subsequent editors of Lysias).

κῆς, τὴν δ' ἄλλην ἅπασαν ὥσπερ ἐχθρὰν κρίνειν καὶ πολεμίαν· οὐδὲ γὰρ καταγελάστους ἀποφήναντα τοὺς ἄλλους ἅπαντας οὕτω καὶ τότε χρὴ Πλάτωνα θαυμάζειν ἀναμεῖναι. τοῦτο γὰρ οὐ Πλάτωνος ἂν εἴη τιμή, ἀλλ' ἀτιμία τῶν ἄλλων μᾶλλον, σχεδὸν δέ τι καὶ αὐτοῦ Πλάτωνος. τὸ γὰρ ἡγεῖσθαι χρηστοῦ τινος ἄλλου κριθέντος μὴ εἶναι τούτῳ πλείονος ἀξίῳ δόξαι
609 πῶς οὐ τοιοῦτόν ἐστιν; ἀλλ' ὥσπερ Ὅμηρος ἐπαινεῖ λέγων

> πρόσθε μὲν ἐσθλὸς ἔφευγε, δίωκε δέ μιν μέγ' ἀμείνων·

καὶ πάλιν

> ἀνδρῶν αὖ μέγ' ἄριστος ἔην Τελαμώνιος Αἴας,
> ὄφρ' Ἀχιλεὺς μήνιεν· ὁ γὰρ πολὺ φέρτερος ἦεν.

καὶ ἑτέρωθι

> κάρτιστοι μὲν ἔσαν καὶ καρτίστοις ἐμάχοντο,
> φηρσὶν ὀρεσκῴοισι, καὶ ἐκπάγλως ἀπόλεσσαν·

οὕτω καὶ ἡμᾶς εἰκός ἐστιν ἔχειν πρὸς τοὺς ἐπαίνους, πρεσβεύειν μὲν ὃν ἂν βουλώμεθα καὶ ὃν ἂν ᾖ δίκαιον, μὴ διασύρειν δὲ οὓς οὐκ ἄξιον, μηδὲ νομίζειν τὴν πρὸς τοὺς ἑτέρους ἀπέχθειαν ἀφορμὴν τῆς πρὸς τοὺς ἑτέρους πίστεως εἶναι, ἀλλ' ἡγεῖσθαι παραπλήσιον

alone in Attica, and to regard the whole of the rest of it as hostile and enemy territory; nor when someone has shown everyone else to be ridiculous should he then by this means expect people to admire Plato. That would not be an honoring of Plato, but rather a dishonoring of the rest, and more or less a dishonoring of Plato himself as well. Because how can it not be something of the kind to think that if someone else is judged to be good it is impossible for him to be thought more valuable still? No, the way 609
Homer bestows praise with the words

> in front a good man fled, and there pursued him a
> much better,[484]

or again

> of men by far the best was Telamonian Ajax,
> as long as Achilles was enraged; for he was far
> superior,[485]

and in another passage

> they were the mightiest and fought with the
> mightiest,
> with centaurs who lived in the mountains, and
> terribly they destroyed them,[486]

is the proper model for our own attitude to praise: we should give precedence to whoever we wish and whoever it is right to give precedence to, but not ridicule those who do not deserve to be ridiculed, or think that hatred toward one set of people provides a basis for solidarity with the rest. We should take it that what I am now doing is like

[484] *Il.* 22.158. [485] *Il.* 2.768–69. [486] *Il.* 1.267–68.

νῦν ἡμᾶς ποιεῖν, ὥσπερ ἂν εἴ τις ἐν συμποσίῳ φίλων κοινῶν μαχομένων συστασιάζειν μὲν μηδετέροις ἀξιοίη, μηδ᾽ οὓς ἀδικεῖσθαι νομίζοι, πραΰνειν δ᾽ ἐπιχειροίη τοὺς ὑπάρξαντας καὶ διαλλάττειν εἰς τὸ δυνατόν. εἰ γὰρ τοῦ Πλάτωνα κακόν τι λέγειν ἀφέμενοι τοῖς ἀνδράσι τὰ πρέποντα ἀπεδώκαμεν, οὐκ ἀδικοῦμεν οἶμαι. ταῦτα γὰρ καὶ πολιτικὰ καὶ ἀνθρώπινα καὶ θεοῖς ἀρέσκοντα ἐκ τοῦ παντὸς χρόνου.

610 δεῖ γὰρ καὶ τραγῳδίαν, ὦ Πλάτων, ἐπίστασθαι ἐπαινέσαι καὶ κωμῳδίαν γε ἃ προσήκει καὶ διθύραμβον καὶ χορούς, οὐδ᾽ ἂν ὅ γε Ἀπόλλων ἱστάναι χοροὺς προσέταττεν, εἰ πάντῃ φαῦλον ἦν, οὐδέ γε, ὃ τούτου μεῖζόν ἐστι, τὸν ἀποκτείναντα Ἀρχίλοχον, ὃς τὸ πάντων †ἔξοχον[175] καὶ δυσχερέστερον εἶδος τῆς ποιήσεως μετεχειρίζετο, τοὺς ἰάμβους, ἐξεῖργεν ἂν τοῦ νεώ, φάσκων οὐκ εἶναι καθαρόν, καὶ ταῦτ᾽ ἐν πολέμῳ τοῦ φόνου συμβάντος. ἀλλ᾽ ὅμως ἐτίμησεν τὸν Ἀρχίλοχον καὶ Μουσάων γε θεράποντα προσεῖπεν,
611 ἀλλ᾽ οὐκ ἀνθρώπων διάκονον οὐδενός. οὐ τοίνυν οὐδ᾽ Ἀρχίλοχος περὶ τὰς βλασφημίας οὕτω διατρίβων τοὺς ἀρίστους τῶν Ἑλλήνων καὶ τοὺς ἐνδοξοτάτους ἔλεγεν κακῶς, ἀλλὰ Λυκάμβην καὶ Χειδὸν[176] καὶ τὸν δεῖνα τὸν μάντιν, καὶ τὸν Περικλέα τὸν καθ᾽ αὑτόν, οὐ τὸν πάνυ, καὶ τοιούτους ἀνθρώπους ἔλεγεν κακῶς.

175 ἔσχατον *dubitanter* Reiske *an* αἴσχιον?
176 Χαρίλαον Liebel

someone at a symposium who, when his shared friends are fighting, decides not to side with either party, even the ones he thinks are being wrongly treated, but instead attempts to calm down those who started the quarrel and to reconcile them as far as possible. Because if while refraining from speaking ill of Plato I have also given the Four their due, I think I have done no wrong, since this has counted as civilized and humane and pleasing to the gods since the beginning of time.

Plato, one should know how to praise tragedy, and 610
comedy as far as is appropriate, and the dithyramb and
choruses. Apollo of all gods would not have commanded
the institution of choruses if they had been something
entirely worthless, nor more significantly would he have
barred from his temple the man who killed Archilochus—
Archilochus, who worked in iambus, which is the
most . . .[487] and disagreeable of all genres of poetry—saying that he was polluted, even though the murder had
taken place in wartime; yet even so Apollo honored Archilochus and called him "servant of the Muses," rather than
the lackey of any human master.[488] Nor indeed did Archi- 611
lochus himself, though so intent on defaming people,
abuse the best and most celebrated of the Hellenes, but
rather Lycambes and Cheidos and So-and-So the seer, and
Pericles (his contemporary, not the famous one), and such

[487] The Greek text is corrupt at this point; a word meaning "shameful" or "disgraceful" seems to be called for.

[488] The murderer was one Calondas, nicknamed Corax ("Crow"): Plut. *De sera* 17.560e; Dio Chrys. 33.12.

612 μὴ τοίνυν ἡμεῖς ἐκεῖνον ὑπερβαλώμεθα, μηδὲ Τιμοκρέοντος τοῦ σχετλίου πρᾶγμα ποιῶμεν, ἀλλ' εἰδῶμεν εὐφημεῖν τὰ γιγνόμενα, καὶ ταῦτα παντὸς μᾶλλον δυνάμενοι, καὶ τὸ τοῦ Ὁμήρου νομίζωμεν εὖ ἔχειν

οὐ μὲν γὰρ τιμή γε μί' ἔσσεται οὐδ' ἠβαιόν.

ἀλλὰ κἂν ἄλλο τι τοιοῦτον εἴη; διὸ τῆς ἐπιβαλλούσης μερίδος δικαίως ἂν μεταλαμβάνοι. εἰ δ' ἄρ' ἐπαινεῖν μὴ ἔχοιμεν, ἀλλὰ σιωπᾶν γε δήπουθεν ἔξεστιν.

613 εἰ δ' οὖν καὶ τἄλλα πάντα ἀτιμάζομεν, ἀλλ' οὐ πρὸς ῥητορικὴν εἰκὸς ἦν οὕτω φιλονίκως οὐδὲ πικρῶς ἔχειν· εἰ δέ τοι καὶ πρὸς τοὺς ἄλλους ῥήτορας, ἀλλ' οὐ πρός γε τοὺς ἀρίστους τῶν Ἑλλήνων, οὐδ' οἷς μέγιστα ἀντὶ μεγίστων ὀφείλεται, καὶ οὐ μόνον παρὰ τῶν κατ' ἐκείνους ἢ μετ' ἐκείνους εὐθὺς γενομένων, ἀλλὰ καὶ παρὰ τῶν ὕστερον ὡς εἰπεῖν ἁπάντων.
614 ἔπειτα τῆς μὲν κωμῳδίας κατηγορεῖς, αὐτὸς δὲ κωμῳδεῖς Ἱππίαν, Πρόδικον, Πρωταγόραν, Γοργίαν, Εὐθύδημον, Διονυσόδωρον, Ἀγάθωνα, Κινησίαν,[177] πάντας ἀνθρώπους. καὶ τὸ μὲν τοὺς ἄλλους ἔλαττον· ἀλλ' αὐτὸν τὸν Ἀριστοφάνη τίς ἔσθ' ὁ κωμῳδῶν; ὅτῳ πολὺ

177 Κινησίαν Stephanus κιχησίαν *codd.*

---

489 See frr. 172–81 *IEG* (Lycambes), 13 and 16 (Pericles); "Cheidos" may perhaps be a slip for "Charilaos" (fr. 168 *IEG*), and the unnamed seer may be the Batusiades of fr. 182 *IEG*.

490 Timocreon of Rhodes, a lyric poet of the early fifth century

men as that.[489] Let us then not go further than him and let 612
us not behave like the wretched Timocreon,[490] but instead let us know how to give praise where praise is due (all the more because we are in the best possible position to do so) and let us acknowledge the validity of Homer's declaration that

> there will not be one and the same degree of honor,
> even in the slightest.[491]

Might there however be something else that is comparable? For that very reason it could rightly claim its proper share. If on the other hand we are unable to give praise, it is surely at least possible to keep silent.

So, even if we scorn everything else, it was not reason- 613
able to have such a bitter and competitive attitude toward oratory; and even if that was a reasonable attitude to have to other orators, it certainly was not to the best of the Hellenes, to whom the greatest debt is owed on the strength of the greatest benefactions, not only from their contemporaries and those who came immediately after them, but also from just about all subsequent generations.
Moreover, although you condemn comedy, you yourself 614
satirize Hippias, Prodicus, Protagoras, Gorgias, Euthydemus, Dionysodorus, Agathon, Cinesias, and everyone on earth.[492] Satirizing the others is less serious, but when it comes to Aristophanes himself—well, who is this who is satirizing him? Someone who himself has a rich vein of

BC, who had vitriolic things to say about both Themistocles and Simonides: Plut. *Vit. Them.* 21.2–5, with *PMG* 727–34 and *Anth. Pal.* 7.384.

[491] A combination of *Il.* 24.66 and 2.380.

[492] As in *Protagoras, Gorgias, Symposium*, and *Euthydemus*.

615 τῆς κωμῳδίας, φαίη τις ἄν, περίεστιν. καὶ τὴν μέν
γε τραγῳδίαν λοιδορεῖς, πάλιν δ' ἐπαινῶν τι τῶν
συγγραμμάτων τῶν σαυτοῦ, τοὺς Νόμους οἶμαι, τραγῳδίαν προσείρηκας, καὶ ἀρίστην τῶν τραγῳδιῶν
ἐτίθεις, καὶ αὐτὸς ὁμολογεῖς τραγῳδίας εἶναι ποιητής, ἀληθῆ λέγων, ὡς ἐγὼ φαίην ἄν. ἀλλ' εἴ τι
φαῦλόν γε ἡ τραγῳδία καὶ φαύλων ἀνθρώπων, πῶς
σε φῶμεν τραγῳδίαν ποιεῖν; οὐ γὰρ τό γε ὅλως αἰ-
616 σχρὸν οὐδαμῶς ἔνι δήπου ποιῆσαι καλόν. καὶ λέγεις
μὲν ὡς οὐ χρὴ μιμεῖσθαι τοὺς φαύλους οὐδ' ἀφομοι-
οῦν αὑτὸν τοῖς χείροσιν, αὐτὸς δ' οὐ πάνυ χρῇ τούτῳ
διὰ τέλους, ἀλλὰ μιμῇ σοφιστάς, μιμῇ συκοφάντας,
μιμῇ Θρασύμαχον τὸν οὐδεπώποτε ἐρυθριάσαντα,
θυρωρούς, παιδία, μυρίους. ἀλλ' οἶμαι τὸ τῆς φύσεως
Ἑλληνικὸν καὶ εὔκολον καὶ εὔχαρι καὶ ποικίλον καὶ
θεῖον ἐφ' ἅπαντα ταῦτ' ἄγον σε ποιεῖ μαρτυρεῖν ὅτι
καὶ τούτων ἑκάστου χρῆσίς ἐστι καιρὸν ἔχουσα καὶ
χάριν ἐμμελῆ.

ὁρῶ δ' ὅτι κἀν τῇ σεμνοτάτῃ τῶν πολιτειῶν μνη-
σθείς τι καὶ περὶ τούτου Ἑλληνίδα τὴν πόλιν ἀξιοῖς
εἶναι. δεῖν γὰρ αὐτὴν φῂς ὥς τι διάφορον δηλονότι.
617 οὐκοῦν ταῦτά γε τῶν Ἑλλήνων ἐπιχώρια. καίτοι πῶς
εἰκὸς ὑπὲρ μὲν τῶν ἀδήλων τὴν Πυθίαν κελεύειν ἐπε-
ρωτᾶν, ἃ δ' ἡ Πυθία πολλάκις ἤδη καὶ πολλοῖς

---

[493] *Leg.* 817a–b. [494] *Resp.* 395c–96b.
[495] *Resp.* 350d. [496] *Prt.* 314c–e. [497] For example, Charmides, or the sons of Nicias and Laches in *Laches*.

comedy in him, one might well say. And although you rail 615
at tragedy, you did on the other hand in praising one of your own works, the *Laws* I think, call it "a tragedy," and considered it "the best of tragedies," and confessed to being "a tragic poet" yourself (and were right to do so, in my view).[493] But if tragedy is something worthless and the work of worthless individuals, how can we say that you are writing tragedy? It is certainly not possible by any stretch of the imagination to make what is utterly shameful into
something fine. You also say that one should not depict 616
worthless characters or make oneself like one's inferiors,[494] but you do not yourself consistently adhere to this, and instead depict sophists, informers, Thrasymachus who had never yet blushed for shame,[495] doorkeepers,[496] children,[497] and countless others. But I think the truly Hellenic and good-natured and charming and versatile and inspired element of your genius, in bringing you to all this, also makes you testify that each of these instances has a practical function that is both timely and pleasingly appropriate.

I also observe that in your most revered of republics, when you make some mention of this matter, you require your city to be Hellenic.[498] Evidently, when you say that she has to be, you mean this as a distinguishing feature. Your city's features, then, are native Hellenic characteristics. But how can it be reasonable on the one hand to tell 617
people to consult the Pythia over obscure matters,[499] while on the other willfully overlooking and refusing to take ac-

[498] *Resp.* 470e.
[499] *Resp.* 427b–c, 461e, 540b–c; *Leg.* 738b, 759c, 947d.

*ἀνεῖλεν ὑπερβαίνειν ἑκόντα καὶ μὴ ἐθέλειν λογίζε-
σθαι; τί οὖν ἀνεῖλεν ἐκείνη πολλάκις ἤδη καὶ πολλοῖς; νόμῳ πόλεως πράττοντας ὀρθῶς ἂν πράττειν.*
618 *μὴ τοίνυν ἡμεῖς κινῶμεν τὰ περὶ ταῦτα νόμιμα, ἄλλως
τε καὶ αὐτοὶ πολλάκις αὐτοῖς χρώμενοι καί τιν' εὐδο-
κιμοῦντες τρόπον καὶ τούτων ἕνεκα· ἐπεὶ καὶ τὸν διθύραμβον δόξειε μὲν ἄν τῳ ψέγειν, φαίνεται δ' οὕτω
τιμῶν ὥστε καὶ χρῆσθαι, καὶ ὅ γ' ἔτι τούτου κάλλιόν
ἐστιν, ὅτι καὶ αὐτὸς ὁμολογεῖ. φησὶ γάρ που λέγων*
619 *οὐ πόρρω διθυράμβων φθέγγεσθαι. καίτοι εἰ καθάπαξ αἰσχρὸν ὁ διθύραμβος καὶ ἀγεννὲς καὶ ἀνελεύθερον, τί σὺ ποιεῖς διθυράμβους, εἰ δὲ μή, μιμῇ γε, καὶ
ταῦτ' εἰς τοὺς πεζοὺς τελεῖν ταχθείς; ἢ τί σοι βούλεται τὸ μὴ πόρρω διθυράμβων φθέγγεσθαι; οὐ γὰρ δὴ
τοῦτο λέγεις, μὴ πόρρω τῶν κολάκων καὶ τῶν διακόνων φθέγγεσθαι, οὔτε σὺ φαίης ἂν τοῦτό γε οὔθ'
ἡμεῖς κατὰ σοῦ πιστεύσομεν, ἢ κομιδῇ πάντ' ἄνω καὶ
κάτω γίγνοιτ' ἄν.*

620 *ἡγοῦμαι μὲν τοίνυν καὶ διθυράμβων εἶναι Πλάτωνα
ποιητὴν ἄριστον· πῶς γὰρ οὔ; οὐ μὴν οὐδὲ τῶν Πινδάρου διθυράμβων ὅτι χρὴ καταγνῶναι τοιοῦτον οἷον
Πλάτων ἐπητιάσατο ἔγωγ' ἔχω,*[178] *οὐ μόνον αὐτὸ
τοῦτο τοὺς διθυράμβους σκοπῶν ἀνδρειότερον δήπου-*

[178] *ἔχω* <*συνιδεῖν*> Reiske *an* <*εἰπεῖν*>?

count of the answer the Pythia often gave to many of her inquirers? What was this answer that she often gave to many of her inquirers? That in acting in accordance with their city's customs they would be acting correctly.[500] Let 618
us then not disturb customary practices in this area, especially when we ourselves have often followed them and indeed enjoyed some degree of good repute precisely on their account. I say this because in the case of the dithyramb too, Plato might give the impression to some of criticizing it, but also clearly respects it enough to employ it himself, and what is better still, confesses that he does: somewhere in his work he says that his "utterances are not far from being dithyrambs."[501] Yet if the dithyramb were 619
something flatly shameful and ignoble and base, why are you composing dithyrambs, or if not that, imitating them, when your proper place is among the prose writers? Or what is it that you do mean by saying that your "utterances are not far from being dithyrambs"? You certainly do not mean that your utterances are not far from those of flatterers and lackeys: you would not say this, nor would we believe it against you, or the world really would be turned upside down.

I believe then that Plato is an excellent composer of 620
dithyrambs too—how could I not?—but at the same time I cannot agree that one ought to condemn Pindar's dithyrambs as roundly as Plato's accusation suggested. I say this not simply from looking at the dithyrambs themselves and seeing that they have too virile and robust

[500] For example, in the responses cited by Demosthenes in *Orr.* 21.52 and 43.66.

[501] *Phdr.* 238d.

θεν ἔχοντας καὶ στερεώτερον ἢ ὡς ἐκεῖνόν τῳ[179] δοκεῖν ὑποπίπτειν, ἀλλ' ὅτι κἀν τοῖς ὕμνοις διεξιὼν περὶ τῶν ἐν ἅπαντι τῷ χρόνῳ συμβαινόντων παθημάτων τοῖς ἀνθρώποις καὶ τῆς μεταβολῆς τὸν Κάδμον φησὶν ἀκοῦσαι τοῦ Ἀπόλλωνος "μουσικὰν ὀρθὰν" ἐπιδεικνυμένου. [οὕτω καὶ Πίνδαρος τῆς ὀρθῆς μουσικῆς ἐραστής ἐστι. τὸ δ' ἐραστής ἐστι τὴν ὀρθὴν μουσικὴν μεταχειρίζεται.][180] οὐ γὰρ δήπου τῷ μὲν Ἀπόλλωνι ταύτην προστίθησιν, αὐτὸς δ' ἑτέραν διώκει ταύτην ἀφείς, καὶ ταῦτ' ἀεὶ τὸν Ἀπόλλω καὶ τὰς Μούσας καλῶν.

621 εἶτα λέγεις ὅτι πάντες οὗτοι τοῦ πρὸς ἡδονὴν ἐξήρτηνται. πότερον οὖν σε φῶμεν ἔλαττον τοῦ δέοντος λέγειν ἢ πλέον; ὅτι μὲν γὰρ καὶ τοῦ πρὸς ἡδονὴν φροντίζουσιν ὁμολογεῖται, ὥσθ' ὅσον προσθεῖναι προσῆκεν, τοσοῦτον ἀφελὼν ἔλαττον παρὰ τοῦτ' εἴρηκας.[181] ὅτι δ' αὐτοῖς κολακείαν ἐπενηνόχεις ἐκ τούτου πῶς οὐκ ἔξω τοῦ δέοντος εἴρηκας, ἢ πῶς οὐ ταύτῃ
622 πλέον αὖ τοῦ δέοντός ἐστιν ἔχων ὁ λόγος; εἶεν. αὐτὸς δὲ σὺ πρὸς Διὸς οὐ πώποθ' ἡμῖν οὐδὲν πρὸς ἡδονὴν οὔτ' εἶπας οὔτ' ἐποίησας, οὐ συνέθηκας, οὐ διέθου λόγον, οὐκ ἀνέπαυσας, οὐκ ἐπεισήγαγες, ἀλλ' ἁπλῶς οὑτωσὶ τὴν ἀπὸ Σκυθῶν ἡμῖν διαλέγῃ; ἐγὼ μὲν οὐκ ἐνέτυχον εἰς τήνδε τὴν ἡμέραν ἡδίονι τούτου καὶ πρὸς

[179] τῳ Reiske τό Q τῷ *cett.*
[180] *del.* Trapp (τὸ δ' . . . μεταχειρίζεται *iam* Behr)
[181] ὥσθ' ὅσον . . . εἴρηκας *del.* Behr

a character for their author to be thought to be subservient to anyone, but also because in his hymns too when he is reviewing the sufferings and the change that have befallen mankind through the whole of time he says that Cadmus heard Apollo performing "music true."[502] It surely cannot be that he assigns this kind of music to Apollo but abandons it himself and pursues another, especially as he is always invoking Apollo and the Muses.

621 Can you really then say that all these people are devoted to what promotes pleasure? In that case, should we say that you are saying less than you ought to or more? It is agreed that they do also have a concern for what promotes pleasure; so that in withholding whatever it was appropriate to add to this you have thereby said less. But in imputing flattery to them on these grounds, how can you not have gone beyond what you ought to have said, and how can your argument in this respect not contain more than it ought to? Well then: tell me, have you your- 622
self for heaven's sake never said or done anything with a view to giving pleasure—never composed anything, never structured an argument, never devised an ending, never brought in extra material—but do you just address us in pure Scythian style?[503] I for my part have never to this day read an author who gives more pleasure than this one, and

[502] Fr. 32 Sn-M. The next two sentences in the Greek text, bracketed opposite, look like a couple of reader's notes: "Thus Pindar too is a lover of 'music true.' The word 'lover' means that he practices music true."

[503] Scythian speech, as represented, e.g., by the sage Anacharsis, was thought of as notably spare and direct: e.g., Hdt. 4.127; Lucian *Toxaris* 35; Max. Tyr. 25.1.

αὐτοὺς τοὺς διθυραμβοποιοὺς καὶ τοὺς τραγῳδιοποι-
623 οὺς εἶπον ἄν, εἴ τις αὐτῶν ἤρετο. εἶτ' αὐτὸς ὅμοιον τῷ Νέστορι φθεγγόμενος, εἰ δὴ κἀκεῖνον τοιοῦτόν τι χρὴ φθέγξασθαι δοκεῖν, ἐγὼ μὲν γὰρ καὶ τὰς Σειρῆνας ἂν εἶξαί σοι δοκῶ, τῶν ἄλλων εἴ τι καὶ πρὸς ἡδονὴν λέγουσι κατηγορεῖς; ὅρα μὴ παίζοντα μᾶλλον τιθῇ σέ τις ἢ σπουδάζοντα καὶ φιλονεικοῦντα, ὅς γε καὶ ἐν αὐτοῖς τούτοις τοῖς λόγοις, ἐν οἷς διασύρει ταῦτα τὰ ἔθνη τοσοῦτον χαρίτων καὶ ἡδονῆς εἰσηνέγκατο, ὅσον οἷόν τ' ἦν πλεῖστον ὡς ἐν ἀηδεῖ λέγω τῷ παντὶ λόγῳ καὶ τραχεῖ.

624 τὸ μὲν οὖν μείζω τῶν ἄλλων Πλάτωνα φρονεῖν οὐ νεμεσῶ, τὸ δὲ τοὺς ἄλλους, εἰ μὴ πικρὸν εἰπεῖν, προπηλακίζειν, κἂν αὐτῷ συνών τε καὶ συμβουλεύων ἀφαιρεῖν οὐκ ἀδικεῖν ἂν ἡγοῦμαι. οἶμαι δὲ καὶ Σωκράτει τὸν Ἀπόλλω τοῦτο κελεύειν, κελεύοντα μουσικὴν ποιεῖν, ἀφελεῖν τὴν φιλαπεχθημοσύνην τὴν περὶ τοὺς λόγους, ὡς ἐκείνου γ' ἄλλο μὲν οὐ ῥᾴδιον εὑρεῖν ὅ τί τις κατηγορήσει. τοῦτο δ' ἤδη τινὲς ᾐτιάσαντο, ἀμέλει καὶ πρὸς τὸν ἀγῶνα ὃν ἔφυγεν τοῦτο μάλιστ' αὐτὸν βλάψαι δοκεῖ. καὶ ὅπως μή τίς μοι τῶν σοφιστῶν ὑπολήψεται, ἀλλ' οὐδέν γ' ἐβλάβη Σωκράτης, ἐπεὶ κἂν ἄλλος ἔχοι πρὸς τοῦθ' ὑπολαμβάνειν, ἀλλὰ βλαβῆναί γ' αἴτιος ἐγένετο τῶν δικαστῶν τοῖς κατα-

504 *Il.* 1.247–49 (on the strength of which Nestor was regularly regarded as a model of the "middle" or "flowery," Isocratean, style of oratory: e.g., Quint. *Inst.* 12.10.64); cf. §427 above.

I would have said as much to the dithyrambic poets and the tragedians, if any of them had asked. So although you 623
yourself give tongue like Nestor—if we should believe that he too gave tongue in some such way as this,[504] though for myself I think that even the Sirens would yield to you[505]—do you condemn everyone else if they say anything with a view to giving pleasure? Take care that people do not suppose that you are joking rather than being serious and competitive, seeing that in the very works in which you satirize these categories of people you have incorporated the greatest possible degree of charm and entertainment, allowing that is to say for the harsh and disagreeable nature of the work overall.

What makes me indignant is not that Plato is prouder 624
of himself than the others are; it is his vulgar abuse for the others, if that is not too cutting a way of putting it, and I do not think I would be doing wrong in advising him personally to do away with it. I think this was what Apollo was telling Socrates to do when he told him to "make music,"[506] namely to do away with the fondness for making enemies that he showed in his discourses, since it is not easy to find anything else that one might condemn in him. But this was something that people had already faulted him for, and indeed it was this that seems to have done him the most harm in the court case that he had to defend. And let no quibbling sophist retort to me "But Socrates did not suffer any harm,"[507] since anyone would be in a position to fire back "He was at all events responsible for

[505] *Od.* 12.186–88, 192; for the Sirens as models of enthralling eloquence, cf. Lucian *Nigr.* 3. [506] *Phd.* 60e.

[507] A claim based on *Ap.* 30c–d and 41c–d.

625 ψηφισαμένοις, εἴπερ γε μὴ τὰ δίκαια ἔγνωσαν. χωρὶς δὲ τούτων εἰ μὲν ὅλως ἐπεθύμει θανάτου, πρῶτον μὲν τί τοσοῦτον ἦν αὐτῷ; ἔπειτ᾽ οὐδ᾽ ἀπολογεῖσθαι προσῆκε τὴν ἀρχήν. εἰ δ᾽ οὐκ ἂν ἀηδέστερον ἀπέφυγεν, τοῦτ᾽ ἦν τὸ κωλῦσαν, τὸ πολλοῖς ἐκ τοῦ κακῶς
626 λέγειν προσκροῦσαι. ἔοικεν δὲ καὶ Ὅμηρος ἐκ πολλοῦ ταῦτα χρησμῳδεῖν καὶ προλέγειν, ἅτε τοῦ Ἀπόλλωνος θεράπων οἶμαι καὶ πάρεδρος ὤν. ἃ γὰρ ἐν Λιταῖς Ὀδυσσεὺς λέγει πρὸς Ἀχιλλέα, Πηλέως τοῦ πατρὸς αὐτοῦ φάσκων παραίνεσιν εἶναι, ταῦθ᾽ Ὁμήρου παράκλησιν εἶναι πᾶσιν ὡς κοινοῦ πατρὸς ἡγεῖσθαι προσήκει,

> ληγέμεναι δ᾽ ἔριδος κακομηχάνου, ὄφρα σε μᾶλλον
> τίωσ᾽ Ἀργείων ἠμὲν νέοι ἠδὲ γέροντες.

δεινὴ γὰρ ἡ σφοδρὰ ἔρις καὶ τὴν ὑπάρχουσαν εὔνοιαν μεταστῆσαι καὶ τοὺς οὐκ ὄντας ἀγῶνας ἐπισπάσασθαι.

[*(v) The Gratuitous Superfluity of the Attack on the Four (627–45)*]

627 ἐγὼ μὲν οὖν ὡς μέχρι τῆς ῥητορικῆς κατέθει καὶ τοὺς τυράννους ἤλεγχεν καὶ τἄλλα διεξήρχετο, εἰπόμην ὥσπερ εἰκὸς ἦν, εἰδὼς μὲν ὅτι οὐδὲν τούτων ἔλεγχός

harm being done to those of the jurors who voted for his
condemnation, if it is true that their decision was an unjust
one." But quite apart from that, if he wholeheartedly de- 625
sired to die, in the first place, why did it matter so much
to him? And secondly, he should not have offered a defense in the first place. But if it would not have displeased
him to be acquitted, this is what prevented it, offending
so many people by abusing them. It even looks as if Homer 626
long before prophesied and predicted this, thanks I believe to his role as Apollo's servant and assistant. Because
what Odysseus says to Achilles in Book 9, claiming it as
the advice of his father Peleus, we ought to think of as
Homer's advice to us all as our common father:

> Desist from the strife that brings about ill, so that all the more
> the Argives may honor you, young and old alike.[508]

Intense strife is horribly adept at doing away with existing goodwill and dragging in contests where there were none before.

(v) The Gratuitous Superfluity of the Attack on the Four (627–45)

For my part, then, for as long as Plato was running down 627
the art of oratory and confuting tyrants and making his way
through the rest of his argument, I followed him as you
might expect me to; I knew that none of this counted as a

[508] *Il.* 9.257–58.

ἐστι ῥητορικῆς, ἀλλ' ἔχων τὸν δικαιότατον λόγον ἀντιθεῖναι, ὅμως δὲ[182] τῆς γε τόλμης ἠγασάμην καὶ τὴν δεινότητα καὶ τὴν εὐπορίαν ἐθαύμασα, καὶ εἰ χρὴ κατ' αὐτὸν εἰπεῖν οἷον λέοντος σκιρτῶντος ἔννοιάν τιν' ἐλάμβανον καὶ μόνον οὐκ ἐθεώμην τὸν ἄνδρα ἐν τοῖς λόγοις. εἰ δὲ δεῖ καὶ τοῦτο προσθεῖναι, καὶ ὁ Μέλης οὐκ ἀηδής μοι καὶ ὁ Κινησίας, ἀλλ' ἀπέλαυον τοῦ γελοίου καὶ συνεχώρουν ἄχρι τούτου καὶ ὀνομαστὶ[183]
628 κωμῳδῆσαι. πάντως οὐχ οὗτοί μοι τὰ φίλτατα. ἐπεὶ δὲ καὶ ἐπὶ Μιλτιάδην καὶ Θεμιστοκλέα καὶ τοὺς περὶ τούτους ἀφίκετο καὶ τὸ χαίρειν ἀφεὶς τούτους ἔκρουε τὴν αὐτὴν ἁρμονίαν, καὶ τὸν Θεαρίωνα προσῆπτεν, καὶ πάντα ἐμίγνυ καὶ γελοῖα καὶ σπουδαῖα ὑπὲρ τοῦ τοὺς ἄνδρας ἐλέγχειν, καὶ οὐδ' ὁτιοῦν ὑπεστέλλετο, ἀλλ' ἀνέδην ἔλεγεν κακῶς, ἐνταῦθ' ἤδη τι προσίστατό μοι καὶ ὡσπερεὶ προδοσία τις ἐφαίνετο τοὺς ἄνδρας προλιπεῖν.

629 τί λέγεις; οὐ περαίνεις αὐτὸν ἐφ' αὑτοῦ τὸν λόγον, ἀλλ' ὀνόμαθ' ἡμῖν εἰς τὸ μέσον φέρεις καὶ τὸ πρᾶγμ'
630 ἀφεὶς τὸν δεῖνα καὶ τὸν δεῖνα λέγεις κακῶς; καὶ ὁ μὲν τοῦ Σόλωνος νόμος οὐδὲ νόμον ἐπ' ἀνδρὶ γράφειν ἐᾷ, σὺ δ' ἐπ' ἀνδράσι βίβλον ποιεῖς; καὶ Σωκράτης μὲν καὶ Πυθαγόρας οὐδ' αὐτοὺς τοὺς λόγους ἐν οἷς ἔζων συνέγραψαν, ἀλλ' ἐφ' αὑτῶν ἐφιλοσόφουν, σὺ δὲ τῶν

182 δέ Trapp γε *codd. del.* Iunt., *edd.* γε τῆς τε Lenz
183 ὀνομαστί *edd.* ὀνόματι *codd.*

refutation of the art of oratory and that I had the most impeccably justified counterarguments to hand, but even so I admired his daring and marveled at his forcefulness and his fluency, and if it is permissible to speak in his own style, I had an impression as of an exuberant lion and all but saw the man himself in his words.[509] And if I may add this too, I was not annoyed by his Meles and his Cinesias,[510] but enjoyed the joke and up to this point even went along with his satirizing them by name; at all events, these men were not what I held most dear. But when he came 628
to Miltiades and Themistocles and their associates, and without a word of greeting proceeded to play the same tune over them too, and added in Thearion,[511] and produced a farrago of all kinds of comic and serious elements aimed at discrediting these men, and did not hold back at all, but let rip with his abuse, then at last I was offended and it seemed to me that it would be a kind of betrayal to abandon them.

Plato, what are you saying? Are you declining to com- 629
plete the argument on its own proper terms, but instead bringing out a set of names to present to us, and abandoning the issue simply to heap abuse on this person or that? When the law of Solon does not allow even a law to be 630
written to deal with a single individual,[512] can you write a whole book against these men? When Socrates and Pythagoras did not even write down the very principles by which they lived, but practiced their philosophies in their

[509] Aristides is perhaps thinking of Plato's characterization of Thrasymachus in *Resp.* 336b and 314.

[510] *Grg.* 502a, as in §231 above.

[511] *Grg.* 518b.

[512] This law is cited by Demosthenes in *Orr.* 23.86 and 24.59.

631 Ἑλλήνων κωμῳδεῖς τὰ ἀγάλματ᾽ ἐν μέσῳ; καὶ κωμῳδίας μὲν ἤδη ποιηταὶ τῶν ὀνομάτων ἀπέσχοντο καὶ ἠδυνήθησαν ἄνευ τοῦ ὀνομαστὶ κωμῳδεῖν τὸ δρᾶμα ἀπεργάσασθαι, σὺ δὲ τῶν Ἑλλήνων τοὺς ἄκρους τὸν Ἀριστοφάνους ἀλλαντοπώλην πεποίηκας, καὶ ταῦτα εἰκῇ καὶ πρὸς οὐδεμίαν χρείαν ἔτι τοῦ λόγου;

632 ἀπειρηκότος γὰρ ἤδη τοῦ Καλλικλέους καὶ συγχωροῦντος τῷ Σωκράτει τί πρᾶγμ᾽ ἦν ἔτι τούτων μεμνῆσθαι, ὅπου γ᾽ εἰ καὶ ὁ Καλλικλῆς ἔτυχεν περὶ αὐτῶν ὑπολαβών[184]—ἔστι μὲν οἶμαι γέλως πᾶν τοῦτο. τίς γὰρ οὐκ οἶδεν ὅτι καὶ ὁ Σωκράτης καὶ ὁ Καλλικλῆς καὶ ὁ Γοργίας καὶ ὁ Πῶλος πάντα ταῦτ᾽ ἐστὶν Πλάτων, πρὸς τὸ δοκοῦν αὐτῷ τρέπων τοὺς λόγους;—εἰ δ᾽ οὖν καὶ τῷ ὄντι ἐκεῖθεν ἀφῖκτο ὁ λόγος καὶ ὁ Καλλικλῆς ἐξεπίτηδες ἐμνήσθη περὶ τῶν ἀνδρῶν ἐπ᾽ ἐλέγχῳ τοῦ Σωκράτους, ἐξῆν ὡδὶ δέχεσθαι καὶ μηδὲν βλάσφημον λέγειν· ἄξιον δ᾽ εἴπερ τῳ καὶ τούτῳ προ-
633 σέχειν. οὑτωσὶ γὰρ ἐγίγνετό που τὰ δεύτερα, ὥς γέ μοι φαίνεται, "οὐκοῦν εἰ μὲν καὶ τούτους, ὦ φίλε Καλλίκλεις, κόλακάς τινας εἶναι λέγεις καὶ τῶν πρὸς ἡδονὴν δημηγορούντων, τίθει μοι καὶ κατὰ τούτων ταῦτ᾽ εἰρῆσθαι. οὐδὲν γὰρ βέλτιον ἥ γε δήπου κολακεία διὰ Μιλτιάδην καὶ Περικλέα καὶ ὃν ἂν εἴπῃς· πῶς γὰρ ὅ γ᾽ ἐστὶ φαῦλον φύσει; ὥστε τὸ Εὐριπίδου γίγνεται, 'σὺ λέγεις ταῦτ᾽, οὐκ ἐγώ,' ὡς ἄρα οὐδὲν οὗτοι βελ-

[184] *lac. post* ὑπολαβών Reiske

own persons, can you publicly satirize the icons of Hellenism? When in the past comic poets held back from nam- 631
ing names and were yet able to complete their dramas without satirizing their victims by name,[513] have you turned the greatest of the Hellenes into Aristophanes' sausage seller,[514] and what is more done so purposelessly and without any benefit to your argument?

What I mean is this. When Callicles had already given 632
up and agreed with Socrates,[515] what point still was there in mentioning these men, given that, even if Callicles had happened to offer a reply on this point—I think the whole business is in fact a joke: because who does not know that Socrates and Callicles and Gorgias and Polus are all Plato, turning the argument whichever way he pleases?—but anyway, if the argument really had reached that point and Callicles had deliberately mentioned the Four as a means of refuting Socrates, it would have been possible to respond to him in the following spirit without insults—and this if anything is worth paying attention to. This is how I 633
think the rejoinder might perhaps have gone: "If then, my dear Callicles, you are saying that these men too were flatterers and belonged to the number of those who made their speeches in order to give pleasure, then please take it that my denunciation includes them too. Flattery is certainly not made any better by Miltiades and Pericles and whoever else you mention: how could this be with something that is worthless in its very nature? In which case, to quote the Euripidean tag, 'it is you not I who says,'[516] that in fact these men were no better than the men of

[513] Cf. §8 above, with n. 7. [514] The central character in *Knights*. [515] *Grg.* 513c. [516] *Hipp.* 352.

τίους τῶν νῦν. εἰ δὲ τῆς ἑτέρας ἦσαν μερίδος καὶ τὸ βέλτιστον ἀντὶ τοῦ πρὸς ἡδονὴν ᾑροῦντο, καὶ οὗτοι κατηγοροῦσιν, ὡς ἔοικε, φαύλους εἶναι περὶ ὧν διειλέγμεθα, καὶ οὐδὲν βελτίων ἡ ῥητορικὴ διὰ τούτους, ἣν σὺ μέχρι τούτου ἐπῄνεσας καὶ ἣν ἐμοὶ προξενεῖς, ἀλλὰ καὶ παρὰ τούτοις κριταῖς αἰσχρόν, καὶ φαίνεῃ δὴ τούτοις κατ' ἐμοῦ μάρτυσι χρώμενος, οἷς ταὐτὰ δοκοῦντα ἅπερ κἀμοὶ φαίνεται."

634 οὕτως ἐξῆν οἶμαι διαλύειν τὸν λόγον, βλασφημίας δ' οὐδὲν προσέδει. οὐδὲν γὰρ ἐξωτέρω προὔβαινεν ὁ λόγος, ἀλλ' ἐπὶ τῶν αὐτῶν εἱστήκει. τί γάρ φησιν πρὶν ἐλθεῖν ἐπὶ τοὺς ἄνδρας;

> ἐξαρκεῖ. εἰ γὰρ καὶ τοῦτ' ἐστὶν διπλοῦν, τὸ μὲν ἕτερον αὐτοῦ κολακεία ἂν εἴη καὶ αἰσχρὰ δημηγορία, τὸ δ' ἕτερον καλόν·

635 περὶ τῆς ῥητορικῆς δήπου λέγων. καίτοι ὅτε τοῦτ' ἐξήρκει, ‹ἐξήρκει›[185] καὶ περὶ τούτων σιωπᾶν. οὐδὲν γὰρ ἐκώλυεν διπλοῦν εἶναι τὴν ῥητορικὴν τὸ τούτους γε χρηστοὺς εἶναι συγχωρῆσαι, ἀλλὰ καὶ σφόδρ' ἐκείνῳ τῷ λόγῳ συνέβαινεν. οἱ μὲν γὰρ ἦσαν κόλακες, οἱ δ' οὔ. εἰ μὲν γὰρ οὐ διπλοῦν ἡ ῥητορική, τί διῃροῦ; εἰ δὲ τοιοῦτον, τί πλέον τούτους ἐλέγχειν;
636 ἀλλὰ μὴν ὅτε καὶ τούτων κατηγορήσας ἄλλον αὖθις

[185] *add.* Reiske

today. If on the other hand they belonged to the other party and chose what was best rather than what gave pleasure, then they too, it seems, condemn the people we were talking about as worthless, and the art of oratory, which you up till now have been praising and which you recommend me to take up too, is no better because of them, but in the eyes of these judges as well it is something shameful, and you are clearly trying to use as witnesses against me men who evidently think the same as I do."

That is how I think the argument could have been 634
brought to a conclusion, and there would have been no need to add in any insults; it would not have ranged any further afield, but would have kept to the same terms. Because what does Socrates say before coming to the Four?

> That is all I need, because even if this is a twofold phenomenon, one form of it would be a kind of flattery and shameful haranguing, even if the other was something fine,[517]

meaning the art of oratory, of course. But of course if that 635
was sufficient, then it would also have been sufficient to keep quiet about these men, since conceding that they at least were good people would have done nothing to prevent the art of oratory from being twofold, but in fact would have been in strong agreement with that proposition. Some people were flatterers and some were not. If the art of oratory is not twofold, why did you make the distinction? If it is, what is the advantage in discrediting
these men? Given that having condemned these men he 636

[517] *Grg*. 503a.

ἐπῄνει, οὐδὲν τῷ λόγῳ προσελάμβανεν. ὥστ' εἶχεν ἂν πάλιν ὁ Καλλικλῆς εἰς τὰς αὐτὰς λαβὰς ἐπανελθεῖν, τί λέγων; "ἐξαρκεῖ. εἰ γάρ ἐστι διπλοῦν, καὶ τοὺς μὲν ἐπαινεῖς, τοὺς δὲ ψέγεις, τί σοι προκέκοπται, πλὴν εἰ τούτοις ἄλλως ἀηδῶς εἶχες."

637 φέρε γὰρ πρὸς θεῶν, εἰ ὁ Καλλικλῆς εὐθὺς ἐν ἀρχῇ τὸν Ἀριστείδην προὐτείνατο, ἤτοι μόνον εἰπὼν ἢ καὶ μετ' ἐκείνων, ἡνίκ' αὐτὸν ἤρετο Σωκράτης εἴ τινα τῶν παλαιῶν εἰπεῖν ἔχει, πῶς ἂν αὐτὸν ἐδέξατο, ἢ τί τὸ συμβαῖνον ἔμελλεν ἔσεσθαι περὶ τὸν λόγον; εἰ μὲν γὰρ κἀκεῖνον ἂν ὥσπερ καὶ τούτους εἶπεν κακῶς, οὕτω καὶ τούτων ἕκαστον, ὡς ἔοικεν, εἴρηκεν. ὥσθ' ὃν ἐπῄνεσεν, εἶπεν ἄν, εἰ συνέβη, κακῶς. εἰ δ' οὐχ οἷόν τ' ἦν αἰτιάσασθαι, τί ταύτης ἔδει τῆς φιλονικίας, "εἴ τινα τῶν παλαιῶν ἔχεις εἰπεῖν;" ὁπότε γὰρ μὴ ἐνῆν ἅπαντας ἐλέγχειν, τί χρῆν κατὰ πάντων προκαλεῖ-
638 σθαι; καὶ μὴν εἴ γε μηδὲν βλάβος ἦν τῷ λόγῳ μὴ ἐλέγξαι τὸν Ἀριστείδην, οὐδὲ τούτους ἐπάναγκες ἦν κακῶς εἰπεῖν. εἰ τοίνυν τὸν μὲν ἐπῄνεσεν, τὸν δ' ἔψεξεν αὐτῶν, τί πλέον προσεγίγνετ' ἂν αὐτῷ; τὸ γὰρ ἀρχαῖον ἐκεῖνο ἔμενεν, τὸ ἐξαρκεῖ καὶ τὸ διπλοῦν ἐστιν. οὐ γὰρ δὴ προῄδει γ' ὁ Σωκράτης ὅτι πάντων μᾶλλον ἢ 'κείνου μνησθήσοιτο ὁ Καλλικλῆς καὶ διὰ τοῦτ' ἠρώτα θαρρῶν, ἀλλ' ἐξῆν καὶ μόνον εἰπεῖν καὶ

then went and praised another man, he certainly added
nothing to his argument. Callicles could therefore have
resorted to the same hold. By saying what? "That is all I
need: if it is a twofold phenomenon, and you praise some
while criticizing others, what progress have you made, unless you have some other grounds for disliking these men?"

Look, for heaven's sake, if Callicles had suggested Aris- 637
tides right at the outset, citing him either on his own or
along with the others, when Socrates asked him if he could
name anyone from among the men of old, how would Socrates have responded to him, and what would the likely
consequences for the argument have been? If Socrates
had denigrated Aristides too just as he did the others,
then, as it would seem, if things had fallen out like this, he
would have been in the position of having spoken about
each of them in such a way as to denigrate the man who
in fact he praised. If however it had not been possible to
bring any charge against Aristides, what need was there
for that aggressive question about "naming anyone from
among the men of old"? Because if there was no possibility of discrediting them all, what need was there to challenge Callicles over all of them? Certainly if it indeed 638
would have done no harm to the argument not to discredit
Aristides, it was not necessary to denigrate these other
men either. And if Socrates had praised some of them and
criticized others, what advantage would he have derived?
There would still have been those statements "that is all I
need" and "it is twofold," just as before. Socrates certainly
did not know in advance that Callicles was going to mention everybody rather than Aristides, and question him
confidently for that reason; it was open to Callicles both
to mention Aristides alone, and to mention him too along

μετὰ τῶν ἄλλων κἀκείνου μνησθῆναι, καὶ οὕτως ἐξεχεῖτ᾽ ἂν ἅπασα ἡ περιβολή.

639 τί δὴ φήσομεν διαφέρειν ἢ μετ᾽ ἐκείνων ἀναμὶξ αὐτὸν ἐπαινεῖσθαι κακῶς ἀκουόντων καὶ τοῦ Καλλικλέους εἰς μέσον ἐξ ἀρχῆς ἐνεγκόντος, ἢ μετὰ τὴν ἐκείνων κατηγορίαν τοῦτόν γ᾽ ἐπαινεῖσθαι καὶ τὸν μεμνημένον αὐτοῦ Σωκράτη αὐτὸν εἶναι; ἐγὼ μὲν οὐδὲν φήσαιμ᾽ ἂν διαφέρειν πρός γε τὸ συγχεῖσθαι τὸν
640 λόγον. καὶ μὴν εἴ γε μόνου τις ἐμνημόνευσεν, οὐκ ἂν εἶχεν οὔτ᾽ ἐκεῖνον δήπου οὔτε τούτους εἰπεῖν κακῶς. οὕτως οὐκ ἀνάγκη τούτους εἰπεῖν κακῶς. ἀλλ᾽ οἶμαι τοιοῦτόν ἐστιν, ᾧ καὶ μάλιστα δῆλός ἐστι τῶν ἀνδρῶν κατηγορῆσαι προθυμηθεὶς ἤδη Πλάτων καὶ πρῶτον εἰπεῖν τὸν Ἀριστείδην καὶ μόνον, καὶ προεώρα τὸν ἄνδρα ἐξ ἀρχῆς, καὶ οὐδεὶς αὐτὸν Καλλικλῆς παρὼν ἐτάραττεν, οὐδ᾽ ἐκώλυεν τὸ μὴ ὅπως
641 βούλεται περαίνειν τὸν λόγον. εἰ μὲν οὖν, οἶμαι, κατ᾽ ἀρχὰς εὐθὺς ἐμνήσθη τοῦ Ἀριστείδου, οὐκ ἂν εἶχεν ἀφορμὴν τοῦ κατὰ τούτων λέγειν, ἀλλ᾽ ἅμα τ᾽ ἀπώλλυε τοὺς λόγους τούτους καὶ τὸ πρᾶγμα εἰς τοὐναντίον αὐτῷ περιίστατο, πρὸς τὸ μηδ᾽ ὁτιοῦν ἀνύτειν πλέον. νῦν δ᾽ ἵνα τούτων κατηγορήσειεν, τὸν Ἀριστεί-
642 δην ὑπεξείλετο. εἶθ᾽ ὅτε δὴ διεξῆλθεν ἃ ἐβούλετο, ἵνα μὴ δοκῇ παντελῶς φιλονίκως ἔχειν, ὃν οὐχ οἷόν τ᾽ ἦν ἐν ἀρχῇ κακῶς εἰπεῖν, τοῦτον ἐν τοῖς τελευταίοις ἐπήνεσεν, ὡς ἐξὸν ἤδη, μάλ᾽ ἀρχαίως καὶ ἀφελῶς, ὡς ἄν τῳ δόξαι. καὶ τὸ δὴ στερεώτατον, ὅτε γὰρ διεξῆλθεν

with the others, and in that case the whole sweep of the
argument would have gone to waste.
What difference shall we say there is between on the 639
one hand having Callicles bring Aristides into the discussion at the outset, and his praise being mixed in together
with abuse for the others, and on the other hand having
Socrates bring him up, and his praise follow their denunciation? I for one would say that it made no difference, at
least to the confounding of the argument. Moreover, if 640
someone had mentioned Aristides alone, he would surely
not have been able to denigrate either him or them, and
that shows just how unnecessary it was to denigrate them.
But, well, the argument is as it is, which makes it all too
clear that Plato was already keen to condemn the Four and
to be the first and only person to mention Aristides, and
that he had the man in his sights from the outset, and no
Callicles by his presence was going to disconcert him or
prevent him completing the argument as he wanted to. If, 641
then, he had mentioned Aristides right at the beginning,
I do not think he would have had any basis for speaking
against the Four, but at a stroke he would have undone his
arguments and found his whole case had been turned
against him, leaving him utterly unable to achieve anything further. But as it was he spirited Aristides away so as
to be able to attack these men. Then when he said as much 642
as he wanted to, so as not to seem motivated by pure
competitiveness, when it was now possible to do it, he
praised in his concluding remarks the man he could not
speak ill of at the outset, and one might well think he did
so in a very simplistic and offhand manner. And here is the
kernel of the matter. When he had finished his indictment

τὴν ἐκείνων κατηγορίαν, ἐπὶ τελευτῇ πάλιν νεανιευσάμενος καὶ ἐπειπὼν ὅτι

ἀληθεῖς ἄρα, ὡς ἔοικεν, οἱ ἔμπροσθεν λόγοι ἦσαν, ὅτι οὐδένα ἡμεῖς ἴσμεν ἄνδρα ἀγαθὸν γεγονότα τὰ πολιτικὰ ἐν τῇδε τῇ πόλει.

ταῦτ᾽ εἰπὼν καὶ προσεπισφραγισάμενος μετὰ πολλοὺς ἔτι τῶν λόγων μέσους τὸν Ἀριστείδην ἐπέθηκεν ἐπαινῶν. τοσοῦτον πλέον ἐστὶ τὸν Σωκράτη, ἀλλὰ μὴ τὸν Καλλικλέα τὸν εἰρηκότ᾽ εἶναι περὶ αὐτοῦ.

643 οὐκοῦν οὔτ᾽ ἐξ ἀνάγκης ἦν αὐτῷ κακῶς λέγειν τοὺς ἄνδρας οὔθ᾽ ὅ τι ἄν τις φήσειεν ἐκ περιουσίας εἶναι σώσας φαίνεται, τὸ μηδ᾽ ἀγαθὸν τῶν παλαιῶν γεγενῆσθαι μηδένα. ἀλλὰ μὴν ὅτε καὶ αὐτὸν τὸν Καλλικλέα, πρὸς ὃν ἦσαν οἱ λόγοι, τοῦ μηδενὸς ἄξιον ὄντα ἤλεγξεν τὰ πολιτικά, ἀνερωτῶν ἅπαντα ἐκεῖνα ἃ ἤρετο, ὅτε ταῦτα ἐλήλεγκτο, τί τῶν παλαιῶν προσέδει κατηγορίας; εἰς γὰρ τὸ κάλλιστον δήπου καὶ ὃ μάλιστα προσῆκεν ὁ λόγος ἐτελεύτα, τὸ τὸν ἀντιλέγοντα καὶ τὸν προτρέποντα εἰς τὴν πολιτείαν ἢ διακονίαν ἀποφῆναι φαῦλον ὄντα καὶ μὴ γιγνώσκοντα ὑπὲρ ὧν λέγει· καὶ τοῦτο δ᾽ αὐτὸ δήπου σὺ φῂς ἐξαρκεῖν αὐτὸν πρὸς ὃν ἂν ποιῇ τοὺς λόγους ὁμολογοῦντα παρέχε-
644 σθαι. ἐκεῖνος τοίνυν, ὡς ἔοικεν, οὐ μόνον συνεχώρει τῷ λόγῳ, ἀλλὰ καὶ ἐκ τῶν ἑαυτῷ προσόντων ἠναγκάζετο· ὥστ᾽ εἶχεν τελευτὴν προσήκουσαν ὁ λόγος, καὶ

of the Four, in a further burst of juvenile assertiveness at the end he added the comment that

> it would seem after all that what we said earlier was true, that we do not know of anyone who lived in this city who was a good man in respect of political activity.[518]

It was only after he had said this by way of setting an extra seal on his argument, and after some further intervening discussion, that he finally added Aristides with some words of praise. That is the extent of the advantage there is in its having been Socrates and not Callicles to speak about him!

Thus neither was it necessary for Socrates to have 643
abused the Four, nor, clearly, did he carry the point (which
one might say was superfluous), that none of the men of
old was a good person either. Indeed, given that he had
demonstrated that his addressee Callicles was worthless as
a politician, by asking him all those questions that he
posed to him, once that point had been proved, what need
was there to accuse the men of old as well? The argument
would surely have reached its best and most appropriate
conclusion in the demonstration that his interlocutor, the
man who was encouraging him to take up a life of politics
(or menial service), was worthless and did not understand
what he was advocating. This is surely what you yourself
say, that it is enough to secure the agreement of the individual you are talking to.[519] Well, this interlocutor appar- 644
ently not only agreed with the proposition, but was even
compelled to do so on the strength of his own personal
characteristics. Thus the argument would have an appro-

[518] *Grg*. 516e–17a.

[519] *Grg*. 472b–c.

οὐκ ἦν ἴσον Καλλικλέα ταῦτ᾽ ἀκούειν καὶ Περικλέα ἢ Θεμιστοκλέα. πόθεν; ὁ δὲ καὶ τοῦτ᾽ ἐσπούδασεν ἐξ ἴσου τοῦτον ἐκείνοις καταστῆσαι. ἔστι δ᾽ οὐ ταυτόν, ὦ τᾶν, Ἰφικλῆς τε καὶ Ἡρακλῆς.

645 ἔτι μὴν πλέον οἶμαι τὸ μέσον Καλλικλέους τε καὶ τούτων· ὥστ᾽ εἰκὸς ἦν τούτων γε φείσασθαι. καὶ γὰρ εἰ μὲν ζώντων ἐγίγνονθ᾽ οἱ λόγοι, τάχ᾽ ἄν τις ἔφησεν νουθεσίας ἕνεκ᾽ αὐτοὺς λέγεσθαι· τεθνεῶσι δ᾽ ἐπιτιμᾶν τίς ὁ καιρός; ὅπου γὰρ εἰ καὶ ζῶντας ἐλέγχειν ἐβούλετο, οὐκ ἀπόντων γε κατηγορεῖν εἰκὸς ἦν, οὐδὲ πρὸς ἄλλους τινάς, ἀλλὰ πρὸς αὐτοὺς λέγειν, ἦ που τό γε παντελῶς οὕτως ἐρήμην ἀγωνίσασθαι ἀωρία. ὁπότε γὰρ καὶ τοὺς οἰκείους τοὺς ἐκείνων αἰδεῖσθαι προσῆκεν δι᾽ ἐκείνους, πῶς γε οὐ καὐτοὺς εἰκὸς ἦν;

[*(vi) Plato's Lack of Respect for the Great Dead (646–62)*]

646 ἐνθυμηθῶμεν δὴ καὶ τὸν τοῦ Σόλωνος νόμον ὡς ἥμερος, μὴ λέγειν κακῶς τὸν τελευτήσαντα, μηδ᾽ ἂν
647 αὐτὸς ἀκούσῃ ὑπὸ τῶν αὐτοῦ παίδων. οὐκοῦν τό γε μήθ᾽ ὑπὸ παίδων, φαίη τις ἄν, μήθ᾽ ὑπ᾽ ἄλλου του τῶν

priate conclusion, and it is not the same for Callicles to have had this said of him as it is for Pericles or Themistocles. How could it be? Yet Socrates was keen to do this too, and put him on all fours with them. But, my dear sir, Iphicles and Heracles are not the same thing.[520]

I think in fact that the difference between Callicles and 645
the Four is still greater, to the extent that it would have been reasonable to spare them entirely. If the discussion had been taking place while they were still alive, then one might perhaps have said that it was taking place in order to admonish them; but what was the point of reproving them once they were dead? Seeing that, if he had wanted to expose their failings while they were still alive, the reasonable course would have been not to accuse them in their absence, or to speak to others rather than to them, then it was certainly out of season to pursue a completely undefended case like that. Considering that it was appropriate to revere those men's relatives because of them, how can it not have been reasonable to revere them too?

(vi) Plato's Lack of Respect for the Great Dead (646–62)

Let us reflect also on the civilized character of the law of 646
Solon, that one should not speak ill of a dead man, even if
he was ill spoken of by his own children.[521] One might well 647
say, then, that to make such strenuous efforts to prove the

[520] Iphicles was Heracles' less distinguished half brother, son of Alcmene by Amphitryon rather than by Zeus.

[521] As also mentioned in a similar context in Dem. *Or.* 20.104; cf. Plut. *Vit. Sol.* 21.

ἐκείνοις προσηκόντων προακούσαντας[186] τοσαύτην
σπουδὴν ποιήσασθαι κακοὺς ἀποφῆναι πολὺ τοῦ νό-
648 μου τούτου κεχώρισται. καὶ μὴν οὐδ' ἐκεῖνό γ' εἰκὸς
ἐναντίον μὲν ἂν τῶν παίδων ὀκνεῖν αὐτοὺς λοιδορεῖν,
ἐν ἅπασι δὲ καὶ ἐκγόνοις καὶ πολίταις καὶ ξένοις
τοιαῦτα ψέγειν, καὶ τῶν μὲν ἐν Σικελίᾳ τετελευτηκότων τοὺς παῖδας αἰδεῖσθαι καὶ περὶ δωρεῶν αὐτοῖς
πολιτεύεσθαι, τῶν δ' εἰς τὰ μέγιστα τῇ πόλει καὶ τοῖς
Ἕλλησιν ὑπαρξάντων μηδὲ τῶν ὀνομάτων φείσα-
649 σθαι. καὶ εἰ μὲν εἰκόνας αὐτῶν τοῦ δήμου στήσαντος
ἐκίνει, πᾶς ἄν τις ἔφη νεμεσητὸν εἶναι, ἐπεὶ δ' ὃ τοῦ
πλέονος ἄξιον ἦν αὐτοῖς, τὴν δόξαν τὴν ἀγαθὴν ἀναι-
ρεῖ, τί χρὴ φῆσαι; καὶ ζωγράφος μὲν ἂν ὢν ἐπὶ τὰ
αἰσχίω καὶ γελοιότερ' αὐτοὺς μιμούμενος οὐ καλῶς
ἂν ἐδόκει τὴν τέχνην δεικνύναι· ἐπεὶ δ' ἐν τοῖς λόγοις
ἐπὶ τὰ φαυλότατ' ἐξηγεῖται καὶ τὰς ἀληθεῖς εἰκόνας
αὐτῶν τῆς διανοίας διαφθείρει καὶ τοῖς μηδὲν προσ-
ήκουσιν ὁμοιοῖ, πῶς εἰκός ἐστι συνήδεσθαι; καὶ εἰ μὲν
ἐπ' εἰκόνων ἢ μνημάτων αὐτοῖς ἐπόντα ἐπιγράμματα
ἐξεκόλαπτεν ἢ μετεποίει βλάσφημ' ἀντ' εὐφημιῶν,
ὅτι τούτους ὁ δῆμος κολακείας ἕνεκα καὶ κακίας <ἐκ-
βάλλει>,[187] πολλὴν ἄν τις ἔφη τὴν ὕβριν καὶ τὴν ἀτι-
μίαν εἶναι· εἰς σύγγραμμα δ' οὕτω σπουδαῖον τοιαῦτ'
ὀνείδη κατακλείσας, καὶ ταῦτ' ἀντὶ τῆς πρόσθεν ὑπαρχούσης εὐφημίας αὐτοῖς ἀντιγραψάμενος, καὶ

[186] *προακούσαντας* Trapp *προακούσαντα codd.*
[187] *add.* Iunt.

villainy of people who had not previously been ill spoken of either by their children or by anyone else related to them is a far cry from this law. Nor indeed is it reasonable 648
to be reluctant to revile them in the presence of their children, yet to criticize them so severely before everybody including their descendants, and fellow citizens and foreigners alike, or again to revere the children of those who died in Sicily and promote measures to see them rewarded,[522] yet to spare not even the names of those who did their city and the whole of Greece the highest possible service. If the people had erected statues in their honor 649
and Plato were removing them, everyone would say that it was a disgrace, but given that what he is actually doing away with is what mattered more to them than anything else, their good name, what are we to say? If he had been a painter and had represented them as more ugly and ridiculous that they really were, it would have been thought that he was giving a sorry demonstration of his skill; but if in fact what he is doing is offering an account that belittles them, corrupting their true images, which are those of their characters, and likening them to people with whom they have no connection at all, how can it be reasonable to applaud him? If he were chiseling off the inscriptions on their statues or memorials, or revising them to carry slanders rather than compliments, to the effect that the people were expelling them because they were flatterers and villains, one would say that this was a great outrage and a great insult; if what he has in fact done is include reproaches of this kind in so serious a work, writing them moreover in direct contradiction to their existing good

[522] As in *Ep.* 7.355c–d, cf. §§272–74 above.

παραδοὺς ἅπασιν ἀκούειν, μή τῳ δοκεῖ σφόδρα τῆς
αὑτοῦ μουσικῆς εἰργάσθαι;[188]
650 καὶ Θεμιστοκλῆς μὲν Ἄρθμιον ἐστηλίτευσεν, ὅτι
τὸν ἐκ Μήδων χρυσὸν εἰς Πελοπόννησον ἤνεγκεν,
Πλάτων δὲ Θεμιστοκλέα καὶ Μιλτιάδην καὶ οὓς μετ᾽
αὐτῶν ἠξίωσεν καταλέξαι στηλίτας οὑτωσὶ πεποίη-
651 κεν. καίτοι τὴν μὲν κατ᾽ ἐκείνου στήλην τοῖς προσοι-
κοῦσι μόνοις ὁρᾶν ἦν καὶ τοῖς εἰσαφικνουμένοις, σὺ
δ᾽ εἰς ἅπαντας ἀνθρώπους καὶ πανταχοῦ γῆς καὶ
θαλάττης τὰς κατὰ τούτων βλασφημίας ἐκδέδωκας.
καὶ τῶν μὲν οἰκετῶν οὐδένα πώποτ᾽ ἔστιξας τῶν σαυτοῦ, τῶν δ᾽ Ἑλλήνων τοὺς ἐντιμοτάτους καὶ τοὺς ὑπὲρ
τῆς κοινῆς ἐλευθερίας ἀγωνιζομένους ἴσα καὶ στίξας
γεγένησαι, καὶ Γοργίου μὲν ἐφείσω, καὶ λέγει που
Σωκράτης "ὀκνῶ Γοργίου ἕνεκα λέγειν, ἵνα μή με
ὑπολάβῃ διακωμῳδεῖν αὐτοῦ τὴν τέχνην," Περικλέους
δὲ οὐκ ἐφείσω τεθνηκότος καὶ ταῦτα· ἀλλὰ τῷ μὲν
Γοργίᾳ νέμεις αἰδῶ παρὰ τὸν Καλλικλέα, τῷ δὲ Θεμιστοκλεῖ καὶ τοῖς ἄλλοις οὐ νέμεις, ἀλλ᾽ ἐξ ἴσου
πάντας αὐτοὺς ποιεῖς, μᾶλλον δὲ καὶ πλείω κακὰ
τούτους ἢ ᾽κεῖνον εἴρηκας, καὶ ταῦτ᾽ εἰδὼς ὅτι ἅπας
μὲν λόγος, ἐπειδὰν ἅπαξ γραφῇ, κυλινδεῖται, μεταχειρίζεται δ᾽ αὐτὸν ὁ βουλόμενος ὁμοίως ἐπαΐων καὶ
μή, ἂν δέ τις μὴ καλῶς ἀκούειν ἐπίστηται, δέος ἐστὶ
διαφθαρῆναι· οἷον καὶ περὶ τούτους ἄν τις συνίδοι
τοὺς λόγους ὄν. εἰ γὰρ καὶ τὰ μάλιστα Πλάτων

188 εἴργεσθαι VQ² εἰργάσθαι <ἔξω> Lenz

name, and then publish them for all to hear, how could anyone think he has acted completely in line with his own proper brand of music?[523]

Themistocles held Arthmius up to general opprobrium 650
on an inscribed slab, because he conveyed Persian gold to
the Peloponnese,[524] and Plato made a similarly public ex-
hibition of Themistocles and Miltiades and those he saw
fit to list along with them. But the inscription denouncing 651
Arthmius was visible only to those who lived in the area and to visitors arriving from abroad, whereas you, Plato, have published your slanders against the Four everywhere on land and sea, to the whole of humanity. You have never branded any of your own slaves, yet you have as good as branded the most honored of the Greeks and those who fought for the common freedom of them all. You spared Gorgias—Socrates somewhere says "I hesitate on Gorgias' account to say this, lest he suppose that I am making fun of his art"[525]—but you did not spare Pericles, even though he was dead. You show respect for Gorgias in comparison to Callicles, but not for Themistocles and the rest; instead you treat them all on a level, or rather you have heaped more abuse on them than on him, even though you are well aware that any discourse, once it is committed to writing, rolls about the place for anybody who wishes to pick up, no matter whether he understands it or not,[526] and if someone does not know how to listen to it properly, the risk is that it he will be corrupted. Which is just what one might observe happening with this particular set of arguments, because even if it was utterly true that Plato

523 That is, philosophy: cf. *Phd.* 61a.
524 Cf. §334 above.
525 *Grg.* 462e (paraphrased).
526 Alluding to *Phdr.* 275e.

αὐτοῖς[189] ἐπὶ πᾶσι δικαίοις κέχρηται, ὃ πολλοῦ δεῖν εἴποι τις ἂν οὕτως ἔχειν, ἀλλ' οὖν ἀνάγκη γ' ἀπ' αὐτῶν θρασυτέρους καὶ τραχυτέρους γίγνεσθαι καὶ ἰταμωτέρους καὶ τοιούτους, οἵους ῥᾳδίως ἐπιπηδᾶν καὶ ἄρχουσι καὶ πρεσβυτέροις καὶ οἷστισι δεῖ συγκε-
652 χωρῆσθαι. εὖ γὰρ ὁ τῶν Λακεδαιμονίων ἔχει νόμος καὶ λυσιτελῶς [ἀμαθῶς][190] εἰσάπαξ ὑποχωρεῖν τοῖς πρεσβυτέροις, οὐχ ὡς πάντως δήπου βελτίους καὶ δικαιοτέρους τοὺς πρεσβυτέρους ὄντας ἅπαντας, ἀλλὰ τῆς μελέτης ἕνεκα καὶ ὅπως ἡ τάξις μὴ συγχέοιτο. κἂν τοῖς λόγοις καλὸν τὸ φείδεσθαι τῶν προηκόντων ἐπιεικῶς εἰς ὅσον ἔξεστιν, ὅπως μή τις εὐχέρεια τοῖς πολλοῖς ἐνδύηται καὶ συνήθεια τοῦ προπηλακίζειν οὓς αὐτοῖς προσήκει τιμᾶν. ὅταν γὰρ οἱ μέγιστοι καὶ σεμνότατοι ῥᾳδίως κακῶς ἀκούωσιν, καὶ ταῦθ' ὑπὸ τῶν σοφωτάτων εἶναι δοκούντων, ὀλιγωρία τοῦ νόμου τοῖς φαύλοις ἐγγίγνεται, ὥστε οὐδὲν ὠφελοῦνται τοσ-
653 οῦτον ὅσον βλάπτονται. καὶ μὴν σύ γ' ἐλαύνεις Ὅμηρον οὐχ ὡς πάντα δήπου λέγοντα κακῶς οὐδ' ὡς τοῖς ὅλοις ἁμαρτάνοντα, ἀλλ' ὡς οὐκ ἀσφαλῶς ἐχόντων τοῖς νέοις γ' ἐνίων ἀκούειν, οὐδ' ἂν κατ' ἄλλο τι δεξιῶς ἔχῃ τὰ λεγόμενα· ἡμεῖς δ' ἐλαύνειν μέν σε πολλοῦ τινος δέομεν, ὅτι μὴ κἂν εἰς τὸν θρόνον ἐγκαθίζοιμεν, εἰ βούλει, τοὺς δὲ τοιούτους τῶν λόγων ὑπεξαιρούμεθα· οὐδὲ γὰρ τούτους ὡς ἐξαλείψομεν φήσομεν, οὐχ οὕτως ἡμεῖς εὐχερεῖς.

189 αὐτοῖς a² Canter αὐτός *codd.*

190 *del.* Valckenaer

employed them with full justification, which one might say is far from being the case, it was nonetheless inevitable that under their influence people should become bolder, more abrasive, more impetuous, and the sort to find it easy to lay into magistrates and elders and everybody they
ought to defer to. The Spartan custom of categorical def- 652
erence to one's elders is a good and beneficial one,[527] not on the understanding that all members of the older generation are always better and more just, but because it is good practice, and in order to prevent a breakdown in the social hierarchy. In words too it is a good thing to spare one's forebears pretty much as far as can be done, so as to prevent the masses from becoming offhand and accustomed to insult those whom they ought to honor. When the greatest and most revered are casually abused, and what is more abused by those who are supposed to be the wisest of all, a contempt for law and custom is engendered in the masses, with the result that they are not benefited
so much as harmed. You, Plato, expel Homer not of course 653
on the grounds that everything he says is bad or that he gets absolutely everything wrong, but because some of his contents are not safe for the young to hear, even if in some other respect what he says may be brilliant;[528] I on the other hand am a long way from expelling you—indeed I might even enthrone you, if you like—but I do insist on setting aside that kind of talk (I will not say that that I will "expunge" it,[529] since I am not as irresponsible as that).

527 As described in Hdt. 2.80.
528 *Resp.* 377a–91e, 397e–98b.
529 *Resp.* 386c.

654 καὶ μὴν οὐδ' ἐκεῖνό γε οὔτε Πλάτωνα λαθεῖν εἰκὸς ἦν οὔτε τῶν ἄλλων οὐδεὶς ἀγνοεῖ δήπου ὅτι ἡ τῶν λαμπρῶν καὶ μεγάλων ἀνδρῶν εὐδοξία καὶ μνήμη χωρὶς τῆς εἰς τὸ παρὸν φιλοτιμίας καὶ πρὸς τὰς ὕστερον τύχας ἀποθήκην ἔχει ταῖς πόλεσιν, καί τινες ἤδη διὰ τὸν δεῖνα καὶ τὸν δεῖνα τῶν παλαιῶν ἐπιείκειάν τιν' εὕροντο ἐν ταῖς συμφοραῖς, ὅπερ καὶ τοῖς Ἀθη-
655 ναίοις αὐτοῖς ὑπάρξαι δοκεῖ πολλάκις. ὁ δὲ καὶ τούτου φαίνεται τὸ καθ' αὑτὸν ἀποστερῶν τὴν πόλιν. εἰ γὰρ ἑκάστῳ τοῦτ' ἐν τῇ ψυχῇ παρασταίη καὶ τοῦτο πάντες πεισθεῖεν, μὴ ὅτι Μιλτιάδης καὶ Θεμιστοκλῆς καὶ Περικλῆς καὶ Κίμων καὶ ὅτιπερ κεφάλαιον τῶν Ἀθηναίων, οὐδὲν τῶν ὀψοποιῶν οὐδὲ τῶν σιτοποιῶν ἄρα βελτίους ἦσαν, ἀλλὰ "κἀγώ τινας ἐν τοῖς οἰκέταις κέκτημαι τοιούτους τὴν φύσιν, οἳ τὸν αὐτὸν τρόπον θεραπεύουσιν ἐμὲ ὅνπερ ἐκεῖνοι τὸν δῆμον τῶν Ἀθηναίων ἐθεράπευον, τοσοῦτον τούτων διαφέροντες, ὅτι πολλοὺς ἀνθ' ἑνὸς δεσπότας ἐκέκτηντο," εἰ ταύτην ἔχοιεν κατ' ἐκείνων τὴν δόξαν καὶ μὴ λογίσαιντο ὅτι λόγος ἄλλως ταῦτ' ἦν καὶ πρὸς τὸ παρὸν φιλονικία τις καὶ ὑπερβολή, σχολῇ γ' ἂν ἄλλους τινὰς αἰδεσθεῖεν, ἢ τιμῆς τινος ἀξιώσαιεν δημοσίᾳ διὰ τούτους, οἷς αὐτοῖς οὐδ' ὁτιοῦν αἰδοῦς ὠφείλετο ὡς ἐκ τοῦ λόγου.

656 οὐκοῦν ἀλγεινὸν εἰ Λακεδαιμόνιοι μὲν ᾐσχύνθησαν τὸν Μιλτιάδην καὶ τὸν Θεμιστοκλέα καὶ τῆς πόλεως κρατήσαντες ἐφείσαντο τῆς ἐκείνων πολιτείας μνησθέντες, σὺ δὲ ταῦτα πάντ' ἀναιρεῖς τοῖς λόγοις.

What is more, it was not reasonable even for Plato to be unaware, nor certainly does anyone else not know, that the glorious memory of great and distinguished men, besides the honor it brings in the present, is also a valuable resource to help their cities deal with their subsequent fortunes; history is full of instances of people who have discovered reserves of virtue in times of disaster thanks to one or another of the men of old. We are told that this was the case for the Athenians many times over. But Plato is manifestly doing his best to deprive the city of this too. For imagine that each and every person had the thought in their minds and everyone were convinced of it, not only that Miltiades, Themistocles, Pericles, and Cimon and all the leading lights of Athens, were after all no better than caterers and bakers, but also that "I too have people with characters like that among my house slaves, who look after me in the same way as they looked after the Athenian people, differing only to the extent that they had many masters instead of one." If people had such a discreditable impression of our men and could not entertain the idea that Plato's is mere idle talk, a piece of exaggerated *ad hoc* competitiveness, they would hardly be ready to respect anyone else, or to think that anyone else deserved public honor because of men who themselves, on this line of argument, did not deserve the slightest respect either. 654
655

It is therefore distressing that the Spartans should have respected Miltiades and Themistocles and spared their city when they conquered it because they remembered their political achievements,[530] but that you should tear all 656

530 Cf. Xen. *Hell.* 2.2.19–20 (but without explicit mention of Miltiades and Themistocles).

657 καὶ μὴν εἰ μηδὲ τείχη μηδὲ νεώρια μηδὲ συμμάχους
αὐτοῖς ἐξεπόρισας, τὸ δοκεῖν διακονεῖν αἰσχυνθείς,
ἀλλ' ὑπερεῖδες πάντων ὡς ἐλαττόνων σαυτοῦ, τοῦτό
γε δήπου προσῆκεν ἀφεῖναι τῇ πατρίδι ἀφορμὴν τοῦ
μέλλοντος χρόνου, καὶ τὸ δοκεῖν ἐπιεικείας τινὸς
ἀξίαν εἶναι. ἢ παρὼν μὲν ἂν αὐτοῖς ἀτυχήσασί που
καὶ μέλλουσι διαφθαρήσεσθαι, εἰ κύριος ἦσθα, παρ-
αιτήσασθαι οὐκ ἂν ὤκνησας, ἀλλὰ καὶ πρὸς τῶν
ἱερῶν καὶ πρὸς τῶν τάφων καὶ πρὸς αὐτοῦ τοῦ ἐδά-
φους συνέπραττες ἂν ὅ τι οἷός τ' ἦσθα, κἂν εἴ τι
κατηγορεῖν εἶχες, τὴν δὲ τῶν ἐπιτηδειοτάτων παραι-
τήσασθαι δόξαν καθαιρῶν, τοῦτ' ἐκεῖνο ὃ σπουδάζεις
658 τῇ πολιτικῇ τί προσῆκον πράττειν δοκεῖς; εἶεν. ἄνευ
δὲ τῆς τοιαύτης χρείας εἰς τὴν συνεχῆ παρὰ πάντων
εὐμένειαν καὶ τὸ ταῖς γνώμαις συγκεκρᾶσθαι τῇ
πόλει, πόσον τι δοκεῖν χρὴ συντελεῖν τὴν τῶν ἀνδρῶν
τούτων μνήμην φυλαττομένην ἐφ' οἷσπερ καὶ παρ-
659 εδόθη τὸ ἐξ ἀρχῆς; οὐκοῦν τοῦτό γε παντὶ προσῆκεν
φάσκοντί γ' εἶναι χρηστῷ, ἐάν τ' ἰδιωτεύῃ ἐάν τε δη-
μοσιεύῃ λέγω, παρασκευάζειν ὡς δυνατὸν πλείστην
εὔνοιαν παρὰ πάντων τῇ πατρίδι· εἰ δὲ μή, τήν γ'
ὑπάρχουσαν μὴ διαφθείρειν. οὐ γάρ πω καὶ τούτῳ
διακονία τις πρόσεστιν ἀγεννὴς οὐδ' ἀνελεύθερος.
660 θαυμάζω δὲ Πλάτωνος εἰ χοὰς μὲν ἀποστερῆσαι τοὺς
ἄνδρας οὐκ ἄν ποτε ἠξίωσεν ἑκὼν εἶναι, τὴν δὲ μνή-

this down with your words. If you did not furnish the 657
people of Athens with walls or shipyards or allies,[531] because you would have been ashamed to be thought a lackey, and instead despised them all as inferior to yourself, you ought at least to have allowed your homeland to hold onto this as a resource for the future, and with it the possibility of being thought to deserve some degree of clemency. If you had been there yourself when the people of Athens had met with disaster and were on the point of being annihilated, and you had had the necessary authority, you would not have hesitated to plead on their behalf, and would have done what you could in the name of the shrines and tombs and the very soil of Attica, even if you did have some charge to bring against them; so what on earth do you think you are doing for the art of politics by devoting such energy to destroying the good name of the
people best placed to plead for their country? Well, then. 658
What does the preservation of these men's memory in the condition in which it was bequeathed to us add, should we think, without that sort of usefulness to the city in securing
the continued goodwill of all and a unity of purpose? It 659
was therefore the duty of anyone who claims to be a good man, whether a private citizen or a participant in public life, to secure the greatest possible degree of goodwill from everybody for his homeland, or failing that not to destroy such goodwill as there already was; not the slightest suggestion of base and ignoble servitude attaches to
such a man. I am amazed that Plato of his own free will 660
would never have seen fit to deprive these men of their funerary libations, and yet thought that when he obliter-

531 Cf. *Grg.* 519a.

μην καὶ τὴν ὑπὸ πάντων εὐφημίαν συγκεχωρημένην αὐτοῖς ἀφανίζων ἑαυτοῦ τὸ ἕρμαιον ἡγήσατο.

661 *καὶ μὴν εἰ τὸ συμμέτρους τὰς τιμωρίας ποιεῖσθαι πολιτικόν, ἥ γ' ἀτιμία τοῖς ἀνδράσιν αὐτὴ τὸ σύμμετρον παρελήλυθεν. οἶμαι γάρ, εἴ τις ἐστὶν αἴσθησις τοῖς τελευτήσασιν, μὴ ὅτι τῶν νομιζομένων, ἀλλὰ μηδ' αὐτῶν τῶν μνημάτων ἀποστερηθέντας ἂν αὐτοὺς μηδ' εἰς τοὺς ἐκγόνους τὰ ἔσχατα πάντων ἀτυχήσαντας τοσαύτην ἂν ποιήσασθαι τὴν συμφοράν, ὅσηνπερ εἰ κολακείαν αὐτῶν οἱ Ἕλληνες καταγνοῖεν, καὶ ἃ ζῶντες ἔφυγον καὶ ὑπὲρ ὧν ὅπως αὐτοῖς μὴ ἔνοχοι γένοιντο πάντα καὶ λέγειν καὶ πράττειν ὑπέστησαν, ταῦτα τεθνηκότες καὶ ἐπ' ἐξειργασμένοις οἷς διενοήθησαν φέροιντο τὰ τῆς δουλείας ὀνείδη, ὁ δὲ ταῦτα πείθων εἴη Πλάτων, ὁ μόνος κοσμῆσαι τὰς ἐκείνων ἀρετὰς κατ' ἀξίαν δυνάμενος, καὶ μέντοι καὶ κεκο-*
662 *σμηκώς. ἀλλὰ μὴν εἴ γε τοὖθ' ἕπεται φύσει τοῖς ἀγαθοῖς ἀνδράσιν, τὴν ἀγαθὴν δόξαν διώκειν, πῶς οὐκ ἀδικεῖσθαι φαίη τις ἂν αὐτούς, εἰ κινδυνεύειν μὲν καὶ πάσχειν ὁτιοῦν ᾤοντο δεῖν ἐπὶ τῷ καλλίονι τῶν λόγων, εἰ δὲ μή, μέρος γέ τι καὶ διὰ τοῦτο, ἐχόντων δὲ πέρας καὶ τῶν λόγων καὶ τῶν ἔργων αὐτοῖς καὶ προσέτι καὶ τοῦ βίου, τὴν ἐναντίαν δόξαν οἴσονται, καὶ πῶς ἂν μᾶλλον ἀποστεροίημεν τὸν μισθὸν αὐτούς, ὃς μόνος τοῖς ἐπιεικέσι παρὰ τῆς φύσεως ὑπάρχει, καὶ ταῦτα συμφάσκοντες εἶναι δεῖν τοῖς ἀγαθοῖς καὶ ζῶσιν καὶ τελευτήσασιν. ἐξῆν γάρ, ὦ γενναῖε, καὶ τοὺς νέους δικαίους εἶναι προτρέπειν καὶ τοῖς πρεσβυ-*

ated their memory and the good name accorded them by all, he was the one who had landed the windfall.

Again, if it is statesmanlike to make punishments pro- 661
portionate, the dishonor inflicted on these men exceeds all proportion. For I think that, if the dead have any perception, being deprived not only of the customary rites but even of their very gravestones, and having the worst possible ill luck in respect of their descendants would not have been such a catastrophe for them, as it would have been for the Greeks to find them guilty of flattery, and for them to bear in death, when their purposes had been achieved, those reproaches of servitude that they had shunned in life and would have brought themselves to say and do anything in order not to lay themselves open to, and for the one urging this to be Plato, the only man with the ability to honor their virtues as they deserved, who
indeed actually did so honor them. If it is in the very na- 662
ture of good men to pursue a good reputation, how could it be denied that they are being wronged if, when they themselves thought it their duty to risk and suffer anything for the fairer kind of repute, or at any rate in part for this reason, they will, now that their words and deeds and indeed their very lives are at an end, endure the opposite reputation? And what more could we do to deprive them of the one reward that nature furnishes for the virtuous, especially when we ourselves agree that it should attach to the good both in life and in death? It would have been possible, my dear fellow, both to encourage the young to be just and to give the elder generation their due.

τέροις τὰ πρέποντα ἀποδοῦναι. καὶ γὰρ εἰ μηδὲν εἴχομεν ἐπαινεῖν αὐτούς, ἀλλ᾽ ἐξῆν γε δήπου παρελθεῖν σιωπῇ, καὶ οὐκ ἔμελλες ὀφλήσειν ἀλογίου.

[*Excursus: Plato's Bad Example to Modern Critics of Oratory (663–91)*]

663 ἀλλὰ γὰρ οὐκ εἰ Πλάτων ὁ τῶν Ἑλλήνων τοσοῦτον ὑπερφέρων καὶ δικαίως μέγιστον ἐφ᾽ ἑαυτῷ φρονῶν κατηγορῆσαί τινων ἠξίωσεν μεγέθει τινὶ καὶ ἐξουσίᾳ φύσεως, τοῦτο καὶ μάλιστ᾽ ἄν τις ἀγανακτήσειεν, ἀλλ᾽ ὅτι καὶ τῶν κομιδῇ τινὲς οὐδενὸς ἀξίων ἀφορμῇ ταύτῃ χρώμενοι μελέτην ἤδη τὸ πρᾶγμα πεποίηνται καὶ τολμῶσιν καὶ περὶ Δημοσθένους, ὃν ἐγὼ φαίην ἂν Ἑρμοῦ τινος λογίου τύπον εἰς ἀνθρώπους κατελ-
664 θεῖν, ὅ τι ἂν τύχωσιν βλασφημεῖν. καίτοι τίς ἂν εἰς ζῶντας τελῶν τούτων ἀνάσχοιτο, οἳ πλείω μὲν σολοικίζουσιν ἢ φθέγγονται, ὑπερορῶσι δὲ τῶν ἄλλων ὅσον αὐτοῖς ὑπερορᾶσθαι προσήκει, καὶ τοὺς μὲν ἄλλους ἐξετάζουσιν, αὐτοὺς δὲ οὐδεπώποτ᾽ ἠξίωσαν, καὶ σεμνύνουσι μὲν τὴν ἀρετήν, ἀσκοῦσι δ᾽ οὐ †πᾶσι,[191]

[191] πάνυ UR^2 πᾶσι *cett. del.* Lenz (*vel* παντάπασι)

---

[532] Aristides here contrives a paradox by means of an untranslatable play on words: the Greek for "prosecution for failing to submit accounts" (*dikê alogiou*) sounds as if it might also mean "prosecution for not speaking."

[533] Compare §§577 and 586 above.

Even if we had no praise to bestow on them, it would at least have been possible to pass over them in silence, and you would not have laid yourself open to a charge of failing to submit accounts.[532]

Excursus: Plato's Bad Example to Modern Critics of Oratory (663–91)

It is not, however, the fact that Plato, who excels all other 663
Greeks by so much and quite justifiably has the highest opinion of himself, should have seen fit, in the greatness of his genius and with the license this allows him,[533] to denounce certain individuals, that should especially arouse our indignation. It is rather the fact that certain other completely worthless characters, taking this as their starting point, have now made a regular exercise of the thing and even dare hurl whatever insults come to hand against Demosthenes, the man who I would say came down to earth as the very image of Hermes, god of eloquence.[534] How could any man alive put up with this, 664
seeing that, although these people utter more solecisms than words, they still despise others as much as they themselves ought to be despised, subject others to examination without ever seeing fit to do the same to themselves, and exalt virtue but do not practice it? They wander uselessly

534 The identity of these "completely worthless individuals" is harder to pin down than has sometimes been thought. Although initially they look just like Cynics, as depicted in other second-century sources, in §§672 and 683 they start to take on characteristics of school philosophers as well. See further Introduction, xiii–xiv.

περιέρχονται δὲ ἄλλως βροτῶν εἴδωλα καμόντων,
Ἡσιόδου κηφῆνες, Ἀρχιλόχου πίθηκοι, δύο μορφὰς
ἔχοντες ἀντὶ τριῶν[192] τῆς τραγικῆς βοός, τῶν ἱματίων
τῶν ἠπημένων οὐδὲν διαφέροντες, τὰ μὲν ἔξω σεμνοί,
τὰ δ' ἔνδον ἄλλους[193] <ἂν>[194] εἰδείη τις, οὐδὲ μεθ'
ἡμέραν σώφρονες, ὡς Δημοσθένης φησίν, ἀλλ' αὐτοῖς
καὶ ἡμέρα καὶ νὺξ ταὐτόν ἐστι δυνηθεῖσιν· οἳ τοῦ μὲν
Διὸς οὐδὲν χείρους φασὶν εἶναι, τοῦ δ' ὀβολοῦ τοσοῦτον ἡττῶνται· ὀνειδίζουσι δὲ τοῖς ἄλλοις, οὐ τῶν
πραγμάτων κατεγνωκότες, ἀλλὰ φθονοῦντες ὅτι αὐτοὶ
665 ταῦτα πράττειν οὐ δύνανται. εἰ δέ τις αὐτῶν περὶ τῆς
ἐγκρατείας διαλεγομένων ἀπαντικρὺ σταίη ἔχων ἔν-
θρυπτα καὶ στρεπτούς, ἐκβάλλουσι τὴν γλῶτταν
ὥσπερ ὁ Μενέλεως τὸ ξίφος. αὐτὴν μὲν γὰρ ἐὰν ἴδωσι
τὴν Ἑλένην—Ἑλένην λέγω; θεράπαιναν μὲν οὖν
ὁποίαν ἐποίησεν Μένανδρος τὴν Φρυγίαν—τῷ ὄντι
παιδιὰν ἀποφαίνουσι τοὺς σατύρους τοῦ Σοφοκλέους.
666 ἀλλὰ μὴν τήν γ' ἀπληστίαν[195] καὶ πλεονεξίαν αὐτῶν
οὐδὲν δεῖ γνῶναι παρακαταθέμενον, αὐτοὶ γὰρ λαμβάνουσιν ὅ τι ἂν δυνηθῶσιν· οἳ τῷ μὲν ἀποστερεῖν

192 <τῶν> τριῶν Keil
193 ἄλλους Behr ἄλλως UA^{2}R^2 ἄλλος *cett.*
194 *add.* Oporinus
195 ἀπληστίαν Canter ἀπιστίαν *codd.*

---

535 Hom. *Od.* 11.476.
536 *Op.* 303–7.
537 Fr. 185 *IEG*.
538 Euripides' *Seers*, or *Polyidus*, quoted from by Plato in another connection in *Grg.* 492e; in this play the seer Polyidus correctly interprets the portent of a calf in King Minos' herd

around like "shades of dead mortals,"[535] Hesiod's drones,[536] Archilochus' apes,[537] with two forms rather than the three of the ox in the tragedy,[538] for all the world like patched-up cloaks, impressive on the outside but (you would find) another story on the inside. They are unable to control themselves even in the daytime, in Demosthenes' phrase,[539] but day and night are all the same to them when they get the opportunity. They say that they are no whit inferior to Zeus,[540] yet are completely overwhelmed by an obol. They reproach others not because they condemn their behavior, but because they are jealous that
they cannot do the same. If when they are discoursing on 665
self-control somebody were to stand in front of them holding tipsy-cakes and pastries,[541] their tongues would hang out like Menelaus' sword;[542] and if they ever see Helen—what do I mean Helen? a serving girl like the Phrygian in Menander[543]—they make Sophocles' satyrs look like a
kindergarten.[544] Indeed, you do not need to have en- 666
trusted anything to them to understand their insatiability and greed, since they actively take whatever they can, hav-

changing color daily from white to red to black (Apollod. *Bibl.* 3.3.1; Hyg. *Fab.* 136; Eur. fr. 395 *TrGF*; Ath. *Deipn.* 2.51d).

539 Dem. 45.80.

540 A characteristic claim of (or on behalf of) Cynic philosophers: Lucian *De mort. Peregr.* 4; Arr. *Epict. diss.* 3.22.95.

541 A phrase copied from Dem. *De cor.* (18) 260.

542 That is, hanging down like Menelaus' sword, after the sight of Helen's beauty had overcome his resolve to kill her (as described in Eur. *Andr.* 627–31 and Ar. *Lys.* 155–56; cf. *Little Iliad* fr. 17 Allen).

543 Fr. 432 Kassel-Austin.

544 Perhaps in Sophocles' play *The Marriage of Helen* (frr. 181–84 *TrGF*), if this was indeed a satyr drama.

κοινωνεῖν ὄνομα τέθεινται, τῷ δὲ φθονεῖν φιλοσοφεῖν,
τῷ δ' ἀπορεῖν ὑπερορᾶν χρημάτων. ἐπαγγελλόμενοι
δὲ φιλανθρωπίαν ὤνησαν μὲν οὐδένα πώποτε, ἐπη-
667 ρεάζουσι δὲ τοῖς χρωμένοις. καὶ τοὺς μὲν ἄλλους οὐδ'
ἀπαντῶντας ὁρῶσιν, τῶν δὲ πλουσίων ἕνεκα εἰς τὴν
ὑπερορίαν ἀπαίρουσιν, ὥσπερ οἱ Φρύγες [οἳ][196] τῶν
ἐλαῶν ἕνεκα τῆς συλλογῆς, καὶ προσιόντων εὐθὺς
ὤσφροντο καὶ παραλαβόντες ἄγουσι, καὶ τὴν ἀρετὴν
668 παραδώσειν ὑπισχνοῦνται. καὶ τοὺς μὲν ἄλλους οὐδὲ
προσειπόντας ἀντιπροσείποιεν ἂν εὐμενῶς, τοὺς δὲ
τῶν πλουσίων ὀψοποιοὺς καὶ σιτοποιοὺς καὶ τοὺς
ἐν ταῖς ἄλλαις τάξεσιν πόρρωθεν εὐθὺς ἀσπάζονται,
πρὶν εὖ καὶ καλῶς ὀφθῆναι, ὥσπερ τούτου χάριν ἐξ
εὐνῆς ἀναστάντες· κἂν τοῖς προθύροις καλινδοῦνται,
πλείω τοῖς θυρωροῖς συνόντες ἢ τοῖς δεσπόταις
αὐτῶν, ἀναιδείᾳ τὴν κολακείαν ἐπανορθούμενοι, ἓν
τοῦτο σύμβολον κεκτημένοι τοῦ μὴ πρὸς χάριν τοῖς
ἀνθρώποις ὁμιλεῖν, ὅτι πάντας[197] ἀποκναίουσιν ἀηδίᾳ
λιπαροῦντες, ὁρώμενοι [πρῶτον][198] ῥᾷον αἰτοῦντες τὰ
μὴ προσήκοντα ἢ ἕτεροι τὰ γιγνόμεν' αὐτοῖς ἀπαι-
τοῦντες. οὗτοι γάρ εἰσιν οἱ τὴν μὲν ἀναισχυντίαν
ἐλευθερίαν νομίζοντες, τὸ δ' ἀπεχθάνεσθαι παρρη-
σιάζεσθαι, τὸ δὲ λαμβάνειν φιλανθρωπεύεσθαι. εἰς
τοῦθ' ἥκουσι τῆς σοφίας ὥστ' ἀργύριον μὲν οὐ πράτ-
τονται, ἀργυρίου δ' ἄξια[199] λαμβάνειν ἐπίστανται·

196 *om.* U *eras.* QR^{2}Ph^{M3} *del.* Dindorf
197 πάντας Reiske πάντα *codd.*
198 *del.* Trapp
199 ἄξια Bernays ἀξίως *codd.*

ing rebranded theft as "sharing," envy as "philosophy," and poverty as "contempt for material possessions." Although they preach benevolence they have never yet done anyone any good, and they rail at those who keep company with them. When other people run into them and say hello, 667
they do not even see them, but for the wealthy they set off for foreign parts like Phrygians heading for the olive harvest; they scent them the moment they approach and intercept them and lead them away, promising as they do so that they will teach them virtue. When other people ad- 668
dress them they won't even give a civil answer, but the chefs and pastry cooks of the rich, and everyone else in their service, they hail when they are still in the distance, before even being fairly and squarely in sight, as if this was what they had gotten out of bed for. They haunt their doorsteps, spending more time with the doorkeepers than with the masters, amending their flattery with impudence. The one indication they can give of not aiming to ingratiate themselves in their dealings with the world at large is that the unpleasantness of their incessant begging wears everybody out, since they are openly more ready to ask for what does not belong to them than others are to request their due entitlement. These are the people who think that shamelessness is "free spiritedness," that offending people is "frank speaking,"[545] and that being given things is "generosity." Their cleverness is of such a high order that, although they do not charge money, they know how to bring in what is worth just as much as money. If it so happens

[545] For "free spiritedness" (*eleutheria*) and "frank speaking" (*parrhêsia*) as Cynic catchphrases, see, e.g., Max. Tyr. 32.9, 36.5; Diog. Laert. 6.69.

κἂν μέν γε τύχῃ τις ἔλαττον πέμψας, ἐνέμειναν τῷ
δόγματι, ἂν δὲ ἁδρότερον τὸ σακκίον αὐτοῖς φανῇ,
669 Γοργόνα Περσεὺς ἐχειρώσατο. καὶ ἡ πρόφασις πάν-
σοφος· τὰ γὰρ παιδία καὶ ἡ γυνή. ὦ δυστυχέστατε
τῆς οἰκίας. εἶτα καπηλεύεις τούτων ἕνεκα; τί οὖν οὐ
καὶ τῇ γυναικὶ συγχωρεῖς λαμβάνειν ὅθεν ἂν δύνηται
670 ῥᾷόν γε θρέψεσθαι; καινότατον δέ μοι δοκοῦσι τρόπον τὴν μεγαλοψυχίαν ὁρίζεσθαι, οὐκ εἰ μεγάλα δώ-
σουσιν, ἀλλ᾽ εἰ μὴ μικρὰ λήψονται [ἤδη. οὐ γὰρ τῷ
μεγάλα δωρεῖσθαι δεικνύουσιν αὐτήν, ἀλλὰ τῷ μεγάλα ἀξιοῦν λαμβάνειν].[200] ἤδη δέ τινες καὶ τοῦτο, ὡς
ἀκούω, δόγμα πεποίηνται, προσίεσθαι μὲν τὸ διδόμε-
νον, λαμβάνοντες δὲ λοιδορεῖν.
671 μόνους δὲ τούτους οὔτ᾽ ἐν κόλαξιν οὔτ᾽ ἐν ἐλευθέροις ἄξιον θεῖναι. ἐξαπατῶσι μὲν γὰρ ὡς κόλακες,
προπηλακίζουσι δ᾽ ὡς κρείττονες, δύο τοῖς ἐσχάτοις
καὶ τοῖς ἐναντιωτάτοις ἔνοχοι κακοῖς ὄντες, ταπει-
νότητι καὶ αὐθαδείᾳ, τοῖς ἐν τῇ Παλαιστίνῃ δυσσε-
βέσι παραπλήσιοι τοὺς τρόπους, [καὶ γὰρ ἐκείνοις
τοῦτ᾽ ἐστὶ σύμβολον τῆς δυσσεβείας, ὅτι τοὺς κρείττους οὐ νομίζουσι, καὶ οὗτοι τρόπον τινὰ ἀφεστᾶσι
τῶν Ἑλλήνων, μᾶλλον δὲ καὶ πάντων τῶν κρειτ-

200 *del.* Lenz

546 A proverbial phrase (Apostol. *Prov.* 5.58) for a great achievement, here used ironically to satirize the greed of these false philosophers.

that someone sends too little, they stay faithful to their doctrine, but if the purse looks fatter to them, Perseus has defeated the Gorgon.[546] They have an utterly ingenious 669
excuse—a wife and children. How desperately unlucky you are in your family circumstances! So have you set up in trade to support them? Why don't you allow your wife to make money from an easier source of subsistence too?
It seems to me that they have a most novel way of defining 670
magnanimity, not as giving away large sums but as not being paid small sums![547] I gather also that some of them have been known to make it a matter of doctrine to accept what is given, but to fling insults as they take it.

These people alone deserve to be counted neither 671
among flatterers nor among the free. They deceive people like flatterers and abuse them as if they were their superiors; falling prey to two of the worst and most contradictory failings, baseness and arrogance, they can only be compared to the infidels of Palestine in their behavior.[548]

[547] The next sentence in the Greek text, bracketed opposite, is clearly a reader's paraphrase and should be expelled ("Because they do not manifest it by giving large sums as gifts, but by demanding to receive large sums").

[548] Probably Christians rather than Jews, given the emphasis on their offensive combination of arrogance with low social status. The next sentence in the Greek, bracketed opposite, should be expelled as a reader's comment ("For the distinguishing mark of those people's impiety is that they do not acknowledge the higher powers, and these ones have in a way defected from the Greek race, or better from all that is higher"). These words break the flow of Aristides' tirade and offer a clumsy and badly positioned précis of the point he is trying to make over §§663–85 as a whole.

672 τόνων][201] τὰ μὲν ἄλλ' ἀφωνότεροι τῆς σκιᾶς τῆς ἑαυτῶν, ἐπειδὰν δὲ κακῶς τινας εἰπεῖν δέῃ καὶ διαβαλεῖν, τῷ Δωδωναίῳ μὲν οὐκ ἂν εἰκάσαις αὐτοὺς χαλκείῳ, μὴ γὰρ ὦ Ζεῦ, ταῖς δ' ἐμπίσι ταῖς ἐν τῷ σκότῳ βομβούσαις· συγκαταπρᾶξαι μέν τι τῶν δεόντων ἁπάντων ἀχρηστότατοι, διορύξαι δ' οἰκίαν καὶ ταράξαι καὶ συγκροῦσαι τοὺς ἔνδον πρὸς ἀλλήλους καὶ φῆσαι πάντ' αὐτοὺς διοικήσειν πάντων δεινότατοι· οἳ λόγον μὲν ἔγκαρπον οὐδένα πώποτ' οὔτ' εἶπον οὔθ' εὗρον οὔτ' ἐποίησαν, οὐ πανηγύρεις ἐκόσμησαν, οὐ θεοὺς ἐτίμησαν, οὐ πόλεσι συνεβούλευσαν, οὐ λυπουμένους παρεμυθήσαντο, οὐ στασιάζοντας διήλλαξαν, οὐ προὔτρεψαν νέους, οὐκ ἄλλους οὐδένας, οὐ κόσμου τοῖς λόγοις προὐνοήσαντο· καταδύντες δὲ εἰς τοὺς χηραμοὺς ἐκεῖ τὰ θαυμαστὰ σοφίζονται, σκιᾷ τινι λόγους ἀνασπῶντες, ἔφης ὦ Σοφόκλεις, τὸν ἀνθέρικον θερίζοντες, τὸ ἐκ τῆς ψάμμου σχοινίον πλέκοντες, οὐκ οἶδ' ὅντιν' ἱστὸν ἀναλύοντες· ὅσον γὰρ ἂν προκόψωσιν τῆς σοφίας, τοσοῦτον ἀνταφαιροῦσιν μεγάλα φρονοῦντες ἐὰν ῥητορικὴν εἴπωσιν κακῶς, ὥσπερ † οὐ καὶ †[202] τοὺς δούλους τοῖς δεσπόταις ὑπ' ὀδόντα πολλάκις καταρωμένους, καὶ μάλιστα δὴ τοὺς μαστιγίας αὐτῶν. ἤδη δέ τις καὶ σάτυρος τῶν ἐπὶ σκηνῆς κατη-

201 *del.* Trapp

202 οὐ $Q^1AR^1EU^1a$ οὖν $TVQ^2R^2U^2Ph^{AM}$ *οἴδαμεν καί* Friedlander *an* οἶμαι?

In other respects they are dumber than their own shadow, 672
but when they have to abuse anyone or slander them, one might compare them not—God forbid!—to the bronze vessel at Dodona,[549] but to gnats buzzing in the dark. They are the most useless of all at cooperating in any of the necessary tasks of life, but the smartest of all at breaking into a house and turning it upside down and setting its inhabitants at odds with each other and saying that they themselves will take control of everything. Yet they have never yet delivered or conceived or composed any productive discourse: they have not brought luster to festivals, or honored the gods or given advice to cities, or consoled the grieving, or reconciled warring factions, or exhorted the young (or anyone else at all), or shown any concern for seemliness of style. Instead they duck down into their lairs and practice their wonderful cleverness there, jerking out their words to a shadow, in your phrase, Sophocles,[550] harvesting asphodel, weaving a rope of sand, unpicking I know not what web.[551] For any progress they may make in wisdom they undo again through their pride in speaking ill of rhetoric, just as slaves often curse their masters under their breath, particularly the hardened offenders among them. It is not unknown for a satyr on stage to curse Her-

549 A proverbial expression for incessant talkers, drawn from a vessel at the oracular site of Dodona that supposedly sounded all day, or at least to a count of four hundred, when struck: Zen. *Prov.* 6.5; Suda s.v.; Callim. *Hymn* 4.286, fr. 483 Pf.; Men. fr. 65 Kassel-Austin; Strabo 7 fr. 3.

550 Describing Ajax in his madness: *Aj.* 301–2.

551 Images for futile (and interminable) activity, the last of them drawn from Homer's Penelope (*Od.* 2.93–109).

ράσατο τῷ Ἡρακλεῖ, εἶτά γ' ἔκυψεν προσιόντος κάτω.
673 εἰκότως δέ μοι δοκοῦσι κακῶς ἅπαντας λέγειν, πολὺ γὰρ τοῦ πράγματος αὐτοῖς περίεστιν, οἵ γε κἂν μηδενὸς ἀνθρώπων μεμνήσονται,[203] λέγουσιν ἃ[204] λέγουσι κακῶς· ὥστ' ἀφ' ὧν ἔχουσι χαρίζονται.

καὶ τολμῶσιν ἤδη τῶν ἀρίστων ἐν τοῖς Ἕλλησι μνημονεύειν, ὥσπερ ἐξὸν αὐτοῖς· ὧν εἴ τις ἐξέλοι τὴν ψευδολογίαν καὶ τὴν κακοήθειαν, ὡσπερεὶ τὰ ἰσχύρ'
674 ἀφῄρηκεν τοῦ βίου. εἶτα τὸ κάλλιστον τῶν ὀνομάτων αὑτοῖς τέθεινται φιλοσοφίαν, ὥσπερ θέαν προκατειληφότες καὶ τοὺς ἄλλους εὐθὺς συγχωρεῖν δέον, ἢ τῇ μεταθέσει τῶν ὀνομάτων τὰ τοιαῦτα κρινόμεν',[205] ἀλλ' οὐ τοῖς πράγμασιν, ὥσπερ ἂν εἰ ὁ Φρυνώνδας ἐκεῖνος Αἰακὸν αὑτὸν μετέθετο, ὡς δὴ †δίδυμος[206] εὐθὺς εἶναι δόξων καὶ κρείττων ἁπάσης αἰτίας, [ἐπιτρεπτικὸν τοῦτο κακουργημάτων, ὥσπερ ἂν εἰ καὶ ὁ κλέπτης[207] ἡγεῖτο κλέψας τὰ βλεπόμενα Ῥαδάμανθυς εἶναι][208] ἢ ὁ Θερσίτης προσεῖπεν ἑαυτὸν Ὑάκινθον ἢ Νάρκισσον, ἢ ὁ Λυκάων Ἕκτορα, ἢ ὁ Κόροιβος Παλαμήδην, ἢ ὁ Μαργίτης Νέστορα, ἢ Βάττος Στέντορα, ὁ περὶ

[203] μεμνήσονται T^1Q^1 *ante corr.* U^1 *post corr.* Thom. Mag. μεμνήσωνται Q^1 *post corr.* VAREU^1 *ante corr.* T^2Ph^{AM} μέμνωνται Dindorf

[204] λέγουσιν ἃ Reiske λέγουσιν δὲ ἅ *codd.*

[205] κρινόμεν' Canter κρίνομεν *codd.*

[206] αἰδέσιμος *aut* ἀοίδιμος Reiske καί Keil *fort.* δίκαιος *aut* Αἰακός (*deleto* Αἰακόν) [207] Εὐρύβατος Keil *e* Σ

[208] *del.* Trapp *post* Behr (*qui* ὥσπερ . . . εἶναι *tantum*)

acles, and then bow low when he approaches.[552] I think it 673
is only to be expected that they should have bad words for everybody—they are particularly strong in this, since even if they are not talking about anybody in particular, they still say what they say badly, so they are simply being generous with what they have.

And now they dare to speak of the best among the Greeks as though they had permission to do so: really, if one were to take out of them their mendacity and their malice, it would be as if one had removed the very core of
their existence. These for goodness' sake are the people 674
who have gone and bestowed on themselves the noblest of all names, philosophy, as if they had bagged front-row seats at the theater and everyone else immediately had to make way for them, or as if issues like these were decided by changes of name rather than by the facts—as if the notorious Phrynondas had changed his name to Aeacus, in the belief that he would straight away be thought † twin † and above all reproach, or Thersites had called himself Hyacinthus or Narcissus, or Lycaon Hector, or Coroebus Palamedes, or Margites Nestor, or Battus—the one who

[552] Heracles is known to have featured in a number of satyr plays, including Aeschylus' *Kerykes* (*Heralds*), Sophocles' *Heracles at Taenarum* and *Cerberus* (if these are not the same play), and Euripides' *Syleus*; a Sophoclean fragment (756 *TrGF*) in which a satyr speaks aggressively about Heracles is quoted at Ath. *Deipn*. 23d.

675 τῆς φωνῆς [τῆς][209] εἰς Δελφοὺς ἀφικόμενος. εἶδον δ' ἔγωγε καὶ ἐν κωμῳδίᾳ[210] θεράποντας ἀλιτηρίους τοῖς τῶν θεῶν ὀνόμασιν κοσμοῦντας ἑαυτούς, ὧν ἀπώναντο τὸ σῶμα ξαινόμενοι, καὶ ἀξίως γ' ἐγίγνοντο μᾶλλον θεοῖς ἐχθροί. οὐκ ἤρκεσεν τῷ Βοσκυπταίχμῳ μεταθέσθαι τοὔνομα, ἀλλ' ὅτ' εὖ καὶ καλῶς Εὐτυχῆ
676 προσεῖπεν ἑαυτόν, ἔτι κρεῖττον ἐδυστύχει. καὶ οὗτοι τὴν τῆς φιλοσοφίας εὐφημίαν προκαλυψάμενοι διὰ ταύτης κλέψειν οἴονται τἄνδοθεν. ἔπειτά γε ἀλώπηξ ἀντὶ λέοντος ὑπέστη κερδαλῆ.

677 ἀρχὴν δὲ οὐδ' εἰδέναι μοι δοκοῦσιν οὐδ' αὐτὸ τοὔνομα τῆς φιλοσοφίας ὅπως εἶχεν τοῖς Ἕλλησιν καὶ ὅτι ἠδύνατο οὐδ' ὅλως τῶν περὶ ταῦτ' οὐδέν. οὐχ Ἡρόδοτος Σόλωνα σοφιστὴν κέκληκεν, οὐ Πυθαγόραν πάλιν, οὐκ Ἀνδροτίων τοὺς Ἑπτὰ σοφιστὰς προσείρηκε, λέγων[211] δὴ τοὺς σοφούς, καὶ πάλιν αὖ Σωκράτη σοφιστὴν τοῦτον τὸν πάνυ; αὖθις δ' Ἰσοκράτης σοφιστὰς μὲν τοὺς περὶ τὴν ἔριν καί τούς,

[209] *om.* U *del. edd.*
[210] κωμῳδίᾳ Boulanger ψαλμῳδίᾳ *codd.*
[211] λέγων Reiske λέγω *codd.*

---

[553] The point of this list of names is clear, even though the text containing it is faulty and has not yet been satisfactorily emended. Phrynondas was a notorious bandit, already proverbial for Plato (*Prt.* 327d) and Old Comedy (Ar. *Thesm.* 861 and perhaps Pherecrates' *Savages*); Thersites was an emblem of deformity and ugliness (Hom. *Il.* 2.212–19), Lycaon one of Priam's less successful sons (*Il.* 21.34–135), Coroebus (Suda s.v., Callimachus fr. 587

went to Delphi to ask about his voice—Stentor.[553] I my- 675
self have seen villainous servants in a comedy decking themselves out with the names of the gods; their reward for this was a physical flogging and it quite rightly put them still more firmly in the gods' bad books. It did not help Boscuptaechmus to change his name:[554] when he had fairly and squarely called himself Eutyches ("Lucky") his
bad luck grew still worse. These people wrap themselves 676
in the good reputation of philosophy and think that by exploiting her they are going to deceive us about what they are like inside. If so, then the fox in its cunning lurks in place of the lion![555]

It seems to me that they do not have the first idea of 677
the status and meaning of the name "philosophy" among Greeks, nor in general about anything at all that bears on this. Did not Herodotus call Solon a "sophist," and also Pythagoras?[556] Did not Androtion talk of the Seven as "sophists," meaning the Sages, and did he not also call the great Socrates a "sophist"?[557] Or again, did not Isocrates give the name "sophists" to devotees of eristic and to those

Pf.) and Margites proverbial idiots, and Battus (Hdt. 4.155) a famous stutterer. In the Greek text, the word translated "twin" (*didymos*) is obviously corrupt (for ? "supremely just"), and the bracketed words, omitted from the translation ("this is an encouragement to misbehavior, as if the thief were to think cheating the whole of creation made him a Rhadamanthys") look like a reader's addition.

554 "Boscuptaechmus" is not otherwise known; the name may have become garbled in the manuscript tradition.

555 Almost, but (deliberately?) not quite an allusion to the Aesopic fable of the fox and the ass in the lion's skin (188 Perry).

556 Hdt. 1.29.1, 4.95.2.

557 Androtion (324) F 69 Jacoby.

ὡς ἂν αὐτοὶ φαῖεν, διαλεκτικούς, φιλόσοφον δ' ἑαυτὸν καὶ τοὺς ῥήτορας καὶ τοὺς περὶ τὴν πολιτικὴν ἕξιν φιλοσόφους; [ὡσαύτως δὲ καὶ τῶν τούτῳ συγγενομένων ὀνομάζουσί τινες.][212] οὐ Λυσίας Πλάτωνα σοφιστὴν καλεῖ καὶ πάλιν Αἰσχίνην; κατηγορῶν οὗτός γε, φαίη τις ἄν. ἀλλ' οὐχ οἵ γε ἄλλοι κατηγοροῦντες ἐκείνων τῶν ἄλλων ὅμως ταυτὸν τοῦτο προσειρήκασιν αὐτούς. ἔτι δ' εἰ καὶ Πλάτωνος ἐξῆν κατηγοροῦντα σοφιστὴν προσειπεῖν, τί τούτους γ' ἂν
678 εἴποι τις; ἀλλ' οἶμαι καὶ σοφιστὴς ἐπιεικῶς κοινὸν ἦν ὄνομα καὶ ἡ φιλοσοφία τοῦτ' ἠδύνατο, φιλοκαλία τις εἶναι καὶ διατριβὴ περὶ λόγους, καὶ οὐχ ὁ νῦν τρόπος οὗτος, ἀλλὰ παιδεία κοινῶς. τεκμηριοῖ δὲ καὶ Δημοσθένης καὶ ἕτεροι μυρίοι. καὶ οὐ μόνον ἐν τοῖς καταλογάδην οὕτω ταῦτ' ἔχοντ' ἐστίν, ἀλλὰ κἀν τοῖς
679 ποιήμασιν. ἤδη μέντοι καὶ τοὺς κακοτεχνοῦντας ἐπισκώπτοντες καὶ τούτους ἔλεγον φιλοσοφεῖν, τὸν αὐτὸν τρόπον ὅνπερ καὶ τὸν σοφιστὴν ἐπὶ τὸ φαυλότερον ἤνεγκαν.

680 αὐτὸς τοίνυν Πλάτων ὁ μάλιστ' ἀνθαψάμενος τούτου τοῦ προσρήματος καὶ φιλοσοφίαν τοῦτ' εἰπών, τό θ' αὑτοῦ[213] καὶ Σωκράτους καὶ πρᾶγμα καὶ γράμμα, ὅμως κατ' ἀμφότερα πεποίηται τοὺς τρόπους

212 ὡσαύτως . . . τινες *secl.* Trapp
213 τό θ' αὑτοῦ Dindorf τό γ' αὑτοῦ UR^{2} τό γ' αὐτοῦ OPh^{M3}

who would describe themselves as dialecticians, and "philosopher" to himself and the orators and those whose
search for wisdom centered on the attributes of the states-
man?[558] Does not Lysias call Plato a "sophist" and also
Aeschines?[559] Well, he was speaking in accusation, you
might say. But the rest of them were not making any accusations against those others and nevertheless called
them the same thing. And moreover, if it was possible to
call even Plato a sophist when attacking him, what could
we call them? No, I think "sophist" was more or less a 678
general term and what "philosophy" meant was a love of
all that is fine and a dedication to words, that is to say
"cultivation" in general rather than the sense of the word
that is now current, as Demosthenes and countless others
testify.[560] This is the case not only in prose authors but also
in poetry. When making fun of the deviously clever poets 679
used to say that they too were "philosophizing," in the
same way as they also applied the word "sophist" in an
uncomplimentary sense.

Plato himself, who was particularly committed to this 680
designation and called "philosophy" what he and Socrates
did and wrote, nevertheless uses the words in both of two

558 For example, Isoc. *Orr.* 13 (*Against the Sophists*), 15 (*Antidosis*), 270–80. The next sentence in the Greek text, bracketed opposite, looks like a reader's addition ("Some of his pupils also use the same nomenclature").

559 Lysias used the word "sophist" of Aeschines in his speech *Against Aeschines the Socratic* (fr. 1 Carey, reported in Ath. *Deipn.* 13.611e–12f); the reference to Plato, otherwise unattested (fr. 449 Carey), may have come in the same speech.

560 [Dem.] 61.40–44.

αὐτῶν. τούς τε γὰρ φιλοκάλους καὶ φιλομαθεῖς ἐπιεικῶς εὕροι τις ἂν αὐτὸν φιλοσόφους ὀνομάζοντα, ἐγγύς τι τῆς τῶν πολλῶν κλήσεως, καὶ πάλιν που διαιρούμενος τούτους ἰδίᾳ προσείρηκεν φιλοσόφους, τοὺς περὶ τὰς ἰδέας πραγματευομένους καὶ τῶν σωμάτων ὑπερορῶντας. οὕτως οὔτε τοὺς ἄλλους ἀφαιρεῖται τοὔνομα, ἀλλὰ δίδωσι κἀκείνοις φιλοσοφεῖν, οἷς τ' ἰδίᾳ ταύτην ἀπέδωκε τὴν ἐπωνυμίαν οὐχ ἅπαντές εἰσιν οἱ φάσκοντες οὗτοι[214] φιλοσοφεῖν, ἀλλ' οἱ νῦν[215] <τῶν>[216] Πυθαγόρου καὶ Πλάτωνος σχεδὸν ὄντες λόγων· ἐπεὶ τούς γε ἄλλους φιλοσωμάτους, ἀλλ' οὐ φιλοσόφους καλοίη τις ἂν ἐν τῇ Πλάτωνος φωνῇ.
681 ἐπεὶ καὶ τὸν σοφιστὴν δοκεῖ μέν πως κακίζειν ἀεί, καὶ ὅ γε δὴ μάλιστα ἐπαναστὰς τῷ ὀνόματι Πλάτων εἶναί μοι δοκεῖ. αἴτιον δὲ τούτου καὶ τῶν πολλῶν αὐτὸν καὶ τῶν κατ' αὐτὸν ὑπερφρονῆσαι. φαίνεται δὲ καὶ ταύτῃ εἰς ἅπασαν εὐφημίαν τῇ προσηγορίᾳ κεχρημένος. ὃν γοῦν ἀξιοῖ σοφώτατον εἶναι θεὸν καὶ παρ' ᾧ πᾶν εἶναι τἀληθές, τοῦτον δήπου τέλεον σοφιστὴν κέκληκεν.

682 ἀλλ' ἐῶ τὸν σοφιστήν· ἀλλ' οὗ χάριν ἐξέβην ἐπὶ ταῦτα, κατ' οὐδετέραν γὰρ τῶν προσηγοριῶν εἰς τούτους γένοιτ' ἂν ἡ φιλοσοφία φωνήν, <οὔτε,>[217] ὥσπερ ἔφην, κατὰ τὴν κοινὴν τῶν Ἑλλήνων· οὐ γὰρ

214 οὕτω UR^2
215 μόνον Monac. 432 *an* ἀλλὰ μόνον οἱ?
216 *add.* Laur. 60.9 217 *add.* Reiske

applications. One can find him often enough giving the
name "philosophers" to lovers of what is fine and lovers of
learning, in a way close to the majority usage,[561] but he
also at times draws a distinction and gives the name philosophers in a restricted sense to those who deal in the
Forms and who regard physical entities as inferior.[562] The
situation is thus both that he does not deprive the others
of the name, but allows them too to count as philosophers,
and that those to whom he gives this name in its special-
ized sense are not all those who claim to be practicing
philosophy more broadly understood, but only those who
affiliate themselves to the arguments of Pythagoras and
Plato, since in Platonic terminology one would call the
others "lovers of physical entities" rather than "lovers of
wisdom."[563] For one way or another he gives the impres- 681
sion of always denigrating "the sophist," and as I see it
Plato is the one who is particularly up in arms against the
word. The reason for this is his contempt both for the
majority of mankind and for his contemporaries. Yet he
also clearly uses this term too in an entirely complimentary sense: at any rate, he certainly called the god whom
he judges the wisest of all and who is the repository of all
truth, "a perfect sophist."[564]

But I will say no more about "the sophist." The reason 682
for this excursus of mine has been to show that "philosophy" would not be the right word for these people in either
of its two senses, neither, as I have said, in its normal

561 For example, *Phdr.* 248d, *Resp.* 376b–c.
562 For example, *Phd.* 61c–69e.
563 *Phd.* 68b.
564 Hades: *Cra.* 403e.

ἀφώριστο τοῦτ' εἶναι τὸ φιλοσοφεῖν, ἀλλὰ παιδεία τις ἦν, ἧς τούτοις οὐδ' ὁτιοῦν μέτεστιν, ἀπ' αὐτῶν τῶν ὀνομάτων ἀρξαμένοις, οὔτ'[218] αὖ κατὰ τὴν Πλάτωνος, ἣν ἰδίᾳ τισὶν ἀξιοῖ σῴζεσθαι. οὐ γὰρ ἅπασι μετέδωκε τῆς προσηγορίας τοῖς ἐπὶ τοῦ προσχήματος, ἀλλ' οἷς
683 εἶπον μόνοις. ἀλλ' ὅμως πρὶν καὶ περὶ αὐτῆς τῆς ἐπωνυμίας ἔχειν εἰπεῖν τι, σεμνύνονται καί φασιν φιλοσοφεῖν καὶ μόνοι τά τε ὄντα καὶ τὰ ἐσόμενα γιγνώσκειν, καὶ πάσας ὑφ' αὐτοῖς καὶ πρὸς αὐτοὺς εἶναι τὰς τέχνας· οὓς οὐδὲν δεῖ κατ' ὄνομα ἐξετάζειν, ἀλλὰ φορμηδὸν ἐφ' ἁμαξῶν ἐκφέρειν, ὥσπερ τοὺς Κερκυ-
684 ραίων νεκρούς. τί γὰρ οὗτοι χρήσιμοι τῷ τῶν ἀνθρώπων γένει, οἷς οὐδὲ φαρμακοῖς, τὸ τοῦ κωμῳδιοποιοῦ, χρήσαιτ' ἄν τις ῥᾳδίως; ἀλλ' ὅμως ἡμεῖς τούτου γ' αὐτοῖς μεταδῶμεν καὶ μὴ φθονῶμεν, πρὸς ἓν τοῦτο ἔστων χρήσιμοι ταῖς πόλεσι, θρέψαντας ἐκρῖψαι. ὡς οὐκ εἶναί γέ τις ἂν φαίη πραγμάτων καὶ κακῶν αὐτοῖς ἀπαλλαγὴν καλλίω καὶ καθαρωτέραν ἢ εἰ τῶν θηρίων
685 τούτων ἀπολυθεῖεν. εἰ δὲ μὴ τῇ κακίᾳ τῆς φύσεως αὐτῶν καὶ τοῖς πονηρεύμασιν ἀσθένειαν καὶ ἀνανδρείαν ὁ θεὸς προσῆψεν, ἅπαντ' ἂν ἀοίκηθ' ὑπ' αὐτῶν ἦν, ὥσπερ Ἡρόδοτος περὶ τῶν ὄφεων ἔφη. νῦν δὲ κἂν ἶβις τούτων κρατήσειεν.

686 καὶ ταῦτα μηδεὶς οἰέσθω βλασφημίαν εἰς φιλοσοφίαν ἔχειν μηδ' ἀηδίᾳ μηδεμιᾷ λέγεσθαι, ἀλλὰ πολλῷ

[218] οὔτ' Reiske οὐδ' *codd.*

Greek sense—this is not how philosophy was defined; it was defined as a kind of cultivation, of which they are entirely innocent, beginning with the meanings of these very words—nor in Plato's sense, which he thinks ought to be kept for a specific class of people, since he did not allow the term to be applied to all who put up an outward appearance of deserving it, but only to those I stated. Yet 683
before they are even able to say anything about the name itself they give themselves airs and say that they are philosophers and the only ones to understand what is now and what will be in the future, and that all the arts and sciences come under their supervision and are their concern. There is no point in naming names as we discuss them; they should be carted away in heaps, like dead Corcyreans.[565]
What use are they to the human race, when, to quote the 684
comic poet, one could not easily use them even as scapegoats?[566] But even so let us be generous and allow them to qualify for this if nothing more: let there be just the one respect in which they are useful to their cities, to be thrown out as soon as they grow up. For it is impossible to specify a better and cleaner release from trouble and suffering than being freed from these pests. Had God not 685
added weakness and cowardice to the baseness and defects of their nature, the whole world would have become uninhabitable because of them, as Herodotus said of the snakes;[567] but as it is, even an ibis could dispose of them.[568]

Let nobody suppose that any of this involves an insult 686
to philosophy or that it is said in any spirit of distaste; let

[565] Thuc. 4.48.4. [566] Ar. *Ran.* 732–33. [567] Hdt. 2.75.

[568] Pointed: besides being known as a snake killer, the ibis was also thought of as a distastefully filthy bird (Strabo 17.2.4).

μᾶλλον ὑπὲρ φιλοσοφίας εἶναι καὶ πρὸς τοὺς ὑβρίζοντας ταύτην εἰρῆσθαι † καὶ συνηγορῶν τῇ φιλοσοφίᾳ νῦν ἡμᾶς ἀναστὰς κατηγορῶν †[219] *εἴπερ τι χρηστὸν αὐτῆς*[220] *εἶναι δοκεῖ.*[221] *ἀναμνησθῶ καὶ τοῦ φαλακροῦ χαλκέως τοῦ τῇ δεσποίνῃ συνοικοῦντος. τοῦτον οὐκ ἀτιμάζων δήπου φιλοσοφίαν ἐποίησεν* Πλάτων, *ἀλλά τινας ὑπὲρ αὐτῆς κάλλιστ' ἀνθρώπων εἰκάζων τοὺς ἐνισταμένους, καὶ ῥᾳδίως αὐτοὺς*[222] *ἀξιοῦντας τῶν*
687 *μειζόνων ἢ κατ' αὐτούς. ἐπεὶ καὶ τοῦτο ἔμοιγε θαυμαστὸν καὶ θεῖον φαίνεται τῆς ἐκείνου φιλοσοφίας, τὸ μὴ πᾶσιν εἰκῇ συγχωρεῖν ἐπικεκινδυνευκόσιν,*[223] *ἀλλ' ἔγκρισιν*[224] *εἶναι τῶν ἀνδρῶν καὶ τὰς φύσεις ἐξετάζεσθαι. οὐδὲ γὰρ τοὺς Ἠλείους* [*αὐτοὺς*][225] *ἔγωγε νομίζω καταλύειν τὸ τῶν Ὀλυμπίων οὐδὲ ἀτιμάζειν, ὅτι οὐ πάντας ῥᾳδίως προσίενται τοὺς τοιούτους ἀγωνιστάς, † ἀλλὰ πρόκρισιν ἐστὶν οὐ ταυτόν †*[226] *ἀλλά*[227] *μοι καὶ μειζόνως αὔξειν δοκοῦσιν καὶ κοσμεῖν τὸν θεσμὸν τῷ τοσοῦτον ἅπασι παριστάναι τὸν φόβον καὶ τῷ τὰ πάντα ἀξιοῦν εἶναι τὸ*[228] *παρὰ σφίσι κηρυκεύεσθαι τὰ μὲν ἀποδύντα τὴν ἀρχὴν ὀφθῆναι, <τὰ δὲ . . . . .>.*[229]

[219] *locum desperatum alius aliter tractat, nemo adhuc satis*
[220] *αὐτῆς* Q^{1}R^1 *edd. αὐτῆς cett.* [221] δοκεῖ Trapp δοκεῖν *codd.* [222] *αὑτούς* U *αὐτούς cett.*
[223] *ἐπικεκινδυνευκόσιν* Reiske *ἐπικεκινδυνευκός codd.*
[224] *ἔγκρισιν* Behr *ἔκκρισιν codd.* (*praeter* UR^2 *ἀλλὰ κρίσιν*)
[225] *αὐτούς del.* Trapp *τοὺς Ἠλείους αὐτούς* T^2 *αὐτοὺς τοὺς* Ἠλείους R^2 *αὐτούς* V *αὐτοὺς εἰς αὐτούς cett.*
[226] *locus nondum sanatus lac. post πρόκρισιν stat.* Dindorf (*fort. e.g.* <ποιοῦνται>) *ἐστὶν οὐ ταυτόν fort. delenda*

it rather be supposed that it is much more a defense of philosophy and addressed to those who violate her † and it is as an advocate for philosophy now stands up and denounces us † if it is thought she has any redeeming feature.[569] Remember also the bald blacksmith cohabiting with his mistress.[570] Plato clearly was not doing philosophy down when he invented him but was instead defending her by producing the most brilliant image conceivable for beginners who rashly suppose themselves capable of feats beyond their abilities. For what strikes me as extraordi- 687
nary and inspired in his philosophy is the fact that it does not casually admit all who have ventured on it, but that there is instead a selection process to choose the personnel through an examination of their natural abilities. I do not think the Eleans either are destroying or dishonoring the spirit of the Olympics in not casually admitting all this sort of contestant † but instead a preliminary selection it is not the same thing †[571] but I think that they actually augment and adorn their institution all the more by instilling such a degree of fear in everybody and by insisting on the all-importance of their own local practice in proclaiming both that a contestant should be seen stripped of his clothing

569 The Greek text of this sentence is faulty and has not yet been satisfactorily repaired.

570 *Resp.* 495e.

571 The Greek text is again faulty and has not yet been satisfactorily repaired; possibly, "it is not the same thing" should be expelled as a reader's note and a verb added to give "not casually admitting . . . but imposing a preliminary selection instead."

---

227 ἀλλά Stephanus ἀλλ' ὅ $T^1Q^1A^1R^1E$ ἀλλ' ὅτι $UaQ^2A^2R^2$
228 τὸ Trapp τά *codd.* 229 *lac. stat.* Behr

688 *οὔτω τοίνυν καὶ ἡμεῖς οὐ φιλοσοφίαν ἀτιμάζομεν,*
ἀλλ᾽ ὑπὲρ φιλοσοφίας ἀμυνόμεθα, ὡς εἰκὸς ἦν. οἶμαι
γὰρ ἔγωγε καὶ Πλάτωνα καὶ Πυθαγόραν αὐτοὺς ἀνα-
στάντας καὶ λαβόντας † σοφιστὴν πόρρω που οὔτω
δὲ † ἂν κελεύειν τούτους καθέζεσθαι καὶ νομίζειν[230]
κάλλιστ᾽ ἂν οὕτως αὐτοῖς ὑπὲρ φιλοσοφίας εἶναι δε-
δογμένον † ὃν καὶ τοὺς κωμάζοντας ἐπ᾽ αὐτὴν ἀπο-
689 *κρῖναι ἐν ᾧπερ οἱ τοὺς τῷ ὄντι κωμάζοντας ἐπ᾽ αὐτὴν*
ἀποκρίνοντες †[231] *καὶ ἡμεῖς οὐχ ἅπαντας δήπου λέγο-*
μεν κακῶς, οὐδ᾽ εἰρήκαμεν, ἀλλ᾽ οἷς τοῦτο προσήκει
τῶν σκηπτούχων καὶ οἵτινες ἂν γνωρίζωσι τὰ λεγό-
μενα, οὔθ᾽ ὅστις αὐτῶν πρῶτος αἰτιάσεται, πρὸς
690 *τοῦτον εἴρηται. ἐπὶ*[232] *φιλοσοφίᾳ.γέ μοι † καὶ αἰσχρὸν*
καὶ μέθην[233] *† ὥσπερ ἂν ἄλλῳ τῳ τοιούτῳ. οἶμαι δὲ*
κἀγὼ συγγενέσθαι τῶν ἐπ᾽ ἐμαυτοῦ φιλοσοφησάντων
τοῖς ἀρίστοις καὶ τελεωτάτοις, καὶ οὐ πολλῶν ἡττᾶ-
σθαι ταύτῃ θνητῶν, καὶ ἐν τροφέων μοίρᾳ γεγόνασί
μοι. ὥστε τοῖς οἴκοι πολεμοίην ἂν <μᾶλλον>[234] *ἢ τοῖς*
φιλοσόφοις. ἀλλὰ μὴ τοῦτο τοιοῦτον ᾖ, ἀλλ᾽ ἔχει τινὰ
καὶ χάριν ἡμῖν ἡ φιλοσοφία.

230 *καὶ νομίζειν* Reiske *καὶ νομίζεσθαι* TUQ^{2}R^2 *om.* Q^{1}VAR^{1}Ea 231 *σοφιστήν . . . δέ et ὃν καί . . . ἀποκρίνοντες nondum sanaverunt edd.* 232 *ἐπεί* Reiske
233 *μετῆν* Scaliger
234 *add.* Iunt. *sed fort. ἢ τοῖς φιλοσόφοις delenda*

572 A clause seems to be missing from the Greek text here.

573 The Greek text here ("got hold of a sophist") is clearly corrupt; something more like "had the opportunity," or "were given the authority," is needed.

at the outset, <and . . . . .>.[572] In the same way, then, I too 688
am not doing philosophy down but fighting back in philosophy's defense, as was only reasonable. I am convinced
that Plato and Pythagoras themselves, if they came back
to life and got hold of . . . ,[573] would order these people to
sit down and would think that the best decision they could
have made on philosophy's behalf was this one † and separate off those trying to burst drunkenly in on her . . . the
ones who are separating off those who are in all reality
trying to burst drunkenly in on her †.[574] I am of course not 689
denigrating all of them, nor have I ever done so, but only
those of the stick carriers[575] who deserve it, and whoever
may recognize what is being said, and my words have not
been directed toward the one among them who will be the
first to press charges. For as far as philosophy itself goes, 690
I †. . . . .†[576] just as for anyone of this kind. I think that in
fact I have studied with the best and most complete of the
philosophers of my time and in this regard have few superiors among men; they have been like foster parents to me,
so that I would rather be at war with my own household
than with philosophers.[577] But perish the thought; in fact
philosophy actually has something to be grateful to me for.

[574] The Greek text here is again faulty and not yet satisfactorily repaired. The overall sense is clear: the "philosophers" Aristides is berating are incompetent interlopers, and Plato and Pythagoras themselves would have joined him in kicking them out.

[575] That is, Cynics, with their distinctive "uniform" of stick and bag.

[576] The Greek text is again faulty at this point and not yet satisfactorily repaired.

[577] The text is uncertain at this point: perhaps instead, "so that fighting them would be like fighting my nearest and dearest."

691 ἐπεὶ καὶ ῥητορικῇ χαίρειν ἂν φαίην εἴπερ τις ἀνθρώπων <. . . . .>[235] καὶ ἐμοί τι μέτεστιν ἴσως τοῦ πολέμου.[236] ἀλλ᾽ οὐ διὰ τοῦτο τοὺς ὑβρίζοντας εἰς αὐτὴν ἐπαινεῖν οἴομαι δεῖν, ἀρχὴν δὲ οὐδὲ καλῶ ῥήτορας· ἀλλ᾽ ὅσῳ μᾶλλον [τε][237] τὴν ῥητορικὴν θαυμάζω τε καὶ ἀσπάζομαι, τοσούτῳ μᾶλλον τοῖς ἀναξίως αὐτῆς ταύτης καταψευδομένοις ἄχθομαι, καὶ ὑπὲρ αὐτῆς τῆς ῥητορικῆς ἥδιστ᾽ ἂν ἀμυνοίμην καὶ πειρῴμην εἰς ὅσον οἷός τ᾽ εἴην δεικνύναι πάντα μᾶλλον ἀκούειν δικαίους ἢ τοῦτο. ἀλλ᾽ οὐ πρὸς Μιλτιάδην γε καὶ Θεμιστοκλέα καὶ Περικλέα καὶ Κίμωνα ταύτην ἔχω τὴν γνώμην.

[*Peroration:* *A Plea for Reciprocal Respect (692–94)*]

692 πρὸς γὰρ σέ, ὦ Πλάτων, ἤδη περιαχθέντας δεῖ τούτους χαίρειν ἐᾶσαι, εἰ δή τι μέτεστιν αὐτοῖς τούτου,
693 οἶμαι δὲ οὐδέν. † ταῦτα μικρόν †.[238] ἡμεῖς δὲ γνωρίζωμεν ἡμᾶς αὐτοὺς καὶ μὴ φυρώμεθα ὥσπερ ἐν νυκτομαχίᾳ,[239] μηδὲ τοῦτό γε ἕν, κακὸν Ἑλληνικόν,

[235] *lac. stat.* Reiske
[236] καὶ ἐμοί . . . πολέμου *del.* Behr
[237] γε Q *om.* UPh^{M3} *del.* Dindorf μᾶλλόν τε *del.* Behr
[238] ταῦτα μικρόν *del.* Behr *lac. ante* ταῦτα *stat. Reiske*
[239] νυκτομαχίᾳ Stephanus ἡμερομαχίᾳ *codd.*

I would say that I love the art of oratory if any man ever 691
did, <. . . . .> and this is a battle that I perhaps have a part in,[578] but I do not for this reason think that those who behave outrageously toward her should be praised, and do not even call them orators at all. Admiring and cherishing the art of oratory as I do, I am all the more angry at those who produce an unworthy counterfeit of it; I would take the greatest pleasure in defending the art itself from them, and in trying to the best of my ability to prove that they deserve to be called anything rather than orators. But this is not my opinion of Miltiades or Themistocles or Pericles or Cimon.

Peroration:
A Plea for Reciprocal Respect (692–94)

Now that these reprobates have been traced back to you, 692
Plato,[579] you ought to send them packing—if indeed they have anything to do with this business, which I think they
really do not. † These things (are) a trivial matter †.[580] For 693
our own part, let us recognize each other and not mix things up as if in a night battle. Let there be at least this

[578] The Greek text is again faulty and not yet satisfactorily repaired; this translation assumes that Reiske is right that some words have dropped out after "ever did." Behr expels "this is a battle that I perhaps have a part in" as an interpolated gloss.

[579] Cf. §663 above.

[580] The Greek text is once more corrupt at this point and not yet satisfactorily repaired; Behr may well be right simply to expel the problem words as a reader's note.

μιμώμεθα, στασιάζοντες περὶ τῆς ἡγεμονίας, ἀλλ' ἐπιχωρήσαντες[240] τῷ θεῷ τὴν κρίσιν παρέχωμεν ἡμᾶς αὐτοὺς ἐν τῷ τεταγμένῳ καὶ γιγνώμεθα τοιοῦτοι περὶ τοὺς πρότερον οἵουσπερ ἂν αὖ τοὺς ὕστερον εἶναι περὶ ἡμᾶς βουλοίμεθα. αἰσχρὸν γάρ, ὥς γ' ἔφη Δημοσθένης, οὓς οὐδ' ἂν τῶν ἐχθρῶν καὶ τῶν πολεμίων οὐδεὶς ἂν ἀποστερήσειεν τῶν εὐφημιῶν, τούτους ὑφ' ἡμῶν, οἳ[241] προσήκομεν αὐτοῖς, μὴ τῆς γιγνομένης αἰδοῦς καὶ φιλανθρωπίας τυγχάνειν.

694 ἐγὼ μὲν οὖν καὶ Πλάτωνι τὴν προσήκουσαν τιμὴν ἀπένειμα καὶ τοῖς ἀνδράσι τὰ πρέποντα ἐβοήθησα, καὶ οὐχὶ προηκάμην. εἰ δέ τις ἀντειπεῖν ἔχει τούτοις, φυλάττων ἐμοὶ τὴν ἴσην εὐφημίαν ὅσηνπερ ἐγὼ Πλάτωνι, τοῦτον ἐγὼ καὶ νῦν καὶ ὕστερον φίλον, οὐκ ἐχθρὸν κρίνω.

240 ἐπιχωρήσαντες Monac. 432 ἐπιτρέψαντες UR^2 ἐπικουρήσαντες *cett.*

241 οἳ Reiske ὅτι *codd.*

one Greek failing that we do not reproduce in ourselves by splitting into factions over who should be leader. Let us instead defer to God's decision, keeping to our posts and behaving toward those who have gone before us as we would wish those who come after us to behave toward us in their turn. As Demosthenes said, it is a shameful thing that those whom not even a single one of their personal enemies or opponents in war would rob of their good name, should not be granted the proper respect and goodwill by us, their own.[581]

I have, then, granted Plato the honor that is due to him, 694
and I have rendered fitting assistance to the Four, and not betrayed them. If there is someone who has a counterargument to bring against my words, while maintaining the same courtesy to me as I have to Plato, I deem him now and in time to come no enemy, but a friend.[582]

581 Dem. 19.313.

582 A concluding nod at *Grg.* 458a: Aristides suggests that he has been more faithful to an important Socratic principle than Plato.

ORATION 4
A REPLY TO CAPITO

4

ΠΡΟΣ ΚΑΠΙΤΩΝΑ

Νῦν σὲ καὶ μᾶλλον φιλοῦμεν οὕτως ἐρωτικῶς τοῦ Πλάτωνος ἔχοντα, ὃν ἐγὼ φαίην ἂν τιμᾶν καθ' Ὅμηρον ἶσον ἐμῇ κεφαλῇ. εἰ γάρ τοι καὶ πάντες φαῦλοι πρὸς ἐκεῖνον, ἀλλ' ἕκαστος τιμιώτατος αὐτὸς ἑαυτῷ, φασίν. καίτοι τί λέγω; οὐκ οἶδα μὲν γὰρ εἰ πιστεύεις, ἀληθὲς δὲ ἐρῶ. εἰ δὲ μὴ ἐγγὺς ἐκεῖνον ἔφησας ἡμῶν εἶναι, οὐκ ἂν οὕτω με εὔφρανας ὡς ὅτι προκατείληψαι δείξας· οὕτως ἐμοὶ φίλος ἀνὴρ καὶ φίλων ἐπέκεινα.

συνέβη δέ μοι καὶ περὶ Δημοσθένη τοιοῦτον ἕτε-
2 ρον, φράσω δὲ καὶ πρὸς σέ. ἀνὴρ τῶν ἐκ τῆς γερουσίας τῆς Ῥωμαίων, Λίβυς τὰ ἀρχαῖα, Μάξιμος τὸ ὄνομα, ἄξιος ὅτου βούλει, φασὶ δὲ οἱ ταῦτα δεινοὶ καὶ ῥήτορα αὐτὸν ἐν πρώτοις εἶναι Ῥωμαίων, οὗτος τοῖς τε Δημοσθένους λόγοις προσέκειτο ὑπερφυῶς καὶ οὐκ οἶδ' ὅντινα τρόπον καὶ τοῖς ἡμετέροις ἑάλω τούτοις· καὶ δὴ οἷα[1] συμφοιτῶν τε εἰς Ἀσκληπιοῦ καὶ φιλο-

[1] οἷα δή Behr

---

[1] *Il.* 18.81–82 (said by Achilles of Patroclus).

[2] Probably Q. Tullius Maximus, subsequently commander of

4
A REPLY TO CAPITO

I love you now more than ever because of this devotion of yours to Plato, whom I would say that I esteem, in Homer's phrase, "as much as I do my own person."[1] (Even if everyone is worthless compared to him, each man is, so they say, supremely valuable in his own eyes.) But what do I mean by this? I don't know if you believe me, but I will tell you the truth all the same. If you had said that Plato came nowhere near me, you would not have delighted me as much as you actually have by showing that he has a prior claim on your allegiance—so true is it that this man is dear and beyond dear to me.

Something similar happened to me with Demosthenes
too, and I shall tell you about it. There was a Roman sen- 2
ator of Libyan extraction called Maximus,[2] as worthy an individual as you could wish, and the experts in this area say that he is also among the leading lights of Roman oratory. This man was both extraordinarily attached to the speeches of Demosthenes and somehow or other also taken by my own, and since he was a fellow habitué of the shrine of Asclepius and a man of impeccable good taste,

the Legio VII Gemina in Spain, governor of Thrace and suffect consul in AD 168: *PIR*[1] 3.340–41 (T279/T280).

καλίας ἐλλείπων οὐδὲν συνῆν ἐμοὶ καθ᾽ἡμέραν ἑκάστην κατὰ τοὺς λόγους· ὥστε τι καὶ περιειργασάμην
3 πρὸς αὐτὸν ὑπὸ τοῦ τοιούτου. ἔτυχεν γάρ μοι λόγος τις πεποιημένος ἐκ τρίτων πρὸς Λεπτίνην ἐξ ἀρχῆς τοιᾶσδε· εἶχον ἐν χερσὶ τὸν λόγον τὸν τοῦ Δημοσθένους, καὶ ὡς ἐγενόμην ἐπὶ τῶν κεφαλαίων ἃ τοῦ Λεπτίνου μέλλοντος ἐρεῖν ὑπετέμνετο, ἀποστήσας ἐμαυτὸν τοῦ Δημοσθένους ὑπ᾽ ἐμαυτοῦ τι συνεώρων. ὡς δὲ εὗρον καὶ δύο καὶ τρία τῶν χρησίμων, ἐνταῦθα πάλιν αὖ ἐπ᾽ ἄλλο τι ἐχώρουν. καί μοι πειρωμένῳ τὸ αὐτὸ ἀεὶ συνέβαινεν. καὶ οὕτω δὴ ἀπὸ τοῦ κρασπέδου θοἰμάτιον, εἰ δὲ βούλει, τὸν λέοντα ἀπὸ τοῦ ὄνυχος
4 ἀπειργασάμην. τοῦτον οὖν αὐτῷ τὸν λόγον δεῖξαι ἐπεχείρησα καὶ μέλλων δείξειν προεῖπον ὅτι τὰ[2] πρὸς Λεπτίνην ἐφευρημένα σὺν τῷ πρὸς Λεπτίνην ἐφευρήσει.[3] μὴ ἀδικῶ γε, ἔφην ἐγώ. καὶ ὃς μὰ Δία εὐγενῶς τε καὶ ὡς ἂν πᾶς ἠράσθη τε καὶ ἠγάσθη ὅστις φιλόλογος, οἶσθα, ἔφη, ὅτι κάθημαι πρὸς τοῦ Δη-

[2] QR[2] Laur. 60.9 Marc. gr. 425 *om. cett.*
[3] *fort.* εὑρήσει Reiske

---

[3] This reference to Maximus as a fellow incubant and to Aristides' oratorical activity dates the episode to the period of his residence (*kathedra*) in the temple of Asclepius at Pergamum in AD 145–147. Whether this also dates the composition of the *Reply to Capito* is unclear (*pace* Behr): Aristides could be looking back on the episode at an interval of some years.

[4] There is a verbal echo here of *Grg.* 500a; Aristides is "the third" because speeches *Against Leptines* had previously been

he was at my side each day in my oratorical pursuits.[3] As a result, I addressed an extra little something to him, in
circumstances of the kind I shall now explain. It just so 3
happened that I had composed a speech against Leptines, making me the third person to do so,[4] and that it had originated as follows: I had the Demosthenic speech in my hands, and when I reached the chapters that forestalled what Leptines was going to say,[5] I parted company with Demosthenes and made up something on my own account. When I had thought up two or three serviceable arguments, I then went back again to another chapter of the speech. Each time I repeated the experiment it was equally successful, and by this means I finished off the whole cloak starting from the fringe, or if you prefer, the
whole lion starting from the claw.[6] Well, I ventured to 4
perform this speech to Maximus and just before I did so, I alerted him to the fact that side by side with the *Against Leptines* he would discover my own freshly invented thoughts against Leptines.[7] "I am not doing anything wrong in this, am I?", I said. And he replied, with real nobility and in a spirit that would win the affection and admiration of every lover of literature, "You know very

composed not only by Demosthenes (*Or.* 20) but also by his co-supporting speaker Phormio (hypoth. to Dem. *Or.* 20).

5 For example, Dem. *Or.* 20.98, 112, 120, 125, 131, 139, 145.

6 Two proverbial expressions for achieving extensive results from modest beginnings: Diogenianus 5.15 (Leutsch-Schneidewin 1.252, with note). The latter seems to go all the way back to Alcaeus (fr. 438 L-P).

7 Not entirely clear: Aristides perhaps means that Maximus needs to have a copy of Demosthenes' speech to hand in order fully to appreciate his new effort.

μοσθένους; κἀγώ, τὸν αὐτὸν ἄρ, ἔφην, ἐμοὶ βουκολεῖς, ὥστ᾽ εἰ νικῴη μ᾽, οὐκ ἐχθρὸς ὁ στεφανούμενος,
5 ἀλλ᾽ ᾧ σύ τε[4] κἀγὼ συσπεύδομεν.[5] ὡς δὲ ἐκέλευεν τὰ βιβλία ἐν μέρει δεικνύναι καὶ τὸ πρᾶγμα πανταχῇ σπουδὴ ἦν, οὑτωσί τοι, ἔφην ἐγώ, σοὶ ταὐτὰ γιγνώσκω περὶ Δημοσθένους, καὶ ἡγοῦμαι ταυτὸν ὅπερ σύ, μὴ ῥᾴδιον εἶναι τὸν ἄνδρα ἐκεῖνον παρελθεῖν. εἰ δ᾽ οὖν τις κἀμοὶ θεῶν ἐπιβοηθήσειεν, πολλὰ δὲ ἐν Ἀσκληπιοῦ τὰ παράδοξα, τί[6] οὐκ ἔδειξας, ἔφην, τἆθλα, ἵνα προθυμότερον ἀγωνιζοίμην; ἀποτυγχάνοντι μὲν γὰρ μανία καὶ μηδὲν ἐπαΐειν περὶ λόγων· ἐὰν δὲ ἄρα, ἔφην, κρατῶ, τί μοι περιέσται; καὶ ὃς ἥσθη τε ἀκούσας, ὥσπερ ἐγὼ ἐκείνου ἀκούσας ἥσθην ὅτι τῷ Δημοσθένει συνεστήκοι, καὶ ἔδωκεν ἄδειαν δεῖξαι τὸν λόγον. καὶ ὅπως ἤδη διετέθη τὰ ἐπὶ τούτοις αὐτὸς ἂν εἰδείη, καὶ σὺ δὲ εἴ που συγγένοιο τῷ ἀνδρὶ καὶ μνησθείης.

6 οὕτως ἐμοὶ κοινῶς μὲν εἰπεῖν τῶν παλαιῶν ἀνδρῶν, δι᾽ ἀκριβείας δὲ τούτων[7] ὑπὲρ πάντας ἔρως δεινὸς καὶ φιλία θαυμαστή τις ἐντέτηκεν ἐκ παιδός. ὥστε καὶ σοὶ νῦν οὐ μόνον οὐ νεμεσῶ τῆς γνώμης ἣν ἔχεις, ἀλλὰ καὶ συγχαίρω, καὶ φιλῶν οὐκ ἀνήσω, ὅτι[8] μὴ καὶ ὅσον οἷόν τε προσθήσω, νομίζων ἀκριβῶς ἑταῖρόν τε ἐμαυτοῦ καὶ στασιώτην εἶναι. οὐ γὰρ εἰς μελάν-

[4] τε *edd.* γε *codd.* [5] συσσπένδομεν Canter *post* a^2 in mrg. [6] τί Keil ὅτι *codd.* [7] τούτοιν U
[8] ὅτι *del.* Behr

well that my loyalty is to Demosthenes." "In that case," I said, "'You tend the same one as I do,'[8] so if I'm beaten by him, the winner of the victor's wreath will not be an enemy, but the man you and I both are devoted to." When 5
he then told me to take my turn and perform my composition, and things with this became really serious, I said "I share your opinion of Demosthenes as warmly as I've said, and just like you I believe he is someone not easy to surpass. All the same, if some god were to help me—many are the miracles in Asclepius' shrine—why don't you tell me what the prize is, to make me compete the more enthusiastically? The penalty for failure is to be thought mad and to know nothing about oratory; but if I win," I said, "what will my reward be?" He was delighted when he heard this, just as I had been delighted to hear him say that he sided with Demosthenes, and he gave me permission to declaim the speech with a clear conscience. How he was affected by what then followed is for him to know, and for you too if you have ever met him and mentioned the subject.

This is how deeply a tremendous love and an extraor- 6
dinary affection, for the ancients in general and above all specifically for these two,[9] has been ingrained in me from boyhood. As a result, I am not only not indignant now at your opinions, but actually congratulate you on them, and I will not let my love for you grow any less, but rather will add to it as far as possible, in the belief that you are in the full sense of the words my companion and a partisan of the same faction. We may not have "slaughtered a bull into a

[8] Ar. *Vesp.* 10. [9] Plato and Demosthenes, compared to somewhat different effect in *Or.* 3.499–510.

δετον σάκος ταυροσφαγοῦντες, ὡς Αἰσχύλος ἐποίησεν, ἀλλ᾽ εἰς τοὺς Πλάτωνος λόγους ἀφορῶντες ὥσπερ τινὰς συναγωγέας † καὶ κοινούς †,[9] εἰκότως ἂν
7 πιστεύειν ἀλλήλοις ἔχοιμεν περὶ ἁπάντων. πάρεστιν δέ σοι γνῶναι ὅτι καὶ ἡμῖν τι προσήκει Πλάτωνος, εἰ καὶ μὴ τοσοῦτον ὅσον τοῖς σοφοῖς, ἀλλ᾽ ὅσον γε ἐπίστασθαι χαίρειν τῷ ἀνδρί. ἥ τε γὰρ ἡμῖν φωνὴ σὺν θεοῖς εἰπεῖν οὐχὶ κώλυμα τὸ μηδὲν ἂν τῶν ἐκείνου δέξασθαι δύνασθαι, οὐδέ τις ἡμᾶς ἀπελαύνει πρόρρησις[10] † εἰ καὶ μυστηρίων †,[11] καὶ τὸν βίον οὐ παντάπασιν ἀπᾴδειν φασὶν τῆς ἐκείνου γνώμης οἱ πεπειραμένοι. ἀλλ᾽ εἴτ᾽ ἐγὼ κατ᾽ ἐκεῖνον ἔφην τότε εἴτ᾽ ἐκεῖνος νῦν κατ᾽ ἐμέ, οὐκ ἄν μοι δοκεῖ μέσος ἐγγενέσθαι <οὐδεὶς>[12] οὐδὲ παρελθεῖν παρὰ τῷ ἑτέρῳ τὸν ἕτερον εὐνοίας ἕνεκα καὶ τοῦ ταὐτὰ γιγνώσκειν περὶ τῶν ὅλων εἰπεῖν.

8 φέρε δὴ πρὸς αὐτοῦ τοῦ φιλίου Διός, ἐπεὶ καὶ Πλάτων τό τε[13] ἀληθὲς ἁπανταχοῦ τιμᾷ καὶ τὰς ἐν τοῖς λόγοις συνουσίας ἀφορμὴν φιλίας ἀληθινῆς ὑπολαμβάνει, σαφέστερον κατίδωμεν τί ποτε ἦν ὅ

9 *nisi delenda vel substantivum (e.g.* διαλλακτάς) *vel appositum expectare licet* 10 πρόρρησις U^{1}R^{2} πρόσρησις *cett.*
11 ὥσπερ μυστηρίων UR^{2} εἰ καὶ μυστηρίων *cett.* ἑκὰς μυστηρίων Canter *an delenda?* 12 *add.* Behr *(sed post* ἄν)
13 τε Reiske γε *codd.*

---

10 *Sept.* 43. 11 The Greek text here is probably faulty; some word like "reconciler" or "mediator" seems to be needed.

black-bound shield," as in Aeschylus,[10] but it would be perfectly reasonable for us to trust each other in anything because we both look to Plato's works as a kind of unifying force and † common property †.[11] You for your part can 7
see that I too have some bond with Plato, and that even though it may not be as intense a one as the philosophers have, it is at least enough for me to know how to enjoy him. My own oratorical ability, if the gods will not look askance on me for saying it, in no way prevents me from being able to accept any of his ideas; there is no preliminary proclamation bidding me keep my distance † even if from the mysteries †;[12] and those who have some acquaintance with my style of life say that it is not entirely discordant with his views. But whether my words then were in agreement with his, or he now is in agreement with me, I do not think that anyone could come between us or that the one of us could outstrip the other in goodwill or in determination to express the same view of the world.[13]

Well then, in the name of Zeus god of Friendship him- 8
self, since Plato everywhere values the truth and supposes spending time together in discussion to be the basis of true friendship,[14] let us work out more clearly what it was that

12 The Greek text is again faulty; the daggered words should perhaps be removed as a reader's note making explicit the imagery in the reference to a prohibitory proclamation.

13 The core claim of *Or.* 2, summarized at §§438–45.

14 Key features of the ideal of dialectic expounded by Plato in the *Gorgias* and exemplified (or at least aspired to) in the dialogues collectively: cf. *Grg.* 458a–b, 473b (truth), 487a–c (friendship).

σοι προσέστη τῶν λόγων, οὓς δὴ πρὸς αὐτὸν ἡμῖν φασί τινες πεποιῆσθαι. ἐγὼ μὲν γὰρ αὐτὸν ἐπειρώμην πανταχοῦ σύμψηφον ὄντα ἐμαυτῷ δεικνύναι· εἴτε γάρ τι ἡμῖν λελήρηται, οὐδὲν δεῖ τῆς Στησιχόρου παλινῳδίας, ἀλλὰ σπογγιὰ ἰάσεται, εἴτε τι καὶ κρεῖττον ἐν τοῖς λόγοις ἔνεστιν ἢ ὡς τοῦτο τὸ ἆθλον πρέπειν αὐτοῖς, σὺ δὲ ἐπαίνει μέν, εἴ σοι μὴ δοκεῖ, μηδὲν μᾶλλον, συγγίγνωσκε δὲ ὅμως· εἰ[14] μὴ καὶ τιμῆς ἀξιοῖς, ἀλλὰ τούτου γε ἂν ἀξιοῖς.

9 ἔφησθα, ὡς ἐγὼ πυνθάνομαι, δυσχεραίνειν ὅτι ἦν ἐν τοῖς λόγοις μνήμη τῆς εἰς Σικελίαν ἀποδημίας αὐτοῦ, καὶ ὅτι τοῦ βίου δὴ καθάπτεσθαι τοῦ Πλάτωνος ἐν τούτοις ἐδοκοῦμεν· ἐχρῆν δὲ ἄρα τοῦτο μὲν χωρίς που εἶναι, τὸν λόγον δὲ ἐλέγχειν, καὶ ταῦτά γε οὐκ ἐραστοῦ μόνον τὰ ἐγκλήματα, ἀλλὰ καὶ σωφρονοῦντος περὶ λόγους.

10 ἀλλ᾽ ὅρα δὴ μὴ ἀναίτιόν με αἰτιᾷ. ἐγὼ γὰρ οὐκ ἔλεγον δήπου Πλάτωνα κακῶς, ὥσπερ ἐν δικαστηρίῳ τινὶ κρίνων, οὐδ᾽ ᾐτιώμην τὰς ἀποδημίας, ἵνα χείρων νομίζοιτο, ἀλλὰ κἀν τούτοις μαρτυρεῖν ἔφασκον ἐμαυτῷ τε καὶ ῥητορικῇ. δῆλον γὰρ ὅτι εἰ μὲν μικροῦ τινος ἄξιον ἦν τὸ ἀδικεῖσθαι, ἢ τὸ δίκην λαμβάνειν ἀδικηθέντα, οὐδ᾽ ἂν ἐκεῖνον ἐπῆρεν οὐδεὶς πέλαγός τε τοσοῦτον πλεῖν καὶ παρὰ ἄνδρα τύραννον ὑπὲρ τῶν

[14] <ὡς> εἰ Keil

offended you in the arguments that some people represent as an attack on him by me. I for my part was trying to show that he was consistently in agreement with me. For there's no call for Stesichorus' *Palinode*,[15] whether I've said something stupid (in which case a sponge will put things right),[16] or whether there is something too substantial in my words for that to be their appropriate reward. You for your part shouldn't be any the more ready to agree with them if you don't see fit, but you should forgive them all the same; even if you don't think they deserve respect, you might at least think that they deserve this.

You said, I am told, that you were offended that in what I said there was a mention of Plato's trip to Sicily, and that in the course of this I gave the impression of criticizing his life.[17] This should have been done separately somewhere else, you thought, and I ought instead to have been showing what was wrong with his argument; this latter was the proper course not just for a lover's accusations, but also for those of someone exercising due restraint in argument. 9

But ask yourself if you are not accusing an innocent man. I was certainly not speaking ill of Plato as if judging someone in court, and I was not bringing charges against his foreign travels in order to make people think the worse of him; I was insisting that in this respect too he testifies in my favor and in favor of the art of oratory. Because it is clear that if being wronged and getting justice when you have been wronged are unimportant matters, no one would ever have inspired Plato to sail on Dion's business 10

[15] As also referred to in *Or.* 3.557 (and 2.234), picking up on Pl. *Phdr.* 234a. [16] A standard means of erasing freshly-written ink: Mart. 4.10.5–8. [17] *Or.* 2.279–98.

Δίωνος πραγμάτων, οὐδέ γε ἐκεῖθεν ἀναστρέψαντα
συμπράττειν ἅπαντα Δίωνι, κατελθεῖν τε βουλομένῳ
καὶ δίκην ὧν ἐπεπόνθει λαμβάνειν. νῦν δὲ ἔργῳ μαρτυρεῖν αὐτὸν ὅτι οὐ φαύλης φύσεως οὐδὲ τῆς τυχού-
σης εἴη δυνάμεως τὸ τοῖς ἀδικεῖν ἐπιχειροῦσιν μὴ
11 ἐπιτρέπειν. καὶ ταῦθ' ὅτι ἀληθῆ εἰσι μὲν οἱ τῶν λόγων
δήπουθεν ἀκούσαντες, εἰσὶ δὲ οἱ λόγοι.[15] καὶ τὰ μὲν
ἄλλα ἐῶ μεθ' ὅσης αἰδοῦς καὶ πραότητος περὶ αὐτῶν
τούτων διειλέγμεθα, τοσοῦτον δεινότητος εἰσφερόμε-
νοι ὅσον μήτε ἐκεῖνον διέβαλλεν κἀμοὶ κρείττω καθ-
ίστη τὸν λόγον, ἀλλ' εἰσεποιήσαμεν ὥσπερ παράβα-
σιν χωρίον ἐξαίρετον αὐτῷ. οὗ σὺ εἰ μὲν ἤκουσας,
ἀναμνήσθητι, εἰ δὲ μὴ ἤκουσας, μὴ προκαταγίγνω-
σκε. φέρε οὖν σοι ὥσπερ οἱ ἐν τοῖς δικαστηρίοις ἀγω-
νιζόμενοι αὐτὰ ἐκ τοῦ βιβλίου παράσχωμαι. [ἐκ τοῦ
βιβλίου][16]

12 μικρὸν δέ τι βούλομαι διαλαβεῖν, μή τις ὅλως οἰηθῇ με τοῖς λόγοις τούτοις κατηγορεῖν Πλάτωνος, ἢ λέγειν κακῶς μετὰ ἀφορμῆς. ἐγὼ γὰρ οὔτε αὐτὸς ἔγκλημα δήπου ποιοῦμαι εἴ που καὶ ὁπωσοῦν ᾠήθη δεῖν Πλάτων ἀποδημῆσαι οὔτ'

[15] *an nomen (e.g.* μάρτυρες) *vel post* ἀκούσαντες *vel post* λόγοι *addendum?* [16] *del.* Lenz

---

[18] "Is testified to" has to be what Aristides means; the relevant word does not feature in the Greek text as it stands and should perhaps be added.

over such an expanse of sea and into the presence of a tyrant, nor on coming back from there to assist Dion in everything that arose from his desire to return home and exact just retribution for what he had suffered. But in fact Plato shows by practical example that preventing those who attempt to do wrong from having their way is the mark of a noble nature and an uncommon ability. That this 11
is the truth is testified to both of course by those who heard my arguments and by the arguments themselves.[18] I will say nothing about the great respect and mildness of tone with which I discussed these same matters elsewhere in the speech, employing only as much forcefulness as was compatible with avoiding insult to Plato while still strengthening my own argument, but I did also insert a special section for him like a kind of *parabasis*.[19] If you heard it, recall it now, and if you did not, do not prejudge the issue. Let me then quote you the exact words from my text, like someone presenting a case in court:[20]

> I should like to pause briefly here, in case anyone 12
> should think I am simply attacking Plato in what I say, or finding an excuse to abuse him. I do not myself count it grounds for accusation if Plato thought it incumbent on him to take a trip anywhere and in

[19] That is, a passage standing outside the main line of argument and commenting on it, like the set-piece address of Chorus Leader to audience in Aristophanic comedy.

[20] *Or*. 2.295, with some minor variants. The manuscripts here, and at relevant points later on, add a note stating the source of the quotation just introduced (here "From the text (book)"). These are clearly editorial matter, not part of Aristides' composition, and should be removed.

εἰ ἄλλος τις προφέρει νοῦν ἔχειν ἡγοῦμαι, οὔθ' ὅλως ἔξω τῶν εἰς τὸν λόγον ἡκόντων οὐδὲν περιεργάζομαι, [ὥστε εἰ δεῖ καὶ τοῦτο εἰπεῖν καὶ ἐν αὐτοῖς τούτοις][17] μή πω τοσούτου μηδὲν ἄξιον ἔστω νικητήριον, ἀλλ' ἅ τε αὐτὸς ἔπραξεν καὶ τίνων ἔπραξεν χάριν [καὶ ἃ][18] αὐτὸς [ἂν][19] καθαρῶς εἴρηκεν, ταῦτα συμβαίνειν φημὶ τοῖς ὑπὲρ τῆς ῥητορικῆς λόγοις· καὶ τοσούτῳ δέω κακίζειν ἐκεῖνον τούτοις, ὥστε εἰ δεῖ καὶ τοῦτο εἰπεῖν, καὶ ἐν αὐτοῖς τούτοις σεμνύνειν αὐτὸν ἡγοῦμαι, εἰ τούτων ἐκείνοις ὑπεναντίως ἐχόντων μὴ τὰ ἔργα μηδὲ τὰς πράξεις αὐτοῦ διαβάλλω, ἀλλ' ἐκ τοῦ βίου καὶ τῶν ἔργων, ἃ μεθ' ἡμῶν καὶ ὧν ἡμεῖς ἀξιοῦμεν εἶναι τίθημι, ταῦθ' ἑτέρως ἔχοντα ἢ ὡς ἄν τις πιστεύσειεν ἀποφαίνω.

13 δοκεῖ σοι ταῦτα κακίζοντος ἐκεῖνον εἶναι, ἤ τινος αὐθαδείας ἢ προπετείας μετασχεῖν; ἐγὼ μὲν οὐκ οἶμαι. ἀλλ' εἰ δεῖ τι τούτοις ἔγκλημα ἐνεγκεῖν, μᾶλλον ἄν τις ἐγκαλέσειεν[20] δικαίως εὐλάβειαν πλείω τῆς προσηκούσης. καίτοι ἐκεῖνός γε ὅπου καὶ μικρὸν ἐλέγχειν ἔχει τινὰ τῶν πρεσβυτέρων,[21] ἢ καὶ τῶν καθ' ἑαυτὸν ἐνδόξων ἀνδρῶν, οὐδὲν ὑφίεται.

14 ἀλλὰ μή πω περὶ τούτων. ἀλλὰ τί χρῆν με ποιεῖν ὦ πρὸς Διός; πότερον μὴ μνησθῆναι τὸ παράπαν τῆς

17 *del.* Dindorf 18 *del.* Behr 19 *del. edd.*
20 ἐγκαλέσειε R^2 καλέσειε(ν) QR^1Ea (TVA)
21 πρεσβυτέρων Reiske πρεσβυτάτων *codd.*

> any manner, nor do I think that anyone else who brings any such charge is being sensible, nor in general am I wasting superfluous effort on something irrelevant to the case in hand;[21] may no victory ever be worth that much! What I am saying is that what he himself did, and the reasons he himself plainly gave for doing it, all agree with the argument in defense of oratory. So far am I from reproaching him on these grounds that, if this really needs saying, I think I am actually doing him an honor in just this respect, if when his words and his deeds are in contradiction with each other I have nothing insulting to say about his deeds and achievements, but instead demonstrate from his life and deeds, which I say are in agreement with me and the claims I am making, that things are otherwise than one might suppose in this matter.

Does it strike you that these are the words of someone abusing Plato, or that they are characterized by any willfulness or imprudence? I certainly don't think so. If there is any charge to be brought against them, they could justifiably be accused of an undue degree of caution. But Plato, where he can find even a slight fault in an authority from previous generations, or in one of the distinguished men of his own time, does not hold back at all. 13

But more about that anon.[22] What ought I to have done, in god's name? Should I not have mentioned his visit 14

21 The Greek text at this point wrongly repeats the words "so if this really needs saying, actually in just this respect" from further on in the quoted passage.

22 See §§29–45 below.

εἰς Σικελίαν ἀποδημίας ὥσπερ τι τῶν ἀπορρήτων μέλλοντα ἐρεῖν; ἀλλ᾽ οὔτε ψήφισμα συνῄδειν ἀπαγορεῦον καὶ τῷ λόγῳ συνέφερεν, καὶ ἅμα ἀληθὲς ἦν· καὶ γὰρ ἔπλευσεν οὐχ ἅπαξ καὶ ὑπὲρ τοῦ Δίωνι γενέσθαι τὰ δίκαια. ἔστω δὲ ταῦτα· ἐφαίνετο δὲ ἐν τοῖς λόγοις [Γοργίου][22] εἰρηκὼς οὐ πολλοῦ τινος ἄξιον τὸ μὴ ἀδι-
15 κεῖσθαι. εἰ δὲ ταῦτα ἀσθενῆ καὶ τοῦ μηδενὸς ἄξια, ἐν μέσῳ μὲν δὴ πρόκειται, λυόντων δὲ οἱ σοφοί, εἰ βούλονται, καὶ κακῶς λέγοντες ἐμέ. πάντως συνηθέστε-
16 ρον κακῶς λέγειν ἢ εὖ. ἀλλὰ σύν τινι ἤθει πραοτέρῳ καὶ σχήματι χρῆν μνησθῆναι περὶ αὐτῶν; οὔκουν[23] ἤκουσας τῆς παραιτήσεως εἰ μὴ τότε, ἀλλὰ νῦν; ὅτι δὲ οὐ τὰς παρὰ σοῦ ταύτας αἰτίας δείσαντες ὕστερον εἰσεποιήσαμεν ταῦτα, ἀλλ᾽ ἀπ᾽ ἀρχῆς ἐνῆν, κάλει τούτων μάρτυρας, εἰ βούλει, τοὺς ἀκούοντας. ἀλλὰ νὴ Δί᾽ ἀνιαρὸν τοῦτο τοῖς Πλάτωνος ἑταίροις. ἕτερος λόγος οὗτος, οὐ πρὸς ἐμέ, ἀλλὰ πρὸς ὀντιναδήποτε.

17 ἢ καὶ τοῦτο ἀδικῶ ὅτι τὰ ἐκ τῶν Νόμων αὐτοῦ παρεγραψάμην; καὶ ὅπως γε, ἐπεὶ καὶ δυσχεραίνουσι, κἀκεῖνο ἐπιδείξουσιν ὡς οὐ τοῖς αὐτὸς αὑτοῦ περιπίπτει λόγοις, ἐπειδάν τι φάσκῃ. [ἐκ τῶν Νόμων][24]

> τοῖς δ᾽ εὐδαιμόνως ζῶσιν ὑπάρχειν ἀνάγκη πρῶτον τὸ μὴ ἀδικεῖν ἄλλους, μήτε αὐτοὺς ὑφ᾽ ἑτέρων ἀδικεῖσθαι. τούτοιν δὲ τὸ μὲν οὐ πάνυ

[22] *del.* Trapp
[23] οὔκουν Keil *οὐκοῦν codd.*
[24] *del.* Lenz

to Sicily at all, as if I were going to reveal a holy secret? I
was not aware of any decree forbidding it. It was in the
best interests of my argument, and at the same time it was
true: he did sail more than once and it was indeed in order
that Dion should have his rights that he did so. Those are
the facts; yet he also clearly stated in his dialogue that not
being wronged is nothing very valuable.[23] If this is a weak 15
and worthless argument, it is out there in the open, so let
the clever people refute it, and speak ill of me as they do
so if they wish. (At all events, speaking ill of people is more
of a habit than praising them.) But in what gentler tone or 16
form should I have mentioned all this? If you did not hear
my words of excuse then, did you not hear them just now?
Please, if you want, call my audience as witnesses to the
fact that I did not insert this passage later because I was
afraid of these accusations of yours, but that it was there
from the start. But, you may say, this is hurtful to Plato's
partisans. That is another question, which cuts against
someone else and not me.[24]

Am I also at fault for inserting the passage from his 17
Laws?[25] Since people do in fact take this badly, let them
also see about proving, for any of his assertions, that he
does not fall foul of his own arguments.

> A happy life requires first and foremost neither wronging others nor oneself being wronged by others. Of these two, the former is not extremely

[23] *Grg.* 469b–c. The Greek text at this point has interpolated a reader's note unnecessarily identifying the dialogue.

[24] Aristides here quotes a phrase from Dem. *De cor.* (18) 44.

[25] *Leg.* 829a, quoted at *Or.* 2.304.

χαλεπόν, τοῦ δὲ μὴ ἀδικεῖσθαι κτήσασθαι δύναμιν παγχάλεπον· καὶ οὐκ ἔστιν αὐτὸ τελέως ἔχειν ἄλλως ἢ τελέως γενόμενον ἀγαθόν.

18 ἐπὶ τούτοις αὖ τοῖς ῥήμασι τί ἡμεῖς ἐφθεγξάμεθα ἐν τῷ βιβλίῳ; [ἐκ τοῦ βιβλίου][25]

ἰοῦ ἰοῦ τῆς μαρτυρίας. τούτων ἐδεόμην. ταῦτα λέγει Πλάτων, ὁ τοῦ ἐπιγράμματος μετέχων καὶ δι᾽ ὃν τὸ Ἀρίστωνος γένος θεῖον ὡς ἀληθῶς. τελέως ἄρα, ὦ δαιμόνιε, [ἡ][26] ῥητορικὴ καλὸν καὶ οὐ πρὸς παντὸς οὔτε λαβεῖν οὔτε κτήσασθαι. φαίνῃ γὰρ καὶ σὺ τοῦτό γε συγχωρῶν, ὅτι ἐπὶ τῷ μὴ ἀδικεῖσθαι τέτακται. οὐκοῦν ὅτε ἀδικεῖν μὲν οὐ προσηνάγκαζεν, ἀδικεῖσθαι δὲ οὐκ ἐᾷ, ὡς δὲ ἐκ τοῦ λόγου συνέβαινεν, οὐδέτερον τούτων ἐᾷ, οὔτε ἀδικεῖν οὔτε ἀδικεῖσθαι, εἰ μὲν [οὖν][27] καὶ τῆς φιλοσοφίας ὁ αὐτός ἐστιν ὅρος, φιλοσοφία τις οὖσα ἡ ῥητορικὴ φαίνεται. εἰ δὲ ἐξαρκεῖ τῇ φιλοσοφίᾳ μὴ ἀδικεῖν, ἡ ῥητορικὴ τελεώτερον· τὸ γὰρ χαλεπώτερον κτήσασθαι καὶ μεῖζον ἤδη προστίθησιν, ὅπως μηδ᾽ αὐτὸς ὑπ᾽ ἄλλων ἀδικήσεται.[28] πῶς οὖν τὸ αὐτὸ ἅμα μὲν τελέως ἀγαθὸν καὶ μέγιστον τῶν ἀγαθῶν, ἅμα δὲ ἔσχατον τῶν κακῶν καὶ κολακεία; ἢ πῶς ἐλάχιστον οἱ ῥήτορες δύνανται, εἴ γε οὗ

[25] *del.* Lenz [26] *del. edd.*
[27] *del. edd.* [28] ἀδικηθήσεται TQ^2

> difficult, but to acquire the power of not being wronged is difficult in the extreme; there is no way to possess it completely other than by being completely good.

What comment did I then make on these words in my text?[26] 18

> Three cheers for this testimony! That is what I needed! So says Plato, the one mentioned in the epigram, who truly conferred divinity on the family of Ariston. Oratory therefore, dear sir, is a fine thing, and not for just anybody to acquire and possess. Because you too clearly agree on this point at least, that its appointed function is preventing people from being wronged. Thus, because it did not compel the doing of wrong, and does not allow people to be wronged, but as has emerged from the argument, allows neither of these things, doing wrong or being wronged, if this is also the definition of philosophy, oratory is clearly a kind of philosophy. But if philosophy requires only abstention from doing wrong, then oratory is more perfect, because it adds what is more difficult to acquire and more important, namely ensuring that one is not wronged oneself by others either. How then can the same thing be simultaneously perfectly good and the greatest of goods, and the worst of evils and a form of flattery? Or how can orators have minimal power

26 *Or*. 2.304–6.

καὶ παγχάλεπον κτήσασθαι δύναμιν, τοῦτ' αὐτοῖς περίεστιν; ἐγὼ μὲν οὐκ ἔχω συμβαλεῖν. εὐδαίμονες ἄρα, οὐκ ἄθλιοι, κατὰ τὸν Πλάτωνος λόγον οἱ ῥήτορες, εἴ γε ὁ μὲν τελέως ἀγαθὸς εὐδαίμων, τοῦτο δὲ οὐκ ἔστιν κτήσασθαι μὴ τελέως ἀγαθὸν γενόμενον.

19 πότερον ταῦτα ὀρθῶς καὶ ἀναγκαίως ἔχει ἐνεγκεῖν εἰς μέσον, ἢ καὶ τοῦτο ἀδικοῦμεν καὶ περιεργαζόμεθα, εἰ μὴ προσκυνοῦμεν, ὡσπερεὶ κίστην[29] ἀπόρρητα κρύπτουσαν; ἐγὼ δὲ οὐ τοῦτο ᾤμην εἶναι τὸ τἀπόρρητα ἐκφέρειν.

20 καὶ ὅπως αὖ μή με φήσεις πικρότερα τοῦ δέοντος λέγειν. οὐ γὰρ ἔγωγέ τις τούτων αἴτιος, ἀλλ' ἔδει δέχεσθαι τὴν πρόκλησιν. αὕτη δὲ τίς ἦν; τολμᾶν ἀκροᾶσθαι ὥσπερ ἐν δικαστηρίῳ ἴσους καὶ κοινοὺς ἀμφοῖν. ἀλλὰ γὰρ ὀρθῶς ἐγὼ περὶ τούτων, ὡς ἔοικεν, προεωρώμην καὶ προὔλεγον ὡς εἰ μή τις ἅπαντος τοῦ λόγου διακούσεται, οὐ μόνον οὐ τιμήσει τὰ πρέποντα, ἀλλ' οὐδὲ εἴσεται τοῦ πράγματος οὐδέν. διὰ ταῦτα ἠξίουν ἀκροᾶσθαι διὰ τέλους ὅστις μέλλει τὸ ἀγώνισμα πᾶν ὄψεσθαι καὶ ψῆφον ὀρθὴν καὶ δικαίαν ἐποί-
21 σειν. οὐδὲ γάρ, ὦ ἄριστε ἀνδρῶν, οἱ δικασταὶ τοῦτον τὸν τρόπον κρίνουσι καὶ προοιμίου τινὸς ἢ διηγήσεως ἀκούσαντες ἀπαλλάττονται, οὐδὲ αὖ[30] ταῦτα παρέντες πρὸς μέρος τι τῶν εἰκότων συνῆλθον, ἢ

[29] ὡσπερεὶ κίστην Canter ὥσπερ οἱ κίστην *vel* ὥσπερ οἰκιστίν *fere codd.* [30] οὐδὲ αὖ Reiske οὐδὲ αὐτά *codd.*

if they have in abundance that which it is extremely difficult to acquire power in? I cannot make it out. Orators are evidently happy not wretched, according to Plato's argument, if the perfectly good person is happy and it is impossible to possess the science of oratory if one is not perfectly good.

Is it necessary and right to bring these issues out into the 19
open, or am I doing another wrong and again exceeding my brief if I do not simply prostrate myself before Plato's words as if they were a casket concealing holy secrets? I did not think that that was what was meant by revealing holy secrets.

Beware too of saying that I am speaking more acerbi- 20
cally than I should. I am not the one who is to blame for this; you should have accepted my challenge. What challenge? To dare to listen to both parties fairly and impartially as if in a court of law.[27] It was quite correct of me, it seems, to take precautions over this and predict that if someone did not listen right through the whole speech, he would not only not value it at its true worth, but would not understand anything of the subject at issue either. That is why I requested anyone who was going to get a full view of the matter under dispute, and cast his vote justly and
correctly, to listen through to the end. My dear fellow, 21
jurors do not judge in this fashion and go away once they have heard a proem or a narrative, nor again do they let those elements pass and concentrate on some part of the arguments from likelihood, or so as to hear just one piece

[27] An echo ("to both parties fairly and impartially") of Dem. *De cor.* (18) 7.

ὅσον μιᾶς τινος μαρτυρίας ἀκοῦσαι ἢ τῆς ἐπανόδου τῶν εἰρημένων, ἀλλ' ἀκούσαντες ἀπ' ἀρχῆς εἰς τέλος οὕτω τὴν ψῆφον φέρουσιν· καὶ τοῦτο κἀκείνοις οἶμαι
22 *λυσιτελεῖ. πρὸς τῶν θεῶν τῶν ὁρκίων οὐδέ γε ὑμεῖς ὅταν ποιῆτε Ὀλύμπια, οὐχ οὕτως ἀγωνοθετεῖτε, τοῦ μὲν ἅπαντα ἀκούσαντες τῶν ἀγωνιστῶν, τοῦ δὲ ὅσον εἰσόδιον, ἢ τῶν μὲν ἐν μέσῳ τι,*[31] *ἢ τῶν ἐν τέλει. πρὸς οὖν τί τοῦτο λέγω; ὅτι μικρῷ τινι τοῦ λόγου μέρει προστυχὼν ἀπὸ τούτου τὸ πᾶν ἔκρινας, προοιμίου δὲ οὐκ ἤκουσας οὐδὲ τῆς ὅλης καταστάσεως,*[32] *ἣν ἐξῆν μηδὲν ἐλάττονος ἀξίαν νομίσαι τοῦ παντὸς ἀγῶνος, ὡς περὶ μέρους*[33] *εἰπεῖν. τὸ γὰρ ἦθος ὅλον ἐνταῦθα ἂν μᾶλλον*[34] *‹. . . . .›*[35] *τὸν ἄνδρα ἢ καθαιρήσοντες*
23 *εἰσῄειμεν. οὕτω πᾶσαν αἰδῶ καὶ τιμὴν ἀπεδώκαμεν αὐτῷ, ὥστε εἰ αὐτὸς πρὸς αὑτὸν ἔμελλεν ἀντερεῖν, οὐκ ἄν μοι δοκοίη μᾶλλον αὑτοῦ φείσασθαι. οἶμαι δὲ εἰ καὶ υἱὸς ἐκείνου ἔμελλεν ἀντερεῖν αὐτῷ, οὐκ ἂν πλείω τὴν παραίτησιν ἐποιήσατο, οὐδ' ἂν περιφανέστερον*

[31] *τι* Canter *τινι codd.*

[32] *καταστάσεως ‹e.g. ἐπήσθησαι›* Reiske

[33] *ὡς περὶ μέρους* TQVAR^{1}a *ὡσπερεὶ μέρους* EU *ὡσπερεὶ μέρος* R^2

[34] *ὅλον ἐν τούτῳ δείκνυται κἀνταῦθα μᾶλλον* UR^2 *post μᾶλλον pergunt ἐν αὐτοῖς γὰρ ἔγνως ὡς ἐπαινέσοντες πλέον τὸν ἄνδρα* aA^2 Barocc. 136

[35] *lac. stat.* Trapp *‹ἐπαινέσοντες›* UT^{2}Q^{2}A^{2}R^2

of testimony or the recapitulation of what has been said, but instead they listen from start to finish and on that basis cast their votes; and I think this is in their interests
too. By the gods who watch over men's oaths, you and your 22
fellow citizens do not administer the games like that either when you are holding your Olympics,[28] listening to everything that one of the contestants says but only to the introduction from another, or just to something in the middle, or at the end. What is my point in saying this? That you have happened on a small part and judged the whole from it, but not given ear to the proem or to the overall set of the speech, which you could have regarded as no less valuable than the case as a whole, if one can say that of a constituent element, since the whole character of the piece is <to be found?> there rather than anywhere else <. . . . .> I came to court <to . . .> the man rather than to
bring him down.[29] So true is it that I granted Plato all re- 23
spect and honor that if he were going to speak against himself, I do not think that he would have treated himself more gently. I believe that even if his son were going to speak against him, he would not have excused himself more copiously nor eulogized him more splendidly before

[28] If, as Behr suggests (*Complete Works* 1.480), the reference is to the Olympia Asclepeia at Pergamum, rather than to the Elean Olympics, the plural "you" here identifies Capito as a Pergamene.

[29] The Greek text is faulty at this point and not yet satisfactorily repaired. Some manuscripts suggest "<to praise> the man rather than to bring him down," which seems sensible; but something is still missing between the mention of the overall "set" (*katastasis* = *stasis*; Latin *constitutio* or *status*) of the speech and the words about Aristides' intentions toward Plato.

ἐκόσμησεν εἰς τοὺς Ἕλληνας. σὺ δὲ τούτων ἀπολειφθεὶς ὅμοιος εἶ τῷ πρὶν ἀμφοῖν ἀκοῦσαι τὸν μῦθον δικάζοντι.

24 καίτοι ἕτερός γ᾽ ἂν ἔχων συνέχειαν ἐπελάθετο καὶ αὐτὸς ἑαυτοῦ, μὴ ὅτι τοῦ ἀντιπάλου, καὶ τὸ προκείμενον δεικνὺς οὐδὲν ἂν πλέον ἐζήτει. ἐγὼ δὲ ὥσπερ δεδοικὼς μὴ φαυλότερος περὶ ταῦτα ἐκεῖνος νομισθῇ, τὸ ἐκείνου σπεύδων παρὰ πάντα τὸν λόγον διαγίγνομαι.
25 καὶ τῆς ἀποδείξεως οὕτω συνεχοῦς καὶ πυκνῆς οὔσης, ἐξέστω γὰρ εἰπεῖν, τὸ σχῆμα τῶν λόγων τῶν πρὸς τὸν ἄνδρα οὐχ ἧττον ἀγαστόν ἐστιν, [καὶ][36] ὅτι οὐχ ἑτέρως μὲν τὴν κρηπῖδα ὑπέθηκα, ἑτέρως δὲ τὸ λοιπὸν ἐπήγαγον, ἀλλ᾽ ἀκολουθεῖ πανταχοῦ τῷ λόγῳ τὸ τοῦ ἀνδρὸς προορώμενον, καὶ δείκνυμεν ὅτι ἀντιλέγοντες τὰ ἀναγκαῖα κοσμοῦμεν ἐκ περιουσίας. καίτοι ἐβουλόμην ἂν ἐκεῖνον οὕτως ἀντειπεῖν μοι δεῦρο γενόμενον, ἀλλ᾽ ἴσως ἧττον ἂν τοῦ τοιούτου ἐμέλησεν αὐτῷ.
26 σκόπει τοίνυν καὶ τὰ ἐπὶ τῆς τελευτῆς τῶν λόγων ὡς ἀκόλουθα τῷ προοιμίῳ· τοῦτο μὲν περὶ τῶν τῷ ὄντι ῥητόρων διαλεγόμενοι, Πλάτων δ᾽ ἡμῖν ποῦ χοροῦ, φαμέν, στήσεται; ἡμεῖς μὲν γὰρ αὐτὸν ἐν τῷ καλλίστῳ τάττειν ἕτοιμοι τοιουτοισί τισι τοῖς ῥήμασιν, οὐ γὰρ τό γ᾽ ἀκριβέστερον μέμνημαι· τοῦτο δὲ ἑτέρων τινῶν ἀνθρωπίσκων μνησθέντες, πρὸς δὲ δὴ Πλάτωνα, τὸν τῶν ῥητόρων πατέρα τε καὶ διδάσκαλον, οὕτως οἶμαι τὸ ἐφεξῆς εἰρήκαμεν, καὶ τοσαῦτά γε

36 *del.* Reiske

a Greek audience. You, however, have failed to register this and so are like someone judging a case before hearing what both sides have to say.

Someone else, not pausing in the development of his 24
argument, might have forgotten himself, to say nothing of his opponent, and once he had proved what he set out to prove might not have looked any further. I however, as if afraid that Plato's reputation might suffer over this, consistently kept his interests vividly in mind through the
whole of my discourse. The texture of my argumentation 25
is then a dense and continuous one (I hope I may be allowed to say this), and the character of the words directed at Plato himself is no less admirable, in that I did not lay the foundations one way and then add on the rest in another, but instead my concern for the man's interests remains a constant throughout the work, and I demonstrate that while advancing the necessary objections I can also praise him abundantly. I might have wished that he could have been here to answer me back in the same spirit, but perhaps that would have mattered less to him than it does
to me. Just look at what is said at the end of the work, and 26
how consistent it is with the proem. For a start, when discussing true orators, I say "And where will we think Plato stands in this company? I am ready to place him in the most distinguished position," or words to that effect, I don't remember more exactly.[30] Then, after mentioning some other contemptible individuals, I think I continued by saying "but for Plato, the father and teacher of orators"[31]—and to go that far is obviously not the mark of

[30] *Or.* 2.428, which Aristides here indeed paraphrases rather than quoting exactly. [31] *Or.* 2.465.

ἐστὶν οὐ τὸν βίον τὸν ἐκείνου καὶ τοὺς λόγους εἰς ὅσον οἷόν τε σεμνύνοντος.

27 καὶ ταυτὶ πάντα ὑπὲρ τῆς ἀληθείας ἀκριβολογοῦμαι καὶ διεξέρχομαι, φησὶ Δημοσθένης, ἐπεὶ τό γε τοῦ Πινδάρου πολλοὶ ὑμνοῦσι

χρὴ δὲ πᾶν ἔρδοντ᾽ ἀμαυρῶσαι τὸν ἐχθρόν.

ἐχθρὸν δέ που λέγει τὸν ἀντίπαλον. καὶ σχεδὸν ἔν τε ταῖς σφαιρομαχίαις καὶ τοῖς γυμνικοῖς αὐτοῖς ἀγῶσι, προσθήσω δὲ καὶ ἱππικοῖς, οὕτως ὁρῶμεν οὐ τοῖς τῶν ἀντιπάλων βουλήμασιν ἀκολουθοῦντας τοὺς περὶ τῆς νίκης ἐρίζοντας, ἀλλὰ τὰ αὑτοῖς συμφέροντα καὶ ποιοῦντας καὶ λέγοντας, ἕως ἂν μή τις περιφανῶς κωλύῃ νόμος. ὥστ᾽ εἰ τὰ μάλιστα μὴ πρὸς ἡδονήν τισιν ἦσαν οἱ λόγοι, ἔλεγχον δὲ εἶχον ἢ τῶν λόγων τῶν ἐκείνου ἢ τοῦ βίου, ἀρχαῖος ὁ νόμος χρῆσθαι τοῖς τοιούτοις, καὶ οὐκ ἐγὼ κατέδειξα αὐτόν, ἀλλὰ παντάπασιν παλαιός ἐστιν· ἢ δέδοικα αὖ λέγειν μὴ
28 Πλάτων ὁ καταδείξας αὐτὸν ᾖ. κἀμοὶ μὲν ἀπολελόγηται μετρίως ὑπὲρ τῆς αἰτίας, ὡς ἐγὼ νομίζω· ὅτι δὲ ἐκεῖνός ἐστιν ὁ οὐ πάνυ φροντίζων εἴ του δέοι καθάπτεσθαι, μάλιστα μὲν εἰκὸς ἄμεινόν σε ταῦτα ἐπίστασθαί τε καὶ μεμνῆσθαι[37] τούτοις σχολάζοντα, ἃ δ᾽ οὖν κἀγὼ μέμνημαι φέρε ἀναμνήσθητι. καὶ ὅπως αὖ μή με φήσεις Πλάτωνος κατηγορεῖν. οὐ γὰρ κατη-

[37] μεμνῆσθαι Bodl. misc. 57 *om. cett.* ἐπίστασθαι ἅτε καὶ τούτοις Reiske

someone honoring his life and works to the best of his ability!

In Demosthenes' words, "it is in the interests of truth that I am going through all this so minutely,"[32] since there are many who sing the praises of Pindar's line 27

One should do anything to crush one's foe.[33]

(And by "foe" he surely means one's opponent.) As a rule in ball-fighting matches[34] and in athletic competitions in general, and in horseracing too, I would add, we see that contestants striving to win do not fall in with their opponents' wishes, but do and say what is to their own advantage, provided no rule manifestly forbids it. Thus however true it may be that what I said was uncongenial to some, with its criticism of Plato's words and his life, it is a time-honored custom to proceed in this manner, one which I did not introduce but is thoroughly ancient. Or (I tremble
to say it) perhaps Plato was the one who introduced it. For 28
my part I have offered what I consider a measured defense in response to the accusation. That Plato is actually the one who is not very concerned about having to attack someone is something it is particularly plausible to expect you to be better at understanding and remembering, since you are a student of these matters; but all the same do remember what I have mentioned as well. And please beware in your turn of saying that I am attacking Plato: it

32 Dem. *De cor.* (18) 21.

33 Pind. *Isthm.* 4.66 (48).

34 The so-called *sphairomachia*. It is unclear which of the two sports that went under this name (boxing with spherical "gloves," or a kind of all-in football) Aristides has in mind here.

γορίας ἕνεκα ἐκείνου, ἀλλὰ ἀπολογίας ἕνεκα παρ' αὐτοῦ χρήσομαι τῷ παραδείγματι. ὅτι δὲ ἄκων εἰς τούτους ἐμπίπτω τοὺς λόγους σχεδὸν οἶσθα. οὐδὲ γὰρ ἐξ ἀρχῆς οὕτως ἐκείνους ἐποίουν τοὺς ὑπὲρ τῆς ῥητορικῆς ὡς ἀπολογίας μοι δεῆσαν.

29 οὐχ ὁ μὲν Ἀλκιβιάδης αὐτῷ βούλεται παράκλησιν τοῖς μέλλουσι πολιτεύεσθαι ἐπιμελείας ἑαυτῶν; προελθὼν δὲ τοῦ λόγου κακίζει Περικλέα οὐ πάνυ τι <. . . . .>[38] οὐδὲ τοῦ πράγματος ἀναγκάζοντος. παρρησιάζομαι γὰρ πρὸς σὲ καὶ πρὸς αὐτὸν Πλάτωνα. σκέψαι δὲ ἐκ τῶν ῥημάτων. [ἐκ τοῦ βιβλίου][39]

> ἀμαθίᾳ γὰρ συνοικεῖς, ὦ βέλτιστε, τῇ ἐσχάτῃ, ὡς ὁ λόγος σου κατηγορεῖ καὶ σὺ σαυτοῦ. διὸ καὶ ᾄττεις ἄρα πρὸς τὰ πολιτικὰ [καὶ][40] πρὶν παιδευθῆναι. πέπονθας δὲ τοῦτο οὐ σὺ μόνος, ἀλλὰ καὶ οἱ πολλοὶ τῶν πραττόντων τὰ τῆσδε τῆς πόλεως, πλὴν ὀλίγων γε καὶ ἴσως[41] τοῦ σοῦ ἐπιτρόπου Περικλέους.

30 ἔστω ταῦτα ἀναγκαῖα, εἰ βούλει, μέχρι τούτου "πέπονθας δὲ τοῦτο οὐ σὺ μόνος, ἀλλὰ καὶ οἱ πολλοὶ τῶν πραττόντων τὰ τῆσδε τῆς πόλεως," τὸ δὲ λοιπὸν ὦ πρὸς θεῶν τί βούλεται τῷ σοφῷ ἀνδρὶ "πλὴν ὀλίγων γε καὶ ἴσως[42] τοῦ σοῦ ἐπιτρόπου Περικλέους;" ἀλλ' ὅτι

[38] <ἐπειγόμενος> Reiske *possis et (e.g.)* <δέον>
[39] *del.* Lenz [40] *om.* U *del.* Dindorf
[41] γε καὶ ἴσως *codd. Plat.* καὶ ἴσως γε *codd.*
[42] γε καὶ ἴσως *codd. Plat.* καὶ ἴσως γε U τε καὶ ἴσως *cett.*

is not in order to attack him, but in order to defend myself that the example I use will be drawn from him. That it is not of my own choice that I have become involved in this new dispute you can take as more or less certain, because it didn't occur to me either when I produced my original case in favor of the art of oratory that I myself might need a defense.

Plato's *Alcibiades* is intended as an exhortation to those about to enter public life to practice care of the self, is it not? Yet when he is some way into the work he slanders Pericles when, to be frank with you and with Plato himself, there is no great need to do so and the subject matter does not necessitate it.[35] Consider this on the evidence of his own words:[36] 29

> You are wedded to stupidity, my fine friend, of the worst kind—the argument charges you with this and you charge yourself with it too—and this apparently is why you dash into politics before you have been educated. You are not alone in this plight, but you share it with most of those who manage our city's affairs, except for just a few, including perhaps your guardian Pericles.

If you like, let it be conceded that he has to say this, up to "you are not alone in this plight, but you share it with most of those who manage our city's affairs"; but for goodness' sake what does our sage mean by "except for just a few, including perhaps your guardian Pericles"? Actually, he 30

35 A word is missing in the Greek text of this sentence, but the overall sense is not in doubt.

36 *Alc. I* 118b–c.

ἡ ἐκβολὴ αὕτη ἐστὶν ἐξεπίτηδες ἐζητημένη ὑπὲρ τοῦ κακῶς εἰπεῖν Περικλέα αὐτὸς μαρτυρήσει.

31 καὶ ὅπως μὴ πάλιν ἀχθεσθῇς ὑπὲρ αὐτοῦ.[43] σκόπει γὰρ αὐτὰ ἃ λέγει. [ἐκ τοῦ Ἀλκιβιάδου][44]

λέγεταί γέ τοι, ὦ Σώκρατες, οὐκ ἀπὸ[45] ταὐτομάτου σοφὸς γεγονέναι, ἀλλὰ πολλοῖς καὶ σοφοῖς συγγεγονέναι, καὶ Πυθοκλείδῃ καὶ Ἀναξαγόρᾳ· καὶ νῦν ὅτι τηλικοῦτος ὢν Δάμωνι σύνεστιν αὐτοῦ τούτου ἕνεκα.—τί οὖν; ἤδη τινὰ εἶδες σοφὸν ὁντιναοῦν[46] ἀδυνατοῦντα ποιῆσαι ἄλλον σοφὸν ἅπερ αὐτός; ὥσπερ ὅς σε ἐδίδαξεν γράμματα αὐτός τε ἦν σοφὸς καὶ σὲ ἐποίησεν τῶν τε ἄλλων ὁντιναοῦν[47] ἐβούλετο; ἦ γάρ;—ναί.—[118d] οὐκοῦν καὶ σὺ ὁ παρ' ἐκείνου μαθὼν ἄλλον οἷός τε ἔσῃ;—<ναί.>[48]—καὶ ὁ κιθαριστὴς δὲ καὶ ὁ παιδοτρίβης ὡσαύτως.—πάνυ γε.—ἱκανὸν[49] γὰρ δήπου τοῦτο τεκμήριον τῶν ἐπισταμένων ὁτιοῦν ὅτι ἐπίστανται, ἐπειδὰν καὶ ἄλλον τινὰ[50] οἷοί τε ὦσιν ἀποδεῖξαι ἐπιστάμενον.—ἔμοιγε δοκεῖ.—τί οὖν ἔχεις εἰπεῖν, Περικλῆς τίνα ἐποίησε σοφὸν ἀπὸ τῶν υἱέων ἀρξάμενος;—[118e] τί δὲ εἰ τὼ Περικλέους υἱέε ἠλιθίω ἐγενέσθην, ὦ Σώκρατες;—ἀλλὰ Κλει-

43 *τοῦ αὐτοῦ* UR^2Ph^{M3} *αὐτοῦ cett.*
44 *del.* Lenz
45 *ἀπό codd. Plat. ὑπό codd.*
46 *ὁτιοῦν codd. Plat.*

himself will provide the evidence that this parenthesis was deliberately contrived in order to insult Pericles.

Please don't get upset all over again on his behalf. Consider what he actually says:[37] 31

> Yes, you know, Socrates, they say he did not get his wisdom spontaneously, but kept company with many wise men, such as Pythoclides and Anaxagoras; and now, old as he is, he still confers with Damon for this same purpose.—Well, have you ever found a man who is wise in anything at all and yet unable to make someone else wise in the same respect as himself? For instance, the man who taught you to read and write was wise himself, and also made you wise, and anyone else he wished to, did he not?—Yes.—[118d] And you too, who learned from him, will be able to make another man wise?—Yes.—And the lyre player and the athletic trainer likewise?—Certainly.—For, I presume, it is adequate proof that those who know something really do know it, when they are able to make someone else manifestly knowledgeable in it too.—I agree.—Well then, can you tell me who Pericles made wise, beginning with his sons?—[118e] But what if the two sons of Pericles were simpletons, Socrates?—

37 *Alc. I* 118c–19a, with some minor variations in phrasing and word order from the text in our manuscripts of Plato.

---

47 ὅντιν' *codd. Plat.*
48 *add.* Dindorf *cum codd. Plat.*
49 καλόν *codd. Plat.*
50 *non habent codd. Plat.*

νίαν τὸν σὸν ἀδελφόν.—τί δ᾽ ἂν αὖ Κλεινίαν λέγοις, μαινόμενον ἄνθρωπον;—ἐπειδὴ τοίνυν Κλεινίας μὲν μαίνεται, τὼ δὲ Περικλέους υἱέε ἠλιθίω ἐγενέσθην, σοὶ τίνα αἰτίαν ἀναθῶμεν, διότι σε οὕτως ἔχοντα περιορᾷ;—ἐγώ, οἶμαι, αἴτιος, οὐ προσέχων τὸν νοῦν.—[119a] ἀλλὰ τῶν ἄλλων Ἀθηναίων[51] δοῦλον ἢ ἐλεύθερον εἰπὲ ὅστις αἰτίαν ἔχει διὰ τὴν Περικλέους συνουσίαν σοφώτερος γεγονώς, ὥσπερ ἐγὼ ἔχω σοι[52] διὰ τὴν Ζήνωνος Πυθόδωρον τὸν Ἰσολόχου καὶ Καλλίαν τὸν Καλλιάδου· ὧν ἑκάτερος Ζήνωνι ἑκατὸν μνᾶς τελέσας σοφός τε καὶ ἐλλόγιμος γέγονεν.—ἀλλὰ μὰ Δί᾽ οὐκ ἔχω.

32 πράγματά σοι παρέχειν ἔοικα; οὐ μέντοι πλείω ἢ ἐμαυτῷ καὶ τῷ ὑπογραφεῖ. περὶ γὰρ λύχνων ἁφὰς ταῦτα ἐζητεῖτο, καὶ ἔδει πρὶν εἰς εὐνὴν ἰέναι τέλος ἔχειν.

33 οὐκοῦν ὃ λέγω σκόπει. ταῦτα εἰ μὲν ἀναγκαῖα τῷ λόγῳ, καὶ τὰ παρ᾽ ἡμῶν εἰς ἐκεῖνον μετέχει τῆς ἀπολογίας, εἰ δὲ μὴ ἀναγκαῖα, ὅρα τὸ περιὸν τῆς εὐγνωμοσύνης. ἐγὼ μὲν γὰρ ἐφαινόμην οὐδ᾽ ἐν αὐτοῖς τοῖς ἀναγκαίοις ἀποτόμως τῷ λόγῳ χρώμενος, ἀλλὰ πεφεισμένως καὶ σχηματιζόμενος τὰ πρέποντα, ὁ δ᾽ ἀνδρὶ τῶν κατ᾽ αὐτὸν ἐνδοξοτάτῳ οὕτω ῥᾳδίως ἀμα-

[51] Ἀθηναίων ἢ τῶν ξένων *codd. Plat.*
[52] σοι εἰπεῖν *codd. Plat.*

> Well, Cleinias, your brother.—Cleinias? Why mention him either—he is a maniac!—Well, if Cleinias is mad and the two sons of Pericles were simpletons, what reason are we to assign, in your case, for his allowing you to be in your present condition?—I believe I am myself to blame for not paying attention to him.—[119a] But name me any other Athenian or foreigner, slave or freeman, who is alleged to have become wiser through keeping company with Pericles, as I can tell you Pythodorus son of Isolochus and Callias son of Calliades did through keeping company with Zeno; each of them paid Zeno a hundred minas, and has become wise and distinguished.—You know, I simply can't!

Does it look as if I am just making work for you? No more than for myself and for my secretary: it is around lamplighting time that I am going into this, and it has to be finished before I go to bed.[38] 32

So, think what I am saying. If this passage was necessary to Plato's case, then my words to him are entitled to the same defense as well; if they were not necessary, just look how excessively courteous he was! I for my part was clearly not brusque in my use of the argument even when it was necessary for me to employ it, but instead used it sparingly and with all due propriety in my presentation; but Plato found it this easy to accuse the most distinguished man of his times of stupidity, and what is more to 33

38 Both the tenses here (imperfects in the Greek) and the reference to the process of composition are consciously epistolary touches.

θίαν ἐγκέκληκεν, καὶ ταῦτα ἀκούοντος μειρακίου ἐπιτηδείου [καὶ][53] καταφρονῆσαι καὶ ὁτουοῦν, καὶ ᾧ θεῖός
34 τε καὶ ἐπίτροπος καὶ ἀντὶ τοῦ πατρὸς [ἂν][54] ἦν. ὥστε ἐγὼ μὲν οὐδὲν ψέγω οὐδ᾽ ἐξελέγχω,[55] δέδοικα δὲ μή τις ἐμοῦ γοργότερον βλέπων φῇ συνῳδὰ ταῦτα εἶναι ταῖς αἰτίαις ἃς Σωκράτης εἶχεν, ὡς ἀναπείθων τοὺς νέους τῶν πρεσβυτέρων καταφρονεῖν. καὶ ἐὰν δὴ λέγω ὅτι Περικλέα φασὶν καὶ τὰ ἴδια οὐδὲν ἀτιμότερον βιῶναι Σωκράτους σεμνότητος ἕνεκα κἂν ταῖς στρατείαις ταῖς κοιναῖς λυσιτελέστερον εἶναι Σωκράτους συμπαρόντα, ἐὰν ταῦτα λέγω, φήσεις με ῥητο-
35 ρεύειν. οὐκοῦν ταῦτα ἐῶ σὴν χάριν. ἀλλὰ τοσοῦτον δέομαι πυθέσθαι, ποῦ ταῦτα ἀναγκαῖον ἐγκαταμῖξαι τοῖς διαλόγοις; οὐ γὰρ ἄν μοι θαυμαστὸν εἴη εἰ μηδεὶς ἔχοι δεῖξαι. τεκμαίρομαι ἑνὶ[56] μικρῷ. εἰ γάρ τις ἅπαν τοῦτο ἐξέλοι, ἀρξάμενος ἀπὸ τοῦ "πέπονθας δὲ οὐ σὺ μόνος τοῦτο, ἀλλὰ καὶ <οἱ>[57] πολλοὶ τῶν πραττόντων τὰ τῆσδε τῆς πόλεως," ἢ καὶ ἔτι ἀπ᾽ ἐκείνου "διὸ καὶ ᾄττεις ἄρα πρὸς τὰ πολιτικὰ πρὶν παιδευθῆναι" μέχρι τοῦ "ἀλλὰ μὰ Δί᾽ οὐκ ἔχω," εἰ τοῦτό τις ἐξέλοι, τί χείρων ὁ λόγος γίγνεται, ἢ τί ἧττον προτρέπει τὸν Ἀλκιβιάδην, ἐὰν οὕτω τὸ συνεχὲς ᾖ "ἀμαθίᾳ γὰρ συνοικεῖς, ὦ βέλτιστε, τῇ ἐσχάτῃ, ὡς ὁ λόγος σοῦ κατηγορεῖ καὶ σὺ σαυτοῦ. εἶεν. τί οὖν διανοῇ

[53] *om.* Ua *eras.* A *del. edd.* [54] *del.* Dindorf
[55] ἐξελέγχω U² ἐξελέγξω *cett.* [56] <δ᾽> ἑνί Reiske
[57] *add.* Dindorf

do so in the hearing of a lad who was prone in any case to be contemptuous of anyone and everyone, and to whom
that man was uncle, guardian, and substitute father. Thus 34
though I myself offer no reproach or criticism, I am afraid that someone else may glare more fiercely than me and say that all this chimes with the charges brought against Socrates of persuading the young to despise their elders.[39] If I go on to observe that Pericles is said in his private life as well to have lived with no less honor and dignity than Socrates, and in the military campaigns in which both participated to have been more useful than Socrates by his presence, you will accuse me of speechifying. So I will let these
points pass in deference to you. But I do at least have to 35
ask where the necessity was for Plato to include all this in his dialogues. It would not surprise me if no one could explain it to me. I infer this from one small indication. If one were to take out the whole passage, beginning with the words "You are not alone in this plight, but you share it with most of those who manage our city's affairs," or indeed with "and this apparently is why you dash into politics before you have been educated," and going up to "You know, I simply can't!"—if one were to take this out, in what respect would the argument be a worse one? Or in what respect would it make a less effective exhortation to Alcibiades if the sequence went like this, "You are wedded to stupidity, my fine friend, of the worst kind–the argument charges you with this and you charge yourself with

[39] The charge of "corrupting the young," as analyzed in Pl. *Ap.* 23c–e and Xen. *Mem.* 1.2.49–55.

περὶ σεαυτοῦ; πότερον ἐὰν ὡς νῦν ἔχεις,[58] ἢ ἐπιμέλειάν τινα ποιεῖσθαι;" τί χείρων ἐγίγνετο ὁ λόγος, εἰ ταῦτα οὑτωσί πως εἶχεν; ἐγὼ μὲν οὐχ ὁρῶ. εἰ γὰρ τῶν ἄλλων τισὶ τῶν πολλῶν ἐβούλετο ἐπιτιμῆσαι προτροπῆς ἕνεκα τοῦ μειρακίου, ἐξῆν ὅπερ εἴρηκα ποιῆσαι.
36 διείλεκται γάρ που καὶ περὶ τούτων ἰδίᾳ, ὡς οὐ χρὴ πρὸς τὸν δεῖνα ὁρᾶν αὐτόν, ἀλλὰ πρὸς τοὺς ἀληθινοὺς ἀνταγωνιστάς. οὔκουν[59] δεινόν, εἰ Πλάτων μὲν κωμῳδεῖ Περικλέα μηδεμιᾶς ἀνάγκης οὔσης, ἡμῖν δὲ μηδὲ τοσοῦτον εἰπεῖν ἄνευ μέμψεως ἐξέσται ὡς ἀπεδήμησε Πλάτων εἰς Σικελίαν; καίτοι τί τοῦτο αἰσχυνόμεθα οἱ φιλοῦντες ἐκεῖνον;

37 Παρμενίδης τοίνυν ἔστιν αὐτῷ σύγγραμμα θεῖον. τί οὖν πρὸς τὸ ἓν καὶ πολλὰ καὶ τὰς πολλὰς ταύτας στροφὰς τὸ γενέσθαι Ζήνωνα παιδικὰ Παρμενίδου; ποῦ τοῦτο ἀναγκαῖον ἦν προφέρειν ἀνδρὶ τηλικούτῳ; ἀλλ' ὅμως εἴρηκε κόσμου τινὸς ἕνεκα τῶν λόγων.

38 ἀλλὰ νὴ Δία ὡς Ὅμηρον μύρῳ χρίσας ἐκπέμπει χελιδόνος τιμὴν καταθείς, οὕτως ἡμεῖς Πλάτωνα ἐκπέμπειν ἐκ τῶν πόλεων ἐκελεύομεν ἢ μετ' ἀδείας τοσαύτης κακῶς αὐτὸν εἰρήκαμεν; ἢ τούτους πάλιν αὖ τοὺς Γοργιείους[60] λόγους παραιτούμεθα μὴ δυσχεραί-

58 ἐὰν ὡς νῦν ἔχεις Dindorf *cum codd. Plat.* ἕως ἂν νῦν (νοῦν) ἔχῃς *codd.* 59 οὔκουν Behr οὐκοῦν *codd.*
60 Γοργιείους Reiske *cum* R^2 Γοργείους *cett.*

---

40 Another Demosthenic turn of phrase: e.g., *De cor.* (18) 284, 3.8, 20.28, etc. 41 *Alc. I* 119d. 42 *Prm.* 127b.

it too. Well, then, what do you intend to do about yourself? To let yourself remain as you now are, or to take some care of yourself?" In what respect would the argument be a worse one, if the passage ran something like this? I at least cannot see any.[40] If Plato had wanted to criticize others from the population at large in order to exhort the lad, he
could have done so, as I have said. In fact there is a place 36
where he did talk specifically about this and say that Alcibiades should look not to some particular individual or other, but to his true opponents.[41] So is it not outrageous that Plato should satirize Pericles when there was no need for it, but that I will not be allowed to say even as much as that Plato traveled abroad to Sicily, without being reproached for it? Yet why should I as a friend of his be ashamed of this?

His *Parmenides* is an inspired piece of writing. So what 37
does the fact that Zeno was Parmenides' boyfriend have to do with unity and multiplicity and all those twists and turns?[42] Where was the necessity to bring this up against a man like that? But all the same he has said it, just for the sake of some sort of ornamentation to his argument.

For goodness' sake, did I really order Plato to be es- 38
corted from the cities of men in just the same way as Plato anoints Homer with myrrh and escorts him on his way, paying out only what one would for a swallow,[43] and have I really abused him with a comparable degree of freedom? Or again, am I asking people not to be upset if I put a line

[43] *Resp.* 398a. In the Rhodian folk ritual known as "swallowing" (*chelidonismos*), described in Ath. *Deipn.* 8.360b–d, trick-or-treaters dressed as swallows were bought off with small gifts of food and drink.

νειν ἐὰν διαγράφωμεν, ὥσπερ ἐκεῖνος βούλεται τὸν Ὅμηρον διαγράφειν, ὡσπερεί τις ἑλλανοδίκης πρὸς
39 ἐπῶν κρίσιν ᾑρημένος; ἀλλὰ τοὺς ἑταίρους τοῦ Πλάτωνος κωμῳδοῦμεν ὥσπερ ἐκεῖνος τοὺς Ὁμήρου, καὶ ταῦτα μέντοι πρὸς θεῶν τί τοῦ λόγου προσαναγκάζοντος αὐτόν; οὐ γὰρ ἔγωγε ἐπινοῶ. οὐκ ἂν οἱ φύλακες καθ' αὑτοὺς ᾤκουν, εἰ μὴ κακῶς Ὅμηρος ἤκουσεν; ἀλλὰ γυναῖκες κοιναὶ ταῦτα ἐπηνάγκαζον; ἀλλ' ἡ χιλιέτης πορεία χεῖρον ἂν εἴρητο αὐτῷ, εἰ μὴ Κρεώφυλος ἤκουσεν κακῶς; ἀλλὰ τί τοῦτο ἐβούλετο αὐτῷ
40 κωμῳδεῖν Ὅμηρον διὰ κενῆς; καὶ μὴν οὐδὲ αὐτό γε τοῦτο παρῃτήσατο εἰς τοσοῦτον οὔτε ἀρχόμενος τῶν πρὸς αὐτὸν λόγων, ὥσπερ ἡμεῖς πολλὰ παρῃτησάμεθα, οὔτε ἐν τοῖς ὕστερον, ἀλλ' ἓν γὰρ τοῦτ' εἶπεν βραχύ, ὡς οὐ πρό γε τῆς ἀληθείας τιμητέος ἀνήρ. ἡ δὲ ἀλήθεια οὐκ ἐπηνάγκαζεν Κρεώφυλον ἄγειν εἰς λόγον. ἢ Πλάτωνι μὲν καὶ ἀπὸ τῶν ὀνομάτων ἐξέσται διασύρειν οὓς βούλεται καὶ διὰ τούτων ἑτέρους πάλιν, ἡμῖν δὲ οὐδὲ ἀπὸ τῶν ἔργων τῶν ἐκείνου τοὺς ἐκείνου
41 λόγους ἐλέγχειν ἐξέσται; καὶ τὸ μὲν δὴ περὶ τῶν ἐπῶν ἀφῶμεν αὐτῷ καταστάσεώς γ' ἕνεκα τῆς πολιτείας διερευνᾶν, καίτοι κἀνταῦθά τις ἂν ἔχοι ὑπολαβεῖν αὐτῷ, "τί δ' ἐστὶ τοιοῦτον; εἰ μὲν γὰρ ὅλως ἔμελλες χρήσεσθαι τῷ ποιητῇ, χρῆν ὅμως[61] ἐξαλείφειν ἅ γε

[61] ὅμως Trapp ὅλως *codd. del.* Reiske

through those Gorgianic arguments, in the same way that
he wants to put a line through Homer,[44] as if he had been
chosen as some sort of Hellenic judge to censor epic poetry? Do I really make fun of Plato's partisans, as he does 39
Homer's,[45] when one might well ask what necessity the
argument places on him to do so? I certainly cannot see
any. Would it be impossible for his Guardians to live as a
separate class to themselves unless Homer were ill spoken
of?[46] Was it necessitated by the common ownership of
women?[47] Would he have given a worse account of the
thousand-year journey if Creophylus had not been in-
sulted?[48] What did he mean by this empty satirizing of
Homer? What is more, he did not even try to excuse him- 40
self to the same extent, either at the beginning of the arguments directed against Homer, as I did at great length at
the beginning of mine, or in what followed; all he did was
make the one brief declaration that we should not revere
a man in preference to the truth.[49] The truth did not compel him to bring Creophylus into the discussion! Or is
Plato going to be allowed to mock whoever he wants for
so much as having the names they do, and others again
through them, while I am forbidden even to use his actions
to refute his arguments? Well, as far as the issue of epic 41
poetry is concerned, let us allow him to investigate it in
the interests of the establishment of his state, even though
here too someone could retort to him, "What on earth is
going on? If you were going to find some overall role for
the poet, you would still have had to censor what you did

[44] *Resp.* 387b. [45] *Resp.* 600a–b. [46] *Resp.* 416d–17b. [47] *Resp.* 457c–d. [48] *Resp.* 600b (Creophylus); 615a, 621d (thousand-year journey). [49] *Resp.* 595c.

μὴ προσίεσο· εἰ δὲ ἁπλῶς ἐκπέμπεις αὐτὸν καὶ οὐδέσιν οὐδὲ ὧν ἐπαινεῖς ἐᾷς ὁμιλεῖν τὴν σαυτοῦ πόλιν, πράγματα σαυτῷ παρέχεις τὰ μὲν ἐξαίρων, τὰ δὲ ἐγκαταλείπων."

42 δῶμεν οὖν, εἰ βούλεται, ἡδύσματος ἕνεκα τῶν λόγων αὐτῷ καὶ διατριβῆς ταῦτ' εἰρῆσθαι; ἢ δεῖ τοῖς πεπολιτευμένοις ἅπασιν αὖθις ἐπ' αὐτὸν ἐπανόδου;[62] ἆρ' οὐ φιλοτιμία λαμπρά; ἤδη γὰρ ἀποκαλύψας ἐγὼ λέγω. [ἐκ τῆς Πολιτείας][63]

43 ὦ φίλε Ὅμηρε, <εἴπερ>[64] μὴ τρίτος ἀπὸ τῆς ἀληθείας εἶ ἀρετῆς πέρι εἰδώλου δημιουργός, ὃν δὴ μιμητὴν ὡρισάμεθα, ἀλλὰ καὶ δεύτερος, καὶ οἷός τε ἦσθα γιγνώσκειν ὁποῖα ἐπιτηδεύματα βελτίους ἀνθρώπους ἢ χείρους[65] ποιεῖ ἰδίᾳ καὶ δημοσίᾳ, λέγε ἡμῖν, τίς τῶν πόλεων διὰ σὲ βέλτιον ᾤκησεν, ὥσπερ διὰ Λυκοῦργον Λακεδαιμόνιοι καὶ δι' ἄλλους πολλοὺς πολλαὶ μεγάλαι τε καὶ σμικραί; [599e] σὲ δὲ τίς αἰτιᾶται πόλις νομοθέτην[66] γεγονέναι καὶ σφᾶς ὠφεληκέναι; Χαρώνδαν μὲν γὰρ Ἰταλία καὶ Σικελία καὶ ἡμεῖς Σόλωνα, σὲ δὲ τίς; ἕξει τινὰ εἰπεῖν;—οὐκ οἶμαί γε, ἔφη ὁ Γλαύκων· οὔκουν λέγεταί γε οὐδ' ὑπ' αὐτῶν Ὁμηριδῶν.—[600a] ἀλλὰ δὴ πόλεμος ἐπὶ Ὁμήρου ὑπ' ἐκείνου ἄρχοντος ἢ συμβουλεύοντος εὖ πολεμηθεὶς μνημονεύεται;—

[62] ἐπανόδου Reiske ἐπάνοδον *codd.* [63] *del.* Lenz
[64] *add.* Stephanus *cum codd. Plat.*

not want to let in; but if on the other hand you are expelling him once and for all and not allowing your city to have to do even with the parts of his work you praise, then you are simply putting yourself to unnecessary trouble in removing some things and leaving others in place."

Should we then grant, if he wants us to, that all this had 42
been said merely as seasoning for his argument and for amusement? Or does in fact the whole of his discussion of politics have to come back to Homer? If so, is this not flagrant competitiveness, to speak now without veiling my words?

> My dear Homer, if in the matter of human excel- 43
> lence you are not the creator of phantoms that we gave as the definition of the mimetic artist, but are actually only at one remove and capable of knowing what pursuits make men better or worse in private or public life, tell us what city was better governed owing to you, as Lacedaemon was because of Lycurgus, and many other cities great and small because of other legislators. [599e] What city credits you with having been a good legislator and having benefited them? Italy and Sicily say this of Charondas and we say it of Solon. But who says it of you? Will he be able to name any?—I think not, said Glaucon; at any rate none is mentioned even by the Homerids themselves.—[600a] Well, is any war in Homer's time remembered as having been well conducted under his command or advice?—

---

65 *ἢ χείρους ἀνθρώπους codd. Plat.*
66 *νομοθέτην ἀγαθόν codd. Plat.*

οὐδείς. ἀλλ' οἷα δὴ εἰς τὰ ἔργα σοφοῦ ἀνδρὸς πολλαὶ ἐπίνοιαι καὶ εὐμήχανοι εἰς τέχνας, ἤ τινες ἄλλαι πράξεις λέγονται, ὥσπερ αὖ Θάλεω πέρι τοῦ Μιλησίου καὶ Ἀναχάρσιος τοῦ Σκύθου;—οὐδαμῶς τοιοῦτον οὐδέν.—ἀλλὰ δὴ εἰ μὴ δημοσίᾳ, ἰδίᾳ τισὶν ἡγεμὼν παιδείας ζῶν αὐτὸς λέγεται Ὅμηρος γενέσθαι, οἳ ἐκεῖνον ἠγάπων ἐπὶ [600b] συνουσίᾳ καὶ τοῖς ὑστέροις ὁδόν τινα παρέδοσαν βίου Ὁμηρικήν, ὥσπερ Πυθαγόρας αὐτός τε ὑπερβαλλόντως ἐπὶ τούτῳ ἠγαπήθη καὶ οἱ ὕστερον ἔτι καὶ νῦν τρόπον τὸν αὐτὸν ἐπονομάζοντες τοῦ βίου διαφανεῖς πῃ δοκοῦσιν εἶναι ἐν τοῖς ἄλλοις;—οὐδ' αὖ, ἔφη, τοιοῦτον οὐδὲν λέγεται. ὁ γὰρ Κρεώφυλος, ὦ Σώκρατες, ἴσως, ὁ τοῦ Ὁμήρου ἑταῖρος, <τοῦ ὀνόματος ἂν γελοιότερος>[67] ἔτι πρὸς παιδείαν[68] φανείη, εἰ τὰ λεγόμενα περὶ Ὁμήρου ἀληθῆ. λέγεται γὰρ <ὡς πολλή τις ἀμέλεια περὶ [600c] αὐτὸν ἦν ἐπ' αὐτοῦ ἐκείνου, ὅτε ἔζη.—λέγεται γὰρ>[69] οὖν, ἦν δ' ἐγώ. ἀλλ' οἴει, ὦ Γλαύκων, εἰ τῷ ὄντι οἷός τε ἦν παιδεύειν ἀνθρώπους καὶ βελτίους ἀπεργάζεσθαι Ὅμηρος, ἅτε περὶ τούτων οὐ μιμεῖσθαι, ἀλλὰ γιγνώσκειν δυνάμενος, οὐκ ἄρ' ἂν πολλοὺς ἑταίρους ἐποιήσατο καὶ ἐτιμᾶτο καὶ ἠγαπᾶτο ὑπ' αὐτῶν; ἀλλὰ Πρωταγόρας μὲν ἄρα ὁ Ἀβδηρίτης καὶ Πρόδικος ὁ Κεῖος καὶ ἄλλοι

67 *add.* Lenz *cum codd. Plat.*

None.—Well, as might be expected of a man wise in practical matters, are many clever inventions in the arts and crafts, or any other sorts of practical activity, reported of him as they are of Thales the Milesian and Anacharsis the Scythian?—Nothing whatever of the sort.—Well, if no public service is credited to him, is Homer reported to have been a guide in education in his lifetime to men who cherished him for [600b] his company, and to have bequeathed to posterity a Homeric way of life, just as Pythagoras was himself especially cherished for this, and his successors to this day, giving his name to the same style of life, are thought somehow to stand out from the rest of mankind?—No, nothing of this sort is reported either, Socrates. Homer had a friend called Creophylus, but if the stories about Homer are true, he would look even more ridiculous than his name as far as culture and education are concerned: it is said that this very individual completely failed to pay Homer any attention [600c] during his lifetime.—Why, yes, that is what is said, said I; but do you suppose, Glaucon, that, if Homer had really been able to educate men and make them better because he had the ability not just to imitate in this domain but to know, he would not have acquired many companions and been honored and cherished by them? Are we to believe that while Protagoras of Abdera and Prodicus of Ceos

---

68 παιδείαν Lenz παιδιάν *codd.*
69 *add.* Dindorf *cum codd. Plat.*

πάμπολλοι δύνανται τοῖς ἐφ'[70] *αὑτῶν παριστάναι, ἰδίᾳ συγγιγνόμενοι,* [600d] *ὡς οὔτε πόλιν οὔτε οἰκίαν*[71] *τὴν ἑαυτῶν διοικεῖν οἷοί τε ἔσονται, ἐὰν μὴ σφεῖς*[72] *αὐτῶν τῆς παιδείας*[73] *ἐπιστατήσωσιν, καὶ ἐπὶ ταύτῃ τῇ σοφίᾳ οὕτω σφόδρα φιλοῦνται ὥστε μόνον οὐκ ἐπὶ τῆς κεφαλῆς*[74] *περιφέρουσιν αὐτοὺς οἱ ἑταῖροι. Ὅμηρον δ' ἄρα οἱ ἐπ' ἐκείνου, εἴπερ οἷός τ' ἦν πρὸς ἀρετὴν ὀνίναι ἀνθρώπους, καὶ*[75] *Ἡσίοδον ῥαψῳδεῖν ἂν περιιόντας [ἂν]*[76] *εἴων, καὶ οὐ μᾶλλον ἂν αὐτῶν ἀντείχοντο <ἢ>*[77] *τοῦ χρυσοῦ καὶ* [600e] *ἠνάγκαζον παρὰ σφίσιν οἴκοι εἶναι, ἢ εἰ μὴ ἔπειθον, αὐτοὶ ἂν ἐπαιδαγώγουν ὅπῃ ᾖσαν*[78] *ἕως ἱκανῶς παιδείας μεταλάβοιεν;—παντάπασιν, ἔφη, δοκεῖς μοι, ὦ Σώκρατες, ἀληθῆ λέγειν.—οὐκοῦν τιθῶμεν ἀπὸ Ὁμήρου ἀρξάμενοι πάντας τοὺς ποιητικοὺς μιμητὰς εἰδώλων ἀρετῆς εἶναι καὶ τῶν ἄλλων περὶ ὧν ποιοῦσιν ἀληθείας*[79] *οὐχ ἅπτεσθαι;*

44 *ταῦτα, ὦ πρὸς τῶν θεῶν, τίνας τὰς ἀνάγκας ἢ τίνα τὴν εὐπρέπειαν ἔχει; τίς ἀνέξεται Χαρώνδαν πρὸ*

70 *ἐφ'* Dindorf *cum codd. Plat. ὑφ' codd.*

71 *οὔτε οἰκίαν οὔτε πόλιν codd. Plat.*

72 *σφεῖς codd. Plat. ὃ φής codd.*

73 *παιδείας* Lenz *cum codd. Plat. οἰκίας codd.*

74 *ταῖς κεφαλαῖς codd. Plat.*

75 *ἤ codd. Plat.*

76 *del.* Behr *cum codd. Plat.*

77 *add.* Dindorf *cum codd. Plat.*

78 *ᾖσαν* Lenz *cum codd. Plat. ἦσαν codd.*

and many others are able by private teaching to impress upon their contemporaries the conviction [600d] that they will not be capable of governing either their cities or even their own homes unless they put them in charge of their education, and are so warmly loved for this wisdom of theirs that their companions all but carry them about on their shoulders, Homer's contemporaries, if he had been able to benefit men in the pursuit of moral excellence, would have allowed him or Hesiod to roam about rhapsodizing and would not have clung to them far more than to their gold, and [600e] compelled them to live with them in their homes, or if they failed to persuade them, would themselves have escorted them wherever they went until they had learned from them as much as they needed?—What you say seems to me to be altogether true, Socrates, he said.—Shall we, then, lay it down that all poets, beginning with Homer, are imitators of shadow images of moral excellence and have no grip on the truth of the other things about which they write?[50]

In heaven's name, what need is there for this? Isn't it 44
completely unbecoming? Who is going to put up with

[50] *Resp.* 599d–600d, with some minor differences in wording and word order from the text in our Plato manuscripts. In the last sentence, their reading ("imitators of shadow images of moral excellence and the other things about which they write, and have no grip on the truth") should perhaps be restored.

---

[79] τῆς δὲ ἀληθείας *codd. Plat.*

Ὁμήρου ταττόμενον καὶ Πρωταγόραν καὶ Πρόδικον καὶ ἄλλους παμπόλλους; ὁ δὲ αὐτὸς οὗτος Πρόδικος ἐν τοῖς αὐτοῦ που[80] κατάκειται μάλα γελοίως καὶ ὁ Πρωταγόρας εἰς τὸν Ἱππίαν παραβλέπει καὶ ὁ Ἱππίας ληρεῖ. τί ταῦτα συντελεῖ, φαίη τις ἄν, τοῖς θαυμαστοῖς αὐτοῦ δόγμασιν; ἀλλ᾽ ὅμως τούτους τοὺς ἑτέρωθι γελοίους ἐνταῦθα ἐν εὐφημίᾳ τέθειται, οὐχ ἵνα τούτους ἐπαινέσειεν, ἀλλ᾽ ἵνα Ὁμήρῳ, ἀηδὲς μὲν εἰπεῖν, τὸ δὲ ἀληθὲς ἀποκρύψασθαι <. . . . .>,[81] ἐπη-
45 ρεάσειεν [λέγω].[82] τίς γάρ ἐστιν ὁ λέγων "καὶ μὴν Τάνταλον εἰσεῖδον" καὶ "τὸν δὲ μέτ᾽ εἰσενόησα;" οὔκουν[83] ἐκείνους μὲν διὰ τῶν Ὁμήρου κωμῳδεῖ, Ὅμηρον δ᾽ αὖ δι᾽ ἐκείνων; παρενθήκη δὲ καὶ Ἡσίοδος αὐτῷ γέγονεν. ὥστ᾽ ἐγὼ θαυμάζω τίνας ἂν τὰς βλασφημίας εἰς αὐτοὺς ἐποιήσατο, εἰ τὴν πόλιν αὐτὴν[84] διέβαλλον, ἢ τὴν πολιτείαν ἀφῃροῦντο, ὁπότ᾽ οὐδὲν ἔχων ἕτερον προφέρειν ἢ ὅτι πλείους ἴσως τοῦ δέοντος ἐπαινοῦσιν, αὐτὸς οὕτως ἀνομοίως αὐτοῖς προσενήνεκται.

46 ἀτάρ, ὦ ἄριστε Καπίτων, ἐνεθυμήθην καὶ τοῦτο μεταξὺ τῶν λόγων ὅτι πάντα εἴδωλά ἐστιν τῷ ἀνδρί, καὶ τοῦτο μὲν οἱ ποιηταὶ "μιμηταὶ εἰδώλων ἀρετῆς," τοῦτο δὲ ἡ ῥητορικὴ "πολιτικῆς μορίου εἴδωλον." "εἰδώλων δὲ πλέον πρόθυρον" φαίη ἂν εἰς αὐτὸν Ὅμη-

[80] που Reiske πολύ *codd.* πολύς Canter *om.* U
[81] ἀποκρύψασθαι οὐ θέμις U
[82] *om.* U *del.* Trapp
[83] οὔκουν Behr οὐκοῦν *codd.*
[84] αὐτοῦ Reiske

Charondas and Protagoras and Prodicus and a whole host of others being ranked before Homer? Somewhere in Plato this same Prodicus lies in bed looking utterly ridiculous, and Protagoras shoots sideways glances at Hippias, and Hippias spouts nonsense.[51] What, one might ask, does this contribute to his wonderful teaching? Yet even so these people who elsewhere are figures of fun he here treats as men of good repute, not so as to praise them but so as—it gives me no pleasure to say it, but it is wrong to conceal the truth—so as to insult Homer. Who is it who 45
says "And I saw Tantalus too" and "After him I spied"?[52] Is he not satirizing them by means of Homer, and then again Homer by means of them? (He also brought in Hesiod as a footnote.) I wonder therefore what insults he would have directed at the poets if they had slandered his city itself or suppressed its constitution, given that when he had nothing else to reproach them with beyond the fact that more people praise them than perhaps should, he himself behaved toward them in such a dissimilar fashion.

Indeed, my dear Capito, the thought occurs to me as I 46
write that in Plato's eyes everything is shadow images: poets are "imitators of shadow images of moral excellence" on the one hand, the art of oratory is "a shadow image of a part of the art of politics" on the other.[53] "The court before your door is full of shades" Homer might say to

[51] *Prt.* 315c–16a, 318e, 337b–38e (cf. 347a–b).

[52] *Prt.* 315b–c, quoting *Od.* 11.582 and 601.

[53] *Resp.* 600e, *Grg.* 463d.

ρος. πότερον ταῦτα θρασύτερα καὶ προπετέστερα,
ἢ τἀμά, ἐν οἷς φημι Πλάτωνα ἀποδημῆσαι ὑπὲρ
†αὐτῶν,[85] *καί φημι ταῦτα λέγειν οὐ τὴν ἀποδημίαν*
κακίζων, ἀλλὰ τῇ ἀποδημίᾳ τὸν λόγον πιστούμενος;
47 *ναί, ἀλλ' ἀπεστερήκαμεν αὐτὸν δόξης φιλοσοφίας.*
ὥσπερ ἐκεῖνος τοὺς μὲν τῆς τραγῳδίας ποιητὰς οὐδὲ
ἐν λόγῳ τίθησιν, Ὅμηρον δὲ τραγῳδιοποιὸν προσ-
είρηκεν, οὐ τοῦτον τούτῳ κοσμῶν, ἀλλὰ τούτους μὲν
διὰ τοῦτον[86] *κολούων, τοῦτον δὲ ᾧ τιμᾷ καθαιρῶν.*
πλέον γὰρ οἶμαι ‹ἢ›[87] *τὴν τραγῳδίαν Ὁμήρῳ συνή-*
δεσαν οἱ Ἕλληνες. ἀλλ' Ἐπίχαρμος δῆτα δικαίως
αὐτῷ κωμῳδίας ἄκρος, ᾧ ταῦτ' ἄριστα φαίην ‹ἂν›[88]
ἔγωγε ἔχειν ὅσα τῆς φωνῆς τῆς Ἀττικῆς ἐστιν ἐγγυ-
τάτω.

48 *οὔκουν*[89] *δεινόν, εἰ οὗτος μὲν καὶ τραγῳδιοποιοὺς*
καὶ κωμῳδιοποιοὺς καὶ πόλιν καὶ πολιτείαν καὶ νό-
μους αὐτῷ καθίστησιν, ἡμῖν δὲ μηδὲ λόγου τινὸς ἐξ-
έσται πρὸς αὐτὸν ἀμφισβητῆσαι, καὶ ταῦτα οὐ μύρῳ
ἐπαλείφουσιν αὐτόν, ἀλλὰ λόγοις τοῖς εὐφημοτάτοις
καὶ ὧν οὐδ' ἂν αὐτὸς μείζους ἠξίωσεν ἀκούειν ὑπὲρ
49 *αὑτοῦ. εἰ γὰρ ἓν μόνον εἴπομεν ἀρχόμενοι τῶν λόγων*
τῶν πρὸς αὐτόν, "καλῶ δὲ ἐπὶ τῷ τολμήματι καὶ Ἑρ-
μῆν λόγιον καὶ Ἀπόλλω μουσηγέτην καὶ Μούσας

[85] *susp.* Lenz *fort.* *τῶν Δίωνος πραγμάτων* (cf. *supra* §10)
[86] *τοῦτον* a^2 Behr *τούτων cett.*
[87] *add.* Lenz
[88] *add.* Dindorf
[89] *οὔκουν* Behr *οὐκοῦν codd.*

him.[54] Are the bolder and hastier remarks Plato's, or mine, when I say that he traveled abroad on their behalf,[55] and assert that when I say this I am not denigrating his travels but using his travels as evidence in favor of my argument? Yes, you will say, but I have denied him his good name as 47
a philosopher. Just as he ranked the tragic poets as entirely negligible, then called Homer a tragic poet, not complimenting him by this, but using him to cut them down to size, while humbling him by the very honor he pays him.[56] For I think the Greeks saw more than just tragedy in Homer. (Plato is however right to say that Epicharmus is the supreme author of comedy,[57] who I would say is at his best in those parts of his work that are closest to Attic dialect.)[58]

Is it not monstrous, then, that Plato for his part should 48
organize tragic poets and comic poets and a city and a republic and laws as he sees fit, but that I should not be allowed to debate even a single one of his arguments with him, even though I anoint him not with myrrh, but with the most complimentary of words, such that not even he would have thought he should have anything more laudatory said about him? If I had said just the one thing at the 49
beginning of my argument against him, "to aid me in this bold venture I call upon Hermes, god of eloquence, Apollo

54 *Od.* 20.355, in a passage cited by Plato in *Ion* 539a.

55 The true reading here may be "in defense of Dion's interests" (cf. §10 above).

56 *Resp.* 595c, 598d, 607a.

57 *Tht.* 152e, where Homer and Epicharmus are named together as the respective leading lights of tragedy and comedy.

58 The relevance of this and the preceding sentence to Aristides' argument is hard to detect; may they in fact be a note by a later reader (a Christian, for whom "Greek" = "pagan"?), wrongly incorporated into the text?

ἀπάσας," εἰ τοῦτο μόνον τὸ ἀπάσας[90] ἐπεθήκαμεν, τίς εἰς τοσοῦτον ἂν ἠρκὼς ἦν Πλάτωνα; μὴ γάρ τοι νομίσῃς ῥῆμα ἄλλως ἐφόλκιον εἶναι τοῦτο, ὥσπερ Ὁμήρῳ ἐστὶ "Μοῦσαι δ' ἐννέα πᾶσαι," ἀλλ' εἰ περὶ τῶν ἑαυτοῦ λέγειν ἔξεστιν, ἀμήχανον ὅσον ἐστὶ τὸ τῆς προσθήκης.

50 νὴ Δί', εἴποι τις ἄν, ἀλλ' ἐν τούτοις μόνοις ἡμῶν
πλείω περιεργάζεται, τὰ δ' ἄλλα μεστὸς εὐλαβείας
ἀνήρ;[91] οὐκ Ἀριστοφάνει μὲν λύγγα προσάπτει, οὐδὲν
πρὸς λόγον, μᾶλλον δὲ καὶ παντελῶς πρᾶγμα ἄχαρι
καὶ ἀπᾷδον τῶν περὶ ἔρωτος λόγων, τοσοῦτον δὲ ἀπέχει τοῦ τἀναγκαῖα ἢ τοῦ τἀληθῆ λέγειν ὥστε ὅλην
δήπου τὴν συνουσίαν ἔψευσται καὶ τοὺς τεθνεῶτας ὡς
ζῶντας συμπλάττει; γνοίης δ' ἂν ἐξ αὐτῶν τῶν λεγο-
51 μένων. Μαντινεῖς μὲν γάρ, ὧν ἐν τῷ λόγῳ μέμνηται
λέγων ὡς [ἐπὶ][92] Ἀρκάδων, διῳκίσθησαν ἐπὶ τοῦ δεῖ-
νος ἄρχοντος, Σωκράτης δὲ ἐτεθνήκει πρὸ τόσου καὶ
τόσου, ὁ δὲ Ἀριστοφάνης αὐτῷ λύζει τε καὶ λέγει
ταῦτα πρὸ[93] τοῦ Σωκράτους. εἶτ' ἐκείνῳ μὲν ἔνια καὶ
μηδαμῇ συμβαίνοντα ἔξεστι συμπλάττειν, κἂν ἔξω
φανερῶς ᾖ τοῦ λόγου, ἡμῖν δὲ ἄρα τίς μνησικακήσει
εἴ τι τῶν ὑπ' αὐτοῦ πραχθέντων ἠνέγκαμεν εἰς μέσον;

[90] ἀπάσας Behr πάσας *codd.* [91] ἀνήρ Dindorf ἀνὴρ *codd.*
[92] *del.* Keil περί Behr [93] πρό Trapp πρός *codd.*

---

[59] *Od.* 24.60 (the only place in Homer where the Muses are referred to as nine).

[60] In the *Symposium*, 185c–e and 189a, as also noted, equally indignantly, by Aristides in *Or.* 3.579–81.

Mousagetes, and all the Muses," if I had done no more than apply that adjective "all," who could ever have exalted Plato so highly? Do not assume, I mean, that this word has just been idly drafted in, as with Homer's "all the nine Muses";[59] if I may be allowed to say so about my own composition, it is an enormously important addition.

For heaven's sake, one might well add, is it really in this 50
instance alone that the man is guilty of greater excesses
than me, while in other respects being full of restraint?
Doesn't he afflict Aristophanes with hiccups,[60] when this
has no relevance to the argument, or rather is utterly
charmless and out of tune with the discussion of Love, and
doesn't he stray so far from saying what is needful or true
that he actually makes up the whole gathering and falsely
depicts the dead as living?[61] You can see this from the 51
contents of the speeches themselves. The Mantineans, whom he speaks of as Arcadians when he mentions them in the speech,[62] were dispersed during the archonship of X,[63] while Socrates died *n* years previously,[64] yet his Aristophanes hiccups and says all this before Socrates has his turn.[65] Is he then allowed to invent things that are completely incompatible with each other, even if they are manifestly irrelevant to the argument, while I am resented for exposing just one of his actions to general scrutiny?

61 Aristides' point, made more fully in *Or.* 3.579–80, is that it was chronologically impossible for Aristophanes, Socrates, a young Agathon, and a young Alcibiades to have met as they are depicted as doing in the *Symposium*.

62 *Symp.* 193a.

63 Dexitheus, 385–384 BC.

64 Fourteen years previously, in 399 BC.

65 Cf. again *Or.* 3.579–82.

INDEX

Abdera, 4.43
Academy, 3.441, 608
Achaea/Achaeans, 3.67, 105, 120, 296, 325, 470–71, 477–78
Achilles, 3.463, 467, 471, (497–98), 609, 626
Acropolis, 3.17, 106, 234
Admetus, 3.383
Adrastus, 3.37
Aeacus, 3.245, 674
Aegina/Aeginetans, 3.183, 237, 382
Aegospotami, 3.200
Aeschines (orator), 3.500
Aeschines (Socratic), 3.348, 351, 511, 575, 577, 677
  Fr. 5 Dittmar = 46 [fr. 5] Giannantoni: (3.575)
  Fr. 7 Dittmar = 49 [fr. 8] Giannantoni: 3.575
  Fr. 8 Dittmar = 50 [fr. 9] Giannantoni: 3.348, 575
  Fr. 9 Dittmar = 51 [fr. 10] Giannantoni: (3.576)
Aeschylus, 3.65, 466, 607; 4.6
  Septem 43: 4.6
  Fr. 182 *TrGF*: (3.479)
  Fr. 303 *TrGF*: 3.607
Aesop, (3.593)
  188 Perry = 199 Hausrath: (3.676)
  276 Perry = 273 Hausrath: 3.424
  356 Perry: (3.593)
Agamemnon, 3.213, 479
Agathon, 3.579, 580, 582, 614
Agesilaus, 3.90, 201–2
Ajax (son of Oeleus), 3.469
Ajax (son of Telamon), 3.86, 470, 471, 609
Alcaeus, 3.298
  Fr. 112.10 L-P: (3.298)
Alcibiades, 3.34–35, 38, (119), 234, 348, 434, 438, (543), 572–73, 580–82; 4.35–36
Aleuadae, 3.177
Alexander (of Macedon), 3.331, 333
Alexander (Trojan). *See* Paris
Amphion, 3.515
Amphipolis, 3.263, 486
Anacharsis, 4.43
Anaxagoras, 3.34, 59, 204, 564; 4.31
  B1 DK: (3.582)
Androtion, 3.677
  F69 Jacoby: (3.677)

Anniceris, 3.384
Antalcidas, Peace of, 3.577
Anthedon, 3.301
Antilochus, 3.424
Antiphon, 3.56
Apollo, 3.244, 322, 323, (409), 610, 620, 624, 626; 4.49
Apollodorus, 3.603
Arcadians, 3.579; 4.51
Archelaus, 3.18, 270
Archilochus, 3.610–11, 664
  Fr. 185 *IEG*: (3.664)
Archytas, 3.377
Ares, 3.140
Argives, 3.219, 224, 626
Aristides, 3.(99), 123, 194, 253–54, 506, 532, 534, 541, 551, 553, 555–56, 567, 637–42
Ariston, 3.488; 4.18
Aristophanes, 3.(51), 65, 79, (447), 579–82, 614, 631, (684); 4.50–51
  Ach. 531–33: 3.79
  Nub. 961–65, 967–69, 972–73, 985–86: 3.155
  Ran. 91: 3.65
  Equ.: (3.631)
  Vesp. 10: 4.4
Artemisium, 3.141, 238, 246, 556
Arthmius, 3.334, 650–51
Asclepius, 4.2, 5
Asia, 3.140, 180–81, 213
Aspasia, 3.(45), 56–58
Athena, 3.(155), 247, 322, 469
Athens/Athenians, 3.3, 11–510 *passim*, 533, 541, 543, 546, 550, 553–54, 558–60, 567–69, 654–55; 4.31, 45
Athos, 3.217
Attica, 3.94–96, 189, 224, 254, 293, 301, 608, 657
Atticism, 4.47

Babylon, 3.246, 473
barbarians, 3.109, 137–42, 175–78, 198, 202, 212–13, 220, 224–25, 229, 232–33, 235–36, 238, 243–44, 246–47, 254, 256, 258, 261, 272–73, 276, 278, 280, 284–85, 287, 304, 309, 315–16, 342, 344, 370–71, 392, 461, 463, 577
Battus, 3.674
Bellerophon, 3.308
Boeotia/Boeotians, 3.219, 246–47, 296, 328
Boscuptaechmus, 3.675
Brasidas, 3.486
Byzantines, 3.104

Cadmean victory, 3.92
Cadmus, 3.620
Callaeschrus, 3.434
Calliades, 4.31
Callias, 4.31
Callicles, 3.3–6, 501, 513, 515, 536, 539–40, 632–33, 636–45, 651
Calondas, (3.610)
Caria/Carians, 3.74, 136
Carthage/Carthaginians, 3.33, 104, 371
centaurs, 3.37, 609
Ceos/Ceans, 3.97; 4.43
Cephallenians, 3.322
Chabrias, 3.443
Chaerephon, 3.311

Charondas, 4.43–44
Charybdis, 3.306
Cheidon, 3.611
Chimera, 3.308
Christians, 3.671
Cimon, 3.1, 128–49, 207, 258, 259–60, 262, 360, 378, 408, 410, 413, 416, 418, 420, 437, 442, 462, 490, 553–54, 556, 570, 602, 604, 655, 691
Cinesias, 3.614, 627
Cleinias, 3.434; 4.31
Cleisthenes, 3.402
Cleon, 3.203, (439), 448, 486–87
Cleophon, 3.203
Codrus, 3.395
Colonus, 3.188
comedy, 3.8, 50–52, 605, 610, 614, 628, 631; 4.47–48
Corcyreans, 3.219, 224, 683
Corinth/Corinthians, 3.92, 577–78, 582
Coroebus, 3.674
Cratinus, (3.51)
Creophylus, 4.39–40, 43
Cretans, 3.82, 224
Critias, 3.434, 438, 453
Cyclops, 3.389
Cyprus/Cypriots, 3.139, 556
Cyrene, 3.275
Cythera, 3.391

Daedalus, 3.309
Damon, 4.31
Darius, 3.72, (158), 209–10
Datis, 3.157, 196
Delium, 3.263
Delphi/Delphians, 3.219, 234, 236, 311, 315, 674
Demeter, (3.320)
Demosthenes, 3.76, 499–511, 663–64, 678, 693; 4.1–5, 27
Or. 3.21: 3.506
Or. 13.34: (3.97, 184, 300)
Or. 18.7: (4.20), 18.21: 4.27, 18.44: (4.16), 18.237: (3.504), 18.306: (3.77), 18.314: 3.500, 18.316: 3.505, 18.317: 3.502
Or. 19.313: (3.693)
Or. 20: 4.3–4
Or. 45.80: (3.664)
Or. 61.40–44: (3.502)
Demosthenes (of Aphidna), (3.506)
Demostratus, (3.51)
dialectic, 3.509–10, 677; 4.7. *See also* philosophy/philosophers
Diomedes (king of Thrace), 3.405
Diomedes (son of Tydeus), 3.470
Dion, 3.272, 280, 282–83, 307, 384, 392; 4.10, 14
Dionysius (Elder), 3.284, 369–71, 377–79, 381, 384–85, 391–92, 411, 440
Dionysius (Younger), 3.284, 369–71, 385, 388, 440
Dionysodorus, 3.614
(Dionysus, 3.320)
Dioscuri, 3.276
Diotima, 3.44–45
dithyramb, 3.386, 391, 605, 610, 681–20, 622

Dodona, 3.672
Dolopians, 3.157
Dorians, 3.327

Egesta, 3.36
Egypt/Egyptians, 3.180, 216, 583
Eleans, 3.687
Elysian Fields, 3.580
Enyalius, 3.463–64
Epicharmus, 4.47
Eretria/Eretrians, 3.158, 181–82
Euboea/Euboeans, 3.74, 141, 181, 243, 264
Euboulides, 3.578
Eumelus, 3.467–69
Euneus, 3.105
Eupolis, (3.51, 365, 487)
  Demes: (3.365)
  Fr. 102 KA: 3.51
  Fr. 103 KA: 3.51
Euripides, 3.65, 267, (585), 633
  Cresphontes fr. 449 *TrGF*: 3.267
  Hippolytus 352: 3.633
  Polyidus: (3.664)
Europe, 3.140, 181, 213, 560
Eurybates, 3.270
Eurybiades, 3.243, 253
Eurymedon, 3.140
Eurytion, 3.37
Euthydemus, 3.614
Eutyches, 3.675

flattery (*kolakeia*), 3.3, 25, 31, 41, 118, 125, 131, 207–8, 250–51, 262, 330, 349, 415, 513–15, 517, 521, 523–24, 526, 529, 532, 538, 543, 552, 557–58, 565, 567, 605, 619, 621, 633–35, 649, 661, 668, 671; 4.19

Gela, 3.370
Gelon, 3.219
Geryon, 3.167
Glaucon, 4.43
Glaucus, 3.301
Gordius, 3.37
Gorgias, 3.614, 632, 651; (4.38)
Gorgon, 3.668; 4.38

Hades, 3.602, 605, (681)
Hector, 3.463, 674
Helen, 3.425, 665
Hellespont, 3.217
Helots, 3.137
Heracles, 3.68–69, 186, 191, 276, 602, 644, 672
Heraclidae, 3.325, 327
Hermes, 3.192, 464, 583–84, 663; 4.49
Hermocrates, 3.369, 440
Hermopolis, 3.(583), 584
Herodotus, 3.677, 685
  (6.131.2: 3.97)
Hesiod, 3.70, 123, 188, 664; 4.43, 45
  Op. 122–23: 3.188
  (*Op.* 303–7: 3.664)
  Op. 493: 3.70
  Op. 763–64: 3.123
Hippias (sophist), 3.602, 614; 4.44

Hippias (tyrant), 3.177
Homer, 3.42, 127–28, 143, 164–65, 184, 213, 245, 290, 322, 359, 388, 424, 463, 467, (469), 471, 473, 570, 605–6, 609, 612, 626, 653; 4.1, 38–47, 49
Iliad
1.267–68: 3.609
2.213–14: 3.67
2.380: 3.612
2.764: 3.467
2.768: 3.471
2.768–69: 3.609
3.39: 3.463
5.531: 3.143
7.473: 3.105
8.81–86: 3.425
8.369: 3.377
9: 3.626
9.257–58: 3.626
9.443: 3.128
9.593–94: 3.134
9.648: 3.377
10.511: 3.42
(11.218–20: 3.213)
12.270–71: 3.167
13.278: 3.226
13.321: 3.471
14.521–22: 3.469
(15.189–92: 3.220)
15.678: 3.470
15.685–86: 3.86
(16.112–13: 3.213)
17.32: 3.388
17.98: 3.315
17.279: 3.471
18.81–82: 4.1
18.309: 3.463
20.198: 3.388
20.250: 3.42
22.158: 3.609
(22.359–60: 3.463)
(23.304–50: 3.424)
23.395: 3.468
23.536: 3.467
23.774: 3.469
(23.777: 3.469)
(23.850–83: 3.472)
24.66: 3.612
Odyssey
2.276–77: (3.149), 359
8.329: 3.474
(10.495: 3.604)
11: 3.602
11.469–70: 3.471
11.476: 3.664
11.582: 3.602; 4.44
11.601: 3.602; 4.44
(19.209–12: 3.251)
20.355: 4.46
24.60: 4.49
Homeric, 3.126
Homeridae, 3.365; 4.43
Hyacinthus, 3.674
Hyperbolus, 3.203
Hystaspes, 3.72

Iacchus, 3.320
Iolaus, 3.69
Ionios, 3.245
Iphicles, 3.644
Iphicrates, 3.443
Isles of the Blessed, 3.498
Isocrates, 3.677
Isolochus, 4.31

Isthmus, 3.246, 316, 325–26, 338
Italy/Italians, 3.33, 224, 274, 303, 371, 377; 4.43

justice, 3.18, 39, 122–23, 155, 158, 160, 174, 179, 184, 195, 213, 221, 253, 257, 270, 279, 307, 309, 330, 363–64, 369, 444, 448, 454, 489, 498, 518–20, 532, 547, 595–600; 4.10, 17–18, 43

Laches, 3.47, 264, 578
Laconia, 3.342
law. *See* legislation
Lechaeum, 3.577–78, 582
legislation, 3.17–18, 28, 68, 71, 79, 133, 135–36, 153, 158, 162–63, 172, 184, 250, 270, 369, 380, 387, 477, 546–47, 549–50, 558–64, 595–600, 615, 630, 646–47, 652; 4.20–21, 48
Leontini, 3.370
Leptines, 4.3–4
Libya, 3.33, 180, 371, 384; 4.2
Locri/Locrians, 3.328, 585
Lycambes, 3.611
Lycaon, 3.674
Lycurgus, 3.162–63, 202; 4.43
Lysander, 3.200, 202
Lysias, 3.607, 677
Lysimachus, 3.194

Macedon, 3.331
Magnesia, 3.348
Mantinea/Mantineans, 3.45, 579; 4.51
Marathon, 3.151, 154–55, 182, 195, 198, 209–10, 215, 237, 259, 295, 304, 336, 556
Mardonius, 3.210, 331, 332
Margites, 3.674
Maximus, 4.2–5
Medes, 3.140, 199, 219, 334–35, 650
medicine, 3.44, 134, 236, 254, 270–71, 362, 475, 537, 588–94, 597–600; 4.5
Megara/Megarians, 3.74, 79, 549
Meleager, 3.97, 134
Meles, 3.231, 627
Melesippus, 3.84
Menander, 3.(133), 665
  Fr. 506 KA: (3.133)
  Fr. 432 KA: 3.665
Menelaus, 3.389, 479, 665
Messenians, 3.181
Miletus, 3.45; 4.43
Miltiades, 3.1, 9, 149–208 *passim*, 210–12, 258–60, 265, 269, 282, 360, 402, 404, 408, 410, 420–22, 436–38, 442–43, 462, 482, 490, 553, 556, 570, 602, 604, 628, 633, 650, 655–56, 691
Minos, 3.245
Mithaecus, 3.25, 123, 127, 250, 270, 368–69
Molionidae, 3.405
Molossians, 3.383
Muses, 3.155, 213, 313, 610, 620; 4.49

music, 3.155, 159, 242, 359, 466, 620, 624, 649; 4.31
Mycale, 3.328
Myrcinus, 3.486
Myrrhine, 3.573

Narcissus, 3.674
Naucratis, 3.583–84
Naupactus, 3.317
navigation, 3.87, 183–87, 462, 474–75, 537, 591
Nestor, 3.67, 424, 426–28, 623, 674
Niceratus, 3.542
Nicias, 3.506–7, 542–46
Nisaea, 3.120

Odysseus, 3.67–68, 251, (322), 385, 389, 478, 626
Oenophyta, 3.328
Olorus, 3.20
Olympia/Olympic Games, 3.149, 186, 465, 687
Olympian (nickname of Pericles), 3.123–24
Olympics (games), 3.465, 687
Olympics (?Pergamene festival), 4.22
oratory, 3.47, 51–59, 62, 64, 66, 99, 128, 174, 193, 195, 203, 428, 487, 500, 509–10, 513–14, 517–18, 521, 524–41, 548–49, 557, 565–66, 567, 600, 604, 613, 627, 633–35, 691; 4.3–5, 7, 18, 26, 46, 49
Orestes, 3.205, 323
Orontes, 3.468
Orpheus, 3.252
Orph. Fr. 334 Kern, 3.50

Paeania, 3.499
Palamedes, 3.477–78, 480–82, 674
Palestine, 3.671
Pallas, 3.155
Pamphylia, 3.139, 556
Pan, 3.191–92, 194
parabasis, 4.12
Paris, 3.425, 463
Parmenides, 4.37
Patroclus, 3.424, 467, (498)
Pausanias, 3.195, 197–98, 200, 202, 259–60, 262, 418
Pegae, 3.120
Pegasus, 3.308
Peleus, 3.37, 471, 626
Peloponnese/Peloponnesians, 3.22, 23, 74–75, 77, 80, 91, 94, 96, 120, 137, 243–44, 296, 325, 327, 334, 650
Pericles, 3.1, 11–127 *passim*, 153, 360, 365, 401–2, 406, 408, 410, 420–23, 427–29, 431, 436–37, 439, 441–45, 448–49, 481–82, 484, 486–87, 490, 506–7, 553, 556, 564–75, 602, 604, 633, 644, 651, 655, 691; 4.29–31, 34, 36
Pericles (contemporary of Archilochus), 3.611
Persephone, (3.320)
Perseus, 3.668
Persia, 3.80

Persians, 3.180, 184, 196, 229, 309, 380, 460, 468, 473, 558, 560
Phaedrus, 3.573
Philocles, 3.466
philosophy/philosophers , 3.85, 99, 135, 172, 243, 258, 289, 324, 335, 368, 370, 408, 526, 537, 543, 630, 663–91, 677–79, 681. *See also* dialectic
Philoxenus, 3.386, 391
Phocis/Phocaeans, 3.328
Phoenicians, 3.139–40
Phormio, 3.317
Phrygia/Phrygians, 3.665, 667
Phrynondas, 3.270, 674
Pindar, 3.37, 191, 238, 466, 478, 620; 4.27
  Isthmia 4.66: 4.27
  Fr. 32 Sn-M: 3.620
  Fr. 38 Sn-M: 3.466
  Fr. 48 Sn-M: 3.37
  Fr. 77 Sn-M: 3.238
  Fr. 260.7 Sn-M: 3.478
Piraeus, 3.80
Pisistratids, 3.177, 415
Pisistratus, 3.17
Plataeans, 3.152
Platea, 3.195, 197–99, 224, 259, 261, 309, 328
Plato, 3 and 4 *passim*
  Alcibiades I
    118b–c: 4.29
    (118b–19a: 3.572)
    118c–19a: 4.31
    (119d: 4.36)
  Apologia, 3.477
    28b: 3.496
    28b–c: 3.497, 519
    (30c–d: 3.387)
    31e–32a: 3.489
    (41b: 3.477)
  Cratylus
    (398a: 3.188)
    (398d: 3.510)
    403e: 3.681
    (408d: 3.192)
    (436c–d: 3.600)
  Critias
    (112c: 3.12)
  Epistula II
    314c: 3.587
  Epistula VII
    (345c: 3.306)
    355d: 3.272
    355e–56a: 3.280
    356a–b: 3.284
  Euthydemus
    (298c: 3.98)
  Gorgias, 3 and 4 *passim*
    (462c: 3.651)
    463d: (3.538, 549), 4.46
    (463e–64c: 3.63)
    (464b–e: 3.270, 597)
    (468a: 3.522)
    (469b–c: 4.14)
    (470d–71d: 3.270)
    (472a: 3.542)
    (472b–c: 3.103, 643)
    (473a: 3.26)
    (474a: 3.27)
    (476a: 3.27)
    (479d–e: 3.270)
    (486d: 3.227)
    (500a: 3)
    (501e–2a: 3.605)
    (502a: 3.231, 391, 627)

(502c: 3.548)
502e: 3.536
503a: 3.536, 538, 634
503b: 3.538, 540
(503c: 3.539)
(503d–4a: 3.144)
(506b: 3.515)
(508a: 3.38, 62, 144, 369, 445, 546)
(511b–13a: 3.265)
(511d: 3.183)
513a: 3.3
(513c: 3.632)
513e–14a: 3.6
(515e: 3.41, 82, 98, 539)
(515e–16c: 3.569)
516a: 3.401, (423)
(516a–17a: 3.354)
516d: 3.(146), 151, (570)
516e: 3.401, (421)
516e–17a: 3.642
517a: 3.513
(517b–18b: 3.270)
(518b: 3.127, 250, 368, 605, 628)
(518c–e: 3.36)
(518e–19a: 3.241)
(519a: 3.279, 546, 559)
519b–c: 3.520
520a: 3.600
(520b: 3.588, 595, 600)
(523e–25a: 3.110)
526a: 3.551
(526b: 3.532, 555)

Laches
(191b–c: 3.309)

Leges
(685b–e: 3.327)
689b–c: 3.560, 561
(692e–93a: 3.558)
699b: 3.562
699c: 3.562
(705a: 3.294)
(706c: 3.288)
709b: (3.474), 482
(709e–10b: 3.135)
(717b: 3.269)
(803c: 3.474)
(817a–b: 3.615)
829a: 4.17
(950b–c: 3.123)

Lysis
(206a: 3.5)

Menexenus
(235d–36a: 3.56–57)
(240c–46a: 3.556)
(245b: 3.577)
(245e: 3.577)
(247e–48a: 3.195)

Parmenides
(127b: 4.37)

Phaedo
60e: 3.624
(68b: 3.680)

Phaedrus
(234d: 3.266)
(236b: 3.315)
238d: 3.618
(263d: 3.192)
268e: 3.306
269e: 3.567
(269e–70a: 3.59)
270a: 3.564
(274c: 3.583)
(276c–d: 3.33)

Protagoras
(311e–12a: 3.603)
(314c–e: 3.616)

315b–d: 3.602–3; (4.45)
(315b–16a: 4.44)
(317c: 3.603)
(318e: 4.44)
(326d: 3.111)
(328a: 3.361)
(337b–38a: 4.44)
Respublica
(350d: 3.616)
(351c: 3.97)
(374a ff.: 3.136)
(386b–c: 3.653)
(387b: 3.277; 4.38)
(394b–d: 3.605)
(395c–96b: 3.616)
(398a: 3.605; 4.38)
(416d–17a: 3.103, 335; 4.39)
(416d–21c: 3.136)
(457a: 3.332)
(457c–d: 4.39)
(468b–e: 3.136)
(473c–e: 3.135)
(495e: 3.686)
(496d: 3.288)
(522d: 3.480)
(595c: 4.40)
599d–600d: 4.43
(600a–b: 4.39)
(600b: 4.39)
600e: 4.46
Symposium
(185c: 3.579)
(185c–e: 4.50)
(189a: 4.50)
(193a: 3.579; 4.50)
(198a: 3.579)
(201d: 3.44)
(212d: 3.580)
(220e–21b: 3.263)
Theaetetus
143d: 3.275)
(152e: 4.47)
Timaeus
(21b–c: 3.548)
Plato Comicus, (3.69)
Fr. 202 KA: 3.69
Pnyx, 3.195, 221
Pollis, 3.379–82, 384
Polus, 3.538, 599, 632
Polycrates, 3.377
Polydamas, 3.465
Polypoetes, 3.470
Pontus, 3.183
Poseidon, 3.218, 276, 290, 338, 424, 462
Potidaea, 3.263
Prodicus, 3.602, 614; 4.43–44
Protagoras, 3.361, 602, 603, 614; 4.43–44
Protesilaus, 3.365
Pylos, 3.121, 487
Pythagoras, 3.630, 677, 680, 688; 4.43
Pythagoreans, 3.377
Pythia, 3.311, 316, 617
Pythian (Apollo), 3.244, 323
Pythoclides, 4.31
Pythodorus, 4.31
Pythonax, 3.334

Radamanthys, 3.110
Rhium, 3.325

Salamis, 3.189, 210, 234–35, 247, 251, 253, 297, 304,

318–21, 326, 332, 348, 556
Samos/Samians, 3.74
Sarambus, 3.(127), 250, 322
Saron, 3.301
satyrs, 3.665, 672
Scyros, 3.409
Scythians, 3.180, 309, 380, 622; 4.43
Seven Sages, 3.677
Siceliots, 3.224
Sicily/Sicilians, 3.21, 32–33, 35–36, 234, 250, 272, 274, 306–7, 368–69, 370–71, 377, 379, 383, 385, 389, 440, 543, 548, 648; 4.9, 14, 36, 43
Simonides, 3.(97), (140), 151
  Fr. 582 *PMG*: (3.97)
  Ep. 2 Page (*Anth. Pal.* 7.26): (3.140)
Sirens, 3.623
Socrates, 3.3, 16, 33–34, 70–71, 99, 109, 116, 119, 184, 204, 253, 263–64, 311, 348–49, 351, 434–35, 437–39, 444, 446, 448, 453, 477, 488, 492, 496–97, 538, 543, 575, 577–80, 582, 587, 599, 603, 605, 624, 630, 632, 634, 637–39, 642–44, 651, 677, 680; 4.31, 34, 43, 51
Solon, 3.(107), 162, 189, 402, 546–50, 630, 646, 677; 4.43
sophists, 3.16, 352, 439, 444, 600–604, 616, 624; 4.43–45
Sophocles, 3.65, 376, 466, 585, 665, 672
  Aias 301–2: (3.672)
  Aias Locros, fr. 14 *TrGF*: (3.549)
  OC 267: (3.376)
  OT: 3.466
Sparta/Spartans, 3.77, 80, 85 89–90, 121, 131, 137, 142, 170, 177, 181, 198–99, 201, 224, 231, 239–40, 242–44, 278, 309, 317, 328, 333, 341–42, 344, 348, 379–80, 384, 408, 418, 486, 543, 558, 579, 605, 652, 656; 4.43
Spartiate, 3.202, 379, 384
sphaeromachia, 4.27
Stentor, 3.674
Stesichorus, 3.557; 4.8
  Fr. 192 *PMG*: (3.557; 4.8)
Styx, 3.377
Syracuse/Syracusans, 3.284, 286, 385

Tantalus, 3.602, 604; 4.45
Telamon, 3.470, 471, 609
Tempe, 3.244
Terpander, 3.231, 242
Teucer, 3.395, 472
Thales, 4.43
Thearion, 3.25, 123, 127, 270, 628
Thebans, 3.90
Themistocles, 3.1, 9, 141, 209–351 *passim*, 360, 365, 383, 406, 408, 410, 413, 416, 418–20, 436–37, 442, 490,

553–54, 556, 570, 575–76, 602, 604, 628, 644, 650–51, 655–56, 691
Theodotus, 3.578
Thermopylae, 3.141, 244, 261, 326
Thersites, 3.67, 674
Theseus, 3.276, 408–9
Thespiae, 3.224
Thessaly/Thessalians, 3.170, 177, 213, 219, 224, 244, 467
Thetis, 3.497
Theuth, 3.583
Thibron, 3.202
Thrace, 3.177, 405
Thrasymachus, 3.97, 616
Thucydides (historian), 3.20, 24, 55, 57, 507, 511
Thucydides (politician), 3.13
Timocreon, 3.612
tragedy, 3.65, 480, 605, 610, 615, 622; 4.47–48
Tritogeneia (Athena), 3.312
Troezen, 3.120, 247, 313
Troy/Trojans, 3.42, 86, 213, 463, 470, 480, 497–98

Xenophon, 3.109, 111
Xerxes, 3.209–10, 254–55, 301

Zelea, 3.334
Zeno, 4.31, 37
Zeus, 3.123, 245, 312, 322, 392, 424, 469, 664; 4.8